Lecture Notes in Computer Scie

Commenced Publication in 1973
Founding and Former Series Editors:
Gerhard Goos, Juris Hartmanis, and Jan van Leeuwen

Yingshu Li   Dung T. Huynh   Sajal K. Das
Ding-Zhu Du (Eds.)

Wireless Algorithms, Systems and Applications

Third International Conference, WASA 2008
Dallas, TX, USA, October 26-28, 2008
Proceedings

 Springer

Volume Editors

Yingshu Li
Georgia State University, Department of Computer Science
34 Peachtree Street, Suite 1413, Atlanta, GA 30303, USA
E-mail: yli@cs.gsu.edu

Dung T. Huynh
University of Texas at Dallas, Department of Computer Science and Engineering
EE/CS Building, Richardson, TX 75083, USA
E-mail: huynh@utdallas.edu

Sajal K. Das
University of Texas at Arlington, Department of Computer Science and Engineering
P.O. Box 19015, Arlington, TX 76019, USA
E-mail: das@cse.uta.edu

Ding-Zhu Du
University of Texas at Dallas, Department of Computer Science and Engineering
EE/CS Building, Richardson, TX 75083, USA
E-mail: dzdu@utdallas.edu

Library of Congress Control Number: Applied for

CR Subject Classification (1998): F.1, F.2, D.1, D.2, D.4, C.2, C.4, H.4

LNCS Sublibrary: SL 1 – Theoretical Computer Science and General Issues

ISSN   0302-9743
ISBN-10   3-540-88581-1 Springer Berlin Heidelberg New York
ISBN-13   978-3-540-88581-8 Springer Berlin Heidelberg New York

Springer is a part of Springer Science+Business Media

springer.com

© Springer-Verlag Berlin Heidelberg 2008
Printed in Germany

Typesetting: Camera-ready by author, data conversion by Scientific Publishing Services, Chennai, India
Printed on acid-free paper   SPIN: 12543076   06/3180   5 4 3 2 1 0

Preface

Recent advances in cutting-edge wireless communication and computing technologies have paved the way for the proliferation of ubiquitous infrastructure and infrastructureless wireless networks. These emerging networks are enabling a broad spectrum of applications ranging from critical infrastructure protection and security, to environment monitoring, health care, and quality of life. The need to deal with the complexity and ramifications of the ever-growing mobile users and services, however, is intensifying the interest in the development of sound fundamental principles, novel algorithmic approaches, rigorous and repeatable design methodologies, and systematic evaluation frameworks for next-generation wireless networks.

The Third International Conference on Wireless Algorithms, Systems and Applications (WASA) was held in Dallas, TX, USA during October 26–28. The objective of WASA is to address the research and development efforts of various issues in the area of algorithms, systems and applications for current and next-generation infrastructure and infrastructureless wireless networks. The conference is structured to provide a forum for researchers and practitioners, from the academic, industrial, and governmental sectors, with a unique opportunity to discuss and express their views on the current trends, challenges, and state-of-the-art solutions addressing various issues related to current and next-generation wireless networks. Following a rigorous review process, the Program Committee selected an outstanding set of 35 papers for publication in the proceedings and oral presentations at the conference. The program of WASA 2008 also included three keynote talks by Lionel Ni, Ty Znati, and Jie Wu along with 15 invited papers.

Finally, we would like to express our gratitude to all the authors of the submissions, all the members of the Program Committee, all the members of the Organizing Committee, and the keynote speakers for making WASA 2008 possible and successful.

October 2008

Yingshu Li
Dung T. Huynh
Sajal K. Das
Ding-Zhu Du

Organization

General Co-chairs

Sajal K. Das   University of Texas at Arlington
Dung T. Huynh   University of Texas at Dallas

Program Committee Co-chairs

Ding-Zhu Du   University of Texas at Dallas
Yingshu Li   Georgia State University

Steering Committee

Xiuzhen Susan Cheng   The George Washington University
David Hung-Chang Du   US National Science Foundation
Ding-Zhu Du   University of Texas at Dallas
Wei Li   University of Toledo
Eun K. Park   US National Science Foundation
Jie Wu   US National Science Foundation
Wei Zhao   Rensselaer Polytechnic Institute
Ty Znati   US National Science Foundation

Publicity Chair

Yiwei Wu   Georgia State University

Local Arrangements Chair and Webmaster

Donghyun Kim   University of Texas at Dallas

Finance Chair

Feng Zou   University of Texas at Dallas

Program Committee

Dharma Agrawal   University of Cincinnati
Raheem Beyah   Georgia State University
Amiya Bhattacharya   New Mexico State University
Jiannong Cao   Hong Kong Polytechnic University,
     Hong Kong

Ionut Cardei   Florida Atlantic University
Mihaela Cardei   Florida Atlantic University
Guohong Cao   Penn State University
Maggie X. Cheng   University of Missouri, Rolla
Xiuzhen Cheng   George Washington University
Baek-Young Choi   University of Missouri, Kansa City
Jorge A. Cobb   University of Texas at Dallas
Cherita L. Corbett   Sandia National Laboratories
Jun-Hong Cui   University of Connecticut
Bhaskar DasGupta   University of Illinois at Chicago
Murat Demirbas   SUNY at Buffalo
Mohammad
  Taghi Hajiaghayi   Massachusetts Institute of Technology
Ruhan He   Wuhan University of Science and Engineering,
                               China
Tian He   University of Minnesota
Chih-Hao Huang   City University of Hong Kong, Hong Kong
Yan Huang   University of North Texas
Xiaohua Jia   City University of Hong Kong, Hong Kong
Yoo-Ah Kim   University of Connecticut
Santosh Kumar   University of Memphis
Fei Li   George Mason University
Jianzhong Li   Harbin Institute of Technology, China
Minming Li   City University of Hong Kong
Xiangyang Li   Illinois Institute of Technology
Xinrong Li   University of North Texas
Yonghe Liu   University of Texas at Arlington
Ion Mandoiu   University of Connecticut
Manki Min   South Dakota State University
Lionel M. Ni   Hong Kong University of Science and
                               Technology, Hong Kong
Hung Ngo   SUNY at Buffalo
Dan Popa   University of Texas at Arlington
Ivan Stojmenovic   Ottawa University, Canada
Violet R. Syrotiuk   Arizona State University
Amin Teymorian   George Washington University
My T. Thai   University of Florida
Limin Sun   Chinese Academy of Sciences, China
Peng-Jun Wan   Illinois Institute of Technology
Feng Wang   Arizona State University at the West Campus
Jie Wang   University of Massachusetts Lowell
Xiaoming Wang   Shaanxi Normal University, China
Xinbing Wang   Shanghai Jiaotong University, China
Yu Wang   University of North Carolina at Charlotte
Hongyi Wu   University of Louisiana at Lafayette

Weili Wu	University of Texas at Dallas
Neal N. Xiong	Georgia State University
Kuai Xu	Yahoo
Guoliang Xue	Arizona State University
Qiang Ye	UPEI, Canada
Alex Zelikovsky	Georgia State University
Zhao Zhang	Xinjiang University, China
Sheng Zhong	SUNY at Buffalo

Table of Contents

Research Challenges in Complex Large Scale Networks and Cyber Physical Systems

Ty Znati

National Science Foundation, USA
tznati@nsf.gov

Abstract. Unprecedented advances in technology are revolutionizing the use and scale of distributed and networked systems, ushering in a variety of global-scale, data intensive applications. Furthermore, as computers become ever-faster and communication bandwidth ever-cheaper, computing and communication capabilities are penetrating every facet of our physical world, giving rise to a new class of Cyber Physical Systems (CPS). The operations of these physical and engineered systems are monitored, coordinated, controlled and seamlessly integrated by an intelligent computing core. This intimate coupling between the cyber and physical will transform how we interact with the physical world. The talk will discuss future research trends, grand challenges, opportunities, and initiatives in computing and networking with a focus on future networking technology and Cyber Physical Systems.

Y. Li et al. (Eds.): WASA 2008, LNCS 5258, p. 1, 2008.

China's National Research Project on Wireless Sensor Networks

Lionel M. Ni

Department of Computer Science and Engineering
The Hong Kong University of Science and Technology
Clear Water Bay, Kowloon, Hong Kong
ni@cse.ust.hk

Abstract. This talk will give an overview of the 5-year National Basic Research Program of China (also known as 973 Program) on Wireless Sensor Networks launched in September 2006 sponsored by Ministry of Science and Technology. This national research project involving researchers from many major universities in China and Hong Kong with an aim to tackle fundamental research issues rose in three major application domains: coal mine surveillance, water pollution monitoring, and traffic monitoring and control. The distinctive feature of the project is that it will present a systematic study of wireless sensor networks, from node platform development, core protocol design and system solution development to critical problems. This talk will address the research challenges, current progress, and future plan.

Y. Li et al. (Eds.): WASA 2008, LNCS 5258, p. 2, 2008.
© Springer-Verlag Berlin Heidelberg 2008

A Utility-Based Routing Scheme in Ad Hoc Networks

Jie Wu

National Science Foundation, USA
jwu@nsf.gov

Abstract. To efficiently address the routing problem in ad hoc networks, we introduce a new utility metric, maximum expected social welfare, and integrate the cost and stability of nodes in a unified model to evaluate the optimality of routes. The expected social welfare is defined in terms of expected benefit (of the routing source) minus the expected costs incurred by forwarding nodes. Based on this new metric, we design an optimal and efficient algorithm, and implement the algorithm in both centralized (optimal) and distributed (near-optimal) manners. We also look at several extensions in improving benefit, all optimal routes, incentive compatible routing, and applications of this new model.

Y. Li et al. (Eds.): WASA 2008, LNCS 5258, p. 3, 2008.
© Springer-Verlag Berlin Heidelberg 2008

Delivery Guarantee of Greedy Routing in Three Dimensional Wireless Networks

Yu Wang[1,*], Chih-Wei Yi[2,**], and Fan Li[3]

[1] University of North Carolina at Charlotte, USA
yu.wang@uncc.edu
[2] National Chiao Tung University, Taiwan
yi@cs.nctu.edu.tw
[3] Beijing Institute of Technology, China
fli@bit.edu.cn

Abstract. In this paper, we investigate how to design greedy routing to guarantee packet delivery in a three-dimensional (3D) network. In 2D networks, many position-based routing protocols apply face routing on planar routing structure as a backup method to guarantee packet delivery when greedy routing fails at local minimum. However, in 3D networks, no planar topology can be constructed anymore. Even worse, a recent result [6] showed that there is no deterministic localized routing algorithm that guarantees the delivery of packets in 3D networks. Therefore, we propose to set up the transmission radius large enough to eliminate local minimum in the 3D network. In particular, we study the asymptotic critical transmission radius for greedy routing to ensure the packet delivery in randomly deployed 3D networks. Using similar techniques in [12], we theoretically prove that for a 3D network, formed by nodes that are produced by a Poisson point process of density n over a convex compact region of unit volume, $\sqrt[3]{\frac{3\beta_0 \ln n}{4\pi n}}$ is asymptotically almost surely (abbreviated by a.a.s.) the threshold of the critical transmission radius for 3D greedy routing, where $\beta_0 = 3.2$. We also conduct extensive simulations to confirm our theoretical results.

1 Introduction

Most existing wireless systems and protocols are based on two-dimensional (2D) design, where all wireless nodes are distributed in a two dimensional plane. This assumption is somewhat justified for applications where wireless devices are deployed on earth surface and where the height of the network is smaller than transmission radius of a node. However, 2D assumption may no longer be valid if a wireless network is deployed in space, atmosphere, or ocean, where nodes of a network are distributed over a 3D space and the difference in the third dimension is too large to be ignored. In fact, recent interest in ad hoc and sensor networks (such as underwater sensor networks [2])

---

* This work of Yu Wang is supported in part by the US National Science Foundation (NSF) under Grant No. CNS-0721666.
** This work of Chih-Wei Yi is supported in part by the NSC under Grant No. NSC95-2221-E-009-059-MY3, by the ITRI under Grant No. 7301XS2220, and by the MoE ATU plan.

Y. Li et al. (Eds.): WASA 2008, LNCS 5258, pp. 4–16, 2008.

hints at the strong need to design 3D wireless networks. Most current research in 3D networks [11,3,13] primarily focuses on coverage and connectivity issues. In this paper, we study 3D localized position-based routing.

Localized position-based routing makes the forwarding decision based solely on the position information of the destination and local neighbors. It does not need the dissemination of route discovery information and the maintenance of routing tables. Thus, it enjoys the advantages of lower overhead and higher scalability than other traditional routing protocols. The popular localized routing is *greedy routing*, where a node finds the next relay node whose distance to the destination is the smallest among all neighbors. It is easy to construct an example to show that greedy routing will not succeed to reach the destination but fall into a local minimum (a node without any "better" neighbors). There are two ways to guarantee the packet delivery for greedy routing in 2D networks: (1) applying face routing, or (2) using large enough transmission power. Many position-based routing protocols [5,8,9] applied face routing as a backup method to get out of the local minimum after simple greedy heuristic fails. The idea of face routing is to walk along the faces which are intersected by the line segment st between the source s and the destination t. To guarantee the packet delivery, face routing requires the underlying routing topology to be a planar graph (*i.e.*, no link/edge intersection). The other way to guarantee packet delivery is letting all nodes have sufficiently large transmission radii to avoid the existence of local minimum. Recently, Wan *et al.* [12] studied the *critical transmission radius* (CTR) of greedy routing to guarantee the packet delivery in randomly deployed 2D networks.

Though some protocols for 2D networks can be directly extended to 3D networks, the design of 3D networks is surprisingly more difficult than that of 2D. In case of position-based routing, the simple greedy routing can be easily extended to 3D. Several 3D routing protocols [10, 14] specifically designed for underwater sensor networks are just variations of simple greedy routing. However, to guarantee the packet delivery of 3D greedy routing is not straightforward and very challenging.

In 3D networks, there is no planar topology concept any more, thus, face routing can not be applied directly to help the greedy routing getting out of local minimum. Fevens *et al.* [7, 1] proposed several 3D position-based routing protocols and tried to find a way to still use face routing to get out of the local minimum. Their basic idea is projecting the 3D network to a 2D plane (or multiple 2D planes), then applying the face routing in the plane. However, as shown in Figure 1 [7], a planar graph cannot be extracted from the projected graph. It is clear that removing either $v_3'v_4'$ or $v_1'v_2'$ will break the connectivity. In fact, Durocher *et al.* [6] have recently proven that *there is no deterministic localized routing algorithm for 3D networks that guarantees the delivery of packets.*

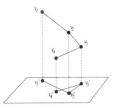

Fig. 1. A projection causes intersections

Therefore, in this paper, we adopt the second way to achieve delivery guarantee and provide a completed theoretical study on the critical transmission radius of 3D greedy routing that guarantees the delivery of packets between any source-destination pairs. We prove that for a 3D network, formed by nodes that are generated by a Poisson point process of density n over a convex compact region of unit volume, the critical transmission radius for 3D greedy routing is a.a.s. at most $\sqrt[3]{\frac{3\beta \ln n}{4\pi n}}$ for any $\beta > \beta_0$ and at least $\sqrt[3]{\frac{3\beta \ln n}{4\pi n}}$ for any $\beta < \beta_0$. Here, $\beta_0 = 3.2$.

2 Preliminaries

2.1 Critical Transmission Radius for Greedy Routing

In any greedy-based routing, the packet may be dropped by some intermediate node u before it reaches the destination t when node u could not find any of its neighbors that is "better" than itself. One way to ensure that the routing is successful for every source-destination pairs is during the topology control (or power control) phase each wireless node is set with a sufficiently large transmission radius such that each intermediate node u will always find a better neighbor. Critical transmission radius for routing algorithm is first studied by [12]. Here, we review its definition as in [12]. Assume that V is the set of all wireless nodes in the network and each wireless node has a transmission radius r. Let $B(x, r)$ denote the open disk of radius r centered at x. Let

$$\rho(V) = \max_{\substack{(u,v) \in V^2 \\ u \neq v}} \min_{w \in B(v, \|u-v\|)} \|w - u\|.$$

In the equation, (u, v) is a source-destination pair. Since $w \in B(v, \|u - v\|)$, we have $\|w - v\| < \|u - v\|$. It means w is closer to v than u. If the transmission radius is not less than $\|w - u\|$, w might be the one to relay packets from u to v. Therefore, for each (u, v), the minimum of $\|w - u\|$ over all nodes on $B(v, \|u - v\|)$ is the transmission radius that ensures there is at least one node that can relay packets from u to v, and the maximum of the minimum over all (u, v) pairs guarantees the existence of relay nodes between any source-destination pair. Clearly, if the transmission radius is at least $\rho(V)$, packets can be delivered between any source-destination pairs. On the other hand, if the transmission radius is less than $\rho(V)$, there must exist some source-destination pair, e.g., the (u, v) that yields the value $\rho(V)$, such that packets can't be delivered. Therefore, $\rho(V)$ is called the *critical transmission radius* (CTR) for greedy routing that guarantees the delivery of packets between any source-destination pair of nodes among V. By assuming the nodes are randomly deployed in a unit area region, Wan *et al.* [12] proved that $\sqrt{\frac{\beta_1 \ln n}{\pi n}}$ is asymptotically almost surely the threshold of $\rho(V)$ for greedy routing in 2D networks, where $\beta_1 = 1/(\frac{2}{3} - \frac{\sqrt{3}}{2\pi})$.

2.2 Assumptions and Notations

In this paper, we consider the deliverability by the asymptotics of $\rho(V)$, where V is given by a Poisson point process. By proper scaling, we assume the wireless devices are represented by a Poisson point process of density n over a unit-volume cube $\mathbb{D}$. $Po(n)$ denotes a Poisson RV with mean n, and $\mathcal{P}_n(A)$ represents a Poisson point process of density n over a region A. Especially, $\mathcal{P}_n$ is shorthand for $\mathcal{P}_n(\mathbb{D})$. In what follows, $\|x\|$ is the Euclidean norm of a point $x \in \mathbb{R}^3$ and $\|x - y\|$ is the Euclidean distance between two points $x, y \in \mathbb{R}^3$. For a countable and finite set S, we use $\#(S)$ to denote its cardinality. $|A|$ is shorthand for the volume of a measurable set $A \subset \mathbb{R}^3$. All integrals considered will be Lebesgue integrals. For a set $A \subset \mathbb{R}^3$, $diam(A)$ denotes the diameter of A, and ∂A denotes the topological boundary of A. Let $B(x, r)$ denote the open sphere of radius r centered at x. For any two points $u, v \in \mathbb{R}^3$, the intersection of two spheres of radii $\|u - v\|$ centered respectively at u and v, denoted by L_{uv}, is called the *biconvex* of u and v, i.e. $L_{uv} = B(u, \|u - v\|) \cap B(v, \|u - v\|)$, and $\|u - v\|$ is called the depth of the biconvex. An event is said to be *asymptotic almost sure* (a.a.s.) if it occurs with a probability converges to one as $n \to \infty$. To avoid trivialities, we tacitly assume n to be sufficiently large if necessary.

2.3 Geometric Preliminaries

We first provide several geometric lemmas which will be used in the proof of our result in next section. However, due to the space limit, we ignore the detailed proofs of them.

If $\|u - v\| = 1$, a straightforward calculation yields that $|L_{uv}| = \frac{5\pi}{12}$. The volume of a biconvex with respect to two unit-volume balls is $\frac{5\pi/12}{4\pi/3} = \frac{5}{16}$. Let $\beta_0 = \frac{16}{5} = 3.2$. Then, the volume of a biconvex with depth r is $\frac{1}{\beta_0}\left(\frac{4}{3}\pi r^3\right)$. The following lemma gives a lower bound of the volume of two intersecting biconvexes.

Lemma 1. *Assume $R > 0$ and $a_1, b_1, a_2, b_2 \in \mathbb{R}^3$. Let $z_1 = \frac{1}{2}(a_1 + b_1)$, $r_1 = \|a_1 - b_1\|$, $z_2 = \frac{1}{2}(a_2 + b_2)$, and $r_2 = \|a_2 - b_2\|$. If $r_1, r_2 \in \left[\frac{1}{2}R, R\right]$, $\|z_1 - z_2\| \le \sqrt{3}R$, $a_1, b_1 \notin L_{a_2 b_2}$, and $a_2, b_2 \notin L_{a_1 b_1}$, there exist a constant c such that*

$$|L_{a_1 b_1} \cup L_{a_2 b_2}| - |L_{a_1 b_1}| \ge cR^2 \|z_1 - z_2\|.$$

For any convex compact set $C \subset \mathbb{R}^3$, C_{-r} denotes the set of points in C that are away from ∂C by at least r. Next lemma gives a lower bound of the volume of C_{-r}.

Lemma 2. *Given a convex compact set $C \subset \mathbb{R}^3$ with diameter at most d, $|C_{-r}| \ge |C| - \pi d^2 r$.*

An ε-tessellation is a technique that divides the 3D space by vertical planes perpendicular to either x-axis or y-axis and horizontal planes perpendicular to z-axis into equal-size cubes, called cells, in which cells are with width ε. Without loss of generality, we assume the origin is a corner of cells. In a tessellation, a polycube is a collection of cells intersecting with a convex compact set. The x-span (and y-span, z-span, respectively) of a polycube is the distance measured in the number of cells in the x-direction (and y-direction, z-direction, respectively). If the span of a convex compact set is s and the width of cells is l, the span of the corresponding polycube is at most $\lceil s/l \rceil + 1$.

Lemma 3. *If a convex compact set S consists of m cubes and τ is a positive integer constant, the number of polycubes with span at most τ and intersecting with S is $\Theta(m)$.*

Next, we introduce a technique to obtain the Jacobian determinant in the change of variables that will be implicitly used in Subsection 3.2. Assume a tree topology is fixed over $x_1, x_2, \cdots, x_k \in \mathbb{R}^3$. Without loss of generality, we may assume (x_{k-1}, x_k) is one of edges. Let $z_{k-1} = \frac{1}{2}(x_{k-1} + x_k)$ and (r, ϕ, θ) be the spherical coordinate of x_k with the origin at z_{k-1}. In other words, $(x_k - z_{k-1})_X = r \sin \phi \cos \theta$, $(x_k - z_{k-1})_Y = r \sin \phi \sin \theta$, and $(x_k - z_{k-1})_Z = r \cos \phi$. For $1 \leq i \leq k - 2$, we use $p(x_i)$ to denote x_i's parent in the tree rooted at x_k, and let $z_i = \frac{1}{2}(x_i + p(x_i))$. Let $\mathbf{I}_3$ and $\mathbf{0}_3$ denote a 3×3 identity matrix and a 3×3 zero matrix respectively, and

$$\mathbf{J} = \begin{bmatrix} \sin \phi \cos \theta & r \cos \phi \cos \theta & -r \sin \phi \sin \theta \\ \sin \phi \sin \theta & r \cos \phi \sin \theta & r \sin \phi \cos \theta \\ \cos \phi & -\sin \phi & 0 \end{bmatrix}$$

be the Jacobian matrix corresponding to changing variables from the Cartesian coordinate to the spherical coordinate. Then, the Jacobian determinant for changing variables $x_1, \cdots, x_{k-1}, x_k$ by $z_1, \cdots, z_{k-1}, (r, \phi, \theta)$

is
$$\left| \frac{\partial(x_1, \cdots, x_{k-1}, x_k)}{\partial(z_1, \cdots, z_{k-1}, r, \phi, \theta)} \right| = \left| \frac{\partial(x_1 + p(x_1), \cdots, x_{k-1} + p(x_{k-1}), x_k)}{\partial(z_1, \cdots, z_{k-1}, r, \phi, \theta)} \right| = 8^{k-1} \left| \frac{\partial \left(\frac{x_1 + p(x_1)}{2}, \cdots, \frac{x_{k-1} + p(x_{k-1})}{2}, x_k \right)}{\partial(z_1, \cdots, z_{k-1}, r, \phi, \theta)} \right|$$

$$= 8^{k-1} \left| \frac{\partial \left(\frac{x_1 + p(x_1)}{2}, \cdots, \frac{x_{k-1} + p(x_{k-1})}{2}, x_k \right)}{\partial(z_1, \cdots, z_{k-1}, r, \phi, \theta)} \right|$$

$$= 8^{k-1} \left| \frac{\partial(z_1, \cdots, z_{k-1}, x_k - z_{k-1})}{\partial(z_1, \cdots, z_{k-1}, r, \phi, \theta)} \right| = 8^{k-1} \begin{vmatrix} \mathbf{I}_3 & \cdots & \mathbf{0}_3 & \mathbf{0}_3 \\ \vdots & \ddots & \vdots & \vdots \\ \mathbf{0}_3 & \cdots & \mathbf{I}_3 & \mathbf{0}_3 \\ \mathbf{0}_3 & \cdots & \mathbf{0}_3 & \mathbf{J} \end{vmatrix} = 8^{k-1} r^2 \sin \phi.$$ In the first

equality, each non-root variable is added by its parent variable. The equality stands since the Jacobian determinant is equal to 1 as we add one variable to another. Note that $\int_0^\pi \sin \phi \, d\phi = 2$.

2.4 Probabilistic Preliminaries

Let ϕ be the function over $(0, \infty)$ defined by $\phi(\mu) = 1 - \mu + \mu \ln \mu$. A straightforward calculation yields $\phi'(\mu) = \ln \mu$ and $\phi''(\mu) = 1/\mu$. Thus, ϕ is strictly convex and has the unique minimum zero at $\mu = 1$. Let $\phi^{-1} : [0, 1) \to (0, 1]$ be the inverse of the restriction of ϕ to $(0, 1]$. We define a function $\mathcal{L}$ over $(0, \infty)$ by

$$\mathcal{L}(\beta) = \begin{cases} \beta \phi^{-1}(1/\beta) & \text{if } \beta > 1, \\ 0 & \text{otherwise.} \end{cases}$$

It can be verified that $\mathcal{L}$ is a monotonic increasing function of β. The following lemma from [12] gives an estimation of the lower-tail distribution of Poisson RV's.

Lemma 4. *For any $\mu \in (0, 1)$, $\lim_{\lambda \to \infty} \Pr(Po(\lambda) \leq \mu \lambda) = \frac{1}{\sqrt{2\pi}} \frac{1}{\sqrt{\mu(1-\mu)}} \frac{1}{\sqrt{\lambda}} e^{-\lambda \phi(\mu)}$.*

The next lemma gives a lower bound for the minimum of a collection of Poisson RVs. Due to space limit, we ignore its detailed proof.

Lemma 5. *Assume that $\lim_{n \to \infty} \frac{\lambda_n}{\ln n} = \beta$ for some $\beta > 1$. Let $Y_1, Y_2, \cdots, Y_{I_n}$ be I_n Poisson RVs with means at least λ_n. If $I_n = o\left(n^s \sqrt{\ln n}\right)$ for some real number $s \in (0, 1]$, then for any $1 < \beta' < \beta$, $\min_{i=1}^{I_n} Y_i > s\mathcal{L}\left(\frac{1}{s}\beta'\right) \ln n$ a.a.s..*

At last, we state the Palm theory [4] on the Poisson process.

Theorem 1 ([4]). *Let $n > 0$. Suppose $k \in N$, and $h(\mathcal{Y}, \mathcal{X})$ is a bounded measurable function defined on all pairs of the form $(\mathcal{Y}, \mathcal{X})$ with $\mathcal{X} \subset \mathbb{R}^3$ being a finite subset and $\mathcal{Y}$ being a subset of $\mathcal{X}$, satisfying $h(\mathcal{Y}, \mathcal{X}) = 0$ except when $\mathcal{Y}$ has k elements. Then*

$$\mathbf{E}\left[\sum_{\mathcal{Y} \subseteq \mathcal{P}_n} h(\mathcal{Y}, \mathcal{P}_n)\right] = \frac{n^k}{k!} \mathbf{E}[h(\mathcal{X}_k, \mathcal{X}_k \cup \mathcal{P}_n)]$$

where the sum on the left side is over all subsets $\mathcal{Y}$ of the random Poisson point set $\mathcal{P}_n$, and on the right side the set $\mathcal{X}_k$ is a binomial process with k nodes, independent of $\mathcal{P}_n$.

We need to estimate the number of subsets with some specified topology, for example, two nodes are local minima w.r.t. each other. But it is not so easy to estimate this among Poisson point processes. The Palm theory allows us to place a set of random points first and then estimate the expectation over the Poisson point process. This technique will be used in Subsection 3.2 to prove Theorem 2(2).

3   Main Result: Critical Transmission Radius for 3D Greedy

The main result of our paper is the following theorem whose proof will be given in next two subsections.

Theorem 2. *Let $\beta_0 = 3.2$ and $n\left(\frac{4}{3}\pi r_n^3\right) = (\beta + o(1))\ln n$ for some $\beta > 0$. Then,*

1. *If $\beta > \beta_0$, then $\rho(\mathcal{P}_n) \leq r_n$ is a.a.s..*
2. *If $\beta < \beta_0$, then $\rho(\mathcal{P}_n) > r_n$ is a.a.s..*

To simplify the argument, we ignore boundary effects by assuming that there are nodes outside $\mathbb{D}$ with the same distribution. So, if necessary, packets can be routed through those nodes outside $\mathbb{D}$.

3.1   Upper Bound of Theorem 2

The upper bound in Theorem 2 is going to be proved through a technique called minimal scan statistics. For a finite point set V and a real number $r > 0$, we define $S(V, r) = \min_{u,v \in \mathbb{D}, \|u-v\|=r} \#(V \cap L_{uv})$. $S(V, r)$ is the minimal number of nodes of V that can be covered by a biconvex with depth r. We claim that the event $S(\mathcal{P}_n, r_n) > 0$ implies the event $\rho(\mathcal{P}_n) \leq r_n$. Assume to the contrary that $\rho(\mathcal{P}_n) > r_n$. Then there exist a pair of nodes u and v such that u is a local minimum w.r.t. to v. In other words, $\|u - v\| > r_n$ and no other nodes of $\mathcal{P}_n$ are in $B(u, r_n) \cap B(v, \|u - v\|)$. Let w be the intersection point of the segment uv and the sphere $\partial B(u, r_n)$. Since $L_{uw} \subset B(u, r_n) \cap B(v, \|u - v\|)$, this implies that L_{uw} contains no nodes of $\mathcal{P}_n$. Thus, $S(\mathcal{P}_n, r_n) = 0$, which is a contradiction. So, our claim is true.

   To have the lower bound of minimal scan statistics, we apply the tessellation technique to discretize the scanning process. We tessellate the deployment region by properly choosing cell size such that: (1) each copy of the biconvex contains a polycube with volume at least $\eta \frac{\ln n}{n}$ for some $\eta > 1$, and (2) the number of polycubes is $O\left(\frac{n}{\ln n}\right)$. Then, the next lemma follows Lemma 5.

Lemma 6. *Suppose that* $n\left(\frac{4}{3}\pi r_n^3\right) = (\beta + o(1))\ln n$ *for some* $\beta > \beta_0$. *Then for any constant* $\beta_1 \in (\beta_0, \beta)$, *it is a.a.s. that* $S\left(\mathcal{P}_n, r_n\right) > \mathcal{L}\left(\frac{\beta_1}{\beta_0}\right)\ln n$.

PROOF. Let $d = \sqrt{3}r_n$ which is the largest distance between any two points in a bi-convex. For a given β_1, choose a constant $\beta_2 \in (\beta_1, \beta)$, and let $\varepsilon = \frac{4}{27\beta_0}\left(1 - \frac{\beta_2}{\beta}\right)$. Consider an εd-tessellation. (Note that ε is chosen such that each copy of the bicon-vex contains a polycube with volume at least $\eta\frac{\ln n}{n}$ for some $\eta > 1$.) To prove this inequality, it is sufficient to show that any biconvex of two points in $\mathbb{D}$ that are sepa-rated by a distance of r_n contains a polycube with span at most $\frac{1}{\varepsilon}$ and volume at least $\frac{\beta_2}{\beta_0}\left(\frac{4}{3}\pi r_n^3\right)\frac{1}{\beta}$.

For a biconvex L, let P denote the polycube induced by $L_{-\sqrt{3}\varepsilon d}$. Then, $P \subseteq L$, and the span of P is at most $\left\lceil\frac{d - 2\sqrt{3}\varepsilon d}{\varepsilon d}\right\rceil + 1 < \frac{1}{\varepsilon}$. By Lemma 2 and the fact that $|L| = \frac{4}{3}\pi r_n^3\frac{1}{\beta_0} = \frac{4}{9\sqrt{3}}\pi d^3\frac{1}{\beta_0}$, we have $|P| \geq \left|L_{-\sqrt{3}\varepsilon d}\right| \geq |L| - \pi d^2\left(\sqrt{3}\varepsilon d\right) = |L| - \sqrt{3}\varepsilon\pi d^3 = |L| - \frac{27\beta_0}{4}\varepsilon|L| > |L|\left(1 - \frac{27\beta_0}{4}\varepsilon\right) = \frac{\beta_2}{\beta}|L| = \frac{\beta_2}{\beta_0}\left(\frac{4}{3}\pi r_n^3\right)\frac{1}{\beta}$.

Let I_n denote the number of polycubes in $\mathbb{D}$ with span at most $\frac{1}{\varepsilon}$ and volume at least $\frac{\beta_2}{\beta_0}\left(\frac{4}{3}\pi r_n^3\right)\frac{1}{\beta} = \left(\frac{\beta_2}{\beta_0} + o(1)\right)\frac{\ln n}{n}$, and Y_i be the number of nodes on the i-th poly-cubes. Then Y_i is a Poisson RV with rate at least $\left(\frac{\beta_2}{\beta_0} + o(1)\right)\ln n$. Since the number of cells in $\mathbb{D}$ is $O\left(\left(\frac{1}{\varepsilon d}\right)^3\right) = O\left(\frac{n}{\ln n}\right)$, by Lemma 3, $I_n = O\left(\frac{n}{\ln n}\right)$. By Lemma 5, it is a.a.s. that $\frac{\min_{i=1}^{I_n} Y_i}{\ln n} \geq \mathcal{L}\left(\frac{\beta_2}{\beta_0}\right) > \mathcal{L}\left(\frac{\beta_1}{\beta_0}\right)$. Thus, $S\left(\mathcal{P}_n, r_n\right) \geq \min_{i=1}^{I_n} Y_i$. $\qquad\square$

3.2   Lower Bound of Theorem 2

Theorem 2(2) can be proved by showing that if $r_n = \sqrt[3]{\frac{3\beta\ln n}{4\pi n}}$ for any $\beta < \beta_0$, there a.a.s. exists local minima. The space is going to be tessellated into equal-size cube cells. For each cell, an event that implies the existence of local minima in the cell is introduced, and a lower bound for the probability of the event is derived. Since these events are identical and independent over cells, we can estimate a probability lower of existence of local minima. By showing the lower bound is a.a.s. equal to 1, we prove Theorem 2(2). The detail is given below.

Let β_1 and β_2 be two positive constants such that $\max\left(\frac{1}{8}\beta_0, \beta\right) < \beta_1 < \beta_2 < \beta_0$. In addition, let R_1 and R_2 be given by $n\left(\frac{4}{3}\pi R_1^3\right) = \beta_1\ln n$ and $n\left(\frac{4}{3}\pi R_2^3\right) = \beta_2\ln n$, respectively. Since $\frac{1}{8}\beta_0 < \beta_1 < \beta_2 < \beta_0$, we have $\frac{1}{2}R_2 \leq R_1 \leq R_2$. Divide $\mathbb{D}$ by $\left(4\sqrt[3]{\frac{\ln n}{n\pi}}\right)$-tessellation. Let I_n denote the number of cells fully contained in $\mathbb{D}$. Here we have $I_n = O\left(\frac{n}{\ln n}\right)$. For each cell fully contained in $\mathbb{D}$, we draw a ball of radius $\frac{1}{2}\sqrt[3]{\frac{\ln n}{n\pi}}$ at the center of the cell. For $1 \leq i \leq I_n$, let E_i be the event that there exists two nodes $X, Y \in \mathcal{P}_n$ such that their midpoint is in the i-th ball, their distance is between R_1 and R_2, and there is no other node in L_{XY}. For any two nodes u and v with $\|u - v\| > r_n$, if there are no other nodes in L_{uv}, u and v are local minima w.r.t. each other. So, E_i implies existence of local minimum, and

$$\Pr\left[\rho\left(\mathcal{P}_n\right) > r_n\right] \geq \Pr\left[\text{at least one } E_i \text{ occurs}\right].$$

Let o_i denote the center of the i-th ball, and u, v be two points such that $\frac{1}{2}\left(u + v\right)$ is in the i-th ball and $R_1 \leq \|u - v\| \leq R_2$. By triangle inequality, for any point $w \in L_{uv}$, we have $\|w - o_i\| \leq \|w - \frac{1}{2}\left(u + v\right)\| + \|o_i - \frac{1}{2}\left(u + v\right)\| < \frac{\sqrt{3}}{2}\sqrt[3]{\frac{3\beta_0 \ln n}{4n\pi}} + \frac{1}{2}\sqrt[3]{\frac{\ln n}{n\pi}} <$ $2\sqrt[3]{\frac{\ln n}{n\pi}}$. Since the width of cells is $4\sqrt[3]{\frac{\ln n}{n\pi}}$, u, v, and L_{uv} are contained in the i-th cube. Therefore, $E_1, \cdots, E_{I_i}$ are independent. In addition, $E_1, \cdots, E_{I_i}$ are identical. Then,

$$\Pr\left[\text{none of } E_i \text{ occurs}\right] = \left(1 - \Pr\left[E_1\right]\right)^{I_n} \leq e^{-I_n \Pr(E_1)}.$$

If $I_n \Pr\left(E_1\right) \to \infty$, we may have $\Pr\left[\rho\left(\mathcal{P}_n\right) > r_n\right] \to 1$, and Theorem 2(2) follows. Next, we will prove that $I_n \Pr\left(E_1\right) \to \infty$.

First, we introduce several relevant events and derive their probabilities. Let A denote the disk with radius $\frac{1}{2}\sqrt[3]{\frac{\ln n}{n\pi}}$ at the center of the first cube. Assume V is a point set and $T \subset V$. Let $h_1\left(T, V\right)$ denote a function such that $h_1\left(T = \{x_1, x_2\}, V\right) = 1$ only if $\frac{1}{2}\left(x_1 + x_2\right) \in A$, $R_1 \leq \|x_1 - x_2\| \leq R_2$, and there is no other node of V in $L_{x_1 x_2}$; otherwise, $h_1\left(T, V\right) = 0$. In addition, under Boolean addition, for any $\{x_1, x_2, x_3\} \subseteq V$, let $h_2\left(\{x_1, x_2, x_3\}, V\right) = h_1\left(\{x_1, x_2\}, V\right) \cdot h_1\left(\{x_1, x_3\}, V\right) + h_1\left(\{x_2, x_1\}, V\right) \cdot h_1\left(\{x_2, x_3\}, V\right) + h_1\left(\{x_3, x_1\}, V\right) \cdot h_1\left(\{x_3, x_2\}, V\right)$; for any $\{x_1, x_2, x_3, x_4\} \subseteq V$, let $h_3\left(\{x_1, x_2, x_3, x_4\}, V\right) = h_1\left(\{x_1, x_2\}, V\right) \cdot h_1\left(\{x_3, x_4\}, V\right) + h_1\left(\{x_1, x_3\}, V\right) \cdot h_1\left(\{x_2, x_4\}, V\right) + h_1\left(\{x_1, x_4\}, V\right) \cdot h_1\left(\{x_2, x_3\}, V\right)$.

E_1 is the event that there exists two nodes $X, Y \in \mathcal{P}_n$ such that $h_1\left(\{X, Y\}, \mathcal{P}_n\right) = 1$. In the remaining of this subsection, we use X_1', X_2', X_3' and X_4' to denote elements of $\mathcal{P}_n$. Let $F_1'\left(\{X_1', X_2'\}\right)$ be the event that $h_1\left(\{X_1', X_2'\}, \mathcal{P}_n\right) = 1$; $F_2'\left(\{X_1', X_2', X_3'\}\right)$ be the event that $h_2\left(\{X_1', X_2', X_3'\}, \mathcal{P}_n\right) = 1$ which is the indicator of the event and $F_3'\left(\{X_1', X_2', X_3', X_4'\}\right)$ be the event that $h_3\left(\{X_1', X_2', X_3', X_4'\}, \mathcal{P}_n\right) = 1$. Applying Boole's inequalities, we have

$$\Pr\left[E_1\right] \geq \sum_{\{X_1', X_2'\} \subseteq \mathcal{P}_n} \Pr\left[F_1'\left(\{X_1', X_2'\}\right)\right] - \sum_{\{X_1', X_2', X_3'\} \subseteq \mathcal{P}_n} \Pr\left[F_2'\left(\{X_1', X_2', X_3'\}\right)\right]$$
$$- \sum_{\{X_1', X_2', X_3', X_4'\} \subseteq \mathcal{P}_n} \Pr\left[F_3'\left(\{X_1', X_2', X_3', X_4'\}\right)\right]. \tag{1}$$

For the sake of clarity, we use X_1, X_2, X_3 and X_4 to denote independent random points with uniform distribution over $\mathbb{D}$ and independent of $\mathcal{P}_n$. Let F_1 be the event that $h_1\left(\{X_1, X_2\}, \{X_1, X_2\} \cup \mathcal{P}_n\right) = 1$, F_2 be the event that $h_2(\{X_1, X_2, X_3\}, \{X_1, X_2, X_3\} \cup \mathcal{P}_n) = 1$, and F_3 be the event that $h_3(\{X_1, X_2, X_3, X_4\}, \{X_1, X_2, X_3, X_4\} \cup \mathcal{P}_n) = 1$. According to the Palm theory (Theorem 1), we have

$$\sum_{\{X_1', X_2'\} \subseteq \mathcal{P}_n} \Pr\left[F_1'\left(\{X_1', X_2'\}\right)\right] = \mathbf{E}\left[\sum_{\{X_1', X_2'\} \subseteq \mathcal{P}_n} h_1\left(\{X_1', X_2'\}, \mathcal{P}_n\right)\right]$$
$$= \frac{n^2}{2!}\mathbf{E}\left[h_1\left(\{X_1, X_2\}, \{X_1, X_2\} \cup \mathcal{P}_n\right)\right] = \frac{n^2}{2}\Pr\left[F_1\right]; \tag{2}$$

$$\sum_{\{X_1',X_2',X_3'\}\subseteq\mathcal{P}_n} \Pr\left[F_2'\left(\{X_1',X_2',X_3'\}\right)\right] = \mathbf{E}\left[\sum_{\{X_1',X_2',X_3'\}\subseteq\mathcal{P}_n} h_2\left(\{X_1',X_2',X_3'\},\mathcal{P}_n\right)\right]$$

$$= \frac{n^3}{3!}\mathbf{E}\left[h_2\left(\{X_1,X_2,X_3\},\{X_1,X_2,X_3\}\cup\mathcal{P}_n\right)\right] = 3\frac{n^3}{3!}\Pr\left[F_2\right] = \frac{n^3}{2}\Pr\left[F_2\right]; \qquad (3)$$

$$\sum_{\{X_1',X_2',X_3',X_4'\}\subseteq\mathcal{P}_n} \Pr\left[F_3'\left(\{X_1',X_2',X_3',X_4'\}\right)\right] = \mathbf{E}\left[\sum_{\{X_1',X_2',X_3',X_4'\}\subseteq\mathcal{P}_n} h_3\left(\{X_1',X_2',X_3',X_4'\},\mathcal{P}_n\right)\right]$$

$$= \frac{n^4}{4!}\mathbf{E}\left[h_3\left(\{X_1,X_2,X_3,X_4\},\{X_1,X_2,X_3,X_4\}\cup\mathcal{P}_n\right)\right] = 3\frac{n^4}{4!}\Pr\left[F_3\right] = \frac{n^4}{8}\Pr\left[F_3\right].$$

$$(4)$$

From Eq. (1), (2), (3), and (4), we have

$$\Pr\left[E_1\right] \geq \frac{n^2}{2}\Pr\left[F_1\right] - \frac{n^3}{2}\Pr\left[F_2\right] - \frac{n^4}{8}\Pr\left[F_3\right]. \qquad (5)$$

In the next, we will derive the probabilities of F_1, F_2, and F_3. Let S_1 denote the set $\left\{(x_1,x_2)\,\middle|\,\frac{1}{2}(x_1+x_2)\in A, R_1\leq\|x_1-x_2\|\leq R_2\right\}$. We have

$$\Pr\left[F_1\right] = \int\int_{S_1} \Pr\left[F_1\mid X_1=x_1, X_2=x_2\right]dx_1dx_2$$

$$= \int\int_{S_1} e^{-n|L_{x_1x_2}|}dx_1dx_2 = \int\int_{S_1} e^{-n\frac{1}{\beta_0}\left(\frac{4}{3}\pi\|x_1-x_2\|^3\right)}dx_1dx_2.$$

Let $z=\frac{x_1+x_2}{2}$ and $r=\frac{1}{2}\|x_1-x_2\|$. Then,

$$\Pr\left[F_1\right] = \int_{z\in A}\int_{r=\frac{R_1}{2}}^{\frac{R_2}{2}} e^{-\frac{n}{\beta_0}\frac{32}{3}\pi r^3}32\pi r^2 drdz = \int_{z\in A}\int_{r=\frac{R_1}{2}}^{\frac{R_2}{2}} e^{-\frac{n}{\beta_0}\frac{32}{3}\pi r^3}d\left(\frac{32}{3}\pi r^3\right)dz$$

$$= -\left(\frac{\beta_0}{n}e^{-\frac{n}{\beta_0}\frac{32}{3}\pi r^3}\bigg|_{r=\frac{R_1}{2}}^{\frac{R_2}{2}}\right)|A| = \frac{\beta_0}{6n^2}\left(n^{-\frac{\beta_1}{\beta_0}} - n^{-\frac{\beta_2}{\beta_0}}\right)\ln n. \qquad (6)$$

Let S_2 denote the set $\left\{(x_1,x_2,x_3)\,\middle|\,\begin{array}{l}\frac{x_1+x_2}{2},\frac{x_1+x_3}{2}\in A;\\ R_1\leq\|x_1-x_2\|\leq R_2; x_1,x_2\notin L_{x_1x_3};\\ R_1\leq\|x_1-x_3\|\leq R_2; x_1,x_3\notin L_{x_1x_2}\end{array}\right\}$. Applying Lemma 1, if $(x_1,x_2,x_3)\in S_2$, we have

$$\Pr\left[F_2\right] = \int\int\int_{S_2} \Pr\left[F_2\,\middle|\,\begin{array}{l}X_i=x_i\\ \forall i=1,2,3\end{array}\right]dx_1dx_2dx_3$$

$$\leq 3\int\int\int_{S_2} e^{-n|L_{x_1x_2}\cup L_{x_1x_3}|}dx_1dx_2dx_3$$

$$\leq 3\int\int\int_{S_2} e^{-n\left(\frac{1}{\beta_0}\frac{4}{3}\pi\|x_1-x_2\|^3+cR_2^2\left\|\frac{x_1+x_2}{2}-\frac{x_1+x_3}{2}\right\|\right)}dx_1dx_2dx_3.$$

Let $z_1 = \frac{x_1 + x_2}{2}$, $z_2 = \frac{x_1 + x_3}{2}$, $r = \frac{\|x_1 - x_2\|}{2}$, and $\rho = \|z_1 - z_2\|$. Then,

$$
\begin{aligned}
\Pr[F_2] &\leq 3 \int_{z_1 \in A} \int_{r=\frac{R_1}{2}}^{\frac{R_2}{2}} \int_{z_2 \in A} e^{-n\left(\frac{1}{\beta_0} \frac{32}{3} \pi r^3 + cR_2^2 \|z_1 - z_2\|\right)} \cdot 256\pi r^2 \, dr \, dz_1 \, dz_2 \\
&\leq 24 \int_{z_1 \in A} \int_{r=\frac{R_1}{2}}^{\frac{R_2}{2}} e^{-\frac{n}{\beta_0}\left(\frac{32}{3}\pi r^3\right)} d\left(\frac{32}{3}\pi r^3\right) dz_1 \cdot \int_{z_2 \in A} e^{-cnR_2^2 \|z_1 - z_2\|} dz_2 \\
&\leq 24 \int_{z_1 \in A} \int_{r_1 = \frac{R_1}{2}}^{\frac{R_2}{2}} e^{-\frac{n}{\beta_0}\left(\frac{32}{3}\pi r^3\right)} d\left(\frac{32}{3}\pi r^3\right) dz_1 \cdot \int_{\rho=0}^{\infty} e^{-cnR_2^2 \rho} 4\pi \rho^2 \, d\rho \\
&= 24 \left(\frac{\beta_0}{6n^2}\left(n^{-\frac{\beta_1}{\beta_0}} - n^{-\frac{\beta_2}{\beta_0}}\right) \ln n\right) \left(\frac{8\pi}{(cnR_2^2)^3}\right) \\
&= \frac{32\pi \beta_0}{c^3 \left(nR_2^3\right)^2 n^3} \left(n^{-\frac{\beta_1}{\beta_0}} - n^{-\frac{\beta_2}{\beta_0}}\right) \ln n.
\end{aligned}
\tag{7}
$$

Let S_3 denote the set $\left\{ (x_1, x_2, x_3, x_4) \,\middle|\, \begin{array}{l} \frac{x_1 + x_2}{2}, \frac{x_3 + x_4}{2} \in A; \\ R_1 \leq \|x_1 - x_2\| \leq R_2; x_1, x_2 \notin L_{x_3 x_4}; \\ R_1 \leq \|x_3 - x_4\| \leq R_2; x_3, x_4 \notin L_{x_1 x_2} \end{array} \right\}$. Applying Lemma 1, if $(x_1, x_2, x_3, x_4) \in S_3$, we have

$$
\begin{aligned}
\Pr[F_3] &= \int \int \int \int_{S_3} \Pr\left[F_3 \,\middle|\, \begin{array}{l} X_i = x_i, \\ \forall i = 1, 2, 3, 4 \end{array}\right] dx_1 dx_2 dx_3 dx_4 \\
&\leq 3 \int \int \int \int_{S_3} e^{-n|L_{x_1 x_2} \cup L_{x_3 x_4}|} dx_1 dx_2 dx_3 dx_4 \\
&\leq 3 \int \int \int \int_{S_3} e^{-n\left(\frac{1}{\beta_0} \frac{4}{3}\pi \|x_1 - x_2\|^3 + cR_2^2 \left\|\frac{x_1 + x_2}{2} - \frac{x_3 + x_4}{2}\right\|\right)} \cdot dx_1 dx_2 dx_3 dx_4.
\end{aligned}
$$

Let $z_1 = \frac{x_1 + x_2}{2}$, $r_1 = \frac{\|x_1 - x_2\|}{2}$, $z_2 = \frac{x_3 + x_4}{2}$, $r_2 = \frac{\|x_3 - x_4\|}{2}$, and $\rho = \|z_1 - z_2\|$. Then,

$$
\begin{aligned}
\Pr[F_3] &\leq 3 \int_{z_1 \in A} \int_{r_1 = \frac{R_1}{2}}^{\frac{R_2}{2}} \int_{z_2 \in A} \int_{r_2 = \frac{R_1}{2}}^{\frac{R_2}{2}} e^{-n\left(\frac{1}{\beta_0} \frac{32}{3} \pi r_1^3 + cR_2^2 \|z_1 - z_2\|\right)} \cdot \left(32\pi r_1^2 dr_1 dz_1\right) \left(32\pi r_2^2 dr_2 dz_2\right) \\
&\leq 3 \left(\int_{z_1 \in A} \int_{r_1 = \frac{R_1}{2}}^{\frac{R_2}{2}} e^{-\frac{n}{\beta_0} \frac{32}{3} \pi r_1^3} d\left(\frac{32}{3}\pi r^3\right) dz\right) \left(32\pi \left(\frac{R_2}{2}\right)^2 \left(\frac{R_2}{2} - \frac{R_1}{2}\right) \int_{\rho=0}^{\infty} e^{-cnR_2^2 \rho} 4\pi \rho^2 d\rho\right) \\
&= \frac{16\pi^2 \beta_0}{c^3 \left(nR_2^3\right) n^4} \left(1 - \frac{R_1}{R_2}\right) \left(n^{-\frac{\beta_1}{\beta_0}} - n^{-\frac{\beta_2}{\beta_0}}\right) \ln n.
\end{aligned}
\tag{8}
$$

Put Eq. (5), (6), (7) and (8) together. We have

$$
\begin{aligned}
\Pr[E_1] &\geq \left(\frac{\beta_0}{12} - \frac{16\pi \beta_0}{c^3 \left(nR_2^3\right)^2} - \frac{2\pi^2 \beta_0}{c^3 \left(nR_2^3\right)} \left(1 - \frac{R_1}{R_2}\right)\right) \left(n^{-\frac{\beta_1}{\beta_0}} - n^{-\frac{\beta_2}{\beta_0}}\right) \ln n \\
&\sim \frac{\beta_0}{12} \left(n^{-\frac{\beta_1}{\beta_0}} - n^{-\frac{\beta_2}{\beta_0}}\right) \ln n.
\end{aligned}
$$

Since $I_n = \Omega\left(\frac{\ln n}{n}\right)$, we have $\Pr[E_1] = \Omega\left(\left(n^{-\frac{\beta_1}{\beta_0}} - n^{-\frac{\beta_2}{\beta_0}}\right) \ln n\right)$, and $I_n \Pr[E_1] = \Omega\left(n^{1 - \frac{\beta_1}{\beta_0}}\right) \to \infty$. This complete the proof of Theorem 2(2).

4   Simulation

We have analyzed the theoretical bounds of the critical transmission radius for 3D greedy routing. To confirm our theoretical analysis, we conduct several simulations to see what is the practical value of transmission radius (r) such that greedy can guarantee the packet delivery with high probability in random networks.

Critical Transmission Radius for Random Networks: We randomly generate 1000 networks with n wireless nodes in a $20 \times 20 \times 20$ cubic region, where n is from 100 to 500. For each network V, we compute the critical transmission radius $\rho(V)$ by definition (the equation in Section 2.1). Figure 2 gives the histograms of the distribution of $\rho(V)$ for 1000 random networks. Figure 4(a) shows the probability distribution function of $\rho(V)$. It is clear that the critical transmission radius satisfies a transition phenomena, i.e., there is a radius r_0 such that the greedy can successfully deliver the packet when $r > r_0$ and can not deliver the packet when $r < r_0$. We also find that the transition becomes faster when the number of nodes increases. Notice that the practical value of $\rho(V)$ is larger than the theoretical bound in our analysis. Remember the theoretical bound is true for $n \rightarrow \infty$. However, the practical value will approach the theoretical bound with the increasing of n. When $n = 500$, it already becomes very near the theoretical bound. When $n = 500$, the theoretical bound is $\sqrt[3]{\frac{3\beta_0 \ln n}{4\pi n}} \times 20 = 0.212 \times 20 = 4.24$ for a $20 \times 20 \times 20$ cubic region.

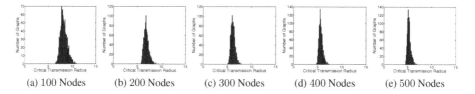

| (a) 100 Nodes | (b) 200 Nodes | (c) 300 Nodes | (d) 400 Nodes | (e) 500 Nodes |

Fig. 2. The distribution of $\rho(V)$ for random networks with 100-500 nodes

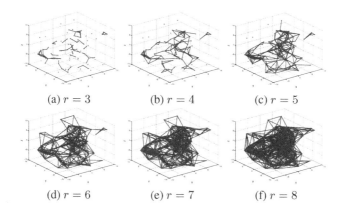

| (a) $r = 3$ | (b) $r = 4$ | (c) $r = 5$ |

| (d) $r = 6$ | (e) $r = 7$ | (f) $r = 8$ |

Fig. 3. Network topologies with 100 nodes when r is from 3 to 8

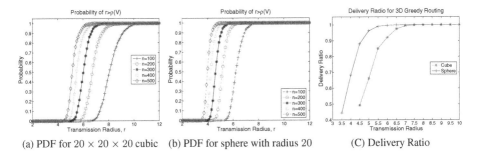

(a) PDF for $20 \times 20 \times 20$ cubic   (b) PDF for sphere with radius 20   (C) Delivery Ratio

Fig. 4. (a) and (b): the probability distribution function of $\rho(V)$ for cubic and sphere networks; (c): delivery ratio for 100-node random networks with various r

Delivery Ratio of Greedy Routing with Various Transmission Radii. We implement the 3D greedy routing in our simulator. By setting various transmission radii, we generate 100 random networks with 100 wireless nodes again in a $20 \times 20 \times 20$ cubic region. Figure 3 shows a set of examples when the transmission radius r is from 3 to 8. Notice that when $r \leq 5$, the network is not connected. In this simulation, we only consider the connected networks. We randomly select 100 source-destination pairs for each connected network and test the 3D greedy routing. Figure 4(c) (the blue curve marked by crosses) illustrate the average delivery ratio of 3D greedy routing. Clearly, the delivery ratio increases when r increases. After r is larger than a certain value, it always guarantee the delivery. This also confirms our theoretical analysis. In addition, from Figure 3 and Figure 4(c), we can conclude that the CTR for greedy routing (approaching 100% delivery ratio when r is around 7 in Figure 4(c)) is just a little bit larger than the CTR for connectivity (network becomes connected when r is around 6 in Figure 3).

Besides deploying random networks in a cubic region, we also performed simulations for networks deployed in a spherical region (with 20 as its radius). Figure 4(b) gives the probability distribution function of $\rho(V)$ and Figure 4(c)(the red curve marked by stars) illustrates the average delivery ratio of 3D greedy routing. The conclusions from these simulations are consistent with the simulations for random network deployed in cubic region.

5 Conclusion

In this paper, we study the critical transmission radius for 3D greedy routing which leads to a delivery-guaranteed 3D localized routing. We theoretically prove that for a random 3D network, formed by nodes that are generated by a Poisson point process of density n over a convex compact region of unit volume, the critical transmission radius for 3D greedy routing is a.a.s. $\sqrt[3]{\frac{3\beta_0 \ln n}{4\pi n}}$, where $\beta_0 = 3.2$. This theoretical result answers a fundamental question about how large the transmission radius should be set in a 3D networks, such that the greedy routing guarantees the delivery of packets between any two nodes. We also conduct extensive simulations to confirm our theoretical results.

References

1. Abdallah, A., Fevens, T., Opatrny, J.: Power-aware 3D position-based routing algorithm for ad hoc networks. In: Proc. of IEEE ICC (2007)
2. Akyildiz, I.F., Pompili, D., Melodia, T.: Underwater acoustic sensor networks: research challenges. Ad Hoc Networks 3(3), 257–279 (2005)
3. Alam, S.M.N., Haas, Z.J.: Coverage and connectivity in three-dimensional networks. In: Proc. of ACM Mobicom (2006)
4. Baccelli, F., Bremaud, P.: Elements of Queueing Theory: Palm-Martingale Calculus and Stochastic Recurrences. Springer, Heidelberg (2003)
5. Bose, P., Morin, P., Stojmenovic, I., Urrutia, J.: Routing with guaranteed delivery in ad hoc wireless networks. ACM/Kluwer Wireless Networks 7(6) (2001)
6. Durocher, S., Kirkpatrick, D., Narayanan, L.: On routing with guaranteed delivery in three-dimensional ad hoc wireless networks. In: Rao, S., Chatterjee, M., Jayanti, P., Murthy, C.S.R., Saha, S.K. (eds.) ICDCN 2008. LNCS, vol. 4904, pp. 546–557. Springer, Heidelberg (2008)
7. Kao, G., Fevens, T., Opatrny, J.: Position-based routing on 3D geometric graphs in mobile ad hoc networks. In: Proc. of CCCG 2005 (2005)
8. Karp, B., Kung, H.: GPSR: Greedy perimeter stateless routing for wireless networks. In: Proc. of the ACM Int'l Conf. on Mobile Computing and Networking (2000)
9. Kuhn, F., Wattenhofer, R., Zollinger, A.: Worst-Case Optimal and Average-Case Efficient Geometric Ad-Hoc Routing. In: Proc. of ACM MobiHoc (2003)
10. Pompili, D., Melodia, T.: Three-dimensional routing in underwater acoustic sensor networks. In: Proceedings of ACM PE-WASUN 2005, Montreal, Canada (October 2005)
11. Ravelomanana, V.: Extremal properties of three-dimensional sensor networks with applications. IEEE Transactions on Mobile Computing 3(3), 246–257 (2004)
12. Wan, P.-J., Yi, C.-W., Yao, F., Jia, X.: Asymptotic critical transmission radius for greedy forward routing in wireless ad hoc networks. In: Proc. of ACM Mobihoc (2006)
13. Wang, Y., Li, F., Dahlberg, T.: Power efficient 3-dimensional topology control for ad hoc and sensor networks. In: Proc. of IEEE GlobeCom (2006)
14. Xie, P., Cui, J.-H., Lao, L.: VBF: Vector-based forwarding protocol for underwater sensor networks. In: Proceedings of IFIP Networking 2006 (2006)

Landmarks Selection Algorithm for Virtual Coordinates Routing

Sergey Baskakov

Information Systems and Telecommunications Department
Bauman Moscow State Technical University
Moscow, Russian Federation
sergey.baskakov@mail.ru

Abstract. In this paper, we propose a distributed, self-organized land-marks selection algorithm which ensures different patterns of landmarks spread throughout deployment area of a wireless sensor network. The algorithm is highly scalable through decentralized implementation with low time and memory complexity. The proposed technique represents an optimal complexity algorithm for virtual coordinates routing protocols in large-scale wireless sensor networks, and our simulations show that it improves significantly virtual coordinates routing protocols performance, preserving simplicity and high scalability of this routing method.

1 Introduction

Routing in wireless sensor networks (WSN) is one of the most challenging and actual research areas, since routing protocol performance has a significant impact on overall network efficiency. Many emerging WSN applications and data dissemination methods (e.g. data-centric storage) require scalable and reliable point-to-point routing service. Such service could be implemented with either real or virtual coordinates routing techniques.

Geographic routing protocols, e.g. GPSR [1], use physical space location information, the real coordinates, for greedy packet forwarding. The protocols have been considered as one of the most promising solutions for providing point-to-point routing in large-scale WSNs, because they operate via only local interactions between neighboring nodes and require constant per-node state. However, geographic routing protocols efficiency degrades under realistic operation in presence of voids and localization errors.

Recently, Virtual Coordinates Routing (VCR) approach has been proposed to retain the stateless point-to-point routing ability and to eliminate the shortcomings of the traditional geographic routing technique. VCR protocols such as BVR [2], LCR [3,4], Hop ID [5], VCap [6] and HGR [7] assign each node virtual coordinates - a vector of hop counts to a small fixed set of reference nodes called landmarks (also called beacons or anchors). Virtual coordinates serve as geographic locations for greedy forwarding by minimizing the distance between the current node and the destination. In case a local minimum is reached, the protocols use a backtracking mode to guarantee packet delivery at the expense of path length increase.

Y. Li et al. (Eds.): WASA 2008, LNCS 5258, pp. 17–28, 2008.

Virtual coordinates are based on connectivity information and not on physical positions and distances; therefore, VCR protocols are insensitive to voids and location errors. Moreover, a routing protocol may automatically adapt to network topology dynamics through a periodic refresh of virtual coordinates.

Known VCR protocols vary by details such as virtual distance metric, landmarks count and their selection scheme, as well as backtracking mode algorithm. The overall protocol efficiency is predetermined primarily by greedy forwarding success rate, which depends on distance metric and landmarks distribution pattern. In this paper, we cover in detail the landmarks selection problem, a challenging issue that has been only minimally addressed by other works on VCR.

The landmarks selection problem is to find such a landmark placement over network deployment area that will result in a high success rate of greedy routing. Obviously, it is desirable to use as fewer landmarks as possible in order to minimize overhead due to storage (per-node state) and transmission (per-packet state) of virtual coordinates. Moreover, since no manual configuration is possible in most application scenarios, the self-organizing nature of WSN requires automatic landmarks selection from normal nodes.

Beacon Vector Routing [2] and Hop ID [5] protocols select landmarks randomly. Such scheme has simple implementation, but it cannot guarantee uniform landmark distribution. For this reason, we should use more landmarks (up to several dozens) to reduce the protocol's sensitivity to a randomly sampled reference nodes placement. Thus, the random landmarks selection approach yields stable greedy mode efficiency at the expense of the protocols' higher overhead.

Works such as [4,6,7] propose usage of boundary nodes as landmarks and show that such placement improves VCR protocol performance as compared to the random selection scheme.

In [6], boundary nodes are automatically found by a special algorithm. However, the algorithm is capable to select only 3 landmarks; its expansion for a larger number of landmarks requires more complicated heuristics.

The original paper on LCR [3] assumes that landmarks are manually placed at the boundaries of the deployment area. Obviously, manually controlled landmarks selection complicates large-scale WSN deployments or is even impossible in many applications scenarios. Hence, in the later work [4], authors proposed a distributed and self-organized algorithm that allows selecting any necessary number of landmarks along the network perimeter. Later we show, however, that the LCR landmarks selection algorithm's drawback is dependence of its memory complexity on the network scale.

Thus, algorithms, proposed in other works besides [4], do not provide automatic selection of any fixed number of landmark nodes in wireless mesh network. In this paper, we fill in the gap by proposing a distributed algorithm for automatic landmarks selection, taking place both at the network initialization phase and after possible landmarks failures during the operation. Depending on a chosen version, the algorithm ensures that landmarks are evenly spread throughout the deployment area or placed uniformly along the topology boundary. At the same time, our algorithm has lower memory complexity than the analogue from [4].

2   Landmarks Selection Algorithm

We consider wireless sensor network consisting of n nodes randomly placed on a plane covering A m^2 area. We assume that network topology is static and nodes have a radio communication range of r m. Thus, the average network density, i.e. the average neighborhood size, is $\rho = n\pi r^2/A$ nodes. We estimate the network diameter d - the maximum value among lengths of the shortest paths between all nodes pairs - with the following formula,

$$d \approx \frac{\sqrt{A}}{r} = \sqrt{\frac{\pi n}{\rho}}. \tag{1}$$

Note, if nodes are deployed in 3-dimensional space with volume A_{3D} m^3, the network diameter is given by

$$d \approx \frac{\sqrt[3]{A_{3D}}}{r} = \sqrt[3]{\frac{4}{3}\pi\frac{n}{\rho}}, \tag{2}$$

but anyway the proposed algorithm does not require any revisions.

The landmarks selection algorithm chooses n_L ($n_L \leq n$) landmark nodes from original nodes set V ($|V| = n$), resulting in landmark nodes set V_L ($V_L \subseteq V$). The landmarks selection criterion depends on their desired distribution. Current algorithm versions may produce one of two landmark placement patterns:

- even spread out at maximum distances from each other;
- uniform placement along the network boundary.

At first, we describe briefly the centralized algorithm implementation to show its general idea. Then we give details for its distributed implementation.

2.1   Centralized Algorithm Implementation

General algorithm structure could be divided into 3 sequential phases.

Initiator Node Selection. At this stage, we choose randomly one node that initiates a landmarks selection procedure by broadcasting beacon packets, receiving such packets all other nodes calculate their distances to the initiator node. In this paper, we define distance between the nodes as the shortest path length in a hops count; however, other link metrics are admissible without any need for algorithm modification.

The First Landmark Selection. After all the nodes have measured distances to the initiator, the most distant node is selected as the first landmark, i.e.

$$l_1 = \underset{v \in V}{\operatorname{argmax}}\, h_0(v), \tag{3}$$

where $h_0(v)$ - distance between node v and the initiator node.

The selected node starts to function as the landmark, and the initiator becomes an ordinary node after receiving the first beacon packet from the landmark l_1.

Other Landmarks Selection. Subsequent landmarks selection is based on a special voting function, which value for a node defines its priority to be declared as a landmark.

The voting function may have different appearances depending on the desired landmark placement. In this paper, we offer two voting functions:

$$f_{min}(\boldsymbol{v}, L) = \min_{i \in L} v_i \qquad (4)$$

and

$$f_{prod}(\boldsymbol{v}, L) = \prod_{i \in L} v_i, \qquad (5)$$

where
$\boldsymbol{v}$ - virtual coordinates vector of node $v \in V$, $\boldsymbol{v} = \{v_i\}_{i=1}^{n_L}$;
v_i - i-th coordinate of node v;
L - set of active landmarks indices.

The second and next landmarks are selected sequentially: the k-th landmark is the node with the maximum votes, i.e.

$$l_k = \operatorname*{argmax}_{v \in V} f(\boldsymbol{v}, L_k), 2 \leq k \leq n_L. \qquad (6)$$

This iterative algorithm results in a landmarks set $V_L = \{l_1, l_2, \ldots, l_{n_L}\}$. If we use voting function (4) in (6), landmarks will be evenly spread throughout the deployment area, and function (5) selects landmarks among nodes located at the network boundary.

Figures 1 and 2 demonstrate landmarks selection algorithm output for large-scale dense and small-scale sparse networks. Landmarks are denoted as large circles with indicated assignment sequence numbers.

Placing landmarks at maximum distances from each other prevents their concentration in separate network areas, so both voting functions tend primarily to select landmarks from boundary nodes as these nodes are the most mutually distant ones. Then, however, $f_{min}(v, L)$ function exploits nodes in the network center, such strategy results in uniform landmarks spread throughout the deployment area. On the other hand, voting function $f_{prod}(v, L)$ selects all landmarks from boundary nodes, which causes even placement of the landmarks along the network perimeter.

Voting functions use only those vector components that correspond to landmarks active at the moment of votes calculation. Thus, in case of the sequential selection, active landmarks indices set is equal to $L_k = \{1, 2, \ldots, k - 1\}$.

Obviously, it is possible that several nodes have equal maximum number of votes. Such conflict may be resolved by various techniques. For instance, considering uniqueness of nodes identifiers, or addresses, a node with a higher, or lower, address gets priority.

Landmark Substitution. One or more landmarks may fail during network operation. In such cases, substitution for the m-th landmark can be found with (6) calculated over set $L = \{1, 2, \ldots, m - 1, m + 1, \ldots, n_L\}$.

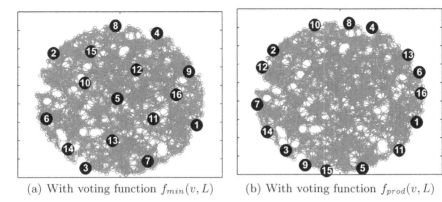

(a) With voting function $f_{min}(v, L)$ (b) With voting function $f_{prod}(v, L)$

Fig. 1. Landmarks selection results for large-scale dense network

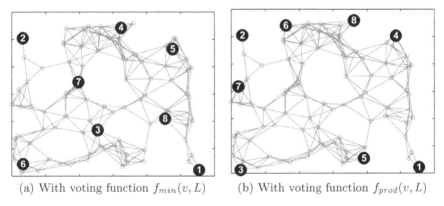

(a) With voting function $f_{min}(v, L)$ (b) With voting function $f_{prod}(v, L)$

Fig. 2. Landmarks selection results for small-scale sparse network

2.2   Distributed Algorithm Implementation

The distributed algorithm implementation is intended for practical use and implies that each node performs the same set of operations without any centralized control.

Initialization. At startup, each node $v \in V$ initializes its virtual coordinates $\boldsymbol{v} = \{v_i = \infty\}_{i=1}^{n_L}$, clears the neighborhood table and sets timers for two independent periodical processes:

- local neighborhood exchange process with period t_n;
- landmarks selection process with period t_{ls}.

At this moment, all nodes are equal, there are no landmarks in the network and nodes should select among themselves n_L landmarks in a distributed manner.

Local Neighborhood Exchange Process. In Local Neighborhood Exchange process nodes periodically broadcast special beacon packets to discover their neighbors and to update connectivity information according to the actual topology state. Beacon packets broadcasting is used for virtual coordinate system construction like in any VCR protocol, and we just put into such packets some additional information described further. Local neighborhood exchange period t_n defines reactivity to topology dynamics, and thus it can be considered as the VCR protocol parameter independent of the network scale.

Landmarks Selection Process. This process means that each node checks with period t_{ls} the necessity to vest itself with a function of landmark. Every time the timer expires each node $v \in V$ executes the following algorithm.

If v is already the landmark (or initiator), or all n_L landmarks are elected, it stops current iteration and resets the timer.

If v does not know any landmarks, i.e. $L(v) = \emptyset$, it declares itself as the initiator node and also exits this procedure.

If the initiator node or some landmarks ($|L(v)| < n_L$) are already active, then the index of the next selected node is

$$k = \min \{i : 1 \le i \le n_L, i \notin L(v)\} \tag{7}$$

and node v calculates its votes to become the k-th landmark:

$$p(v, L(v)) = \begin{cases} h_0(v), & \text{for } k = 1; \\ f(v, L(v)), & \text{for } 1 < k \le n_L. \end{cases} \tag{8}$$

Similarly, node v takes count of votes for its neighbors from the subset $\{w : w \in N(v), L(w) = L(v)\}$ (where $N(v)$ is the total set of v's one-hop neighbors) and finds neighbor q with maximum votes count $p(q, L(q))$. If inequality

$$p(v, L(v)) > p(q, L(q)) \tag{9}$$

holds, v declares itself as the k-th landmark. If v and q have an equal number of votes, we also can use their addresses for conflict resolution as described above.

In its beacon packets, the landmark includes a votes count and set $L(v)$ that took place at the moment of its election. We denote these values as $\hat{p}_i$ and $\hat{L}_i$ for the i-th landmark.

Obviously, the described landmarks selection procedure could be executed both periodically and asynchronously on detection of landmark failure, but t_{ls} value should be such that all nodes have enough time to compute distance to the recently selected landmark. The minimum permissible value of t_{ls} is equal to the worst case delay of beacon packet propagation from a landmark to all other nodes.

Landmarks Priorities Rules. A situation where several landmarks present with equal indices is obviously unavoidable, because nodes analyze only local information while making a decision about the landmarks selection. Therefore, we propose the landmarks prioritizing algorithm to suppress redundant landmarks in a distributed manner.

As described above, nodes periodically broadcast beacon packets, and at reception of such packet from neighbor q node v gets the following information about q:

- virtual coordinates vector $\boldsymbol{q} = \{q_i\}_{i=1}^{n_L}$;
- set of known to q landmarks indices $L(q)$;
- for each i-th landmark $l_i(q)$ known to q, i.e $i \in L(q)$:
  - number of votes $\hat{p}_i(q)$ at the moment of $l_i(q)$ appointment;
  - known landmarks indices set $\hat{L}_i(q)$ at the moment of $l_i(q)$ appointment.

After reception of beacon packet from q, node v executes the following procedure for each i-th landmark.

If v and $l_i(q)$ are both i-th landmark, but v had fewer votes, i.e. $\hat{p}(v) < \hat{p}_i(q)$, it stops functioning as a landmark and becomes ordinary node.

If ordinary, i.e. non-landmark, node v has no information about i-th landmark, it accepts node $l_i(q)$ as a landmark only in case of a lower votes count, i.e. the inequality $p(v, \hat{L}_i(q)) < \hat{p}_i(q)$ is checked. Notice that we use $\hat{L}_i(q)$ set to calculate v's votes for such comparison.

If v already knows another i-th landmark, it agrees to accept $l_i(q)$ as the new one only if $l_i(q)$ had more votes than $l_i(v)$ at the moment of appointment, i.e. in case the inequality $\hat{p}_i(v) < \hat{p}_i(q)$ holds.

3   Algorithm Complexity Analysis

In this section, we estimate time and memory complexity of the distributed algorithm implementation. Time complexity stands for the total time required to select n_L landmarks in a newly deployed network. Memory complexity is the amount of each node's memory resources required to maintain the algorithm state.

We assume that the initiator node selection overhead is negligible. The first and the following landmarks are selected in sequence with time steps proportional to the worst case delay of beacon packet propagation $O(dt_n)$, but the distributed algorithm implementation requires additional time reserve to suppress duplicate landmarks. Therefore, taking into account that t_n is the routing protocol setting parameter independent of network scale, we get an equation for the algorithm time complexity:

$$T = O\left(2n_L d\right). \tag{10}$$

The (10) is the convergence time of the distributed algorithm and relates to any network topology and arbitrary (not only uniform) nodes placement over deployment area.

On average, each node has ρ one-hop neighbors and should maintain information about them in order to decide about declaring itself as the landmark. Thus, the algorithm memory complexity is equal to

$$M = O\left(n_L \rho\right), \tag{11}$$

because per-neighbor state overhead is $O\left(n_L\right)$.

In general, VCR protocols set n_L as a constant independent of total nodes count n, and in the majority of cases the relation $n_L \ll n$ holds. Therefore, we have the following algorithm complexity estimates for large-scale networks:

$$\tilde{T} = O(d), \tag{12}$$

$$\tilde{M} = O(\rho). \tag{13}$$

Obviously, any VCR protocol (regardless of landmarks assignment method) requires $O(d)$ time to construct a virtual coordinates system, because such time is necessary for beacon packets to propagate throughout the network, and $O(\rho)$ memory to store the neighborhood table. Hence, if some distributed landmarks selection algorithm has $O(d)$ execution time, uses $O(\rho)$ memory to maintain data about one-hop neighbors and results in both landmarks selected and virtual coordinates calculated by every node, then such algorithm is *optimal* for application in VCR protocols.

Therefore, the proposed landmarks selection algorithm is optimal for VCR protocols in large-scale networks, in which $n_L \ll n$ and n_L is a constant.

4   Comparison with LCR Algorithm

Cao et al. proposed originally Logical Coordinate Routing protocol in [3] and they complemented it with distributed landmarks selection algorithm in [4]. Their algorithm also allows to assign any fixed number of landmarks from boundary nodes but uses different voting function and selection procedure.

The LCR landmarks selection algorithm and the proposed here one, when used with voting function $f_{prod}(v, L)$ (5), induce almost similar placement of landmarks, but differ in time and memory complexity. Therefore, we compare only algorithmic complexity of these two landmarks selection techniques. Unfortunately, there is no algorithm complexity analysis in [4], so we have performed the analysis ourselves and here present only the final results for large-scale networks, omitting the detailed algorithm description for brevity purposes.

Assuming the inequality $n_L \ll n$ holds and n_L is a constant, the LCR landmarks selection algorithm time and memory complexity are equal to

$$\tilde{T}_{LCR} = O(d), \tag{14}$$

$$\tilde{M}_{LCR} = O(\rho + n/\rho) = O(\rho + d^2) \tag{15}$$

for 2D-space placement and

$$\tilde{M}_{LCR} = O(\rho + n/\rho) = O(\rho + d^3) \tag{16}$$

for 3D-space deployment.

Time complexity of both algorithms is proportional to network diameter d, because $O(d)$ is the worst-case propagation delay of a beacon packet; however, our algorithm executes in $2n_L$ times longer (see (10)) than the LCR landmarks selection algorithm as we select landmarks in series. However, in case of the large-scale networks, its time complexity could also be estimated as $O(d)$. Thus, both algorithms are optimal for VCR protocols in terms of time complexity.

In terms of memory complexity our algorithm is absolutely scalable as its memory requirements depend only on nodes deployment density ρ and are not affected by total nodes count n or network diameter d. Algorithm exploits only local information about one-hop neighborhood that is also required by any VCR protocol, so in a sense of memory complexity, it is optimal for virtual coordinates routing.

On the other hand, according to (15) and (16) the LCR landmarks selection algorithm memory complexity depends linearly on network size n and quadratically (or in third-degree for 3D-space deployment) on diameter. Therefore, it does not have the scalability property to the full extent, and its application in large-scale networks may entail implementation difficulties.

5   Simulations

We implemented basic virtual coordinates routing framework and distributed version of the proposed landmarks selection algorithm in discrete event simulation system, OMNeT++ ver. 3.2 combined with Mobility Framework ver. 2.0, to study expedience of algorithm introduction into VCR protocols. We simulate performance of only a network layer, not taking into account such issues as packet losses due to errors, collisions, buffers overflows, etc.

In our simulations, we generate random network topologies according to given parameters (nodes count n, network density ρ and diameter d). Nodes are uniformly distributed over the deployment square field with area A m^2 and communication range $r = 50$ m. We randomly choose 100 nodes to be source and destination pairs, so the results of each simulation run are averaged over 9900 paths. If network size is less than 100 nodes, all of them exchange packets. Ordinary Euclidean norm is used as a virtual distance metric.

We compare effectiveness of virtual coordinates routing technique under 3 different landmarks placement strategies:

- random placement;
- uniform spread throughout deployment area (Fig. 1(a));
- network boundary placement (Fig. 1(b)).

Figure 3(a) shows greedy mode packets delivery success rate under variable nodes count n under fixed network density $\rho = 10$ nodes (network diameter varies from 8 to 35 hops). Figure 3(b) demonstrates impact of one-hop neighborhood size ρ under fixed network diameter $d = 10$ hops (nodes count varies from 23 to 358).

The number of landmarks n_L is set to 4 and 8. If landmarks count is 4, the algorithm gives almost the same landmarks placement for both voting functions (see Fig. 1), therefore, results, obtained for uniform and boundary placement of 4 landmarks, are shown in common plots.

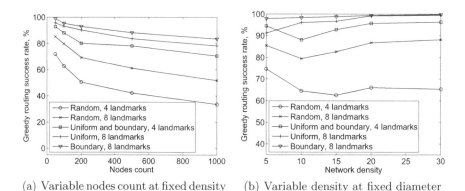

(a) Variable nodes count at fixed density   (b) Variable density at fixed diameter

Fig. 3. Packets delivery success rate as a function of network parameters

For all strategies of landmarks distribution success rate decreases monotonically as the network size grows (Fig. 3(a)), but at uniform or boundary placement the slope is smaller than at random landmarks selection. The reason for such a success rate decrease is that network extension under fixed density causes growth of network diameter and average path length. As a result, there arises a probability of a local minimum occurrence during packet delivery process.

On the other hand, as network density increases, the routing protocol performance improves, saturating at $\rho > 20$ nodes (Fig. 3(b)). If landmarks are spread out uniformly through the deployment area or placed along the network boundary, the greedy routing success rate reaches values of more than 95% at 4 landmarks and above 99% at $n_L = 8$, whereas for random landmarks selection these values are 66% and 87% respectively.

The second VCR protocol performance metric is path stretch - the ratio of found routing path length to the shortest path length. Although it is known that the shortest path is not always optimal under unreliable and asymmetric links, we use here hop count metric because of accepted ideal PHY and MAC layers assumption. If greedy forwarding fails due to the local minimum, we use backtracking mode from [2]. It is significant to mention that delivery success rate is 100% under all settings provided that backtracking mode is enabled.

The results, presented in Fig. 4, demonstrate direct relationship between greedy mode success rate and routing paths length. Low success rate means a high probability of a local minimum, hence routing protocol switches to backtracking mode more frequently resulting in paths stretching. At 4 landmarks placed according to the algorithm, paths are 9% to 25% shorter than paths under random landmarks selection, whereas at 8 landmarks the advantage is slightly lower, 4% to 19%.

Thus, the introduction of the proposed landmarks selection algorithm into VCR protocols improves significantly efficiency of greedy forwarding over virtual coordinates. At the same time, greedy routing success rate dispersion is much lower than in random landmarks placement; therefore, VCR protocol performance will be more stable and predictable.

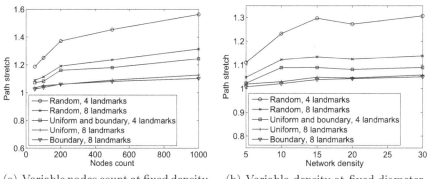

(a) Variable nodes count at fixed density   (b) Variable density at fixed diameter

Fig. 4. Path stretch as a function of network parameters

Our simulations also reveal that landmarks placement over the network boundary produces better results than uniform spread throughout the deployment area.

6   Conclusion

We proposed a distributed and self-organized algorithm intended for automatic selection of any fixed number of landmarks both at network initialization phase and after possible landmarks failures during operation. Described voting functions provide two different landmarks distribution strategies, even spread throughout deployment area and uniform network boundary placement. Other voting functions could also be introduced into the algorithm framework to obtain alternative desired landmarks placement patterns.

The algorithm complexity analysis showed that it is both time and memory complexity optimal for large-scale WSNs, whereas the memory complexity of its analogue from [4] depends considerably on the network size.

We demonstrated through simulations that introduction of the proposed landmarks selection algorithm into virtual coordinates routing protocol improves efficiency of greedy forwarding, preserving simplicity and high scalability of this routing technique.

We suppose that the proposed algorithm could be also useful in other WSN research areas (for example, improving accuracy of distributed localization methods), but it is a subject of future work.

References

1. Karp, B., Kung, H.: GPSR: greedy perimeter stateless routing for wireless networks. In: Proceedings of the 6th annual ACM/IEEE international conference on mobile computing and networking, Boston, Massachusetts, USA, pp. 243–254 (2000)
2. Fonseca, R., Ratnasamy, S., Zhao, J., Ee, C., Culler, D., Shenker, S., Stoica, I.: Beacon vector routing: scalable point-to-point routing in wireless sensornets. In: Proceedings of the 2nd symposium on networked systems design and implementation, Boston, Massachusetts, USA (2005)

3. Cao, Q., Abdelzaher, T.: A scalable logical coordinates framework for routing in wireless sensor networks. In: Proceedings of the 25th IEEE international real-time systems symposium, pp. 349–358 (2004)
4. Cao, Q., Abdelzaher, T.: Scalable logical coordinates framework for routing in wireless sensor networks. ACM Transactions on Sensor Networks 2(4), 557–593 (2006)
5. Zhao, Y., Li, B., Zhang, Q., Chen, Y., Zhu, W.: Efficient hop ID based routing for sparse ad hoc networks. In: Proceedings of the 13th IEEE international conference on network protocols (2005)
6. Caruso, A., Chessa, S., De, S., Urpi, A.: GPS free coordinate assignment and routing in wireless sensor networks. In: Proceedings of the 24th annual joint conference of the IEEE computer and communications societies, vol. 1, pp. 150–160 (2005)
7. Liu, K., Abu-Ghazaleh, N.: Aligned virtual coordinates for greedy routing in WSNs. In: Proceedings of the 3rd IEEE international conference on mobile ad-hoc and sensor networks, Vancouver, BC, Canada, pp. 377–386 (2006)

Energy Efficient Broadcast Routing in Ad Hoc Sensor Networks with Directional Antennas*

Deying Li[1,2], Zheng Li[1,2], and Lin Liu[1,2]

[1] Key Laboratory of Data Engineering and Knowledge Engineering
(Renmin University of China), MOE, Beijing,China
[2] School of Information, Renmin University of China, Beijing, China

Abstract. Different from omni-directional antennas, directional antennas model allows that each sensor can adjust the beam-width from θ_{min} to 360° and steer the antenna orientation to any desired direction [1], [2]. In this paper, we discuss the energy efficient broadcast problem with the directional antenna model in ad hoc sensor networks. The problem of our concern is: given n nodes and a broadcast request from s, each node equips a directional antenna with at least minimum angle θ_{min}, find a broadcast tree rooted at s and spanning all other nodes, in which each submitting node selects its propagation area, such that the total energy cost of the broadcast tree is minimized. We propose a greedy algorithm for this problem, and extensive simulation results have demonstrated the performance of our algorithm is more efficient than D-BIP algorithm[2].

Keywords: wireless sensor networks, energy efficient, broadcast routing, directional antenna, greedy algorithm.

1   Introduction

Wireless sensor network (WSN) has drawn extensive attention to researchers in recent years due to its wide range of applications such as habit monitoring, forest fire detection, healthcare and military surveillance etc. [3]. Wireless sensor network consists of a collection of sensor nodes dynamically forming a temporary network without the use of any existing network infrastructure. A communication session is achieved either through a single-hop transmission or through multiple hops by relaying through intermediate nodes. In such network, each node is powered by batteries that may not be possible to be recharged or replaced during a mission. Consequently, the limited energy resource imposes a constraint on the network performance and makes the energy efficiency becomes one of the primary issues in ad hoc sensor networks.

---

* This work was supported in part by the National Natural Science Foundation of China under Grant No. 10671208 and 863 High-tech Project under grant 2008AA01Z133.

There have been a lot of works on energy efficient broadcast routing in ad hoc/sensor networks [4-18]. However, most of the existing works assume that each node equips the omni-directional antenna. In this paper, we consider the energy efficient broadcast routing problem in wireless ad hoc sensor networks with directional antennas model and we aim at, for each broadcast request, finding a broadcast tree that has the minimum energy consumption. Note that the directional characteristic discussed in this paper is from the point of view of the sending, but not from receiving (i.e. the receiving area is omni-directional).

Previous researches have shown that the use of directional antennas can further reduce the energy consumption and the radio interference, improve the throughout, but increases the complexity of the problem. In practice, the beam is generated only toward a certain direction, it creates less interference to other nodes that are outside the beam, which enables greater information transmitting capacity in such network [2]. Besides, since nodes outside the beam coverage cannot receive the source's signal, security concerns associated with omni-directional broadcast can be somewhat alleviated [4]. As a result, it is expected that the use of directional antennas has a great potential in wireless ad hoc sensor networks.

In this paper, we address energy efficient broadcast routing problem with directional antennas. We assume that each sensor node equips a directional sending antenna and an omni-directional receiving antenna, and the propagating area of the antenna of a sensor node is a sector of the disk centered at the node with a propagating radius. By adjusting the beam-width from θ_{min} to $360°$ and steering the antenna orientation to any desired direction, a node's propagation area (i.e. antenna beam) can be effectively controlled. Broadcast routing is to find a broadcast tree, which is rooted at the source and spans all other nodes. When omni-directional antennas are used, every transmission by a node can be received by all nodes within its transmission range, which is named of "wireless multicast advantage" [2]. Using directional antennas, only the nodes located within the transmitting node's propagating area can receive the signal, thus the effect of the wireless multicast advantage is possibly lowered by using directional antennas. In addition, We assume the reception of signals cost no extra energy. Since only the non-leaf nodes need to transmit messages in a broadcast tree, the energy cost of a broadcast tree is the sum of energy cost of all the non-leaf nodes in the tree [5].

The rest of the paper is organized as follows: In Section 2, we briefly summarize some related work. In Section 3, we formulate the directional antennas model, the network model and problem specification. In Section 4, we give a greedy algorithm to the problem. Finally, we simulate on proposed algorithm in Section 5 and conclude the paper in Section 6.

2   Related Work

Most of the previous studies on efficient broadcast/multicast are focused on omni-directional antennas. The solutions [5], [7], and [8] are mainly based on geometry features of the nodes in the plane. Some energy-efficient broadcast algorithms were proposed in [9], namely BIP, MST and SPT. The proposed algorithms were evaluated through simulations. The authors in [10] firstly gave the quantitative characterization of performances of these three greedy heuristics. Some other works applied graph theory and techniques to construct the broadcast tree, such as in [11], [12], and [13].

Different from the scenarios of omni-directional antennas, using directional antennas can further reduce the energy consumption while increasing the complexity of the problems. Compared to the problems for omni-directional antenna networks, heuristic algorithms for the problem of finding the broadcast routing with directional antennas have not been studied extensively over the last few years [6]. The most famous and initial work was produced in [1], [2], where two heuristic algorithms, RB-BIP (Reduced Beam BIP) and D-BIP (Directional BIP) were proposed as various extensions of the BIP algorithm [9]. The RB-BIP algorithm included two steps, one is to construct a energy efficient broadcast tree by any algorithms for the omni-directional antenna scenario, then reduce each transmitting node's beam-width to the smallest possible angle (between θ_{min} and 360°) that can cover all this node's downstream neighbors. D-BIP algorithm outperforms RB-BIP; D-BIP is similar to the BIP, the only difference between D-BIP and BIP is in the computation of the incremental power. Unlike to the BIP in which computing the incremental power only involves the transmission range, the D-BIP also involves the antenna orientation and beam-width. Guo et al. in [4] proposed the D-MIDP (Directional MIDP) algorithm which used the manner of local searching. The authors also constructed the MILP (Mixed Integer Linear Programming) for the problem with directional antennas model, which can obtain the optimal solution in the case of small network scale. Some researchers also developed the localized algorithms for the broadcast routing problem with directional antennas model. Cartigny et al. extended the LBIP for directional communications using localized algorithms D-RBOP [14] and A-DLBOP [15] which based on the RNG and the LMST respectively.

The problem considered in this paper is similar to works in [1], [2], where each node equips a directional antenna which can adjust the beam-width from θ_{min} to 360° and steer the antenna orientation to any desired directions. We propose a greedy algorithm for the problem. When each node has a limited maximum transmission power, the algorithms in [1], [2] may not create a tree, but our algorithm has higher success rate for creating a broadcast tree than the algorithm [2].

3   Network Communication Model and Problem Formulation

In this section, we first introduce the directional antennas model and give some preliminaries. Then we formally define *the minimal energy broadcast routing with directional antennas* problem (DMEB). Since the energy efficient broadcast tree problem with omni-directional antennas, which is NP-hard [16], is a special

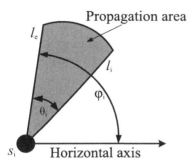
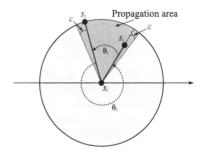

Fig. 1. Propagation model   **Fig. 2.** An example for the beam-width

case of DMEB problem, so the DMEB problem is NP-hard. We try to design approximation algorithm for this problem.

3.1   The Directional Antenna Model

Unlike to the omni-directional antennas, directional antennas model allows that each sensor can adjust the beam-width from θ_{min} to 360° and steer the antenna orientation to any desired direction. For simplicity, we assume that all nodes use directional antennas when it transmits and omni-directional antennas when it receives. The directional antennas can provide energy savings by concentrating propagation energy on where it is needed. In this way, messages can be received by node v from node u only when v is located within the transmitting node u's propagation area.

We use an idealized directional antenna communication model as shown in Fig. 1. All nodes have different locations. The propagation area of node s_i's antenna is a sector shown by the hatching area in Fig. 1, which is between initial line l_i and end line l_e with the propagation radius. The propagation area of a sensor s_i can be denoted by a 4-tupe $(L_i, r_i, \varphi_i, \theta_i)$ [19], where L_i is the location of the sensor node s_i, r_i is the propagation radius, the antenna orientation φ_i $(0 \leq \varphi_i \leq 2\pi)$ of node s_i is defined as angle measured counter-clockwise from the horizontal axis to the end line of the propagation area, and θ_i $(\theta_{min} \leq \theta_i \leq 2\pi)$ is the angle of beam-width. We assume that for each node s_i, the transmitted energy is concentrated uniformly in the beam-width θ_i, ignoring the possibility of side-lobe interference and the energy consumption in the antennas steering. By rotating the propagation area's initial line l_i and end line l_e, adjusting the beam-width and steering the antenna orientation can be proceeded accurately. Fig. 2 shows an example for the beam-width. $\angle s_1 s_i s_2$ denotes the θ_1, $\angle s_2 s_i s_1$ denotes the θ_2. For convenience of expression, we adopt the simplified 4-tupe $(L_i, r_i, \varphi_i, \angle s_1 s_i s_2)$ to denote the propagation area which cover s_1 and s_2 instead of the more realistic one $(L_i, r_i, \varphi_i + \varepsilon, \varepsilon + \angle s_1 s_i s_2 + \varepsilon)$, where ε is a very small angle that is additional and necessary beam-width for the communication from s_i to s_1 and s_2 .

3.2   Network Model

Given n sensors $V = \{s_1, s_2, ..., s_n\}$ in 2-D plane. Suppose the maximum transmission power of each node in V is P_{max}. And θ_{min} is a threshold angle of beamwidth to support transmission between any two nodes. Based on this communication model, the transmitted power needed by a node with a particular propagation area $(L_i, r_i, \varphi_i, \theta_i)$ is:

$$p(s_i) = \begin{cases} r_i^\alpha \cdot \theta_i/2\pi & \theta_{min} \le \theta_i \le 2\pi \\ r_i^\alpha \cdot \theta_{min}/2\pi & \theta_i < \theta_{min} \end{cases}$$

where α is the transmitting loss factor, $2 \le \alpha \le 4$.

We define set $S(s_i) = \{(L_i, r_{ik}, \varphi_{ik}, \theta_{ik})|1 \le k \le K_i\}$ contains all feasible and unduplicated propagation areas of node s_i. If node s_j is within the propagation area of s_i, s_j is covered by s_i. Each node $s_i \in V$ is associated with a transmission power $p(s_i)$ with respect to its propagation area.

Given the propagation area for each sensor, a sensor network can be modeled by a directed graph $G(V, A)$, while V represents a set of sensors; A is a set of directed arcs. For any two nodes s_i and s_j, if s_j is within the propagation area of s_i, there is an arc $(s_i, s_j) \in A$(i.e. a directed link from s_i to s_j).

In this paper, we focus on the problem of establishing minimum-energy broadcast tree in terms of logical level rather than implementation of a practical protocol. We assume node locations are static or change slowly.

3.3   Problem Definition

Given a broadcast request from source s, let T is a broadcast tree rooted at s. There are two kinds of nodes in T: the nodes that need to transmit/relay broadcast messages and the nodes that only receive broadcast messages. We assume that a node costs energy only when it does transmissions. Let $NL(T)$ denote the set of nonleaf nodes in T. The total energy cost of T can be represented as:

$$C(T) = \sum_{s_i \in NL(T)} p(s_i)$$

The problem is formally represented as following:

Minimum energy broadcast routing with directional antennas problem: Given a broadcast request sourced at s and each node $s_i \in V$ equips a directional antenna, find a broadcast tree T rooted at s by adjusting the beamwidth and steering the antenna orientation such that the total energy cost $C(T)$ of the tree is minimized.

4   Algorithm

In this section, we propose a greedy algorithm for the problem. We first define three different sets before getting into details of the algorithm. The first one is cover-set C that consists of non-leaf nodes in the broadcast tree and it is initialized to empty set. The nodes in C will transmit broadcast messages during broadcasting and each of them can cover its neighbors. In the algorithm, we aim at finding the "energy efficient" set C that covers all other sensor nodes in the network. The second set is candidate-set N, which is union of neighbors of all nodes in C. Each time in the algorithm a node in N will be selected to be included in C. By expanding C in this way, it maintains $G[C]$ (a subgraph induced by node set C) as a tree structure. The third set is uncovered-set U.

This greedy algorithm grows the broadcast tree from s. Initially, let C be empty and U be $V - \{s\}$. N contains only s. Then, a node in N is selected to be included in C (the selection criteria is given below), and its neighbors are removed from U and added into N. This operation is repeated until U becomes empty, which means all nodes in N have been covered by set C and the nodes in C are the non-leaf nodes of the broadcast tree. The broadcast tree is thus obtained.

In order to select nodes added into cover-set and choose their propagation area such that the total energy cost defined is minimized, we use the following function to evaluate every propagation area of a candidate node.

For $\forall (L_i, r_{ik}, \varphi_{ik}, \theta_{ik}) \in S(s_i)$, $1 \leq k \leq K_i$:

$$f(r_{ik}, \theta_{ik}) = \frac{|V_{ik} \bigcap U|}{p(s_{ik})}$$

where V_{ik} is the neighbors set of s_i and $p(s_{ik})$ is transmitted power of s_i respect to the kth propagation area $(L_i, r_{ik}, \varphi_{ik}, \theta_{ik})$. Then we use the following function to evaluate every candidate node $s_i \in N$:

$$f(s_i) = \max\{f(r_{ik}, \theta_{ik}) | \forall (L_i, r_{ik}, \varphi_{ik}, \theta_{ik}) \in S(s_i), 1 \leq k \leq K_i\}$$

4.1   The Greedy Algorithm

The function $f(r_{ik}, \theta_{ik})$ represents the number of uncovered nodes that a candidate can cover per energy unit with a node's k^{th} propagation area. The larger value is, the more efficient a propagation area $(L_i, r_{ik}, \varphi_{ik}, \theta_{ik}) \in S(s_i)$ covers the uncovered nodes. Each iteration, a candidate node in N with the largest value (i.e. $\max\{f(s_i) | s_i \in N\}$) will be selected and put into the Cover-Set C. Firstly, we need to choose the propagation area $(L_i, r_{ik}, \varphi_{ik}, \theta_{ik})$ with the largest $f(r_{ik}, \theta_{ik})$ for $\forall s_i \in N$, then select node s_i with the largest $f(s_i)$ in the candidate set N. We call this process as the *Antenna Selection Process*. We describe the detail of this process separately in next subsection. As a result, the total energy cost of the broadcast tree can be made as small as possible.

The *Greedy Algorithm* is formally as the following:

Input: V, P_{max}, θ_{min} and a broadcast request from s

Output: T: a broadcast tree rooted from s.

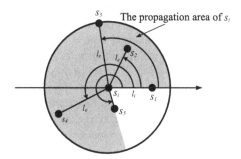

Fig. 3. The **Antenna Selection Process** of the Greedy algorithm

$C = \emptyset$;
$U = V - \{s\}$;
$N = \{s\}$

While $(U \neq \emptyset)$ **do**

Call the **Antenna Selection Process** to choose the propagation area $(L_i, r_{ik}, \varphi_{ik}, \theta_{ik})$ for node s_i and select a node in N with the largest $f(s_i)$;
$C = C \bigcup \{s_i\}$
$U = U - V_{ik}$
$N = N \bigcup V_{ik}$

End While

Construct the broadcast tree T from C.

4.2 The Antenna Selection Process in the Greedy Algorithm

At first, we have the candidate-set N for relay nodes for broadcasting. We consider the characteristics of directional antenna model: The beam-width can be adjusted from θ_{min} to $360°$ and the antenna orientation can be steered to any desired direction. There are different strategies to select the propagation area $(L_i, r_{ik}, \varphi_{ik}, \theta_{ik})$ with the largest value of $f(r_{ik}, \theta_{ik})$, which can produce different effective solutions with different time complexities.

We provide a method to select node s_i in N with the largest $f(s_i)$. We give the following example in Fig.3 to see how the *Antenna Selection Process* works. Each iteration, the strategy of choosing the propagation area $(L_i, r_{ik}, \varphi_{ik}, \theta_{ik}) \in S(s_i)$, $1 \leq k \leq K_i$, of node s_i with the largest value of $f(r_{ik}, \theta_{ik})$ can be described as follows:

For each $s_i \in N$, we select a node from the Uncover-Set U arbitrarily (without loss of generality, we assume the selection is s_i) and then let initial line l_i and end line l_e of the propagation area of s_i's antenna coincide with the axis $\overrightarrow{s_i s_1}$. Then we execute the *counterclockwise-rotating-select-process* for s_i and s_1:

Firstly, we adjust s_i's propagation area to cover only s_1, i.e., $(L_i, r_i, \varphi_i, \theta_i)$ is set to $(L_i, r_{i1}, \varphi_{i1}, \theta_{i1}) = (L_i, d(s_i, s_1), \varphi_{i1}, \theta_{min})$. $V_{i1} = \{s_1\}$ and $p(s_i) = r_{i1}^{\alpha} \cdot \theta_{i1}/2\pi$.

The value of $f(r_{i1}, \theta_{i1})$ can also be calculated, and set $f(s_i, s_1) = f(r_{i1}, \theta_{i1})$. Secondly, we rotate the end line l_e of s_i's propagation area counterclockwise to extend the beam-width to θ_{i2}, such that next node (i.e. s_2) can also be covered by propagation area. Now the propagation area of s_i is set to $(L_i, r_{i2}, \varphi_{i2}, \theta_{i2}) = (L_i, \max\{d(s_i, s_1), d(s_i, s_2)\}, \varphi_{i2}, \angle s_1 s_i s_2)$. $V_{i2} = \{s_1, s_2\}$, $p(s_i) = r_{i2}^{\alpha} \cdot \theta_{i2}/2\pi$. If $f(r_{i2}, \theta_{i2})$ is greater than $f(s_i, s_1)$, set $f(s_i, s_1) = f(r_{i2}, \theta_{i2})$. Then do the same rotating operations until the end line l_e coincides with the initial line l_1. After *counterclockwise-rotating-select-process* for s_i and s_1 has been done, we select another node s_2 and do the identical *counterclockwise-rotating-select-process* for s_i and s_2. And do *counterclockwise-rotating-select-process* continually for s_i and any other nodes in U.

When all nodes in Uncover-Set U have been dealt with, we can obtain the propagation areas set $(L_i, r_{ik}, \varphi_{ik}, \theta_{ik}), 1 \leq k \leq K_i$, the positive integer K_i is at most $|U|^2$. And get $f(s_i) = \max\{f(s_i, s_j)|s_j \in U\}$ and corresponding the propagation area $(L_i, r_{ik}, \varphi_{ik}, \theta_{ik})$. Doing *the Antenna Selection Process* for any node in N can return the node s_i with the largest $f(s_i)$ in N and the corresponding propagation area $(L_i, r_{ik}, \varphi_{ik}, \theta_{ik})$ and neighbor set V_{ik}.

Theorem. Given V, a source node s and θ_{min}, the Greedy Algorithm in subsection 4.1 can output a broadcast tree rooted at s in time $O(n^4)$.

Proof. It is easy to know that the Greedy Algorithm can output a broadcast tree. In the While-loop, there are at most n loops. The time complexity of finding the node with maximum value $f(s)$ and the corresponding propagation area, which is determined by the Antenna Selection Process, is $O(n^3)$. In addition, the construction of a broadcast tree in the last step takes times $O(n)$. Therefore, we can conclude that the whole algorithm ends in times $O(n^4)$.

5   Simulations

In simulations, we compare our greedy algorithm with the D-BIP algorithm [2] for broadcast request. We study how the total energy cost is affected by varying two parameters over a wide range: the number of nodes in the network (N) and the minimum value of the beam-width θ_{min}.

The simulation is conducted in a 100×100 2-D free-space by randomly allocating N nodes ($100 \leq N \leq 200$). Each node can adjust its antenna to any desired direction with an antenna beam-width $\theta(\theta_{min} \leq \theta \leq 360°)$. We assume that transmission power (p) relates to the node radius (r) and beam-width (θ) with function: $p = r^{\alpha} \cdot \theta/2\pi$. We can get different topologies by varying N and θ. In this simulations, we consider $\alpha = 2$.

We present averages of 100 separate runs for each result shown in the figures. In each run of the simulation, for given N, θ_{min}, we randomly place N nodes in the square. And we randomly choose any node as the source node for broadcast request. Then, we run the Greedy algorithm and D-BIP algorithm on this network.

Fig. 4 shows the total energy cost versus the number of nodes. From the curves in Fig. 4, our greedy algorithm performs much better than D-BIP when

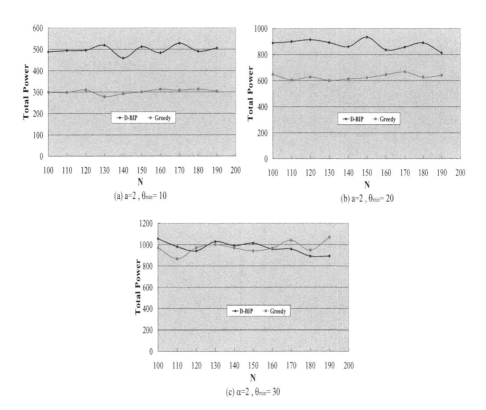

Fig. 4. The total energy cost versus N

$\theta_{min} < 30°$. And the Greedy algorithm and D-BIP become close as θ_{min} increases.

In the above simulations, nodes have no constraint for the maximum transmission power P_{max} such that it ensures the greedy algorithm and D-BIP can get a broadcast tree. The following simulations show the success rate which the algorithms can get the broadcast tree when nodes have limited maximum transmission power. In the following, we assume that all nodes in the network have an identical limited maximum transmission power P_{max}. Clearly, a node's maximum propagation radius is equal to $\sqrt[\alpha]{P_{max}}$ by using omni-directional antennas.

Fig. 5 shows the success rate (i.e. the ratio of the success times of constructing a broadcast tree in 100 broadcasting requests to 100) versus the maximum transmission power P_{max}. Fig. 5a shows the success rate versus N. In Fig.5a, P_{max} is restricted to 225 such that the maximum propagation radius is equal to 15 when using omni-directional antennas. Fig. 5b shows also the success rate versus N, and the maximum propagation radius is equal to 20 when using omni-directional antennas. Fig. 5c and Fig. 5d are the success rate versus P_{max}. The simulation results show that success rate of the Greedy algorithm is more than success rate of D-BIP algorithm. Through the results, we can see that our proposed algorithm is more reliable and efficient than the D-BIP algorithm.

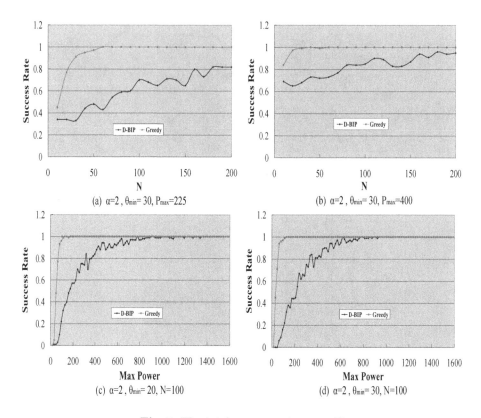

Fig. 5. The total energy cost versus N

6 Conclusion

We have studied the broadcast routing problem with the directional antennas model in wireless ad hoc sensor networks. A number of algorithms designed for omni-directional antenna model may not be suitable for directional scenarios. We propose a greedy algorithm and simulation results have demonstrated that our Greedy Algorithm outperforms the famous D-BIP algorithm [2].

References

1. Wieselthier, J.E., Nguyen, G.D., Ephremides, A.: Energy-Limited Wireless Networking with Directional Antennas: The Case of Session-Based Multicasting. In: Proc. IEEE Infocom Conf., pp. 190–199 (2002)
2. Wieselthier, J.E., Nguyen, G.D., Ephremides, A.: Energy-Aware Wireless Networking with Directional Antennas: The Case of Session-Based Broadcasting and Multicasting. IEEE Trans. Mobile Computing 1(3), 176–191 (2002)
3. Akyildiz, I.F., Su, W., Sankarasubramaniam, Y., Cayirci, E.: A Survey on Sensor Networks. ACM Trans. on Multimedia Computing, Communications and Applications, 102–114 (August 2002)

4. Guo, S., Yang, O.: Minimum-energy Multicast in Wireless Ad Hoc Networks with Adaptive Antennas: MILP Formulations and Heuristic Algorithms. IEEE Transactions on Mobile Computing 5(4), 333–346 (2006)

5. Cagalj, M., Hubaux, J., Enz, C.: Minimum-energy Broadcast in All-Wireless Networks: NP-completeness and Distribution Issues. In: ACM MobiCom, Atlanta, GA, USA, pp. 172–182 (2002)

6. Guo, S., Yang, O.: Energy-Aware Multicasting in Wireless Ad Hoc Networks: A Survey and Discussion. Elsevier Computer Communications 30(2007), 2129–2148

7. Cheng, X., Sun, J., Min, M., Du, D.-Z.: Energy Efficient Broadcast and Multicast Routing in Ad Hoc Wireless Networks. In: Proc. 22nd IEEE Int'l Performance, Computing, and Comm. Conf. (2003)

8. Kang, I., Poovendran, R.: A novel Power-Efficient Broadcast Routing Algorithm Exploiting Broadcast Efficiency. In: Proceeding of IEEE Vehicular Technology Conference (VTC), Orlando, October 2003, pp. 2926–2930 (2003)

9. Wieselthier, J.E., Nguyen, G.D., et al.: On the Construction of Energy-efficient Broadcast and Multicast Trees in Wireless Networks. In: IEEE INFOCOM 2000, pp. 585–594 (2000)

10. Wan, P., Calinescu, G., Li, X., Frieder, O.: Minimum-energy Broadcast Routing in Static Ad Hoc Wireless Networks. In: INFOCOM 2001, vol. 2, pp. 1162–1171 (2001)

11. Liang, W.: Constructing Minimum-Energy Broadcast Trees in Wireless Ad Hoc Networks. In: Proceedings of 3rd ACM International Symposium on Mobile Ad Hoc Networking and Computing, Lausanne, Switzerland, June 2002, pp. 112–122 (2002)

12. Egecioglu, O., Gonzalez, T.F.: Minimum-Energy Broadcast in Simple Graphs with Limited Node Power. In: Proc. IASED Int'l Conf. Parallel and Distributed Computing and Systems (PDCS 2001), August 2001, pp. 334–338 (2001)

13. Cagalj, M., Hubaux, J.P., Enz, C.: Minimum-Energy Broadcast in All-Wireless Networks: NP-Completeness and Distribution Issues. In: Proc. MOBICOM (2002)

14. Cartigny, J., Simplot-Ryl, D., Stojmenovic, I.: Localized energy efficient broadcast for wireless networks with directional antennas. In: IFIPMED-HOC-NET (Mediterranean Ad Hoc Networking) Workshop, Sardegna, Italy (2002)

15. Cartigny, J., Simplot-Ryl, D., Stojmenovic, I.: An adaptive localized scheme for energy-efficient broadcasting in ad hoc networks with directional antennas. In: Niemegeers, I.G.M.M., de Groot, S.H. (eds.) PWC 2004. LNCS, vol. 3260, pp. 399–413. Springer, Heidelberg (2004)

16. Li, D., Jia, X., Liu, H.: Energy Efficient Broadcast Routing in Ad Hoc Wireless Networks. IEEE Transactions on Mobile Computing 3(2), 144–151 (2004)

17. Kang, I., Poovendran, R.: S-GPBE: A Power-Efficient Broadcast Routing Algorithm Using Sectored Antenna. In: Proceeding of Wireless and Optical Communications (2003)

18. Dai, F., Wu, J.: Efficient Broadcasting in Ad Hoc Wireless Networks Using Directional Antennas. IEEE Transactions on Parallel and Distributed Systems 4(17) (2006)

19. Ma, H., Liu, Y.: Some problems of directional sensor networks. International Journal of Sensor Networks 2(1/2), 44–52 (2007)

DTN Routing with Probabilistic Trajectory Prediction

Ionut Cardei, Cong Liu, Jie Wu, and Quan Yuan

Department of Computer Science and Engineering,
Florida Atlantic University, Boca Raton, FL 33431, USA
icardei@cse.fau.edu, cliu8@fau.edu, jie@cse.fau.edu, qyuan@fau.edu

Abstract. Many real-world DTN application involve vehicles that do not have a purely random mobility pattern. In most cases nodes follow a predefined trajectory in space that may deviate from the norm due to environment factors or random events. In this paper we propose a DTN routing scheme for applications where the node trajectory and the contact schedule can be predicted probabilistically. We describe a technique for contact estimation for mobile nodes that uses a Time Homogeneous Semi Markov model. With this method a node computes contact profiles describing the probabilities of contacts per time unit, and uses them to select the next hop such that the delivery ratio is improved. We develop the Trajectory Prediction DTN Routing algorithm and we analyze its performance with simulations.

Keywords: DTN; delay tolerant networking; routing protocols; message scheduling; Markov process.

1   Introduction

Regular MANET routing protocols work on the assumption that there exists at least one path between endpoints, and will,therefore, fail route discovery. Proactive routing protocols (e.g. DSDV, OLSR) will also fail to converge due to rapid topology changes or lack of stable connectivity.

To mitigate these issues a new class of Delay Tolerant Networks (DTN) has been defined in [4]. Connectivity in DTNs relies on nodes physically delivering messages between disconnected partitions, similar to how the postal service delivers packages. This store-carry-forward approach for end-to-end message delivery exploits the increased user mobility instead of being hindered by it. If a message reaches a node that has no link to the next hop towards the destination, it will be buffered until a contact occurs with the next hop. In this way a message can be delivered from a source to its destination even when there never exists an instantaneous path between the two endpoints. In some DTNs the waiting time between successive contacts may be very large (hours for interplanetary networks) and variable, so applications must be designed to tolerate long delivery latencies.

The intermittent nature of end-to-end connectivity and the variable delay require a new approach for routing. The local decision of selecting the next

Y. Li et al. (Eds.): WASA 2008, LNCS 5258, pp. 40–51, 2008.

hop for a message depends on available information on current connectivity and on future opportunities to establish links with other nodes (contacts). Hence, routing also may involve scheduling transmissions for future contacts in addition to selecting the next hop. To optimize the network performance, such as delivery ratio or latency, DTN routing must select the right contact to transmit the message. If a contact is not available when a message is received from the upper layer, the DTN transport layer will buffer it until a proper contact begins and transmission time becomes available, or until the message expires and is dropped.

In this paper we propose a Trajectory Prediction DTN Routing scheme (TPDR) for applications where the node trajectory and the contact schedule can be predicted probabilistically. Most sensing applications with mobile nodes define trajectories that are far from random. Node movement is typically controlled such that sensing quality of service is optimized to increase application lifetime, coverage, or to reduce latency. DTN message routing can be employed to extend the operational range of vehicles beyond communication range and to mitigate intermittent connectivity. For instance, Autonomous Underwater Vehicles (AUVs) in a littoral surveillance application follow a scan pattern that provides full sonar coverage of the sea bed (Figure 1). In these networks it is possible to predict nodes trajectories and contact schedules. Due to events affecting the mission plan and environmental factors (such as ocean currents), contact schedules can not be known with 100% accuracy. We describe a technique for trajectory prediction and contact estimation for mobile nodes that uses a Time Homogeneous Semi Markov model. With this method we compute contact profiles for pairs of nodes that describe the probability of a contact per time unit. We develop the Trajectory Prediction DTN Routing algorithm and we analyze its performance with simulations.

This paper continues in Section 2 with a presentation of the application and network models, and the routing architecture. Section 3 describes related work in routing for Delay and Disruption Tolerant networks. Section 4 presents results from performance evaluations using simulations. The paper concludes in Section 5 with some comments.

2   DTN Routing with Trajectory Prediction

This section begins with a description of the application and the network models considered in this paper for the DTN routing algorithm with contact prediction.

The applications addressed in this paper consider small and medium size networks where nodes are mobile, with trajectories that can be predicted for a certain time horizon and where the communication topology is mostly disconnected. Such a scenario is not thoroughly addressed by the DTN research community. More specifically, the proposed routing solution applies to applications where nodes are location aware and also have available enough information on the mobility pattern, such as the velocity vector and mission status, that they can approximate when contacts begin and end. Contact prediction of this nature is possible in applications where node operation is coordinated either centrally

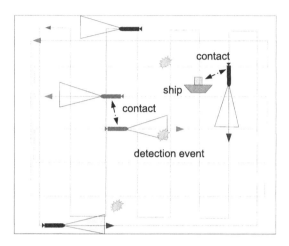

Fig. 1. DTN network scenario with autonomous underwater vehicles scanning an area and reporting to a controller ship

(mass transit, trains) or autonomously (mobile sensing). In mobile sensing applications, such as subsea monitoring [13], sensor–actor networks [1,11], position status and movement data is disseminated to the network. In mobile sensing applications location updates can be broadcasted with low data rate to reach the entire network, while mission payload data can be forwarded on a high speed wireless link with shorter range during contacts. When a broadcast channel is not available, status (position and velocity) updates is propagated throughout the network in the typical DTN store-and-carry fashion, although with considerably higher delays. For all practical reasons it is nor feasible, neither useful to predict contacts for the whole application duration. It is considerably cheaper to limit trajectory and contact predictions to a finite time horizon.

To support the contact prediction and the node state dissemination mechanisms it is necessary for all nodes to have their system clocks synchronized. In networks where the contact duration/link data rate fraction is large, precise node time synchronization is not required. Otherwise, if the contacts are very short, maybe due to high vehicle speed, or if the link data rate is very high, precise time synchronization is important to pinpoint contact begin times to avoid wasting unused transmission time. In most cases broadcast beacon protocols can serve for synchronization.

An application that fits the above description involves underwater littoral monitoring with Autonomous Underwater Vehicles (AUV). As described in [12], the high costs of equipment and deployment make feasible applications with only a relatively small number of AUVs. Increased coverage is achieved by designing the vehicle trajectory to scan the target area. Characteristics of the underwater acoustic communications channel, such as long propagation delays, low data rates and short transmission range, limit the operational capability of AUVs. A store-and-carry delay tolerant approach is an economic solution to improve coverage at the cost of higher delays. The availability of an out-of band slow long-range acoustic channel used to broadcast vehicle status updates brings up the possibility of predicting nodes' trajectories and contact opportunities. A short range high data rate acoustic link forwards sensor data (e.g. sonar or video) during contacts.

Figure 1 shows a notional AUV scenario with vehicles executing repeatedly a closed monitoring path. To simplify the presentation, the application defines two trajectories, a horizontal combing pattern and a vertical one. Several vehicles can follow the same trajectory with a delay between them.

We assume that each node moves according to a predetermined pattern at a constant speed monitoring the environment. Periodically, onboard sensors generate images (from a camera or a sonar) that have to be forwarded towards the controller station on the ship. From time to time pattern recognition algorithms running on sensor data on each AUV will trigger a *detection event*. This event causes the AUV to autonomously interrupt its current trajectory and gather extra data before it continues on its original path. The vehicles report sonar measurement messages to the base station located on a non-moving ship using the acoustic high data rate link, following the DTN store-and-carry bundle forwarding approach if a connected contemporaneous multihop path is not available.

2.1 Network Model and Trajectory Prediction

The monitored area is overlayed on a $w \times w$ square grid. Grid coordinates x, y are numbered between 1 and w. Each cell is assigned a unique cell ID $s(x, y)$ given by the following mapping:

$$s(x, y) = (y - 1)w + x$$

This cell numbering is equivalent to assigning successive numbers to cells from left to right, top to bottom, beginning with the origin cell, $(1,1)$. The set of all cells is denoted with S. The size of set S is $m = w^2$.

Time in this model is discretized. The trajectory followed by a vehicle u up to time unit t is a sequence of cells $S_{1,t}^i = \{s\}_{1..t} = \{(x, y)_{1..t}\}$. We describe this trajectory for an individual vehicle, as it evolves in time, as a Markov process. The set of Markov states is represented by the set of cells on the grid S.

As a vehicle enters a state (grid cell) i, it stays there for a time called *state holding time*, and then leaves to the next state j. The selection of j can be described by a transition probability matrix P^e, $P_{ij}^e = P(\text{transition from } i \text{ to } j)$. Let T_n be the time of the nth transition, $n \geq 0$, and $T_0 = 0$. The state holding time for the nth transition is $T_n - T_{n-1}$. The probability distribution of the state holding time depends on the states involved in the transitions. We believe it is not realistic to assume that the state holding times have the memoryless Markov property, with a geometric distribution.

We model the system with a Time Homogeneous Semi-Markov Process (TH-SMP). The state holding times can have arbitrary distributions – with the constraints that they are i.i.d. and do not change in time (time-homogeneous). The

TH-SMP is defined by the tuple $\{(S_n, T_n)|n \geq 0\}$, where S_n is the nth state reached. The TH-SMP *kernel Q* describes the process evolution in time:

$$Q_{ij}(t) = P(S_{n+1} = j, T_{n+1} - T_n \leq t \mid S_n = i) = P_{ij}^e H_{ij}(t) \tag{1}$$

We assumed that the selection of the next state (given by P^e) is independent of the state holding time distribution function when the model transitions from state i to state j (denoted with H_{ij}).

$$H_{ij}(t) = P(T_{n+1} - T_n \leq t \mid S_{n+1} = j, \ S_n = i).$$

The state holding time effectively depends on the vehicle speed that we assume is constant in our application. We also assume a vehicle is delayed in a state by a constant time d_{ev} when a detection event occurs. The probability of a detection event per time unit per state is a constant, p_{ev} .

A vehicle geometric path on the grid is defined by the matrix P^e that forms the embedded Markov chain of the TH-SMP, as we observe that $P_{ij}^e = \lim_{t \to \infty} Q_{ij}(t) = P(S_{n+1} = j \mid S_n = i)$.

The state holding time irrespective of the next state is defined as $D_i(t) = P(T_{n+1} - T_n \leq t \mid S_n = i)$. This is the c.d.f. of the time it takes the vehicle to traverse a grid cell i regardless where it goes next. $D_i(t)$ can be computed as:

$$D_i(t) = \sum_{j=1}^{m} Q_{ij}(t) \tag{2}$$

To predict the future vehicle trajectory, we define the stochastic process $X = (X_t, t \in \mathbf{N})$, where $X_t \in S$ is the vehicle state at time t. The distribution of X_t is given by $\phi_{ij}(t) = P(X_t = j \mid X_0 = i)$. If we know that a vehicle is now in state i, after t time units in the future it will be in state j with probability $\phi_{ij}(t)$. As a special case $\phi_{ij}(0) = \delta_{ij}$, where δ is Kronecker's symbol.

To determine $\phi_{ij}(t)$ one can use the distributions for $D_i(t)$ and $Q_{ij}(t)$, which can be derived from P^e and $H_{ij}(t)$, both easy to determine from the application domain.

To determine $\phi_{ij}(t)$ we start with a special case when the process stays in state i between time 0 and t, with no transitions.

$$P(X_t = i | X_0 = i \text{ and } T_1 \geq t) = P(T_1 - T_0 \geq t \mid X_0 = i) = (1 - D_i(t)).$$

If the process makes at least a transition between times 0 and t, conditioned on the time of the first transition (at time k) from i, and on the state l to which the process moves after state i, we obtain:

$$P(X_t = j \mid X_0 = i \text{ and at least one transition}) = \sum_{l=1}^{m} \sum_{k=1}^{t-1} \dot{Q}_{il}(k) \phi_{lj}(t - k),$$

where $\dot{Q}_{il}(k) = \frac{dQ_{il}(k)}{dk} = Q_{il}(k) - Q_{il}(k-1)$ is the time derivative of Q. Putting it together, we obtain:

$$\phi_{ij}(t) = (1 - D_i(t))\delta_{ij} + \sum_{l=1}^{m} \sum_{k=1}^{t-1} \dot{Q}_{il}(k) \phi_{lj}(t - k) \tag{3}$$

ϕ can be calculated iteratively, as $\phi_{ij}(t)$ depends on probabilities $\phi_{lj}(t-k)$ computed in the previous steps.

This approach was inspired by the work in [7] that looked at the problem of predicting access point handoffs in WLANs. Our Markov model (state space, transitions) is defined differently and the prediction is extended to handle inter-node contacts.

2.2   Contact Prediction and the Forwarding Decision

The *contact profile* $C_{ab}(t) = P(a \leftrightarrow b$ contact at time $t)$ for two nodes a and b can be determined from the TH-SMP behavior given by ϕ and from the *neighborhood map* N_s. For each state $s \in S$, N_s is the set of states $z \in S$, s.t. a vehicle in state s can communicate with a vehicle in z. The neighborhood map can be computed based on underwater topography maps, channel characteristics, and on the technical properties of the communication device. For the simple disk model, with distance $d()$, $N_s = \{z \in S \mid d(s,z) \le r\}$.

The contact profile at time t depends on having the two nodes a and b in each other's neighborhood, and it is expressed as:

$$C_{ab}(t) = \sum_{s_a \in S} P(X_t^a = s_a) \sum_{s_b \in N_{s_a}} P(X_t^b = s_b) = \sum_{s_a \in S} \phi_{i_a s_a}^a(t) \sum_{s_b \in N_{s_a}} \phi_{i_b s_b}^b(t) \quad (4)$$

i_a and i_b are the states of nodes a and b, respectively, found out most recently. Note that the contact prediction works with relative time. Different time offsets can be applied as parameters to $\phi(t)$. We note that the contact profile is not a proper pdf and is not normalized, as $\sum_t C_{ab}(t)$ may exceed 1.

Each message has a time-to-live (TTL) field. When the TTL expires, the message is dropped. A nodes buffers messages until a contact begins. Then, the TPDR protocol decides whether to forward a message intended for destination d in a greedy way.

Suppose at time t the current node a is in contact with a set of nodes $\{b_i\}$. Assume the current node a receives periodic updates with the current state s_{b_i} for all nodes b_i over the secondary channel. Node a removes from the set $\{b_i\}$ all nodes that have already received a message node a buffers and has to forward. This can be accomplished either by storing the message path in its header, by query, or by summary vector exchange, as in Epidemic Routing. After that node a computes the following:

- the contact profile for the destination node d: $C_{ad}(t)$, indicating the probabilities of direct contact and delivery to the destination node
- the contact profiles of nodes b_i with the destination d: $C_{b_i d}(t)$. These give the probabilities that the next hop (one of nodes b_i) will be in contact with the destination d in the future.

The prediction window for which the contact profiles are computed is limited by the remaining message time-to-live. Then the routing algorithm at node a takes the following steps:

1. pick the node $c \in \{a\} \cup \{b_i\}$ that maximizes the probability of contact with the destination: $c = \mathrm{argmax}_{u \in \{a\} \cup \{b_i\}} \mathrm{max}_{t=1..TTL} C_{ud}(t)$
2. if $c = a$, continue buffering the message. There is no forwarding.
3. else forward the message to next hop c since c has a higher probability of a contact with the destination than the current node a.

Discussion. Routing cycles are avoided by preventing forwarding to nodes that have seen a message before. This routing algorithm has several simplifying assumptions. First, it assumes that during a contact all queued messages can be forwarded to the next hop. Then, it assumes infinite buffers and an ideal communications channel during a contact. With the affordability of memory capacity, the infinite buffer assumption is not out of line for most applications. The first assumption applies to cases where the message load is low, the data rate is very high, or the contact duration is very long. For the AUV application, the latter case is more realistic due to the reduced vehicle speed.

In terms of effective implementation, it is worthwhile to note that matrices $\phi_{ij}(t)$ that give the trajectory prediction, must be computed just once, at the beginning of the application runtime, provided the other involved distribution (state holding time H) and the state transition probabilities P^e do not change.

While the number of states (w^4) in the TH-SMP can be daunting, matrices ϕ, H, Q, and P^e are very sparse. For the area combing patterns in Figure 1, the fill factor for these matrices is about $\frac{1}{w^3}$. Sparse matrices support efficient storage and matrix arithmetic operations.

The Trajectory Prediction DTN Routing algorithm could be expanded in many directions. We investigate an extension for a shortest path routing algorithm that uses contact profiles. Similar work has been described in [5]. Our approach benefits from the ability of specifying arbitrary distribution functions for the state holding time $H_{ij}(t)$, which is more realistic. This also supports better the use of recorded historic data on trajectory traces.

3 Related Work

In this section we present a brief overview of DTN routing techniques relevant to our problem. For a comprehensive overview of DTN routing, the reader should consult [17].

One of the first thorough analysis of communications in networks with intermittent connectivity is done by Fall in [4]. Fall proposes a new delay/disruption tolerant architecture, later updated by Cerf et. al. in [3]. The DTN architecture defines a *bundle layer* operating above the transport layer, that offers end-to-end delivery service to applications. The bundle layer forms an overlay network used for transfer of message *bundles* with the option of hop-by-hop custody transfer (delivery responsibility) and optional delivery with end-to-end confirmation.

Routing has better performance when more information are available on the current state of the network topology and on its future evolution. At one end of the spectrum is *deterministic routing*, where the current topology is known and future changes can be predicted. With deterministic routing, message forwarding can be scheduled to optimize network performance and to reduce resource utilization using single-copy forwarding. In contrast, *stochastic routing* techniques assume node mobility is random or unknown and therefore must rely on multicopy forwarding to increase the end-to-end delivery probability.

Deterministic DTN routing techniques are based on formulating models for time-dependent graphs and finding a space-time shortest path in DTNs by converting the routing problem to classic graph theory. These techniques are appropriate for scenarios with predictable topology (e.g. space networks) or where node mobility is tightly controlled, such as unmanned air vehicles (UAVs) and Autonomous Underwater Vehicles . A major problem facing deterministic routing protocols remains the distribution of network state and mobility profiles under sporadic connectivity, long delays, and sparse resources.

Jain et al. present in [6] a routing framework that takes advantage of increasing levels of information on topology, queue state and traffic demand. Four *knowledge oracles* are defined. The *contacts summary oracle* provides time-invariant aggregate or summary statistics on inter-node contacts, such as average waiting time until a next contact. The *contact oracle* provides full information for all contacts, such as start time and duration, enough to build a time-varying contact multigraph. The *queuing oracle* answers for the instantaneous queue state and current waiting times at all nodes. The *traffic demand oracle* gives information on any present and future messages injected in the network. The authors adapt the Dijkstra shortest path algorithm to run in a time-varying multigraph where the edge cost functions is determined with the available oracles. The edge cost function is the total estimated edge delay, consisting of the sum of the signal propagation delay (computed from node location information), the contact waiting time (given by the contact oracle), and the transmission queuing delay (available from the queuing oracle). A *complete knowledge* centralized linear program optimization is presented that uses the traffic demand oracle to more accurately characterize transmission times. This serves as a benchmark for performance evaluations. Due to the sparse connectivity in DTNs, estimating current queue state across the network and implementing edge capacity reservation are difficult. Simulation results point out that in scenarios with limited resources (buffer space and edge capacity) the benefits from using the additional knowledge from the queuing oracle are not significant.

When network state is too uncertain, *stochastic routing* techniques forward messages randomly hop-by-hop with the expectation of *eventual delivery*. In between, there are routing mechanisms that may predict contacts using prior state, or that adjust the trajectory of mobile nodes to serve as message ferries. Stochastic routing techniques rely on replicating messages and controlled flooding for improving delivery rate, trading off resource utilization against improved routing performance in absence of accurate current and future network state.

Passive routing techniques do not interfere with node mission, do not change the node trajectory and react to a changing topology. Passive routing techniques rely in general on flooding multiple copies of the same message with the objective of *eventual delivery* [14,15,16]. These protocols trade off delivery performance against resource utilization. By sending multiple copies on different contact paths (such as in epidemic routing [16]), the delivery probability increases and the delay drops at the cost of additional buffer occupancy during message ferrying and higher link capacity usage during contacts. This approach is appropriate when nothing or very little is known about mobility patterns.

Some passive stochastic routing protocols use *delivery estimation* to determine a per contact probabilistic metric for successful delivery based on recorded history of prior contacts ([8,10]. These protocols are useful when contacts cannot be accurately predicted and when nodes follow non-random trajectories.

Active routing techniques ([2,9,18]) rely on controlling the trajectory of some ferry nodes to pick up messages and ferry them in preparation for a contact with the destination node. Active routing techniques provide lower delays with the additional cost of increased protocol and system complexity. They also rely on the availability of mobile message ferries that could be reassigned from their original mission.

4   Performance Evaluation

In this section we present the simulation performance evaluation for the TPDR algorithm described in this paper. The results are compared with other routing protocols for DTNs, Direct Delivery and Epidemic Routing [16]. With Direct Delivery, the source node buffers a message until it is delivered during a contact with the destination node. The simulated scenario involves 4 to 10 AUVs, plus one ship, deployed in a 1 km square area divided in a 20×20 grid. The dynamics of the AUV vertical and horizontal scan patterns are modeled by the transition probability matrix P^e and the state holding time distribution matrix $H_{ij}(t)$. The state holding time is 1 with probability $1 - p_{ev}$ and 3 with probability $p_{ev} \in \{0.01, 0.05, 0.1\}$. This models the random detection events that trigger a delay for taking additional sonar measurements. These detection events also generate new messages intended for the ship node. The message TTL is varied between 40 and 100 time units. 100 is also the upper bound for trajectory prediction.

We simulated this topology with a packet-level simulator written in Matlab. The simulation assumed an ideal channel with no delay, as we wanted to focus mostly on the effectiveness of the prediction element on the overall routing performance metrics — message end-to-end delay and delivery ratio. Half of AUVs use the horizontal scan and the others use the vertical pattern.

The quality of the contact prediction is of great interest. In Figure 2 we overlap the computed predicted contact profile between AUV_2 and the ship node ($C_{21}(t)$) with the actual contact trace between these two nodes that was captured during the simulation. The contact prediction accurately indicates future contacts with higher probability values.

Tables 1 a) and b) show the variation of the delay and the delivery ratio depending on the AUV count: 6, 8, and 10. One can notice that the delivery

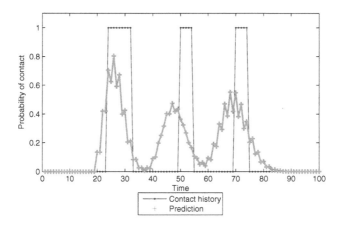

Fig. 2. Predicted contact profile and actual contact trace between AUV_2 and the ship

Table 1. End-to-end message delay and delivery ratio for 6, 8, and 10 AUVs

	6	8	10			6	8	10
Direct	18.77	18.74	16.63		**Direct**	0.37	0.4	0.43
Epidemic	21.02	19.31	17.48		**Epidemic**	0.77	0.75	0.74
TPDR	21.02	20.47	18.89		**TPDR**	0.67	0.68	0.68

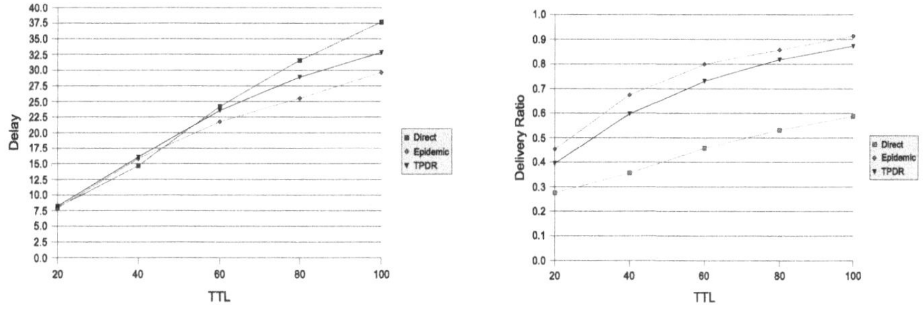

a) Message delay   b) Delivery ratio

Fig. 3. Protocol performance depending on the message TTL field

ratio comes within 10% of Epidemic Routing, which is a multi-copy routing approach. The delay is not better, as the routing decision picks the next hop with the highest probability of contact with the destination. We also note the better delay for the Direct Delivery protocol. This happens because most messages for this protocol get dropped due to expired TTL from lack of connectivity, and they do not contribute negatively to lower the average delay.

In the next experiment shown in Figure 3, the AUVs and the ship use message TTL that changes from 40 to 100. Figure 3 a) illustrates the variation of the message delay depending on TTL. As expected, a larger TTL increases the average delay, but also improves the delivery ratio. TPDR performs well for delay, but excels for delivery ratio. For higher TTLs, TPDR closes on the Epidemic Routing's delivery ratio, which is maximal, reaching above 80%.

5   Conclusions

In this paper we presented an approach for probabilistic DTN routing that uses prediction of the trajectory of mobile nodes. The prediction mechanism models the geographic rectangular grid as a Time-Homogeneous Markov Process, where the states map to grid cells, and the transitions between cells reproduce vehicle movement. This approach does not depend on the memoryless property for correct state estimation and supports arbitrary state holding time probability distributions that are i.i.d. and time-homogeneous (i.e. do not change over time). Based on the state transition prediction, we developed contact estimation using contact profiles. The profile gives the probability for a contact between two nodes in a particular time unit, regardless of the grid location. A DTN forwarding algorithm was developed, that selects the next hop based on the highest contact probability. Simulations have demonstrated the effectiveness of this algorithm.

References

1. Akyildiz, I.F., Kasimoglu, I.H.: Wireless sensor and actor networks: research challenges. Ad Hoc Networks, Elsevier 2, 351–367 (2004)
2. Burns, B., Brock, O., Levine, B.N.: Mv routing and capacity building in disruption tolerant networks. In: IEEE INFOCOM 2005, vol. 1, pp. 398–408 (2005)
3. Cerf, V., et al.: Delay tolerant network architecture. draft-irtf-dtnrg-arch-05.txt (March 2006)
4. Fall, K.: A delay-tolerant network architecture for challenged internets. Technical report, Intel Research, IRB-TR-03-003 (2003)
5. François, J.-M., Leduc, G.: Predictable disruption tolerant networks and delivery guarantees. CoRR, abs/cs/0612034 (2006)
6. Jain, S., Fall, K., Patra, R.: Routing in a delay tolerant network. In: SIGCOMM 2004. Proceedings of the 2004 conference on Applications, technologies, architectures, and protocols for computer communications, vol. 34, pp. 145–158. ACM Press, New York (2004)
7. Lee, J.-K., Hou, J.C.: Modeling steady-state and transient behaviors of user mobility: formulation, analysis, and application. In: MobiHoc 2006. Proceedings of the 7th ACM international symposium on Mobile ad hoc networking and computing, pp. 85–96. ACM, New York (2006)
8. Leguay, J., Friedman, T., Conan, V.: Evaluating mobility pattern space routing for dtns. In: INFOCOM 2006 (2006)
9. Li, Q., Rus, D.: Communication in disconnected ad hoc networks using message relay. J. Parallel Distrib. Comput. 63(1), 75–86 (2003)

10. Lindgren, A., Doria, A., Schelén, O.: Probabilistic routing in intermittently connected networks. In: SIGMOBILE: Mobile Computing Communications Review, vol. 7, pp. 19–20. ACM Press, New York (2003)
11. Melodia, T., Pompili, D., Akyildiz, I.F.: A Communication Architecture for Mobile Wireless Sensor and Actor Networks. In: Proceedings of IEEE SECON 2006, Reston, VA (September 2006)
12. Partan, J., Kurose, J., Levine, B.N.: A survey of practical issues in underwater networks. In: Proc. ACM International Workshop on UnderWater Networks (WUWNet), September 2006, pp. 17–24 (2006)
13. Rice, J.: Seaweb acoustic communication and navigation networks. In: The International Conference of Underwater Acoustic Measurements: Technologies and Results, Heraklion, Crete, Greece (July 2005)
14. Shah, R.C., Roy, S., Jain, S., Brunette, W.: Data mules: Modeling a three-tier architecture for sparse sensor networks. In: IEEE International Workshop on Sensor Network Protocols and Applications, May 2003, pp. 30–41 (2003)
15. Spyropoulos, T., Psounis, K., Raghavendra, C.S.: Spray and wait: an efficient routing scheme for intermittently connected mobile networks. In: The ACM SIGCOMM workshop on Delay-tolerant networking, pp. 252–259. ACM Press, New York (2005)
16. Vahdat, A., Becker, D.: Epidemic routing for partially connected ad hoc networks. Technical report, Duke University, CS-200006 (April 2000)
17. Zhang, Z.: Routing in intermittently connected mobile ad hoc networks and delay tolerant networks: Overview and challenges. In: IEEE Communications Surveys, vol. 8 (2006)
18. Zhao, W., Ammar, M., Zegura, E.: Controlling the mobility of multiple data transport ferries in a delay-tolerant network. In: INFOCOM 2005. 24th Annual Joint Conference of the IEEE Computer and Communications Societies. Proceedings IEEE, vol. 2, pp. 1407–1418 (2005)

A Simple Yet Effective Diversifying Improvement of the Minimum Power Multicast Tree Algorithms in Wireless Ad Hoc Networks*

Manki Min

Dept. of Electrical Engineering and Computer Science
South Dakota State University
Brookings, SD 57007, USA
Manki.Min@sdstate.edu

Abstract. In this paper, we present an iterated algorithm framework that can be implemented with heuristics in the literature for the minimum energy multicasting problem in wireless ad hoc networks to improve the solution quality. We investigate three iterated algorithm implementations, IBIP, IOMEGa, ISOR, that are based on BIP, OMEGa, SOR. The algorithms run iterations to find better solutions of the problem and in each iteration, fixing the source node's transmission power, the algorithm finds the intermediate solutions. And after all the iterations, the algorithm prunes the broadcast tree into a multicast tree and gives the output of the best solution so far. By fixing the source node's transmission power we can achieve the diverse solution search without hurting the original algorithm's theoretical performance bound. The experimental results confirm that the iterated algorithms significantly improve the solution quality.

1 Introduction

In wireless ad hoc networks, each device runs on its own battery, and hence conservation of the battery power is essential to prolong the whole network lifetime. The recent literature finds the studies about the multicast trees that minimizes the energy consumption in wireless ad hoc networks ([1], [2], [3], [5], [6], [7], [9], [11], [12], [8]). For unicast communications, we can adapt the traditional shortest path method to find the energy optimal path. But the multicast communications do not work well with the shortest path method. One interesting property of wireless communications is so-called WMA (wireless multicast advantage [11]) and it is the overlapping property of wireless communications.

The minimum energy multicast tree problem is NP-hard and hence, in the literature, we see two different types of approaches:

1. developing heuristics that efficiently compute good, but in most cases not optimal, solutions ([1], [2], [5], [6], [9], [11]) mostly based on WMA property, or

---

* Research is supported by NSF Award CCF-0729182.

2. developing mathematical formulations that are used to compute the optimal solutions exhaustively, but with some intelligence ([3], [7], [12], [8]) .

However, to our best knowledge, no explicit study of mixing the two different approaches has been found in the literature, except [7]. In [7], we used our efficient heuristic SOR [6] in our iterated algorithm to find the optimal solutions. In [7], in each iteration we used mathematical formulation to find an optimal solution with the help of heuristic solutions. Using fairly good solutions from the heuristic SOR as upper bounds for the solution value, we saw significant cut-offs of the search space. The optimization technique-based approach is designed to solve the broadcast problem and cannot solve the multicast tree problem. Our contribution in this paper is to explore the other way to combine the heuristics and the optimization techniques for the multicast tree problem by importing the optimization techniques for multicast tree problem into the heuristics to improve the solution quality. Evidently, there must be trade-offs between the solution quality improvement and the increase of running time and we investigate the trade-offs of the mixed approach.

In this paper, we present the iterated algorithm framework that can be applied to heuristics in the literature and compare the performance of algorithms applied to three heuristics, BIP ([11], OMEGa [5], SOR [6]). The comparison is made mainly on the perspective of the quality of the solution and running time issues. We claim that the theoretical performance bound of a heuristic is still valid for its iterated version. And the experimental results show the notable improvement on the solution quality.

The rest of this paper consists as follows. In section 2, related work including heuristics and optimization techniques in the literature are reviewed. section 3 presents our iterated algorithm framework. The computational results are discussed in section 4 and section 5 concludes this paper.

2   Related Work

In this section, we briefly review related work on minimum energy multicast tree problem in wireless ad hoc networks in two directions: heuristic approaches and optimization techniques.

In wireless networks, the network connectivity depends on the transmission power and the received signal power varies as $r^{-\alpha}$, where r is the range and α is a parameter that typically takes on a value between 2 and 4, depending on the characteristics of the communication medium. Based on this model, the transmission power p_{ij} required for a link between two nodes i and j separated by distance r is proportional to r^{α}. Ignoring the constant coefficient, we can model as $p_{ij} = r^{\alpha}$. For the computations, we used 2 as the value of α.

For multicasting communication, there exist a source node and destination nodes (called as multicast group) consisting of some nodes other than the source node. We assume that for any multicast request there is only one source node. One multicast tree rooted at the source node will be generated as a solution to the problem. In a multicast tree, there must be at least one path from the root to any node in the multicast group, and the sum of the transmission power of the tree should be minimized. Cagalj *et al* [1] provided the definition of the *Geometric Minimum Broadcast Cover (GMBC)* problem and shows its $\mathcal{NP}$-completeness by reduction from the *Planar 3-SAT problem* [4]. GMBC is to decide the power assignment for each node in the network represented as a two-dimensional Euclidean metric space such that the total power consumption is at most a constant amount and each node has a path from the source node. The multicast tree with the minimum transmission power will consume minimum energy and hence the minimum energy multicast tree problem in wireless ad hoc networks belongs to $\mathcal{NP}$-hard.

2.1 Heuristic Approaches

In this section, we review heuristics in the literature, specifically the ones used in our experiments.

Wieselthier *et al* presented the well known BIP (Broadcast Incremental Power algorithm) [11]. To improve energy-efficiency, BIP constructs a tree rooted at the source node by adding nodes with *minimum additional cost*. This algorithm is based on Prim's algorithm with iterative modifications of the link costs. The link costs will be updated at each step as follows:

$$p'_{ij} = p_{ij} - P(i) \tag{1}$$

where $P(i)$ is the power level at which node i is already transmitting. Most incremental heuristics use this concept of additional transmission power (Eq. 1) as the metric for the transmission selection to increment the tree ([1], [2], [5], [6], [9], [10], [11]). The authors also proposed two procedures: pruning phase and a local improvement phase called *sweep*. After a broadcast tree is obtained, the tree is pruned to a multicast tree by removing transmissions not included in any paths from the root to the multicast group. And the sweep operation reduces the power sum of the tree by removing redundant transmission energy. The redundancy of a transmission happens when removal of the transmission does not break the tree structure.

In our previous work [5], we presented a heuristic named *OMEGa* (Optimistic Most Energy Gain). OMEGa uses optimistic energy gain which is an estimation of energy gain when a transmission is used to build the tree. The actual energy gain is hard to compute, and its estimation by lower bound or upper bound of lower bound is used. At every iteration, we compute the optimistic energy gain of every possible pair of two nodes, one in the tree and the other not in the tree, and select the largest energy gain pair. In this way, OMEGa utilizes the WMA property which is essential to minimize the energy consumption. OMEGa also works for multicasting with small modification such that a node not in the multicast group will added with a low probability. After a broadcast tree is obtained, OMEGa prunes unnecessary transmissions, i.e., the transmissions of nodes that do not reach any node in the multicast group. In [6], we presented another heuristic named *SOR* (Shrinking Overlapped Range). SOR tries to change the current tree structure at the point when new nodes are added to the tree. The tree structure is changed by shrinking the overlapped transmission range based on WMA property. SOR also works for multicasting by means of the penalty function which ensures the node not in the multicast group can be selected as a relaying node only if it has a very close neighbor which is in the multicast group.

2.2   Optimization Techniques

In this section, we review the optimization techniques in the literature to solve the minimum energy broadcast tree problem. The techniques reviewed in this section are based on IP (Integer Programming).

IP has been used in [3], [12] as an optimization technique to solve the minimum energy broadcast tree problem. Five different IP formulations are proposed in [3], [12]. The main difficulty of the problem comes from the constraints of connectivity, or cycle prevention. The IP formulation should represent the constraints which ensure the existence of a path from the root to any node in the tree and this is the part which increases the complexity of the problem. The constraints are represented either by using sequential numbers on each node, or by using flow constraints. The power assignment is represented in two ways: find links and determine the minimum power of a node that can cover all the links that come out of the node, or find direct transmission destination and deal with the hidden link (which comes from WMA property).

Our previous experimental results in [7] show that all those formulations in [3], [12] find the optimal solutions very slowly even for small-sized problem with 10 or 20 nodes. Our results show that power assignment by finding direct transmission destination and cycle prevention by using flow constraints gives the fastest solution. This finding suggests strong connection between the optimal solution structure and the discrete power assignments. However, when the number of nodes increases, the computation time is exponentially slow and it is practically not feasible to use the IP to solve the problem. Two interesting and important points about IP formulations are that the power assignment by finding direct transmission destination gives tighter LP relaxation value and that flow constraints use less memory and converge faster. In addition to the IP formulations, we presented two iterated algorithms which make use of relaxed IP sub-formulations which describes the problem without the connectivity constraints. We showed our IP formulation finishes the computation at least 10 times faster than any other formulations and our iterated algorithms run in time less than 0.5 % of running time of our efficient IP formulation.

For IP formulations, it is assumed that we can reuse the formulation by adjusting the multicast group constraints. However, for the best performing iterated algorithms, further careful investigation is required and the work presented in this paper will be the first step towards the optimal algorithm for the multicast problem.

3   Iterated Algorithm Framework

In this section, we describe our iterated algorithm framework and explain its application to three heuristics BIP, OMEGa, SOR.

3.1   Basic Idea

It is intuitive that the diverse search of the solution space will give a better solution than the narrow search does. If we can extend the diversity to exhaustiveness, then the search will end up with an optimal solution and our previous work [7] is one of such approaches. In this paper we are going to try mixing the diverse search and the narrow search so that the mixed approach can provide improvement of the solution quality. Evidently when we increase the diversity, the running time will increase accordingly. We present a simple iterated algorithm framework that can improve the solution quality without dramatically increasing the running time.

The exhaustive search is to examine every possible multicast tree and see which requires the minimum energy. However this approach easily grows the running time exponentially and it's not practical to use the approach. Instead of examining every possible multicast tree, our framework will examine the multicast tree with a fixed source node's transmission power. More specifically, at the first iteration, set the transmission power of the source node to be the smallest among all the possible values and compute the multicast tree T_1 by using a heuristic for broadcast and then pruning. At the second iteration, increase the transmission power of the source node to be the second smallest and compute the multicast tree T_2. Now the two trees T_1 and T_2 may or may not have the same power sum. In either case we can choose the one with the smaller power sum as the current best tree T^*. And we continue until the transmission power of the source node becomes larger than the power sum of T^*. This part resembles the cut-offs by upper bounds used in our previous work [7]. The simple yet effective iterated algorithm framework works with any heuristics with a small modification such that the heuristic does not change the transmission power of the source node.

3.2   The Framework

Before describing the framework, we begin with notations and definitions used in the framework.

Let src be the source node of the multicast and k be the number of possible transmission powers of src. $k < n$, where n is the number of the nodes in the network and possibly k can be strictly less than $n-1$ if more than one nodes are at the same distance from the root. We assume $p_1, p_2, \ldots, p_k$ is the sorted list of all the possible transmission powers of src. For any multicast tree T, define $C(T)$ to be the sum of the transmission powers of all the transmitting nodes. Let T_i be the multicast tree computed after the i-th iteration and T^* be the current

Initialization
1. Run the original heuristic H to compute a multicast tree T_H.
2. Set $T^* = T_H$.
3. Sort the possible transmission powers of src that is not greater than $C(T^*)$ and list them as $p_1, p_2, \ldots, p_k$.
Iteration Do the following for every $i \in \{1, \ldots, k\}$:
4-i. Set the transmission power of src to be p_i.
4-ii. Run the modified heuristic H' to compute a broadcast tree and prune it into a multicast tree T_i.
4-iii. If $C(T_i) < C(T^*)$, then replace T^* with T_i.

Fig. 1. The iterated algorithm framework

best multicast tree with the minimum power sum found so far. Then after all the iterations we have, clearly,

$$C(T^*) \leq C(T_i), 1 \leq i \leq k$$

Let H be the original heuristic for multicast that will be implemented in the iterated algorithm and H' be the modified heuristic for broadcast such that H' behaves in just the same way as H except that H' does not change the src's transmission power. Let T_H be the multicast tree resulting from H. After all the iterations, we want to have $C(T^*) \leq C(T_H)$ and this can be achieved by first running H at the beginning of the iterated algorithm and use the solution value as the initial upper bound of the solution quality.

Now we are ready to describe the iterated algorithm framework (see Figure 1).

The broadcast tree T^* at the end of the execution of the algorithm is the final solution and $C(T^*) \leq C(T_H)$ since T^* will be replaced only when the power sum has decreased. Note that H' does not change the source node's transmission power to achieve more diversity. If the original algorithm H is purely incremental, i.e., increments the multicast tree without changing the previous tree structure, then the diversity obtained from using modified algorithm H' can be minimal. However, for a transformative algorithm such as SOR which changes the previous tree structure, we can expect more diversified search space than using only one algorithm H. Due to the extensive structure changes in the transformative algorithms, if we use the same algorithm H for two different, but consecutive transmission powers of src, then we may end up with the same transmission power of src and moreover the two multicast trees may be the same tree. On the contrast, if we use H' which doesn't change the transmission power of src, then the two tress for two different transmission powers of src will always have different transmission powers of src and therefore those two trees will always be different. Note that in the framework we only consider the possible transmission powers of src and the consecutive transmission powers of src mean a transmission power p_1 of src and the smallest transmission power p_2 for src to reach at least one new node in addition to the nodes reachable by p_1.

3.3   Analysis of the Framework

In this section, we theoretically analyze the proposed iterated algorithm framework.

The proposed framework can be implemented with any heuristic which incrementally finds the solution. Any heuristic that preserves the feasibility of the solution, such as EWMA, requires a further thorough investigation.

Theorem 1. *The iterated algorithm implemented with a heuristic H has the theoretical upper bound for the approximation ratio less than or equal to that of H.*

The iterated algorithm implemented with a heuristic H will produce a solution with the value of at most that of the solution of H. So, the iterated algorithm will have the theoretical upper bound for the approximation ratio less than or equal to that of H. This theoretical bound is not tight enough and more study is expected for thorough examination of the tighter bound.

Theorem 2. *Let H be the heuristic that is implemented in the framework and $t(H)$ be the running time complexity of H. Then the iterated algorithm implemented with H has time complexity of $O(n \cdot t(H))$, where n is the number of nodes in the network.*

Since the iterated algorithm will run at most $n - 1$ iterations by increasing the source node's transmission power. Hence, it is clear that the implemented iterated algorithm will have the running time complexity of $O(n \cdot t(H))$.

4   Computational Results

In this section, we present the computational results of six algorithms: BIP, OMEGa, SOR, IBIP, IOMEGa, and ISOR. IBIP, IOMEGa, and ISOR are the iterated algorithms for BIP, OMEGa, and SOR, respectively. In this work, we only consider static network environments. More practical settings such as dynamic topology, node failures are to be studied in future work.

For the tree computation, we generate 100 nodes located randomly in a 100 × 100 area with identical transmission range of 142. In this way, every node can communicate directly with any other node. The node firstly generated is set as the source node and the multicast group is determined randomly. For one node placement, multicast groups of four different sizes are generated: 25 % of the total number of nodes, 50 %, 75 %, and 100 % (broadcast). The power sum is normalized so that the minimum heuristic solution has the normalized value 1. All the results presented here are averaged numbers over 26 sets.

Figure 2 shows the simulation results of six algorithms: BIP, IBIP, OMEGa, IOMEGa, SOR, ISOR. The power sum is normalized and in most cases (except 25 % multicast group), ISOR generates the minimum among all the heuristic solutions. The bar graphs in (a) shows the solution quality of IBIP, IOMEGa, and ISOR. For the 25 % multicast group, IOMEGa generates the best solution on average. IOMEGa's solution shows 1.039 which means about 3.9 % away from the

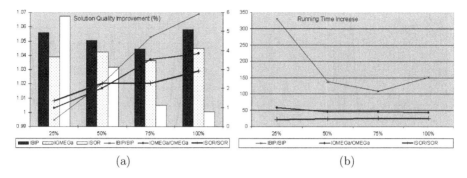

Fig. 2. Comparison of solution quality between the original heuristics and their iterated algorithms

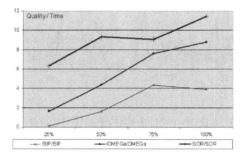

Fig. 3. Trade-offs between solution quality improvements and running time increase

heuristic minimum solutions. However, as the multicast group size grows, ISOR outperforms the other algorithms. It shows 1.032, 1.005, and 1.001 ratios to the heuristic minimum solutions for 50 %, 75 %, and 100 % (broadcast) multicast group. The line graphs in (a) shows the solution quality improvements of the iterated algorithms against the original algorithms. ISOR shows stable ratio for all multicast group sizes (between 1.35 and 2.92). However, the other two algorithms, expecially IBIP shows steep growth in the ratio (from 0.35 to 5.92). Even though the iterated algorithm framework can work with any incremental algorithms, the results show that IBIP may not be a good choice, especially for smaller size multicast groups. Moreover, in (b) which shows the running time increases, IBIP dramatically increases the running time compared to BIP. IBIP takes at least 109 times more than BIP while ISOR takes about 25 times more than SOR.

Figure 3 depicts the ratio of solution quality improvement over the running time increase. From the graph, we see that ISOR provides the best and the most stable performance. The graph should read as follows: ISOR will reduce the power sum by 0.115 % for each doubling of computation time for broadcast trees. This metric shows the feasibility of iterated framework for the algorithms

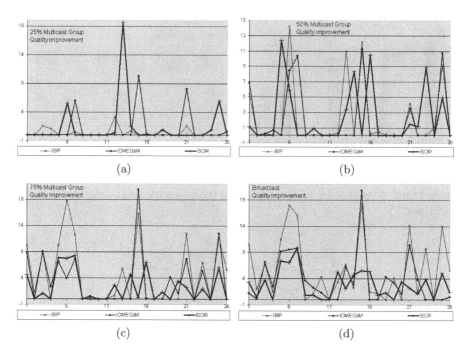

Fig. 4. Solution quality improvement of IBIP, IOMEGa, and ISOR for different multicast group sizes

and from the low ratio value $(0.001 \% \sim 0.039 \%)$ of IBIP, we can see that IBIP computation is not efficient enough. Figure 4 shows the solution quality improvements of each iterated algorithm against the original algorithm. The figures show the results of each run out of 26 runs. The higher y value means the better improvement. For example, in (a), ISOR cuts nearly 20 % of the power sum of the SOR solution. For the numeric representation of the results, please refer to Table 1.

5   Discussion

In this paper, we presented the iterated algorithm framework that can be used to improve the solution quality of any incremental approach heuristic for the minimum energy multicast tree problem. The simple, yet powerful diversification of search space provides significant solution quality improvement. We compared three incremental approach heuristics, BIP, OMEGa, and SOR. The results show ISOR, the iterated algorithm implementation of SOR, gives the best quality solution at the highest efficiency in terms of the trade-offs between quality improvement and running time increase. A more careful and thorough examination of the trade-offs will be helpful for better understanding of wireless communications and is one of the future works. Other future works include the study of

Table 1. Computational results

	25 %	50 %	75 %	100 %
Quality improvement (%)				
IBIP	0.3515	2.2512	4.7024	5.9182
IOMEGa	0.9630	2.0076	3.5112	3.8571
ISOR	1.3508	2.2728	2.2850	2.9197
Running time increase				
IBIP	331.1538	138.0385	108.3077	151.1154
IOMEGa	57.9519	45.9506	46.1083	43.9551
ISOR	21.2804	24.3615	25.2438	25.4927
Quality / Time (%)				
IBIP	0.1061	1.6308	4.3417	3.9164
IOMEGa	1.6617	4.3691	7.6150	8.7752
ISOR	6.3477	9.3294	9.0516	11.4532

tighter theoretical upper bound of the approximation ratio and the fine-tuning of the framework and also the extension of the framework to the optimization approach to find the optimal solution to the minimum energy multicast tree problem in wireless ad hoc networks.

References

1. Cagalj, M., Hubaux, J.-P., Enz, C.: Minimum-Energy Broadcast in All-Wireless Networks: NP-Completeness and Distribution Issues. In: Proceedings of the international conference on Mobile computing and networking, pp. 172–182 (2002)
2. Cheng, M.X., Sun, J., Min, M., Du., D.-Z.: Energy-efficient Broadcast and Multicast Routing in Ad Hoc Wireless Networks. In: Proceedings of the IEEE International Conference on Performance, Computing, and Communications Conference, pp. 87–94 (2003)
3. Das, A.K., Marks, R.J., El-Sharkawi, M., Arabshahi, P., Gray, A.: Minimum Power Broadcast Trees for Wireless Networks: Integer Programming Formulations. In: Proceedings of INFOCOM 2003 (2003)
4. Garey, M.R., Johnson, D.S.: Computers and Intractibility: A Guide to the Theory of NP-completeness. W.H. Freeman, San Francisco (1979)
5. Min, M., Pardalos, P.M.: OMEGa: an Optimistic Most Energy Gain Method for Minimum Energy Multicasting in Wireless Ad Hoc Networks (in submission, 2006)
6. Min, M., Pardalos, P.M.: Total Energy Optimal Multicasting in Wireless Ad Hoc Networks. Journal of Combinatorial Optimization (accepted, 2006)
7. Min, M., Prokopyev, O., Pardalos, P.M.: Optimal Solutions to Minimum Total Energy Broadcasting Problem in Wireless Ad Hoc Networks. Journal of Combinatorial Optimization, Special Issue on Wireless Network Applications 11, 59–69 (2006)
8. Montemanni, R., Gambardella, L.M.: Minimum Power Symmetric Connectivity Problem in Wireless Networks: A New Approach. In: Proceedings of IEEE International Conference on Mobile and Wireless Communication Networks (2004)
9. Wan, P.-J., Calinescu, G., Li, X.-Y., Frieder, O.: Minimum-Energy Broadcasting in Static Ad Hoc Wireless Networks. Wireless Networks 8, 607–617 (2002)

10. Wan, P.-J., Calinescu, G., Yi, C.-W.: Minimum-Power Multicast Routing in Static Ad Hoc Wireless Networks. IEEE/ACM Transactions on Networking 12, 507–514 (2004)
11. Wieselthier, J.E., Nguyen, G.D., Ephremides, A.: Energy-Efficient Broadcast and Multicast Trees in Wireless Networks. Mobile Networks and Applications 7, 481–492 (2002)
12. Yuan, D.: Computing Optimal or Near-Optimal Trees for Minimum-Energy Broadcasting in Wireless Networks. In: Proceedings of International symposyum on Modeling and Optimization in Mobile, Ad Hoc, and Wireless Networks, pp. 323–331 (2005)

Analytical Study of the Expected Number of Hops in Wireless Ad Hoc Network

Shadi M. Harb and Janise McNair

Department of Electrical and Computer Engineering,
University of Florida, FL 32611
sharb@tec.ufl.edu, mcnair@ece.ufl.edu

Abstract. Due to the randomness and mobility of ad hoc networks, estimating the average number of hops becomes very essential in multi-hop ad hoc networks, which is used as a key metric for performance comparison between multi-hop routing protocols; however, most current research derives the average number of hops based on simulations and empirical results, lacking the theoretical analysis of this essential metric. This paper presents a theoretical study of the expected number of hops between any two random nodes using typical modeling assumptions -an N-node randomly Poisson distributed connected network (i.e. for any two random nodes, they are connected by at least one path). The proposed theoretical analysis studies the relationship between the average number of hop counts and other critical ad hoc network parameters such as transmission range (r_0), node density (ρ), and area (A). At last, simulation results will be given to verify the theoretical analysis.

Keywords: Ad hoc Network, connectivity, expected number of hops, routing protocols, mathematical model.

1 Introduction

Ad hoc networks have many advantages over the traditional cellular radio systems. They have the ability to be rapidly deployed to support emergency requirement, short term needs and coverage in undeveloped areas [1]. In this environment, as network size grows, multi-hopping over several intermediate devices to reach the final destination becomes prevalent, because of obstacles, spatial spectrum reuse and power saving considerations. Moreover, mobility is common in ad hoc networks, because of the nature of the applications, which are diverse, ranging from small, static networks that are constrained by power sources, to large-scale, mobile, highly dynamic networks. However, due to the complexity and randomness of these networks, most current research focuses on delivering simulations and quantitative results to understand the behavior of these networks and a little has been done with regard to the theoretical analysis.

In ad hoc networks, the average number of hops is considered as one of the essential parameters, which is used as key metric for performance comparison between different multi-hop routing protocols. Besides, it can predict the delay that a packet

Y. Li et al. (Eds.): WASA 2008, LNCS 5258, pp. 63–71, 2008.
© Springer-Verlag Berlin Heidelberg 2008

takes to reach destination. Furthermore, the impact of hop counts on the network performance has been widely studies in literature. In [2], it is shown by simulations that the end-to-end throughput is degraded inversely with the number of required hop counts for the path due to mutual interferences between adjacent links. In [3], an analytical study has been done to show the significance of hop counts on the network capacity. In addition, the impact of hop counts in the tradeoffs between throughput and end-to-end delay in multi-hop wireless networks is presented in [4]. In [5], it is shown that the hop count also affects the target searching cost and latency in most existing ad hoc routing protocols. The expected per-hop progress in multi-hop wireless networks has been discussed in literature under certain assumptions [6-8], but the path connectivity probability has never been developed.

This paper presents a theoretical analysis of the expected number of hops for any random source and destination. Furthermore, the proposed theoretical study presents a derived model that shows the relationship between the average number of hops and different ad hoc network parameters such as transmission range (r_0), node density (ρ), and area (A). Moreover, it can be shown that the expected number of hops and the average distance between nodes are related to each other [9].

This paper is organized as follows: Section 2 presents the theoretical analysis. Simulation results are presented in section 3. A conclusion is given in section 4.

2 Theoretical Analysis

For our analysis, we assume a Poisson distributed nodes model, and all nodes in the ad hoc network have the same transmission range (r_0). In order to derive our presenting equations of the proposed analytical approach, let's define the probability of multi-hop counts between any two random nodes in the network, i.e., $P(1$-hop), $P(2$-hop), $P(3$-hop), ..., $P(m$- hop), where m is the maximum hops distance in the network. Consequently, we could formulate a mathematical expression of the expected number of hops as follows:

$$E(h) = \sum_{h=1}^{m} h \cdot P(h) = P(1) + 2 \cdot P(2) + \cdots + m \cdot P(m), \tag{1}$$

where m is the maximum hops distance in the network.

Thus, let's define the probability for the one-hop and two-hop cases, and generalize the formula for the m-hop case as described in the following sections:

2.1 One-Hop Connection

The probability of 1-hop connection can be derived as follows; we assume that the source and destination nodes are within the transmission range of each other (i.e., the source and destination are only 1-hop away). For this assumption, we consider the geometry given in Fig. 1.

Thus, the probability opy of a 1-hop count can be given as the probability that the destination is a direct neighbor to the source (i.e., $P(0<r\leq r_0)$), where r is the link distance between the source and destination.

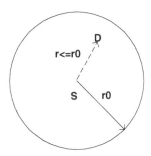

Fig. 1. Geometry of 1- Hop Connection

The probability density function for the shortest link distance [10-12] between two nodes is presented as follows:

$$f(r) = 2\pi\rho r * e^{-\rho\pi r^2},$$ (2)

where r is the distance, and ρ is the node density,

Hence, the probability of a 1-hop connection can be derived as follows:

$$P(1-hop) = \int_0^{r_0} f(r)dr = \int_0^{r_0} 2\pi\rho re^{-\rho\pi r^2} dr$$

$$P(1-hop) = 1 - e^{-\rho\pi r_0^2}$$ (3)

2.2 Two-Hop Connection

Similarly, we can derive the probability of a 2-hop count, let's assume that the destination for this case will lie in the second tier with respect to the source transmission range, thus, we can define that the 2-hop connection between source and destination nodes can exist if both of the following conditions are met:

- The positions for source and destination nodes are such that the distance between the nodes is greater than the transmission range r_0 but less than $2r_0$.
- There is at least one node that should be within the two nodes ranges.

The geometry of the 2-hop connection is illustrated in Fig. 2 by assuming S(x1,y1) is the source node, D(x2,y2) is the destination node, I(x3,y3) is the intermediate node, which is within both transmission ranges of the source and destination, and R(Circle Radius)= r_0 (transmission range).

Given the positions (x1,y1) and (x2,y2), the two circles with radius R intersect but their centers are greater than R apart; the position of the relay node (x3,y3) must lie within the intersection area of the two circles.

The probability of number of nodes (n_0) in a certain area for a Poisson distribution model [11] can be presented as follows:

$$P(n_0, A) = \frac{(\rho A)^{n_0} e^{-\rho A}}{n_0!},$$ (4)

where n_0 is number of nodes, and A is the area.

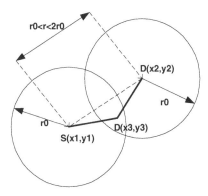

Fig. 2. Geometry of a two-hop connection

Furthermore, the probability of not having any node in a certain area can be described as follows:

$$P(n_0 = 0, A) = e^{-\rho A} \tag{5}$$

Thus, the probability of a 2-hop connection can be formulated as follows:

$$P(2 - hop) = P(r_0 < r < 2r_0) * P(n_0 > 0, A), \tag{6}$$

where A is the intersection area

Hence, the probability of a 2-hop connection can be derived as follows:

$$P(2 - hop) = \int_{r_0}^{2r_0} 2\pi\rho r * e^{-\rho\pi r^2} dr * [1 - p(n0 = 0, A)]$$

$$P(2 - hop) = \left[e^{-\rho\pi r_0^2} - e^{-4\rho\pi r_0^2} \right] * \left[1 - e^{-\rho A} \right], \tag{7}$$

where, $A = r_0^2 \left[2\cos^{-1}\left(\dfrac{r}{2r_0}\right) - \sin\left(2\cos^{-1}\left(\dfrac{r}{2r_0}\right)\right) \right]$, as shown in appendix A

Similarly, we can derive the probability of a 3-hop connection, as described in the following equations:

$$P(3 - hop) = P(2r_0 < r < 3r_0) * P(n_0 > 0, A) \tag{8}$$

where A is the intersection area

$$P(3 - hop) = \left[e^{-4\rho\pi r_0^2} - e^{-9\rho\pi r_0^2} \right] * \left[1 - e^{-\rho A} \right]^2 \tag{9}$$

Consequently, the probability of m-hop connection can be generalized as follows:

$$P(m - hop) = \left[e^{-(m-1)^2 \rho\pi r_0^2} - e^{-m^2 \rho\pi r_0^2} \right] * \left[1 - e^{-\rho A} \right]^{m-1} \tag{10}$$

Base on equations (1) and (10), the expected number of hops can be derived as follows:

$$E(h) = \sum_{h=1}^{m} h * \left[e^{-(h-1)^2 \rho\pi r_0^2} - e^{-h^2 \rho\pi r_0^2} \right] * \left[1 - e^{-\rho A} \right]^{h-1} \tag{11}$$

As shown in equation (11), the derived equation defines the relationship between the expected number of hops, transmission range, node density and area.

3   Simulation

A wireless ad hoc network environment with a shortest path routing algorithm has been implemented in Matlab 7 as shown in Fig. 3. The following assumptions and constraints have been considered for simulation purposes and summarized in Table 1:

Table 1. Simulation setup and assumptions

Random distribution function is used to scatter nodes over a finite area A=1500 × 1500 m²
Transmission range (r_0) varies from 100-900m   Node density (ρ) varies from 100-500 nodes.
The shortest hop distance between any two nodes is considered

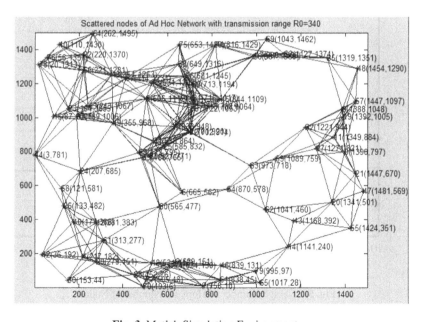

Fig. 3. Matlab Simulation Environment

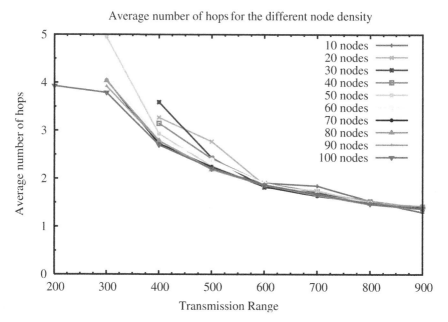

Fig. 4. Average Number of Hops vs. Transmission Range

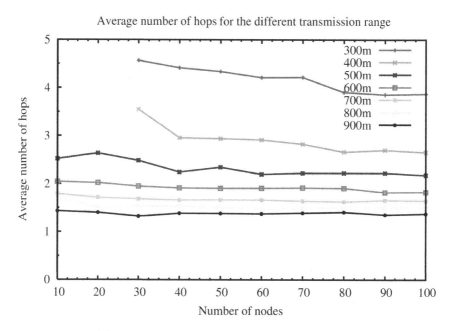

Fig. 5. Average Number of Hops vs. Number of Nodes

The conducted simulations show the effect of varying the transmission range and number of nodes on the average number of hops. Fig. 4 shows a significant decrease in the average number of hops as the transmission range increases for a fixed number of nodes and area. The presented graph also shows that the simulated network with less number of nodes have a relatively high average number of hops compared to the network with large number of nodes. On the other hand, the average number of hops decreases slightly as the number of nodes increases given a fixed transmission range as shown in Fig. 5. Finally, our analytical results are verified as shown in Fig. 6. The analysis results match our simulation results very well and show an appropriate parametric relationship between the expected number of hops, transmission range, node density, and area.

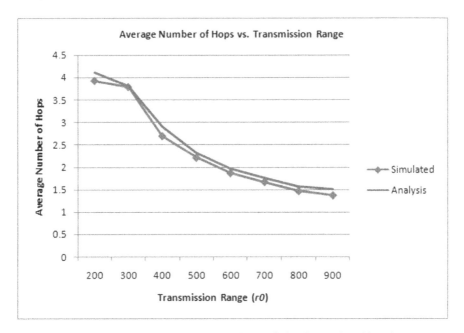

Fig. 6. Average Number of Hops vs. Transmission Range for 100 nodes

4   Conclusion

In ad hoc networks, the average number of hops can be used as key metric for performance comparison between multi-hop routing algorithms, besides; it can be used to predict the routing delay for a packet to reach destination. In this paper, we presented a mathematical model for the expected number of hops based on a Possion randomly distributed network. The proposed analysis shows the relationship between the expected number of hops with other ad hoc parameters such as transmission range, node density, and area. Matlab simulations have been conducted to verify the mathematical model, which measures the expected number of hops between any random source and destination based on a shortest hops distance algorithm. Furthermore, the derived model matches our simulation results very well and shows an appropriate parametric relationship between the expected number of hops, transmission range, node density, and area, which meets our expectations based on the simulated results.

References

1. Perkins, C.E. (ed.): Ad hoc networking. Addison-Wesley, Reading (2000)
2. Li, J., Blake, C., Couto, D., Lee, H., Morris, R.: Capacity of ad hoc wireless networks. In: Proc. ACM MobiCom, pp. 61–69 (2001)
3. Jun, J., Sichitiu, M.: The nominal capacity of wireless mesh networks. IEEE Wireless Commun. 10(5), 8–14 (2003)
4. Gamal, A., Mammen, J., Prabhakar, B., Shah, D.: Throughput–delay trade-off in wireless networks. In: Proc. IEEE Infocom, pp. 464–475 (2004)
5. Cheng, Z., Heinzelman, W.B.: Flooding strategy for target discovery in wireless networks. In: Proc. ACM MSWiM, September 2003, pp. 33–41 (2003)
6. Kleinrock, L., Silvester, J.: Optimum transmission radii for packet radio networks or why six is a magic number. In: Proc. IEEE Nat. Telecommun. Conf., Birmingham, AL, December 1978, pp. 4.3.1–4.3.5 (1978)
7. Hou, T.C., Li, V.O.K.: Transmission range control in multi-hop packet radio networks. IEEE Trans. Commun. COM-34(1), 38–44 (1986)
8. Nagpal, R., Shrobe, H., Bachrach, J.: Organizing a global coordinate system from local information on an
9. Li, D.Y.: A statistical study of Neighbor Node properties in Ad hoc network. In: International Conference on Parallel Processing Workshops, pp. 103–108 (2002)
10. Cressie, N.A.C.: Statistics for Spatial Data. John Wiley & Sons, Chichester (1991)
11. Bettstetter, C.: On the Minimum Node Degree and Connectivity of a Wireless Multi-hop Network. In: Proceedings of the 3rd ACM international symposium on Mobile Ad hoc networking & computing, pp. 80–91 (2000)
12. Miller, L.E.: Distribution of Link Distances in a Wireless Network. NIST J. of Research (Spring 2001)
13. Dousse, O., et al.: Connectivity in ad hoc and hybrid networks. In: Proc. Infocom (2002)
14. Papoulis, Probability, random variables, and stochastic processes. McGraw–Hill, New York (1984)
15. The MathWorks: http://www.mathworks.com
16. Diestel, R.: Graph Theory, 2nd edn. Springer, Heidelberg (2000)
17. Bollob´as, B.: Modern Graph Theory. Springer, Heidelberg (1998)
18. Johnson, D.B., Maltx, D.A.: Dynamic Source Routing in Ad hoc Wireless Network. In: Tmielinski, T., Korth, H. (eds.) Mobile Computing, ch. 5, Kluwer Academic, Dordrecht (1996)
19. Johnson, D.B., Maltx, D.A.: The Dynamic Source Routing Protocol for Mobile Ad hoc Network (DSR) (April 2003)
20. Perkins, C.E., Royer, E.M.: Ad hoc On-Demand Distance Vector Routing. In: Proceeding of 2nd IEEE Workshop on Mobile Computing Systems and Applications, pp. 90–100 (February 1999)
21. Perkins, C.E., Royer, E.M.: Ad hoc On-Demand Distance Vector Routing (AODV) (July 2003), http://www.ietf.org/rfc/rfc3561.txt
22. Scalable Networks Technologies, http://www.scalable-networks.com/
23. GloMoSim, http://pcl.cs.ucla.edu/projects/glomosim/

24. Chang, N., Liu, M.: Revisiting the TTL-based controlled flooding search: Optimality and randomization. In: Proc. ACM MobiCom, September 2004, pp. 85–99 (2004)
25. Bruno, R., Conti, M., Gregori, E.: Mesh networks: Commodity multi-hop ad hoc networks. IEEE Commun. Mag. 43(3), 123–131 (2005)

Appendix A: Intersection Area between Two Circles

As illustrated in the figure below, the intersection area between two circles can be formulated as follows:

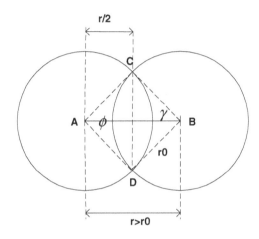

$$\theta = 2\gamma, \cos\gamma = \frac{r}{2r_0}$$

$$\gamma = \cos^{-1}\frac{r}{2r_0}$$

$$\theta = 2\gamma = 2\cos^{-1}\left(\frac{r}{2r_0}\right)$$

$$A = 2[Area(Sector(ACD)) - Area(Triangular(ACD))]$$

$$A = 2\left[\frac{1}{2}(\theta)r_0^2 - \frac{1}{2}r_0^2 * \sin\theta\right]$$

$$A = 2\left[\frac{1}{2}\left(2\cos^{-1}\left(\frac{r}{2r_0}\right)\right)r_0^2 - \frac{1}{2}r_0^2 * \sin\left(2\cos^{-1}\left(\frac{r}{2r_0}\right)\right)\right]$$

$$A = r_0^2\left[2\cos^{-1}\left(\frac{r}{2r_0}\right) - \sin\left(2\cos^{-1}\left(\frac{r}{2r_0}\right)\right)\right]$$

HoP: Pigeon-Assisted Forwarding in Partitioned Wireless Networks⋆

Hui Guo[1], Jiang Li[1], and Yi Qian[2]

[1] Department of Systems and Computer Science
Howard University, Washington DC, 20059, USA
[2] National Institute of Standards and Technology
Gaithersburg, Maryland, 20899, USA
hguo@networks.howard.edu, lij@scs.howard.edu, yqian@nist.gov

Abstract. Due to the mobility, limited radio range and low density of mobile devices, the mobile *ad-hoc* and sensor networks are vulnerable to be partitioned into a group of clusters. In our work, we propose using a set of messengers (called pigeons) that relay messages among clusters. Each cluster in networks owns multiple dedicated pigeons moving around the plane to deliver messages to their destinations. We name this form as homing-pigeon (HoP) based messaging scheme. The proposed scheme is different from the preceding work such as Message Ferry and Data Mules that it is a dedicated messenger scheme. Our goal is to exploit an optimized pigeon scheduling algorithm that can promote cooperation among multi-pigeons, enhance the system performance and reduce the cost. Using simulations, we evaluate the algorithms under different scenarios. The results can be used for better understanding the impact of algorithms on system performance.

Keywords: Homing-pigeon system, Delay-tolerant networks, Scheduling algorithms, Wireless networks.

1 Introduction

Wireless *ad-hoc* networks allow nodes to communicate with each other without any existing infrastructure. Traditional routing algorithms such as DSR, AODV view the network as a connected graph over which end-to-end paths always exists. In most of real situations, however, due to node mobility, limited radio range, sparse node deployment, etc., the networks are often vulnerable to be partitioned into isolated entities. Each entity is composed of a group of connected nodes, named as cluster. These clusters have end-to-end paths between nodes within each cluster. However, the inter-cluster communication path is not available due to long distance. The paradigm of partitioned wireless network belongs to the general category of Delay-Tolerant Networks (DTNs) [1] where most of the time there does not exist a complete path from a source to a destination. Presently, what all existing

---

⋆ The work was funded in part by NSF grant CNS-0832000 and the Mordecai Wyatt Johnson Program at Howard University.

Y. Li et al. (Eds.): WASA 2008, LNCS 5258, pp. 72–83, 2008.

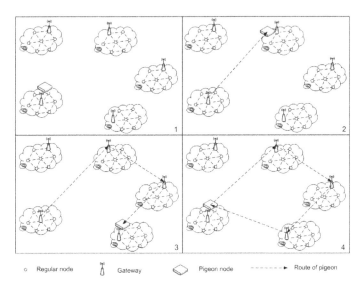

| ○ Regular node | Gateway | Pigeon node | -------► Route of pigeon |

Fig. 1. An example of HoP based messaging system

transmission approaches in DTNs share in common is that physical movement of nodes must be exploited to carry messages around the network to overcome path disconnection, which refers to *store-carry-and-forward* scheme [2].

In our work, we use controlled mobility to overcome network partitions. Specifically, a set of special mobile messengers called *pigeons* are responsible for carrying data among isolated clusters by moving around the deployment area along scheduled routes. Each cluster in networks owns multiple dedicated pigeons, and the cluster that a pigeon is dedicated to is called the home of that pigeon. When the nodes in a cluster have messages for destination nodes in other clusters, the messages are bundled together (i.e., message bundles [1]) and then uploaded to the pigeon, the pigeon will have a round trip starting from its home, through the destination clusters and return to home, disseminating the messages on its way. An example is shown in Fig. 1. In this figure, we suppose each cluster elects a most suitable node as its gateway (e.g., nodes with more energy resource, higher communication capacity). The gateway is responsible for collecting messages from one or more nodes in the same cluster and uploading them to the pigeon. When a pigeon passed by, the gateway is responsible for downloading received messages from the pigeon and distributing the messages to their respective destination nodes. The intra-cluster communication among nodes can resort to existing *ad-hoc* routing algorithms.

As the proposed strategy is similar to ancient messaging system using homing pigeons, we name it homing-pigeon (HoP) based messaging system. HoP scheme can be used in many practical scenarios that networks are partitioned into several entities. For example, in message transportation among several battlefields, communication between multiple disaster rescue groups, field hospitals or remote disconnected villages. A requirement of HoP delivery scheme is that pigeons know the location of other clusters. This requirement is reasonable as the current location of a cluster could be transmitted to the pigeons through various long-distance communication technologies, such as GPS.

The contribution of this paper is to present a new way for message delivering in partitioned wireless networks, which is practical and efficient to overcome network disconnections. The major difference with previous related approaches such as Message Ferry [6], DataMule [7] is that it propose the ownership conception of messengers (pigeons). Under multiple pigeons scenario, how to schedule these pigeons to promote their cooperation, maximize system performance and reduce the cost is a challenge issue. In this work, we propose a heuristic scheduling algorithm and compare it with other more intuitive algorithms. Our goal is to find out an effective way to deliver data in this challenging network environments and design a more reasonable and intelligent scheduling algorithm for pigeons. Using simulations, we can better understand the system performance in term of delay, cost and efficiency.

The rest of this paper is organized as follows: the next section discusses related work. In Section 3, we describe the network model and assumptions. Section 4 describes the algorithms in detail. The results are evaluated by simulations in Section 5. Finally, conclusions are drawn in Section 6.

2 Related Work

Depending on whether node movement is controlled or not, the message transmission mechanisms falls into two categories. One utilizes the inherent movements of nodes (reactive), while the other enforces artificial node moving patterns (proactive). There has been work in both directions. Some examples of the work in the first category can be found in [3], [4] and [5]. Schemes of this kind have the advantages of without disturbing the behavior of existing nodes and not adding extra nodes. On the contrary, the second category intervenes in node movement. Usually, auxiliary nodes are added into the network, and their movements are controlled to facilitate messages relaying among existing nodes. This kind of schemes are suitable for critical applications that require system performance is predictable and controllable, e.g., military applications, disaster recovery. Our proposed HoP based messaging system falls into this category. Most of existing schemes of this kind, e.g., Message Ferry [6], Data Mules [7], have auxiliary nodes shared by all source nodes (shared messenger scheme). That is, an auxiliary node can carry messages on behalf of any source nodes, which differs from HoP scheme described in this paper where pigeons (auxiliary nodes) only serve their home nodes and completely under control of the home node (dedicated messenger scheme).

Our previous work [8] have investigated the system performance of HoP scheme through modeling the message delivery process as a queueing system. However, the discussion is based on a couple of simplistic assumptions such as each cluster owns single pigeon, the pigeon carries fixed number of messages at each trip. In this article, we relax these assumptions to make the model more realistic and practical.

3   The Model

We consider the scenarios when the networks are partitioned into several clusters. Each cluster is composed of a group of nodes, and there is a end-to-end path between any two nodes within the same cluster. The nodes in different cluster, however, can not communicate directly due to long distance and nonexistence of communication infrastructure. In real scenarios, the clusters could either be mobile, such as in battlefields, search/rescue groups, or be stationary, such as in field hospital or remote disconnected villages. For simplicity, in this work we only consider the cases that clusters are stationary. The cases of mobile clusters leave in our future research. For ease of description, we denote the term **node** as a partitioned cluster in our following discussion. We model the system as following:

- The destination nodes are stationary and uniformly distributed around the deployment area;
- The data generation at each node follows a Poisson process. All of nodes have the same average rate of λ;
- The traffic falls into uniform pattern. That is, all of recipient nodes have an equal probability of acting as destination of a message;
- Each node owns multiple pigeons for message delivery. The pigeons move around with a stable speed of v;
- The size of messages comply with normal distribution with expectation of δ.

Table 1. Symbols of system parameters

Symbols	Definition
n	total number of destination nodes in deployment area
k	the number of available pigeons at home node
v	traveling speed of the pigeon
λ	average message arrival rate at source node
δ	average size of messages
T	the next pigeon comes back at time T
m	m number of messages queuing at home for delivery
t	the $(m+1)$-th (next) message arrive at time t

We try to model the system close to realistic environments. The objective is to propose a more reasonable and adaptive scheduling algorithm for pigeons to enhance system performance and promote the cooperation among pigeons. Through simulations we can provide guidance and forecast for the performance of such system. The symbols and notations used in our analysis are summarized in Table 1.

4   Algorithms

In homing-pigeon based messaging system, data is transported via pigeons mobility. Therefore, the design of movement of pigeons have significant impact on network performance. As we know, the movement of each pigeon is a round trip starting from its home node, we expect to get a shortest path that passing through all of the destinations to minimize data delivery delay. To compute the pigeon route, we can resort to the solutions for well-studied traveling salesman problem (TSP) [9]. Hence the route design of pigeon is not a key issue in our work. Our concern is that given a number of available pigeons at source (home) node, how to schedule these multiple pigeons to get a higher system performance. In addition, suppose there is a cost for movement of pigeon, we compare the costs introduced by different scheduling strategies. In this section we present two intuitive scheduling algorithms, On-Demand and Periodic at first, then we describe our Adaptive Pigeon Scheduling (APS) algorithm in detail.

4.1   On-Demand Scheduling

The pigeons will start out to deliver messages as soon as their home nodes exist any message need to be delivered. Specifically, when a pigeon returns to its home node, if there are messages queuing at the home node to wait for being delivered, the pigeon will departure immediately to deliver these messages. Otherwise, the pigeon will wait until the first message delivering request arrive and then start out.

4.2   Periodic

The periodic algorithm means that pigeons inter-departure time is fixed, which is denoted as T_0. Suppose the elapsed time from the last pigeon's departure to current pigeon's arrival is η. When a pigeon returns, if $\eta < T_0$, the pigeon will wait for a longer time of $T_0 - \eta$ before start out. Otherwise, if $\eta > T_0$, the pigeon will depart its home immediately. This strategy is similar to a shuttle system where shuttles leave their starting point periodically. The determination of value of T_0 have a trad-off between system performance and pigeon traveling cost. For example, a larger value of T_0 will achieve a smaller pigeon traveling distance in total but will lead to longer messages delay. The range of T_0 can be figured out as following. Suppose a pigeon costs the time of t_a for passing through all destinations, and costs the time of t_0 for passing through a single node. If there are k pigeons at source node, the T_0 should be $t_0/k < T_0 < t_a/k$.

4.3   Adaptive Pigeon Scheduling (APS)

The adaptive pigeon scheduling (APS) algorithm is target for reducing average messages waiting time, i.e., the period from the generation of a message to its departure time from the source node. As message waiting time act as an important part of message delivery delay, we believe that reducing average messages waiting time can achieve reduced average messages delivery delay. In APS algorithm, the pigeon has a self-determination mechanism to decide whether leave its home immediately or wait for a longer time before leave, which is adapt to specific conditions. The algorithm is to promote the cooperation of multiple pigeons to reduce the average messages delivery delay.

We consider the situation when a pigeon comes back. At this time the pigeon has two choices: The first case, the pigeon start out immediately, do not waiting for the $(m+1)$-*th* message's arrival (suppose there are m number of messages queuing at the home for delivery); The second case, the pigeon will wait until the $(m+1)$-*th* message arrived, or until the time of T' elapsed (T' will be described later), then start out. Suppose current time (the time when doing calculation) is always 0, the next pigeon will comes back at time T (T is certainly can be calculated as the route of pigeon has been predetermined before pigeon start out). Suppose the waiting time for each of the m messages is t_i, $i = 1, 2, ..., m$, and the $(m+1)$-*th* message will arrive at t. If $t <= T$, in the first case, the $(m+1)$-*th* message have to wait at that source (home node) until the next pigeon return, its waiting time is at least $T - t$. Thus the average waiting time of the group of $m + 1$ messages is at least

$$\overline{T_{w1}} = (t_1 + t_2 + ... + t_m + T - t)/(m + 1) \tag{1}$$

In second case, the current pigeon will wait until $(m+1)$-*th* message arrive then start out immediately. In this case the $(m+1)$-*th* message's waiting time is 0. However, the previous m number of messages must wait for a longer time of t. The average waiting time of the $m + 1$ messages is

$$\overline{T_{w2}} = (t_1 + t_2 + ... + t_m + mt)/(m + 1) \tag{2}$$

If the pigeon choose to wait for a while before start out, it should be $\overline{T_{w2}} < \overline{T_{w1}}$, i.e., $t < T/(m + 1)$, that waiting for a longer time (until the arrival of $(m+1)$-*th* message) can achieve a smaller average waiting time than starting out immediately. In case of $t > T$, it is obvious that the $(m+1)$-*th* message should be delivered by the next pigeon, i.e., the current pigeon should leave immediately. Therefore, we do not need to discuss this case. We only consider the case of $t <= T$.

We define $T' = T/(m + 1)$. From previous analysis we can get the conclusion that: If the $(m+1)$-*th* message will arrive before T' (i.e., $t < T'$), waiting for the arrival of $(m+1)$-*th* message will achieve a smaller average waiting time. Otherwise, if the $(m+1)$-*th* message will arrive after T' ($t > T'$), waiting for the arrival of $(m+1)$-*th* message will introduce a larger average waiting time. The APS algorithm is to compare the probability of these two different cases to make a decision. As the inter-arrival time of messages falls into exponential distribution, the probability of the next message will arrive before $T/(m + 1)$ (i.e., $t <= T'$) is

$$P(t < T') = \int_0^{T'} \lambda e^{-\lambda t} dt = 1 - e^{-\lambda T'} \tag{3}$$

Also, we have

$$P(T' < t < T) = \int_{T'}^{T} \lambda e^{-\lambda t} dt = e^{-\lambda T'} - e^{-\lambda T} \tag{4}$$

Notations

λ: average messages arrival rate

k: number of available pigeons

m: number of messages queuing at home for delivery

v: speed of pigeons

$\mathbb{C}_{dest}$: set of coordinates of destination nodes

L_i: shortest length of a TSP route for pigeon i

t_i: returning time of pigeon i

t_{cur}: current time (the time when doing calculation)

$\mathbb{T}_k$: set of pigeons' returning time

T: the duration from now to next pigeon's return

input : λ, k, v, and nodes coordinates.

output: scheduling strategy for pigeons.

```
1  for i ← 1 to k do
2  │   C_dest ⇐ coordinates of destination nodes for pigeon i;
3  │   L_i ← TSP(C_dest);
4  │   t_i ← L_i/v+t_cur;
5  │   T_k ⇐ t_i;
6  end
7  while (1) do
8  │   if a pigeon (pigeon i) comes back to home then
9  │   │   m ← Update(m);
10 │   │   while pigeon i stay at its home do
11 │   │   │   t_i ← ∞;
12 │   │   │   T ← Min(T_k) − t_cur;
13 │   │   │   T' ← T/(m + 1);
14 │   │   │   if e^{−λT'} < (1+e^{−λT})/2 then
15 │   │   │   │   t_old ← t_cur;
16 │   │   │   │   while (1) do
17 │   │   │   │   │   if a message arrived then
18 │   │   │   │   │   │   m ← m + 1; break;
19 │   │   │   │   │   end
20 │   │   │   │   │   if t_cur ≥ t_old + T' then
21 │   │   │   │   │   │   break;
22 │   │   │   │   │   end
23 │   │   │   │   end
24 │   │   │   end
25 │   │   │   else
26 │   │   │   │   pigeon i start out right now;
27 │   │   │   end
28 │   │   end
29 │   end
30 end
```

Algorithm 1. adaptive pigeon scheduling algorithm

If $P(t < T') > P(T' < t < T)$, i.e., $e^{-\lambda T'} < \frac{1+e^{-\lambda T}}{2}$, the pigeon will choose to wait. Otherwise, the pigeon start out immediately.

If the pigeon choose to wait, it will wait until the (m+1)-*th* message arrival or wait for at most the time of T' at this round. Once the (m+1)-*th* message arrived, or once the duration of T' expired (i.e., no message arrived during the period of T'), the pigeon will conduct the same judgments again to decide whether leave right now or wait for a longer time for the next round. The judgment should be conducted repeatedly at each time when a new message request arrived or until the period of T' elapsed. This loop will continue until $P(t < T') < P(T' < t < T)$. Note that the value of T (current time to return time of next pigeon), m and T' ($T/(m + 1)$) should be updated before calculation at each round. The algorithm is described in *Algorithm 1*.

5   Simulations

We evaluate the homing-pigeon based transportation system under various parameter settings, with a focus on the following important metrics: average messages delivery delay, pigeons traveling cost and efficiency. We also compared our proposed APS algorithm with other two intuitive algorithms, On-Demand and Periodic.

5.1   Simulation Setup

We have implemented the prototype of HoP messaging system in OPNET Modeler [10] to extensivly evaluate our design. In our simulations, 50 nodes (each node represents a cluster in real network) are randomly distributed around 6 $km \times$ 6 km area. We choose one of the nodes as observation node to understand system performance. The observation node acts as a source node, which generates sending messages with the average rate of λ. Each message chooses one of other nodes as its destination with equal probability. The source node owns k number of pigeons that moving around the deployment area at a speed of v. The transmission range of both the nodes and the pigeons is 200 m and the data rate is 10 $Mbps$. As we expect that the pigeon would visit the destinations with shortest path, we use the solutions of well-studied traveling salesman problem (TSP) [9]. Specifically, we use the bio-inspired Ant Colony Optimization (ACO) algorithm [11] to compute the pigeons routes. ACO algorithm has been proved to be a successful and low-cost solution to solve the TSP problem. Given node coordinates and parameters described above, we use the proposed algorithms discussed before to schedule multiple pigeons. In periodic algorithm, pigeons inter-departure time is fixed as 1200 seconds, which is based on one-fourth of average round-trip time of a pigeon in single pigeon system (as the default number of pigeons is 4). The simulation duration at each time is 12 hours. Simulation parameters are summarized in Table 2. The default values of parameters are used for all experiments unless otherwise stated. The value range of parameters are used to evaluate the impact of value's variation on simulation results.

Table 2. Simulation parameters in OPNET

Parameters	Normal Value	Value Range
Topology	6 $km\times$ 6 km	N/A
Simulation time	12 hours	N/A
# of nodes	50	N/A
# of pigeons	4	2 - 10
Pigeon speed	10 m/s	5 - 40 m/s
Message arrival rate	0.05 message/s	0.01 - 2.05
Average message size	9 kBytes	8k - 4096 kBytes
Periodic time	1200 sec	N/A
Communication range	200 m	N/A
Data rate	10 Mbps	N/A

5.2   Result and Analysis

The average messages delay (AMD) is an important performance metric for partitioned networks. In Fig. 2, we compare the AMD under different algorithms. We can see that our proposed APS algorithm achieves lowest delay at all kinds of scenarios, while the periodic algorithm incurred highest delay, which is the result we expected. Fig. 2(a) shows the impact of changing number of pigeons on AMD. We can see that in both APS and On-Demand schemes, the messages delay decreases dramatically with the increase of pigeons. This result demonstrates that these two algorithms achieve good system scalability. In periodic scheme, however, the increase of pigeons does not have much influence on performance. The reason is that pigeon's departure time is based on a fixed periodic time rather than available pigeons. Fig. 2(b) presents the impact of increasing λ (messages arrival rate) on AMD. We make the following observations. First, AMD increases with the increase of λ for all algorithms. Second, with the increase of λ, larger than 0.11, the AMD remains steady state approximately. Third, the difference between periodic and the other two algorithms is dramatically when λ is small. It is because that when λ is small, there are small number of messages delivered by pigeon at one trip, thus the pigeon could return quickly. In periodic algorithm, the pigeon have to wait for a longer time before start out again because the period from departure of the last pigeon to arrival of current pigeon is smaller than a fixed inter-departure time. Fig. 2(c) shows the results of AMD as a function of speed of pigeon. It is obvious that AMD decreases with the increase of speed of pigeon. We can see that in APS and On-Demand schemes, the AMD decreases more quickly than periodic scheme, and with the continuously increase of the speed (larger than 25 m/s), the decrease of AMD is not dramatically for all algorithms. We can conclude that when speed of pigeon is small, the increase of speed has more effect on system performance than the cases when speed of pigeon is already large enough.

Another issue we are concerning about is the cost of movement of pigeon movement. We suppose there are traveling cost of pigeons, and the cost is proportional to its traveling distance. For simplicity, we consider the traveling

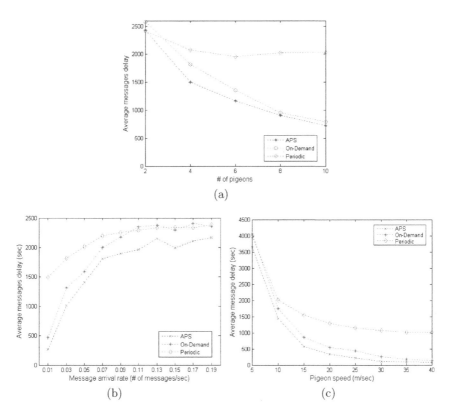

Fig. 2. Average messages delay under different algorithms

distance of pigeon as the cost in our experiments. Fig. 3 shows the total traveling distance of pigeons (4 pigeons) during 12 hours simulation time with different values of λ. We can see that the On-Demand algorithm achieves the largest pigeons traveling distance, while the periodic algorithm is the smallest one. We conclude that the periodic algorithm consumes the least of cost for movement of pigeon. The reason is because that in periodic algorithm, the pigeons would carry more messages at once trip. While in On-Demand algorithm, the pigeons would start out immediately as soon as there are messages queueing at source node, therefore they carry smaller number of messages at each trip, which cause larger travel distance totally. In addition, we observe that in APS algorithm, the variation of λ does not have much influence on traveling distance of pigeon.

Next we examine the traveling distance of pigeons for a given number of delivered messages with different algorithms. Fig. 4 shows the results. Basically, the traveling distance of pigeons increases linearly with the increase of delivered messages. Similarly, the period algorithm always achieves the smallest cost (i.e., traveling distance of pigeons). Given the traveling distance of a pigeon, we wish the pigeon could carry data as much as possible. In our work, we define efficiency of a pigeon as the ratio between the amount of delivered data by the pigeon and

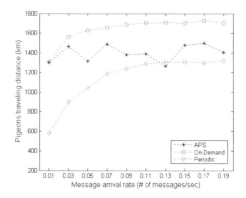

Fig. 3. Pigeons traveling distance with different λ

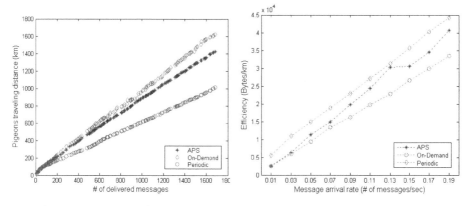

Fig. 4. Pigeons traveling distance as a function of delivered messages

Fig. 5. Pigeons traveling efficiency in different λ

its traveling distance (Bytes/km). Fig. 5 shows the results of average efficiency of a pigeon as a function of λ. We can see that the efficiency increases linearly with the increase of λ, and the periodic algorithm achieves the best efficiency among the three algorithms. This is because that in periodic algorithm, the pigeon would wait for a period of time before its departure. Therefore the pigeon can carry more messages at one trip, which achieves higher efficiency.

6   Conclusions

In this work, we have investigated a message transmission scheme for partitioned networks, where each cluster in networks owns multiple dedicated relay nodes (named as pigeons) that can deliver the messages to their destinations. The specific issue we have explored is how to schedule departure time of pigeons that can achieve a lower delivery delay. We have evaluated three different scheduling algorithms under a variety of network conditions using simulation. The results demonstrate that our proposed APS algorithm achieves the best performance (lowest delay). Whereas, if we focus on the cost and efficiency of a pigeon, the periodic algorithm is more suitable. Our future work will investigate the tradeoff between the efficiency and message delay and consider how to apply current algorithms to the scenario when partitioned clusters are mobile and dynamic.

References

1. Fall, K.: A Delay-Tolerant Network Architecture for Challenged Internets. In: ACM SIGCOMM, Karlsruhe, Germany (August 2003)
2. Jain, S., Fall, K., Patra, R.: Routing in a Delay Tolerant Network. In: ACM SIG-COMM, Portland, OR, USA (August 2004)
3. Vahdat, A., Becker, D.: Epidemic Routing for Partially Connected Ad hoc Networks. Technical Report CS-200006, Duke University (April 2000)
4. Lindgren, Doria, A., Schelen, O.: Probabilistic Routing in Intermittently Connected Networks. In: 1st International Workshop on Service Assurance with Partial and Intermittent Resources (August 2004)
5. Spyropoulos, T., Psounis, K., Raghavendra, C.: Spray and Wait: An Efficient Routing Scheme for Intermittently Connected Mobile Networks. In: 1st Sigcomm workshop on WDTN (2005)
6. Zhao, W., Ammar, M., Zegura, E.: Controlling the Mobility of Multiple Data Transport Ferries in a Delay-tolerant Network. In: IEEE Infocom (2005)
7. Shah, R.C., Roy, S., Jain, S., et al.: Data MULEs: Modeling a Three-tier Architecture for Sparse Sensor Networks. In: IEEE International Workshop on Sensor Network Protocols and Applications (May 2003)
8. Guo, H., Li, J., Washington, N.A., et al.: Performance Analysis of Homing Pigeon based Delay Tolerant Networks. In: IEEE MILCOM 2007, Orlando, Florida (October 2007)
9. Bentley, J.: Fast Algorithms for Geometric Traveling Salesman Problems. ORSA Journal on Computing 4, 387–411 (1992)
10. OPNET Technologies, Inc., http://www.opnet.com/
11. Dorigo, M., Maniezzo, V., Colorni, A.: Ant system: Optimization by a Colony of Cooperating Agents. IEEE Transactions on Systems, Man, and Cybernetics - Part B 26(1), 29–41 (1996)

Load-Based Metrics and Flooding
in Wireless Mesh Networks

Sameh Gobriel[1,*], A.S. Krishnakumar[2], P. Krishnan[2], and Shalini Yajnik[2]

[1] Intel Research Labs, Hillsboro, OR 97124
[2] Avaya Labs, 233 Mt. Airy Rd., Basking Ridge, NJ 07920
sameh.gobriel@intel.com, {ask,pk,shalini}@avaya.com

Abstract. On-demand routing protocols in wireless ad-hoc (mesh) networks use route requests to search for a routing path. To determine a
route that optimizes a metric function, an intermediate node retransmits
a route request that has a lower metric value. This can create *flooding
waves*, where a large number of route requests are retransmitted through
the network. In this paper, we study different classes of node load-based
metric functions that are useful in sensor networks and telephony applications. We tackle the problem of determining optimal routes while
minimizing flooding waves. We define a notion of *efficient flooding* and
show that an online algorithm can discover an optimal metric path while
achieving efficient flooding for a *sum load* metric, but this is not possible for a *min-max* load metric. We simulate an online algorithm that
is provably efficient in terms of flooding for some classes of metrics and
analyze its performance for different load-based metric functions.

Keywords: Wireless mesh; Routing; Load metrics; Flooding; Optimal.

1 Introduction

Deployments of wireless ad-hoc (or mesh) networks [1,2] consist of wireless devices spread over an area. These devices connect to each other in an ad-hoc
manner and form a network that allows data to flow from one device to another
with intermediate devices acting as relays for the traffic. The path along which
to send data is determined using a routing protocol. Routing in wireless mesh
networks has been a well-studied area of research [3,4,5,6,7]. Routing protocols
for mobile ad-hoc/mesh networks can be generally categorized into *proactive*
and *reactive* routing protocols. Proactive routing protocols like DSDV [7] try
to maintain correct routing information to all the network nodes at all times.
Such protocols are table-driven, with topology changes handled through periodic broadcast of routing table updates. In contrast, reactive (or *on-demand*)
routing protocols like AODV [5] and DSR [6] obtain a route only when needed.
Generally speaking, although on-demand routing protocols have a larger route
setup overhead, they can support node mobility, larger networks and frequent
topology changes. Since mesh networks can be large and dynamic, on-demand
routing has been the preferred choice.

---

* This work was done while the author was visiting Avaya Labs Research.

Y. Li et al. (Eds.): WASA 2008, LNCS 5258, pp. 84–95, 2008.
© Springer-Verlag Berlin Heidelberg 2008

The basic function of a routing protocol is to discover a path from a source to a destination that optimizes a specified metric. On-demand routing protocols have been traditionally presented in terms of a *hop-count* metric where the goal of minimizing end-to-end delay is mapped to minimizing path length. Other communication-oriented link-based metrics have also been studied [3,8,9].

One application of wireless mesh is for sensor networks [10], where small CPU and power-constrained devices like sensors collaborate to relay data through the network. Another application is small-business IP telephony [11], where phones with limited capacity create a mesh network to enable telephony deployments with low installation costs. In such networks, each node has a limited capacity for relaying traffic. For maintaining QoS and minimizing packet losses it is important for the routing protocol to ensure that no node gets overloaded. Such a requirement can be modeled by assigning each node a *load* and optimizing some appropriate function of the node loads. We refer to this class of metrics as node load-based metrics. On-demand routing protocols are useful in this context since node load makes the network conditions dynamic. Paths optimizing the node-load metric (also called load-balanced routing [12,13,14]) could have more hops than the shortest path based on a hop-count metric [15].

An on-demand routing protocol (like DSR [6]) operates by sending a route request (RREQ) from the source to a destination. When intermediate nodes receive an RREQ, they update the metric value in the request and retransmit it, if necessary. In particular, to determine the best metric path, if an intermediate node receives an RREQ with a lower metric value (perhaps along another path), it will retransmit the RREQ with the lower metric value. Such route request retransmissions can however cause *flooding waves* in the network, where the network gets inundated with a large number of route requests. An efficient routing protocol implementation would minimize route request retransmissions. Mitigating flooding waves was first studied in the context of energy-efficient routing and a technique was presented for a specific power-related metric [16]. In this paper, we investigate more general node-load based metrics, and study efficient flooding techniques through analysis and simulations. One of the main contributions of this paper is to analyze how routing protocols can discover optimal metric paths while *simultaneously minimizing flooding waves (overhead)*, and study the *fundamental dependence of flooding waves on the chosen metric*. To minimize flooding waves, the approach uses *metric-aware delays* of RREQs at nodes.

The rest of the paper is organized as follows. In Section 2 we motivate different types of node-load based metrics. In Section 3 we present the criterion used to evaluate routing protocol performance and introduce an intuitive notion of efficiency for flooding waves. We study node load-based metrics in Section 4 and analytically prove their influence in achieving efficient flooding. We present simulation results in Section 5 and conclude in Section 6.

2 Node Load-Based Metric

An ad-hoc network can be expressed as a graph $G(V, E)$ with the ad-hoc nodes being the node set V of the graph, and the communication links being the edge set E. The problem of finding a routing path in the network is equivalent to finding a path in the graph that matches a required criterion. A popular metric used in the literature is to minimize the hop count (i.e., the number of edges or hops) between the source and destination. A node load-based metric can be considered as a generalization of the hop-count metric where a *load* with value greater than zero is assigned to each node and/or edge of the graph. Depending on the network environment, the desired path would optimize a metric that is a function of these assigned loads. We call these classes of metrics as *load-based* metrics. For ease of exposition, in the rest of the paper we assume that only the nodes have loads. Generalizing the metric to when the edges or both nodes and edges have loads is possible. Conceptually, while a node accounts for node load during packet transmission, it accounts for edge load at packet reception; further discussion on this is omitted for brevity.

Two typical node load-based metric functions are the *sum load* and *min-max load* metrics described below.

Sum Load. The sum load metric computes the metric value of a path as the sum of node loads along the path, and chooses the path with minimum metric value. Typical network scenarios use such a metric. For example, if the delay incurred by a packet at a node is proportional to the load on the node, the sum load minimizes the delay in packet reception at the destination. The node load can either be related to the processing required at the node or to the size of the send and receive buffers at the node. Alternatively, by assigning node load proportional to the energy drain at a node, the sum load computes energy efficient paths. The hop-count metric is a special case of the sum load metric where every node in the graph has a node metric value equal to one.

Min-Max Load. The min-max load metric computes the metric value of a path as the maximum load on any node in a path, and chooses a path that minimizes this maximum load. Network scenarios where we do not want any device in the network to be a part of too many chosen paths can use such a metric. Consider, for example, a sensor node or an IP phone that can process only a limited number of streams. Using a min-max load can limit the maximum number of streams through any node.

Mathematically, the metrics described above are *classes* of functions. Assuming that every node has a load greater than zero, then along a path the sum load metric is an increasing function, and the min-max load metric is non-decreasing. A well-known property of a routing metric that ensures convergence to optimal metric paths is *isotonicity* [17]. Essentially, the isotonic property means that a metric should ensure that the order of the weights of any two paths are preserved if they are appended or prefixed by a common third path. The sum load and min-max load metric functions are isotonic. For the sake of mathematical completeness, we can consider an *average load* metric as follows.

Average Load. The average load metric computes the metric value of a path as the average of the node loads along the path, and chooses the path with minimum average cost.

The average load metric value may increase or decrease along a path and is not isotonic. As such, the average load metric may not yield loop-free paths and does not find much use with routing protocols.

Other functions used in the literature [8,9,16] could be mapped to one or a combination of the above. For example, a product (or geometric mean) of n loads can be expressed as a sum (or average) of the logarithms of the n loads.

3   Assumptions and Analysis Model

In this paper, we consider *online* on-demand routing protocols (like DSR and AODV) that do not maintain full knowledge of the network. In other words, the nodes are aware of (at most) their immediate neighbors in the ad-hoc network, but not the complete network topology. In contrast, offline algorithms have full knowledge of the network. During the process of route discovery, an intermediate node may receive a route request with a better metric value after having propagated an earlier one. This better route request will then propagate through the network like a "wave," leading to the problem of *flooding waves* [16,18], where a network gets flooded with a large number of RREQs.

3.1   Flooding Waves and Efficient Flooding

We define the *flooding* F for an RREQ generated by a source node for a given destination as the total number of times the RREQ is forwarded by all the nodes in network. In particular, if $f(v)$ is the number of times the RREQ is forwarded by node v, $F = \sum_{v \in V} f(v)$. Flooding determines the bandwidth utilized by the RREQ while traversing through the network and is an indication of the overhead imposed by the routing protocol on the network.

Ideally, if each node in the path from source to destination gets the RREQ from the best metric path first, each node will forward the RREQ at most once. We call this *efficient flooding*. In particular, with efficient flooding, each node retransmits or *fires* the RREQ at most once, leading to $f(v) \leq 1$. For a network with n nodes, since the destination never fires, efficient flooding implies that $F \leq n - 1$.

Definition 1. *We define* efficient flooding *as the situation where during route discovery, for each node v, $f(v) \leq 1$.*

Note that an algorithm achieving efficient flooding may not find the best metric path. The interesting situation to consider is whether an algorithm can optimize both criteria (i.e., find an optimal metric path with efficient flooding) simultaneously. Under this constraint, our goal in this paper is to understand the requirement for efficient flooding and study its dependence on the chosen metric and network condition. An offline algorithm (i.e., an algorithm with full knowledge of the network) can easily design a rule such that only nodes on the optimal metric path fire. However, we are interested in understanding what online algorithms that do not have full knowledge of the network can achieve. Notice that

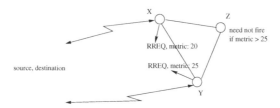

Fig. 1. Example showing $F < n - 1$

even in this context, efficient flooding does not imply minimal number of firings. In some situations, $f(v) = 0$ leading to $F < n - 1$. For example, see Figure 1. If node Z knows that nodes X and Y are its only neighbors and that both have fired, then depending on the load value of node Z it may confirm that it can not be a part of the optimal metric route to the destination and decide not to fire.

3.2   Need for RREQ Manipulation

For simple metrics like hop count that are not node-dependent, the first request that reaches an intermediate node is usually the best and the flooding is contained. To mitigate any flooding waves that might be caused by, for example, propagation delay variance, a routing protocol optimizing the hop count metric waits for a fixed time period at each node before deciding whether to propagate a received RREQ [7]. The intuition behind this is that other RREQs with comparable metric will arrive within this time period, allowing only the RREQ with the best metric to be forwarded.

However, as also pointed out in [16], for metrics that are not hop count-like (e.g., generic node and link load metrics that we are considering here), the fixed delay technique can not always help mitigate flooding waves. This is because there may be no correlation between the delays encountered by the RREQ and the metric it is trying to optimize. One might argue that in cases where the metric is dependent on the send and receive buffer lengths at a node, an RREQ will automatically get delayed and flooding will be minimized. However, the situation is not that simple. When implementing mesh routing protocols, RREQs (considered as control messages) are given priority for transmission. If this is not done, RREQs (and route invalidation messages) may wait behind data packets leading to dependencies that cause timeouts and dropped data packets. In particular, without prioritizing RREQs, an RREQ packet may be held up behind a data packet whose destination is the route being updated by the RREQ. The net effect of RREQ prioritization is that, if the RREQ packets are not explicitly delayed, the only metric for which we could get efficient flooding would be the hop count-like metrics.

The above discussion establishes that RREQ transmission delays must be explicitly manipulated by a routing protocol that wants to minimize flooding. How to do this is the main emphasis of our work presented here. Before analyzing the relationship between minimizing flooding and the metric chosen, we make explicit the tools available to our online algorithm to mitigate flooding.

3.3   On-Line Algorithm Capabilities

As mentioned earlier, we consider online on-demand routing algorithms. The only capability we allow our algorithm is to delay an RREQ at a node by a finite amount, and at the end of the delay period the RREQ is either discarded or forwarded. In particular, the RREQ is discarded if an RREQ with a better metric was received during the delay period. We assume that the decision of how much to delay an RREQ is based only on the available information at the node. More specifically, how much to delay an RREQ is only dependent on the node's load metric, knowledge of its neighbors, the received RREQs, and the information in these RREQs. Some general information about the network like the range of load values and maximum number of nodes in the network may also be available. For simplicity, we only consider deterministic techniques in our description below; our results can be extended to randomized algorithms as well and we omit details for brevity.

4   Dependence of Efficient Flooding on Node Metric

We seek to answer two questions in this section. First, is efficient flooding achievable in any provable sense? Second, how much does an algorithm's ability to achieve efficient flooding depend on the metric being optimized? That is, is there something fundamental in metric functions that makes achieving efficient flooding easy or difficult? We study these questions in the context of the node load-based metrics outlined in Section 2. Generalizing to other metrics can be done using an approach similar to the one described below. As pointed out in Section 3.1, efficient flooding does not always yield optimal metric paths. In this section we restrict ourselves to algorithms that guarantee optimal metric paths.

Efficient flooding as we have defined in Section 3.1 requires any intermediate node to forward an RREQ at most once. Since we are only interested in online algorithms, the efficient flooding requirement will be satisfied if the RREQ traversing the lowest metric value path arrives at an intermediate node before a decision is made to fire. Since, by itself, the delay encountered by RREQs (e.g., propagation delays) are not dependent on the metric being optimized (e.g., sum load), the online algorithm must actively delay RREQs in an intelligent way to ensure their reception in the desired order. This delay might increase the route discovery time, but can be minimized by choosing appropriate delay functions. In the rest of the section, we will describe how such a metric-dependent delay function can be defined.

4.1   No Propagation Delays

To motivate our approach, let us first assume that there are no propagation delays in the network. (This assumption is not practical, and will be relaxed in the next section.) The no propagation delay assumption implies that a transmission from node v will be immediately received by its neighbors, and transmissions can be made at any desired instant.

Consider a simple delay function $d(\cdot)$, such the $d(l) = k \cdot l$, for load l, where k is a constant. Let node v have a metric value of $l(v)$. Let an RREQ with metric value $l(p)$ be received at a node v along path p. After incorporating node v into the path, the metric value of the updated path $p \oplus v$ is denoted by $l(p \oplus v)$. In particular, for the sum load metric, $l(p \oplus v) = l(p) + l(v)$, and for the min-max metric, $l(p \oplus v) = \max(l(p), l(v))$. Consider algorithm D_1 that delays the RREQ at node v by $d(\Delta l) = k \cdot \Delta l$, where $\Delta l = l(p \oplus v) - l(p)$ is the change in the metric value at node v. We can verify the following observation.

Observation 1. *Assuming no propagation delay, algorithm D_1 ensures efficient flooding for any isotonic metric function, and in particular, the sum load and min-max load metric functions.*

The observation can be easily verified since the delay function $d(\cdot)$ ensures the following invariant: at any node v, RREQs arrive at the node in non-decreasing order of metric value. In particular, assume that two paths p_1 and p_2 with metric values $l(p_1)$ and $l(p_2)$ respectively, join at node v. The RREQ that traverses path p_1 will encounter a delay equal to $k \cdot l(p_1)$, and the RREQ traversing path p_2 with metric value $l(p_2)$ will encounter a delay equal to $k \cdot l(p_2)$. If $l(p_1) \leq l(p_2)$, the delay $k \cdot l(p_1) \leq k \cdot l(p_2)$. Hence, the RREQ traversing the path with lower metric value will encounter lower delay. Since both the sum load and min-max load metrics are non-decreasing, the invariant holds. Note that from a practical perspective a smaller value of k will lead to faster path discovery. The delay function does not have to be linear as depicted above. There are several classes of delay functions that can achieve the desired goal of efficient flooding in this case.

The amount by which an RREQ is delayed at a node by algorithm D_1 is dependent on the path traversed by the RREQ and the value of the metric at the node. We can also consider an algorithm D which delays an RREQ at a node by a value dependent only on the metric value at the node. This algorithm is independent of the path traversed by the RREQ and hence is memoryless.

Definition 2. *We denote by D an algorithm that delays an RREQ at node v by $d(l(v))$.*

Algorithm D is the same as algorithm D_1 for the sum load metric. From the argument used to prove Observation 1, it can be verified that algorithm D achieves efficient flooding for the sum-load metric but not for the min-max metric. Being memoryless, algorithm D is easy to implement in practice and is used in our simulations described later in Section 5.

4.2   Propagation Delays

Let us now consider the situation where there are link propagation[1] delays. We assume that a link has a propagation delay of at most δ. It is obvious that

---

[1] We include contention and transmission delays in the propagation delay but ignore queuing delay within the node since we assume RREQs are given priority.

algorithm D_1 described above cannot ensure efficient flooding in this case, since it does not account for link delays. However, we can show that there exists a delay function $\widehat{d}(\cdot)$ that ensures efficient flooding *for the sum load metric, but not the min-max metric*. The intuition behind the delay function $\widehat{d}(\cdot)$ is that the delay at a node compensates for the link delay; i.e., the amount of time an RREQ is delayed at a node is reduced by the link delay already encountered by the RREQ.

Let node v_i receive an RREQ from its neighbor node v_j. Let $t(v_j, v_i)$ be the propagation delay from node v_j to node v_i. Let $l_m > 0$ be the minimum of the load values on any node. Define a function $\widehat{d}(\cdot)$ of load l, such that $\widehat{d}(l) = \widehat{k} \cdot l$, where $\widehat{k} \geq \delta/l_m$ to preserve causality. We claim that algorithm D_2 that delays an RREQ received at node v_i from node v_j by $\widehat{d}(l(v_i)) - t(v_j, v_i)$ ensures efficient flooding for the sum load metric. This is easy to verify since we are allocating a "delay budget" of $\widehat{d}(l(v_i))$ to node v_i. Since the RREQ was already delayed by $t(v_j, v_i)$, node v_i reduces this amount from its delay budget.

In particular, the invariant maintained by algorithm D_2 is that if an RREQ traverses path p_1 which has a sum load metric value of $l(p_1)$, it will encounter a delay equal to $\widehat{k} \cdot l(p_1)$. Since the delay budget at any node is at least $\widehat{k} l_m$, and $\widehat{k} \geq \delta/l_m$, the delay budget is at least the maximum link delay δ. This implies that algorithm D_2 will only encounter situations where it has to delay an RREQ by an amount greater than or equal to zero for the sum load metric. The argument does not hold for the min-max metric, since the metric value may not change at a node but the RREQ may be delayed due to the link delay. This may lead to the RREQ being delayed beyond its allocated "budget." We summarize this observation below.

Observation 2. *Algorithm D_2 ensures efficient flooding for the sum load metric, even in the presence of propagation delays.*

Algorithm D_2 delays the RREQ at a node by an amount that depends on where it was received from. More precisely, the delay depends on how long it took to receive the RREQ from the neighbor. It is not necessary for the delay function to be linear. Any increasing function that has a slope at load l of at least δ/l would be sufficient to ensure efficient flooding.

While we have argued that algorithm D_2 does not ensure efficient flooding for the min-max metric, it is possible that some other clever delay function might ensure efficient flooding. We point out below that this is not possible.

Observation 3. *Given any node delay function $h(\cdot)$, in the presence of link propagation delays it is possible to construct a graph that ensures multiple firings by a node for any online algorithm using the min-max metric.*

The proof uses a constructive technique. Consider a graph segment shown in Figure 2. Assume two paths $p_1 = (s, v, t)$ and $p_2 = (s, u_1, u_2, \ldots, u_{n-1}, t)$. The load $l(v) > l(u_i) > 0$, $\forall i$. This ensures that path p_2 has a lower min-max load metric value than path p_1. Let $p_i(x)$ denote the prefix of node x along path p_i. Notice that n is not yet specified and will be determined as part of the construction.

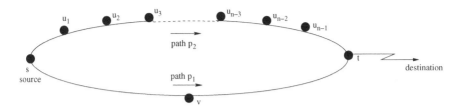

Fig. 2. Example showing multiple firings with a min-max metric

Let the node delay function $h(\cdot)$ delay an RREQ received at node x along path p_i by $h(x, p_i(x))$. The delay for the RREQ along path $p_1(t)$ is at most $h(v, p_1(v)) + 2\delta$, where δ is the maximum propagation delay on any edge of the graph. Similarly, by assigning a delay of δ for each edge along path p_2, we see that the delay for the RREQ along path $p_2(t)$ is $n\delta + \sum_i h(u_i, p_2(u_i))$. The construction first ensures that $n > (h(v, p_1(v)) + 2\delta)/\delta$, which implies that the RREQ along path p_1 will arrive at node t first. Since we are considering online algorithms, the quantity $h(t, p_1(t))$ is well-defined and *independent of the RREQ traversing path* p_2. By setting $n > (h(v, p_1(v)) + 2\delta + h(t, p_1(t)))/\delta$, the construction ensures that the RREQ along path p_2 will reach t *after node t has forwarded the RREQ received along path* p_1, since p_1 was the path with best metric received until then. Node t will then have to retransmit the lower metric value RREQ received on path p_2 leading to multiple firings and inefficient flooding.

4.3   Summary of Analysis

In this section we observe that to achieve efficient flooding, the delay function employed by the routing algorithm should take into account the routing metric function. Furthermore, a simple delay function can achieve efficient flooding for some metric functions like sum load, and simultaneously find the optimal metric path. Interestingly, we observe that for metrics like min-max for which optimal metric routes can be determined, we can encounter situations where we cannot simultaneously achieve efficient flooding. Our construction uses the situation when there are propagation delays in the network.

5   Simulations

In order to study the practical impact of different metrics on the efficiency of flooding waves in real networks, we performed several simulations with algorithm D described in Definition 2. The main objective of our simulation was to study the effect of the delay imposed by algorithm D on efficient flooding.

We simulated a network of 150 nodes distributed uniformly over a 50 meter by 50 meter area. The simulations were done using network simulator ns2 [19]. The metric value (load) at each node was distributed uniformly over the range $[0, 1]$. Network propagation delays modeling small office environments were simulated using standard ns2 models. Route requests (RREQs) were generated randomly

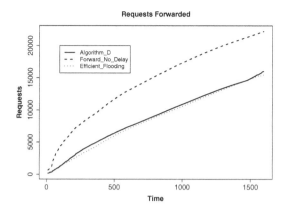

Fig. 3. Efficiency of flooding waves

due to both connection setup and route errors. As mentioned earlier in Definition 2, algorithm D delays a route request at node v by $k \cdot l(v)$, where $l(v)$ is the metric value at node v and k is a constant. The constant k was chosen such that the delay at each node was bounded by 500 milliseconds.

The simulations were run for 1600 seconds. In the first quarter of the simulation time (i.e. 400 seconds) route requests for connections were generated randomly according to a uniform distribution. Termination of connections was done in the last quarter of the simulation time, with each termination giving rise to an RREQ. Route invalidations were randomly generated throughout the simulation period resulting in more RREQs.

5.1   Impact of Delay on Efficient Flooding

We compared our algorithm D with the following.

- Basic DSR, where an intermediate node forwards the first RREQ it receives and drops all subsequent RREQs even if they show a better quality metric. We call this version as *Efficient_Flooding* since it meets our definition of efficient flooding, although it may not find the best metric path.
- DSR modified so that an intermediate node forwards all RREQs with better metrics. We call this *Forward_No_Delay*.

Figure 3 shows the cumulative number of RREQs forwarded through the network using a sum load metric. The *Forward_No_Delay* algorithm incurs a high flooding overhead that varies from 1.4–4.5 times that of Efficient_Flooding. Algorithm D with its simple delay function achieves near-efficient flooding. Recall that algorithm D is provably efficient in the absence of propagation delays. The simulation results show that algorithm D performs close to efficient flooding in practice even in the presence of propagation delays.

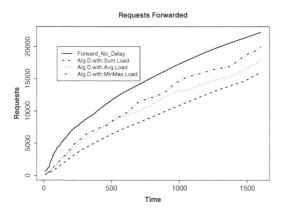

Fig. 4. Impact of metric on efficiency of flooding waves

5.2   Impact of Metric on Efficient Flooding

We now look at how algorithm D impacts flooding efficiency when used with other types of metric functions like the min-max and average load metric. The average load metric is used for illustration purposes only, and in our simulation an intermediate node retransmits an RREQ received with lower average load. In general, an average load metric is non-isotonic and the optimal metric path may not be well-defined.

Figure 4 shows the number of requests forwarded during the simulation for different metrics. As shown in Figure 3, algorithm D applied to the sum load metric shows close to efficient flooding. Algorithm D applied to the other two metrics (min-max-load and the average-load) yields more flooding, while still significantly better than the *Forward_No_Delay* technique. The results also show that use of a delay function not designed specifically for a metric can lead to inefficient flooding.

6   Conclusions

In this paper, we study the problem of mitigating flooding waves when used with load-based routing metrics. We defined the concept of efficient flooding and studied the problem of simultaneously optimizing the routing metric while achieving efficient flooding by intelligently delaying route requests at nodes. We have shown analytically that for some types of isotonic metric functions (exemplified by sum load-like metrics), it is possible to design online delay functions that simultaneously optimize both criteria. However, for other metric functions (like min-max that is also isotonic), there are situations (e.g., in the presence of propagation delays) when this simultaneous optimization is not possible. We also analyzed and simulated a simple algorithm D that employs a memoryless delay function. Our simulations confirmed our analysis, and also demonstrated that not tuning the delay function to the routing metric results in performance penalties.

References

1. IEEE 802.11s Wireless Mesh Networking Project Status Update,
   `http://grouper.ieee.org/groups/802/11/Reports/tgs_update.htm`
2. Akyildiz, I., Wang, X.: A survey of wireless mesh networks. IEEE Radio Communications (September 2005)
3. Draves, R., Padhye, J., Zill, B.: Comparisons of routing metrics for multi-hop wireless networks. In: Proceedings of ACM SIGCOMM, pp. 133–144 (August 2004)
4. Royer, E., Toh, C.K.: A review of current routing protocols for ad-hoc mobile wireless networks. IEEE Personal Communications Magazine, 46–55 (April 1999)
5. Perkins, C.E., Royer, E.M.: Ad-hoc on-demand distance vector routing. In: Proceedings of the 2nd IEEE Workshop on Mobile Computing Systems and Applications, New Orleans, LA, pp. 90–100 (February 1999)
6. Johnson, D.B., Maltz, D.A.: Dynamic source routing in ad hoc wireless networks. In: Imielinski, Korth (eds.) Mobile Computing, vol. 353, Kluwer Academic Publishers, Dordrecht (1996)
7. Perkins, C., Bhagwat, P.: Highly dynamic destination-sequenced distance-vector routing (DSDV) for mobile computers. In: ACM SIGCOMM 1994 Conference on Communications Architectures, Protocols and Applications, pp. 234–244 (1994)
8. Yang, Y., Wang, J., Kravets, R.: Designing routing metrics for mesh networks. In: IEEE Workshop. on Wireless Mesh Networks (WiMesh) (2005)
9. DeCouto, D., Aguayo, D., Bicket, J., Morris, R.: A high throughput path metric for multi-hop wireless routing. In: ACM Mobicom (2003)
10. Akyildiz, I., Su, W., Sankarasubramaniam, Y., Cayirci, E.: A survey on sensor networks. IEEE Commun. Mag. 40(8), 102–114 (2002)
11. Gobriel, S., Krishnakumar, A.S., Krishnan, P., Yajnik, S.: Self-configuring multi-hop ad-hoc wireless telephony for small enterprises. In: Proc. WCNC (March 2007)
12. Hassanein, H., Zhou, A.: Routing with load balancing in wireless ad hoc networks. In: Proc. of ACM international workshop on Modeling, analysis and simulation of wireless and mobile systems, pp. 89–96 (2001)
13. Lee, S., Gerla, M.: Dynamic load-aware routing in ad-hoc networks. In: Proc. of ICC (2001)
14. Kyasanur, P., So, J., Chereddi, C., Vaidya, N.H.: Multi-channel mesh networks: Challenges and protocols. IEEE Wireless Communications (April 2006)
15. Gobriel, S., Krishnakumar, A.S., Krishnan, P., Yajnik, S.: When the long way is not the wrong way. In: Proc. of WLANMesh (2007)
16. Gobriel, S., Melhem, R., Mosse, D.: Mitigating the flooding waves problem in energy-efficient routing for MANETs. In: Proc. of ICDCS (2006)
17. Sobrinho, J.L.: Algebra and algorithms for QoS path computation and hop-by-hop routing in the internet. IEEE/ACM Trans. Netw. 10(4), 541–550 (2002)
18. Tseng, Y.C., Ni, S.Y., Chen, Y.-S., Sheu, J.P.: The broadcast storm problem in a mobile ad-hoc network. ACM Wireless Networks 8(2), 153–167 (2002)
19. Network Simulator 2, `http://nsnam.isi.edu/nsnam/index.php/Main_Page`

New Approximation for Minimum-Weight Routing Backbone in Wireless Sensor Network

Ning Zhang, Incheol Shin, Bo Li, Cem Boyaci, Ravi Tiwari, and My T. Thai

Dept. of Computer and Information Science and Engineering,
University of Florida, Gainesville, FL 32611
{nzhang,ishin,boli,cboyaci,rtiwari,mythai}@cise.ufl.edu

Abstract. Our problem formulation is as follows. Given a weighted disk graph G where the weight of edge represents the transmission energy consumption, we wish to determine a dominating tree T of G such that the total weight of edges in T is minimized. To the best of our knowledge, this problem have not been addressed in the literature. Solving the dominating tree problem can yield a routing backbone for broadcast protocols since: (1) each node does not have to construct their own broadcast tree, (2) utilize the virtual backbone to reduce the message overhead, and (3) the weight of backbone is minimized.

Our contributions to this problem is multi-fold: First, the paper is the first to study this problem, prove the hardness of this problem and propose an approximation framework. Second, we present a heuristic to approximate the solution with low time complexity. Third, a distributed algorithm is provided for practical implementation. Finally, we verify the effectiveness of our proposal through simulation.

Keywords: Dominating Tree, Approximation Algorithm, General Graph, Distributed Algorithm, Time Complexity, Wireless Sensor Network.

1 Introduction

Given an undirected weighted general graph $G = (V, E, w)$ representing a Wireless Sensor Networks (WSN), where V is the set of the nodes in this network, E includes all the undirected links in the network and w is a non-negative *weight* assigned on each undirected edge $e = (u, v)$ and $w(e)$ is the weight of the edge between u and v. Our objective is to construct a Dominating Tree T of G such that: (1) each node in V is either in T or has at least one neighbor in T, (2) the total weight of edges in T is minimum. Since all nodes are at most one hop away from the tree, a message can be first forwarded to the closest node in tree. Then the message can be routed within the DT until it reaches to its destination. For example, in Fig. 1, nodes (0,5) are a DT, since other nodes (6,2,7,3,4,1) are dominated by (0,5), and (0,5) is a tree.

Recently, the probabilistic routing protocols on MANET, Delay Tolerant Networks (TDN), and Intermittently Connected Mobile Ad hoc Networks (ICMAN) have gained much attention [14]-[16]. In this approach, a given network is modeled as a probabilistic graph where each edge weight represents the contact

Y. Li et al. (Eds.): WASA 2008, LNCS 5258, pp. 96–108, 2008.

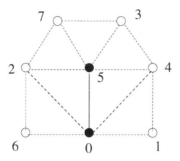

Fig. 1. An example for Dominating Tree

probability of two nodes coming within each other radio range during the entire observed time window. Under this context, it is also important to find a tree with a maximum delivery probability such that all nodes can utilize this tree for their broadcast operation. In the probabilistic graph, our DT can yield a routing backbone with maximum probability space.

From a theoretical point of view, DT problem, which is formally defined in Section 3, has several applications in network design and network routing. For example, multicasting involves the distribution of same data from a central sever to several nodes in the network and the problem is to choose a set of edges (or communication links) of minimum weight for the sever to route the data. Therefore, the connection between this problem and DT problem is clear. However, no non-trivial approximation algorithm were known for DT problem and no literature has proved the NP-hardness of it. In Section 4, we are the first to prove the NP-hardness of this problem and propose an approximation framework in general case.

The rest of this paper is organized as follows. Section 2 briefly describes some related research works. The wireless communication model, some preliminaries, and the formal problem definition are presented in Section 3. Section 4 gives the approximation framework for DT problem, and a heuristic algorithm with low time complexity is presented in Section 5. The progressive heuristic algorithm is developed in Section 6 and the simulations are discussed in Section 7. Section 8 ends this paper with a conclusion.

2   Related Work

From a practical view of energy in WSN, since the sensor nodes usually have no plug-in power, we have to conserve power so that each sensor node can operate for a longer period of time. Many solutions for constructing a routing backbone with minimum energy consumption have been proposed [5]-[8]. However, in these approaches, energy is only associated with each node. In addition, the energy consumption at each link between nodes in communication, which directly effects the energy consumption of routing, was not considered.

In the theory community, there are some work [9]-[11] studying the tree cover problem. The tree cover problem is defined as a connected edge dominating set with total minimum edge weights. Arkin *et al.* first solved this problem in [9]. Later, in [10], this problem can be approximated within a factor of $3 + \epsilon$. In [11], the author presented a fast, purely combinatorial 2-approximation algorithm for the tree cover problem. In contrast to the above work, DT is defined as node dominating sets, not edge dominating sets. Usually, DT always produces a smaller number of links and weight than tree cover, and it is proved to be harder than tree cover problem. Therefore, the two problems are obviously different.

3   Wireless Communication Model and Preliminaries

In this paper, a WSN is modeled as an undirected general graph $G = (V, E, w)$ in a 2-dimensional plane, where V is the set of the nodes in this network, E includes all the undirected links in the network and w is a non-negative *weight* assigned on each undirected edge $e = (u, v)$ and $w(e)$ is the weight of edge between u and v. Then the weight of a DT T is $w(T) = \sum_{e \in T} w(e)$. Theoretically, the DT problem is formally defined as follows:

Definition 1. *Dominating Tree (DT) Problem:* *Given an undirected weighted general graph $G = (V, E, w)$ representing a network, construct a DT T such that: (1) each node in V is either in T or has at least one neighbor in T, (2) $w(T)$ is minimum.*

4   Approximation Framework and Analysis

First, we prove that DT problem is NP-hard. Since DT problem is a general extension of Connected Dominating Set (CDS) problem, we can reduce the CDS problem to it in polynomial time and show that DT problem is also NP-hard. Consider an instance of CDS problem, we can assign the weight of all edges to be 1. In such graph, the DT with minimum weight can be obtained if and only if it is a CDS with minimum size. Therefore, DT problem can be reduced from minimum CDS problem in polynomial time, which has been proved to be NP-hard [2].

In this section we first give some basic definitions and lemmas concerning the partial solutions for DT problem. Then, an approximation framework is analyzed with performance ratio of $i(i-1)2n^{1/i}$ in time $O(n^{3i})$ for any fixed $i \geq 1$, where n is the number of nodes in given graph.

Definition 2. *Directed Steiner Tree (DST):* *In a directed graph $G = (V, E)$ with weight associated with each edge, given a root $r \in V$ and a set $D \subseteq V$, the Directed Steiner tree is to construct a tree rooted at r, ensuring that there is at least a path from the root to each node in the set D and making the total weight minimum.*

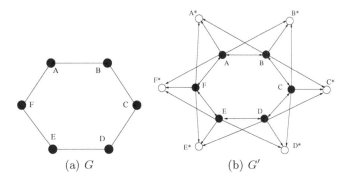

Fig. 2. An Example of Reduction from G to G'

We will show that DT problem can be reduced to the DST problem in polynomial time. And the algorithm for DST can be applied to the DT problem preserving the same performance ratio. For DT problem, in the graph $G = (V, E, w)$, we introduce a dummy node v^* for each real node $v \in V$, then we add the directional edges from all the neighbors of v (including v itself) to dummy node v^*, and we set the weight zero for all these newly added edges. Also for the original edges, we make the edge bidirectional and keep the weight the same as the edge in the original graph. In the new directed graph $G' = (V', E', w')$, if we pick an arbitrary $v \in V$ as a root r, and let all dummy nodes as terminals, we can obtain a DST rooted at r through existing DST algorithm [12]. It is clear that the reduction is completed in linear time and obtaining a DST in G' also obtains a DT in G. This reduction is shown as an example in Fig. 2.

Lemma 1. *If r is in the optimal DT, then the DT introduced by DST will get the same optimal weight. Also, using the approximation algorithm for DST problem will get the same approximation ratio for the DT problem.*

Proof: Suppose there is an optimal dominating tree DT^*, we can make all the nodes in DT^* appear in the DST. Since r is in DT^*, for each node in DT, at least one of its neighbors must be in DT, and for any terminal, we can add a directed edge from that neighbor to it. And we know that these edges are zero weighted, so the weight of that DST is $w(DT^*)$. Suppose there is an optimal DST ST^*, then we have $w(DT^*) \geq w(ST^*)$. Also, for the optimal DST, we can eliminate all these zero weighted edges. Since all the terminal nodes have a path from r to them, each node will have at least one of its neighbor appearing in that tree, which means it is a DT. So we have $w(ST^*) \geq w(DT^*)$. In conclusion, we have $w(DT^*) = w(ST^*)$. This in turn implies, we can get the same performance ratio for DT problem as we have for the DST. $\qquad \square$

In [12], the authors provided a polylogarithmic approximation for DST problem in quasi-polynomial time. Then we have an algorithm to get this ratio for DT problem as well:

Algorithm 1. Approximation Algorithm for DT

1: INPUT: An undirected weighted general graph $G = (V, E, w)$
2: OUTPUT: A DT of G
3: Initialize a list to save the DT and its weight
4: Find a node u in G with minimum degree
5: Transform G into $G' = (V', E', w')$ by using the transformation technique
6: **for** each node v that $(u, v) \in E$ **do**
7:     Run the DST algorithm [12] in G' and make v as the root r to get a DT
8:     Save the DT and its weight in the list
9: **end for**
10: Return the DT with minimum weight in the list

Algorithm 1 is based on the idea to transform DT problem to DST problem, and then use the algorithm in [12] to solve DST problem. Note that after the transformation, we need to find the right root to applying that algorithm, since the ratio for DST is maintained if and only if r is in the optimal DT. This can be done by enumerate the neighbors of the node with minimum degree, since at least one of the neighbors should be in optimal DT. Therefore, from lemma 1, we can obtain the same approximation ratio for DT problem.

Finally, since the terminal nodes in G' are those dummy nodes which have no outgoing edges, then we can simply remove these dummy nodes and those edges incident to them to get a DT. By setting $i = \lg n$, the algorithm will obtain an $O(\lg^2 n)$ approximation in quasi-polynomial time which is $n^{O(\lg n)}$.

5   Heuristic Algorithm and Analysis

In the previous section, we introduced the approximation framework. However, the time complexity is exponentially high, since it is well known that constructing a DST usually results in a long running time. From this point of view, a heuristic with low time complexity is highly expected.

Before we introduce the algorithm, we need to give the following definitions: Given a tree, an edge is called a *leaf edge* if it directly connects to a leaf node. An *internal edge* is an edge which is a non-leaf edge. Clearly, all the non-leaf nodes in the tree are called *internal nodes*.

5.1   Algorithm Description

The heuristic algorithm (HeurDT) is illustrated in Algorithm 3. Given a network $G = (V, E, w)$, the algorithm consists of five main steps:

1. Build a Minimum Spanning Tree (MST) T_{MST} of G.
2. Sort all the internal edges of T_{MST} in non-increasing order based on the weight of edge.

3. Identify each internal edge of T_{MST} in the sorted order if it is a candidate to be a leaf edge.
4. For each candidate in the sorted order, switch to a leaf edge if possible.
5. Trim all the leaf edges of the resultant T_{MST} and the remaining T_{MST} is a DT.

Intuitively, an MST without leaf edges appears to be a DT. (We will compare the performance of our proposed algorithms with that of MST without leaf edges in simulation.) So, our motivation is to minimize the the total weight of internal edges in T_{MST} by using a sequence of search rules. The main idea of search rules is to switch internal edges to leaf edges as many as possible if there is a net gain. The resulting T_{MST} has less weight and size than the MST of G after trimming all the leaf edges.

We now elaborate on how search rules work. The search rules described in Fig. 3 are executed to test the leaf nodes associated to an *active* internal node u. These rules are applied as follows. If a leaf node v explores its neighbors and find an internal node w, then the rule shown in Fig. 3(a) marks (w, v) as a temporary new link for v. Otherwise, if v only has leaf node w (no internal node) as its neighbor, then the rule shown in Fig. 3(b) marks (w, v) as a temporary new link for v and $w(e')$ is summed up to the total weight for compensation, since we put e' into DT in order to switch e to leaf edge. The rule shown in Fig. 3(a) has Priority 2 (P2) and the rule in Fig. 3(b) has Priority 1 (P1). Each leaf node is tested in sequence from P2 to P1. The algorithm for search rules is described in Algorithm 2.

As shown in some examples, the resulting T_{MST} returned by HeurDT still has some redundant nodes, if we drop off those redundant nodes and the associated edges, T_{MST} will have less weight after pruning. The basic idea of this strategy is to check if a leaf node is removed from T_{MST}, the nodes not in T_{MST} are still dominated. If yes, the leaf node and the associated edge can be removed. This procedure is repeated until all leaf nodes in T_{MST} have been checked. The algorithm for this pruning technique is described in Algorithm 4.

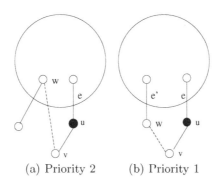

(a) Priority 2   (b) Priority 1

Fig. 3. Search Rules (Dotted line and black nodes represent the temporary new link and *active* internal nodes respectively)

Algorithm 2. SearchRules($Weight, v$)

1: INPUT: $(v, Weight)$
2: OUTPUT: $Weight$
3: **if** v has a neighbor w which is an internal node **then**
4:     Mark (w, v) as a temporary new link for v. /*Priority 2*/
5: **else**
6:     **if** v has a neighbor w which is a leaf node **then**
7:         Mark (w, v) as a temporary new link for v. /*Priority 1*/
8:         $Weight = Weight + w(e')$ /* $w(e')$ is the compensation for switching e to a leaf edge*/
9:     **else**
10:         $flag = 0$; /* e can not switch to a leaf edge*/
11:     **end if**
12: **end if**
13: Return $Weight$

Algorithm 3. Heuristic Algorithm for DT (HeurDT)

1: INPUT: An undirected weighted general graph $G = (V, E, w)$
2: OUTPUT: A DT of G
3: Create MST T_{MST} in G by Kruskal's Algorithm [3]
4: Sort all internal edges of T_{MST} in non-increasing order by Merge Sort algorithm [3]
5: Change the states of internal nodes to *active* if they have exactly one internal edge adjacent to it
6: **for** each internal edges e of T_{MST} in the sorted order **do**
7:     **if** there exists one *active* node u on e **then**
8:         $flag = 1$; /* $flag$ is a global value to indicate if e can switch to leaf edge or not*/
9:         $Weight = 0$; /* $Weight$ is the sum of weights that compensates for switching e to leaf edge */
10:         **for** each leaf node v that connects to u **do**
11:             $Weight = SearchRules(Weight, v)$
12:         **end for**
13:         **if** $flag == 1$ and $Weight \leq w(e)$ **then**
14:             Add new links marked in $SearchRules$ into T_{MST} and destroy the old links /* e has switched to a leaf edge*/
15:         **end if**
16:         Set v to *inactive* /* u has been processed */
17:     **end if**
18: **end for**
19: Trim all the leaf edges in T_{MST}
20: Return T_{MST} where T_{MST} is a DT

5.2   Runtime Complexity

Based on the following variables: n-number of nodes, m-number of edges, Δ-the maximum degree of node, the runtime of each step is listed as follows:

1. The runtime for building an MST by Kruskal's Algorithm in Step 1) is $O(m \log n)$ [3].
2. The complexity of Merge Sort algorithm in Step 2) is $O(n \log n)$ [3].
3. In Step 3), for each internal node u, all its neighbors are checked to see if u has exactly one adjacent internal edge. The number of internal node is $O(n)$ and the complexity of this step is $O(n\Delta)$.
4. For each *active* internal node, all adjacent leaf nodes are tested by *Search − Rules*, which runs at most $O(\Delta)$ time complexity. Therefore, the total complexity for Step 4) is at most $O(n\Delta^2)$.
5. Trimming all the leaf edges only takes linear time.

From the above analysis, the total runtime complexity is dominated by the runtime complexity of Step 3). If the graph is dense enough ($\Delta \approx O(n)$), the runtime of HeurDT is at most $O(n^3)$.

Algorithm 4. Pruning (T_{MST})

1: INPUT: A DT with some redundant nodes
2: OUTPUT: A DT with smaller weight and size
3: Color the nodes in T_{MST} in black and all other nodes in white
4: Sort all leaf edges (not internal edges) of T_{MST} in non-increasing order
5: **for** each leaf edge e of T_{MST} in the sorted order, x is the leaf node of e **do**
6:     **for** each node $u \in T_{MST} - x$ **do**
7:         **for** each u's neighbor v, $v \notin T_{MST}$ **do**
8:             Color v in red
9:         **end for**
10:     **end for**
11:     **if** all nodes not in T_{MST} are red **then**
12:         Remove e from T_{MST}
13:     **end if**
14:     Reset all red node to white
15: **end for**
16: Return T_{MST}

---

6   Progressive Heuristic Algorithm

In this section, we introduce a progressive heuristic algorithm (ProgDT) that under some conditions, can be executed in distributed way.

6.1   Algorithm Description

The basic idea of ProgDT is similar to HeurDT, the major differences are described as follows. (1) The performance of ProgDT can be controlled manually by a user-defined value β, where β is defined as the maximum number of leaf nodes attached to an internal node. (2) Only Priority 2 in Algorithm 2 is employed in ProgDT to reduce the complexity. (3) Every node can be regarded as a processor to run ProgDT simultaneously. During the construction of DT, nodes communicate with each other through exchanging the following messages:

• $FIND$. If node u sends this message to its neighbors, this indicates that u wants to switch to leaf node.

• $SUCCESS$ and $FAIL$. After receiving the $FIND$ message from node u, the leaf node starts to explore if it has a neighbor that is an internal node. If yes, the leaf node sends $SUCCESS$ message back to u. Otherwise, sends $FAIL$ message back to u.

• $ATTACH$. If node u sends this message to its neighbors, this indicates that u is qualified to switch to leaf node. When a leaf node receives this message, it creates a new link and removes the old link from DT.

A distributed algorithm for constructing an MST is proposed in [13]. After an MST is built, the following operations may be conducted at each *active* node:

• An *active* node u sends $FIND$ messages to its neighbors.

• Upon receiving a $FIND$ message, a leaf node v checks all its neighbors to see if an *inactive* internal node w exists. If yes, v sends $SUCCESS$ message back to the sender of message to indicate that it has found a new temporary link (w, v). Otherwise, it informs the sender of message with a $FAIL$ message.

• Upon receiving $(\Delta - 1)$ $SUCCESS$ messages (Δ is the degree of u), u sends $ATTACH$ message to its neighbors. Then, u sets *inactive* to itself.

• Upon receiving $ATTACH$ message, the leaf node v uses the new link (w, v) and destroys the old link (u, v).

• Upon receiving $FAIL$ messages, u sets *inactive* to itself.

When ProgDT satisfies β, all leaf nodes identify themselves simultaneously and destroy the links associated to them, the resultant tree is a DT. Note that each node maintains a global value B and β, where B and β are integers and $B = 1$ initially. The whole procedure of ProgDT is illustrated in Algorithm 5.

We note that if $\beta = 1$, then the algorithm can be partially executed in parallel, which is a distributed algorithm. The reason is that all *active* nodes can perform the operations of switching and cutting off leaf nodes at the same time and the algorithm on longer needs a centralized control. Therefore, it is very scalable in distributed computing.

Theoretically, we can adjust β to control the performance of ProgDT, because a larger β will result in more sophisticated explorations, therefore a DT with less weight can be obtained. However, we may not improve the performance further when β is larger than a threshold. We will evaluate this fact through simulation in the next section.

6.2   Runtime Complexity

Theorem 1. *The ProgDT has an $O(n^2)$ time complexity and $O(n \log n + m)$ message complexity.*

Proof: Constructing an MST by distributed algorithm in [13] produces $O(n \log n + m)$ message complexity and $O(n \log n)$ time complexity. The message complexity of the rest of operations is at most $O(n)$, i.e., to exchange the messages

Algorithm 5. Progressive Heuristic Algorithm for DT (ProgDT)

1: INPUT: An MST T and $G = (V, E, w)$ and a user-defined value β
2: OUTPUT: A DT of G
3: Each node in G is initialized *inactive*
4: Set *active* to internal nodes with exactly B leaf node(s)
5: The *active* node u sends $FIND$ message to its neighbors
6: Upon receiving $FIND$ message, the leaf node v explores all its neighbors to see if an *inactive* internal node w exists. If true, it sends $SUCCESS$ message to the sender of message. Otherwise, it sends back $FAIL$ message
7: Upon receiving $(\Delta - 1)$ $SUCCESS$ messages, u sends $ATTACH$ message to its neighbors and sets *inactive* to itself (Δ is the degree of u)
8: Upon receiving $FAIL$ message, u set *inactive* to itself
9: Upon receiving $ATTACH$ message, the leaf node v creates a new link (w, v) and destroys the old link (u, v)
10: If there is no *active* node in G, increase B by 1
11: If B is larger than the β, then algorithm terminates

through the link between two nodes, which may be sent up to $O(n)$ times. For time complexity, it is dominated by testing each *active* node. Since for each *active* node, all neighbors are explored, and for each leaf node, all possible links are scanned. Thus, the total time and message complexities are $O(n^2)$ and $O(n \log n + m)$.   □

7   Simulation Results

In this section, we conducted the simulation experiments to measure the weight of DT constructed by HeurDT, ProgDT and MST without Leaf edges (MST-L). In addition, since the smaller size (number of nodes) of DT often leads to the reduced message overhead in transmission, it is promising to have a DT with smaller size. Therefore, this factor is tested in simulation as well. Moreover, we are interested in comparing the DT returned by ProgDT by setting different values for β. In the above sections, since the complexities for HeurDT and ProgDT has been discussed, we also would like to verify the running time of these algorithms in practice.

In the simulation, for each edge $e = (u, v)$, we set its weight $w(u, v) = C_v \cdot d_{uv}^\gamma$, where d_{uv} is the Euclidean distance between u and v, and γ is fixed to 2, which is a typical value for unobstructed environment, and C_v is a random constant.

7.1   Simulation for HeurDT, ProgDT and MST-L

To evaluate the performance of these algorithms under different number of nodes, we randomly deployed n nodes to a fixed area of 1,000m x 1,000m. n changed from 100 to 300 with an increment of 10. For ProgDT, since we want to run it in parallel, β is set to 1. For each value of n, 1,000 network instances were investigated and the results were averaged.

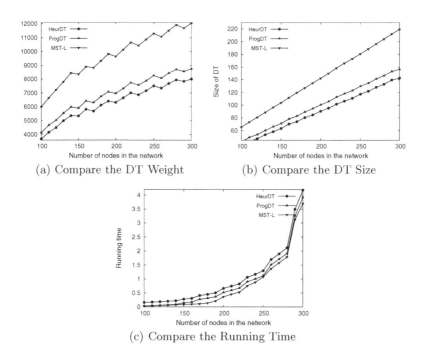

(a) Compare the DT Weight

(b) Compare the DT Size

(c) Compare the Running Time

Fig. 4. Simulation Results for HeurDT, ProgDT and MST-L

Fig. 4(a) compares the weights of DT. It is shown that, under different number of nodes deployed in networks, the DT built by HeurDT has the smallest weight. This is because HeurDT employs more sophisticated technique to reduce the weight. The gap between HeurDT and ProgDT is not big. For example, when 200 nodes are deployed in network, the DT returned by ProgDT has only 9.5% more weight than HeurDT. As expected, MST-L produces a DT with much larger weight, the difference between MST-L and our proposed algorithms is very clear that proves the effectiveness of Search Rules technique in reducing the weight. For all algorithms, when the number of nodes in the network increases, DT admits more edges, hence the weights increase as well.

In Fig. 4(b), the three curves increase with the number of nodes. Also, considering the same number of nodes, MST-L returns a much larger size than ProgDT and MST-L. Again, we learn that Search Rules technique can decrease the size of DT as well.

We also present the runtime for the proposed algorithms in Fig. 4(c). As the complexity analysis indicates, the runtime of HeurDT and ProgDT is higher than MST-L. This is due to the time spent on Search Rules technique to remove redundant edges. Therefore, the trade-off between runtime and size/weight exists in the three algorithms. On the other hand, we show in Fig. 4(c) that the runtime of ProgDT is lower than HeurDT, since ProgDT can be executed parallel. Therefore, ProgDT is more applicable with acceptable performance.

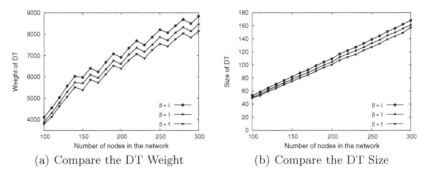

(a) Compare the DT Weight   (b) Compare the DT Size

Fig. 5. Effects of the User-defined Value

7.2   Effects of the User-Defined Value

Now, we compare the size and weight of ProgDT by different values of β. To evaluate the performance, we use the same parameters as the above experiment. We set $\beta = 1$, 3 and 5 respectively. It is shown in Fig. 5 that when $\beta = 5$, ProgDT generates a smaller size and weight of DT than other cases, since more internal nodes switch to leaf nodes and they are trimmed at the end. But, we learned that the performance can not be better than a threshold by increasing β. Theoretically, if we have n nodes in network, the maximum possible value for β is $(n - 3)$. Through extensive simulations, we found that if $\beta \geq 5$, the performance will not be improved anymore.

The simulation results can be summarized as follows: (1) HeurDT outperforms ProgDT and MST-L on size and weight of DT, however, the runtime of MST-L is much faster than ProgDT and HeurDT. Thus, it is clear to see the trade-off. (2) Although ProgDT does not outperform HeurDT in terms of size and weight, the gaps are small and acceptable. Moreover, the distributed algorithm is more applicable. (3) For ProgDT, we can control the performance by adjusting β, and we analyze the effective values of β through simulation.

8   Conclusions

In this paper, we investigate a new NP-hard problem of how to construct a DT with minimum weight in WSN. We propose an approximation framework to solve the DT problem. However, due to the high runtime complexity of DST, a more faster heuristic algorithm is proposed. We also present a progressive heuristic algorithm, which can be implemented in distributed way under certain circumstance.

References

1. Karp, R.M.: Reducibility among combinatorial problems. In: Miller, R.E., Tatcher, J.W. (eds.) Complexity of Computer Computations, pp. 85–103. Plenum, NewYork (1972)
2. Garey, M.R., Johnson, D.S.: Computers and Intractability. A guide to the Theory of NP-completeness. Freeman, New York (1979)

3. Leiserson, C.E., Rivest, R.L., Cormen, T.H., Stein, C.: Introduction to Algorithms. MIT Press and McGraw-Hill Book Company (1976)
4. Rappaport, T.S.: Wireless communications: principles and practice. Prentice-Hall, Englewood Cliffs (1996)
5. Kim, B., Yang, J., Zhou, D., Sun, M.: Energy-Aware Connected Dominating Set Construction in Mobile Ad Hoc Networks. In: Proc. 14th International Conference on Computer Communications and Networks, pp. 229–234 (2005)
6. Wu, J., Dai, F., Gao, M., Stojmenovic, I.: On Calculating Power-Aware Connected Dominating Sets for Efficient Routing in Ad Hoc Wireless Networks. Journal of Communications and Networks 4(1), 1–12 (2002)
7. Agarwal, M., Cho, J.H., Gao, L., Wu, J.: On Calculating Connected Dominating Set for Efficient Routing in Ad Hoc Wireless Networks. In: Proc. of the 3rd Int'l Workshop on Discrete Algorithms and Methods for Mobile Computing and Commun., pp. 7–14 (1999)
8. Ambühl, C., Erlebach, T., Mihalák, M., Nunkesser, M.: Constant-factor Approximation for Minimum-weight (Connected) Dominating Sets in Unit Disk Graphs. In: Díaz, J., Jansen, K., Rolim, J., Zwick, U. (eds.) APPROX 2006 and RANDOM 2006. LNCS, vol. 4110, pp. 3–14. Springer, Heidelberg (2006)
9. Arkin, E.M., Halldorssom, M.M., Hassin, R.: Approximating the tree and tour covers of a graph. Inform. Process. Lett. 47, 275–282 (1993)
10. Fujito, T.: On approximability of the independent/connected edge dominating set problems. Inform. Process. Lett. 79(6), 261–266 (2001)
11. Fujito, T.: How to Trim an MST: A 2-Approximation Algorithm for Minimum Cost Tree Cover. In: ICALP (1), pp. 431–442 (2006)
12. Charikar, M., Chekuri, C., Cheung, T., Dai, Z., Goel, A., Guha, S., Li, M.: Approximation Algorithms for Directed Steiner Tree Problems. Journal of Algorithms 33, 73–91 (1999)
13. Gallager, R.G., Humblet, P.A., Spira, P.M.: A Distributed Algorithm for Minimum-Weight Spanning Trees. ACM TOPLAS 5(1), 66–77 (1983)
14. Lindgren, A., Doria, A., Schelen, O.: Poster Probabilistic routing in intermittently connected networks. In: Proc. MobiHoc 2003 (June 2003)
15. Jain, S., Fall, K., Patra, R.: Routing in a delay tolerant network. In: Proc. ACM SIGCOMM 2004 (September 2004)
16. Ghosh, J., Ngo, H.Q., Yoon, S., Qiao, C.: On a Routing Problem within Probabilistic Graph. In: Proc. INFOCOM 2007 (May 2007)

Ant Colony Optimization-Based Location-Aware Routing for Wireless Sensor Networks

Xiaoming Wang[1,3,*], Qiaoliang Li[2,3], Naixue Xiong[3], and Yi Pan[3]

[1] School of Computer Science, Shaanxi Normal University, Xi'an 710062, China
[2] School of Computer Science and Communication, Hunan University,
Changsha 410082, China
[3] Department of Computer Science, Georgia State University, Atlanta 30319, USA
wangxmsnnu@hotmail.com, lqlbox@163.com, nxiong@cs.gsu.edu

Abstract. The routing for Wireless Sensor Networks (WSNs) is a key and hard problem, and it is a research topic in the field of WSN applications. Based on Ant Colony Optimization (ACO), this paper proposes a novel adaptive intelligent routing scheme for WSNs. Following the proposed scheme, a high performance routing algorithm for WSNs is designed. The proposed routing scheme is very different from the existing ACO based routing schema for WSNs. On one hand, in the proposed scheme, the search range for an ant to select its next-hop node is limited to a subset of the set of the neighbors of the current node. On the other hand, by fusing the residual energy and the global and local location information of nodes, the new probability transition rules for an ant to select its next-hop node are defined. Compared with other ACO based routing algorithms for WSNs, the proposed routing algorithm has a better network performance on aspects of energy consumption, energy efficiency, and packet delivery latency.

Keywords: WSN, routing, ACO, pheromone, transition probability, simulation.

1 Introduction

1.1 Background

With the rapid growth of modern electronic and wireless communication techniques, wireless sensor networks (WSNs) become more and more effective in many fields, such as battlefield surveillance, biological monitor, smart space, intrusion detection and tracking for temperature, object movement, sound and light [1,2,3,4]. Typically, a WSN consists of a large number of sensors. Each sensor is also called a node, and the nodes have the capability of communicating with each other and the base station (sink node) by multi-hop mode. The sink

* Supported by National Natural Science Foundation of China (NSFC) under Grant No.60773224, and 10571052, the Key Research Project of Ministry of Education of China under Grant No.107106, and the 111 Project of China under Grant No.111-2-14.

node may be considered as the center for processing data. Each node collaborates with its neighboring nodes in a distributed manner to sense the physical parameters in the environment surrounding this node. Then, as data packets, the nodes process and deliver the sensed data to their neighbors. Some neighbors continue to process and deliver the data packets toward the sink node by the same mode, that is, the multi-hop mode. In WSNs, the energy of nodes is usually provided by micro-batteries with the very limited power. A large number of nodes are usually deployed in the remote, harsh or hostile environment. Hence, it is usually impossible to recharge or replace the batteries of nodes. However, the lifetime of a WSN significantly depends on the batteries of nodes, and a long lifetime is vital in most of WSN applications. Therefore, the energy efficiency routing is a challenge to large-scale WSN applications. In addition, some WSN applications also require a timely data delivery. For instance, when a moving target enters an area of interest, it may be very critical to reduce the delivery delay of the sensed data from the source node (target) to the sink node. If the sensed data is not received by the sink node within a certain acceptable period of time, the sensed data may become useless. Hence, preserving energy efficiency and reducing delivery delay are key issues in the applications of large-scale WNSs. In recent years, more and more attention has been paid to these issues. Due to the limited communication range of nodes, the data packets are delivered from the source node to the sink node through some mediate nodes in a WSN. The routing refers to select an energy-saving and short delivery delay route from the source node to the sink node. Formally, a WSN may be considered as a weighted undirected graph. It is usually a complex combinatorial optimization problem to select a shortest route from the source node to the sink node, while considering many factors, such as energy consumption, packet delivery delay, and energy efficiency, and it has been proved to be an NP-complete problem [4] [8]. Considering the frequent change of the topology of a WSN, the location-aware routing is needed. Due to some new characteristics of large-scale WSNs, such as high density, limited energy and multi-hop communication, the routing becomes very complex. The traditional routing protocols can not satisfy the requirements for WSN applications, especially large-scale WSN applications. Hence, researchers are trying to propose novel routing protocols for WSNs.

Although some routing schemes for WSNs have been proposed based on the graph theory and the greedy search algorithm in the literature [1,2], the high performance routing is still a research topic. Recently, the routing based on Ant Colony Optimization (ACO) has drawn the attention from many researchers [3,4], and the ACO based adaptive routing has shown promising results in solving routing problem [3]. In fact, since the ACO model was proposed by Dorigo [5,6], and it has been successfully applied in solving some complex optimization problems, such as the routing of traffic in busy telecommunication networks, the asymmetric traveling salesman problem, and the graph coloring problem [12]. By using ants as models, we can design soft agents to solve the complex routing problem in large-scale WSNs. Although the capability of each ant is very limited and the cognitive system of each ant is also too simple to acquire the global knowledge of the environment surrounding the ant, the collective behavior of ants emerges a natural model for solving the distributed parallel problem without any extra centralized coordination [5,6].

1.2 Contribution

Our routing scheme is very different from the existing ACO based routing schema for WSNs. Firstly, in our scheme, when an ant is at the node s_i and selects its next-hop node, the search range of the ant is limited to a subset of the set of s_i's neighbors, instead of the total set of s_i's neighbors. On one hand, this guarantees that the data packets are delivered toward the sink node. On the other hand, many useless searches for an ant to select its next hop node are effectively avoided. Secondly, we propose a novel formula to calculate the transition probability with which ants select their next hop nodes. Thirdly, we propose a novel model to determine the amount of the pheromone which an ant will lay on the route traveled by the ant. This diversifies the solutions that ants found, and the probability of the local convergence of the proposed routing algorithm is decreased. In addition, we also propose a novel scheme to evaporate the pheromone on the different segments of a certain route according to the residual energy and the location information of nodes. This also effectively increases the diversity of the solutions found by ants. The simulation results show that the proposed ACO based routing algorithm has a better performance than other ACO based routing algorithms for WSNs [4,7].

The remainder of the paper is organized as follows. In Section 2, the related work is introduced. The novel ACO based routing scheme and the corresponding algorithm for WSNs are proposed in Section 3. The simulation results are presented in Section 4. Section 5 concludes this paper.

2 Related Work

The biological research has shown that ants communicate with each other by sensing the density of pheromone. The pheromone is a chemical substance which ants lay on the routes traveled by themselves. Each ant prefers to moving toward the route with a high density of pheromone. The more the ants which travel a certain route are, the more the accumulated pheromone on this route is, thus the greater the probability with which the other ants select this route is. As a result, the amount of pheromone is gradually increased on this route. However, pheromone may be evaporated over time. Biological experiments have shown that each ant just interacts with the environment surrounding the ant, and independently selects the route without any global knowledge. In the system organized by a group of ants, ants can quickly find the shortest route by sensing the density of pheromone on the routes from the nest to the food node. Inspired by the real ant colony system, Dorigo et al [5,6] first proposed artificial ant colony algorithms, namely Ant Colony Optimization (ACO), to solve complex combinatorial optimization problems [12].

The ACO is particularly suitable for large-scale distributed self-organization systems [4]. Recently, the ACO based adaptive routing draws the attention from many researchers [3,4]. Despite that several ACO based routing algorithms for WSNs have been proposed, those algorithms are based on the framework proposed by Dorigo [5,6]. In fact, the core idea of ACO based routing lies in two key points. One is to define the formula to calculate the transition probability with which an ant selects its next-hop node, and the other is to determine the rules used to update the pheromone on the routes. According to different WSN applications, researchers defined the different formula to calculate the transition probability, and modified the rules to update the amount of pheromone. In this paper, we define a novel formula to calculate the transition probability under the framework of the ACO based routing proposed by Dorigo, and we also define novel rules to update the amount of pheromone on the routes. Following the proposed scheme, we design a new ACO based routing algorithm for WSNs. Simulation results show that the proposed algorithm has a better comprehensive performance than other ACO based routing algorithms for WSNs [4,7].

3 ACO Based Location-Aware Routing for WSNs

3.1 Problem Description

A WSN consists of m static and identical wireless sensors. Each sensor is called a node. The nodes are uniformly distributed in a flat region, as shown in Fig.1. The nodes are equipped with omni-directional antennas, and the communication range of each node is a circle area whose radius is r. A WSN is formally described as a weighted undirected graph $G(V, E, L)$. Here, $V=\{s_1, s_2, ..., s_m\}$, and each $s_i \in V$ represents a sensor node in a WSN. E is the set of edges, L is the

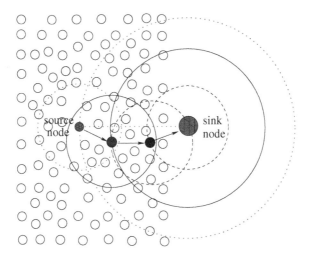

Fig. 1. Ant colony optimization-based location-ware routing for WSNs

set of weights, and $E \subset V \times V \times L$. At any instant t, for any $s_i, s_j \in V$, $i \neq j$, the locations of s_i and s_j are denoted as (x_i, y_i) and (x_j, y_j), respectively. The distance between s_i and s_j is denoted as d_{ij}, and d_{ij} is calculated by the following formula.

$$d_{ij} = \sqrt{(x_i - x_j)^2 + (y_i - y_j)^2} \ . \tag{1}$$

For any $s_i, s_j \in V$, if $d_{ij} \leq r$, and s_i and s_j both are active, that is, s_i and s_j both are working, then there is an undirected edge $(s_i, s_j, \psi_{ij}(t)) \in E$. Here, the weight $\psi_{ij}(t) \in [0, 1]$ is the cost to deliver a data packet from s_i to s_j at instant t. For any $s_i \in V$, the residual energy of s_i is denoted as $e_i(t)$ at instant t. Traditionally, the set of s_i's neighbors is defined as follows.

$$N(s_i) = \{s_j \mid s_j \in V, d_{ij} \leq r\} \ . \tag{2}$$

In this paper, s_0 is the source node, and s_b is the sink node. The set of s_i's next-hop neighbors is defined as follows.

$$C(s_i) = \{s_j \mid s_j \in N(s_i), d_{jb} \leq d_{ib}\} \ . \tag{3}$$

The problem to be solved is to find the best optimal route from the source node s_0 to the sink node s_b, such that a given data packet may be delivered from s_0 to s_b, while energy consumption is minimized and packet delivery latency is minimized. This is a hard combinatorial optimization problem. As shown in Fig. 1, before a given data packet is delivered from the source node to the sink node, we need to find the best optimal route from the source node to the sink node. In this paper, we propose a novel ACO based routing algorithm to effectively solve this problem.

3.2 The Basic Principal of ACO

In the following, the basic principal of ACO is introduced based on the practical procedure that ants find food. Similar to [3], suppose that there are three ants a_1, a_2 and a_3 at the nest node (source node) s_0, and that there are three routes ϕ_1, ϕ_2 and ϕ_3 from the nest node s_0 to the food node (sink node) s_b. The length of ϕ_1 is greater than the length of ϕ_3 and the length of ϕ_3 is greater than the length of ϕ_2. The route ϕ_1 includes four nodes s_0, s_1, s_2 and s_b, the route ϕ_2 includes three nodes s_0, s_3 and s_b, and the route ϕ_3 includes five nodes s_0, s_4, s_5, s_6 and s_b. Here, it is noted that the number of the nodes included in a route is not generally related to the length of the route.

The procedure for ants to find the shortest route from s_0 to s_b is described as follows. Initially, at s_0, the three ants have no knowledge about the routes from s_0 to s_b. Each ant selects one of the three routes in a random mode. Suppose that a_1 selects ϕ_1, a_2 selects ϕ_2 and a_3 selects ϕ_3, and that the three ants move at the same speed. At the initial instant t_0, the three ants start to move from s_0 to s_b along the three routes. Clearly, due to the shorter length of ϕ_2, a_2 first reaches s_b, then a_3 reaches s_b, and a_1 finally reaches s_b. Once an ant reaches

s_b, the ant immediately returns toward s_0 along the route from which the ant just comes. While returning, the ants will lay a different amount of pheromone on the route traveled by themselves. At instant t, the pheromone on the route from s_i to s_j is denoted as $\psi_{ij}(t)$, here s_i and s_j are two neighboring nodes. The pheromone which the ant k lays on the route from s_i to s_j is denoted as $\Delta\psi_{ij}^k(t)$. If the ant k does not pass the route from s_i to s_j, then $\Delta\psi_{ij}^k(t)$ is equal to 0. Usually, the value of $\Delta\psi_{ij}^k(t)$ is inversely proportional to the length of the route traveled by the ant k from s_0 to s_b. Let the length of the route found by the ant k be L^k at instant t. When a_2 return to s_0 before a_1 and a_3, the value of $\psi_{03}(t)$ is immediately set to $1/L^2$. Similarly, when a_3 return to s_0 before a_1, the value of $\psi_{04}(t)$ is immediately set to $1/L^3$. When a_1 return to s_0, the value of $\psi_{01}(t)$ is immediately set to $1/L^1$. When all the three ants return to s_0, we say that these ants complete a round travel. Next, the ants start the second round travel. At s_0, the ants prefer to choosing the route with a high density of pheromone. Since $1/L^2 > 1/L^3 > 1/L^1$, ϕ_2 is chosen by the ants. When the ants complete the second round travel, the density of pheromone on ϕ_2 is much greater than that on ϕ_1 or ϕ_2. Hence, ϕ_2 is the shortest route from s_0 to s_b.

In the above example, any ant at s_0 will be able to choose the optimal route once other ants return to s_0. If the ant k is at s_i, and there is no pheromone on any route from s_i to s_i's next-hop neighbors, the ant k makes a random decision to select one route with the probability of 0.5. However, when there is pheromone on routes, the ant k will select the route with a higher density of pheromone. It is noted that there are other types of ants that use pheromone to communicate with each other in different modes. Hence, there are still other ACO approaches [3]. In addition, the pheromone on a route may be evaporated over time. According to the different problems, different rules to lay or evaporate pheromone are defined to effectively solve these different problems.

3.3 The Proposed Routing Scheme for WSNs

To select the best optimal route from the source node to the sink node, suppose that each node in a WSN has a memory block in which the residual energy of the node and its neighbors, the location information of the node, its neighbors and the sink node are stored. Each ant is a mobile agent that has a contraindication list to memory the nodes traversed by the ant in a round travel. The contraindication list may help each ant avoiding to select the nodes which have been traversed by the ant. Furthermore, each ant may avoid to cycle on the same route. In addition, when the ant k is at s_i at instant t, the ant k will select the node $s_j \in C(s_i)$ as the next-hop node in a probability mode, as shown in Fig. 2. We believe that the location information of nodes significantly influences the probabilities with which the ant k selects s_j as the next-hop node. Hence, we define the location function ξ_{ij} as follows.

$$\xi_{ij} = \left(\frac{d_{0b}}{d_{0i} + d_{ij} + d_{jb}}\right) \times \left(1 - \frac{d_{ij}}{\sum\limits_{s_l \in C(s_i)} d_{il}}\right) . \tag{4}$$

Where d_{ij} is the distance from s_i to s_j, d_{0b} is the distance from s_0 to s_b, d_{0i} is the distance from s_0 to s_i, and d_{jb} is the distance from s_j to s_b. Clearly, $0 \leq \xi_{ij} \leq 1$. The greater the value of ξ_{ij} is, the greater the probability with which ants select s_j as the next-hop node is. If there is not any next-hop neighbor to select, that is, $C(s_i) \backslash \{s_i\}$ is empty, then the ant k returns to the previous-hop node of s_i. Let the previous-hop node of s_i be s_l. Before the ant k makes a reselection at s_l, s_i is added to the contraindication list of the ant k, so that the ant k does not select s_i as the next-hop node again.

In addition, we believe that the residual energy of nodes influences the probabilities with which the ant k selects s_j as the next-hop node. Therefore, we define the energy function $\eta_{ij}(t)$ as follows.

$$\eta_{ij}(t) = \frac{e_j(t)}{\sum\limits_{s_l \in C(s_i)} e_l(t)} \quad . \tag{5}$$

Where $e_l(t)$ is the residual energy of s_l at instant t. The greater the value of $\eta_{ij}(t)$ is, the greater the probability with which the ant k selects s_j as the next-hop node is. To comprehensively consider the location information and the residual energy of nodes, we define the novel transition probability with which the ant k at the node s_i selects $s_j \in C(s_i)$ as the next-hop node at instant t as follows.

$$p_{ij}^k(t) = \frac{[\psi_{ij}(t)]^\alpha \times [\xi_{ij}]^\beta \times [\eta_{ij}(t)]^\gamma}{\sum\limits_{s_l \in C(s_i)} [\psi_{il}(t)]^\alpha \times [\xi_{il}]^\beta \times [\eta_{il}(t)]^\gamma} \quad . \tag{6}$$

Where α, β and γ are the adjustable weights of $\psi_{ij}(t)$, ξ_{ij} and $\eta_{ij}(t)$, respectively. Hence, the routing selection of ants may be tuned according to the different values of α, β and γ. A higher value of α increases the chance for ants to choose the route with a higher pheromone, a higher value of β increases the chance for ants to choose the route with a shorter length, and a higher value of γ increases the chance for ants to choose the node with more residual energy. In general, different values of α, β and γ are selected for different situations. When a WSN is not stable, a lower value of α is generally preferred. This is because the pheromone on a route may not necessarily reflect the optimality of the route at that time. As a WSN becomes stable, a higher value of α is preferred. If a lower latency of packet delivery is needed, a higher value of β is preferred. This is because a higher value of β means a shorter route to select. When the energy of nodes is not uniformly distributed, a lower value of γ is generally preferred. In fact, it may improve the performance of ants' cooperative routing to dynamically change the values of α, β and γ [3].

For each ant, it starts to move from s_0 to s_b. When the ant k reaches s_b, the ant k finds a route R^k from s_0 to s_b. Suppose R^k includes the nodes s_0, s_i, s_j and s_b, denoted as $R^k(s_0, s_i, s_j, s_b)$. Then, the ant k immediately starts to return to s_0 from s_b along the route R^k. While returning, the ant k orderly updates the pheromone ψ_{jb}, ψ_{ij} and ψ_{0i}. Suppose that there are n ants in a WSN. We call it a round travel that n ants reach s_b from s_0, and then return to s_0 from s_b along the routes from which the ants just come, respectively. Suppose that it takes a unit time for ants to finish a round travel. The rule used for updating the pheromone on the route R_{ij} (the segment between s_i and s_j) is defined as follows.

$$\psi_{ij}(t+1) = (1 - \rho(t)) \times \psi_{ij}(t) + \Delta\psi_{ij} \ . \tag{7}$$

Where $\rho(t)$ is the pheromone evaporating rate at instant t, and $0 \leq \rho(t) \leq 1$. $\rho(t)$ is calculated by the following formula.

$$\rho(t) = (1 - \eta_{ij}(t)) \times (1 - \xi_{ij}) \ . \tag{8}$$

The above formula implies that the pheromone evaporating rate $\rho(t)$ is a function of the residual energy and the location information of nodes, instead of a constant. This scheme has a better adaptivity to the frequent change of the topology of a WSN. In Formula (7), $\Delta\psi_{ij}$ is the pheromone increment on the route between s_i and s_j in the current round travel. $\Delta\psi_{ij}$ is calculated by the following formula.

$$\Delta\psi_{ij} = \sum_{k=1}^{n} \Delta\psi_{ij}^k \ . \tag{9}$$

Where $\Delta\psi_{ij}^k$ is the pheromone that the ant k laid on the route between s_i and s_j in the current round travel. $\Delta\psi_{ij}^k$ is calculated by the following formula.

$$\Delta\psi_{ij}^k = \begin{cases} \frac{d_{0b} \times Q}{(d_{0i} + d_{ij} + d_{jb})L^k} & \text{if ant } k \text{ passed from } s_i \rightarrow s_j \\ 0 & \text{otherwise} \end{cases} \ . \tag{10}$$

Where Q is a constant, d_{0i}, d_{0b}, d_{ij} and d_{jb} have the same meaning as that of Formula (4), respectively. L^k is the length of the route that is found by the ant k in the current round travel.

3.4   The Proposed Routing Algorithm for WSNs

Our algorithm (ACLR) is composed of two phases. In the first phase, for each ant k, following the proposed routing scheme, the ant k starts to look for an optimal route from the source node s_0 to the sink node s_b. When the ant k reaches the sink node s_b, a route R^k from the source node to the sink node is found by the ant k. Let the length of R^k be L^k. In the second phase, each ant k returns to the source node from the sink node along the route R^k. At the meantime, following the proposed pheromone updating rules, the ant k updates the pheromone on each segment of R^k. Let the total number of ants be n, and the total number of nodes in a WSN be m. num is the number of the round travels which the ants complete in finding optimal routes. Γ^k is the contraindication list of the ant k at instant t. The ACLR is described as follows.

1: Initialize the numbers n, num of ants and round travels, $\psi_{ij}(0)$, and $t \Leftarrow 0$
2: **while** the end iteration condition is not met **do**
3:     $t \Leftarrow t + 1$
4:     **for** $k = 1$ to n **do**
5:         Ant k is positioned on the source node s_0
6:         $s_i \Leftarrow s_0$; $R^k \Leftarrow \varnothing$; $\Gamma^k \Leftarrow \varnothing$
7:         **while** $s_i \neq s_b$ **do**
8:             **if** $C(s_i) - \Gamma^k \neq \varnothing$ **then**
9:                 Select s_j from $C(s_i) - \Gamma^k$ to move according to the probabilistic transition rules
10:                 $R^k \Leftarrow R^k \cup \{s_i\}$; $\Gamma^k \Leftarrow \Gamma^k \cup \{s_i\}$; $i \Leftarrow j$
11:             **else**
12:                 Return to the previous-hop of s_i; $\Gamma^k \Leftarrow \Gamma^k \cup \{s_j\}$
13:             **end if**
14:         **end while**
15:         Compute the length L^k of R^k by Formula (1)
16:         Calculate $\Delta\psi_{ij}^k$ by Formula (10), here (s_i, s_j) is a segment of R^k
17:     **end for**
18:     Update the pheromone $\psi_{ij}(t)$ by Formula (7)-(10)
19:     Compare and update the best solution set
20: **end while**
21: Return(the best optimal solutions)
22: End.

---

4   Simulation Results

Through simulations, we compare the proposed algorithm (ACLR) with the following four algorithms: Basic Ant Routing (BAR), Sensor-driven Cost-aware Ant Routing (SCAR), Flooded Piggybacked Ant Routing (FPAR) [7], and the IAR [4], which are classical ACO based routing algorithms for WSNs. For different algorithms, we mainly compare energy consumption, packet transmission delay and energy efficiency.

4.1   Simulation Environment

The simulations were conducted with the network simulation software OPNET to evaluate the performance of algorithms. We compare ACLR with BAR, SCAR, FPAR and IAR. The network area is set to 200×300 (m^2), 10000 sensors are uniformly deployed in this region, and the wireless communication radius of sensors is 30m. The data rate at MAC layer is 2Mbps. $\alpha = 3, \beta = 3, \gamma = 3$, and $Q = 100$J. For any node s_i, suppose that s_j is any next-hop node of s_i. The initial pheromone on the route between s_i and s_j is set to $\psi_{ij}(0) = 0.01$. The total number of ants are 20.

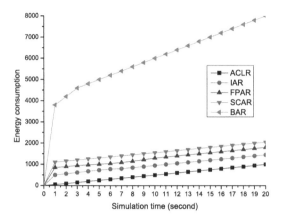

Fig. 2. Energy consumption of different algorithms

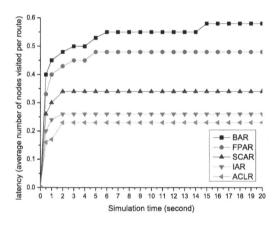

Fig. 3. Packet delivery latency of different algorithms

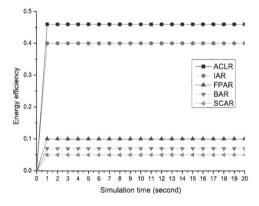

Fig. 4. Energy efficiency of different algorithms

For each case, by randomly choosing the locations of the source node, we simulate each algorithm 50 times so as to get the average results.

4.2 Energy Consumption

Energy consumption refers to the used energy in the process of data packet delivery. Similar to [4], we assume that it consumes one unit energy to directly deliver a data packet between two nodes. Hence, the total energy consumption may be defined as the total number of the data packets which are directly sent between nodes. Fig.2 shows that the energy consumption of ACLR is the smallest. The main reason is that, for ACLR, the least number of redundant data packets are delivered. Therefore, the least amount of energy is consumed.

4.3 Packet Delivery Latency

The packet delivery delay refers to the used time to transmit a data packet from the source node to the sink node, that is, end-to-end delay. For each data packet, suppose that the total time for each node to receive, process and send a data packet is uniform. Since the delay time when a data packet is in a wireless channel is much smaller than the time for a node to receive, process and send the data packet, the delay time when the data packet is delivered in a wireless channel may be neglected. Furthermore, we can use the average number of the nodes included in a route to estimate the data packet delay time in different algorithms [4]. Fig.3 shows that the data packet delivery delay of ACLR is smallest.

4.4 Energy Efficiency

In a WSN, energy efficiency refers to the ratio of the number of data packets received at the sink node by the total consumed energy [9]. A higher energy efficiency means that a specific WSN has a better energy-saving feature. Fig.4 shows that ACLR has the highest energy efficiency among all the five algorithms. We believe that the main reason is the search range of ants is effectively limited in ACLR.

5 Conclusion

The routing for WSNs has been a topic in the field of WSN applications for a long time. In this paper, we proposed a novel routing scheme for WSNs based on Ant Colony Optimization (ACO). We define a novel formula to calculate the transition probability with which an ant selects its next-hop node, and we also propose some novel rules to update the pheromone on the routes traveled by ants. By defining the transition probability as a function of the location information of nodes, the residual energy of nodes and the pheromone on routes, we effectively achieve the balance between node energy and packet transmission delay. Moreover, we define the pheromone evaporating rate as a function of the residual energy and location information of nodes to overcome the disadvantage that the constant rate of pheromone evaporating poses. The simulation results show that the proposed algorithm has a better performance than that of BAR, SCAR, FPAR proposed in [7], and IAR proposed in [4].

References

1. Akyildiz, I.F., Su, W., Sankkarasubramaniam, Y., Cayirci, E.: Wireless sensor networks: a survey. Journal of Computer Networks 38(4), 393–424 (2002)
2. Al-karaki, J.N., Kamal, A.E.: Routing techniques in wireless sensor networks: a survey. IEEE Wireless Communications 11(6), 6–28 (2004)
3. Iyengar, S.S., Wu, H.-C., Balakrishnan, N., Changand, S.Y.: Biologically inspired cooperative routing for wireless mobile sensor networks. IEEE Systems Journal 1(1), 29–37 (2007)
4. Aghaei, R.G., Rahman, M.A., Gueaieb, W., Saddik, A.E.: Ant colony-based reinforcement learning algorithm for routing in wireless sensor networks. In: 2007 IEEE Instrumentation and Measurement Technology, pp. 1–6. IEEE Press, New York (2007)
5. Dorigo, M., et al.: Ant system optimation: a colony of cooperating agents. IEEE Transactions on System, Man, Cybernetics Part B. 26(1), 29–41 (1996)
6. Dorigo, M., Gambadella, L.M.: Ant colony system: a cooperative learning approach to the tranveling salesman problem. IEEE Transactions on Evolutionary Computation 1(1), 53–66 (1997)
7. Zhang, Y., Kuhn, L.D., Fromherz, M.P.J.: Improvements on ant routing for sensor networks. In: Dorigo, M., Birattari, M., Blum, C., Gambardella, L.M., Mondada, F., Stützle, T. (eds.) ANTS 2004. LNCS, vol. 3172, pp. 154–165. Springer, Heidelberg (2004)
8. Shen, C., Jaikaeo, C.: Ad hoc multicast routing algorithm with swarm intelligence. Journal of Mobile Netwotks and Applications 10(1,2), 47–59 (2005)
9. Akkaya, K., Younis, M.: A survey on routing protocols for wireless sensor networks. Journal of Ad Hoc Networks 3(3), 325–349 (2005)
10. Caro, G.D., Dorigo, M.: AntNet: distributed stigmergetic control for communications networks. Journal of Artificial Intelligence Research 9, 317–365 (1998)
11. Dorigo, M., et al.: Special section on ant colony optimization. IEEE Transactions on Evolutionary Computation 6(4), 317–319 (2002)
12. Chakrabarty, K., Iyengar, S.S.: Scalable infrastructure for distributed sensor networks. Springer, Heidelberg (2005)
13. Stuetzle, T., Dorigo, M.: A short convergence proof for a class of ACO algorithms. IEEE Transactions on Evolutionary Computation 6(4), 358–365 (2002)
14. Schoonderwoerd, R., Holland, O., Bruten, J., Rothkrantz, L.: Ant-based load balancing in telecommunications networks. Adaptive Behavior 5(2), 169–207 (1996)

Multi-path GEM for Routing in Wireless Sensor Networks

Qiang Ye[1], Yuxing Huang[2], Andrew Reddin[3], Lei Wang[4], and Wuman Luo[5]

[1,2,3] Dept. of Computer Science and Information Technology, UPEI, Charlottetown, PE,
Canada C1A 4P3
[4] School of Computer Science, Beihang University, Beijing, P.R. China 100083
[5] School of Software Engineering, Univ. of Elec. Science & Tech of China, Chengdu, Sichuan,
P.R. China 610054
{qye,yuxhuang,afreddin}@upei.ca, wanglei@buaa.edu.cn,
amy_lwm@uestc.edu.cn

Abstract. Wireless sensor networks are expected to be used in many different applications such as disaster relief and environmental control. Efficient routing protocols need to be thoroughly studied before wireless sensor networks are widely deployed. GEM is an ingenious routing algorithm that is based on the idea of graph embedding. Using a well designed virtual coordinate system, GEM provides a remarkably simple route selection mechanism. However, GEM does not survive edge failures well. In this paper, we propose R-GEM and S-GEM that use the idea of GEM and improve its reliability performance significantly. Both of them outperform GEM in all of the experimental scenarios. Specifically, in the case that 2% of all edges in the network fail to transfer packets, when only disjoint pairs are taken into consideration, GEM leads to a path error rate of 10% while R-GEM and S-GEM only result in a path error rate of 2%.

Keywords: Graph Embedding, Multi-Path, Reliability, Sensor Networks.

1 Introduction

Wireless sensor networks are composed of spatially distributed wireless nodes that are equipped with sensors. Using sensors, these wireless nodes can cooperatively monitor environmental conditions, such as temperature, sound, vibration, pressure, etc. The wireless nodes can also configure themselves into an efficient wireless network for data delivery. Wireless sensor networks are expected to be used in many different applications such as disaster relief, environmental control, and intelligent buildings.

Routing for wireless sensor networks has been studied over the past decade [1-5]. Haas *et al.* proposed a "rumor mongering" algorithm: once a sensor node receives a new packet, it randomly chooses one of its neighbors to propagate this packet on a periodic basis; it stops after a sufficient number of neighbors have received the packet [1]. Scott *et al.* came up with an energy-efficient algorithm that is based on Dijkstra's algorithm [2]. It tries to obtain routes with minimal total transmission power. Greedy Perimeter Stateless Routing (GPSR) uses the right-hand rule to recover from a labyrinth [3]. That is, to escape a labyrinth, we can simply place the right hand on the wall

Y. Li et al. (Eds.): WASA 2008, LNCS 5258, pp. 121–133, 2008.
© Springer-Verlag Berlin Heidelberg 2008

and keep walking. This way, all the walls of the labyrinth will be visited and finally we will be able to find the destination.

GEM [6] is an ingenious routing algorithm that is based on the idea of graph embedding [7]. It first maps a polar coordinate system, Virtual Polar Coordinate Space (VPCS), to the physical network. Then routing decision will simply be made in the polar coordinate system. GEM routing is remarkably straightforward once the virtual polar system has been established. Furthermore, the construction of VPCS does not depend upon actual physical coordinates and can be done with acceptable overhead. However, GEM does not survive physical edge failures well. In this paper, we propose two multi-path GEM variants in order to improve the reliability performance of GEM.

The reset of the paper is organized as follows. Section 2 gives an introduction to graph embedding and GEM routing in wireless sensor networks. Section 3 explains how the proposed multi-path GEM variants work. The details of our simulation are described in Section 4 and the experimental results are summarized in Section 5. The paper closes with our conclusions and recommendations in Section 6.

2 Graph Embedding and GEM

Graph Embedding is a technique in graph theory that can be applied to varied areas [7]. Particularly, its effectiveness has been proven in various network projects [8, 9]. GEM is also a successful application of Graph Embedding to routing in wireless sensor network.

GEM [6] uses VPCS to facilitate routing in wireless sensor networks. With VPCS, a tree, the guest graph, is mapped to the physical host graph. The mapping is accomplished by assigning each node in the physical network:

1) A *level* that is the number of hops to the root of the tree;
2) A *virtual angle range* that is unique to a node at a certain level.

In GEM, a tree generation algorithm is used to build the tree and determine level/virtual angle range. Each GEM tree has one root node and usually the root node has a few subtrees. The angle range of the root is $[0, 2\pi]$. The root assigns to its children varied angle ranges that are proportional to the subtree sizes corresponding to these children. Fig. 1 is a sample GEM tree. Mathematically, the range of $[0, 2\pi]$ is straightforward and clear. However, when it is divided many times, the resulting ranges will involve fractions. To solve this problem, in real systems, we can use a large integer range, such as $[0, 2^{16}-1]$ or $[0, 2^{32}-1]$, to replace the original $[0, 2\pi]$. Fig. 2 shows an example GEM tree that uses integer ranges.

After angle range is assigned to each node, GEM is ready for node-to-node routing. Generally, when a source node S tries to send a packet to a destination node D, the packet is first routed up the tree to the root R along the path from S to R; then the packet is routed down the tree to the destination along the path from R to D. Fig. 3 includes a very simple example, illustrating how GEM is used to route packets from node S to node D. The dashed arrows in Fig. 3 indicate the route that is chosen by GEM.

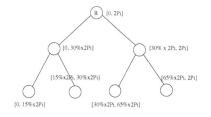

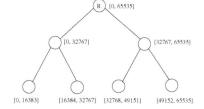

Fig. 1. GEM Tree: Polar Coordinate System

Fig. 2. GEM Tree: Integer Angle Range

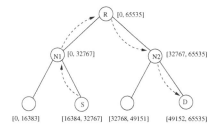

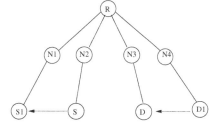

Fig. 3. GEM Routing

Fig. 4. Multi-Path GEM

3   Random and Shortest Multi-path GEM

GEM is a simple but efficient routing algorithm for wireless sensor networks. However, it is extremely vulnerable to potential edge failures. Whenever a single edge on the path from the source to the destination fails, the communication cannot continue any more. Multi-Path Routing has been studied in both traditional wired networks and wireless networks to improve reliability [5, 10]. The idea is to establish two or more physically-disjoint paths between the source and the destination. By "physically disjoint", we mean that the established paths do not share any edge in the network. This way, although an edge failure leads to the malfunction of the path that contains the edge, it does not have an impact on the alternative path connecting the source and the destination.

To add recovery capability to GEM, we proposed Multi-Path GEM, a routing algorithm that attempts to find two physically disjoint paths between a pair of nodes in the GEM tree. Since GEM already provides a straightforward route for any pair of nodes, our task is actually to find another disjoint path. The key problem is that the alternative path should be physically disjoint of the path generated by GEM.

One intuitive solution is to find an alternative path through the neighbor nodes of the source and destination. Assume that for a given pair of nodes, the source node S has a neighbor node N_S and the destination node D has a neighbor node N_D. Then we found that if N_S, N_D, S, and D do not share level-1 ancestors (ancestors that are at level 1 in the GEM tree), the GEM path from N_S to the root R will be disjoint of the GEM path from S to R, and the GEM path from R to N_D will be disjoint of the GEM path from R to D. Thus, the problem of finding disjoint paths can be converted to the problem of finding neighbors that do not share level-1 ancestors with the source node and destination node. This is the idea behind Multi-Path GEM.

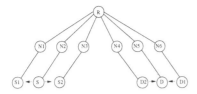

Fig. 5. Random Multi-Path GEM

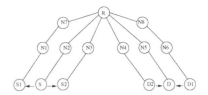

Fig. 6. Shortest Multi-Path GEM

The details of Multi-Path GEM are summarized as follows. Formally, Multi-Path GEM has the following two assumptions:

1) Every node in the GEM tree knows who its level-1 ancestor is. This can be accomplished by adding an extra step to the GEM tree generation process. Namely, after the GEM tree is generated, all level-1 nodes could send out their angle ranges to their children, then the information is passed along various paths in the tree until every leaf node receives it.

2) Every node in the GEM tree knows who the level-1 ancestors of its neighbors are. This can be done in advance when the GEM tree is generated. Or when necessary, the source and destination node can query their neighbors and receive the level-1 ancestor information of their neighbors on the fly.

Once these two assumptions are implemented in wireless sensor networks, Multi-Path GEM can be used to find a disjoint path from the source to the destination by checking the level-1 ancestors of the source's and destination's neighbors. This disjoint path and the original GEM path will serve as two disjoint paths connecting the source and destination. If one path fails, the other path can be used to keep transferring packets. Fig. 4 includes a simple example that illustrates the operation of Multi-Path GEM. In this example, (S, N2, R, N3, D) is the original GEM path and (S, S1, N1, R, N4, D1, D) is the physically disjoint path.

Note that when there are more than two disjoint paths, there should be a mechanism to make the selection. For instance, in Fig. 5, S1 and S2 are the neighbors of S, they do not share level-1 ancestor with S and D; DS1 and DS2 are the neighbors of DS, they do not share level-1 ancestor with S and D. In this case, there could be at least three disjoint paths available: (S, N2, R, N5, D), (S, S1, N1, R, N6, D1, D), and (S, S2, N3, R, N4, D2, D). This leads to a revised version of Multi-Path GEM.

Definition 1 *Random Multi-Path GEM*: Aside from the basic GEM path, when there are two or more alternative disjoint paths from the source node to the destination node, one of the disjoint paths could be randomly selected as the backup for the GEM path. This version of Multi-Path GEM is called "Random Multi-Path GEM". We use "R-GEM" to denote Random Multi-Path GEM in this paper.

R-GEM is used to choose one disjoint path in addition to the GEM path. For the example in Fig. 5, if R-GEM is the routing protocol, either (S, S1, N1, R, N6, D1, D) or (S, S2, N3, R, N4, D2,D) will be selected as the backup for (S, N2, R, N5, D). R-GEM solves the problem associated with multiple disjoint paths in a simple manner. However, when path length and the number of hops associated with the path are taken into account, R-GEM is far from being optimal. For example, in Fig. 6, there are also at least three disjoint paths: (S, N2, R, N5, D), (S, S2, N3, R, N4, D2, D), and (S, S1,

N1, N7, R, N8, N6, D1, D). If R-GEM is used, despite that the length of (S, S2, N3, R, N4, D2, D) is 6 and that of (S, S1, N1, N7, R, N8, N6, D1, D) is 8, either of them could be chosen as the backup path. From the perspective of power assumption, the former path should always be chosen over the latter one. To make sure that the shorter path is selected, we revised R-GEM and arrived at the following routing algorithm.

Definition 2 *Shortest Multi-Path GEM*: Aside from the basic GEM path, when there are two or more disjoint paths from the source node to the destination node, the path whose length is the shortest should be chosen. If the length of several disjoint paths is the same, then one of them is selected in a random fashion. This version of Multi-Path GEM is called "Shortest Multi-Path GEM". We use "S-GEM" to denote Shortest Multi-Path GEM in this paper.

With S-GEM, in the above example, (S, S2, N3, R, N4, D2,D) will be chosen over (S, S1, N1, N7, R, N8, N6, D1, D), the path whose path length is longer. Compared with R-GEM, S-GEM is more efficient in terms of path length. However, it has to calculate the length of each disjoint path when the selection is made. At this moment, it is hard to conclude which one is more appropriate. This is because R-GEM is less efficient in terms of path length, but it involves less computation; S-GEM is more efficient, but it requires extra operations. Our experimental results will help determine their effectiveness in realistic environments.

4 Simulation

Our simulation is carried out using our own customized simulator. Table 1 summarizes the major parameters used in the simulation. In a 400m x 400m area, the network topology is generated by placing the root node at the center and distributing the remaining nodes over the area randomly. In our research, we consider five different scenarios in which there are be 400, 500, 600, 700, and 800 nodes in the network, respectively. This relatively high density guarantees that the generated topologies are well connected and there exist enough disjoint paths among randomly chosen pairs. In our simulation, for the case of 400 and 500 nodes, occasionally one or two nodes are not connected to the rest of the network; for the case of 600, 700, and 800 nodes, it is very rare to see disconnected nodes.

Disjoint path availability is vital to R-GEM and S-GEM. And it is closely related to node density in the network. If node density is so low that only few pairs have disjoint paths, then both R-GEM and S-GEM will be less effective. At the extreme, when there is no alternative path between any pair in the network, R-GEM and S-GEM will essentially be the same as GEM. Table 2 illustrates this relationship quantitatively. In our simulation, as the number of nodes in the network changes from 400 to 800, the average number of pairs that have disjoint paths increases from 360.7 to 648. Intuitively, R-GEM and S-GEM should perform better in the case of 800 nodes than in the scenario of 400 nodes. The detailed experimental results will be presented later.

To study the reliability performance of R-GEM and S-GEM, we purposely introduce random edge errors to the networks under investigation. The random edge errors introduced in our simulation satisfy uniform distribution. Thus, every edge in the

Table 1. Simulation parameters

Parameter	Value
Network Size	400 m x 400 m
Transmission Range	40 m
Node Number	400, 500, 600, 700, 800
Neighborhood	1 hop
Edge Error Distribution	Uniform

Table 2. The number of disjoint pairs in varied scenarios

Scenario	400 Nodes	500 Nodes	600 Nodes	700 Nodes	800 Nodes
Disjoint Pairs	360.7	450.2	563.8	578	648

network has an equal probability of being erroneous. In our simulation, we consider the error rate range of 0-20% with an increment of 1%. Namely, the edge error rate could be 0, 1%, 2%, ..., 19%, or 20% in varied scenarios.

An edge error leads to a path error if the edge is part of the path. When GEM is the routing algorithm used in network, if a path error occurs, then the session using the path will simply be terminated. However, if R-GEM or S-GEM is deployed, one path error does not stop the packet flow. Only when all the disjoint paths selected by R-GEM or S-GEM fail will the current session be destroyed completely. In our research, the impact of random edge errors on routing algorithms is used to evaluate the reliability performance of R-GEM and S-GEM. The detailed experimental results are presented later.

Note that the edge error rate is directly related to the path error rate. In the case of uniformly distributed edge errors, when the edge error rate is e_E and a path is composed of n edges, the path success rate s_P can be calculated using the following equation:

$$s_P = (1 - e_E)^n \tag{1}$$

We can further arrive at the path error rate e_P using the following equation:

$$e_P = 1 - (1 - e_E)^n \tag{2}$$

Apparently, for a particular path in a specific scenario, once the path length and the edge error rate is fixed, the corresponding path error rate will stay put.

The detailed simulations runs are summarized as follows. In the case of 400 nodes, we study the performance of R-GEM/S-GEM in 21 different scenarios. These scenarios correspond to the 21 different edge error rates, 0, 1%, 2%, ..., 19%, and 20%. For each of these scenarios (e.g., the scenario of 1% error rate), we generate 10 different topologies altogether. For each of these 10 topologies, we generate 20 different edge error distributions (every distribution satisfies the 1% error rate in the example scenario of 1% error rate, but different edges are randomly chosen as "erroneous" in each distribution). For each of these 20 topologies, we also randomly choose 1000 pairs of nodes as the sample pairs to study the reliability performance of R-GEM/S-GEM. Our experimental results will show, despite the existing edge errors, more pairs (among these 1000 pairs) can still communicate with each other when R-GEM/S-GEM, instead of GEM, is used as the routing protocol.

Note that in the case of 400 nodes, we need to execute simulation 21 x 20 x 20 = 8400 times. For the case of 500, 600, 700, and 800 nodes, we repeated the same procedure to gather the experimental results.

5 Experimental Results

This section presents the reliability performance of R-GEM and S-GEM in terms of Average Path Length and Path Error Rate.The performance of R-GEM and S-GEM in terms of Average Path Length is first summarized as follows. There are two reasons why path length plays an important role in wireless sensor networks. First of all, the longer the path is, the greater the number of hops will be. Each hop consumes a certain amount of energy. In energy-constraint environments like sensor networks, we should try to reduce path length whenever possible. Secondly, path length is related to path error rate. As mentioned previously, when the edge error rate is eE and a path is composed of n edges, the path error rate eP is equal to 1-(1- eE)n. Apparently, the greater n is, the larger the resulting path error rate will be. From this perspective, if there are multiple paths available, we should also choose the shorter one. Ideally, R-GEM and S-GEM can find a disjoint path that is used as the backup for the basic GEM path and this backup path should not be too long.

Table 3 summarizes the results for the pairs that have disjoint paths in our simulation. For example, in the case of 800 nodes, around 648 pairs among the 1000 candidates have disjoint paths. Then only the path length information about these 648 pairs is presented in Table 3. In our research, these pairs are called "disjoint pairs" and other pairs among the 1000 candidates are called "non-disjoint pairs". For disjoint pairs, assume that:

1) The source node is S and the destination node is D.
2) S_R is the adjacent node of S on the disjoint path generated by R-GEM and D_R is the adjacent node of D on the same path. Apparently, S_R is a neighbor of S and D_R is a neighbor of D.
3) S_S is the adjacent node of S on the disjoint path generated by S-GEM and D_S is the adjacent node of D on the same path. Obviously, S_S is a neighbor of S and D_S is a neighbor of D.

Then we can have the following definitions for varied paths from S to D:

1) GEM Basic Path: It refers to the path from S to D that is generated by GEM.
2) GEM Shortest Path: We mentioned previously that GEM maps a tree to a physical network. The physical network is actually a connected graph from the perspective of graph theory. Thus, Dijkstra's algorithm, one of the shortest path generation methods in graph theory, can be used to find the theoretically shortest path from S to D in the physical network. This path is denoted as "GEM Shortest Path".
3) R-GEM Disjoint Path: It refers to the path generated by R-GEM. It starts from S, goes through S_R, then possibly crosses other intermediate nodes, finally arrives at D via D_R.
4) R-GEM Shortest Path: Dijkastra's algorithm can be used to calculate the theoretically shortest path from S_R to D_R. Then this path plus the edge from S to S_R and the edge from D_R to D will be the theoretically shortest path from S to D via S_R and D_R. It is defined as "R-GEM Shortest Path".

Table 3. Average path length for disjoint pairs in varied scenarios

Scenarios	GEM Basic Path	GEM Shortest Path	R-GEM Disjoint Path	R-GEM Shortest Path	S-GEM Disjoint Path	S-GEM Shortest Path
400 Nodes	5.541001	3.123731	7.556657	5.123731	7.082368	5.123731
500 Nodes	5.496659	2.929532	7.486617	4.929532	6.952778	4.929532
600 Nodes	5.568626	3.088292	7.57249	5.088292	6.979353	5.088292
700 Nodes	5.450609	3.03341	7.471305	5.03341	6.884506	5.03341
800 Nodes	5.423286	2.991247	7.439743	4.991247	6.793542	4.991247

Similarly, we can define S-GEM Disjoint Path and S-GEM Shortest Path. Table 3 presents the related results in our research. Note that the average length for a certain type of path is almost fixed (despite slightly fluctuations) in the cases of 400 to 800 nodes. For example, GEM Basic Path is always around 5.5, indicating that no matter what node density is, the average path length is consistently about 5.5. GEM Shortest Path, R-GEM Disjoint Path, R-GEM Shortest Path, S-GEM Disjoint Path, and S-GEM Shortest Path are fixed at around 3.0, 7.5, 5.0, 7.0, and 5.0, respectively.

Since R-GEM Disjoint and Shortest Path both include two pre-assigned edges ("S to S_R" and "D_R to D"), intuitively, they should be longer than GEM Basic and Shortest Path, respectively. This also applies to S-GEM Disjoint and Shortest Path. Our experimental results confirmed this reasoning. The average length of R-GEM Shortest Path and that of S-GEM Shortest Path are similar. And they are both about 2 hops longer than GEM Shortest Path. R-GEM and S-GEM Disjoint Path are both longer than GEM Basic Path. However, S-GEM Disjoint Path is around 0.5 hop shorter than R-GEM Disjoint Path. This is not a surprise since S-GEM tries to choose the neighbor that is closer to the root. As mentioned previously, path length is closely related to path error rate. This relationship can be clearly observed in the experimental results presented later.

Now we consider the performance of R-GEM and S-GEM in terms of Path Error Rate. So far we have talked about path error in general. To present our experimental results clearly, we use the following definitions in our research:

1) GEM Path Error: For GEM, there is only one path from the source S to the destination D. Whenever an edge on the path fails, the path will stop working. This is denoted as a "GEM Path Error".

2) R-GEM Disjoint Path Error: In the case of R-GEM, for non-disjoint pairs, there is only one GEM path from S to D and the failure of this path is simply a GEM Path Error; for disjoint pairs, there are two disjoint paths from S to D, the failure of the GEM path is counted as a GEM Path Error, and the failure of the alternative disjoint path is denoted as "R-GEM Disjoint Path Error". Similarly, we can define "S-GEM Disjoint Path Error".

3) R-GEM Combined Path Error: In the case of R-GEM, for disjoint pairs, there are two disjoint paths from S to D, the failure of both the basic GEM path and the alternative disjoint R-GEM path is denoted as "R-GEM Combined Path Error". Similarly, we can define "S-GEM Combined Path Error".

4) All-Disjoint Combined Path Error: In the case of R-GEM or S-GEM, for disjoint pairs, there could be two or more disjoint paths from S to D, the failure of both

the basic GEM path and all other disjoint paths is denoted as "All-Disjoint Combined Path Error". For a certain pair of nodes, when All-Disjoint Combined Path Error occurs, there is simply no way for the pair of nodes to communicate with each other. For comparison purposes, we can include another routing algorithm in our simulation. This algorithm sends packets through the basic GEM path and all other disjoint paths and it is called "All-Disjoint" in this paper.

5) R-GEM Overall Path Error: In the case of R-GEM, for non-disjoint pairs, GEM Path Error could occur; for disjoint pairs, R-GEM Combined Path Error could take place. Both of these errors are considered "R-GEM Overall Path Errors". Obviously, R-GEM Overall Path Error is a general term that is used to describe the connectivity between any pair of nodes when R-GEM is used as the routing algorithm. Similarly, we can define "S-GEM Overall Path Error".

6) All-Disjoint Overall Path Error: In the case of All-Disjoint, for non-disjoint pairs, GEM Path Error could occur; for disjoint pairs, All-Disjoint Combined Path Error could take place. Both of these errors are considered "All-Disjoint Overall Path Errors". Obviously, All-Disjoint Overall Path Error is a general term that is used to describe the connectivity between any pair of nodes when All-Disjoint is used as the routing algorithm.

We use e_G, e_{RD}, e_{SD}, e_{RC}, e_{SC}, e_{AC} e_{RO}, e_{SO}, and e_{AO} to denote the probability of GEM Path Error, R-GEM Disjoint Path Error, S-GEM Disjoint Path Error, R-GEM Combined Path Error, S-GEM Combined Path Error, All-Disjoint Combined Path Error, R-GEM Overall Path Error, S-GEM Overall Path Error, and All-Disjoint Overall Path Error. e_G, e_{RC}, e_{SC}, e_{RO} and e_{SO} can be used to evaluate the reliability performance of GEM, R-GEM, and S-GEM. The lower the rate is, the more reliable the routing algorithm is. e_{AC} and e_{AO} are the lower-bound error rates that various routing algorithms should try to reach when GEM tree is the structure used for routing. Both of them serve as the baseline for comparison purposes.

e_G, e_{RD}, and e_{SD} can be calculated using *Eq.* (2) once edge error rate and path length are available. For a specific pair, e_{RC} and e_{SC} can be calculated using the following equations:

$$e_{RC} = e_G \times e_{RD} \tag{3}$$
$$e_{SC} = e_G \times e_{SD} \tag{4}$$

For the randomly-chosen pairs of nodes in a specific network configuration, the number of disjoint pairs is fixed. Assume that the total number of pairs is n_T and the number of disjoint pairs is n_D, then e_{RO} and e_{SO} can be calculated using the following equations:

$$e_{RO} = e_{RC} \times [n_D / n_T] + e_G \times [(n_D - n_T) / n_T] \tag{5}$$
$$e_{SO} = e_{SC} \times [n_D / n_T] + e_G \times [(n_D - n_T) / n_T] \tag{6}$$

Since the number of alternative paths among node pairs is uncertain, it is impossible to use an equation to calculate e_{AC} and e_{AO} precisely. However, through simulation, the particular values of e_{AC} and e_{AO} in each specific case can be collected.

We first consider the impact of R-GEM and S-GEM on disjoint pairs among the 1000 candidates. For example, in the case of 800 nodes, only around 648 pairs have disjoint paths, we only consider the impact on these pairs at this moment. The

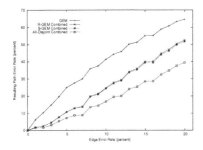

Fig. 7. Combined Path Error Rate: 400 Nodes

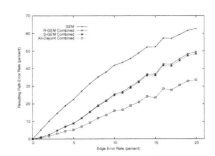

Fig. 8. Combined Path Error Rate: 500 Nodes

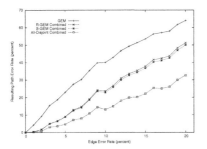

Fig. 9. Combined Path Error Rate: 600 Nodes

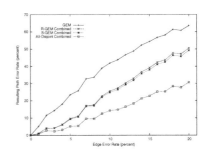

Fig. 10. Combined Path Error Rate: 700 Nodes

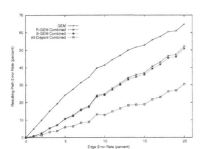

Fig. 11. Combined Path Error Rate: 800 Nodes

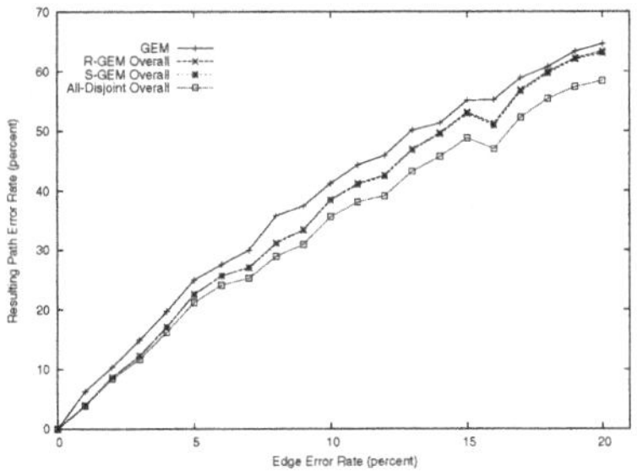

Fig. 12. Overall Path Error Rate: 400 Nodes

experimental results in the case of 400 to 800 nodes are summarized in Fig. 7 to Fig. 11. Each of these figures corresponds to one of the scenarios of 400 to 800 nodes. In each figure, e_G, e_{RC}, e_{SC}, and e_{AC} under different edge error rates (from 0 to 20%) are presented.

In terms of resulting path error rate, All-Disjoint is much better than R-GEM and S-GEM in all different cases. This is not a surprise since All-Disjoint attempts to use every available disjoint path. It is very reliable at the cost of introducing much

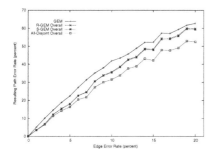

Fig. 13. Overall Path Error Rate: 500 Nodes

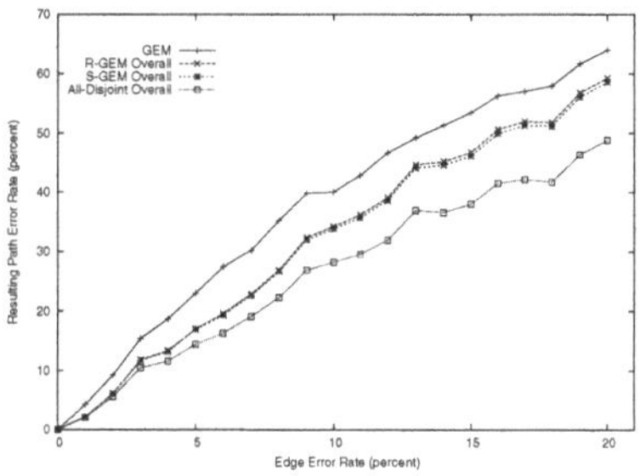

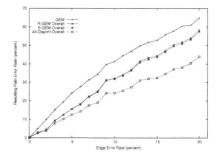

Fig. 14. Overall Path Error Rate: 600 Nodes

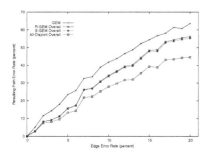

Fig. 15. Overall Path Error Rate: 700 Nodes

Fig. 16. Overall Path Error Rate: 800 Node

redundant traffic into the network. R-GEM and S-GEM are both much better than GEM in all varied scenarios. Specifically, when edge error rate is 1%, e_G is equal to 5%, but e_{RC} and e_{SC} are only around 1%; when edge error rate is 2%, e_G is equal to 10%, but e_{RC} and e_{SC} are only around 2%. Hence, in terms of reliability, R-GEM and S-GEM outperforms GEM significantly. In addition, according to the results in Fig. 7 to Fig. 11, performance wise, R-GEM and S-GEM are very similar. Thus, R-GEM should be a more realistic routing algorithm since it is as almost good as S-GEM in terms of reliability and it does not require the extra operation of disjoint path selection.

Note that from 400 nodes to 800 nodes, the e_G curves are very similar. This is reasonable because according to *Eq.* (2), when edge error rate and path length are fixed, the resulting path error rate is also determined. We mentioned previously that from 400 to 800 nodes, the average length of GEM paths is fixed at around 5.5. Then for a certain error rate, no matter how many nodes are in the networks, the average path error rate does not change. According to *Eq.* (3) and *Eq.* (4), e_{RC} and e_{SC} also remain the same in the case of 400 to 800 nodes. As the result, the e_{RC} and e_{SC} curves are also very similar. The e_{AC} curves in Fig. 7 to Fig. 11 are different since theoretically, the higher the node density is, the greater the number of disjoint paths will be, which leads to lower e_{AC}. Thus, from 400 to 800 nodes, the resulting e_{AC} becomes lower and lower.

Now we consider the influence of R-GEM and S-GEM on all 1000 candidate pairs. The experimental results in Fig. 12 to Fig. 16 illustrate whether, overall, R-GEM and

S-GEM improve network reliability significantly. As expected, All-Disjoint leads to the lowest error rate, namely, best reliability. And e_{AO} decreases with the number of nodes in the network. The reliability performance of R-GEM and S-GEM are still similar since the two types of curves are very close. However, both of them outperform GEM significantly. For example, in the case of 800 nodes, when edge error rate is 2%, e_G is equal to 10%, e_{RO} and e_{SO} are both around 4%. In addition, we found that that as the number of nodes increases from 400 to 800, e_{RO} and e_{SO} becomes lower and lower, indicating that R-GEM and S-GEM both performs better when node density increases. This actually can also be proved theoretically. We know that from 400 to 800 nodes, e_{RC} and e_{SC} do not change much, and they are both lower than e_G. Also, among the 1000 candidate pairs, the number of disjoint pairs increases with node density. In our simulation, e_{RC}, e_{SC}, and e_G do not change much, n_T is fixed at 1000, n_D increases with node density. According to *Eq.* (5) and *Eq.* (6), of course, e_{RO} and e_{SO} will be lower when node density is higher.

6 Conclusion

In this paper, we propose R-GEM and S-GEM, two multi-path GEM variants that improve its reliability performance significantly. Both of them outperform GEM in all of the experimental scenarios. Specifically, in the case that 2% of all edges in the network fail to transfer packets, when only disjoint pairs are taken into consideration, GEM leads to a path error rate of 10% while R-GEM and S-GEM only result in a path error rate of 2%. Considering that S-GEM is only slightly better than R-GEM in terms of reliability and it involves the extra operation of shortest path selection, we recommend R-GEM as a reliable routing algorithm for wireless sensor networks.

References

1. Haas, Z.J., et al.: Gossip-Based Ad Hoc Routing. In: IEEE Inforcom, New York, NY, USA (June 2002)
2. Scott, K., et al.: Routing and Channel Assignment for Low Power Transmission in PCS. In: International Conference on Universal Personal Communications, Cambridge, MA, USA (September 1996)
3. Karp, B., et al.: GPSR: Greedy Perimeter Stateless Routing for Wireles Networks. In: The 6th International Conference on Mobile Computing and Networking (ACM Mobicom), Boston, MA, USA (2000)
4. Kranakis, E., et al.: Compas Routing on Geometric Networks. In: The 11th Canadian Conference on Computational Geometry, Vancouver, BC, Canada (August 1999)
5. Hammoudeh, M., et al.: MuMHR: Multi-path, Multi-hop Hierarchical Routing. In: International Conference on Sensor Technologies and Applications (SENSORCOMM 2007), Valencia, Spain, October 14-20 (2007)
6. Newsome, J., et al.: GEM: Graph Embedding for Routing and Data-Ccentric Storage in Sensor Networks without Geographic Information. In: ACM SenSys, Los Angeles, CA, November 5-7 (2003)
7. Rosenberg, A.L., et al.: Graph Separators With Applications. Kluwer Academic/Plenum Publishers (2000)

8. Heath, L.S.: Graph Embeddings and Simplicial maps. Theory of Computer Systems 30, 599–625 (1997)
9. Koch, R., et al.: Work-Preserving Emulations of Fixed-Connection Networks. Journal of the ACM 44, 104–147 (1997)
10. Mueller, S., et al.: Multipath Routing in Mobile Ad Hoc Networks: Issues and Challenges. In: Calzarossa, M.C., Gelenbe, E. (eds.) MASCOTS 2003. LNCS, vol. 2965, pp. 209–234. Springer, Heidelberg (2004)

Construction of Minimum Connected Dominating Set in 3-Dimensional Wireless Network

Feng Zou[1], Xianyue Li[2], Donghyun Kim[1], and Weili Wu[1,*]

[1] Department of Computer Science, University of Texas at Dallas,
Richardson, TX, 75080
{phenix.zou,donghyunkim}@student.utdallas.edu, weiliwu@utdallas.edu
[2] School of Mathematics and Statistics, Lanzhou University,
Lanzhou, Gansu, P.R. China, 730000
lixianyue@lzu.edu.cn

Abstract. Connected Dominating Set (CDS) has been a well known approach for constructing a virtual backbone to alleviate the broadcasting storm in wireless networks. Previous literature modeled the wireless network in a 2-dimensional plane and looked for the approximated Minimum CDS (MCDS) distributed or centralized to construct the virtual backbone of the wireless network. However, in some real situations, the wireless network should be modeled as a 3-dimensional space instead of 2-dimensional plane. We propose our approximation algorithm for MCDS construction in 3-dimensional wireless network in this paper. It achieves better upper bound $(13 + \ln 10)opt + 1$ than the only known result $22opt$. This algorithm helps bringing the research for MCDS construction in 3-dimensional wireless network to a new stage.

1 Introduction

Due to the lack of pre-defined infrastructure, most routing protocols in wireless network involve flooding, which usually cause serious broadcasting storm[8]. Connected Dominating Set (CDS) has been a well known approach for constructing a virtual backbone to alleviate this broadcasting storm in wireless networks. With the help of the CDS, average message burden of the network could be reduced so that routing becomes much easier and can adapt quickly to network topology changes[3]. Furthermore, using a CDS as forwarding nodes can efficiently reduce the energy consumption, which is also a critical concern in wireless networks.

Researchers have proved that it is a NP-hard problem to find the MCDS for a given graph in early 70s[6]. With some known mathematical conclusions in 2-dimensional graphs like unit disk graphs, most previous literatures modeled the wireless network in a 2-dimensional plane and looked for the approximated

---

* Support in part by National Science Foundation of USA under grants CCF-9208913 and CCF-0627233.

Y. Li et al. (Eds.): WASA 2008, LNCS 5258, pp. 134–140, 2008.
© Springer-Verlag Berlin Heidelberg 2008

Minimum CDS(MCDS) distributed or centralized to construct the virtual backbone of the wireless network[5,9,10,11,12]. They have successfully achieved constant approximation ratios for special graphs like unit disk graphs. However, in some real situations, the wireless network should be modeled as a 3-dimensional space instead of 2-dimensional plane. For example, in an three-dimensional under water-Acoustic sensor networks for ocean column monitoring like figure 1, networks of sensors whose depth can be controlled are included. Sensor nodes float at different depths in order to observe a given phenomenon. This kind of network is used for surveillance applications or monitoring of ocean phenomena (eg. ocean bio-geo-chemical processes, water streams, pollution, etc). It is similar for the temperature sensing system in ocean. Obviously, 2-dimensional modeling is far from enough for real applications like these.

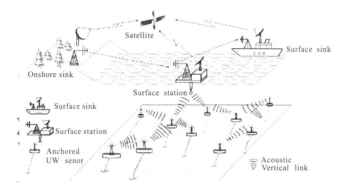

Fig. 1. 3-dimensional Under Water Acoustic Sensor Networks

In this paper, we study the problem of constructing MCDS in 3-dimensional wireless network. We model the 3-dimensional wireless network using unit ball graphs. A graph is a called unit ball graph if its vertices can be represented as points in 3-dimensional Euclidean space and two vertices are adjacent if and only if the distance between the two corresponding points is less than 1. Unit ball graphs have been quite popular in modeling wireless network (eg. ad hoc wireless network) nowadays. It provides a more reasonable representation of a real-life wireless network. As unit disk graphs could be viewed as a subclass of the unit ball graphs and MCDS construction problem in it has been proved to be NP-hard problem[6], it is a NP-hard problem for MCDS in unit ball graphs as well. The only known result for MCDS in 3-dimensional wireless network is given by Butenko et al.[1], which gives a 22-approximation algorithm. We propose our approximation algorithm for MCDS construction in 3-dimensional wireless network in this paper. This algorithm could achieve better approximation ratio of $13 + \ln 10 \approx 15.303$ than Butenko's.

The remainder of this paper is organized as follows. Section 2 discusses the related work of CDS problem and some existing work of MCDS in unit ball graphs. The detailed approximation algorithm and proof are given in section 3. Section 4 concludes the whole work.

2   Related Work

The research of Connected Dominating Set has started from early 80s. It was first introduced as a virtual backbone for routing in Mobile radio network by Ephremides et al.[4]. They thought that it should consist of relatively small number of nodes and remain connected. Meanwhile nodes within it should be able to communicate to points within and outside the central network. Guha and Khuller[5] proposed the first two approximation algorithms for CDSs construction in 1998. In their first algorithm, the CDS is built up at one node first, then they restricted the searching space of the next dominator(s) to the current dominatees. The CDS in this algorithm expands until there is no white nodes. In their second algorithm, all the possible dominators are determined in the first phase, then they are connected through some intermediate nodes in the second phase. Lots of improvements have been done based on it afterwards[5,9,10,12]. Some of them improved the approximation ratio(PR)or computation complexity. For example, Ruan et al.[9] designed a 1-phase greedy algorithm with PR of $2 + \ln \Delta$ where the Δ is the maximum degree in the graph. Some of them implemented distributed versions. For example, Wu and Li[12] proposed a distributed algorithm, which was proved to have a PR of $O(n)$ later.

Recently, a new kind of methodology for constructing CDSs was proposed, which constructed a Maximum Independent Set(MIS) first and then interconnect it into a CDS. Wan et al.[11] proposed two 2-phase distributed algorithms. In these two algorithms, a spanning tree is first constructed. Every node in the spanning tree is then labelled as either a dominator or a dominatee based on a ranking scheme. The algorithms are employed upon Unit Disk Graphs (UDG) to obtain a constant performance ratio of 8. Some other examples are[2,7].

All of these existing research work studied the CDS within the 2-dimensional Euclidean plane R^2 only. They model the network using 2-dimensional graphs, for example, general disk graphs and unit disk graphs. While, in fact, the real network is 3-Dimensional instead of 2-Dimensional. A popular modeling of the 3-Dimensional network is ball graphs, a special case of which is the unit ball graphs(similar to unit disk graphs). Thus CDS construction under ball graphs, especially under unit ball graphs is of great interests nowadays. Few work has been done on this topic as far as we know. The only research result ever known up till now is given by Butenko et al.[1]. They proposed an algorithm in their paper and proved it achieved 22 PR.

3   A 15.303-Approximation Algorithm

We proposed an approximation algorithm for the minimum connected dominating set problem in unit ball graphs in this section, which could achieve a $(13 + \ln 10)$ approximation ratio, better than all other existing algorithms ever known[1].

3.1   Preliminaries

We model the 3 dimensional network using a unit ball graph $G = (V, E)$, in which a vertex represents a point of the network in 3-dimensional Euclidean space $\Re^3$. Two vertices u and v in the graph G are connected by an edge e in E if and only if the balls of radius 1 centered in points u and v have a nonempty intersection. We denote a maximal independent set of the graph G as $MIS(G)$. Meanwhile let opt be the size of the minimum connected dominating set for the unit ball graph G.

3.2   Detailed Algorithm

In our algorithm, we first construct a maximal independent set MIS for the unit ball graph. The detailed process is illustrated in Algorithm 1. For better explanation, we make use of the coloring scheme in this algorithm. Initially, color all nodoes white. Then select a root and color it black and all its neighbors grey. Each round we pick the vertex in the tree that is still white in the graph to add into MIS. By coloring its adjacent nodes grey, we could have a new coloring graph. This algorithm ends when all the vertex in the graph is either in the MIS or grey(adjacent to one of the node in MIS). The size of the MIS constructed by this algorithm, as proved in [1], is bounded by $11opt+1$. Also as a centralized version of MIS constructions, it maintains the property that any pair of complementary subsets of the MIS have a distance of exactly two hops [2,11].

In the second step, we consider the $MIS(G)$ as the terminal set of the graph G, constructing the minimum set of steiner nodes to interconnect them. We employ a greedy approximation algorithm as well, which select the vertex that could connect the maximum number of connected components together each time. We will show that a combination of this greedy approximation and the Algorithm 1 gives the upper bound as $(13 + \ln 10)opt + 1$, which is approximately $15.303opt + 1$.

Algorithm 1. MIS_UBG$(G(V, E))$

1: Color all nodes in V white
2: Randomly select a root node $r \in V$ and color it black and its neighbors grey
3: **while** there is a white node $x \in V$ **do**
4:     Color x in black and all of its white neighbor grey
5: **end while**
6: $M = \emptyset$
7: Put all black nodes in M and return M.

The pseudo-code of the detailed algorithm for the second step is presented in Algorithm 2. With input $MIS(G)$ and $G = (V, E)$, we color vertex in $MIS(G)$ black first and let all other vertices in G remain grey. In the algorithm, we will change some nodes from grey to blue to interconnect the $MIS(G)$. A *black-blue component* is a connected component of the subgraph induced only by black and blue nodes *without considering connections between blue nodes*.

So, the union of the set $MIS(G)$ and S(the result of the Algorithm 2) is the connected dominating set for unit ball graph G.

Algorithm 2. CDS_UBG(MIS(G),G=(V,E))

1: Initialize the set of blue nodes S as Φ
2: **while** there are more than one connected black-blue component exist **do**
3:     choose the vertex v that connects the maximum number of
4:     black-blue components, change it's color from grey to blue
5:     and set $S = S \bigcup v$;
6: **end while**
7: return blue nodes set S.

Theorem 1. *Let opt be the size of the minimum connected dominating set in the unit ball graph G. Then the size of the connected dominating set $MIS(G) \bigcup S$ is up-bounded by $(13 + \ln 10)opt + 1$.*

Proof. Suppose $v_1, v_2, \ldots, v_k$ are selected in turn by the algorithm 2. Let $y_1, y_2, \ldots, y_{opt}$ be a minimum connected dominating set and for any i, $y_1, y_2, \ldots, y_i$ induces a connected subgraph. Denote $C_i = MIS(G) \bigcup \{v_1, v_2, \ldots, v_i\}$ and $C_j^* = \{y_1, y_2, \ldots, y_j\}$.

Let $f(C)$ be the number of connected components of the subgraph induced by vertex set C and $\Delta_y f(C) = f(C \bigcup y) - f(C)$. Since the number of black nodes that y_i could dominate in $C_i \bigcup C_{j-1}^*$ is at most one more than the number of black nodes that it could dominate in C_i. Then we have

$$-\Delta_{y_j} f(C_i \bigcup C_{j-1}^*) + \Delta_{y_j} f(C_i)$$
$$= f(C_i \bigcup C_{j-1}^*) - f(C_i \bigcup C_j^*) + \Delta_{y_j} f(C_i)$$
$$= f(C_i \bigcup C_{j-1}^*) - f(C_i \bigcup C_j^*) + f(C_i \bigcup y_j) - f(C_i)$$
$$\leq 1.$$

As v_{i+1} is the vertex that could connect the maximum number of connected components, $-\Delta_{v_{i+1}} f(C_i) \geq -\Delta_{y_j} f(C_i)$ for all $1 \leq j \leq opt$. Thus,

$$-\Delta_{v_{i+1}} f(C_i)$$
$$\geq (- \sum_{1 \leq j \leq opt} \Delta_{y_j} f(C_i))/opt$$
$$\geq (- \sum_{2 \leq j \leq opt} \Delta_{y_j} f(C_i) - \Delta_{y_1} f(C_i))/opt$$
$$= (-opt + 1 - \sum_{2 \leq j \leq opt} \Delta_{y_j} f(C_i \bigcup C_{j-1}^*)$$
$$- \Delta_{y_1} f(C_i))/opt$$
$$= (-opt + 1 - \sum_{1 \leq j \leq opt} \Delta_{y_j} f(C_i \bigcup C_{j-1}^*))/opt$$
$$= (-opt + 1 - f(C_i \bigcup C_{opt}^*) + f(C_i))/opt$$
$$\geq (-opt - 1 + f(C_i))/opt.$$

So $-f(C_{i+1}) \geq -f(C_i) + \frac{-opt-1+f(C_i)}{opt}$.
Denote $a_i = -opt - 1 + f(C_i)$. Then we have $a_{i+1} \leq a_i(1 - \frac{1}{opt})$, which implies

$$a_i \leq a_0(1 - \frac{1}{opt})_i \leq a_0 e^{-i/opt}.$$

If $a_0 < opt$, then $-opt - 1 + |MIS| < opt$, which means $|MIS| < 2opt + 1 \leq 2opt$. Since for any vertices v_i, it connects at least two black-blue components, the size of S is at most $|MIS| - 1$. Hence, the size of the connected dominating set $MIS(G) \bigcup S$ is up-bounded by $4opt - 1$ now.

Else, choose i to be the largest one satisfying $opt \leq a_i$. So we have $opt \leq a_0 e^{-i/opt}$, which indicates $i \leq opt \ln(a_0/opt)$. Meanwhile,

$$a_k \leq a_{k-1} - 1 \leq a_{k-2} - 2 \leq \ldots \leq a_{i+1} - (k - i - 1)$$

implies that $-opt \leq opt - k + i$ as $a_{i+1} \leq opt - 1$. Furthermore, since $|MIS| \leq 11opt + 1$, $a_0/opt = (-opt - 1 + |MIS|)/opt \leq 10$. We have

$$k \leq 2opt + i$$
$$\leq opt(2 + \ln(a_0/opt)).$$
$$\leq opt(2 + \ln 10)$$
$$= (2 + \ln 10)opt.$$

Hence, $|S| \leq (2 + \ln 10)opt$ and the size of the connected dominating set

$$|MIS(G) \bigcup S| \leq 11opt + 1 + (2 + \ln 10)opt$$
$$= (13 + \ln 10)opt + 1$$

4   Conclusion

Since not much work has been done for MCDS construction in 3-dimensional wireless network, we propose a new approximation algorithm for it in this paper. Compared with the only existing algorithm proposed by Butenko et al., we could achieve a better result of $(13 + \ln 10)opt + 1$ than theirs. This algorithm helps bringing the research for MCDS construction in 3-dimensional wireless network to a new stage.

References

1. Butenko, S., Ursulenko, O.: On minimum connected donimating set problem in unit-ball graphs. Elsevier Science, Amsterdam (2007) (preprint submitted)
2. Cardei, M., Cheng, M.X., Cheng, X., Du, D.-Z.: Connected domination in multihop ad hoc wireless networks. In: International Conference on Computer Science and Informatics (2002)

3. Das, B., Bharghavan, V.: Routing in ad hoc Networks Using Minimum Connected Domianting Sets. In: International Conference on Communications (1997)
4. Ephremides, A., Wieselthier, J., Baker, D.: A design concept for reliable mobile radio networks with frequency hopping signaling. Proc. IEEE 75(1), 56–73 (1987)
5. Guha, S., Khuller, S.: Approximation algorithms for connected dominating sets. Algorithmica 20(4), 374–387 (1998)
6. Garey, M.R., Johnson, D.S.: Computers and Intractability. A guide to the Theory of NP-completeness. Freeman, New York (1979)
7. Li, Y., Kim, D., Zou, F., Du, D.-Z.: Constructing Connected Dominating Sets with Bounded Diameters in Wireless Networks. In: WASA (2007)
8. Ni, S., Tseng, Y., Chen, Y., Sheu, J.: The Broadcast Storm Problem in a Mobile Ad Hoc Network. In: MOBICOM 1999, Washington, USA, August 1999, pp. 152–162 (1999)
9. Ruan, L., Du, H., Jia, X., Wu, W., Li, Y., Ko, K.-I.: A Greedy Approximation for Minimum Connected Dominating Sets. Theoretical Computer Science 329(1-3), 325–330 (2004)
10. Sivakumar, R., Das, B., Bharghavan, V.: An Improved Spine-based Infrastructure for Routing in Ad Hoc Networks. In: IEEE Symposium on Computers and Communications, Athens, Greece (June 1998)
11. Wan, P.-J., Alzoubi, K.M., Frieder, O.: Distributed Construction of Connected Dominating Sets in Wireless Ad Hoc Networks. In: Proc. IEEE Infocom 2002, New York, NY, USA (June 2002)
12. Wu, J., Li, H.: On Calculating Connected Dominating Set for Ecient Routing in Ad Hoc Wireless Networks. In: Proc. the 3rd International Workshop on Discrete Algorithms and Methods for Mobile Computing and Communications, Seattle, USA, August 1999, pp. 7–14 (1999)

Maintaining CDS in Mobile Ad Hoc Networks

Kazuya Sakai[1], Min-Te Sun[2], Wei-Shinn Ku[1], and Hiromi Okada[3]

[1] Auburn University, Auburn, AL 36849-5347, USA
{sakaika,weishinn}@auburn.edu
[2] National Central University, Chung-Li, Tao-Yuan 320, Taiwan
msun@csie.ncu.edu.tw
[3] Kansai University, 3-3-35 Yamate-cho Suita, Osaka 564-8680, Japan
okada@jnet.densi.kansai-u.ac.jp

Abstract. The connected dominating set (CDS) has been generally used for routing and broadcasting in mobile ad hoc networks (MANETs). To reduce the cost of routing table maintenance, it is preferred that the size of CDS to be as small as possible. A number of protocols have been proposed to construct CDS with competitive size, however only few are capable of maintaining CDS under topology changes. In this research, we propose a novel extended mobility handling algorithm which will not only shorten the recovery time of CDS mobility handling but also keep a competitive size of CDS. Our simulation results validate that the algorithm successfully achieves its design goals. In addition, we will introduce an analytical model for the convergence time and the number of messages required by the CDS construction.

1 Introduction

The connected dominating set (CDS) has been used as the virtual backbone for routing [9] and broadcast [1] in MANETs. It is defined as a subset of nodes in a network such that each node in the network is either in the set or a direct neighbor of some node in the set, and the induced graph of the nodes in the set is connected. To reduce the cost of routing table maintenance in the virtual backbone, it is preferred that the size of the corresponding CDS to be as small as possible. Although computing the minimal CDS is known to be NP-hard [3], a number of protocols [8, 5, 10, 2, 11, 7] have been proposed to construct CDS with competitive size. Among these protocols, only few [2, 11, 7] are capable of maintaining CDS under topology changes. For the rest of the protocols, when topology changes cause the CDS to be invalid, they will have to construct CDS from scratch, which in general is a time-consuming process.

In this paper, we augment the CDS construction protocols in [11] and [7] by our Extended Mobility Handling (EMH) algorithm. The algorithm consists of two parts. The first part, namely Height-Reduction (HR), focuses on shortening the recovery time of CDS mobility handling; the second part, namely Initiator-Reduction (IR), keeps the competitive size of CDS while doing mobility handling. The simulation results validate that the algorithm successfully achieves its design

Y. Li et al. (Eds.): WASA 2008, LNCS 5258, pp. 141–153, 2008.

goals. In addition, we introduce an analytical model for the convergence time and the number of messages required by the CDS construction. We have validated that the results obtained from the analytical model match extremely well with the results from the simulation.

The rest of this paper is organized as follows. The existing distributed CDS protocols are reviewed in Section 2. The EMH algorithm is introduced in Section 3. The simulation results are presented and analyzed in Section 4. The analytical model for the convergence time and the number of messages is demonstrated and validated in Section 5. The conclusion and the future work are provided in Section 6.

2   Literature Reviews

While computing the minimum CDS is known to be NP-hard [3], a number of distributed CDS protocols [8, 5, 10, 2, 11, 7] have been proposed to construct a CDS of small size. Both Wan's protocol [8] and Li's protocol [5] obtain CDS by expending the maximal independent set. On the other hand, Wu's protocol [10] obtains CDS by eliminating unnecessary nodes through a number of rules. Although these three protocols are successful in constructing a small size of CDS based on localized information, they lack the mechanism of mobility handling. For MANETs where nodes are roaming freely all the time, it is imperative for the CDS protocol to be adaptive to the changes of topology.

Recently, several practical distributed CDS construction protocols capable of maintaining CDS [2, 11, 7] under the setting of MANETs have been proposed. Dai's protocol [2] extends the pruning rules of Wu's [10] for mobility handling. The problem of Dai's protocol is that it requires the information of two-hop neighbors. When the topology changes, it takes two beacon periods for a node to initiate the adaptation process. In addition, similar to Wu's protocol, Dai's protocol tends to introduce too much communication overhead.

The Single-Initiator (SI) protocol [11] obtains CDS by forming the dominator tree rooted from a single initiator. SI results in small size of CDS and introduces less communication overhead. In addition, SI is able to detect CDS failures caused by nodal mobility by means of transmitting "heartbeat" signals from the initiator and recovery CDS without reconstructing CDS from scratch in most of the failures. However, SI suffers from a single point of failure, i.e., it will still have to reconstruct the whole CDS from scratch should the single initiator fail.

To tackle this issue, a Multi-Initiator (MI) protocol is proposed in [7]. In MI, several initiators are elected. Each initiator generates a dominator tree in exactly the same manner as SI does in [11] and a few nodes (called bridge nodes hence after) are then included to connect the disjoint trees. In MI, the failure of an initiator will only affect the associated dominator tree. The other part of the CDS will remain intact. As each dominator tree is smaller than that of SI, maintaining CDS is much more efficient.

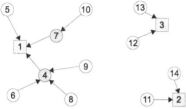

Fig. 1. Original Topology I

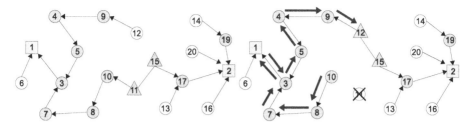

Fig. 2. Mobility Handling of MI on Topology I

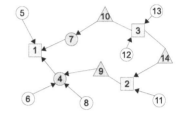

Fig. 3. Original Topology II

Fig. 4. Mobility Handling of MI on Topology II

3 Extended Mobility Handling for SI and MI Protocols

3.1 Motivation

In general, MI and SI are better than Wu's and Wan's protocols, as they incur less communication overhead, result in CDS of competitive size, and adapt to topology changes. SI successfully maintains a CDS under changes of the network topology that include the following four cases: 1) the initiator leaves its dominator tree; 2) a dominator leaves its dominator tree; 3) a new node joins a dominator tree after the tree is constructed. 4) a redundant dominator switches to dominatee status without disconnecting the dominator tree. In addition to the above four cases, MI also deals with the case of 5) a bridge node, a node which connects two trees, leaves its dominator tree.

However, both SI and MI suffer from two issues. First, the CDS recovery time may increase after a period of time. It is because when new nodes join the network, the height of the dominator tree may increase. when a bridge node moves away from the network, in the worst case, the initiator of one of the disconnected trees needs to assign a new bridge node by exchanging control messages between the initiator and nodes in the boundary area. The time to complete this recovery process is in proportion to the height of the tree. Note that during the recovery process, the dominating set will not be connected. Hence, to ensure the CDS to be available for a longer period of time, it is important that the height of the dominator tree to be small.

For instance, in Figure 1, a snapshot of a MANET and its connected dominating set are illustrated. In the figure, a square represents a initiator, a shaded circle is a dominator, a circle is a dominatee, and a triangle is a bridge node. The CDS is formed by the initiators, the dominators, and the bridge nodes. An arrow between two nodes indicates their dominator/dominatee relationship (e.g., node 3 is the dominator of node 5) and a solid line between two bridge nodes means they are neighbors to each other. Assume that the bridge node 11 runs out of power, according to MI, its dominator, node 10, will first look for an alternative bridge to connect to the neighboring tree. When node 10 fails to find such a node, it sends a control message to its initiator, node 1. Then, node 1 designates a new bridge node, node 12, to connect to the neighboring tree. The control message will traverse 9 hops before a new bridge node can connect to the neighboring tree. This message traversal is illustrated in Figure 2.

Another issue of SI and MI mobility handling is the possibility of excessive initiators. When a connected network component breaks into multiple pieces due to mobility, each piece will find at least one initiator. When these pieces are merged, all these initiators will become part of the CDS. In addition, since each initiator generates a dominator tree, more initiators imply more trees, thus more bridge nodes will be needed to connect these trees. This further increases the size of CDS.

For example, in Figure 3, the topology is separated into three pieces, and each piece has its own initiator. After the change of topology, as shown in Figure 4, initiator 2 and 3 move to the proximity of the dominator tree rooted at initiator 1. To connect all these dominator trees, MI protocol will include node 9, 10, and 14 into CDS.

3.2   Extended Mobility Handling

To address the aforementioned issues, we propose the Extended Mobility Handling (EMH) algorithm on top of SI and MI. EMH incorporates two procedures, namely Height-Reduction (HR) and Initiator-Reduction (IR). The following subsections elaborate each of these procedures.

Height-Reduction. To control the height of a dominator tree, a node in the tree needs to know its depth, i.e., the minimum number of hops between its initiator and itself. Recall that in both SI and MI to learn the *status* of the neighboring node, the *status* of a node is encoded in the beacon. By adding an extra *depth* field in the beacon, the *depth* of a node can be obtained without introducing extra messages. When a node receives a beacon from its dominator, it learns and updates its own *depth*, then encodes its *depth* plus one to the *depth* field of its beacon before transmitting it. If a node finds a dominator neighbor which belongs to the same dominator tree and the *depth* of the dominator is smaller than its current dominator, it changes its dominator and updates its *depth* to reduce the height of the tree. The new dominator is able to know that the node becomes its child in the next beacon period. A dominator node which child changes its dominator may no longer have children. If this situation occurs, the dominator changes it *status* to dominatee. The pseudo code of the Height-Reduction procedure is given in Figure 5.

/* Node i executes the following: */
1.   Node i receiving a beacon from j /* change dominator*/
2.   if $(status(j) = dominator \wedge depth(j) < depth(dominator(i)))$ then
3. $dominator(i) \leftarrow j$
4. $depth(i) \leftarrow depth(j) + 1$
5.   if $(status(i) = dominator)$ /* eliminate unnecessary dominator */
6.   if $(\forall j \in N(i), dominator(j) \neq i)$ then
7. $status(i) \leftarrow dominatee$

Fig. 5. Height-Reduction

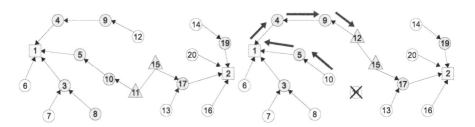

Fig. 6. Topology with Height-Reduction **Fig. 7.** Mobility Handling of MI after Height-Reduction

The following demonstrates how Height-Reduction works for the topology in Figure 1. Assume dominator node 3 is also a direct neighbor of node 8. After receiving beacons from node 3, node 8 knows $depth(3) = 1$ and $depth(7) = 2$. As node 3 is a dominator and closer to the initiator, node 8 changes its dominator to node 3 and updates its *depth*. Then, since dominator node 7 no longer has children, it changes its *status* to dominatee. Similarly, assume dominator node 5 is a direct neighbor of node 10. After node 10 finds that node 5 has a smaller depth, according to Height-Reduction it will switch its dominator to node 5 and update its *depth*. After a few beacon periods, the original dominator tree rooted at node 1 in Figure 1 will be optimized as shown in Figure 6. Now again assume that the bridge node 11 in Figure 6 runs out of power. As illustrated in Figure 7, the loss of the bridge node is handled in the same manner as in Figure 2. As the height of the tree in Figure 7 is smaller than that of Figure 2, the mobility handling for bridge node 11 can be done more efficiently. While MI needs to send 9 messages to recover the CDS, MI with Height-Reduction needs only 5.

Initiator-Reduction. Since each initiator generates a tree, reducing the number of initiators is equivalent to reducing the number of trees. To reduce the number of trees, the small dominator trees can be merged to the large neighboring trees. In essence, if a tree is small, most likely its initiator will also be a boundary node, i.e., the initiator has some neighbor belonging to a different tree. If an initiator finds such a neighbor and its *id* is larger than the initiator *id*

```
/* Node i executes the following: */
1.    if (node i is initiator) /* merge small dominator tree */
2.        if (∃j ∈ N(i) ∧ initiator(j) ≠ i ∧ id(i) > initiator(j)) then
3.            dominator(i) ← j
4.            initiator(i) ← initiator(j)
5.            depth(i) ← dept(j) + 1
4.            if (status(j) = dominatee) then
5.                status(j) ← dominator
6.    Node i receiving a beacon from j /* change initiator id*/
7.        if (dominator(i) = j ∧ initiator(j) ≠ initiator(i)) then
8.            initiator(i) ← initiator(j)
9.            depth(i) ← depth(j) + 1
```

Fig. 8. Initiator-Reduction

of the neighbor, it changes its *status* to dominator, its initiator *id*, and updates its *depth*. The reason to merge the tree with larger initiator *id* to the one with smaller initiator *id* is to avoid the situation that both initiators of neighboring trees try to merge to the other tree simultaneously. After a dominator tree becomes a part of another tree, the children of the merged initiator need to change their *status*. On receiving beacon from its dominator, if a node detects its dominator's initiator *id* is different from its initiator *id*, it updates its initiator *id* and *depth* accordingly. Notice that after Initiator-Reduction procedure is complete, an initiator will not have any neighbor belonging to a different tree. This guarantees that the tree of each initiator including the bridge nodes will be at least two hops in height. The pseudo code of the Initiator-Reduction procedure is provided in Figure 8.

Figure 9 shows how Initiator-Reduction works for the topology in Figure 3. Recall that in Figure 4, initiator 2 and 3 move to the boundary area. The *status* of node 2 is still in initiator, and it has two neighbors 9 and 12 that associate with other initiators. According to the pseudo code, node 2 will switch its *status* to dominator, change its initiator *id*, and update its *depth*. Afterwards, node 9 finds that node 2 become its child, so it will switch its *status* from bridge to dominator. When Node 11 and 14 find that their dominator changed its initiator *id*, they will update their initiator *id* and *depth*. As can be seen, the size of CDS by the MI protocol's mobility handling in Figure 4 is 8, while by MI with Initiator-Reduction in Figure 9 is reduced to 7.

4   Simulation Result

To evaluate the performance of our Extended Mobility Handling (EMH) algorithm, we implemented Dai's [2], SI [11], and MI [7] protocols along with SI with EMH and MI with EMH in C++. In this section, the simulation results of different CDS protocols are reported and analyzed.

4.1 Simulation Configuration

The network topology is randomly generated by placing nodes on a $1000m$ by $1000m$ square field according to uniform distribution. The simulation region is wrapped around vertically and horizontally to eliminate the edge effect. If the generated network is partitioned, it is discarded and a new network topology is generated to ensure the connectivity of the whole network at the beginning of the simulation. The transmission range of a node is set to be $150m$. The number of nodes in the simulation area is set to be 150, which corresponds to 10 neighbors per node, and some nodes are assumed to be mobile. The percentage of the mobile nodes ranges from 20% to 80% with speed up to $5m/s$. For a given simulation configuration, 1000 different network topologies are generated.

The Weighed Way Point (WWP) [4] is adopted as our mobility model. In WWP, the weight of selecting next destination and pause time for a node depends on both current location and time. The value of weights is based on empirical data carried out on University of Southern California's campus [6]. For Dai', SI and MI, the corrupted CDS is recovered according to their mobility handling procedures when the topology changes. The configurations of the heartbeat period in SI, MI, SI with EMH, and MI with EMH are set to be the same as in [7]. Each simulation lasts 1000 rounds of beacon periods. In the simulation, if the network topology is partitioned into disjoint connected components, CDS protocols maintains separate CDS within each component.

To assess the performance of different CDS protocols, four metrics are used, including the percentage of time CDS is alive, the average size of CDS, the number of extra messages, and the average amount of traffic. For MI and MI with EMH, the messages in the tree connection phase and query/response messages in the mobility handling are counted as extra messages. The total amount of time CDS is valid divided by the total simulation period is defined as the percentage of time CDS is alive. For SI, all the information exchanged between nodes are done by beacons. For Dai's protocol, beacons are considered as extra messages since the size of the beacon increases in proportion to the network density and is too large when compared with the standard beacon frame. Each protocol changes the beacon frame format to include additional information. For SI, node id, $status$, $color$, and dominator id are included in the beacon. MI enlarges the beacon of SI to include the initiator id and the minimal id of one-hop neighbors. SI with

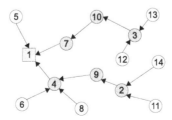

Fig. 9. Topology with Initiator-Reduction

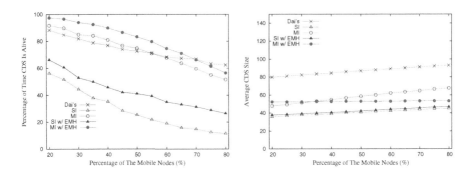

Fig. 10. Percentage of Time CDS is Alive   **Fig. 11.** Average CDS Size

EMH and MI with EMH extend the beacon of SI and MI to add *depth*. The beacon of Dai's protocol includes node *id*, *status*, *marker*, and the list of *id*s for one-hop neighbors.

4.2 Simulation Results

Figure 10 illustrates the percentage of time CDS is alive with respect to the percentage of the mobile nodes. As can be seen in Figure 10, MI with EMH almost always has the highest percentage of CDS alive time than other CDS protocols. Although smaller CDS is generally more vulnerable to topology changes, MI with EMH shows excellent mobility adaptation compared with the other protocols. Only when the percentage of mobile nodes is greater than 70% the percentage of CDS alive time of the MI-EMH becomes slightly lower than that of Dai's due to MI with EMH's smaller CDS size. As pointed out in [8], the time complexity of mobility recovery at each node of Dai's is as high as $O(\Delta^2)$, where Δ is the average number of neighbors. Thus, Dai's protocol takes more time to recover than MI with EMH. SI with EMH also improves the percentage of CDS alive time by at least 10% compared with SI. This clearly demonstrates that EMH is capable of prolonging the time CDS is available to MANETs.

Figure 11 shows the average CDS size with respect to the percentage of the mobile nodes. As illustrated in Figure 11, SI and SI with EMH consistently produces the smallest CDS and Dai's protocol consistently produces the largest CDS. While the size of CDS generated by MI increases slowly in accordance with the percentage of mobile nodes, that of MI with EMH is stable. This is because, by merging trees MI with EMH keeps the number of initiators as a constant, and consequently reduce the CDS size. In general, it is desirable that the size of the CDS is as small as possible for MANETs. From Figure 10 and Figure 11, MI with EMH can quickly adapt to topology changes while keeping CDS size competitive.

Figure 12 presents the number of extra messages to maintain CDS with respect to the percentage of the mobile nodes. As illustrated in Figure 12, SI does not introduce any extra message. MI with EMH introduces less than 25% of extra messages of Dai's. In addition, the numbers of extra messages of MI and SI with

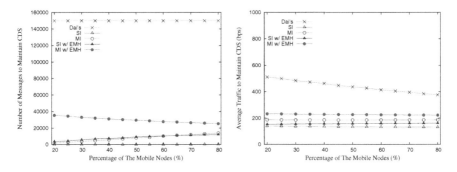

Fig. 12. Number of Messages to Maintain **Fig. 13.** Average Traffic to Maintain CDS
CDS

EMH are roughly the same and are at most 10% of that of Dai's. Compared with MI, MI with EMH introduces more messages. The same can be said to SI and SI with EMH. Unlike the other protocols, the number of extra message created by MI with EMH decreases as the percentage of the mobile nodes increases. This is because IR can better reduce the number of initiators when more initiator moves to the boundary area. By introducing few extra control messages, MI with EMH and SI with EMH become highly adaptive to topology changes, as shown in Figure 10.

Figure 13 shows the average traffic required at each node to maintain CDS with respect to the percentage of the mobile nodes. As can be seen in Figure 13, the average traffic of Dai's protocol is at least twice as much as that of any other protocol. The protocol incorporates EMH has slightly higher traffic than the one without EMH, but the difference is not significant. This is primarily because in EMH the beacon is 4 bit larger to include the depth value. Figure 12 and Figure 13 suggest that the traffic is mostly dominated by the extra bits in the beacon frame.

5 Analytical Model for Convergence Time and Number of Messages

In this section, an analytical model to analyze the convergence time and number of messages that SI and MI require during CDS construction is presented and validated. Note that CDS construction phases of SI and SI with EMH are the same, so are MI and MI with EMH.

5.1 Analytical Model

In the tree construction phase of MI and SI, the defer timer T_d is set to be T_{max}/n_{uc}, where T_{max} is the maximal defer time period and n_{uc} is the number of uncovered neighbors. Since SI is simpler than MI, before we discuss the convergence time of MI, let us first consider the convergence time of SI.

The convergence time of SI should be the product of the number of hops from the initiator to the edge of the tree and the average defer time. To formulate this, let us denote the width and height of the simulation region as l_x and l_y, respectively. The average distance between two nodes, $\bar{d}$, is calculated by Equation 1.

$$\bar{d} = \int_0^r \frac{2\pi x \cdot x}{\pi r^2} dx = \frac{2}{3} r \tag{1}$$

The number of hops, denoted by h, will be the distance from the initiator to the edge of the tree divided by the average distance between two nodes. Assuming $l_x = l_y$, and $S = l_x \cdot l_y$, then the average value of h can be computed by Equation 2.

$$h = \frac{\sqrt{l_x^2 + l_y^2}}{2\bar{d}} = \frac{3\sqrt{2S}}{4r} \tag{2}$$

Next, the average defer time of a node is T_{max} divided by the average number of uncovered neighbors n_{uc}. Let C_A and C_B be the coverage area of two neighboring nodes A and B, and d be the distance between them, the additional area that B forwards a message from node A is $|C_B \setminus C_A| = \pi r^2 - |INTC(r,d)|$, where $INTC(r,d)$ is the intersection of two circle with radius r and their centers separated by d.

$$INTC(r,d) = 4 \int_{d/2}^r \sqrt{r^2 - x^2} dx \tag{3}$$

Thus, the average additional coverage area is

$$\int_0^r \frac{2\pi x (\pi r^2 - INTC(r,x))}{\pi r^2} dx \approx 0.41 \pi r^2 \tag{4}$$

Therefore, the average number of uncovered nodes is 0.41Δ, where Δ is the average number of neighbors in transmission range. In addition, a node at the edge of the tree will wait T_{max} number of beacon intervals before it changes its status into dominatee. Finally, the convergence time of SI is approximately

$$(h - 1) \cdot \frac{T_{max}}{0.41\Delta} + T_{max} \tag{5}$$

The duration of the tree construction phase in MI can be calculated in the similar fashion. In the case of multi-initiator, the number of hops from a initiator to the edge of its tree, h_{mi}, is

$$h_{mi} = \frac{r/\bar{d}}{n_{init}\pi r^2/S} = \frac{3}{2} \cdot \frac{S}{n_{init}\pi r^2} \tag{6}$$

For the tree connection phase in MI, a border node without any uncovered neighbor will wait T_{max} number of beacon intervals before it sends a message to its initiator. Hence, the time required for the tree connection phase is bounded by $2h_{mi} + 1$. The convergence time of MI is the total time spent on the tree construction phase and the tree connection phase, and can be computed as

$$(h_{mi} - 1) \cdot \frac{T_{max}}{0.41\Delta} + 2h_{mi} + T_{max} + 1 \tag{7}$$

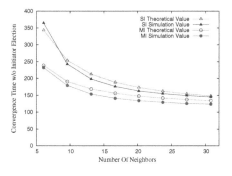 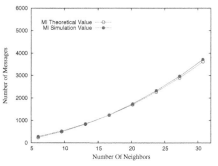

Fig. 14. The Convergence Time w/o Initiator Election

Fig. 15. The Number of Messages

MI does not introduce extra messages except in the tree connection phase. In the tree connection phase, all nodes except initiators forward messages from their children as many times as the number of neighboring trees to their initiator. Thus, the number of message required for MI to construct CDS is

$$0.41\Delta \cdot \frac{n_{init} - 1}{n_{init}} \cdot n \tag{8}$$

5.2 Comparison of Theoretical and Simulation Results

In this subsection, the analytical model are validated by comparing with our simulation results. As the analytical model are the model for CDS construction, we conducted the simulation in static networks. The average network density changes as we change the total number of nodes. The total number of nodes placed in the field ranges from 100 to 450, which corresponds to the network density ranging from approximately 5 to 30 neighbors per node. The other configuration settings are the same as in Section 4.1.

Figure 14 demonstrates the convergence time SI and MI without the initiator election phase with respect to the average number of neighbors. Since the duration of the initiator election phase is fixed for SI and MI (it is 20 beacon periods for SI and 2 beacon periods for MI), our convergence time analysis omits the initiator election phase. The convergence time decreases in proportion to the number of neighbors because the differ timer in the tree construction phase decreases in proportion to the number of uncovered nodes. As can be seen in Figure 14, the theoretical model and simulation results are very close to each other.

Figure 15 shows the number of messages with respect to the average number of neighbors. In the simulation, the control messages in the tree connection phase are traced. Note that since SI forms only one dominator tree, there will be no control messages for tree connection. As can be seen in Figure 15, analytical model again provides a very accurate estimation.

6   Conclusion and Future Work

The CDS protocols proposed in the past either lack the ability to handle nodal mobility, result in large size of CDS, or incur large overhead. In this paper, an Extended Mobility Handling (EMH) algorithm is proposed for single and multi-initiator CDS protocols to optimize their mobility handling mechanism. By adding a few bits of overhead in the beacon frame, EMH can help SI and MI to quickly recover the corrupted CDS caused by nodal mobility. The simulation results show that EMH helps SI and MI to improve the percentage of time CDS is alive and maintain CDS of competitive size under the setting of MANETs. An analytical model is introduced to estimate the time of convergence and the number of messages for SI and MI protocol families. The estimations match extremely well with the simulation results, which validates our analytical model.

With EMH, the remaining shortcoming of SI and MI is the convergence time required in the tree construction phase. In the future, we would like to investigate means to reduce the convergence time for SI and MI. For instance, a different formula can used to replace the current one in SI and MI to achieve shorter differ timer and still allow nodes with more uncovered neighbors to be included in the dominating set earlier.

References

1. Cartigny, J., Simplot, D., Stojmenovic, I.: Localized Minimum-Energy Broadcasting in Ad-hoc Networks. In: Proceedings IEEE Conference on Computer Communications (INFOCOM), March 2003, pp. 2210–2217 (2003)
2. Dai, F., Wu, J.: An Extended Localized Algorithm for Connected Dominating Set Formation in Ad Hoc Wireless Networks. IEEE Transaction on Parallel Distributed Systems 15(10), 908–920 (2004)
3. Hochbaum, D.S. (ed.): Approximation Algorithms for NP-hard Problems. PWS Publishing Co. (1997)
4. Hsu, W.-J., Merchant, K., Shu, H.-W., Hsu, C.-H., Helmy, A.: Weighted Waypoint Mobility Model and its Impact on Ad Hoc Networks. ACM SIGMOBILE Mobile Computing and Communications Review 9(1), 59–63 (2005)
5. Li, Y., Thai, M.T., Wang, F., Yi, C.-W., Wan, P.-J., Du, D.-Z.: On greedy construction of connected dominating sets in wireless networks. Wireless Communicationss and Mobile Compututing 5(8), 927–932 (2005)
6. Mobilab. Community-Wide Library of Mobility and Wireless Networks Measurements, http://nile.usc.edu/MobiLib/
7. Sakai, K., Shen, F., Kim, K.M., Sun, M.-T., Okada, H.: Multi-Initiator Connected Dominating Set for Mobile Ad Hoc Networks. In: Proceedings of International Conference on Communications (ICC) (May 2008)
8. Wan, P.-J., Alzoubi, K.M., Frieder, O.: Distributed Construction of Connected Dominating Set in Wireless Ad Hoc Networks. In: Proceedings of IEEE Conference on Computer Communications (INFOCOM), April 2002, pp. 141–149 (2002)
9. Wu, J.: Extended Dominating-Set-Based Routing in Ad Hoc Wireless Networks with Unidirectional Links. IEEE Transaction on Parallel Distributed Systems 13(9), 866–881 (2002)

10. Wu, J., Li, H.: On Calculating Connected Dominating Set for Efficient Routing in Ad Hoc Wireless Networks. In: Proceedings of the 3rd International Workshop on Discrete Algorithms and Methods for Mobile Computing and Communications (DIALM), August 1999, pp. 7–14 (1999)

11. Zhou, D., Sun, M.-T., Lai, T.: A Timer-based Protocol for Connected Dominating Set Construction in IEEE 802.11 Wireless Networks. In: Proceedings of International Symposium on Applications and the Internet (SAINT), January 2005, pp. 2–8 (2005)

PTAS for Minimum Connected Dominating Set in Unit Ball Graph

Zhao Zhang[1,*] Xiaofeng Gao[2], Weili Wu[2,**], and Ding-Zhu Du[2]

[1] College of Mathematics and System Sciences, Xinjiang University
Urumqi, Xinjiang, 830046, People's Republic of China
[2] Department of Computer Science, University of Texas at Dallas
Richardson, Texas, 75080, USA

Abstract. When sensors are deployed into a space instead of a plane, the mathematical model for the sensor network should be a unit ball graph instead of a unit disk graph. It has been known that the minimum connected dominating set in unit disk graph has a polynomial time approximation scheme (PTAS). Could we extend the construction of this PTAS for unit disk graphs to unit ball graphs? The answer is NO. In this paper, we will introduce a new construction, which gives not only a PTAS for the minimum connected dominating set in unit ball graph, but also improves running time of PTAS for unit disk graph.

Keywords: wireless sensor network, connected dominating set, unit ball graph.

1 Introduction

Virtual backbone in wireless sensor network has a wide range of applications (cf [3] and references there). A virtual backbone is a subset of nodes D such that non-adjacent nodes can communicate with each other though the nodes in D. Modeling the wireless sensor network as a graph, the virtual backbone is exactly a connected dominating set. A *dominating set* of a graph G is a subset D of vertices such that every vertex x in $V(G) \setminus D$ is adjacent to a vertex y in D. Vertex x is said to be *dominated* by y, or y is said to *dominate* x. A vertex $y \in D$ dominates itself. A *connected dominating set* is a dominating set D such that the subgraph of G induced by D, denoted by $G[D]$, is connected. Because of source limitation, it is often required that the size of the virtual backbone is as small as possible. Hence we are faced with a *minimum connected dominating set problem* (MCDS): to find a connected dominating set with the minimum cardinality. The MCDS has been studied extensively in the literatures [2,11,12,14,15,16,18].

* This research is supported by NSFC (60603003), the Key Project of Chinese Ministry of Education (208161) and Scientific Research Program of the Higher Education Institution of XinJiang. The work was completed when the first author was visiting Department of Computing Science, the University of Texas at Dallas.
** This work is supported in part by the National Science Foundation under grant CCF-0514796 and CNS-0524429.

In practice, the sensors are often assumed to be homogeneous, that is, they have omnidirectional antennas with the same transmission range. In this case, the topology of the 3-dimensional wireless sensor network can be modeled as a unit ball graph. In an *unit ball graph* (UBG), each vertex corresponds to a point in the space, two vertices are adjacent if and only if the Euclidean distance between their corresponding points is less than or equal to one. In another word, a vertex u is adjacent with a vertex v if and only if u is within the transmission range of v, which has been scaled to one. When restricted to the plane, a unit ball graph degenerates to a *unit disk graph* (UDG). Compared with the large number of studies on UDGs, the study on UBGs are relatively much less. However, there are cases in which 3-dimensional models are needed, such as under-water sensor systems, outer-space sensor systems, notebooks in a multi-layered buildings, etc.

For MCDS in general graphs, it was proved in [8] that for any $0 < \rho < 1$, there is no polynomial time $\rho \ln n$-approximation unless $NP \subseteq DTIME(n^{O(\ln n)})$, where n is the number of vertices. A greedy $(\ln \Delta + 3)$-approximation [13] and a greedy $(\ln \Delta + 2)$-approximation [8,13] were given, where Δ is the maximum degree of the graph. When restricted to UDG, the MCDS problem is still NP-hard [7]. Hence computing an MCDS in a UBG is also NP-hard. Distributed constant-approximations for MCDS in UDG were studied in [1,5,10,17], etc. Also by distributed strategy, Butenko and Ursulenko [4] gave a 22-approximation for MCDS in UBG. As to centralized algorithm for CDS in UDG, Cheng et al [6] gave a polynomial time approximation scheme (PTAS), that is, for any $\varepsilon > 0$, there exists a polynomial-time $(1 + \varepsilon)$-approximation. The question is: can their method be generalized to obtain a PTAS for MCDS in UBG? The answer is 'no', since their proof depends on a geometrical property which holds in the plane but is no longer true in the space.

In this paper, we present a PTAS for UBG. The method of analyzing the performance ratio is new. In fact, this method can be used to compute CDS for any n-dimensional unit ball graph. Furthermore, when our method is applied to UDG, the running time can be improved, compared with the algorithm presented in [6].

In section 2, the algorithm is presented, the correctness is proved, the time complexity is analyzed. In section 3, we prove that this algorithm is a PTAS. A conclusion is given in section 4.

2   The Algorithm

In this section, we present an algorithm for MCDS in UBG. The algorithm uses partition technique combined with a shifting strategy (which was introduced by Hochbaum and Maass [9]).

Let $Q = \{(x, y, z) \mid 0 \leq x \leq q, 0 \leq y \leq q, 0 \leq z \leq q\}$ be a minimal 3-dimensional cube containing all the unit balls. For a given positive real number $\varepsilon < 1$, let m be an integer with $m = \lceil 300\rho/\varepsilon \rceil$, where ρ is the performance ratio of a constant-approximation for MCDS in UBG, for example $\rho = 22$ by the algorithm given by Butenko and Ursulenko [4]. Set $p = \lfloor q/m \rfloor + 1$, and

$\tilde{Q} = \{(x, y) \mid -m \leq x \leq mp, -m \leq y \leq mp, -m \leq z \leq mp\}$. Divide $\tilde{Q}$ into $(p+1) \times (p+1) \times (p+1)$ grid such that each cell is an $m \times m \times m$ cube. Denote this partition as $P(0)$. For $a = 0, 1, ..., m-1$, $P(a)$ is the partition obtained by shifting $P(0)$ such that the left-bottom-hind corner of $P(a)$ is at the coordinate $(a-m, a-m, a-m)$. For each cell e, the *boundary region* B_e of e is the region contained in e such that each point in this region is at most distance 3 from the boundary of e. The *central region* C_e of e is the region of e such that each point is at least distance 2 away from the boundary of e. Note that B_e and C_e have an overlap.

Algorithm

Input: The geometric representation of a connected unit ball graph G and a positive real number $\varepsilon < 1$.

Output: A connected dominating set D of G.

1. Let $m = \lceil 300\rho/\varepsilon \rceil$.
2. Use the ρ-approximation algorithm to compute a connected dominating set D_0 of G. For each $a \in \{0, 1, ..., m-1\}$, denote by $D_0(a)$ the set of vertices of D_0 lying in the boundary region of $P(a)$. Choose a^* with the minimum $|D_0(a)|$.
3. For each cell e of $P(a^*)$, denote by G_e the subgraph of G induced by the vertices in the central region C_e. Compute a minimum subset D_e of vertices in e, such that

$$\text{for each component } H \text{ of } G_e, G[D_e] \text{ has a connected component dominating } H. \tag{1}$$

4. Let $D = D_0(a^*) \cup \bigcup_{e \in P(a^*)} D_e$.

The following lemma shows the correctness of the algorithm.

Lemma 1. *The output D of the algorithm is a CDS of G.*

Proof. We first show that D is a dominating set. For each vertex $x \in V(G)$, suppose x is in cell e. If $x \in C_e$, then x is dominated by D_e. If $x \in e \setminus C_e$, then x is in the region of e at distance less than two from the boundary of e. If $x \in D_0$, then $x \in D_0(a^*)$. If $x \notin D_0$, then the vertex $y \in D_0$ which dominates x is in $D_0(a^*)$. By the arbitrariness of x, D is a dominating set of G.

Next, we show that $G[D]$ is connected.

Suppose F_1, F_2 are two components of $G[D_0(a^*)]$ which can be connected by D_0 through the central region of some cell e. Then there exist two vertices $x_1 \in V(F_1) \cap B_e \cap C_e$ and $x_2 \in V(F_2) \cap B_e \cap C_e$ such that x_1, x_2 are in a same component H of G_e. By step 3 of the algorithm, x_1 and x_2 are connected through D_e, and thus F_1 and F_2 are also connected through $D_e \subseteq D$. We have shown that any components of $G[D_0(a^*)]$ are connected in $G[D]$.

Let $\tilde{G}$ be the component of $G[D]$ containing all vertices in $D_0(a^*)$. If $\tilde{G} \neq G[D]$, then there exists a cell e and a component R of $G[D_e]$ such that $V(R) \cap D_0(a^*) = \emptyset$ and R is not adjacent with any vertex in $D_0(a^*)$. Let x be a vertex in

D_0 such that x dominates some vertex $y \in V(R)$ (y may coincide with x). Since $x \notin D_0(a^*)$, we have $x \in e \backslash B_e$. Hence $y \in C_e$. Let H be the connected component of G_e containing y. By step 3 of the algorithm, we see that R dominates H. Since $G[D_0]$ is connected, there is a path in $G[D_0]$ connecting x to the other parts of G outside of cell e. Such a path must contain a vertex $z \in D_0 \cap B_e \cap C_e \subseteq D_0(a^*)$. Note that z is also in H. Hence there is a vertex w in $V(R)$ dominating z, contradicting that R is not adjacent with any vertex in $D_0(a^*)$. Hence $\tilde{G} = G[D]$, and thus $G[D]$ is connected. $\qquad\square$

The following lemma is a well-known fact about dominating set and connected dominating set.

Lemma 2. *For any dominating set D in a connected graph, at most $2(|D|-1)$ vertices are needed to connect D. In particular, $|D_2| \le 3|D_1| - 2$, where D_1, D_2 are, respectively, a minimum dominating set and a minimum CDS.*

The next lemma shows that the time complexity of the algorithm is polynomial in n and ε.

Lemma 3. *The above algorithm runs in time $n^{O(1/\varepsilon^3)}$.*

Proof. Clearly, the most time-consuming part is the third step. Since any vertex in a $\sqrt{3}/3 \times \sqrt{3}/3 \times \sqrt{3}/3$ cube dominates any other vertices in the same cube, we see that a minimum dominating set of e uses at most $(\sqrt{3}m)^3$ vertices. By Lemma 2, $|D_e| \le 3(\sqrt{3}m)^3$. Hence the exhaust search takes time at most $\sum_{k=0}^{(3\sqrt{3}m)^3} \binom{n_e}{k} = n_e^{O(m^3)}$ to compute D_e, where n_e is the number of vertices in e. It follows that the total time complexity is bounded by $\sum_{e \in P(a^*)} n_e^{O(m^3)} = n^{O(m^3)} = n^{O(1/\varepsilon^3)}$. $\qquad\square$

3   The Performance Ratio

In this section, we show that our algorithm is a PTAS for CDS in UBG. For this purpose, we need the following two lemmas.

For a path P in G, the length of P, denoted by $len(P)$, is the number of edges in P. Let H be a subgraph of G. For two subgraphs H_1 and H_2 of G, the distance between H_1 and H_2 in H is $dist_H(H_1, H_2) = \{len(P) \mid P$ is a shortest path connecting H_1 and H_2 in $H\}$. In another word, if $dist_H(H_1, H_2) = k$, then H_1 and H_2 can be connected through at most $k-1$ vertices of H. The following lemma can be easily seen from the definition of dominating set.

Lemma 4. *Let H be a connected subgraph of G, and D be a subset of $V(G)$ dominating H. If $G[D]$ does not contain a connected component dominating H, then there exist two components R and K of $G[D]$ such that $dist_H(R, K) \le 3$.*

The following lemma plays an important role in analyzing the performance ratio of the algorithm.

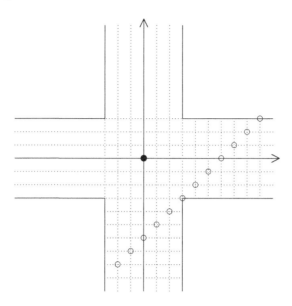

Fig. 1. When the partition shifts, each vertex falls into at most 12 boundary regions

Lemma 5. *For any vertex u in a unit ball graph G, the neighborhood $N_G(u)$ contains at most 12 independent vertices.*

Proof. The result can be obtained by transforming the problem into the famous Gregory-Newton Problem concerning about kissing number [19].   □

Next, we analyze the performance ratio of the algorithm.

Theorem 1. *The algorithm is a $(1 + \varepsilon)$-approximation for CDS in UBG.*

Proof. Let D^* be an optimal CDS of G.

Note that when a runs over $0, 1, ..., m - 1$, each vertex belongs to at most 12 boundary regions of $P(a)$'s (see Fig. 1). Hence

$$|D_0(0)| + |D_0(1)| + ... + |D_0(m - 1)| \leq 12|D_0|,$$

and thus

$$|D_0(a^*)| \leq \frac{12}{m}|D_0| \leq \frac{12\rho}{m}|D^*| \leq \frac{\varepsilon}{25}|D^*|. \tag{2}$$

In the following, we are to add some vertices to D^* such that the resulting vertex set $\tilde{D}$ satisfies:

(i) $|\tilde{D}| \leq |D^*| + 24|D_0(a^*)|$, and

(ii) for each cell e and each connected component H of G_e, $G[\tilde{D} \cap e]$ contains a connected component dominating H.

Before showing how to construct $\tilde{D}$, we first show that as long as this can be done, then the theorem is proved. In fact, since D_e is a minimum subset of e satisfying the requirement (1) and $\tilde{D} \cap e$ satisfies (ii), we have

$$|D_e| \leq |\tilde{D} \cap e|.$$

Then it follows from condition (i) and inequality (2) that

$$
\begin{aligned}
|\bigcup_{e \in P(a^*)} D_e| = \sum_{e \in P(a^*)} |D_e| &\leq \sum_{e \in P(a^*)} |\tilde{D} \cap e| \\
&= |\tilde{D}| \leq |D^*| + 24|D_0(a^*)| \leq (1 + \tfrac{24\varepsilon}{25})|D^*|.
\end{aligned}
\tag{3}
$$

Combining inequalities (2) and (3), we have

$$|D| \leq | \bigcup_{e \in P(a^*)} D(e)| + |D_0(a^*)| \leq (1 + \varepsilon)|D^*|,$$

where D is the output of the algorithm. This proves the theorem.

In the following we show how to construct $\tilde{D}$ satisfying conditions (i) and (ii).

We first claim that for any cell e and any component H of G_e, H is dominated by $D^* \cap e$. In fact, any vertex $x \in V(H)$ is dominated by some vertex $y \in D^*$. Since $x \in C_e$, we have $y \in e$.

Set $\tilde{D}_e^* = D^* \cap e$. Suppose $\tilde{D}_e^*$ does not satisfy condition (ii). Then there is a component H of G_e such that H is not dominated by one connected component of $G[\tilde{D}_e^*]$. By Lemma 4, there are two components R and K of $G[\tilde{D}_e^*]$ such that $dist_H(R, K) \leq 3$. That is, R and K can be connected through at most two vertices in $V(H) \setminus \tilde{D}_e^*$. Add these vertices into $\tilde{D}_e^*$ to merge R and K. Continue this procedure until $\tilde{D}_e^*$ satisfies condition (ii). Suppose k mergences are executed. Then the resulting $\tilde{D}_e^*$ satisfies

$$|\tilde{D}_e^*| \leq |D^* \cap e| + 2k. \tag{4}$$

Next, we use vertices in $D_0(a^*) \cap e$ to compensate for the $2k$ term of inequality (4). Suppose the components are merged in the order that: H_1 is merged with H_2, H_3 is merged with H_4, ..., H_{2k-1} is merged with H_{2k}. To simplify the presentation of the idea, we first assume that the H_i's are all distinct components of the original $G[\tilde{D}_e^*]$. Denote by I_e the region of e between distance 1 and 2 from the boundary of e. For each $i = 1, 2, ..., k$, let x_i be a vertex in $V(H_{2i-1}) \cap I_e$. Such x_i exists since H_{2i-1} dominates some vertex in H which is a component in the central region of e (hence H_{2i-1} is within distance 1 from the central region), and $G[D^*]$ is connected (hence H_{2i-1} is accessible from the outer side of e. Because D_0 is a dominating set of G, there is a vertex $z_i \in D_0$ dominating x_i. Since $x_i \in I_e$, we have $z_i \in B_e$, and thus $z_i \in D_0(a^*) \cap e$. Note that for $i \neq j$, it is possible that $z_i = z_j$. However, in this case, x_i and x_j are independent since they are in different components of $G[\tilde{D}_e^*]$. Hence by Lemma 5, a vertex serves at most 12 times as z_i's. Thus we have shown that

$$k \leq 12|D_0(a^*) \cap e|. \tag{5}$$

Next, consider the case that there are some repetitions among the H_i's. For example, suppose H_3 is the component of the new $G[\tilde{D}_e^*]$ obtained by merging H_1 and H_2. Since x_1 is chosen to be in $V(H_1) \cap I_e$, we can choose $x_3 \in V(H_2) \cap I_e$.

In general, we are always able to choose x_i's such that they are in different components of the original $G[\tilde{D}_e^*]$. Hence (5) holds in any case. Combining (5) with (4), we have

$$|\tilde{D}_e^*| \leq |D^* \cap e| + 24|D_0(a^*) \cap e|. \tag{6}$$

Let $\tilde{D}$ be the union of the modified $\tilde{D}_e^*$'s, where e runs over all cells of $P(a^*)$. Then

$$|\tilde{D}| = \sum_{e \in P(a^*)} |\tilde{D}_e^*| \leq \sum_{e \in P(a^*)} (|D^* \cap e| + 24|D_0(a^*) \cap e|) = |D^*| + 24|D_0(a^*)|.$$

Hence $\tilde{D}$ satisfies requirements (i) and (ii). This completes the proof.   □

4   Conclusion

We presented a construction and an analysis of PTAS for the minimum connected dominating set in unit ball graphs. This construction is different from that in [6] for the minimum connected dominating set in unit disk graphs. In fact, the construction in [6] cannot be extended to 3-dimensional space since a process of merging many parts of connected components into one in boundary area cannot work. Actually, our construction can be applied to unit ball graphs in n-dimensional space for any $n \geq 1$. In addition, when applied to unit disk graph, the $(1 + \varepsilon)$-approximation constructed in this paper runs in time $n^{O(1/\varepsilon^2)}$ while the $(1 + \varepsilon)$-approximation constructed in [6] runs in time $n^{O((1/\varepsilon^2)\ln(1/\varepsilon))}$. Therefore, Our construction also improves the running time.

References

1. Alzoubi, K.M., Wan, P., Frieder, O.: Message-optimal connected dominating sets in mobile ad hoc networks. In: Proceedings of the 3rd ACM international symposium on Mobile ad hoc networking and computing, Lausanne, Switzerland, June 09-11 (2002)
2. Bharghavan, V., Das, B.: Routing in ad hoc networks using minimum connected dominating sets. In: International Conference on Communication, Montreal, Canada (June 1997)
3. Blum, J., Ding, M., Cheng, X.: Applications of Connectd Dominating Sets in Wireless Netwoks. In: Du, D.-Z., Pardalos, P. (eds.) Handbook of combinatorial Optimization, pp. 329–369. Kluwer Academic Publisher, Dordrecht (2004)
4. Butenko, S., Ursulenko, O.: On minimum connected dominating set problem in unit-ball graphs (submitted)
5. Cadei, M., Cheng, M.X., Cheng, X., Du, D.: Connected domination in ad hoc wireless networks. In: Proc. the Sixth International symposium on Mobile ad hoc networking and computing, Lausanne, Switzerland, June 09-11 (2002)
6. Cheng, X., Huang, X., Li, D., Wu, W., Du, D.: A polynomial-time approximation scheme for minimum connected dominating set in ad hoc wireless networks. Networks 42, 202–208 (2003)

7. Clark, B.N., Colbourn, C.J., Johnson, D.S.: Unit disk graphs. Discrete Math. 86, 165–177 (1990)
8. Guha, S., Khuller, S.: Approximation algorithms for connected dominating sets. Algorithmica 20, 374–387 (1998)
9. Hochbaum, D.S., Maass, W.: Approximation schemes for covering and packing problems in image processing and VLSI. J. ACM 32, 130–136 (1985)
10. Min, M., Du, H., Jia, X., Huang, C.X., Huang, S.C., Wu, W.: Improving construction for connected dominating set with Steiner tree in wireless sensor networks. J. Global Optimization 35, 111–119 (2006)
11. Peter Chen, Y., Liestman, A.L.: Approximating minimum size weakly-connected dominating sets for clustering mobile ad hoc networks. In: Proceedings of the third ACM international symposium on Mobile ad hoc networking and computing, Lausanne, Switzerland, June 09-11 (2002)
12. Ramamurthy, B., Iness, J., Mukherjee, B.: Minimizing the number of optical amplifiers needed to support a multi-wavelength optical LAN/MAN. In: Proc. IEEE INFOCOM 1997, April 1997, pp. 261–268 (1997)
13. Ruan, L., Du, H., Jia, X., Wu, W., Li, Y., Ko, K.: A greedy approximation for minimum connected dominating set. Theoretical Computer Science 329, 325–330 (2004)
14. Salhieh, A., Weinmann, J., Kochha, M., Schwiebert, L.: Power Efficient topologies for wireless sensor networks. In: ICPP 2001, pp. 156–163 (2001)
15. Sivakumar, R., Das, B., Bharghavan, V.: An improved spine-based infrastructure for routing in ad hoc networks. In: IEEE Symposium on Computer and Communications, Athens, Greece (June 1998)
16. Stojmenovic, I., Seddigh, M., Zunic, J.: Dominating sets and neighbor elimination based broadcasting algorithms in wireless networks. In: Proc. IEEE Hawaii Int. Conf. on System Sciences (January 2001)
17. Wan, P., Alzoubi, K.M., Frieder, O.: Distributed construction of connected dominating set in wireless ad hoc networks. In: Proc. Infocom 2002 (2002)
18. Wu, J., Li, H.L.: On calculating connected dominating set for efficient routing in ad hoc wireless networks. In: Proceedings of the 3rd ACM International Workshop on Discrete Algorithms and Methods for Mobile Computing and Communications, pp. 7–14 (1999)
19. Zong, C.: Shere pachings. Springer, New York (1999)

A Better Theoretical Bound to Approximate Connected Dominating Set in Unit Disk Graph

Xianyue Li[1,*], Xiaofeng Gao[2], and Weili Wu[2,**]

[1] School of Mathematics and Statistics, Lanzhou University, China
lixianyue@lzu.edu.cn
[2] Department of Computer Science, University of Texas at Dallas, USA
{xxg05200,weiliwu}@utdallas.edu

Abstract. Connected Dominating Set is widely used as virtual backbone in wireless Ad-hoc and sensor networks to improve the performance of transmission and routing protocols. Based on special characteristics of Ad-hoc and sensor networks, we usually use *unit disk graph* to represent the corresponding geometrical structures, where each node has a unit transmission range and two nodes are said to be adjacent if the distance between them is less than 1. Since every Maximal Independent Set (MIS) is a dominating set and it is easy to construct, we can firstly find a MIS and then connect it into a Connected Dominating Set (CDS). Therefore, the ratio to compare the size of a MIS with a minimum CDS becomes a theoretical upper bound for approximation algorithms to compute CDS. In our paper, with the help of Voronoi diagram and Euler's formula, we improved this upper bound, so that improved the approximations based on this relation.

Keywords: Connected Dominating Set, Minimum Independent Set, Unit Disk Graph.

1 Introduction

Wireless Ad-Hoc and sensor network can be widely used in many civilian application areas, including healthcare applications, environment and habitat monitoring, home automation, and traffic control [10,6]. Due to the special characteristics of such networks, we usually use *Unit Disk Graph* (UDG) to represent their geometrical structures (assuming that each wireless node has the same transmission range). A UDG can be formally defined as follows: Given an undirected graph $G = (V, E)$, each vertex v has a transmission range with radius 1. An edge $(v_1, v_2) \in E$ means the distance between vertex v_1 and v_2 is less than or equal to 1, say, $dist(v_1, v_2) \leq 1$.

Compared with traditional computer networks, wireless ad-hoc and sensor networks have no fixed or pre-defined infrastructure as hierarchical structure, resulting the difficulty to achieve scalability and efficiency [2]. To better improve the performance and increase efficiency of routing protocols, a *Connected Dominating Set*(CDS) is selected

---

* This work was done while this author visited at University of Texas at Dallas.
** Support in part by National Science Foundation under grants CCF-9208913 and CCF-0728851.

Y. Li et al. (Eds.): WASA 2008, LNCS 5258, pp. 162–175, 2008.

to form a virtual network backbone. The formal definition of CDS can be shown as follows: Given a graph $G = (V, E)$, a *Dominating Set* (DS) is a subset $C \subseteq V$ such that for every vertex $v \in V$, either $v \in C$, or there exist an edge $(u, v) \in E$ and $u \in C$. If the graph induced from C ($G[C]$) is connected, then C is called a *Connected Dominating Set* (CDS). Since CDS plays a very important role in routing, broadcasting and connectivity management in wireless ad-hoc and sensor networks, it is desirable to find a minimum CDS (MCDS) of a given set of nodes.

Clark et.al. [3] proved that computing MCDS is NP-hard in UDG, and a lot of approximation algorithms for MCDS can be found in literatures [8,7,1,5]. It is well known that in graph theory, a Maximal Independent Set (MIS) is also a Dominating Set (DS). MIS can be defined formally as follows: Given a graph $G = (V, E)$, an Independent Set (IS) is a subset $I \in V$ such that for any two vertex $v_1, v_2 \in I$, they are not adjacent, say, $(v_1, v_2) \notin E$. An IS is called a Maximal Independent Set (MIS) if we add one more arbitrary vertex to this set, the new set will not be an IS any more. Compared with CDS, MIS is much easier to be constructed. Therefore, people usually construct the approximation for CDS with two steps. The first step is to find a MIS, and the second step is to make this MIS connected. As a result, The performance of these approximations highly depends on the relationship between the size of MIS ($mis(G)$) and the size of minimum CDS ($mcds(G)$) in graph G. Such a relation, say, $\frac{mis(G)}{mcds(G)}$ is also called the theoretical bound to approximate CDS.

In our paper, we will give a better theoretical bound to approximate CDS, which is $mis(G) \leq 3.399 \cdot mcds(G) + 4.874$, If there are no holes in the area constructed by the MCDS. The rest of this paper is organized as follows. In Section 2 we introduces the preliminaries and relation between $mis(G)$ and $cds(G)$, including related works. In Section 3 with the help of Voronoi division, we divide the plane into several convex polygons and calculate the area for each polygon under different situations. In Section 4 we use Euler's formula to calculate a better bound for $\frac{mis(G)}{mcds(G)}$, and finally Section 5 gives the conclusion and future works.

2 Preliminary and Related Works

As mentioned in Section 1, we use two steps to approximate a CDS in graph G. The first step is to select a MIS and the second step is to connect this MIS. Let $mis(G)$ be the size of selected MIS, $connect(G)$ be the size of disks that are used to connect this MIS, and $mcds(G)$ be the size of minimum CDS. Then, the approximation ratio for such algorithm is

$$\frac{mis(G) + connect(G)}{mcds(G)} = \frac{mis(G)}{mcds(G)} + \frac{connect(G)}{mcds(G)}.$$

For the connecting part, Min et.al [9] developed a steiner tree based algorithm to connect a MIS, with $\frac{connect(G)}{mcds(G)} \leq 3$, which becomes the best result to connect a MIS. On the other hand, for selecting MIS part, Wan et.al. [12] constructed a distributed algorithm which can select a MIS in graph G with size $mis(G) \leq 4 \cdot mcds(G) + 1$. Later, Wu and her cooperators [13] improved this result into $mis(G) \leq 3.8 \cdot mcds(G) +$

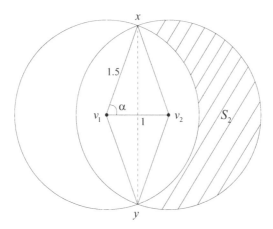

Fig. 1. Two Disks in MCDS

1.2. Funke et.al. [4] discussed the relation between $mis(G)$ and $mcds(G)$ and gave a theorem saying that $mis(G) \le 3.453 \cdot mcds(G) + 8.291$, but the proof lack evidences. In this paper we give a better bound for $mis(G)$ and $mcds(G)$, with a detailed analysis for the approximation ratio.

Actually, $mis(G)$ and $mcds(G)$ have a really close relationship. Given an UDG $G = (V, E)$, let M be the set of disks forming MCDS. If we increase the radius of disks in M from 1 to 1.5, and decrease the radius of the rest disks in $V \backslash M$ from 1 to 0.5, then we can construct a new graph G'. It is easy to know that all the disks in V are located insides the area formed by M. (For disks in M, obviously they are located insides themselves, and for disks in $V \backslash M$, e.g., v_1, since M is a MCDS, there exist a disk $v_2 \in M$ dominating v_2. Therefore $dist(v_1, v_2) \le 1$. Besides, the radius of v_1 is 0.5, while the radius of v_2 is 1.5, so v_1 must locate inside v_2's disk.) If we select a MIS for G, then based on the definition of UDG, the distance between any two disks from MIS should be greater than 1. And since the radius of disks in $V \backslash M$ for G' is 0.5, any of two disks from MIS will not intersect each other. (To simply the conception, we can consider the radius of the disks in both MIS and M as 0.5) Then we can get the conclusion that the sum of maximum area for MIS should be less than the area of MCDS, which is a rough bound for $\frac{mis(G)}{mcds(G)}$. The following theorem gives this bound.

Theorem 1. *The rough bound for $mis(G)$ and $mcds(G)$ is $mis(G) \le 3.748 \cdot mcds(G) + 5.252$.*

Proof. Consider two disks v_1, v_2 in MCDS set M. Both of them have radius 1.5, and $\max(dist(v_1, v_2)) = 1$. If we set v_1 and then add v_2, then the newly covered area will be at most S_2, just shown as the shadow in Fig. 1.

Let $area(xv_1y)$ be the area of sector xv_1y, and $area(\triangle xv_1y)$ be the area of triangle xv_1y. Besides, $cos\alpha = \frac{1}{3}$. Then, the area of S_2 should be:

$$area(S_2) = \pi \cdot 1.5^2 - 2 \cdot (area(xv_1y) - area(\triangle xv_1y))$$

$$= 2.25\pi - 2(\arccos \frac{1}{3} \cdot 1.5^2 - \frac{1}{2}\frac{1}{2} \cdot 2\sqrt{2})$$

$$\approx 2.25\pi - 4.1251$$

If we mimic the growth of a spanning tree for MCDS, then the maximum number of MIS should less than the total areas induced from M divide the area for a small disk with radius 0.5. Consequently, we can get the following inequations.

$$mis(G) \leq \frac{\pi \cdot 1.5^2 + (mcds(G) - 1) \cdot S_2}{\pi \cdot 0.5^2} = \frac{4 \cdot S_2}{\pi} \cdot mcds(G) + \frac{4 \cdot 4.1251}{\pi}$$

$$\approx 3.748 \cdot mcds(G) + 5.252$$

Thus we proved the theorem.

3 Voronoi Division

Based on Theorem 1 we get an upper bound for $\frac{mis(G)}{mcds(G)}$. Now let's analyze the relationship between $mis(G)$ and $mcds(G)$ more specifically. Before our discussion, let's firstly introduce the definition of Voronoi Division, which can be referred from [11].

Definition 1. *Let S a set of n sites in Euclidean space. For each site p_i of S, the Voronoi cell $V(p_i)$ of p_i is the set of points that are closer to p_i than to other sites of S, say,*

$$V(p_i) = \bigcap_{1 \leq j \leq n, \, j \neq i} \{p : |p - p_i| \leq |p - p_j|\}.$$

The Voronoi diagram $V(S)$ is the space partition induced by Voronoi cells.

Similarly, for graph G', let S be the set of selected MIS, then for each disk $w_i \in S$, we can find the corresponding Voronoi cell (the outer boundary is the boundary for MCDS.) Fig. 2 gives an example with $mcds(G') = 2$ and $mis(G') = 7$. It is easy to know that each non-boundary Voronoi cell is a convex polygon, and the area is greater than a disk with radius 0.5. Next let's analyze the area for each kind of polygons under densest situations. For these boundary Voronoi cells, we also consider them as a special kind of polygons with one arc edge.

3.1 Triangle

Assume that we have a Voronoi cell C_i as a triangle including disk w_i. Then the area of C_i is smaller if w_i is its inscribed circle. Besides, among those triangles, the area of equilateral triangle is the smallest. The following lemma gives proof for this conclusion.

Lemma 1. *The equilateral triangle has the smallest area among other triangles with w_i as its inscribed circle.*

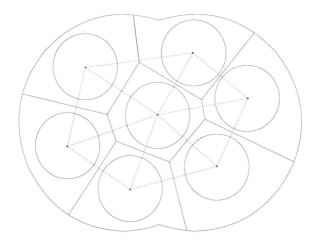

Fig. 2. Example for Voronoi Diagram

Proof. Let a, b, c be the lengths of three edges for triangle C_i, w_i be its inscribed circle, and $r = 0.5$ be the radius of this circle. Then based on Heron's formula, we have

$$area(C_i) = \frac{1}{2}(a + b + c) \cdot r = s \cdot r = \sqrt{s(s - a)(s - b)(s - c)},$$

where $s = \frac{a+b+c}{2}$ is the semiperimeter. Since r is fixed, the smallest area comes when s is smallest. Therefore we have the following model.

$$
\begin{cases}
\min s = \frac{1}{2}(a + b + c) \\
s.t. \ \sqrt{\frac{(s-a)(s-b)(s-c)}{s}} = r = \frac{1}{2}.
\end{cases}
\tag{1}
$$

Based on Lagrange's formula, let

$$F(a, b, c) = (a + b + c) - \lambda \left(\sqrt{\frac{(b + c - a)(a + c - b)(a + b - c)}{a + b + c}} - 1 \right),$$

then (1) can be changed into $\min F(a, b, c)$, and the extreme value comes out when the following partial derivative holds:

$$
\begin{cases}
\partial F/\partial a = 0 \\
\partial F/\partial b = 0 \\
\partial F/\partial c = 0 \\
\partial F/\partial \lambda = 0
\end{cases}
\tag{2}
$$

Then we get that when $a = b = c = f(\lambda, s)$, (2) holds. Therefore the equilateral triangle has the smallest area. Let P_3 denote such kind of triangle, just shown in Fig.3(a).

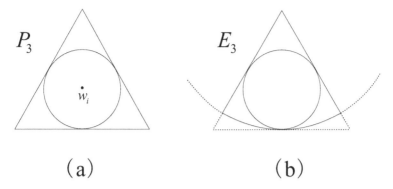

Fig. 3. Example for Triangle Cells

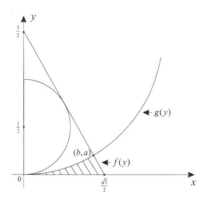

Fig. 4. Compute Area for E_3

Similarly, if C_i is a boundary cell, then the one with smallest area should be an equi-lateral triangle with one side cut by an arc from disks in MCDS at one of its tangency point. An example can be seen from Fig.3(b). Let E_3 denote such pseudo triangle. It is easy to know that $area(P_3) = 6 \cdot \frac{1}{2} \cdot \frac{1}{2} \cdot \frac{\sqrt{3}}{2} \approx 1.299$. To compute the area of E_3, we will use integral. According to Fig.4, $area(E_3) = area(P_3) - 2 \cdot S_3$, where S_3 is the shadow formed by the boundary arc and two edges of P_3. Therefore, we have that

$$
S_3 = f(y) - g(y)
$$
$$
= \int_0^a \left\{ \left(\frac{y}{\tan \frac{2\pi}{3}} + \frac{1}{2} \tan \frac{\pi}{3} \right) - \sqrt{\frac{9}{4} + (y - \frac{3}{2})^2} \right\} dy
$$
$$
\approx 0.0605
$$

where $f(y)$ is the function for intersecting edge of triangle and $g(y)$ is the function for the arc of ICMS. As a consequence, $area(E_3) = 1.1781$.

3.2   Quadrangle, Pentagon and Hexagon

If a non-boundary Voronoi cell C_i has four edges, then using similar conclusion, we can get that a square with w_i as its inscribed circle has the smallest area. Let P_4 be such kind of polygon, just shown as Fig.5(a). If C_i is a boundary Voronoi cell, then under two conditions C_i will have the minimum area. The first condition is when boundary arc cut off one angle of P_3, just shown as Fig.5(b), we name it as A_4; and the second condition is when boundary arc cut off one edge of P_4, shown as Fig.5(c), we name it as E_4. Using similar approach as triangles, we can calculate the area for these quadrangles,

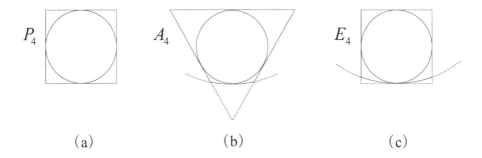

(a)   (b)   (c)

Fig. 5. Example for Quadrangle Cells

and give the result that

$$area(P_4) = 1, \qquad area(A_4) \geq 1.1357, \qquad area(E_4) = 0.9717$$

Repeat the above step for C_i as Pentagon and Hexagon, we can have the following conclusion:

$$area(P_5) = 0.9082, \qquad area(A_5) \geq 0.9499, \qquad area(E_5) = 0.8968$$
$$area(P_6) = 0.8661, \qquad area(A_6) \geq 0.8855, \qquad area(E_6) = 0.8546$$

Fig.6 is examples for pentagons and hexagons. After our calculation, we can get the conclusion that $area(A_i) \geq area(E_i)$ for $i \geq 3$. Therefore, in the next section, we will use E_i as the smallest boundary Voronoi Cell as i pseudo polygon.

3.3   Heptagon and Others

For a non-boundary Voronoi cell C_i, if C_i is a heptagon or n-polygon, $n \geq 7$, we will have the following lemma.

Lemma 2. *The area of non-boundary n-polygon C_i ($n \geq 7$) is greater then $area(P6)$.*

Proof. Firstly, it is easy to know that C_i with 6 adjacent neighbors is the densest situation if any two small disks does not intersect each other, just shown in Fig.7(a). Next,

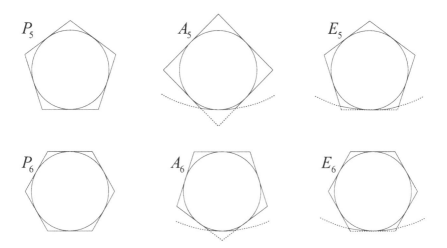

Fig. 6. Examples for Pentagon and Hexagon Cells

if C_i has 7 or more neighbors, then there must exist at least one disk w_j which doesn't touch w_i (w_i is the inner disk for C_i). Hence, the edge for C_i created by w_i and w_j is not the tangent line for w_i. On the consequence, the area covered by C_i is greater than $area(P_6)$. An example of P_7 can be shown in Fig.7(b). If $n > 7$, then the area of C_i will be bigger. Therefore, any Voronoi cell whose edges are more than 6 will have bigger area then P_6.

However, for boundary Voronoi heptagon C_i, when boundary arc cut off one angle of P_6, the area will become minimum. Such pseudo heptagon is A_7 (see Fig.8). After calculation, we have that $area(A_7) = 0.8525$. Similar as Lemma 2, the boundary n-polygon C_i will have bigger area than $area(A_7)$ if $n > 7$.

3.4   Updated Upper Bound

As mentioned above, A_7 is the smallest type of Voronoi cells. Then we can have a better bound for $\frac{mis(G)}{mcds(G)}$.

Theorem 2. $mis(G) \leq 3.453 \cdot mcds(G) + 4.839$

Proof. Similarly as proof for Lemma 1, we have

$$mis(G) \leq \frac{\pi \cdot 1.5^2 + (mcds(G) - 1) \cdot S_2}{area(A_7)} = \frac{S_2}{0.8525} \cdot mcds(G) + \frac{4.1251}{0.8525}$$

$$\approx 3.453 \cdot mcds(G) + 4.839$$

which is almost the same as [4].

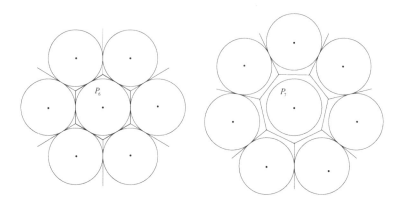

Fig. 7. Compare P_6 and P_7

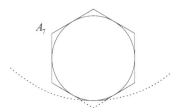

Fig. 8. Example for Heptagon Cells

4   Computing New Upper Bound

In this section, we will compute a better upper bound for $\frac{mis(G)}{mcds(G)}$ using Voronoi division and Euler's formula. Firstly, we give some notations. Let s_i be the minimum area of the non-boundary cell(i-polygon cell) and s_i' that of the boundary cell. From Section 3, we have that

$$s_3 \geq s_4 \geq s_5 \geq s_6 \leq s_7 \leq s_8 \ldots \quad \text{and} \quad s_3' \geq s_4' \geq s_5' \geq s_6' \geq s_7' \leq s_8' \leq s_9' \ldots$$

For convenience, we set $s_i = s_6$ when $i \geq 7$ and $s_i' = s_7'$ when $i \geq 8$. Hence, we get the following equations.

$$s_3 = 1.299, s_4 = 1, s_5 = 0,9082, s_6 = s_7 = \cdots = 0.8661. \tag{3}$$

$$s_3' = 1.1781, s_4' = 0.9717, s_5' = 0,8968, s_6' = 0.8546, s_7' = s_8' = \cdots = 0.8525. \tag{4}$$

4.1   3-Regularization

To simplify our calculation, in the subsection we will modify the Voronoi division such that any vertex of v in Voronoi division has degree exactly 3. For every vertex v, it is

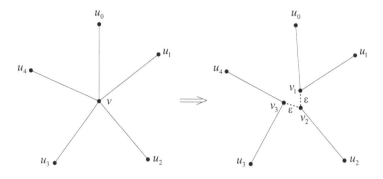

Fig. 9. Regularization when $d(v) = 5$

easy to see that $d(v) \geq 3$. For any vertex v whose $d(v) = d > 3$, let $u_0, u_1, \ldots, u_{d-1}$ be its neighbors in clockwise ordering. Replace this vertex with $d - 2$ new vertices $v_1, \ldots, v_{d-2}$ such that the distance between any v_i and v_j is not more than ε. Then, connect every u_i and v_i and add two edges $u_0 v_1$ and $u_{d-1} v_{d-2}$. Fig.9 gives an illustration when $d(v) = 5$.

After regularization, we can see that every vertex in Voronoi division has degree of exactly 3. Furthermore, if we choose ε sufficiently small, the area of every Voronoi cell will almost remain the same and the number of edges of new Voronoi cell is no less than that of original Voronoi cell. Hence, equations (3) and (4) are also hold.

4.2 Euler's Formula

Let ∂f_{out} be the outer boundary of the area constructed by the MCDS. It is trivial that the inside part of ∂f_{out} together with ∂f_{out} form graph G'. Note that there may exist some holes in G', where each hole means a connected area inside the ∂f_{out}, but not within the area constructed by the MCDS. In this subsection, we firstly suppose there are no holes in G', which means that the wireless transmission range will cover the plane we discuss. Let f_i and f'_i be the number of non-boundary and boundary Voronoi cells with exactly i edges, respectively. Then using Euler's formula, we have $\sum_i (f_i + f'_i) + 1 - m + n = 2$. Since G' is a cubic graph, $2m = 3n$. Hence,

$$\sum_i (f_i + f'_i) + 1 - \frac{1}{2}n = 2. \tag{5}$$

Let $|\partial f_{out}|$ be the number of edges in the outer face. Since every edge is exactly in two faces,

$$\sum_i (i(f_i + f'_i)) + |\partial f_{out}| = 2m = 3n. \tag{6}$$

For any boundary Voronoi cell, it must have at least one edge belonging to the outer face. Hence,

$$\sum_i f'_i \leq |\partial f_{out}|. \tag{7}$$

Combining (6) and (7), we have

$$\sum_i i f_i + \sum_i (i+1) f_i' - 3n \leq 0. \tag{8}$$

Then we combine Euler's formula and (8) together. Let $-1 \times$ (8)$+ 6 \times$ (5), we have

$$3 f_3 + 2 f_3' + 2 f_4 + f_4' + f_5 - f_6' - f_7 - 2 f_7' - \cdots \geq 6. \tag{9}$$

Since all Voronoi cells are contained in the area constructed by the MCDS, consider this area and combining (3) and (4), we have

$$\sum_i (s_i f_i + s_i' f_i')$$
$$= 1.299 f_3 + 1.178 f_3' + f_4 + 0,972 f_4' + 0.9082 f_5 + 0.8968 f_5' + 0.886(f_6 + f_7 + \cdots)$$
$$+ 0.8546 f_6' + 0.8525(f_7' + f_8' + \cdots)$$
$$\leq 2.9435 \cdot mcds(G) + 4.1251.$$
$$\tag{10}$$

Then, $-0.0114 \times$ (9)$+$(10), we obtain

$$1.2648 f_3 + 1.1402 f_3' + 0.9672 f_4 + 0.9492 f_4' + 0.8853 f_5 + 0.8968 f_5'$$
$$+ 0.886 f_6 + 0.8974 f_7 + \cdots + 0.866 f_6' + 0.8753 f_7' + \cdots \tag{11}$$
$$\leq 2.9435 \cdot mcds(G) + 4.2205.$$

From (11), since $mis(G) = \sum_i (f_i + f_i')$, we have

$$0.866 \cdot mis(G) = 0.866 \sum_i (f_i + f_i') \leq 2.9435 \cdot mcds(G) + 4.2205.$$

Hence, $mis(G) \leq 3.399 \cdot mcds(G) + 4.874$. Consequently, we have the following theorem.

Theorem 3. *For any unit disk graph G, let $mis(G)$ and $mcds(G)$ be the number of disks in any maximal independent set and minimum connected dominating set, respectively. If there are no holes in the area constructed by the MCDS, then $mis(G) \leq 3.399 \cdot mcds(G) + 4.874$.*

4.3 Discussion with Holes

Actually, in the real world there may exist some place where the wireless signal cannot reach, and some holes in the area constructed by the MCDS. Therefore, in this subsection we will discuss G' with holes in the following. Let k be the number of the holes in G' and $|\partial f_{hole}|$ be the number of edges in all holes. The equations (5) and (6) alter as

$$\sum_i (f_i + f_i') + 1 + k - \frac{1}{2} n = 2.$$

$$\sum_i (i(f_i + f'_i)) + |\partial f_{out}| + |\partial f_{hole}| = 2m = 3n.$$

For any boundary Voronoi cell, it must have at least one edge belonging to the outer face or one hole. Hence,

$$\sum_i f'_i \le |\partial f_{out}| + |\partial f_{hole}|.$$

Calculate them by the same strategy as the subsection 4.2, we can obtain that

$$\begin{aligned}
& 1.2648 f_3 + 1.1402 f'_3 + 0.9672 f_4 + 0.9492 f'_4 + 0.8853 f_5 + 0.8968 f'_5 \\
& + 0.886 f_6 + 0.8974 f_7 + \cdots + 0.866 f'_6 + 0.8753 f'_7 + \cdots \qquad (12) \\
& \le 2.9435 \cdot mcds(G) + 0.0684k + 4.2205.
\end{aligned}$$

Then we have,

$$mis(G) \le 3.399 \cdot mcds(G) + 0.0790k + 4.874.$$

It is easy to see that $k \le mcds(G)$. Next we can obtain the following theorem.

Theorem 4. *For any unit disk graph G, let $mis(G)$ and $mcds(G)$ be the number of disks in any maximal independent set and minimum connected dominating set, respectively. Then $mis(G) \le 3.478 \cdot mcds(G) + 4.874$.*

Besides, after analyzing the relation between disks in MCDS and based on the characteristics for CDS, we can have the following lemma.

Lemma 3. *For any unit disk graph G, let MCDS be a minimum connected dominating set. To form a hole, there need at least 6 connect vertices in MCDS. Fig.10 is an example for a hole.*

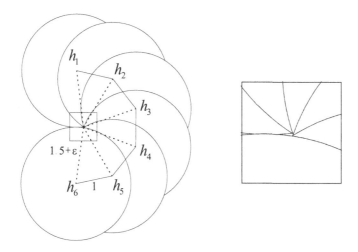

Fig. 10. Example for a Hole

Proof. Let h be a point in a hole and $m_1, \ldots, m_t$ be the vertices in MCDS which can form the hole including h and can induce a connect graph. By the definition of a hole, h can not be covered by any disk from MCDS with radius 1.5. Hence, choosing h as the center and draw a disk D with radius 1.5, any vertex m_i will lie outside this disk D. It is easy to see that if we form a hole with minimum number of vertices, the graph induced by $m_1, \ldots, m_t$ is a path and m_i is sufficiently close to disk D. Let hm_i intersect disk D at h_i. Then the radians of the central angle $\angle h_i h h_{i+1}$ should be

$$\angle h_i h h_{i+1} \leq 2 \arcsin \frac{1/2 h_i h_{i+1}}{h h_i} = 2 \arcsin \frac{1}{3}.$$

Furthermore, since $m_1, \ldots, m_t$ form a hole, the distance between m_1 and m_t is less than 3. Hence, the central angle $\angle h_1 h h_t$ is more than π and $t \geq \lceil \frac{\pi}{2 \arcsin \frac{1}{3}} \rceil + 1 = 6$.

5 Conclusion

In this paper, we presented a better upper bound to compare MIS and MCDS in a given UDG G with the help of Voronoi Division and Euler's Formula. If the area covered by MCDS has no holes, then the best upper bound for MIS and MCDS should be $mis(G) \leq 3.399 \cdot mcds(G) + 4.874$. If there exist some uncovered holes, then the bound will become $mis(G) \leq 3.478 \cdot mcds(G) + 4.874$ by Euler's formula, and $mis(G) \leq 3.453 \cdot mcds(G) + 4.839$ by comparison of area for MCDS and area for smallest Voronoi Cell. Actually, based on the discussion for Lemma 3, we guess that the relation between k and $mcds(G)$ can be $k \leq \frac{1}{3} mcds(G)$, and so comes the result that $mis(G) \leq 3.425 \cdot mcds(G) + 4.839$. The detailed proof becomes a future work which needs thorough discussion.

References

1. Baker, B.S.: Approximation algorithms for NP-complete Problems on Planar Graphs. Journal of the ACM 41(1), 153–180 (1994)
2. Blum, J., Ding, M., Thaeler, A., Cheng, X.Z.: Connected Dominating Set in Sensor Networks and MANETs. Handbook of Combinatorial Optimization, 329–369 (2004)
3. Clark, B.N., Colbourn, C.J., Johnson, D.S.: Unit Disk Graphs. Discrete Mathematics 86, 165–177 (1990)
4. Funke, S., Kesselman, A., Meyer, U.: A Simple Improved Distributed Algorithm for Minimum CDS in Unit Disk Graphs. ACM Transactions on Sensor Networks 2(3), 444–453 (2006)
5. Hochbaum, D.S., Maass, W.: Approximation Schemes for Covering and Packing Problems in Image Processing and VLSI. Journal of the ACM 32(1), 130–136 (1985)
6. Huang, G.T.: Casting the Wireless Sensor Net. Technology Review, 50–56 (2003)
7. Hunt III, H.B., Marathe, M.V., Radhakrishnan, V., Ravi, S.S., Rosenkrantz, D.J., Stearns, R.E.: NC-Approximation Schemes for NP- and PSPACE-hard Problems for Geometric Graphs. Journal of Algorithms 26(2), 238–274 (1998)
8. Marathe, M.V., Breu, H., Hunt III, H.B., Ravi, S.S., Rosenkrantz, D.J.: Simple Heuristics for Unit Disk Graphs. Networks 25, 59–68 (1995)

9. Min, M., Du, H.W., Jia, X.H., Huang, C.X., Huang, S.C., Wu, W.L.: Improving Construction for Connected Dominating Set with Steiner Tree in Wireless Sensor Networks. Journal of Global Optimization 35, 111–119 (2006)

10. Salem, H., Mohamed, N.: Middleware Challenges and Approaches for Wireless Sensor Networks. IEEE Distributed Systems Online 7(3) (2006); art. no. 0603-o3001

11. Voronoi, G.M.: Nouvelles applications des paramètres continus à la théorie des formes quadratiques. deuxième Mémoire: Recherches sur les parallélloèdres primitifs. J. Reine Angew. Math. 134, 198–287 (1908)

12. Wan, P.J., Alzoubi, K.M., Frieder, O.: Distributed Construction of Connected Dominating Set in Wireless Ad Hoc Networks. In: Proceedings of the Third ACM Internat. Workshop on Discrete Algorithms and Methods for Mobile Computing and Communications, pp. 7–14 (1999)

13. Wu, W.L., Du, H.W., Jia, X.H., Li, Y.S., Huang, S.C.: Minimum Connected Dominating Sets and Maximal Independent Sets in Unit Disk Graphs. Theorital Computer Science 352, 1–7 (2006)

Minimum Power Minimum D-Hop Dominating Sets in Wireless Sensor Networks

Trac N. Nguyen, Dung T. Huynh, and Jason A. Bolla

Department of Computer Science
University of Texas at Dallas
Richardson, Texas 75083-0688
{nguyentn,huynh,jason.bolla}@utdallas.edu

Abstract. Clustering structures are used in wireless ad hoc and sensor networks to provide for efficient communications and control. In addition to communications requirements, another important area of concern is power consumption. With that in mind, we would like to find a good network structure that uses a minimum power. In graph theoretic terminology, this paper considers the problem of clustering to be the problem of assigning powers to a set of nodes in the plane, such that we minimize total power and yield a graph that has a dominating set of a desired size. We first show that this problem is NP-complete for planar geometric graphs. We then propose heuristic solutions to the problem, present simulation data for the heuristics, and discuss the results.

1 Introduction

Wireless sensor networks have been widely used in military and civilian applications. Due to the limited power available in each sensor, an important problem in wireless sensor networks is maximizing the network lifetime. Finding techniques to minimize the total power usage of a network while maintaining certain network properties has been the focus of several recent research papers.

Computing dominating sets in a network is one approach to extend the network lifetime as discussed in [3], [4], [6], [5] and [2]. The work in [3] and [4] addresses the use of connected dominating sets in routing or forming a backbone. There are also some studies on how to enhance the connectivity in a network using dominating sets. One way is to ensure that each sensor node is required to connect to at least k dominating sensors as in [5]. Another technique is to create a wake-up schedule for a collection of disjoint (connected) dominating sets as discussed in [6]. The work in [1] also discusses the use of schedules for disjoint dominating sets to provide better coverage. In [2], the author considers the physical characteristic of the battery to schedule a sleep time for sensors in each (connected) dominating set. [7] discusses the construction of a backbone with different adjustable transmission ranges.

Y. Li et al. (Eds.): WASA 2008, LNCS 5258, pp. 176–187, 2008.

In this paper, we study the problem of assigning minimum total power to sensor nodes to form a connected graph that has a dominating set of a desired size. We prove that this problem is NP-complete for planar geometric graphs. In view of known NP-completeness results for WSNs that hold for general graphs only (which is unrealistic), our result is significant as it is derived for the planar geometric graphs which are among the simplest models of WSNs (other simple models include the unit disk graphs which have been extensively studied in the literature). The main contributions of this paper are:

1. The NP-Completeness of the minimum power minimum d-hop dominating set problem for planar geometric graphs (the proof is fairly technical as presented below).
2. The introduction of four heuristics for the minimum total power minimum dominating set problem as well as some simulation results that show how these heuristics perform and illustrate trade-offs between total power usage and dominating set size.

The rest of this paper is organized as follows. Section 2 provides definitions and explanations of models used in this paper. Section 3 contains the NP-completeness proof. The four heuristics described in Section 4 are Shortening Diameter, Shrinking Dominating Set, Shortening All Paths, and Power Level Search. Section 5 describes the simulation results for these heuristics, and Section 6 contains some concluding remarks.

2   Preliminaries

A wireless sensor network is represented as a graph $G = (V, E)$ where each vertex (node) is a sensor node and each edge is a communication link established when two sensors nodes are in the broadcast range of each other. An undirected edge is the combination of two directed edges between two sensor nodes, which are able to transmit and receive information from each other. In this paper, we assume edges are undirected (bidirectional). There are some restricted graph models in wireless networks such as planar graphs, unit disk graphs and planar geometric graphs. A d-hop dominating set (DS) in a graph $G(V, E)$ is a subset S of nodes such that every node is in S or at most d hops away from a node in S.

In our experimental model each node has a broadcast range. The communication between nodes in a network on the plane does not have noise or obstacles. This model of wireless sensor networks forms a geometric graph. A *geometric* graph is defined as a set of points $p_1, .., p_n$ on the plane where each point is specified by its x and y coordinates together with its transmission radius r_i. An edge exists between two points if they are within the transmission radius of each other. A geometric graph is said to be *planar* if it can be arranged so that no edge crosses another. In our simulation, the points $p_1, .., p_n$ are generated randomly on the plane.

3 NP-Completeness of Minimum Total Power Minimum D-Hop Dominating Sets

In this section we prove that the problem of minimizing the total power usage to yield a d-hop dominating set of a bounded size for planar geometric graphs is NP-complete.

Consider a set V of transceivers (nodes) in the plane. Each node u is assigned a power level denoted by $p(u)$. The signal transmitted by node u can only be received by a node v if the distance between u and v, denoted by $d(u,v)$, is $\leq p(u)$. We only consider the bidirectional case in which a communication edge exists between two nodes, u and v, only if both $p(u) \geq d(u,v)$ and $p(v) \geq d(v,u)$. The main problem investigated in this paper is defined as follows. Let $d > 0$ be a fixed integer.

MINIMUM TOTAL POWER MINIMUM D-HOP DOMINATING SETS IN PLANAR GEOMETRIC GRAPHS

Instance: *Given a set of N nodes $V = \{v_1, v_2, ..., v_N\}$ on a plane where each node v_i has a set of power levels $P_i = \{p_1^i, p_2^i, .., p_M^i\}$ at which node v_i can transmit, a positive number Q and a positive integer $K \leq N$.*

Question: *Is there a power assignment to each node that induces a planar geometric graph $G(V, E)$ containing a d-hop dominating set of size $\leq K$ such that the total power usage by the nodes in G is $\leq Q$?*

In the following we show that the problem of assigning minimum power to a set of nodes in the plane in order to obtain a planar geometric graph that has a d-hop dominating set of a desired size is NP-complete.

Theorem 1. The Minimum Total Power Minimum d-hop Dominating Set problem is NP-Complete for planar geometric graphs.

Proof. The Minimum Total Power Minimum d-hop Dominating Set (MTP-MDDS) problem is clearly in NP. Given a set V of nodes v_i in the plane, a set P_i of power levels for v_i, Q, and K, we can nondeterministically assign a power level in P_i to node v_i, nondeterministically select a subset S of nodes, and verify in polynomial time that (1) the power assignment yields a connected and planar geometric graph $G(V, E)$, (2) each node in $G(V, E)$ is either in the set S or d hops away from a node in S (i.e., S is a d-hop DS), (3) S has the size of $\leq K$, and (4) the total power usage of all nodes is $\leq Q$.

To prove the NP-hardness of the MTP-MDDS problem, we construct a polynomial-time reduction from the vertex cover for planar graphs with maximum degree 3 (VC-Deg3) problem, which was proven to be NP-complete in [10]. Given an instance $< G(V, E), K >$ of VC-Deg3, we construct the instance $< V', \{P_1, P_2, ..P_N\}, Q, K' >$ of MTP-MDDS as follows. First, we use Valiant's result [9] to embed the planar graph G into the Euclidian plane:

> *A planar graph with maximum degree 4 can be embedded in the plane using $O(|V|)$ area in such a way that its vertices are at integer coordinates and its edges are drawn so that they are made up of line segments of form $x = i$ or $y = j$, for integers i and j.*

This embedding process can easily be designed to satisfy the additional requirements that each edge must be of length at least 3 units and that every pair of parallel edges in the embedded graph must also be at least 3 units apart.

Let δ be the unit distance in the plane, l_{uv} be the length of the edge connecting two *original* nodes u, v (embedded in the plane), and $d \geq 2$ be the number of hops. Letting $\sigma := \delta/3$, we define three radii r_1, r_2 and r_3 as follows: $r_1 := \sigma/(d+1)$, $r_2 := \sigma + 0.001\delta$ and $r_3 := \sigma * 2$. Every edge (which is a set of line segments) connecting any two *original* nodes is modified by placing additional nodes to create an instance of MTP-MDDS as follows:

1. Keep the *original* nodes at the same locations in the plane.
2. On the edge (u, v) of length l_{uv} connecting two *original* nodes u, v, we add a total of $3 * l_{uv} - 1$ consecutive nodes between u and v such that there is an equal distance of $\delta/3$ from one node to the next. These nodes are called *intermediate* nodes. The two intermediate nodes at the two ends, called *control* nodes, that are adjacent with two *original* nodes will have the exact distance of r_2 to the *original* nodes and the next *intermediate* nodes (also called *interfacing* nodes). This can be accomplished by moving the *control* nodes slightly away from the line segments.
3. Perpendicular to each edge connecting two *orignal* nodes, we attach $(d - 1)$ nodes on each *intermediate*, *control*, and *interfacing* node. We also attach to each *original* node $(d - 2)$ nodes. These nodes are called *auxiliary* nodes. They are added at the distance r_1 from one node to the next starting from the *intermediate*, *control* or *original* node. The *auxiliary* nodes attached on each *interfacing* start at the distance $(2/3) * r_3$ from the *interfacing* node. Moreover, the *auxiliary* nodes added to the *interfacing* nodes surrounding an *original* node are attached so that they do not belong to the same quadrant (defined by the original node and its incident line segments).

Examples of the embedded graphs are shown in Figure 1 for $d = 2$ (left) and $d = 1$ (right). For $d = 2$, A, B, C, D are *original* nodes, whereas c's are *control* nodes and i's are *interfacing* nodes. Nodes between *interfacing* nodes on each edge are *intermediate* nodes. Other nodes are *auxiliary* nodes.

The numbers of additional *intermediate* (I), *control* (C), *interfacing* (I_f) and *auxiliary* (A) nodes added to $G'(E', V')$ can be computed as follows:

$$I = \sum_{(u,v) \in E} (3*l_{uv} - 5), \quad I_f = C = 2*|E|, \quad A = (I + C + I_f)*(d - 1) + |V|*(d - 2)$$

Let V' denote the set of all vertices of G embedded in the plane, and $N := |V|$. To complete the construction of the instance of MTP-MDDS, we define the set of power levels for each node in V, the maximum total power Q, and K' as follows:

Each *auxiliary* node attached to an *interfacing* node at the distance $(2/3)*r_3$ is assigned the power levels $\{0, r_1, r_2, r_3\}$. The power levels assigned to all other *auxiliary* nodes are $\{0, r_1\}$. The set of power levels assigned to each *control* and *intermediate* node is $\{0, r_1, r_2\}$, whereas the set of power levels assigned to each *interfacing* and *original* node is $\{0, r_1, r_2, r_3\}$. Q and K are defined by:

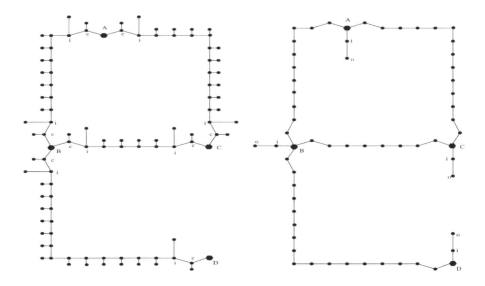

Fig. 1. Construction of $G'(V', E')$ for d=2 (left) and construction of $G'(V', E')$ for d=1 (right)

$$Q = (K+2*I_f)*r_3+((|V|-K)+(I+C))*r_2+(A-I_f)*r_1, \quad K' = K+ \sum_{(u,v)\in E} (l_{uv}-1)$$

where I, I_f, A and C are the numbers of *intermediate*, *interfacing*, *auxiliary* and *control* nodes, respectively, and V is the set of vertices of G. r_1, r_2 and r_3 are the three radii defined earlier.

To prove the correctness of the above polynomial-time reduction, we show that the instance $< G(V, E), K >$ of VC-Deg3 has a vertex cover D of size $\leq K$ if and only if the instance $< V', \{P_1, P_2, .., P_N\}, K', Q >$ of MTP-MDDS has a power assignment that yields a planar geometric graph containing a d-hop dominating set D' of size $\leq K'$, and the total power usage POV is $\leq Q$.

For the only-if direction, suppose that the graph $G(V, E)$ of the VC-Deg3 instance has a dominating set D of size $\leq K$. We define the power assignment for nodes in V' as follows:

- If node $v \in V$ and $v \in D$, assign power level r_3 to the *original* node $v \in V'$.
- If node $v \in V$ and $v \notin D$, assign power level r_2 to the *original* node $v \in V'$.
- Assign the power level r_3 to all *interfacing* nodes and every *auxiliary* node which is at the distance $(2/3) * r_3$ from an *interfacing* node.
- All other auxiliary nodes are assigned the power level r_1.
- Assign the power level r_2 to all other *intermediate* and *control* nodes.

Clearly, the total power assigned to nodes in V' is at most Q and the resulting graph is a planar geometric graph. The d-hop DS D' is constructed as follows:

1. If a node $u \in V$ and $u \in D$, then add the *original* node $u \in V'$ to D'.
2. Given an edge $(u, v) \in E$ with $u \in D$ and $v \notin D$, for every group of 3 consecutive *intermediate* nodes starting from u, we add the *intermediate* node in the middle of the group to D'. The *interfacing* node closest to v is also added to D'.
3. For an edge $(u, v) \in E$ with $u \in D$ and $v \in D$, we add nodes to D' in a manner similar to the previous step.

Clearly, for every set of line segments in E' representing the original edge $(u, v) \in E$, we only add a total of $(l_{uv} - 1)$ non-original nodes to D'. Thus, the total number of nodes in D is $|D'| = |D| + \sum_{(u,v) \in E}(l_{uv} - 1) \leq K' = K + \sum_{(u,v) \in E}(l_{uv} - 1)$.

It is quite straightforward to argue that D' is a d-hop DS. The details are left to the reader. This completes the proof for the *"only-if"* direction.

For the *"if"* direction, suppose that the instance $< V', \{P_1, P_2, ..P_N\}, K', Q >$ has a power assignment with total power $\leq Q$ that yields a connected planar geometric graph $G'(V', E')$ with a d-hop DS D' of size $\leq K'$. Without lost of generality, we may assume that (1) D' is minimal, i.e., D' is not a DS if any node is removed from D', and (2) The power at each node is minimum, i.e., every node uses the least possible power to generate a connected graph. We can construct a vertex cover D with $|D| \leq K$ for $G(V, E)$ based on the following observations:

1. If x is not an original node, there is a unique power level assigned to x to make the resulting graph connected, independent of whether x is in D' or not.
2. For every edge (u, v) in G the number of non-original nodes required to be in D is at least $l_{uv} - 1$ even when one or both of u and v belong to D. From the definition of K, it follows that the number of original nodes in D is $\leq K$. Moreover, the total power usage does not exceed Q even if every original node in D is assigned the power level r_3.
3. Consider an edge (u, v) in G where both of the original nodes u, v do not belong to D. Such an edge (u, v) must have at least l_{uv} non-original nodes in D'. If any two such edges are adjacent and have a common original node, we can add this common *original* node to D', assign to it the power level r_3, and remove one non-original node on each edge from D'. This yields a smaller DS whose size is of course $\leq K'$ and the total power usage is still bounded by Q as pointed out in Observation 2.
4. The *auxiliary* nodes cannot be in D'; otherwise the size of D can be reduced.
5. For each edge $(u, v) \in G'$ with $u \notin D'$ and $v \notin D'$, remove an *intermediate* or *control* node which is closest to u or v, and add u or v to D' with the power level r_3. The size of D' does not change and the total power usage is still $\leq Q$.

From the above observations, we may assume that every edge (u, v) in G must have at least an *original* node and $(l_{uv} - 1)$ non-original nodes in D'. The vertex cover set D is constructed from D as follows: If an *original* node $u \in V'$ belongs to D', add $u \in V$ to D.

Clearly, we only add to D the *original* nodes in G' representing nodes in D'. For each set of line segments in G' representing an edge in G, we remove at least $(l_{uv} - 1)$ nodes from D'. The total number of *original* nodes from D' included in D is at most:

$$|D| \leq |D'| - \sum_{(u,v) \in E} (l_{uv} - 1) \leq K' - \sum_{(u,v) \in E} (l_{uv} - 1) = K$$

From the construction of D, it is clear that every edge in G is covered by a node in D. Thus, D is a vertex cover in G. This completes the proof of Theorem 1 for the case $d \geq 2$.

For $d = 1$, we define the radii r_1 and r_2 by $r_1 := \sigma + 0.001$ and $r_2 := \sigma * 2$, where $\sigma := \delta/3$, and construct the instance of MTP-MDDS as follows:

1. Keep the *original* nodes at the same locations in the plane.
2. On the edge (u, v) of length l_{uv} connecting two *original* nodes u, v, we place a total of $3 * l_{uv} - 1$ consecutive nodes such that there is an equal distance of $\delta/3$ from one node to the next. These nodes are called *intermediate* nodes. The two *intermediate* nodes that are adjacent with two *original* nodes will have the exact distance of r_1 to the *original* and to the next *intermediate* node. This can be accomplished by placing these two *intermediate* nodes slightly away from the line segments. These nodes are called *control* nodes, and their adjacent intermediate nodes are called *interfacing* nodes.
3. We attach to each *original* node two more nodes. The first node is placed at distance r_1 from the *original* node. This node is called the *support* node. The second node, called the *auxiliary* node, is placed at distance r_2 from the *support* node.

The total number of *intermediate* (I), *auxiliary* (A) and *support* nodes (S) can be computed as follows:

$$A = S = |V|, \qquad I = \sum_{(u,v) \in E} (3 * l_{uv} - 1)$$

To complete the construction of the instance of MTP-MDDS for $d = 1$, we define the set of power levels for each node, and the numbers Q and K'. Each *original*, *support* and *control* node has the set of power levels $\{0, r_1, r_2\}$. The *interfacing* nodes are assigned the power levels $\{0, r_2\}$, whereas all other *intermediate* nodes including the *control* nodes are assigned the power levels $\{0, r_1\}$. Furthermore,

$$Q = (K + 2 * |E| + 2 * |V|) * r_2 + (I - 2 * |E|) * r_1, \quad K' = K + |V| + \sum_{(u,v) \in E} (l_{uv} - 1)$$

An example of an instance of MTP-MDDS for $d = 1$ can be found in Fig. 1 (right). Nodes A, B, C, D are *original* nodes, and the i' and o' nodes are *support* and *auxiliary* nodes, respectively.

Observe that each edge (u, v) represented by a set of line segments in G' must have at least $(l_{uv} - 1)$ non-original nodes in D'. Moreover, to dominate each pair of *auxiliary* and *support* nodes, at least one of them has to be in D. Hence, $|D'| = |D| + |V| + \sum_{(u,v) \in E}(l_{uv} - 1)$. The correctness proof for the case $d = 1$ is similar to the case $d \geq 2$. This concludes the proof of Theorem 1.

4   Heuristics

In this section, we describe four heuristics for the minimum total power minimum DS problem along with some supporting algorithms to find graph diameter and compute dominating sets. To compute dominating sets, we use the Progressive Maximum Degree D-Hop Dominating Set (Minimum Dominating Set) algorithm introduced in [8]. The heuristics presented are: Shortening Diameter, Shrinking Dominating Set, Shortening All Paths, and Power Level Search. The Finding Diameter algorithm is a supporting algorithm used by the Shortening Diameter heuristic to find the diameter of a graph.

In the Shortening Diameter heuristic we successively shorten the longest of all shortest paths by increasing the power levels of the nodes along that path, whereas Shortening All Paths increases the power level of all nodes during each

---

MINIMUM DOMINATING SET (G(V,E))

1	Initialize all nodes as uncovered nodes;.
2	Set Dominating Set S to be empty;
3	Do {
4	Pick the uncovered node x with the largest number of uncovered d-hop neighbors;
5	Set node x to be covered and add node x to the dominating set S;
6	Set all uncovered d-hop neighbors of node x to be covered; }
7	Until (all nodes are covered);
8	Return Dominating Set S;

Fig. 2. Minimum Dominating Set Algorithm

SHORTENING ALL PATHS

Input: Distances of every pair of nodes in the plane and the hop number D

1	Call Minimum Spanning Graph algorithm;
2	Do {
3	Call the Minimum Dominating Set algorithm;
4	Calculate the total number of nodes in the dominating set S;
5	If (|S| > 1)
6	For (Every node x in G) {
7	Find all 2-hop neighbors of x;
8	Increase the power of x to reach its farthest 2-hop away neighbor; }
9	For (Every node x in G)
10	Reduce the power level of x to reach its farthest 1-hop neighbor;
11	Calculate the total power usage; }
12	Until (|S| == 1)

Fig. 3. Shortening All Paths Algorithm

```
FINDING DIAMETER
Input:    A graph G(V,E)
Output   The longest of all shortest paths.
1      largest_level = 0;
2      For every node x in G(V,E) {
3              Initialize order level of every node 0 and node x with level 1;
4              d = 1;
5              While (there is still a node with order level = 0) {
6                      Find all d hops away neighbors of x;
7                      For (Each neighbor y of x)
8                              If (y has the order level = 0)
9                                      Set order level of y = d;
10                     d++; }
11             If (d > largest_level) {
12                     Set the largest_level = d;
13                     Store nodes on the path from x to a neighbor that has the order level d;} }
14     Output the longest path;
```

Fig. 4. Finding Diameter Algorithm

```
POWER LEVEL SEARCH
Input:    Distances of every pair of nodes in the plane and hop number D

1      Innitialize  upper_level = the farthest distance of any pair of nodes;
2      Innitialize curr_level = 0 and lower_level = 0;
3      While (upper_level > lower_level) {
4              Using binary search to find the next good power level which makes the graph connected;
5              Initialize Level of every node to be 0 and initialize Mutihome of every node to be 0;
6              If (upper_level > lower_level) {
7                      Call Minimum Dominating Set algorithm and set Level of node in dominating set S to be 0;
8                      For (every node x that is in G but not in S) {
9                              Set Level of x to be the number of hops from x to the closest node in S;
10                             Set Multihome of x to be the total number of node in S that are d hops away from x;}
11                     For (int u = 1; u <= D; u++)
12                             For (Every node x in G) {
13                                     If ( Multihome of x == 1  &&  x is not in S)
14                                             Set the power level of x to reach the closest 1-hop neighbor y that has
                                               the Level lower that x;
15                                     Else If (Multihome of x  > 1  &&  x is not in S  &&  Level of x == 1)
16                                             Set the power level of x to reach the farthest 1-hop neighbor y that has
                                               the Level value of 0 or D-1;
17                                     Else If (Multihome of x > 1  &&  x is not in S   && Level of x > 1)
18                                             Set the power level of x to reach the farthest 1-hop neighbor y that has
                                               the Level lower than x; }
19                     For (Every node in G)
20                             Reduce the power level of x to reach the farthest 1 hop neighbor;
21                     Calculate the total power usage and the total number of nodes in the dominating set S; }}
```

Fig. 5. Power Level Search Algorithm

iteration. In the Shrinking Dominating Set heuristic we increase the power of the nodes of the current DS and obtain a new DS of smaller size. The Power Level Search algorithm simply searches for all power levels that yield DSs of different sizes. All four heuristics and supporting algorithms are described in Figures 2, 3, 4, 5, 6 and 7.

SHORTENING DIAMETER
Input: Distances of every pair of nodes in the plane and the hop number D

1   Call Minimum Spanning Graph algorithm;
2   Do {
3   Call the Minimum D ominating Set algorithm;
4   Calculate the total number of nodes in the dominating set S;.
5   If (|S| > 1) {
6   Call the Finding Diameter algorithm;
7   For (Every node x of the longest path) {
8   Increase the power of x to reach the farthest 2 hops away neighbor y which
                             is also a member of the longest path; } }.
9   For (Every node x in G)
10   Reduce the power level of x to reach its farthest 1 hop neighbor;
11   Calculate the total power usage; }
12   Until (|S| == 1);

Fig. 6. Shortening Diameter Algorithm

SHRINKING DOMINATING SET
Input: Distances of every pair of nodes in the plane and hop number D

1   Initialize total_power = 0 and prev_total_power = -1;
2   Initialize |S| = 0 and prev_ds = -1;
3   Call Minimum Spanning Graph algorithm ;
4   While (total_power != prev_total_power || |S| != prev_ds) {
5   Call the Minimum Dominating Set algorithm;
6   Calculate the total number of nodes in the dominating set S;
7   If (|S| != prev_ds || total_power != prev_total_power)
8   For (Every node x in S)
9   Increase the power level of x to reach the closest node y which is also a
                             member of S;
10   Calculate the total power usage and set it to total_power;
11   Set prev_total_power = total_power;
12   Set prev_ds = |S|;
13   For (Every node x in G)
14   Reduce the power of x to reach its farthest 1 hop neighbor; }

Fig. 7. Shrinking Dominating Set Algorithm

5   Experimental Results

To perform our experiment we randomly generate 5 different sets of 300 nodes on
an area of size 30x30 units. For each set of nodes generated each heuristic is run
several rounds, and each round provides a total power usage and a new minimal
dominating set. We calculate the total power usage and the dominating set size
for each round. The results for 2-hop DSs are presented in Figures 8 and 9.

In terms of the DS size, the Shortening Diameter heuristic gives the greatest
number of choices for DS size and total power usage. The Shortening Diameter
heuristic increases the power of the nodes along the diameter of the current
graph to connect nodes on this diameter that are two hops apart from each
other. As the total power usage increases, the DS size gradually decreases until
it is equal to 1. On the other hand, the Shrinking Dominating Set heuristic

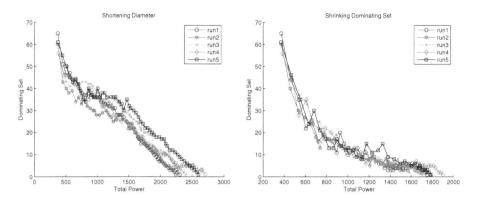

Fig. 8. Power Level w.r.t DS for Shortening Diameter (left) and Shrinking Dominating Set (right)

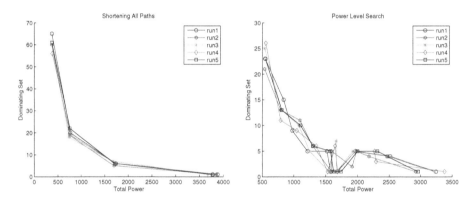

Fig. 9. Power Level w.r.t DS for Shortening All Paths (left) and Power Level Search (right)

concentrates only on the current DS. This heuristic increases the power of nodes in the previous DS to reduce its size. The whole process stops and exits when increasing the power level of previous DS nodes does not change the size or the nodes in the DS.

The Shrinking Dominating Set heuristic provides a few more choices of DS size and total power usage than the Shortening All Paths and Power Level Search algorithms. However, this is still far less than the number of choices provided by the Shortening Diameter heuristic. The Shortening All Paths heuristic increases the power of all nodes to connect every pair of 2 hop neighbors. This reduces the size of the DS rapidly and hence gives the fewest number of choices for the DS size.

The Power Level Search heuristic uses binary search to find a new power level every round. The power level is either decreased or increased each time until a connected graph having a new DS of different size is found. Therefore the Power Level Search gives fewer choices for DS size and total power than the Shrinking Dominating Set heuristic.

The Shortening Diameter heuristic provides significantly more choices for DS size and total power usage than all the others. This is apparently due to the fact that the other heuristics increase the power levels of the nodes in a global fashion whereas Shortening Diameter focuses on nodes along the longest of the shortest paths only. When having more choices is an important factor, it appears that Shortening Diameter is the better choice among the four heuristics.

6   Conclusions

In this paper we show that the Minimum Total Power Minimum D-Hop Dominating Set problem is NP-complete for planar geometric graphs. We also introduce four heuristics and study the trade-offs between DS size and total power usage. From the simulation results for all four heuristics, the Shortening Diameter approach provides significantly more options to find different dominating sets of varying size where total power usage is comparable to the other approaches. The simulation result for Shortening Diameter also provides us an interesting trade-off between total power usage and DS size.

References

1. Cardei, M., MacCallum, D., Cheng, M.X., Min, M., Jia, X., Li, D., Du, D.-Z.: Wireless Sensor Networks with Energy Efficient Organization. Journal of Interconnection Networks 3, 213–229 (2002)
2. Ma, C., Yang, Y., Zhang, Z.: Constructing Battery-Aware Virtual Backbones in Sensor Networks. In: Proceedings of the 2005 International Conference on Parallel Processing, June 2005, pp. 203–210 (2005)
3. Thai, M.T., Du, D.-Z.: Connected Dominating Sets in Disk Graph with Bidirectional Links. IEEE Communication Letters 10(3), 138–140 (2006)
4. Thai, M.T., Wang, F., Liu, D., Zhu, S., Du, D.-Z.: Connected Dominating Sets in Wireless Networks with Different Transmission Ranges. IEEE Transactions on Mobile Computing 6(7) (July 2007)
5. Tang, J., Hao, B., Sen, A.: Relay Node Placement in Large Scale Wireless Sensor Networks. Computer Communications 29, 490–501 (2006)
6. Carle, J., Gallais, A., Simplot-Ryl, D.: Preserving area coverage in wireless sensor networks by using surface coverage relay dominating sets. In: Proceedings. 10th IEEE Symposium on Computers and Communications Issue 27-30, June 2005, pp. 347–352 (2005)
7. Wu, J., Dai, F.: Virtual Backbone Construction in MANETs Using Adjustable Transmission Ranges. IEEE Trans. on Mobile Computing 5(9), 1188–1200 (2006)
8. Vuong, T., Huynh, D.: Connected D-Hops Dominating Sets in Wireless Ad Hoc Networks. SCI 20002/ISAS 2002, Vol IV
9. Valiant, L.: Universality Considerations in VLSI Circuits. IEEE Transactions on Computers C-30, 135–140 (1981)
10. Garey, M.S., Johnson, D.S.: The rectilinear Steiner tree problem is NP-complete. SIAM Journal on Applied Mathematics 32, 826–834

Convex Combination Approximation for the Min-Cost WSN Point Coverage Problem

Zheng Fang and Jie Wang

Department of Computer Science
University of Massachusetts, Lowell, MA 01854
{zfang,wang}@cs.uml.edu
http://www.cs.uml.edu

Abstract. This paper presents a new algorithm for finding better approximation solutions to the min-cost point coverage problem in wireless sensor networks. The problem is to compute a deterministic sensor deployment plan, with minimum monetary cost on sensors, to cover the set of targets spread across a geographical region such that each target is covered by multiple sensors. This is a Max-SNP-complete problem. Our approximation algorithm, called alpha-beta approximation, is a convex combination of greedy LP-rounding and greedy set-cover selection. We show that, through a large number of numerical simulations on randomly generated targets and sites, alpha-beta approximation produces efficiently better approximation results than the best approximation algorithm previously known. In particular, the alpha-beta approximation in our experiments never exceeds an approximation ratio of 1.07, providing up to 14.86% improvement over previous approximation algorithms.

Keywords: sensor deployment, point coverage, minimum set multicover, LP-rounding, approximation algorithm.

1 Introduction

The min-cost point coverage (MCPC) problem is a classic sensor coverage problem in wireless sensor networks. This problem has been studied intensively in recent years (see, e.g., [Vaz01, CIQ+02, SX05, CW04, WZ06, YW07, WZ08]). Given a set of targets in a 3D (or 2D) geographical region, a set of sensor sites in the proximity of targets, and multiple types of sensors with different monetary costs, the problem is to select a set of sensors with minimum monetary cost on sensors, a set of sites, and a mapping of the selected sensors to the selected sites, so that each target under this mapping is covered by multiple sensors.

The MCPC problem is Max-SNP-complete, and so it does not have polynomial-time approximation schemes unless P = NP. On the other hand, there are approximation algorithms for this problem with proven approximation guarantees. These algorithms can be characterized as greedy set-cover selection,

Y. Li et al. (Eds.): WASA 2008, LNCS 5258, pp. 188–199, 2008.

greedy LP-rounding, and randomized LP-rounding. The approximation ratios of these algorithms are based on different attributes that are not directly comparable, and so they provide little insights as how well each of these approximation algorithm would perform in practical applications.

To obtain better insights, it is desirable to compare these algorithms using numerical experiments and this paper takes up this task. In particular, we design and carry out a large number of numerical experiments on randomly generated sensors and sites with various densities. we show that greedy LP-rounding provides better approximation results than both randomized LP-rounding and greedy set-cover selection. We also show that the solutions produced by randomized LP-rounding are unstable. That is, running the randomized LP-rounding algorithm at different times on the same set of data will produce fluctuating results of wide spans, where the cost differences can be as large as 20%.

Next, we devise a new approximation algorithm using a convex combination of greedy LP-rounding and greedy set-cover selection. We call our new algorithm *alpha-beta approximation*. We show that alpha-beta approximation provides feasible solution to the MCPC problem. We then show that, through a large number of experiments on randomly-generated targets and sites with different densities, alpha-beta approximation provides better approximation results than all previous approximation algorithms. In particular, the actual approximation ratios of alpha-beta approximation in our experiments never exceed 1.07, and it provides up to 14.86% improvement over the best approximation using previous algorithms.

This paper is structured as follows. Section 2 describes the MCPC problem, greed set-cover selection, greedy LP-rounding, and randomized LP-rounding. Section 3 presents alpha-beta approximation. Section 4 describes experiment settings and provides numerical results. Section 5 presents final remarks and open problems.

2   Preliminaries

Let R denote a set of targets spread across a 3D (or 2D) geographical region and S a set of sites to place sensors in the proximity of targets, where R and S may or may not intersect. Targets and sites are represented as 3D (or 2D) points.

Let $\langle t_1, \ldots, t_\ell \rangle$ be ℓ types of sensors with sensing radius $\langle r_1, \ldots, r_\ell \rangle$ and monetary costs $\langle c_1, \ldots, c_\ell \rangle$, where $r_1 < \cdots < r_\ell$. We assume that a sensor can only be placed on a point, and each point can only be occupied by at most one sensor. We also assume that there is an unlimited supply for each type of sensor. Moreover, we assume that S is fully usable to R; that is, for every site j there is at least one target i and one sensor type t_v such that i falls in the sensing range of a type-t_v sensor placed at site j.

The basic form of the MCPC problem is to select sensors and sites to place these sensors, such that every target in R is covered by at least σ sensors and that the total monetary cost of the selected sensors is minimum, where $\sigma \geq 1$ is a given integer.

Denote by S_j^v the set of targets that can be covered by a type-t_v sensor placed at site j. Let c_v be the cost of set S_j^v. Then solving the MCPC problem is equivalent to solving the weighted set multicover problem, which is known to be Max-SNP-complete.

Let $|R| = n$ and $|S| = m$. For simplicity, we label targets and sites as $R = \{1, 2, \ldots, n\}$ and $S = \{1, 2, \ldots, m\}$. Denote by $d(i,j)$ the Euclidean distance between target $i \in R$ and site $j \in S$. Let

$$E_v = \{(i,j) \mid 0 \leq d(i,j) \leq r_v, \ i \in R, \ j \in S\}, \ v = 1, \ldots, \ell.$$
$$E_v[i] = \{j \mid (i,j) \in E_v\}, \ i = 1, \ldots, n.$$
$$E_v'[j] = \{i \mid (i,j) \in E_v\}, \ j = 1, \ldots, m.$$

Note that $S_j^v = E_v'[j]$. Solving the MCPC problem is equivalent to solving the following ILP problem, where x_j^v is a 0-1 variable indicating the number of type-t_v sensor placed at site j:

$$\text{Minimize} \ \sum_{j \in S} \sum_{v=1}^{\ell} c_v \cdot x_j^v$$

$$\text{Subject to} \ (\forall i \in R) \sum_{v=1}^{\ell} \sum_{j \in E_v[i]} x_j^v \geq \sigma, \tag{1}$$

$$(\forall j \in S) \sum_{v=1}^{\ell} x_j^v \leq 1. \tag{2}$$

A feasible solution of this ILP model is also referred to as a σ-*cover*.

Greedy set-cover selection, greedy LP-rounding, and randomized LP-rounding approximation algorithms have the following approximation ratio upper bounds r:

1. For greedy set-cover selection [RV99],

$$r = H_d = \sum_{i=1}^{d} \frac{1}{i} = 1 + O(\log d),$$

   where d is the largest number of targets that can be covered by a sensor, namely, $d = \max_{j \in S, \ 1 \leq v \leq \ell} |E_v'[j]|$.

2. For greedy LP-rounding [WZ06, WZ08],

$$r = f - \sigma + 1,$$

   where f is the largest number of sensors that cover a target, namely, $f = \max_{i \in R}(\sum_{v=1}^{\ell} |E_v[i]|)$.

3. For randomized LP-rounding [Vaz01],

$$r = O(\log n).$$

Greedy Set-Cover Selection

We say that a target is σ-*covered* if it is covered by at least σ sensors. The greedy set-cover selection selects the largest set with the smallest cost at each step as follows:

1. Set $C \leftarrow \emptyset$, $S' \leftarrow \{S_j^v \mid 1 \leq j \leq m \text{ and } 1 \leq v \leq \ell\}$, and $A \leftarrow R$.
2. Choose an S_j^v from S' such that $c(S_j^v)/|a(S_j^v)| = \min_{S_i^u \in S'}\{c(S_i^u)/|a(S_i^u)|\}$, where $a(S_j^v) = S_j^v \cap A$ is the set of targets in S_j^v that are still active; namely, these targets are not σ-covered yet at this point.
3. Set $C \leftarrow C \cup S_j^v$, remove from A all the targets that are σ-covered, and remove S_j^v from S'.
4. If $A \neq \emptyset$, go back to Step 2.
5. Output C.

Greedy LP-Rounding

A simple form of greedy LP-rounding is as follows:

1. Solve the LP-relaxation of the ILP model by allowing variables x_j^v to take real values between 0 and 1.
2. Let $S^* = \{x_j^{v,*} \mid x_j^{v,*} > 0, 1 \leq j \leq m, \text{ and } 1 \leq v \leq \ell\}$ be the optimal solution to the LP model. Sort S^* in non-increasing order to produce a sorted list L^*.
3. Select a variable from L^* one at a time, round it to 1, until a σ-cover is obtained, where variables not selected are set to 0.

Randomized LP-Rounding

Treat each value $x_j^{v,*} \in (0,1]$ in the optimal solution S^* to the LP model as a probability. We use a biased coin to select set S_j^v with probability $x_j^{v,*}$ for all j and v; i.e. set $x_j^v = 1$ if its corresponding biased coin toss turns to head, and set $x_j^v = 0$ otherwise. This forms a sub-collection of sets. Repeat this process independently $k \log n$ times and compute the union of all the sub-collections of sets, where k is a constant such that $(1/e)^{k \log n} \leq 1/(4n)$. When $\sigma = 1$, it can be shown [Vaz01] that the resulting collection of sets from the union is, with high probability, a σ-cover with an approximation ratio of $O(\log n)$.

We will show in Section 4.2 that randomized LP-rounding does not produce stable results. In particular, our numerical experiments show that it produces fluctuating results on the same set of data with as much as 20% difference from different executions. Thus, randomized LP-rounding may only have theoretical interests.

3   Alpha-Beta Approximation

We observe that in greedy LP-rounding, we can obtain a better approximation by also considering greedy set-cover selection. In other words, in addition to considering the value of $x_j^{v,*}$, we also consider how many targets a type-t_v sensor placed at site j can cover. Since $|a(S_j^v)|$ may be much larger than 1 and $x_j^{v,*} \leq 1$, we will consider $|a(S_j^v)|/K$ instead of $|a(S_j^v)|$ to balance two greedy strategies, where K is the largest number of targets a sensor can cover. That is,

$$K = \max_{1 \leq j \leq m, 1 \leq v \leq \ell} \{|E_v'[j]|\}.$$

We consider the convex combination of x_j^v and $|a(S_j^v)|/K$, namely, let

$$h(x_j^v) = \alpha \cdot x_j^v + \beta \cdot \frac{|a(S_j^v)|}{K},$$
$$\alpha + \beta = 1,$$
$$\alpha \geq 0,$$
$$\beta \geq 0.$$

We will then select S_j^v if $x_j^{v,*} > 0$ and $h(x_j^{v,*})$ is large.

Alpha-Beta Approximation Algorithm

1. Select values of α and β.
2. Set $C \leftarrow \emptyset$, $A \leftarrow R$ (the set of all targets), and $G \leftarrow \{x_j^v \mid x_j^{v,*} > 0\}$.
3. Let $x_j^v \in G$ and $h(x_j^{v,*}) = \max_{x_i^u \in G}\{h(x_i^{u,*})\}$.
4. Set $C \leftarrow C \cup S_j^v$ and $G \leftarrow G - \{x_j^v\}$.
5. Remove from A all the targets that become σ-covered, and compute $a(S_j^v) = S_j^v \cap A$ for all $1 \leq j \leq m$ and $1 \leq v \leq \ell$.
6. If $A \neq \emptyset$, goto Step 3.
7. Output C.

Clearly, setting x_j^v to 1 for all $x_j^{v,*} > 0$ provides a σ-cover. Thus, the alpha-beta approximation algorithm guarantees a σ-cover.

We note that the alpha-beta approximation is the same as greedy set-cover selection when $\alpha = 0$, and is the same as greedy LP-rounding when $\beta = 0$. When $\alpha \neq 0$ and $\beta \neq 0$, we note that the alpha-beta approximation algorithm may select a variable x_j^v that will not be selected by greedy LP-rounding or greedy set-cover selection. In our numerical experiments, this phenomenon have happened. Thus, it is possible that, by selecting α and β appropriately, the alpha-beta approximation can produce better results than greedy LP-rounding and greedy set-cover selection. Our numerical experiments confirm this observation.

4 Numerical Experiments and Performance Analysis

We describe our settings for numerical experiments and present numerical results on ILP, alpha-beta approximation, greedy LP-rounding, greedy set-cover selection, and randomized LP-rounding.

4.1 Experiment Settings

In our experiments, we use three types of sensors A, B, and C, where $\langle r_A, r_B, r_C \rangle = \langle 15, 25, 40 \rangle$ and $\langle c_A, c_B, c_C \rangle = \langle 200, 350, 580 \rangle$. Targets and sites are generated in a 300×300 area, where targets are generated uniformly and independently at random. For each target generated, 5 sites are generated uniformly and independently at random within the radius of 20 of the target. This allows all three types of sensors to be evenly selected in the optimal solutions. Experiments are carried out with $\sigma = 1, 2, 3$ on a variety of target density for each value of σ, from sparse to dense, with $n = 100, 200, 300, 400, 500,$ and 600.

4.2 Fluctuating Behavior of Randomized LP-Rounding

Figure 1 is a sample of fluctuating behavior of randomized LP-rounding from 20 executions on the same set of 600 targets, where $\sigma = 3$. Our experiments show that, when $\sigma \geq 2$ and $n \geq 200$, there is an up to 20% difference in the results produced by randomized LP-rounding from different executions on the same set of data.

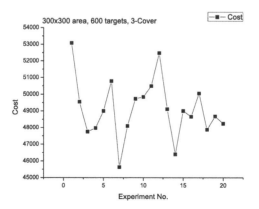

Fig. 1. Fluctuating behavior of randomized LP-rounding

4.3   Cost Curves in Terms of α

The values of α and β determine how much the LP solution and set-cover selection will influence the final decision. We show that, through numerical experiments, the value of α should be roughly reciprocal of K. For example, we observe that, when $K \leq 20$, choosing $\alpha = 0.6$ is better. When $K \geq 25$, choosing $\alpha = 0.2$ is better. Fig. 2 shows two examples of cost curves in terms of α.

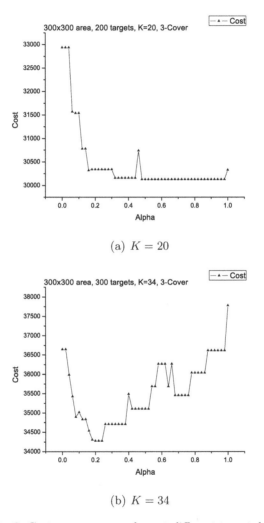

(a) $K = 20$

(b) $K = 34$

Fig. 2. Cost curves vs. α values at different target density

4.4   Variation of Alpha-Beta Approximation

The alpha-beta approximation algorithm runs in polynomial time, but it is slower than greedy LP-rounding. This is because calculating

Table 1. Comparisons of running time and results between original alpha-beta approximation and its variation

number of targets	σ	original time $(10^{-3}$ $s)$	variation time $(10^{-3}$ $s)$	original result	variation result
100	1	40	10	8680	8680
200	1	90	30	10150	10150
300	1	420	410	11950	11950
400	1	920	910	12900	12900
500	1	1720	1720	12940	12940
600	1	2110	2110	12960	12960
100	2	90	10	15940	15940
200	2	470	300	21150	21150
300	2	1400	1340	23370	23370
400	2	1560	1470	24190	23610
500	2	3100	2900	24820	24240
600	2	4570	4420	25200	25200
100	3	200	20	26680	26680
200	3	600	490	30130	30130
300	3	1690	1440	34280	34280
400	3	2720	2510	35500	35500
500	3	5410	4740	37980	37800
600	3	5620	5380	38210	38210

$$h(x_j^{v,*}) = \max_{x_i^u \in G}\{h(x_i^{u,*})\}$$

involves counting active targets for each set. If we can avoid doing this calculation as much as we can without losing accuracy, we can reduce computing time of the algorithm. For example, when $x_j^{v,*}$ is closer to 1 in an LP solution, S_j^v is more likely to be selected in the ILP solution. Thus, we may choose an appropriate threshold value t and select S_j^v directly when $x_j^{v,*} \geq t$.

Our numerical experiments show that when $t = 0.9$ and $\sigma > 1$, the variation of alpha-beta approximation can reduce much running time while producing almost the same result as (and at time even slightly better than) the original alpha-beta approximation. The variation is more effective when the density of targets is low, for there would be more $x_j^{v,*}$ close to 1 in the LP solution. Table 1 compares the running time and results generated by the original alpha-beta algorithm and its variation with $t = 0.9$.

4.5   Performance Comparisons

In all of our experiments, except for greedy set-cover selection, all approximation algorithms generate result is less than 7 seconds. Computing optimal solutions take much longer time and it takes a number of days of running time when n is large. When $\sigma > 1$, the solution produced by alpha-beta approximation has the actual approximation ratio in the range between 1.01 to 1.07.

Table 2. Performance Comparison of all algorithms with $\sigma = 2$

n	LP	OPT	$set\text{-}cover$	r_{sc}	$LP\text{-}round.$	r_{lp}	
100	15760	15760	17680	1.121827	16340	1.036802	
200	19791.61	19880	23800	1.197183	22710	1.142354	
300	21593.5	21980	26810	1.219745	25810	1.174249	
400	21513	22450	27830	1.239644	27730	1.235189	
500	21928.7	23020	28490	1.237619	27810	1.20808	
600	22307.7	23920	29410	1.229515	28840	1.205686	
	$Rand\text{-}LP$ $rounding$	r_{rlp}	$alpha\text{-}beta$ $original$	$r_{\alpha\beta}$	$alpha\text{-}beta$ $variation$	$r'_{\alpha\beta}$	Imp
100	16140	1.024112	15940	1.011421	15940	1.011421	1.24%
200	23640	1.189135	21150	1.063883	21150	1.063883	6.87%
300	29010	1.319836	23370	1.063239	23370	1.063239	9.45%
400	29980	1.335412	24190	1.077506	23610	1.05167	14.86%
500	31060	1.349262	24820	1.078193	24240	1.052997	12.84%
600	32220	1.346990	25200	1.053512	25200	1.053512	12.62%

Table 2 shows the optimal solution and the approximation solution, for $\sigma = 2$, of greedy set-cover selection, greedy LP-rounding, randomized LP-rounding, original alpha-beta approximation, variation of alpha-beta approximation, and the improvement of alpha-beta over LP-rounding. Here r_{sc}, r_{lp}, r_{rlp}, $r_{\alpha\beta}$, and $r'_{\alpha\beta}$ denote, respectively, the approximation ratio of the greedy set-cover selection, greedy LP-rounding, randomized LP-rounding, alpha-beta approximation, and alpha-beta variation. We use Imp to denote the improvement of alpha-beta variation over greedy LP-rounding.

Figure 3 compares the cost from solutions generated by each algorithm, i.e., the ILP model, greedy set-cover selection, the greedy LP-rounding, randomized LP-rounding, and alpha-beta approximation with $\sigma = 1, 2, 3$, respectively. It shows that the alpha-beta approximation provides the best solution than any other approximation algorithm.

Figure 4 shows visualized solutions generated by the ILP model and the alpha-beta approximation for $n = 100$ targets.

5   Final Remarks and Open Problems

This paper presents alpha-beta approximation algorithm for the MCPC problem and provides numerical results that compares performance of the alpha-beta algorithm with other approximation algorithms. We show that alpha-beta approximation algorithm provides better solutions with up to 14.86% improvement over the best approximation algorithm previously known, and it does so efficiently. This indicates that, alpha-beta approximation, i.e., a convex combination of greedy LP-rounding and greedy set-cover selection is a promising new approach. There are a number of issues that warrant a further investigation.

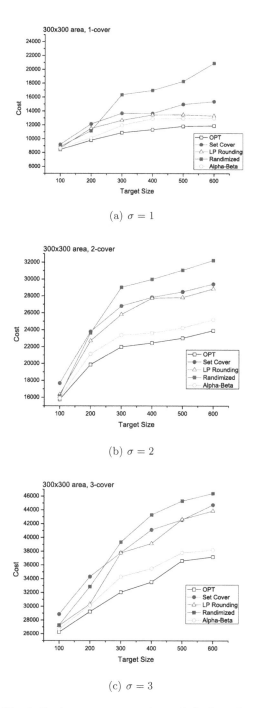

(a) $\sigma = 1$

(b) $\sigma = 2$

(c) $\sigma = 3$

Fig. 3. Performance comparison of all algorithms

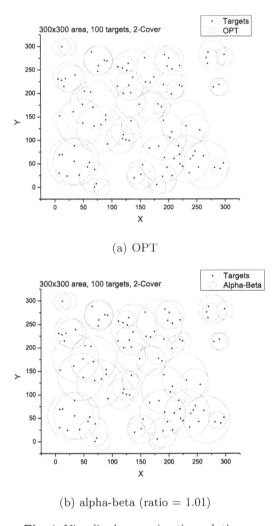

(a) OPT

(b) alpha-beta (ratio = 1.01)

Fig. 4. Visualized approximation solutions

For example, we suspect that the approximation ratio of alpha-beta approxima-tion would depend on the values of α and the approximation ratios of greedy LP-rounding and greedy set-cover selection.

Acknowledgements

This work was supported in part by NSF under grant CNS-0709001. Points of view in this document are those of the authors and do not necessarily represent the official position of NSF.

References

[CW04]   Cardei, M., Wu, J.: Coverage in Wireless Sensor Networks. In: Ilyas, M., Magboub, I. (eds.) Handbook of Sensor Networks, CRC Press, Boca Raton (2004)

[CIQ+02] Chakrabarty, K., Iyengar, S.S., Qi, H., Cho, E.: Grid coverage for surveillance and target location in distributed sensor networks. IEEE Trans. on Comput. 51(12), 1448–1453 (2002)

[Hoc97]   Hochbaum, D.: Approximating covering and packing problems: set cover, vertex cover, independent set, and related problems. In: Hochbaum, D. (ed.) Approximation Algorithms for NP-Hard Problems, PWS Publishing Company (1997)

[RV99]   Rajagopalan, S., Vazirani, V.V.: Primal-dual RNC approximation algorithms for set cover and covering integer programs. SIAM J. on Computing 28, 526–541 (1999)

[SX05]   Sahni, S., Xu, X.: Algorithms for wireless sensor networks. Intl. Jr. on Distr. Sensor Networks 1(1), 35–56 (2005)

[Vaz01]   Vazrani, V.V.: Approximation Algorithms. Springer, Heidelberg (2001)

[WZ06]   Wang, J., Zhong, N.: Efficient point coverage in wireless sensor networks. Journal of Combinatorial Optimization 11, 291–305 (2006)

[WZ08]   Wang, J., Zhong, N.: Minimum-cost sensor arrangement for achieving wanted coverage lifetime. International Journal on Sensor Networks (in press)

[YW07]   Yu, Z., Wang, J.: Reliable sensor arrangement for achieving wanted coverage lifetime with minimum cost. In: Proc. of the 2nd International Conference on Wireless Algorithms, Systems and Applications (WASA 2007), Chicago, August 2007, pp. 95–102. IEEE Computer Society Press, Los Alamitos (2007)

p-Percent Coverage in Wireless Sensor Networks

Yiwei Wu, Chunyu Ai, Shan Gao, and Yingshu Li

Georgia State University, Atlanta, GA 30303
{wyw,sgao,chunyuai,yli}@cs.gsu.edu

Abstract. Due to resource constraint of WSNs, it may be unnecessary or impossible to provide full coverage in many applications. Instead, partial coverage is enough to satisfy user requirements. Meanwhile, by applying partial coverage, network lifetime can be prolonged remarkably which is a primary goal of WSNs. In this paper, we investigate the *p-Percent Coverage Problem* which only requires that $p\%$ of the whole area to be monitored at any time and the *Connected p-Percent Coverage Problem* which enforces connectivity in addition. We propose two algorithms. One is *pPCA* which is a greedy algorithm to solve the *p-*Percent Coverage Problem. The other is *CpPCA-CDS*, which is a total distributed algorithm based on Connected Dominating Set to address Connected *p*-Percent Coverage Problem. The Sensing Void Distance after using *CpPCA-CDS* can be bounded by a constant. Theoretical analysis as well as simulation results are provided to evaluate our algorithms.

1 Introduction

In the near future, sensor nodes will be volume-produced at a very low cost. Low cost and small device size introduce limitations. With the quick improvement on the semiconductor technology, the limitations on computation and storage capabilities will not be concerned as constraints. However, Battery capacity only doubles in 35 years [1]. Therefore, how to conserve energy becomes one of the most important research topics for Wireless Sensor Networks (WSNs). WSNs are designed to collect information from the surveillance area. The sensing coverage is one indication of quality of surveillance. Some applications have strict coverage requirements where the *coverage* indicates how well the area is being monitored, *i.e.*, what is the percentage of the monitored area being watched. On the other hand, for some other applications, strict monitoring may not be necessary and prolonging network lifetime is their first concern. For example, in the rainy seasons, the occurrence possibility of forest fire is much lower than that in dry seasons. Therefore, fully monitoring every point of the monitored area is not necessary and taking care of a few important small regions may be enough so that more sensors could conserve energy. Relaxing the requirement from complete coverage to a percentage of coverage can result in dramatic increase in energy savings. In [2], Zhang and Hou have derived that the upper bound of the lifetime can increase by 15% for 99%-coverage and over 20% for 95%-coverage.

Y. Li et al. (Eds.): WASA 2008, LNCS 5258, pp. 200–211, 2008.

Hence, we also investigate the *p-Percent Coverage Problem* which only requires that *p* percentage of the whole area should be covered, and the *Connected p-Percent Coverage Problem* which requires connectivity in addition.

The rest of this paper is organized as follows. Section 2 surveys the related work. In section 3, we formally define the *p*-Percent Coverage problem (*PC*) and the Connected *p*-Percent Coverage problem (*CPC*). Section 4 presents the *pPCA* algorithm to solve the *PC* problem. In Section 5, *CpPCA-CDS* are proposed to solve the *CPC* problem. And theoretical analysis is also presented in this section as well. The simulation results are illustrated in Section 6. Finally, we conclude this paper in Section 7.

2   Related Work

Much effort has been spent for the full coverage problem of WSNs [3], [4], [5], [6], [7], [11], [9], [10] and [8]. A detailed survey can be found in [8].

Slijepcevic *et al* [3] investigate the full coverage problem by proposing an approach that partitions the sensors into mutually exclusive subsets such that the sensors in each subset can fully cover the monitored region. Their goal is to maximize the number of the subsets and only need to active one subset at any time. Cardei *et al* [4] considered full coverage by proposing an approximation algorithm for partitioning the sensors into the maximum number of disjoint dominating sets, where each disjoint dominating set can fully cover the monitored region. However, all of those works focused only on full coverage without taking into account the connectivity of sensors in each subset.

Another important issue in WSNs is connectivity. Once the sensors are deployed, they organize into a network that must be connected so that the information collected by sensor nodes could be relayed back to data sinks or query controllers. Zhou *et al* [5] generalized the connected, full coverage problem into the connected *k*-coverage problem. They tried to find a set of sensors such that each point in the monitored region is covered by at least *k* sensors in the set of selected sensors. In [6], Zhang *et al* claimed that if the communication range is at least twice the sensing range, a complete coverage of convex area implies connectivity of the working nodes. Wang *et al* in [7] generalized the result of [6] by showing that when the communication range is at least twice the sensing range, a *k*-covered network will result in a *k*-connected network. A new notation, information coverage based on accurate estimation, was proposed by Wang *et al* in [11]. A point is said to be completely information-covered if enough sensors exist to keep the estimation error lower than a predefined threshold. In order to prolong the network lifetime, some papers investigated the sensor scheduling problem. In [9], [10] the Sensor Scheduling for *k*-Coverage *SSC* problem was addressed and several greedy algorithms were proposed.

However, all works mentioned before address the full area coverage problem. There exist several works for the *p*-percent coverage problem. Although the concept of partial coverage was firstly mentioned in [6], their intention is for full coverage. They tried to cover the entire region fully at first, and then reduce the coverage percentage to a given threshold provided when it is impossible to have a full coverage by the living sensors.

Tian *et al* also proposed three location-free schemes in [19], including nearest-neighbor-based, neighbor-number-based and probability-based schemes. All those schemes work in rounds, and each sensor determines its own OFF-duty eligibility according to whether the nearest neighbor's distance, the minimal neighbor number or a randomly generated number is more than a threshold D, K or p respectively, which are chosen based on a statistical calculation given a desired coverage percentage loss. Since the coverage percentage is a statistical concept, it cannot be guaranteed above a desired threshold.

In [18], percentage coverage rather than complete coverage is selected as the design goal, and a location-based Percentage Coverage Configuration Protocol (PCCP) is developed to assure that the proportion of the sensing area after configuration to the original sensing area is no less than a desired percentage.

However, in order to simplify their works, almost all of those papers are based on the assumption that the communication range is at least twice the sensing range to achieve connectivity.

In [17], Liu *et al* studied the connected coverage problem with a given coverage guarantee. They first introduced the partial coverage concept and analyzed its properties for the first time in order to prolong the network lifetime. Then they presented a centralized heuristic algorithm which takes into account the partial coverage and sensor connectivity simultaneously. Initially, active sensors are selected randomly. Within each iteration, nodes in a chosen candidate path with the maximum gain are chosen. The algorithm continues until the whole area is θ-covered.

In [12], the authors proposed a $(1 + \ln(1 - q)^{-1})$-approximation linear programming algorithm for the case where a q-portion ($q\%$) of the monitored area need to be covered. Nevertheless, with a large q, the performance of this algorithm becomes worse and connectivity is not taken care of. Tan proposed a hexagon-based algorithm in [13]. The monitored area is separated into many small hexagon regions. The deployed sensors are grouped together according to the positions of their resident hexagon region. The percentage of the covered area is determined by the size of the hexagons and is unchangeable. Users cannot specify a desired percentage of the monitored area.

In this paper, we propose two algorithms *pPCA* and *CpPCA-CDS* to solve the *PC* and *CPC* problems. The main contribution of our work is that we consider the connectivity of the result set and do not need the assumption that communication range is at least twice the sensing range to achieve connectivity. And we show that the Sensing Void Distance after using *CpPCA-CDS* can be bound by a constant, which means our algorithm can achieve a good distribution of covered area. Also, considering that sensor nodes have very limited resources and unexpected events need to be handled, it is quite necessary to use distributed algorithms instead of centralized ones. Furthermore, Our work is the first one to introduce the concept of *CDS*, which is originally used in constructing routing topology, to address the p-percent coverage problem.

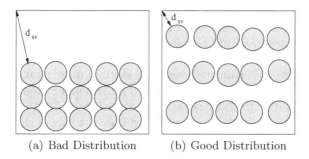

(a) Bad Distribution   (b) Good Distribution

Fig. 1. Distribution of Sensing Void area

3   Preliminaries and Problem Definition

In this section, some basic definitions are given.

Definition 1. *Consider a point t located at (x_t, y_t). If the Euclid distance between t and sensor s_i is less than or equal to s_i's sensing radius, that is, distance $(t, s_i) \leq r_s$, point t is covered by sensor s_i. Similarly, consider an area A and a set of sensors $S = s_1, s_2, \cdots, s_n$. If every point in A is covered by at least one sensor in S, we say that area A is covered by S. If there is a subset $S' \subseteq S$ such that the area covered by S' is not less than p percentage of the area of A, we call S' is a p percent cover of A. That is, A is p percent covered by S'. If the subgraph induced by S' is connected, we call S' is a connected p percent cover of A.*

Definition 2. *Average Region Coverage Degree $D_\varphi = N\pi r^2 / A_\varphi$, where φ is a region, N is the number of nodes deployed in region φ, r is the sensing range of the nodes and A_φ is the area of region φ.*

Definition 3. *Working Nodes Ratio $R_\varphi = n/N$, where n is the number of the working nodes who are currently responsible for the sensing task, and N is the total number of the nodes deployed in region φ.*

Definition 4. *Coverage Increment (CI) of node i C_i is the obtained coverage increment if node i becomes a working node.*

D_φ is used to measure the coverage density of a region. R_φ is an import attribute to measure algorithm performance. The smaller the R_φ, the better the performance. *CI* is another important parameter on selecting which nodes should be activated.

It is inevitable that there are some areas in the monitored region, called *sensing void* [17], in which no point can be covered by any chosen sensor because of the nature of partial coverage. Therefore, we define the sensing void distance to measure the distribution of the covered areas.

Definition 5. *Sensing Void Distance d_{sv} is the distance between a point in a sensing void and the nearest point covered by a active sensor.*

Sensing Void Distance is an important metric in terms of the quality of partial coverage, which will determine the coverage accuracy. As Figure 1 shows, Given the same p percentage, Figure 1(b) has better distribution of sensing void area than 1(a).

In this paper, we are mainly interested in static symmetric multi-hop WSNs. The topology of a network is represented as a general undirected graph, denoted as $G(V, E)$, where V is the node set and E is the edge set. That means two nodes u and v are neighbors in the network if and only if u and v can communicate with each other. We also assume that the whole area can be at least fully covered by all nodes in the network. In other words, there does not exist sensing void area if all nodes are activated. We now formally define the investigated problems as follows.

Definition 6. *p-Percent Coverage problem*: *Given a two-dimensional monitored region* A *whose area is* $\| A \|$ *and a sensor set* S *containing* N *sensors, the problem definition is as follows:*

> *Objective: Minimize* k
> *Subject to: W is a p percent cover of A*
> $k = \mid W \mid$

However, the obtained set W may not be connected. In real applications, it is necessary for W to be connected for data routing and fusion. Therefore, we define the *Connected p-Percent Coverage problem* as follows:

Definition 7. *Connected p-Percent Coverage problem*: *Given a area A, find a connected p percent cover W of A with minimum size.*

> *Objective: Minimize* k
> *Subject to: W is a connected p percent cover of A*
> $k = \mid W \mid$

4   *p*-Percent Coverage Algorithm (*pPCA*)

In this section, we introduce the p-Percent Coverage Algorithm (*pPCA*). In this algorithm, we use a coordinator such as a base station to control the activities of all the nodes. As we know, it is a reasonable strategy to assign one node as a controller and most work also adopt a controller to coordinate the behaviors of nodes in network. We assume every node is aware of its geographic position and sensing range after it is deployed in the monitored area. The base station serves as the coordinator and runs *pPCA* (Algorithm 1) to decide which nodes should be activated. Afterwards, the base station broadcasts this working node list. All nodes in this list stay active and others go to sleep.

Let W denote the cover set *pPCA* plans to construct, and p_s is the percentage specified by application. Each time, the node with the maximum (e_i, C_i) is added to W, where e_i is the remaining energy of node i and C_i is the coverage increment of node i. e_i can be low, medium or high. e_i is given the highest priority because of the observation that the total network lifetime can be extended when the nodes with more remaining energy are used first. ID_i is the ID of node i. It is possible that some redundant nodes present in W. In order to obtain a set W with a smaller size, those redundant nodes should be removed.

Algorithm 1. $pPCA(p_s, S)$

1: Sort nodes in non-increasing order in S based on their (e_i, ID_i)
2: $W \leftarrow \phi$ ▷ Constructing p-Percent Coverage Set W
3: **while** $p < p_s$ **do**
4:     **if** Find a node i with the highest (e_i, C_i) in $S \setminus W$ **then**
5:         $p \leftarrow p + C_i/A$
6:         $W \leftarrow W + i$
7:     **else**
8:         **return false**;
9:     **end if**
10: **end while**
11:   ▷ Optimizing p-Percent Cover W
12: Sort nodes in non-decreasing order in W based on their (e_i, ID_i)
13: Remove node i in W if $p > p_s$ after removing i
14: **return** W

Theorem 1. *The time complexity of* pPCA *is* $O(N^2)$, *where* N *is the number of all the deployed nodes.*

Proof. In *pPCA*, sorting nodes takes $O(N \log N)$ time. At line 4 in Algorithm 1, it needs $O(N)$ time to find node i with the highest (e_i, C_i). The total time of the while loop at line 3 is $O(N^2)$. We also need $O(N^2)$ time to optimize V. Therefore, the time complexity of *pPCA* is $O(N^2)$.

Lemma 1. *For set-cover problem, the Greedy-Set-Cover is a* $(\ln|X| + 1)$-*approximation algorithm, where* X *is the total number of points which are required to be covered.*

Proof. This Lemma has been proved in [14].

Since PC problem is NP-hard, the performance ratio of $pPCA$ is given as follows.

Theorem 2. *Denote the obtained set by* pPCA *as* W *and the optimal solution as* opt. *Then* $|W| \leq (\ln(p\lambda) + 1)|opt|$, *where* λ *is the number of the points in the whole area.*

Proof. Divide the whole monitored area into grids. We assume the grids are small enough such that there exist no grids which are partially covered by any sensor. In this way, grids can be converged into points. We use *point* here instead of *tiny grid* for convenience. Let λ be the number of the points in the whole area. We assume that λ is bounded. As we know, given a λ, pPCA is a Greedy-Set-Cover algorithm. Herein, according to Lemma 1 $|W| \leq (\ln(p\lambda) + 1)|opt|$.

5   Connected p-Percent Coverage Algorithm ($CpPCA$-CDS)

Network connectivity needs to be guaranteed for routing and data querying. However, almost all of the algorithms that considered connectivity were based on the assumption that the communication range is at least twice the sensing range. In our paper, we relax this assumption and claim that communication range is not related to sensing range. This relaxation give our algorithms more flexibility to be used in general WSNs. Before we introduce our algorithm $CpPCA$-CDS, we still need to point out that there exists a naive method, called $CpPCA$-DFS, which is based on the DFS search. The main idea of $CpPCA$-DFS is that nodes with maximum C_i will be explored firstly, till p percentage is satisfied. At the first sight, this scheme is very simple and efficient. However, the major defect of this scheme is that the distribution of covered area is very poor, in other words the Sensing Void Distance, which is an important metric to evaluate the quality of p percent coverage as Figure 1 shows, is very large. In this section, we propose a distributed algorithm to solve the CPC problem, and guarantee that the sensing void distance is bounded by a constant.

Connected Dominating Set (CDS) is originally used in constructing routing topology. Given a graph $G(V, E)$ where V is the node set and E is the edge set, a *Connected Dominating Set (CDS)* C is a subset of V such that every node that is not in C must have at least a neighbor in C and C is connected. The nodes in C are called dominators, the others are called dominatees. According to this definition, intuitively, we know that all covered areas are much distributed in the whole area, that means the Average Sensing Void Distance by using CDS is shorter than others. Furthermore, in the next section, we show that the sensing void distance can be bounded by a constant.

Our algorithm $CpPCA$-CDS has three phases:

1. Construct a CDS using [20]
2. Build a DFS search tree in CDS
3. Add nodes to meet p percent coverage

5.1   Phase 1

There exist some centralized and distributed algorithms for constructing CDSs, such as [15], [16] and [20]. In here, we choose [20], since this algorithm is completely distributed, can be easily implemented and can obtain a CDS with a small size. Now we briefly introduce the basic idea of [20]. The root first builds a BFS tree. After that, the root marks itself black and broadcasts a BLACK message. After receiving either BLACK or WHITE messages from all parents, a node u who has the highest $W(N, ID)$ among its sibling nodes that have not decided their states marks itself white if it receives at least one BLACK message from its parents or siblings. Otherwise, it sends a CONNECT message to its parent who has the highest $W(N, ID)$. Both of the parent node and u mark themselves black and broadcast BLACK messages. After all nodes decide their colors, all black nodes form a CDS.

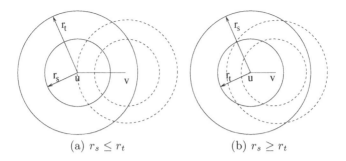

Fig. 2. The Sensing Void Distance can be bounded by a constant

5.2   Phase 2

In this phase, the root which is elected in the phase 1 starts a DFS search, and calculates the p percentage which can be covered so far. However, this DFS search is restrict only in CDS nodes. Then the root passes the token to its CDS children u. The u also augments the p percentage and passes the token to its CDS children, and so on. After all nodes in CDS have been exploited, the root get the token and also know the total p percentage which can be covered by only CDS nodes so far.

5.3   Phase 3

In this phase, the root first checks that p percent coverage is met or not. If p is satisfied, then we are done. Otherwise, the root chooses a dominatee neighbor v with maximum C_i, updates the p percentage and passes the token to v. When v get this token, it still chooses a dominatee neighbor w with maximum C_i if it has one and passes the token to w. Otherwise, v sends this token back to its parent u, and u chooses another dominatee neighbor to augment. This procedure stops when p percentage is satisfied.

Theorem 3. *The set* W *obtained from* CpPCA-CDS *is connected and can* p-*percent cover the whole area.*

Proof. Firstly, we construct a *CDS* W first. According to the property of a *CDS*, one node which is not in W must have a neighbor in W and W is connected. Therefore, whenever a node is added to W, W keeps connected. The phase 2 and 3 guarantee that the W can p-percent cover the whole area.

Theorem 4. *The Sensing Void Distance after using CpPCA-CDS can be bounded by* $|r_{t_{max}} - r_{s_{min}} + r_{s_{max}}|$, *where* $r_{t_{max}}$ *is the maximum transmission range,* $r_{s_{min}}$ *and* $r_{s_{max}}$ *are minimum and maximum sensing range respectively. For a homogeneous network in which every node has the same transmission range and the same sensing range, the sensing void distance can be bounded by* r_t.

Proof. Assume that point q is in a sensing void area. Since the whole area can be fully covered by all nodes in the network, as we mentioned before, there exists a node v that can cover point q. In this situation, v is not a activate node, otherwise, q can not in a sensing void area. Since we build a CDS first, there must exists a dominator node u which dominates node v. Now, We examine four mutually exclusive cases from Figure 2. We are not going to prove all cases, since all methods to prove them is quite same.

- Case 1: $r_s \leq r_t$. In this case, we assume that the sensing range is less than transmission range for both of two nodes u and v. Therefore, the maximum distance d_q from q to the circle, whose centre is u and radius is r_{s_u}, is $l_{uv} - r_{s_u} + r_{s_v}$. Since $l_{uv} \leq \min(r_{t_u}, r_{t_v})$, $d_q \leq \min(r_{t_u}, r_{t_v}) - r_{s_u} + r_{s_v}$.
- Case 2: $r_s \geq r_t$. In this case, we assume that the sensing range is larger than transmission range for both of two nodes u and v. Therefore, the maximum distance d_q from q to the circle, whose centre is u and radius is r_{s_u}, is $r_{s_v} - (r_{s_u - l_{uv}})$, which is less than $\min(r_{t_u}, r_{t_v}) - r_{s_u} + r_{s_v}$

We use the same idea to prove the case 3 in which $r_{s_u} \leq r_{t_u}$ and $r_{s_v} \geq r_{t_v}$, and case 4 in which $r_{s_u} \geq r_{t_u}$ and $r_{s_v} \leq r_{t_v}$. From here, we can show that $d_q \leq |\min(r_{t_u}, r_{t_v}) - r_{s_u} + r_{s_v}|$ for all cases. Therefore, d_q can be bounded by $|r_{t_{max}} - r_{s_{min}} + r_{s_{max}}|$, which is a constant.

Theorem 5. *The time complexity of algorithm* CpPCA-CDS *is* $O(|V| + |E|)$ *and the message complexity is* $O(|V|)$, *where* $|V|$ *is the number of the nodes in the whole network,* $|E|$ *is the total number of edges and* Δ *is the maximum node degree.*

Proof. In [15], the time and message complexities to construct a CDS are$O(Diam)$ and $O((\Delta + 1)|V|)$ respectively. After constructing the CDS, in the phase 2, the maximum running time for a DFS search is $O(|V| + |E|)$, and the message complexity is $O(|V|)$. In phase 3, we still need $O(|V| + |E|)$ running time and $O(|V|)$ messages. Therefore, the total time complexity is $O(|V| + |E|)$, the total message complexity is $O(|V|)$.

6   Simulations and Performance Evaluation

In this section, we present simulation results to evaluate our algorithms. The nodes were randomly and uniformly deployed in an area A of $400m \times 400m$. According to the Definition 2 of D_φ which represent the coverage density, we can determine how many sensors should be deployed. The transmission range and the sensing range of nodes are *100m* and *50m*, respectively. All the results were averaged over 100 simulation runs.

6.1   Results of pPCA, CpPCA-CDS and CpPCA-DFS

Figure 3 shows the relation between working nodes ratio and p under different D_φ. From Figure 3, we can conclude that the average working node ratio of

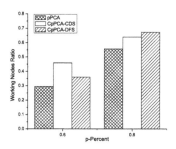 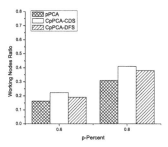

(a) *Working Nodes Ratio* when $D_\varphi = 3$

(b) *Working Nodes Ratio* when $D_\varphi = 5$

Fig. 3. Comparison of *pPCA*, *CpPCA-CDS* and *CpPCA-DFS*

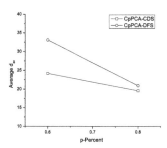 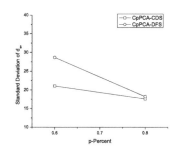

(a) Average Sensing Void Distance

(b) Standard Deviation of Sensing Void Distance

Fig. 4. Comparison of Sensing Void Distance after using *CpPCA-CDS* and *CpPCA-DFS* when $D_\varphi = 5$

pPCA is the smallest among three algorithms because it does not require the connectivity of the working node set. Although *CpPCA-CDS* has a larger average working nodes ratio than *CpPCA-DFS* does, it has an advantage over the latter that it achieve a good distribution of covered area.

When D_φ is fixed, the larger *p*, the larger working nodes ratio. This is obvious since we need more sensors to *p*-percent cover the whole area with large *p*. One can observe from the Figure 3 that there is only 6.8% difference between the working nodes ratio of *pPCA* and its expected value.

6.2 Comparison of Sensing Void Distance After Using CpPCA-CDS and CpPCA-DFS

As we mentioned, the sensing void distance is an important metric to evaluate the quality of the *p* percent coverage. Now, we compare both the average sensing void distance and Standard Deviation of sensing void distance. From Figure 4(a), one can observe that the average sensing void distance after using *CpPCA-CDS* is much smaller than *CpPCA-DFS*. On the other hand, from Figure 4(b), the Standard Deviation of Sensing Void Distance after using *CpPCA-CDS* is also much smaller than *CpPCA-DFS*. From here, we show that distribution of coverd area after using *CpPCA-CDS* is much better than *CpPCA-DFS* especially for low p percentage.

7   Conclusion

In this paper, we investigate the p-Percent Coverage Problem and Connected p-Percent Coverage Problem in WSNs. We propose two distributed algorithms *pPCA* and *CpPCA-CDS* to address the *PC* and *CPC* problems respectively. We introduce the concept of *CDS* to address *CPC* problem for the first time. The Sensing Void Distance after using *CpPCA-CDS* can be bounded by a constant. The simulation results show that our algorithms can obtain good results. Since location is required in most of the work about the partial coverage, it is better to investigate this problem using location-free algorithms. That is an interesting direction for our future work.

Acknowledgement

This work is partly supported by NSF CAREER Award under Grant No. CCF-0545667

References

1. Powers, R.: Batteries for Low Power Electronics. Proceedings of the IEEE (1995)
2. Zhang, H., Hou, J.C.: On Deriving the Upper Bound of α-Lifetime for Large Sensor Networks. In: MobiHoc 2004, Roppongi, Japan, May 2004, pp. 121–132 (2004)
3. Slijepcevic, S., Potkonjak, M.: Power Efficient Organization of Wireless Networks. In: Proc. of IEEE International Conference on Communications (June 2001)
4. Cardei, M., MacCallum, D., Cheng, X., Min, M., Jia, X., Li, D., Du, D.-Z.: Wireless Sensor Networks with Energy Efficient Organization. Journal of Interconnection Networks 3(3-4), 213–229 (2002)
5. Zhou, Z., Das, S., Gupta, H.: Connected K-Coverage Problem in Sensor Networks. In: Proc. of Intl. Conf. on Computer Communications and Networks (ICCCN) (2004)
6. Zhang, H., Hou, J.C.: Maintaining Sensing Coverage and Connectivity in Large Sensor Networks. In: Proc. of the 2004 NSF International Workshop on Theoretical and Algorithmic Aspects of Sensor, Ad Hoc Wireless, and Peer-to-Peer Networks (2004)
7. Wang, X., Xing, G., Zhang, Y., Lu, C., Pless, R., Gill, C.D.: Integrated Coverage and Connectivity Configuration in Wireless Sensor Networks. In: Proc. of 1st ACM Conference on Embedded Networked Sensor Systems (2003)
8. Cardei, M., Wu, J.: Energy-Efficient Coverage Problems in Wireless Ad Hoc Sensor Networks. Computer Communications (2005)

9. Gao, S., Vu, C., Li, Y.: Sensor Scheduling for k-coverage in Wireless Sensor Networks. In: Proceedings of the 2nd International Conference on Mobile Ad-hoc and Sensor Networks (2006)
10. Li, Y., Gao, S.: Designing k-coverage Schedules in Wireless Sensor Networks. Journal of Combinatorial Optimization (2007)
11. Wang, B., Chua, K.C., Srinvasan, V., Wang, W.: Sensor Density for Complete Information Coverage in Wireless Sensor Networks. In: Römer, K., Karl, H., Mattern, F. (eds.) EWSN 2006. LNCS, vol. 3868, Springer, Heidelberg (2006)
12. Berman, P., Calinescu, G., Shah, C., Zelikovsky, A.: Efficient Energy Management in Sensor Networks. In: Ad Hoc and Sensor Networks, ser. Wireless Networks and Mobile Computing, vol. 2, Nova Science Publishers (2005)
13. Tan, H.: Maximizing Network Lifetime in Energy-Constrained Wireless Sensor Network. In: Proceedings of the 2006 international conference on Wireless communications and mobile computing, pp. 1091–1096 (2006)
14. Cormen, T.H., Leiserson, C.E., Rivest, R.L., Stein, C.: Introduction to Algorithms, 2nd edn. McGraw-Hill Book Company, New York (2003)
15. Li, Y., Zhu, S., Thai, M., Du, D.: Localized Construction of Connected Dominating Set in Wireless Networks. In: NSF International Workshop on Theoretical Aspects of Wireless Ad Hoc, Sensor and Peer-to-Peer Networks (2004)
16. Wan, P., Alzoubi, K.M., Frieder, O.: Distributed Construction of Connected Dominating Set in Wireless Ad hoc Networks. In: Preceedings of 21th Annual Joint Conference of the IEEE Computer and Communication Societies (2002)
17. Liu, Y., Liang, W.: Approximate Coverage in Wireless Sensor Networks. In: The IEEE Conference on Local Computer Networks 30th Anniversary (LCN 2005), pp. 68–75 (2005)
18. Bai, H., Chen, X., Ho, Y., Guan, X.: Percentage Coverage Configuration in Wireless Sensor Networks. In: Pan, Y., Chen, D.-x., Guo, M., Cao, J., Dongarra, J. (eds.) ISPA 2005. LNCS, vol. 3758, pp. 780–791. Springer, Heidelberg (2005)
19. Tian, D., Georganas, N.D.: Location and Calculation-Free Node-Scheduling Schemes in Large Wireless Sensor Networks. Ad Hoc Networks 2, 65–85 (2004)
20. Kim, D., Wu, Y., Li, Y., Zou, F., Du, D.-Z.: Constructing Minimum Connected Dominating Sets with Bounded Diameters in Wireless Networks. IEEE Transactions on Parallel and Distributed Systems (accepted, 2008)

Prolonging Network Lifetime for Target Coverage in Sensor Networks

Yuzhen Liu and Weifa Liang

Department of Computer Science, The Australian National University
Canberra, ACT 0200, Australia

Abstract. Target coverage is a fundamental problem in sensor networks
for environment monitoring and surveillance purposes. To prolong the
network lifetime, a typical approach is to partition the sensors in a network for target monitoring into several disjoint subsets such that each
subset can cover all the targets. Thus, each time only the sensors in one
of such subsets are activated. It recently has been shown that the network lifetime can be further extended through the overlapping among
these subsets. Unlike most of the existing work in which either the subsets were disjoint or the sensors in a subset were disconnected, in this
paper we consider both target coverage and sensor connectivity by partitioning an entire lifetime of a sensor into several equal intervals and
allowing the sensor to be contained by several subsets to maximize the
network lifetime. We first analyze the energy consumption of sensors in
a Steiner tree rooted at the base station and spanning the sensors in a
subset. We then propose a novel heuristic algorithm for the target coverage problem, which takes into account both residual energy and coverage
ability of sensors. We finally conduct experiments by simulation to evaluate the performance of the proposed algorithm by varying the number of
intervals of sensor lifetime and network connectivity. The experimental
results show that the network lifetime delivered by the proposed algorithm is further prolonged with the increase of the number of intervals
and improvement of network connectivity.

1 Introduction

Recent advances in microelectronic technology have made it possible to construct compact and inexpensive wireless sensors. Networks consisting of sensors
have received significant attention due to their potential applications from civil
to military domains [1]. The main constraint of sensors however is their low
finite battery energy, which limits the network lifetime and impairs the network
quality. To prolong the network lifetime, energy-efficiency in the design of sensor
network protocols is thus of paramount importance.

In this paper, we consider a sensor network used for monitoring targets. One
efficient method of reducing the energy consumption of sensors and thereby
prolonging the network lifetime is to partition the sensors in the network into
multiple subsets (sensor covers) such that each subset can cover all the targets.

Y. Li et al. (Eds.): WASA 2008, LNCS 5258, pp. 212–223, 2008.

Thus, each time only one sensor cover is activated for a certain period and only the sensors in the active sensor cover are in active mode, while all the other sensors are in sleep mode to save energy. Meanwhile, the communication subgraph induced by the base station and the active sensors must be connected so that the sensed data can be collected at the base station for further processing. Although most of the existing work related to target coverage mainly focused on finding disjoint sensor covers, Cardi *et al* [2] recently presented a novel approach that allows sensor covers not to be disjoint, i.e., a sensor can be included in up to p sensor covers, where $p \geq 1$. Thus, sensor lifetime is partitioned into p equal intervals and each interval corresponds to the duration of the sensor in the active sensor cover. The network lifetime is then the sum of the duration of the sensor covers that can be found in the network. They showed that the network lifetime can be further prolonged by allowing the overlapping among sensor covers. However, they only considered target coverage but sensor connectivity in a sensor cover was not considered.

While taking both target coverage and sensor connectivity into consideration, the energy consumption among the sensors will not be identical, because some sensors consume more energy on both sensing and transmission, whereas the others consume energy on transmission only. This imbalance on energy consumption may result in the situation where no further sensor covers exist but the total residual energy among the sensors in the network is still quite high. For example, consider a network consisting of the base station B, sensors $s_1, s_2, s_3, s_4, s_5, s_6$ and targets t_1, t_2, t_3 (see Fig. 1(a)). Assume that p is 2, both the initial energy capacity and sensor lifetime are 1 units, and each sensor consumes $1/3$ and $2/3$ units of energy for sensing and transmitting data for 1 time unit. A collection of connected sensor covers will be built until there are no further connected sensor covers, where each sensor cover can last at least $1/p$ time units. To built a connected sensor cover, a sensor cover is found first, followed by the construction of a Steiner tree rooted at the base station and spanning the sensors in the cover. The Steiner trees are activated successively and each tree lasts $1/2$ time units. Thus, a terminal node and a non-terminal node in a Steiner tree consume $(1/3 + 2/3) * 1/2 = 1/2$ and $2/3 * 1/2 = 1/3$ units of energy, respectively. In Fig. 1, the trees with dotted edges are the Steiner trees and the values in the brackets are the residual energies of sensors after the trees last $1/2$ time units.

A sensor cover $\mathcal{C}_1 = \{s_1, s_4\}$ can be found and the correspondent Steiner tree is built for data transmission (see Fig. 1(b)). If $\mathcal{C}_2 = \{s_2, s_4\}$ is chosen as a sensor cover after the tree in Fig. 1(b) lasts $1/2$ time units, then no further Steiner trees lasting $1/2$ time units can be found for transmitting the sensed data for target t_1 to the base station, since the sensed data for target t_1 has to be transferred to the base station through sensor s_2 but s_2 has no sufficient residual energy for $1/2$ time units transmission (see Fig. 1(c)). Thus, the network lifetime is 1 time unit since only two connected sensor covers can be found, and the total residual energy left in the network are 3 units. However, we can see that the network lifetime can be further prolonged by balancing residual energy among sensors. One such approach is to include sensors with high residual energy

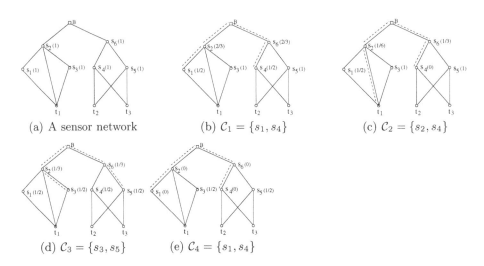

(a) A sensor network   (b) $\mathcal{C}_1 = \{s_1, s_4\}$ (c) $\mathcal{C}_2 = \{s_2, s_4\}$

(d) $\mathcal{C}_3 = \{s_3, s_5\}$ (e) $\mathcal{C}_4 = \{s_1, s_4\}$

Fig. 1. An example for balancing the residual energy among sensors

into sensor covers. Then, there are the other two sensor covers $\mathcal{C}_3 = \{s_3, s_5\}$ and $\mathcal{C}_4 = \{s_1, s_4\}$ (see Fig. 1(d) and (e)) after the tree in Fig. 1(b) has been activated for $1/2$ time units. The network lifetime is thus extended to 1.5 time units and the total residual energy of the sensors is only 1 unit (see Fig. 1(e)).

Motivated by the above example and the work of Cardi *et al* in [2], we here consider both target coverage and sensor connectivity by partitioning sensor lifetime into several equal intervals and allowing a sensor to be contained by more than one sensor cover. However, there are several essential differences between theirs and ours. (i) They only focused on target coverage and whether or not the communication subgraph induced by a sensor cover is connected has not been taken into account, while we consider both target coverage and sensor connectivity. (ii) They only considered the energy consumption on data sensing, and assume that all the sensors in a sensor cover consume the same amount of energy. Such an assumption is reasonable for the case where sensor connectivity is not considered. In practice, this assumption however is inapplicable, because the energy required for data transmission usually is one order of magnitude greater than that for data sensing. Thus constructing a connected sensor cover is challenging, which depends on not only the current coverage ability but also the residual energy of sensors that would not be known in advance. It is crucial to balance the energy consumption on sensing and transmission among the sensors while constructing a connected sensor cover. In this paper, we assume that the data transmission is message-length independent, i.e., each sensor transmits the same volume of data to its parent no matter how much data it received from its children, and both sensed data and transmitted data are a unit-length.

Related work. In recent years, tremendous effort on network lifetime maximization and energy efficiency has been taken for target coverage, sensor connectivity and network fault toleration [3]-[13]. For example, Cardei *et al* [3] dealt with the target coverage problem by organizing sensors into disjoint sensor covers, and allowing only one of the covers to be activated at any given time. The network lifetime is then prolonged through the maximization of the number of sensor covers. Chakrabarty *et al* [4] studied the problem by employing grid coverage and presenting an integer linear programming solution. Wang *et al* [5] investigated the problem by adopting two methods (disk coverage and sector coverage) to explore the sensor density required for guaranteeing a localization error bound over the sensing field. Dong *et al* [6] considered load balancing while guaranteeing that each target is monitored by at least one sensor with an objective to minimizing the maximum energy consumption of sensors for its targets, and proposed centralized and distributed algorithms for it. Cai *et al* [7] studied the problem of multiple directional sensor covers by proving its NP-completeness, followed by proposing heuristic solutions. Wang *et al* [8] studied the target coverage problem by proposing a randomized algorithm, which takes much less time than that of the algorithms in [7]. The connected target coverage problem is considered in [9,10]. Jaggi *et al* [9] proposed an algorithm by decomposing the set of sensors into disjoint subsets such that each subset can guarantee target coverage and sensor connectivity, and their algorithm was within a constant factor of the optimum. Lu *et al* [10] addressed the problem through the adjustment of sensing ranges of sensors and devised a distributed algorithm to determine the sensor range of each individual sensor. By taking routing robustness into account, Li *et al* [11] considered the k-connected target coverage problem by showing its NP-hardness, and they instead designed two heuristic algorithms for the problem. Zhou *et al* [12] introduced the k_1-connected, k_2-cover problem, and proposed a distributed algorithm for the problem by inactivating all the other sensors that are not in the active sensor cover.

2   Preliminaries

System model. A wireless sensor network consisting of n_s homogeneous sensors that are randomly deployed in a region of interest to monitor n_t targets is modelled by an *undirected graph* $G(V, E)$, where $V = V_S \cup V_T$ and $E = E_S \cup E_T$. V_S is the set of sensors and V_T is the set of targets with $|V_S| = n_s$ and $|V_T| = n_t$, and E_S is the set of edges between sensors and E_T is the set of edges between sensors and targets. For each pair of sensors s_i and s_j, there is an edge (s_i, s_j) in E_S if and only if they are within the *transmission range* r_t of each other. For each pair of sensor s and target t, there is an edge (s, t) in E_T if and only if t is within the *sensing range* r_s of s. A *sensor cover* is a set of sensors that can cover all the targets. A *connected sensor cover* is a sensor cover such that the subgraph induced by the base station and the sensors in the cover is connected. *The lifetime of a sensor cover* is the time at which the first sensor in the cover fails due to its energy expiration. *The lifetime of a Steiner tree* is the time when its first node fails. A *sensor cover with lifetime threshold* δ is such a sensor cover that its lifetime is at least δ time units, and similarly *a Steiner tree with lifetime threshold* δ is such a Steiner tree that its lifetime is at least δ time units, where

$\delta > 0$. We assume that each sensor has identical initial energy capacity IE, and e_s and e_t are the energy consumptions for sensing and transmitting a unit-length data respectively, then a sensor can last at least $\tau = IE/(e_s + e_t)$ time units. We further assume that a sensor can participate in at most p sensor covers. Without loss of generality, τ and p are referred to as *sensor lifetime* and *lifetime granularity*, respectively. Thus, the sensor lifetime of a sensor is partitioned into p intervals, and each interval corresponds to the duration of the corresponding sensor cover in which the sensor belongs to.

Problem definition. Given a sensor network $G(V, E)$ consisting of sensors and targets, *the target coverage problem* is to find a collection of connected sensor covers such that the sum of the lifetimes of these sensor covers is maximized. Note that it is not necessary that sensor covers be disjoint, which means that there may exist overlapping between two sensor covers.

3   Algorithm for Target Coverage Problem

In this section, we first provide an overview of the algorithm for the target coverage problem. We then explore the energy consumption of sensors in a Steiner tree corresponding to a connected sensor cover. We finally present a heuristic algorithm for the problem of concern.

Overview of the algorithm. For a given sensor network $G(V, E)$, lifetime granularity p and sensor lifetime τ, we construct a collection $\{\mathcal{C}_1, \mathcal{C}_2, \cdots, \mathcal{C}_q\}$ of connected sensor covers such that the lifetime of each sensor cover is at least δ time units with an objective to maximizing the network lifetime $\delta * q$, where $p \geq 1$, $\delta(= \tau/p)$ is referred to as *lifetime threshold* and $q \geq 0$. Note that each sensor cover is activated for δ time units in order to allow a sensor to participate in more than one sensor cover.

The proposed algorithm proceeds iteratively as follows. The network lifetime is set to be zero initially. Within each iteration, if there is a connected sensor cover with lifetime threshold δ, then the network lifetime increases by δ time units. The construction of a connected sensor cover consists of two phases. Phase one is to find a sensor cover, and phase two is to construct a Steiner tree T' of a directed, edge-weighed auxiliary graph G' rooted at the base station and spanning the sensors in the sensor cover, where the lifetimes of both the sensor cover and the Steiner tree are at least δ time units. A Steiner tree T of G is derived from T'. The residual energy of the sensors in T is updated after T lasts δ time units. The algorithm continues until there are no further connected sensor covers with lifetime threshold δ in the network.

Energy consumption of the sensors in a routing tree. Since the construction of a connected sensor cover depends on the current network status including the residual energy of sensors, we now explore the energy consumption of sensors in a Steiner tree corresponding a connected sensor cover. To guarantee that the lifetime of a Steiner tree is at least δ time units, only those sensors with sufficient residual energy for δ time units sensing and transmission can be included in the tree as terminal nodes, and only the sensors with sufficient residual energy for δ

time units transmission can be included in the tree as non-terminal nodes. Let $\gamma = e_t/e_s$ be the ratio of the transmission energy consumption e_t to the sensing energy consumption e_s for a unit-length data, and $\theta(v) = U(v)/IE$ the energy utility ratio of sensor v, which is the ratio of the consumed energy $U(v)$ of v to the initial energy capacity IE. The introduction of γ and θ significantly simply the assumption related to the energy of sensors, and the following lemma shows the judgement on whether a sensor in the network has sufficient residual energy for δ time units sensing and/or transmission can be reduced to a proposition related only to γ and θ, and the updating of residual energy of sensors in a Steiner tree can be reduced to the updating of θ.

Lemma 1. *Given a sensor network $G(V, E)$, lifetime granularity p and sensor lifetime τ, assume that $\mathcal{C}$ is a sensor cover with lifetime threshold δ, and T is a Steiner tree with lifetime threshold δ rooted at the base station and spanning the sensors in $\mathcal{C}$, where $\delta = \tau/p$. Let $U(v)$ and $U'(v)$ be the consumed energy of sensor v before and after T last δ time units data sensing and transmission. $\theta(v) = U(v)/IE$, $\theta'(v) = U'(v)/IE$, and $\gamma = e_t/e_s$. If v is a terminal node in tree T, then $1 - \theta(v) \geq \frac{1}{p}$, and $\theta'(v) = \theta(v) + \frac{1}{p}$; Otherwise, $1 - \theta(v) \geq \frac{1}{p*(1+\frac{1}{\gamma})}$, and $\theta'(v) = \theta(v) + \frac{1}{p*(1+\frac{1}{\gamma})}$.*

Proof. If v is a terminal node in T, then v is in sensor cover $\mathcal{C}$, and v serves for both sensing and transmission for δ time units. The energy consumption of v is
$$\delta * (e_s + e_t) = \frac{\tau}{p} * (e_s + e_t) = \frac{\frac{IE}{e_s + e_t}}{p} * (e_s + e_t) = \frac{IE}{p}.$$
Since the lifetime of T is at least δ time units, the residual energy of sensor v is no less than the amount of energy $\frac{IE}{p}$, i.e. $IE - U(v) \geq \frac{IE}{p}$. Then, we have
$$1 - \theta(v) = 1 - \frac{U(v)}{IE} = \frac{IE - U(v)}{IE} \geq \frac{1}{p},$$
and
$$\theta'(v) = \frac{U'(v)}{IE} = \frac{U(v) + \frac{IE}{p}}{IE} = \frac{IE*\theta(v) + \frac{IE}{p}}{IE} = \theta(v) + \frac{1}{p}.$$
Otherwise, sensor v in T serves only for transmitting data from its children to its parent for δ time units. The transmission energy consumption of v is
$$\delta * e_t = \frac{\tau}{p} * e_t = \frac{\frac{IE}{e_s + e_t}}{p} * e_t = \frac{IE}{p*(1+\frac{e_s}{e_t})} = \frac{IE}{p*(1+\frac{1}{\gamma})}.$$
Similarly, the residual energy of sensor v is no less than the amount of energy $\frac{IE}{p*(1+\frac{1}{\gamma})}$, i.e. $IE - U(v) \geq \frac{IE}{p*(1+\frac{1}{\gamma})}$. Then, we have
$$1 - \theta(v) = 1 - \frac{U(v)}{IE} = \frac{IE - U(v)}{IE} \geq \frac{1}{p*(1+\frac{1}{\gamma})},$$
and
$$\theta'(v) = \frac{U'(v)}{IE} = \frac{IE*\theta(v) + \frac{IE}{p(1+\frac{1}{\gamma})}}{IE} = \theta(v) + \frac{1}{p(1+\frac{1}{\gamma})}.$$

Target coverage algorithm. For a given lifetime granularity p, how to construct connected sensor covers in the network to maximize the number q of the connected sensor covers is critical to prolong the network lifetime, since the network lifetime is $\delta * q$. On one hand, it is expected that the total energy consumption in a sensor cover be minimized so that more sensor covers can be found. On the other hand, balancing the residual energy of sensors in the network by adding the sensors with high residual energy to a sensor cover can result in a larger q as shown by the example in Fig. 1. Thus, we focus on finding a connected sensor cover with lifetime threshold δ such that the total energy consumption in the cover is minimized and the minimum residual energy among the sensors is maximized.

Let $\mathcal{C}$ be a sensor cover in construction at phase one. To minimize the energy consumption of the sensors in $\mathcal{C}$, we should include a sensor into $\mathcal{C}$ if it covers a larger number of uncovered targets by $\mathcal{C}$. On the other hand, to maximize the minimum residual energy of the sensors in $\mathcal{C}$, we should include a sensor that has more residual energy into $\mathcal{C}$. However, a sensor covering a larger number of uncovered targets may have small residual energy, while another sensor covering few uncovered targets may have substantial residual energy. It has been shown that a heuristic based on the exponential function of energy utility at nodes is very useful in the design of algorithms for unicasting and multicasting in ad hoc networks [14,15], which can balance the energy consumption among nodes. We here use an exponential function of energy utility at sensors and propose a heuristic function that tradeoffs residual energy and coverage ability of sensors. For a sensor $v \in V_S - \mathcal{C}$, we define $gain_{\mathcal{C}}(v)$ as the ratio of an exponential function of the energy utility at v to the number of uncovered targets by $\mathcal{C}$ as follows. If $N_{\mathcal{C}}(v) \neq 0$, $gain_{\mathcal{C}}(v) = a^{\theta(v)}/N_{\mathcal{C}}(v)$, otherwise, $gain_{\mathcal{C}}(v) = \infty$, where $a > 1$, and $N_{\mathcal{C}}(v)$ is the number of uncovered targets by $\mathcal{C}$, i.e., $N_{\mathcal{C}}(v) = |\{t \mid t \in V_T, (v,t) \in E, \forall_{v' \in \mathcal{C}} (v',t) \notin E\}|$. It can be seen that a sensor v with more residual energy and a larger number of uncovered targets has a smaller value of $gain_{\mathcal{C}}(v)$. Thus, a sensor with smallest value of $gain$ has the highest priority to be included in $\mathcal{C}$.

The construction of a sensor cover with lifetime threshold δ proceeds greedily. It maintains a subset $\mathcal{C}$ of V_S and a set $T_{\mathcal{C}}$ that consists of the targets covered by $\mathcal{C}$. Initially, both $\mathcal{C}$ and $T_{\mathcal{C}}$ are empty sets. Each time a sensor v is selected and added to $\mathcal{C}$ if it has the smallest value of $gain_{\mathcal{C}}(v)$ among the sensors that are not in $\mathcal{C}$ and sufficient residual energy for at least δ time units sensing and transmission, i.e., $1 - \theta(v) \geq 1/p$, following Lemma 1. The iteration continues until $\mathcal{C}$ is a sensor cover or no more sensors can be added to $\mathcal{C}$.

Having a sensor cover $\mathcal{C}$ with lifetime threshold δ, we construct a Steiner tree with lifetime threshold δ rooted at the base station and spanning the sensors in $\mathcal{C}$. Since the residual energy among the sensors in the network is non-identical, the data transmission between a pair of neighboring sensors may be asymmetry. For example, sensor u may have sufficient residual energy to transmit data to sensor v but v has no sufficient residual energy for transmitting data to u for at least δ time units, given an edge $(u,v) \in E_S$. Thus, we introduce a directed, edge-weighted auxiliary graph $G'(V', E', w')$ based on the residual energy of the sensors in the network $G(V, E)$, which is constructed as follows. $V' = V$. For each $(u,v) \in E_S$, a directed edge $\langle u, v \rangle$ is added to E' if v has sufficient residual energy for at least δ time units sensing and/or transmission, that is, (i) $v \in \mathcal{C}$, since the lifetime of $\mathcal{C}$ is at least δ time units and thus each sensor in $\mathcal{C}$ has sufficient residual energy for at least δ time units sensing and transmission; or (ii) $v \notin \mathcal{C}$ and $1 - \theta(v) \geq 1/(p * (1 + \frac{1}{\gamma}))$, i.e., v is not in $\mathcal{C}$ but has sufficient residual energy for at least δ time units transmission, following Lemma 1. Since the tree is rooted at the base station, the direction of data transmission is reverse to that of the directed edges in the tree. The weight $w'(u, v)$ assigned to edge $\langle u, v \rangle$ is an exponential function $b^{\theta(v)}$, where $b > 1$. After a directed, edge-weighted auxiliary graph G' has been constructed, an approximate, minimum edge-weighted Steiner tree T' of G' rooted at the base station and spanning the sensors in $\mathcal{C}$ is built. A tree T of G used for data sensing and transmission is then derived from T' and the connected sensor cover is composed of the sensors in T. The detailed algorithm, referred to as algorithm TC, is as follows.

Algorithm $\mathtt{Target\_Coverage}$ (G, p)
Input: sensor network G; lifetime granularity p; sensor lifetime τ.
Output: network lifetime $lifetime$.
begin
1. $lifetime = 0$;
2. while $(true)$ do
3. $\mathcal{C} = \emptyset$; /* the sensor cover */
4. $T_{\mathcal{C}} = \emptyset$; /* the set of targets covered by $\mathcal{C}$ */
5. $flag = true$;
6.   while $(flag \wedge (T_{\mathcal{C}} \neq V_T))$ do
7.   find a sensor $v_0 \in V_S - \mathcal{C}$ such that
                $1 - \theta(v_0) \geq \frac{1}{p}$ and $gain_{\mathcal{C}}(v_0) = min\{gain_{\mathcal{C}}(v) \mid v \in V_S - \mathcal{C}\}$;
8.   if v_0 exists then
9. $\mathcal{C} = \mathcal{C} \cup \{v_0\}$; /* v_0 is included in $\mathcal{C}$ */
10. $T_{\mathcal{C}} = T_{\mathcal{C}} \cup \{t \mid (v_0, t) \in E\}$;
          /* add the uncovered targets by $\mathcal{C}$ into $T_{\mathcal{C}}$ */
       else
11. $flag = false$;
       endif;
    endwhile;
12. if $(flag)$ then /* a sensor cover is found */
13.   construct the auxiliary graph $G'(V', E', w')$;
14.   find an approximate, minimum, edge-weighted Steiner tree T' of G'
          rooted at the base station and spanning the sensors in $\mathcal{C}$;
15.   if $(\mathrm{T}'$ *does not exist*$)$ then
16.   return $lifetime$;/* no further connected sensor covers can be found */
          endif;
17. $V(\mathrm{T}) = V(\mathrm{T}')$;
18. $E(\mathrm{T}) = E(\mathrm{T}')$;
19. $lifetime = lifetime + \frac{\tau}{p}$;
20.   if v is a terminal node in tree T then
21. $\theta(v) = \theta(v) + \frac{1}{p}$;
          else
22. $\theta(v) = \theta(v) + \frac{1}{p*(1+\frac{1}{\gamma})}$.
          endif /* update the energy utility ratio at nodes */

else
23.   return $lifetime$; /* no sensor covers can be found */
    endif
    endwhile
end

4   Performance Evaluation

We evaluate the performance of algorithm TC in terms of the network lifetime through experimental simulations. We first compare the network lifetime delivered by the algorithm for different lifetime granularities. We then evaluate the algorithm for various network connectivity among sensors. We finally analyze the impact of the connectivity between targets and sensors on the network lifetime.

Simulation environment. We assume that the monitored region is a $10m \times 10m$ square in which n_s sensors and n_t targets are deployed randomly by using the NS-2 simulator [16], where n_s is set to be 100 and n_t varies from 10 to 50 with increment of 10. We also assume that the transmission range r_t of sensors is 3, 4, 5, 6 or 7. Each target in the sensor network is randomly connected to the sensors and has a node degree between $l_b * n_s$ and $u_b * n_s$, where l_b varies from 0.1 to 0.25 with increment of 0.05 and u_b is set to be 0.3. We further assume that sensor lifetime τ is 1000 time units and lifetime granularity p is 1, 4 or 8. In addition, γ, a and b in the definition of function $gain$ and w' are set to be 2.

We generate 10 different topologies for n_s sensors and 10 different topologies for n_t targets randomly. For each of the 10 target topologies, each of the sensor topologies is applied to it and thus 100 different network topologies are generated for the given n_s and n_t. The value of the network lifetime in all figures is the mean of the network lifetimes delivered by applying the proposed algorithm to 100 different network topologies.

Performance evaluation of various algorithms. We first evaluate the network lifetime delivered by the algorithm for different lifetime granularities when $r_t = 3$, $l_b = 0.1$ and $u_b = 0.3$. It can be seen from Fig. 2, that the algorithm with

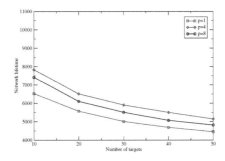

Fig. 2. Comparison of network lifetime delivered by algorithm TC for various lifetime granularities when $r_t=3$, $l_b = 0.1$ and $u_b = 0.3$

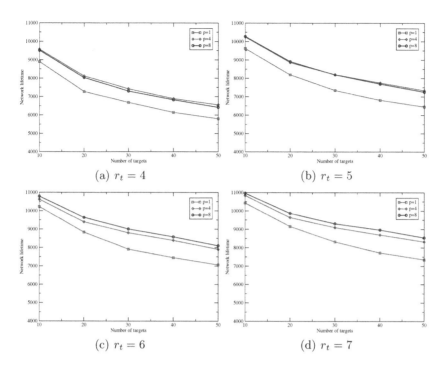

(a) $r_t = 4$ (b) $r_t = 5$

(c) $r_t = 6$ (d) $r_t = 7$

Fig. 3. Comparison of network lifetime delivered by algorithm TC for various lifetime granularities and transmission ranges when $l_b = 0.1$ and $u_b = 0.3$

lifetime granularity $p > 1$ outperforms the algorithm with $p = 1$. For example, the network lifetime delivered by the algorithm with $p = 4$ or $p = 8$ increases by around 20% or 14% when $n_t = 10$, compared the case where $p = 1$. The reason behind is that the sensor covers found when $p = 1$ are disjoint, whereas a sensor can be included in more than one sensor cover as long as they have sufficient residual energy for at least δ time units sensing and/or transmission when $p > 1$. It also can be seen from this figure that the network lifetime delivered by the algorithm with $p = 4$ is longer than that with $p = 8$, which implies that the network lifetime is not necessarily proportional to the value of p for all network topologies. There are two factors that can cause the shorter network lifetime in algorithm TC. One is the sensor cover failure in Step 23 of the algorithm, where no further sensor covers can be found. The other is the connected sensor cover failure in Step 16 of the algorithm, where no further connected sensor covers exist. In our simulations, we found that more network disfunction is caused by the connected sensor cover failure when $p = 8$ than $p = 4$. For example, the percentage of network disfunction caused by the connected sensor cover failure is 76% when $p = 8$, whereas only 50% of the network disfunction is caused by the connected sensor failure when $p = 4$ for the case of $n_t = 10$. Thus, the network connectivity among the sensors is the bottleneck of the network lifetime for a finer lifetime granularity. We then evaluate the algorithm for various p and

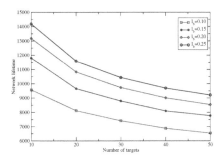

Fig. 4. Network lifetime delivered by algorithm TC for various connectivity between sensors and targets when $r_t = 4$, $p = 4$ and $u_b = 0.3$

network connectivity by increasing the transmission range r_t, i.e., improving the network connectivity among the sensors. As shown in Fig. 3, the performance of the algorithm is improved with the growth of the transmission range from 4 to 7 for various p. Particularly, the difference of the network lifetimes delivered by the algorithm with $p = 4$ and $p = 8$ drops with the growth of the transmission range, and the algorithm with $p = 8$ outperforms that with $p = 4$ for the case where the transmission range r_t is 6 or 7 (Fig. 3(c) and (d)). This is due to the fact the percentage of network disfunction caused by the connected sensor cover failure drops, with the improvement of network connectivity among the sensors, and the network lifetime delivered by the algorithm with larger p can be prolonged. In addition, similar to the case where $r_t = 3$ in Fig. 2, the network lifetime delivered by the algorithm with $p = 1$ is not as long as that with $p = 4$ or $p = 8$. We finally analyze the impact of the connectivity between sensors and targets on the network lifetime delivered by the algorithm when $r_t = 4$ and $p = 4$. We change l_b from 0.1 to 0.25 with the increment of 0.05 while u_b keeps 0.3. Fig. 4 shows that the network lifetime is prolonged further for the networks with improved network connectivity between sensors and targets, since the degree increase of each target results in the size decrease of each sensor cover and thereby more sensor covers can be found.

5   Conclusions

In this paper, we considered the target coverage problem in sensor networks by partitioning the sensor lifetime into p equal intervals and allowing the overlapping among sensor covers. We first analyzed the energy consumption of sensors in a Steiner tree corresponding to a connected sensor cover. We then proposed a novel heuristic algorithm for the problem of concern that took into account both residual energy and coverage ability of sensors. We finally conducted experiments by simulation to evaluate the performance of the proposed algorithm for various lifetime granularities p and network connectivity. The experimental results showed that the algorithm with $p > 1$ outperforms that with $p = 1$, and the network lifetime delivered by the proposed algorithm is further prolonged with the increase of lifetime granularity and improvement of network connectivity.

Acknowledgement. It is acknowledged that the work by the authors is fully funded by a research grant No:DP0449431 by Australian Research Council under its Discovery Schemes.

References

1. Akyildiz, I.F., Su, W., Sankarasubramaniam, Y., Cayirci, E.: A Survey on Sensor Networks. IEEE Communications Magazine 40(8), 102–114 (2002)
2. Cardei, M., Thai, M.T., Li, Y., Wu, W.: Energy-Efficient Target Coverage in Wireless Sensor Networks. IEEE INFOCOM, 1976–1984 (2005)
3. Cardei, M., Du, D.-Z.: Improving Wireless Sensor Network Lifetime through Power Aware Organization. Wireless Networks 11(3), 333–340 (2005)
4. Chakrabarty, K., Iyengar, S., Qi, H., Cho, E.: Grid Coverage for Surveillance and Target Location in Distributed Sensor Networks. IEEE Trans. on Computers 51(12), 1448–1453 (2002)
5. Wang, W., Srinivasan, V., Wang, B., Chua, K.: Coverage for Target Localization in Wireless Sensor Networks. IEEE Trans. on Wireless Communications 7(2), 667–676 (2008)
6. Dong, Q., Shukla, A., Shrivastava, V., Agrawal, D., Banerjee, S., Kar, K.: Load Balancing in Large-Scale RFID Systems. IEEE INFOCOM, 2281–2285 (2007)
7. Cai, Y., Lou, W., Li, M.: Target-Oriented Scheduling in Directional Sensor Networks. IEEE INFOCOM, 1550–1558 (2007)
8. Wang, J., Niu, C., Shen, R.: Randomized Approach for Target Coverage Scheduling in Directional Sensor Networks. In: Lee, Y.-H., Kim, H.-N., Kim, J., Park, Y.W., Yang, L.T., Kim, S.W. (eds.) ICESS 2007. LNCS, vol. 4523, pp. 379–390. Springer, Heidelberg (2007)
9. Jaggi, N., Abouzeid, A.: Energy-Efficient Connected Coverage in Wireless Sensor Networks. In: The Forth Asia International Mobile Computing Conf., pp. 77–86 (2006)
10. Lu, M., Wu, J., Cardei, M., Li, M.: Energy-Efficient Connected Coverage of Discrete Targets in Wireless Sensor Networks. In: Lu, X., Zhao, W. (eds.) ICCNMC 2005. LNCS, vol. 3619, pp. 43–52. Springer, Heidelberg (2005)
11. Li, D., Cao, J., Liu, M., Zheng, Y.: K-Connected Target Coverage Problem in Wireless Sensor Networks. IEEE INFOCOM, 1976–1984 (2005)
12. Zhou, Z., Das, S., Gupta, H.: Fault Tolerant Connected Sensor Cover with Variable Sensing and Transmission Ranges. In: IEEE Commmications Society Conference on Sensor and Ad Hoc Communications and Networks, pp. 594–604 (2005)
13. Wang, W., Srinivasan, V., Chua, K., Wang, B.: Energy-Efficient Coverage for Target Detection in Wireless Sensor Networks. In: The Sixth International Symposium on Information Processing in Sensor Networks, pp. 313–322 (2007)
14. Kar, K., Kodialam, M., Lakshman, T.V., Tassiulas, L.: Routing for Network Capacity Maximization in Energy-Constrained Ad Hoc Networks. IEEE INFOCOM, 673–681 (2003)
15. Liang, W., Guo, X.: On-line Multicasting for Network Capacity Maximization in Energy-Constrained Ad Hoc Networks. IEEE Transactions on Mobile Computing 5(9), 215–1227 (2006)
16. The Network Simulator-ns-2, http://www.isi.edu/nsnam/ns

An Environmental Monitoring System with Integrated Wired and Wireless Sensors

Jue Yang, Chengyang Zhang, Xinrong Li, Yan Huang,
Shengli Fu, and Miguel Acevedo

University of North Texas, Denton, Texas 76207, USA
{jy0074,cz0022,xinrong,huangyan,fu,acevedo}@unt.edu

Abstract. Wireless sensor networks (WSN) technology has great potential to revolutionize many science and engineering domains. We present a novel environmental monitoring system with a focus on the overall system architecture for seamless integration of wired and wireless sensors for long-term, remote, and near-real-time monitoring. We also present a unified framework for sensor data collection, management, visualization, dissemination, and exchange, conforming to the new Sensor Web Enablement standard. Some initial field testing results are also presented.

1 Introduction

Environmental monitoring applications have become major driving forces for wireless sensor networks (WSN) [1,2]. Ecological and environmental scientists have been developing a cyber infrastructure in the form of environmental observatories, consisting of a variety of sensor systems, sophisticated computational resources and informatics, to observe, model, predict, and ultimately help preserve the health of the natural environment. Such an infrastructure becomes more important as we recognize that the natural world is inextricably linked to the human society to form an extremely complex ecosystem. WSN-based environmental monitoring systems promise to enable domain scientists to work with data sets of unprecedented fine spatial and temporal resolution.

In this paper, we present a novel environmental monitoring cyber infrastructure that features (1) soil moisture monitoring with flexible spatial coverage and resolution, (2) seamlessly integrated wired and wireless sensors, (3) long-term autonomous remote near-real-time monitoring, (4) publicly available web services for sensor data visualization and dissemination, and (5) remote system monitoring and maintenance. Despite significant advances in recent years, there are still many challenging issues to be addressed to fulfill the full potential of the emerging WSN technology. The importance of empirical study of WSN has been widely recognized by the research community and considerable efforts have been put into the development and deployment of WSN testbed for various practical applications, including environmental monitoring [1,2,3,4,5,6,7,8]. However, there are many limitations in the existing WSN testbed deployments. For example, many deployments are in controlled environments, instead of real-life

Y. Li et al. (Eds.): WASA 2008, LNCS 5258, pp. 224–236, 2008.

application environments. Most of the deployments are designed for short-term experiments or proof-of-concept demonstration purposes, instead of long-term autonomous operation to support ongoing work by domain scientists and practitioners. Most of the deployments are stand-alone WSN-only system, monitoring very few environmental parameters, instead of being a part of the ever-growing environmental monitoring cyber infrastructure. As a result, it is difficult to consolidate a broad range of sensor data systematically to study the cross-correlation among various environmental parameters.

In this research, we intend to fill the aforementioned gaps in WSN research by developing a soil moisture monitoring WSN system and integrating it into the Texas Environmental Observatory (TEO) infrastructure [9] for long-term operation. The new WSN-based soil moisture monitoring system will mainly support long-term hydrologic monitoring and modeling research. Increasing urbanization brings changes to the land cover of a given drainage area, which in turn increase the quantity of water flowing overland and decrease the amount of time to reach peak flow [10], increasing in some cases the risk of flash floods. Hydrologic models are helpful in predicting how changes in land cover in rapidly urbanizing areas translate into changes in the stream flow regime. These models require inputs that are difficult to measure over large areas, especially variables related to storm events, such as soil moisture antecedent conditions and rainfall amount and intensity. The new monitoring system that we are developing is ideally suited for such applications.

The rest of the paper is organized as follows. In Section 2, we identify key design requirements for the new environmental monitoring system. The overall system architecture is described in Section 3. Then, in the next three sections, we describe three major components of the new system, including WSN for soil moisture monitoring, gateway and telemetry system for remote near-real-time environmental monitoring, and web services for data visualization and dissemination. In Section 7, some initial field test results are presented. At last, the paper is closed with a summary and future work in Section 8.

2   Design Requirements

In this research, we develop a new environmental monitoring system to significantly improve the capability and usability of the system that is currently deployed at the Greenbelt Corridor (GBC) Park, operated by Texas Parks and Wildlife Departments, Denton, Texas. Some key design requirements are identified in this section.

Soil moisture monitoring with flexible spatial coverage and resolution: In the existing system, all sensors are deployed inside a small fence-enclosed area, a situation typical of many environmental monitoring systems. There is a need to provide flexibility to extend the spatial coverage and adjust the spatial resolution of soil moisture sensors. The spatial coverage of the system is limited by the physical limitation on the length of the cable connecting the sensors to the datalogger. In contrast, the spatial coverage and resolution of WSN can be conveniently configured to be meaningful to domain scientists.

Integration of WSN with existing environmental observatories: Despite its limitations, traditional environmental monitoring systems with various wired sensors are capable of accomplishing many monitoring tasks, and substantial investments are in place to monitor temperature, wind speed and direction, rainfall, and solar radiation. Drastically replacing existing systems with an immature technology such as WSN is considered unacceptable to many domain scientists and practitioners. Therefore, it is important to introduce the new WSN technology without disrupting ongoing operation of environmental observatories through seamless integration of wired and wireless sensors.

Long-term, autonomous, remote, near-real-time environmental monitoring: It has been recently recognized that many ecological and environmental studies should implement long-term data collection and management. In addition, many environmental observatories are deployed in remote areas that are inconvenient to access for data retrieval and system deployment and management. Thus, environmental monitoring systems need to be survivable in extreme environmental and weather conditions for long-term operation with limited human intervention, which makes energy harvesting and energy efficiency major design considerations. Near-real-time sensor data collection is another important feature of monitoring systems to support time-sensitive environmental studies, which necessitates a convenient yet reliable long-haul wireless link.

Publicly available web services for sensor data visualization and dissemination: It is important to make data publicly available to benefit a broad range of entities such as environmental researchers, local citizens and government policy makers, and K-12 teachers and students. In addition, explosive growth of environmental data collected by a variety of sensors in long-term operation necessitates a unified framework for data collection, management, integration, visualization, and dissemination. Such a framework should conform to standards, such as the Sensor Web Enablement (SWE) standard proposed by the Open Geographic Consortium (OGC) [11], to enable data exchangeability and interoperability.

Remote system status monitoring and management: For environmental monitoring systems deployed in remote areas, remote monitoring of system status is extremely useful for system development, debugging, and maintenance purposes. Thus, various system status data need to be carefully defined and collected together with environmental sensor data. Furthermore, it is important to remotely adjust system configurations, update and upgrade software programs.

3   Overall System Architecture

The new environmental monitoring system can be divided into four major layers as shown in Fig. 1, including physical data layer, logical data layer, web presentation layer, and user layer. Such a layered approach makes it possible to implement the system in a flexible, extensible, and efficient way. At the physical data layer, a variety of sensors are employed to monitor environmental parameters. Sensor

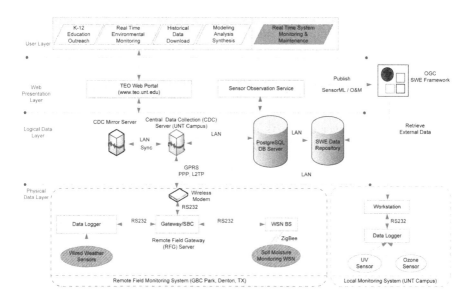

Fig. 1. System architecture of the integrated environmental monitoring system

data are transmitted from monitoring site to a Central Data Collection (CDC) Server. To address the design requirements, we incorporate a GPRS modem for wireless telemetry, a single-board computer (SBC) operating as a Remote Field Gateway (RFG) Server, and WSN for distributed soil moisture monitoring. The RFG Server provides effective control, management, and coordination of two relatively independent sensor systems, i.e., a traditional datalogger-based wired sensor system and the WSN-based wireless sensor system. The Linux-based RFG Server also supports remote login to allow maximum remote manipulation of the devices in the field such as the SBC, datalogger, and WSN.

At the logical data layer, sensor data collected from distributed monitoring stations are stored in a PostgreSQL Database (DB) Server. The CDC Server acts as an intermediate component to hide the heterogeneity of different physical layer devices and support data validation required by the DB Server. The CDC Server and its mirror server also archive raw data on local file systems. Daemon programs running on the CDC Server pre-process the data before it is inserted into the database, and periodically perform synchronization tasks. A SWE-compliant data repository is installed to enable data exchange, accepting data from both internal DB Server and external sources through the OGC web services.

The web presentation layer consists of a web portal, TEO Online [9], and a sensor web implementation. The web portal serves as a user-friendly interface to perform data visualization, analysis, synthesis, modeling, and K-12 educational outreach activities. It also provides useful capabilities for system developers and operators to remotely monitor system status and remotely update software and system configuration, which greatly simplifies system debugging and maintenance tasks. We also implement Sensor Observation Services (SOS) at this layer, conforming to the SWE standard to facilitate data exchange. The standard Sensor ML/O&M data representation makes it easy to integrate our sensor data into the existing Geographic Information Systems (GIS) web services and exchange the data with many other organizations. The SOS web service will be published to a catalog service in the OGC SWE framework to make it publicly accessible on the Internet.

Finally, the user layer abstracts a variety of needs for education, outreach, research, and system development and management purposes.

4   Wireless Sensor Networks for Soil Moisture Monitoring

The WSN hardware platform employed in our current design is the MICAz mote from Crossbow [12]. The MICAz mote provides a highly integrated, cost-effective hardware solution for low-power WSN applications. At each sensor node, a soil moisture sensor probe is connected to an optional MDA300 data acquisition board. The base station (BS) node is installed on an extension board MIB510, which interfaces with the RFG Server through RS232 serial ports. Data collected by each sensor node are periodically transmitted to the BS node through multi-hop communications. Then, BS transmits aggregated data package to the RFG Server through RS232 serial communication.

To accomplish long-term operation with minimum human intervention, motes are powered by solar cells and rechargeable batteries. The capacities of the rechargeable battery and solar cell are determined through power budget analysis of the system (see Section 5 for more details of such analysis). To survive extreme weather conditions, motes are packaged in weatherproof boxes and the boxes are installed 4 feet above the ground on top of metal poles to avoid flooding water and prevent fallen leaves from covering solar cells.

In general, in environmental monitoring applications, every sensor node needs to periodically carry out three main tasks as shown in Fig. 2, including data generation through sensing, data processing, and data reporting through multihop wireless communications. To accomplish the data generation task, sensor readings are collected periodically, at certain desired frequency, and sensor data are time-stamped upon sampling, which necessitates global time synchronization in the network. Then, to perform data processing task, sensor nodes calibrate, aggregate, summarize, and compress data. For example, complex data aggregation and summarization techniques such as the E2K method proposed in [13] may be employed to reduce wireless communications by exploiting the spatial and temporal correlation properties that are inherent in many sensor data. Lastly, during the data reporting task, sensor data are transmitted to the BS node through multihop wireless communication. The data reporting task is enabled by a variety of software services as shown in Fig. 2, which implements essential timing, communication, and networking protocols for energy-efficient multihop sensor data collection in distributed networks.

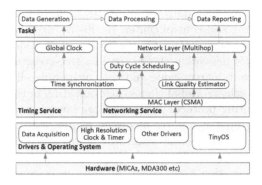

Fig. 2. Functional block diagram of sensor node

As discussed in Section 2, energy efficiency is one of the major design considerations. In wireless networks, Media Access Control (MAC) layer protocols are broadly categorized into two groups: schedule-based and contention-based methods [14]. In schedule-based protocols such as time, frequency, and code division multiple access methods, wireless devices are scheduled to occupy different channels that are physically or logically independent. In contrast, in contention-based protocols such as the carrier-sense multiple access (CSMA) method, wireless devices compete for a single shared channel. A schedule-based protocol could completely eliminate collision in wireless communication but it may not be able to adapt to the rapidly changing channel conditions whereas a contention-based protocol is highly autonomous but relatively energy-inefficient due to high collision rate in the shared channel. In this research, we develop a hybrid MAC layer protocol that integrates CSMA and duty-cycle scheduling. The hybrid protocol employs a distributed duty-cycle scheduling algorithm to coordinate sensor nodes' sleeping. The duty cycle of each node is scheduled by its parent. Sensor nodes remain asleep until their own reporting period; during reporting period, CSMA is employed to avoid any unexpected collision due to overlapping reporting periods of different sub-trees. Thus, the hybrid protocol strives to retain the flexibility of contention-based protocols while improving energy efficiency in multihop networks. Such a design is similar to the S-MAC protocol proposed in [14]. However, S-MAC does not maintain a network-wise global time so that sensors must adopt schedules from multiple virtual clusters.

The performance of schedule-based methods depends on the accuracy of time synchronization. The flooding time synchronization protocol (FTSP) proposed in [15] time-stamps synchronization messages at the MAC layer, which removes the non-deterministic delay at both sender and receiver caused by uncertain processing time in the operating system for context switches, system call overhead, interrupt handling, and other essential operations. FTSP is able to synchronize multiple receivers with a single broadcast message. Such a flooding-based method is also insensitive to topological changes. In environmental monitoring applications, distributed sensor nodes typically form a spanning-tree structure, rooted in a single data-collection BS node serving as a gateway to the remote monitoring and control center. In this research, a modified FTSP is developed to better suit environmental monitoring applications by exploiting the unique tree-structured network architecture. In a tree-structured network, every node synchronizes to its parent node and thus ultimately all nodes synchronize to the root node to achieve global time synchronization in the network.

The multihop routing protocol at the network layer is responsible for establishing and keeping up the routing hierarchy in distributed WSN. While the routing structure in environmental monitoring applications is a simple tree and the data flow is almost one-directional, the dynamic and unreliable nature of the wireless communication poses great difficulty in organizing and maintaining a reliable multihop routing hierarchy. In this research, we implement an exponential weighted moving average (EWMA) estimator-based link quality estimator [16]. The weight used here is the normalized received signal strength of the synchronization packet, which will then be halved in each cycle. Such an estimator reacts quickly to potentially large changes in link quality yet is stable enough when changes are small. The multihop routing protocol makes use of the link quality estimate to maintain a reliable routing topology.

5   Wireless Telemetry System

To seamlessly integrate a variety of devices in the field, as shown in Fig. 1, we implement a RFG Server using a rugged ultra-low-power SBC TS-7260 from Technology Systems, Inc [17]. To minimize energy consumption, the monitoring system is automatically switched between active and sleep modes. The sleep mode of the SBC is enabled by the optional battery backup board TS-BAT3, which also serves as an embedded uninterruptible power supply (UPS). The devices deployed in the field are commonly equipped with RS232 serial port, including data loggers, wireless modem, and WSN BS node. Thus, with five serial ports onboard, the SBC is well suited to serve as gateway server.

The long-haul wireless link from the field to the CDC Server is implemented using a GPRS modem. The GPRS, standing for General Packet Radio Service, is a packet oriented mobile data service available to the subscribers of GSM cellular networks. The GPRS link is maintained by the SBC, using Point-to-Point (PPP) protocol, a data link protocol commonly used to establish a direct connection between two nodes over serial cable, phone line, cellular phone, or dial-up network. Once the SBC boots up, it will automatically dial to GPRS network, and keep the link alive during the entire active period. To enable secure system access, the Layer 2 Tunneling Protocol (L2TP) is used to support virtual private network that establishes a secure point-to-point connection between the RFG Server and the CDC Server through the public Internet. To be energy-efficient, wireless modem is powered off during the system's sleep period.

Wireless telemetry system in the field is powered by solar energy with a large solar panel and rechargeable battery. The required capacities of rechargeable battery and solar panel are determined through power budget analysis. In such analysis, average power consumption of each power load device is determined by measuring or estimating the average current draw and the time spent in each of its operating modes. In practice, a lead-acid battery cannot be 100% discharged repeatedly. Therefore, it is necessary to de-rate the battery by some amount, generally 25% [18]. To survive extreme weather conditions in long-term operation, we target at supporting the system with a fully charged battery for at least a week without recharging. In general, the capacity of a solar panel should be 10 times the average power consumption of the load [18].

The CDC Server receives data through either pull or push operations. In a pull operation, the CDC Server periodically connects to the data source and pulls the data. In a push operation, the CDC Server opens a port, such as File Transfer Protocol (FTP) port, through which the data can be pushed by the data source. Such a mechanism allows the CDC Server to flexibly adapt to different types of data sources. The sensor data collected by the CDC Server is first archived in the local file system. For each data source, a back-end data handler (daemon program) is used to check the integrity of the data. Based on a set of predefined validation rules, the data are cleaned up before sending to the PostgreSQL DB Server. Data handler may also require the RFG Server to recollect and retransmit missing data packets. Data handlers are running on separate user spaces to avoid conflict among different data sources. A new data handler is added for each new data source with minimal change in the database and web visualization layers. Therefore, the system scalability and extensibility are greatly enhanced.

Emphasis on system extensibility drives sensor database design because of the need to handle large volume of sensor data collected from heterogeneous sources in long-term operation. All sensor information is contained in one relation or table, while each observation is stored in a separate relation. When more sensors are deployed as the system expands, they are registered as new records in the sensor relation by data handlers on the CDC Server. Observations from new sensors are added as new tables. The observations and sensors are linked through unique sensor identification codes. Thus, they will be automatically recognized by the upper layer web applications once being added to the database. Such a design allows flexible system development and web interface design. It also facilitates conversion of the data to SensorML [19] to enable sensor data exchangeability and interoperability through web services.

6   Sensor Data Visualization and Dissemination

As an integral part of the new environmental monitoring system, we have developed a dedicated web portal, TEO Online [9], with a set of publicly available web services for sensor data visualization and dissemination. In designing data visualization framework, we take full advantage of the flexible Google Maps API facility to associate sensors with their geographical locations intuitively on the satellite-view map interface. Each sensor is represented by a KML (Keyhole Markup Language [20]) placemark and displayed as an interactive marker that links to a drilldown information page for detailed observation charts. Such an

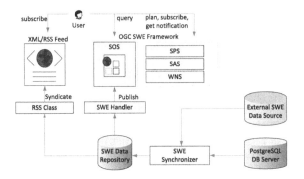

Fig. 3. Sensor data dissemination and exchange framework

interface provides direct visualization of spatial distribution of sensors and sensors data, which is an important aspect of environmental studies.

Real-time and historical sensor data as well as their temporal variation statistics may be viewed in several different formats. Depending on the type of natural phenomenon, various types of single and multi-series charts are provided. For a single series chart, users can adjust the data reporting interval and the zooming level of time range to view data trends at different temporal granularities. Several predefined functions allow the analysis of data statistics such as average and maximum values. With a multi-series chart, users can compare readings reported from sensors deployed at different locations to analyze spatial distribution characteristics of natural phenomena.

In this research, we develop a flexible framework to share sensor data with other parties through Extensible Markup Language (XML) data exchange, Really Simple Syndication (RSS) feed, and Sensor Observation Services (SOS) as shown in Fig. 3. The sensor data exchangeability is achieved by a dedicated SWE data repository as well as web services built upon the repository. RSS feed is a format that has been widely used to publish frequently changing data and allow users to subscribe such data. In our system, the RSS feed items and links are stored in an RSS table in the repository, while the live data is encapsulated in the RSS page by web layer RSS class functions. We also provide a more powerful data exchange interface through the OGC's SWE framework. SWE is a new standard that specifies interoperability interfaces and metadata encodings to enable real-time integration of heterogeneous sensor data [11]. The major encoding standards include SensorML that describes sensor system information, and O&M (Observations and Measurements) that encode actual live observations [19]. The interoperability interface standards include SOS (Sensor Observation Services) that allows near real-time retrieval of sensor data, SAS (Sensor Alert Services) that allow publish and subscription of the data, SPS (Sensor Planning Services) and WNS (Web Notification Services).

Our database is syndicated using sensor table, which automatically enables the conformation to the SWE standard. Thus, the SWE data repository can be easily synchronized with the DB Server through a SWE synchronizer. Meanwhile,

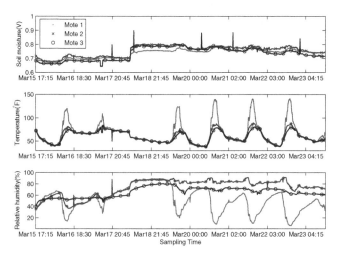

Fig. 4. Sample sensor data collected in field testing

the SWE synchronizer can also retrieve external data from any SWE-compatible data sources and confederate our repository. The data in the SWE repository is converted to SensorML and O&M format by an SWE handler, which then feed the information to the upper layer web services.

7   System Deployment and Field Testing Results

The GBC weather and soil moisture station in Denton, Texas, has been operational for nine years with temperature, solar radiation, rain gauge, wind speed and direction, and soil moisture sensors, all connected to dataloggers. In March 2008, we expanded the GBC station by deploying a wireless modem, a SBC, and a pilot WSN to implement the integrated system shown in Fig. 1. In the current setup, the RFG Server wakes up every 15 minutes for data collection with a duty cycle of about 12%. The wireless modem is powered-off during inactive periods. Eight motes are deployed in the surrounding area of the station and each mote collects data from a soil moisture sensor (connected by wire to the mote), and onboard temperature and relative humidity sensors. Motes wake up every 5 minutes for time synchronization and networking operations, but transmit sensor data only every 15 minutes following the same schedule as the RFG Server. The duty cycle of motes is about 1%. Soil moisture data is kept in raw format while other data are converted into engineering units before transmission.

Figure 4 shows sample data collected by three motes during field testing. On March 18, GBC area experienced heavy rainfall and a significant drop of temperature. The rain event was monitored by a rain gauge connected to datalogger. The variation of weather condition was also captured by the sensors on motes as shown in Fig. 4. The soil moisture exhibits a jump on that day while temperature was falling. The difference among three soil moisture sensors' data reveals spatial variation characteristics of the soil moisture condition in that area, which is an invaluable input to the hydrologic modeling research. As a part of the field testing shown in Fig. 4, we installed motes in two different boxes to test packaging alternatives. Mote 1 is installed in a transparent box to put a solar cell inside the box while Mote 2 and Mote 3 are installed in non-transparent boxes with the solar cell installed outside the box. From the results, we can observe that Mote 1 experiences significantly higher temperature during the day than the other two as a result of the greenhouse effect inside the transparent box, which also results in much lower relative humidity for Mote 1. The temperature may become very high in Texas in the summer. MICAz mote is designed to operate in harsh environment, but the rechargeable NiMh batteries cannot tolerate high temperature. Thus, we are currently evaluating more packaging options for survivable long-term deployment in the field.

The web portal [9] has been operational since March 2008 with most of the basic web services implemented. Various environmental sensor data and system status data from several monitoring sites can be viewed and downloaded from the web portal. Currently, the sensor data are being shared with the City of Denton and the National Weather Service in Fort Worth for various monitoring, modeling, and prediction purposes, which is made extremely convenient by the new data exchange framework described in Section 6.

8   Summary and Future Work

A remote near-real-time environmental monitoring system that is developed to support long-term environmental studies is presented in this paper with a focus on the overall system architecture for seamless integration of the emerging WSN-based system and the legacy wired sensor system. A unified framework for sensor data collection, management, dissemination, and exchange is also presented. Due to space limitation, many technical details of the system components are not covered in this paper; more design and implementation details of the soil moisture monitoring WSN and web services for sensor data visualization, management, dissemination, and exchange will appear in separate publications.

Currently, with support from the National Science Foundation (NSF), we are in the early stage of scaling-up the soil moisture monitoring WSN at the GBC site to around 100 motes to have a much larger geographic coverage than the current eight-mote deployment [9]. In addition, in cooperation with the City of Denton, the current remote monitoring system with WSN and wireless telemetry will be replicated at five other weather stations across the North Texas area. We are also deploying a large-scale WSN of around 100 motes in the GBC site to serve as an open research infrastructure for the WSN research community. To fulfill this goal, secure web services will be developed for remote over-the-air programming and configuration of WSN. Access to such web services will be provided to interested researchers who may carry out experimental studies of WSN from thousands of miles away.

Acknowledgments

This research is supported in part by NSF under Grants OCI-0636421, CNS-0709285, and EEC-0431818, and by Texas Advanced Research Program under Grant 003594-0010-2006. The authors would like to thank David Hunter (City of Denton), Sonny Solis (Texas Parks and Wildlife), Bob Carle (National Weather Service), and members of the TEO Research Group at UNT, especially Rudi Thompson (Biology), Duane Gustavus (CITC), Adam Skelton (EE MS student), Sanjaya Gurung (EE MS student), and Liping Chen (Applied Geography MS student) for their contributions to the development of the TEO system.

References

1. Culler, D., Estrin, D., Srivastava, M.: Overview of sensor networks. IEEE Computer, 41–49 (August 2004)
2. Martinez, K., Hart, J.K., Ong, R.: Environmental sensor networks. IEEE Computer, 50–56 (August 2004)
3. Mainwaring, A., Polastre, J., Szewczyk, R., Culler, D., Anderson, J.: Wireless sensor networks for habitat monitoring. In: Proc. of the ACM Int'l Workshop on Wireless Sensor Networks and Applications (WSNA) (September 2002)
4. MoteLab: Harvard Sensor Network Testbed,
   http://motelab.eecs.harvard.edu
5. ExScal: Extreme Scale Wireless Sensor Networking,
   http://cast.cse.ohio-state.edu/exscal
6. Kansei: Sensor Testbed for At-Scale Experiments,
   http://ceti.cse.ohio-state.edu/kansei
7. CitySense: An Open, Urban-Scale Sensor Network Testbed,
   http://www.citysense.net
8. SCADDS: Scalable Coordination Architectures for Deeply Distributed Systems,
   http://www.isi.edu/scadds/testbeds
9. Texas Environmental Observatory, http://www.teo.unt.edu
10. Cheng, S., Wang, R.: An approach for evaluating the hydrological effects of urbanization and its application. Hydrological Processes 16, 1403–1418 (2002)
11. Sensor Web Enablement WG, OGC Inc., http://www.opengeospatial.org
12. Crossbow Inc., http://www.xbow.com
13. Harrington, B., Huang, Y.: A two round reporting approach to energy efficient interpolation of sensor fields. In: Papadias, D., Zhang, D., Kollios, G. (eds.) SSTD 2007. LNCS, vol. 4605, pp. 130–147. Springer, Heidelberg (2007)
14. Ye, W., Heidemann, J., Estrin, D.: An energy-efficient MAC protocol for wireless sensor networks. In: Proc. of the 21st Int'l Annual Joint Conference of the IEEE Computer and Communications Societies (INFOCOM), vol. 3, pp. 1567–1576 (June 2002)
15. Maroti, M., Kusy, B., Simon, G., Ledeczi, A.: The flooding time synchronization protocol. In: Proc. of the ACM Conference on Embedded Networked Sensor Systems (SenSys) (November 2004)

16. Woo, A., Tong, T., Culler, D.: Taming the underlying challenges of reliable multihop routing in sensor networks. In: Proc. of the Int'l Conference on Embedded Networked Sensor Systems (SenSys) (November 2003)
17. Technologic Systems Inc., `http://www.embeddedarm.com`
18. NovaLynx Corporation, Power Budget Calculations, `http://www.novalynx.com`
19. SensorML, UAH VAST, `http://vast.uah.edu/SensorML`
20. Keyhole Markup Language, Google, `http://code.google.com/apis/kml`

An Energy-Efficient Object Tracking Algorithm in Sensor Networks*

Qianqian Ren, Hong Gao, Shouxu Jiang, and Jianzhong Li

College of Computer Science and Technology,
Harbin Institute of Technology, Harbin, China
{Qqren,Hongao,Jzli}@hit.edu.cn

Abstract. Object tracking needs to meet certain real-time and precision constraints, while limited power and storage of sensors issue challenges for it. This
paper proposes an energy efficient tracking algorithm (*EETA*) that reduces energy consumption in sensor network by introducing an event-driven sleep
scheduling mechanism. *EETA* gives tradeoffs between real time and energy efficiency by making a maximum number of sensor nodes outside tracing area
stay asleep. *EETA* reduces the computation complexity on sensors to $O(N)$ by
formulating the location predication of an object as a state estimation problem
of sensor node, instead of building a complex model of its trajectory. *EETA* lo-
cates the object using modified weighted centroid algorithm with the complexity of $O(N)$. We evaluate our method with a network of 64 sensor nodes, as well
as an analytical probabilistic model. The analytical and experimental results
demonstrate the effectiveness of proposed methods.

Keywords: sensor network; object tracking; energy-efficiency; sleep scheduling; weighted centroid.

1 Introduction

Energy efficiency is a fundamental issue in wireless sensor networks (*WSNs*). Especially in applications of object tracking, energy determines a system's lifetime. Object
tracking is widely used in many areas, such as disaster predication, emergency response and battle-field [1], where returning the object's accurate location information
timely is a major concern, meanwhile, the characteristics of *WSNs* can not be neglected. First, the power of sensor nodes is limited. So it's a waste of energy to let all
nodes work all the time to make response to the object. Second, limits of sensors'
computation and storage require a distributed tracking algorithm with low complexity.
Therefore, tradeoffs between real-time and energy-efficiency, location precision and
computation complexity are efficient solutions.

---

* This paper has been supported by the National Grand Fundamental Research 973 Program of
China under Grant No. 2006CB303000; Key Program of the National Natural Science Foun-
dation of China under Grant No. 60533110; The National Natural Science Foundation of
China under Grant No. 60703012; Program for New Century Excellent Talents in University
under Grant No. NCET-05-0333 and Heilongjiang Province Fund for Young Scholars under
Grant No.QC06C033.

Y. Li et al. (Eds.): WASA 2008, LNCS 5258, pp. 237–248, 2008.

These tradeoffs have hence received some attentions in the literatures. To obtain the tradeoff between real-time and energy-efficiency, the idea of minimizing nodes that participate in communicating or working is proposed [2,3,4,5]. These methods conserve the energy of network to a certain extent. However, the nodes that do not participate in tracking still consume energy when they are idle. It costs sensor nodes nearly 99% of energy when they are waiting for mobile objects in idle state [1]. Therefore, making maximum nodes that do not participate in tracking sleep can conserve more energy. In this paper, a sleeping mechanism based tracking algorithm is presented, which reduces energy cost largely, with guarantee of real time.

To obtain the tradeoff between location precision and computation complexity, developing a tracking algorithm with higher accuracy and lower complexity is necessary. A typical tracking algorithm includes location predication and location computation. Most existing location predication algorithm need to model the object's trajectories, some proposed modeling method such as Bayesian filters, Kalman filters and Particle filters [6, 7, 8] are too complex to be performed on sensor nodes with limited power of computation and storage. Instead of building the object's trajectory model, this paper formulates modeling problems as problems of estimating sensors' state, which just needs $O(N)$ time.

The main contributions of the paper are following. 1) This paper proposes an event-driven sleep scheduling mechanism, which gives guarantee of real time and energy-efficiency for the object tracking. 2) Formulating problems of modeling objects' trajectories as problems of sensors' state estimation, which reduces the complexity of the location predication algorithm on sensors to O(N). 3) Modified weighted centroid algorithm is given to locate the object with the complexity of O(N). 4) We carried out a lab-scale demonstration using sensor nodes with light sensors for a validation of *EETA*, meanwhile impacts of configuration parameters on the performance of the method is analyzed.

The remainder of this paper is structured as follows. The most related work is reviewed in Section 2. Section 3 gives data model of our method. In Section 4, we describe our event-driven sleep scheduling mechanism and give a real time analysis. Section 5 describes tracking algorithm. Section 6 provides the experimental set up and analyzes experimental results. We conclude the paper in Section 7.

2   Related Work

The issue of object tracking in *WSN*s has been explored by many prior references. These proposing approaches use sensor's multiple capabilities including computation, storage, sensing and communication. *DCTC* [9] is a distributed tracking algorithm using dynamic conveying tree structure for node collaboration. These applications generally track objects consistently, while they can not necessarily prolong the network lifetime if they have to achieve long-term surveillance.

In order to conserve the energy of the network, energy efficiency arouses many interests. ZhaoF et al [3] propose a information-driven approach, which decides the sensor collaboration on constraints of information, cost and resource consumption. *MCTA* [2] gives a minimal contour tracking algorithm to minimize the number of working sensor nodes. These methods are efficient for conserving energy in the network; however, neither of them considers the real time requirement of the object tracking. Lee J et al [5] suggest a distributed energy efficient tracking method, which conserves energy by reducing the number of transmitted messages. The effect of only cutting transmission is limited. Because transmitting the object's information periodically is still necessary.

VigilNet [4] is a sleeping mechanism based tracking system, which achieves end-to-end tracking deadline through sub-deadline guarantee. However, this system does not give a tracking algorithm suitable for its sleeping mechanism.

3 Data Model

In this section, we give a *WSNs* model, a sensor nodes model and an object trajectory model, which are bases of *EETA*.

3.1 *WSNs* Model

Assume that the network consists of N nodes deployed in a grid of $n \times m$ at known positions. Each cell is an $a \times b$ rectangle. Nodes in a cell organize theirselves into a same cluster, cluster-heads rotate among the sensors in each cell. All nodes in *WSNs* fall into two classes: *sentry nodes* and *tracking nodes*. Each cluster head plays a role of sentry node, while member nodes are set as tracking nodes. Fig. 1 shows the *WSNs* model. For the simplify of presenting the core algorithm, this paper just describes the case of tracking one object.

3.2 Sensors Model

The nodes in network carry sensors to detect a certain object. We assume that each sensor has a sensing region of radius R, let C_i denotes the sensing region of node i.

Definition (*Influenced node*). The influenced node is the tracking node that can detect the object.

Sensor nodes are represented in the format of:

$$S_t = \{x^i, y^i, A_t^i, \vec{v}\} \tag{1}$$

Where t is a discrete time-step, (x^i, y^i) are position coordinates of node i. A_t^i indicates whether node i is an influenced node at time step t, A_t^i has two values, that's $A_t^i = 1$ denoting node i is an influenced node and $A_t^i = 0$ indicating it is not. $\vec{v}$ denotes the velocity vector of a mobile object. We suppose that $\vec{v}$ is known or can be measured.

3.3 Tracking Trajectory Model

In real applications, a mobile object can walk random, so its trajectory is not regular. We use the piecewise line approximation method to model tracking trajectory based on literary [10]. This method defines a historical data window, and then uses a line to approximate the trajectory of this window. The approximation accuracy is determined by sensors' sample rate and the object's speed.

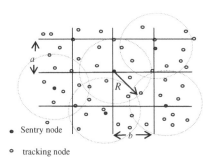

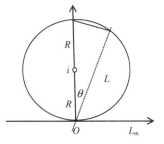

Fig. 1. *WSN* model   **Fig. 2.** The trajectory model of the object

It is obvious that node i may detect the object only if there is the overlapping between its sensing region and the object's trace. We use L to represent the length of above overlapping. An object can enter C_i from any direction, as shown in Fig. 2. The direction determines the time that the object stays in C_i. It is supposed that, at time t, an object enters into C_i at location O, with the direction angle θ, then L is $2R\cos\theta$. The random variable θ has a uniform distribution over $(-\frac{\pi}{2},\frac{\pi}{2})$. The density function of θ equals

$$f(\theta) = \begin{cases} \dfrac{1}{\pi}, & -\dfrac{\pi}{2} < \theta < \dfrac{\pi}{2} \\ 0, & else \end{cases} \tag{2}$$

Let X denote the random variable of the length of the overlapping between the object's approximated trace and C_i, and $P(X \leq L)$ denotes the probability that the length of overlapping equals to or less than L, then the probability distribution function of X is

$$F(L) = P(X \leq L) = \int_{-\theta}^{\theta} f(\theta)d\theta = \int_{-\theta}^{\theta} \frac{1}{\pi}d\theta = \frac{2\theta}{\pi} = \frac{2}{\pi}\arccos\frac{L}{2R} \tag{3}$$

Suppose that the time an object lapses in the sensing region of node i is Δt, then $L=\vec{v}\Delta t$. The expected distance of L can be expressed as

$$L_e = \int_0^L L\frac{d}{dL}F(L)dL = \int_0^L \frac{2L}{\pi}\frac{d}{dL}\arccos\frac{L}{2R}dL = \int_0^L \frac{2L}{\pi}\frac{1}{\sqrt{4R^2-L^2}}dL \tag{4}$$

We can use L_e to approximate the distance that the object walks in the sensing region of node i.

4   Event-Driven Sleeping Scheduling

Let T_{SP} be a sentry node's execution period, where its sleeping period is T_{SS} and its work period is T_{SW} ($T_{SS}+T_{SW}=T_{SP}$). The ratio of T_{SW} and T_{SP} is *duty cycle*. The sentry node periodically goes to sleep and wakes up. When it stays at work state and detects the object, it remains awake before completing its tracking assignment. After that, the sentry node returns to the original cycle.

Let T_{TP} be a tracking node's execution period, and T_{TC} be its detection period. The tracking node maintains sleep state and wakes for a short time to detect the awakening message. When receiving a awakening message, the tracking node turns to awake state. If receives a sleeping message, the tracking node returns to original sleep schedules. In following paragraphs, we will incorporate the sleeping schedules with the tracking procedure.

At time-step t, when an object enters into the area D, the sentry nodes that detect the object sends awaking messages to influenced nodes to awake them. As soon as the influenced nodes detect the awaking message, they turn to work state and sample tracking data periodically, then report data to their sentry nodes (cluster head). They won't stop doing it till receive sleeping messages.

The sentry node collects sensor data from its member nodes and computers the object's location, which will be transmitted to the base station. After receiving the object's location measurement, the base station updates object's trajectory model, computes the influenced nodes of next epoch and then transmits the information to all sentry nodes. The sentry node sends awakening messages to new influenced nodes, and sleeping message to ones that are not influenced nodes any more. If all its member nodes are not influenced nodes, it returns to the original sleep schedules.

4.1 Real-Time Constraints of Tracking

In order to transmit an object's location information to the client timely and efficiently, the tracking algorithm need to meet certain real time constraints. VigilNet[1] defines the real-time constraint as a tracking deadline. However, in a tracking procedure with sleeping mechanism, that the object can be detected timely is an essential requirement. For instance, if the object completes the process of entering into and leaving a node's sensing region during the time that the node is sleeping, then this node can not detect it. Furthermore, if the case happens to most nodes around the object, then the object tracking won't be achieved. To guarantee the object's being detected, this paper gives following two constraints.

It is supposed that at time t, an object moves into area D_t, the tracking system asks sensor nodes (including sentry nodes and tracking nodes) to get the object's location before it moves out area D_t. The real time constraints include:

- Constraints of sentry nodes: There at least exists one sentry node detecting the object with a given probability (such as no less than 90%).
- Constraints of tracking node: There at least exist m tracking nodes being awakened to track the object.

In this section, we discuss the factors that influence *EETA*, furthermore tradeoff these factors to guarantee the real-time and energy efficient of *EETA*.

4.2 Real Time Analysis of *EETA*

Real time analysis of sentry nodes. A sensor node, including sentry nodes and tracking node, can detect the object in its sensing region with the probability of η. η is determined by sensors' physical attributes, and it can be learnt from historic data. Here we assume it is known.

The probability that a sentry node detects the object can be represented as:

$$P_S = \frac{\Delta t}{T_{SS}}\eta = \frac{L_e / \bar{v}}{T_{SS}}\eta = \frac{2(2R - \sqrt{4R^2 - L^2})}{\pi \bar{v} T_{SS}}\eta \tag{5}$$

When $\Delta t \geq T_{SS}$, the object is detected with the probability of η, so P_S only depends on sensor s' attributes.

When sensors have the sensing region of the circle with a radius R, we name the circle centered at the object with a radius $2R$ is *efficient area*. All nodes in the efficient area can detect the object [10]. We assume the average density of sentry nodes per unit area is ρ, thus there are $2\rho\pi R^2$ sentry nodes in an efficient area. The probability that at least one sentry node detects the object is:

$$P_{MS} = 1 - (1-p)^{2\rho\pi R^2} = 1 - (1 - \frac{2(2R - \sqrt{4R^2 - L^2})}{\pi \bar{v} T_{SS}}\eta)^{2\rho\pi R^2} \tag{6}$$

From formula 5, we can see that P_{MS} is determined by sentry node density ρ, sensing radius R, sleeping period T_{SS} and the object's speed. For a given object, increasing ρ and R, or reducing sleeping period bring higher P_{MS}, but also leads to more energy consumptions. Therefore we can adjust these parameters to obtain a balance between real-time and energy efficiency.

Real time analysis of tracking nodes. If the object moves in and then moves out an influenced node's sensing region during T_{TC}, it can't be detected. We can represent the probability that an influenced node detects the object as:

$$P_T = \frac{\Delta t}{T_{TC}}\eta = \frac{L_e / \bar{v}}{T_{TC}}\eta = \frac{2(2R - \sqrt{4R^2 - L^2})}{\pi \bar{v} T_{TC}}\eta \tag{7}$$

When $\Delta t \geq T_{TC}$, the object is detected with the probability of η, so P_T is decided only by the sensor's attributes. When $\Delta t < T_{TC}$, P_T depends on T_{TC}, R, ρ and $\bar{v}$. The probability that at least m influenced nodes track the object is:

$$P_{MT} = \binom{2\rho\pi R^2}{m} p_T{}^m (1 - p_T)^{(2\rho\pi R^2 - m)} \tag{8}$$

From formula 8, we can see that P_{MT} is determined by ρ R, detecting period T_{TC} and the object's speed. Given the object's speed, ρ and R, we can obtain higher P_{MT} by reducing T_{TC}, but detecting medium frequently certainly results in more energy cost. Therefore, we can optionally adapt these parameters to best accommodate the tracking performance.

5 Tracking Algorithm

The tracking procedure consists of two parts: predicating the object's and localize the object.

Predicating the object's area is to identify which nodes should be awakened to participate tracking, that's specify the influenced nodes. In our *EETA*, instead of constructing a complex object's modal, we format it as the problem of estimating tracking nodes' state.

Locating the object can use existing localization method. In this paper, we modify the weighted centroid algorithm, which is introduced by Wooyoung Kim [10], to suit for our sleeping mechanism.

5.1 Identifying the Influenced Nodes

In *WSN*s, each tracking node has two states: influenced node or not influenced node. From time step t to time step $t+1$, the tracking may have four critical state: maintaining not influenced node state, transforming to influenced node state from not influenced node, transforming to not influenced node state from influenced node and maintaining influenced node state. The probability that a node stays at each state can be presented as:

$$P_{00} = P\{A_i^t = 0 \mid A_i^{t-1} = 0\} \qquad P_{01} = P\{A_i^t = 1 \mid A_i^{t-1} = 0\}$$
$$P_{11} = P\{A_i^t = 1 \mid A_i^{t-1} = 1\} \qquad P_{10} = P\{A_i^t = 0 \mid A_i^{t-1} = 1\} \tag{9}$$

Let X_n be the state of a tracking node at time n, if we say that a tracking node is in state 0 when it is an influenced node and state 1 when it is not an influenced node, the preceding of a tracking node changing its state is a two-state Markov chain. We use i and j denote an tracking node's state respectively, then

$$P\{X_{n+1} = j \mid X_n = i, X_{n-1},..., X_1\} = P_{ij} \text{ for all } n \geq 1 \tag{10}$$

According to the characteristics of Markov chain, the present state X_n at time n, depends only on the state X_{n-1} at time $n-1$ and is independent of the past states. Thus, formula (9) can be represented again as:

$$P\{X_{n+1} = j \mid X_n = i\} = P_{ij} \tag{11}$$

Let P denote the matrix of one step transition probabilities P_{ij}, it is given by

$$P_{2\times2} = \begin{Vmatrix} P_{00} & P_{01} \\ P_{10} & P_{11} \end{Vmatrix} \tag{12}$$

The value P_{ij} can be learned from historic data using Baum-Welch method [11]. Having this transition probability matrix, we obtain the nodes satisfying the condition $p(A_{n+1}^i = 1) \geq P_{Threshold}{}^1$, which are influenced nodes. The procedure is described in Algorithm 1, of which the time complexity is $O(N)$, and the space complexity is $O(N)$.

---

[1] $P_{Threshold}$ can be set as the precision demand.

Algorithm 1. Identify _ InfluencedNodes

1: calculate a circle D_{t+1} centered of (x_t, y_t), with the radius of the value of $\bar{v}_t$

2: find each node i whose sensing range has overlapping with D_{t+1}

3: compute the probability p that i stays
   at the state of being a influenced node

4: if p is larger than the threshold

5: then node i is a influenced node

5.2 Modified Weighted Centroid Algorithm

EETA can use existing localization algorithms. We modified weighted centroid algorithm in [10], to adaptive the sleeping mechanism in *EETA*. The weighted centroid localization algorithm does not need to extra hardware cost, and is based on piecewise line approximation trajectory modal. While the algorithm in [10] is developed on binary sensor and not designed for sleeping scheduling system. Algorithm 2 gives a modified algorithm.

Algorithm 2. Modified_Weighted Centroid

1: compute the weight of each node $w_i = \dfrac{L_{ei}}{\sum\limits_{j=1}^{m} L_{ej}}$

2: $x = \sum\limits_{i=1}^{m} w_i x_i$, $y = \sum\limits_{i=1}^{m} w_i y_i$

3: (x, y) is the location of the object

In algorithm 2, L_e is computed at base station, and sent to sentry nodes with influenced nodes information together, so its time complexity is $O(N)$.

6 Experiments and Evaluations

To validate *EETA*, a small experiment using 64 sensors with light sensors is set up. These sensor nodes are arranged in a 8×8 grid with 30 centimeters distance. The sensor node offers a MSP430 processor and nRF905 wireless communication component. These nodes run on the TinyOS operating system, programmed in NesC language. The sensing range of the sensor is set to 50 centimeters and wireless communication distance is adjusted to 60 centimeters. All nodes work at the period of 500 milliseconds. We use an electronic car as the mobile object.

In our experiments, the network are divided into 3×3, 3×4 and 4×4 grid, respectively. Correspondingly, the number of sentry nodes is 9, 12 and16. This section presents the performance of *EETA* and evaluates the impacts of different system configurations on its performance. We consider parameters of detection latency, energy dissipation of the whole network and trajectory approximation. These parameters are key factors that determine the performance of tracking.

6.1 Detection Latency

Detection latency is the difference between the time at which the object enter into an area and the time at which it is first detected. Here we consider average detection latency, that's the average of all nodes during a certain time. With a certain deployment density, the average detection latency is determined by the number of sentry nodes, duty cycle and tracking nodes' detection period T_{TC}.

The results of average detection latency for different sentry nodes and duty cycle are shown in Fig. 3. The detection latency for 9 sentry nodes is slightly longer than that for 12 sentry nodes and 16 sentry nodes. As shown in the figure, the more the duty cycle is, the shorter the average detection latency is. The reason is that increasing sentry node makes each area be covered by more sentry nodes, so the object has more chance to be detected. In addition, the increase of duty cycle makes nodes have less sleeping time, they have much time to work and monitor the object.

Fig. 4 illustrates the detection latency versus T_{TC} varying duty cycle from 25% to 100%. As shown in figure, increasing duty cycle or decreasing T_{TC} lead to shorter detection latency. Because the influenced nodes have more chance to be awakened timely.

6.2 Energy Dissipation

Energy dissipation is the sum of all nodes consuming energy, including nodes state switch, sampling sensor data, computes the object's location, communication by wireless and retain work/sleeping state. We compute the consumed energy as literature [4].

Fig. 5 and Fig. 6 show the energy dissipation of *EETA* and the tracking system without sleeping mechanism (*Normal*). In these figures, coordinate Y denotes the average energy dissipation of all nodes in the network. We note that *EETA* conserves system's energy significantly, moreover, its energy consumption should be proportional to average sleeping time (the sleeping time of sentry nodes and tracking nodes is different) theoretically. However, node state converting, sending waking message and sleeping message cause extra energy cost. When the number of sentry nodes is 9, duty cycle is 25% and T_{TC} is 150*ms*, *EETA* only costs half energy of the tracking system without sleeping mechanism.

Fig. 5 pays attention to the impact of sentry nodes number and duty cycle on energy dissipation. We observe that it increases monotonically with the duty cycle. The reason is that the increase of duty cycle leads to longer work time of sentry nodes, and more awakening information being sent. The energy cost of communication is 160 times much than that of idle state [4]. The increase of sentry node number also brings more energy cost, as the energy consumption of sentry nodes is bigger than that of tracking nodes. While the ratio of sentry nodes in the entire network is lower, the influence is not obvious.

Fig. 6 plots the influence of duty cycle and T_{TC} on energy dissipation, with sentry nodes number is 12. Varying duty cycle influences the energy cost more obviously, which determines the corresponding ratio of sleeping time and work time of sentry nodes. While the energy consumed at work time is 11 timers bigger than that at sleeping time [4]. As the increase of T_{TC}, energy dissipation reduces evidently. For the

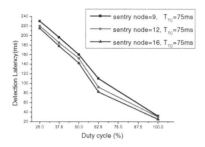

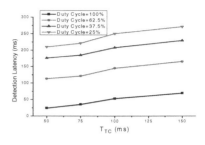

Fig. 3. Impact of sentry nodes num, duty cycle on average detection latency

Fig. 4. Impact of duty cycle and T_{TC} on average detection latency

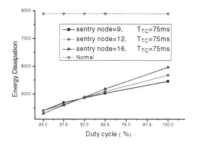

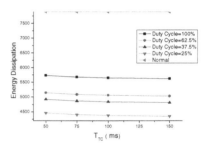

Fig. 5. Impact of sentry nodes num, duty cycle on energy dissipation

Fig. 6. Impact of duty cycle and T_{TC} on energy dissipation

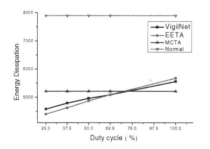

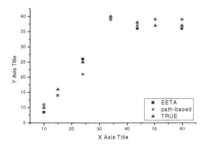

Fig. 7. Energy dissipation of *EETA* , *MCTA* and VigilNet algorithm

Fig. 8. Tracking result of *EETA* vs *path-based* algorithm

increase of T_{TC} reduces periodical detection times. In other word, there is less chance to awake the sleeping nodes, which conserves system energy efficiently.

Fig. 7 compares the energy dissipation of *EETA* with other excellent tracking algorithms including VigilNet and *MCTA*. We observe that, when the duty cycle is no more than 75%, the performances of *EETA* and VigilNet are better, for their taking good advantage of the sleeping mechanism. However, as the increase of duty cycle, this advantage becomes weaker. *MCTA*, which is based on minimizing nodes that participate in communication, is not influenced by duty cycle, so behave better when duty cycle is higher.

6.3 Trajectory Approximation

Trajectory approximation not only relies on localization algorithm, but also depends on the number of tracking nodes and detection latency. Fig. 8 illustrates the tracking results of *EETA* and *path-based* algorithm [10](*TRUE* is the real trajectory). We observe that two methods model the object efficiently. The difference between *EETA* and *path-based* is small, which proves that introducing sleeping mechanism does not bring obviously influence on tracking precision. The efficiency of *EETA* is steadier than that of *path-based* algorithm, because *path-based* algorithm is based on the binary sensor model, which depends on the network's reliability.

7 Conclusions and Future Work

This paper suggests a new tracking algorithm called *EETA*, which balances the requirement of real-time and energy efficiency, location precision and computation complex. The first idea is to introduce an event-driven sleeping mechanism, which makes maximum nodes stay asleep to conserve the energy consumption. We give a probability model to analysis the impact of configuration parameters on real time detection. In order to realize object's location predication in the distributed manner, the second idea is to estimate nodes' state using Markov chain theory to model the object's location area. In addition, we modify the weighted centroid algorithm to suit our sleeping mechanism based tracking. We construct a network of 64 sensor nodes in an experiment environment to validate our approach. The results demonstrate the effectiveness of *EETA* and illustrate influences of several parameters on the system.

As our future work, we will extend our tracking algorithm to multiple objects tracking.

References

1. He, T., Vicaire, A.P., Yan, T., Luo, L., Gu, L., Zhou, G., Stoleru, R., Cao, Q., Stankovic, J.A., Abdelzaher, T.: Achieving Real-Time Target Tracking Using Wireless Sensor Networks. ACM Transaction on Embedded Computing System (2007)
2. Jeong, J., Hwang, T., He, T., Du, D.: Target Tracking Algorithm based on Minimal Contour in Wireless Sensor Networks. In: IEEE 26th Conference on Computer Communications (2007)
3. Zhao, F., Shin, J., Reich, J.: Information-driven dynamic sensor collaboration for tracking applications. IEEE Signal Processing Magazine (2002)
4. He, T., Vicaire, P., Yan, T., Cao, Q., Zhou, G., Gu, L., Luo, L., Stoleru, R., Stankovic, J.A., Abdelzaher, T.: Achieving Long-Term Surveillance in VigilNet. In: IEEE 25th Conference on Computer Communications (2006)
5. Lee, J., Cho, K., Lee, S.: Distributed and energy-efficient target localization and tracking in wireless sensor networks. Elsevier Computer Communications (2006)

6. Ashwin, D., Akbar, S.: Collaborative signal processing for distributed classification in sensor networks. In: Zhao, F., Guibas, L.J. (eds.) IPSN 2003. LNCS, vol. 2634, pp. 193–208. Springer, Heidelberg (2003)
7. Li, D., Wong, K., Hu, Y., Sayeed, A.: Detection, classification and tracking of targets in distributed sensor networks. IEEE Signal Processing Magazine, 19(2), 17–29 (2002)
8. Donal, M., Shrikanth, N.: Distributed detection and tracking in sensor networks. In: 36th Asilomar Conference of Signals, Systems and Computers (2002)
9. Zhang, W., Cao, G.H.: DCTC: Dynamic convey tree-based collaboration for target tracking in sensor networks. IEEE Transactions on Wireless Communication (2004)
10. Kim, W., Mechitov, K., Choi, J.Y., Ham, S.K.: On Tracking Objects with Binary Proximity Sensors. In: Conference on Information Processing in Sensor Networks (2005)
11. Oh, S., Sastry, S.: Tracking on a Graph. In: Conference on Information Processing in Sensor Networks (2005)

Sensor Deployment for Composite Event Detection in Mobile WSNs

Yinying Yang and Mihaela Cardei*

Department of Computer Science and Engineering
Florida Atlantic University
Boca Raton, FL 33431
yyang4@cse.fau.edu, mihaela@cse.fau.edu
http://www.springer.com/lncs

Abstract. In wireless sensor networks, sensors can be equipped with one or more sensing components. An atomic event can be detected using one sensing component. A composite event is the combination of several atomic events. The monitored area is divided into grids. To achieve high reliability, the composite event must be k-watched in each grid. Otherwise, a detection breach occurs. In this paper, we study the movement-assisted sensor deployment for minimum-breach composite event detection. Given the initial deployment, our goal is to relocate sensors to minimize the breach for all regions. We also impose a limit on the maximum distance that a sensor can move. A centralized approach and a localized algorithm are proposed. Simulation results are presented to validate the performance of our algorithms.

Keywords: wireless sensor networks, composite event detection, sensor deployment, reliability, sensor mobility.

1 Introduction

Sensors are used to monitor and control the physical environment [1]. In mobile sensor networks, sensors can move via springs [2], vehicles [4], and robots [3]. A wireless sensor network (WSN) can detect single (or *atomic*) events or *composite* events [6].

Let us consider a single sensing component first, for example, the temperature. If the sensed temperature value rises above a predefined threshold, we say that an *atomic* event occurred. A *composite* event is the combination of several *atomic* events. For example, the composite event fire may be defined as the combination of the temperature and light. The *composite* event fire occurs only when both the temperature and the light rise above some predefined thresholds.

A large number of sensors can be distributed in mass by scattering them from airplanes, or rockets [1]. In that case, the initial deployment is hard to control. However, a good deployment is necessary to improve coverage or reliability.

---

* This work was supported in part by the NSF grants CCF 0545488 and CNS 0521410.

Y. Li et al. (Eds.): WASA 2008, LNCS 5258, pp. 249–260, 2008.

In this paper, the square monitored area is divided into grids. To achieve a reliable surveillance, a *composite event* has to be k-watched in each grid (region). Otherwise, a detection *breach* occurs. We propose the movement-assisted sensor deployment for minimum-breach composite event detection (MDCED) problem. Given the initial deployment of a sensor network, our goal is to relocate sensors after the initial deployment such that to minimize the maximum breach among all regions. Sensors are energy constrained devices. To avoid consuming too much energy in moving, we limit the maximum distance a sensor can move.

In our paper, we study reliable composite event detection such that the composite event is k-watched in each region. We propose a centralized integer programming approach and a localized algorithm as solutions for the MDCED problem. We analyze their performance through simulations.

2   Related Works

Recent research works [5][6] focus on sensor collaboration to detect composite events. In [5], a tree is built using a scheme similar to the publish-subscribe communication model. In [6], Vu *et al.* propose an algorithm to construct a set of detection sets satisfying the k-watching requirement in a greedy manner. Different detection sets work alternatively to achieve energy efficiency.

[2][7][10] focus on improving the initial deployment using sensors' mobile ability. In [2], a mechanism based on the minimum cost maximum flow algorithm is proposed to achieve the maximum coverage. In [7], Wang *et al.* present VEC, VOR, and Minimax to maximize the coverage. In VEC, sensors that are too close to each other will be pushed away. In VOR and Minimax, sensors are pulled to the sparser area. Yang *et al.* present a localized method to achieve load balancing in [10]. Regions with underload and overload find a matching between them.

Unlike [5] and [6], which focus on static sensors, this paper focuses on relocating mobile sensors. [2][7][10] study the single event detection, however, the composite event detection in this paper is more complex.

3   Network Model and Problem Definition

The main notations used in the paper are introduced in Table 1. Sensors are randomly deployed in a square monitored area, divided into $r \times r$ grids (see Fig. 1). We assume that there is at least one sensor in each region. Otherwise, a mechanism similar to [8] can be applied, where regions with more than one sensor donate their sensors to regions with no sensors. To ensure sensor coverage (a sensor can monitor the whole region), we choose r such that $r \leq \frac{\sqrt{2}}{2}R_s$, where R_s is the sensing range of the sensor. Each region has a *representative* which takes care of communication with representatives of the neighbor regions and with the sink. It can be chosen according to the sensor's residual energy or contribution. To ensure the communication between adjacent representatives (left, right, top, and bottom), we require that $r \leq \frac{R_c}{\sqrt{5}}$, where R_c is the sensor communication range.

Table 1. Notations

M	The number of atomic events which form the composite event
x_j	The sensing component which detects atomic event j
$n_i^{x_j}$	The total number of sensing components x_j in region i
k	Fault tolerance level
d_{max}	The maximum moving distance of a sensor
$d(i,j)$	The Manhattan distance between region i and region j
R	The total number of regions in the monitored area
P	The number of sensing combinations using one or more sensing components
X_{st}^l	The number of sensors equipped with sensing combination l which move from region s to region t
w_s^l	The number of sensors equipped with the sensing combination l in region s
σ	The number of extra rounds the algorithm could run after the kth round, $\sigma \geq 0$
φ_i	The contribution of sensor i

A sensor can move to its neighbor regions (left, right, top, and bottom). We consider that sensors have limited mobility capabilities due to the energy constraints. d_{max} denotes the maximum Manhattan distance a sensor can move, computed as $\Delta x + \Delta y$. In Fig. 1, the Manhattan distance between regions 2 and 3 is $d(2,3) = \Delta x + \Delta y = 1 + 1 = 2$.

Sensors can have single or multiple sensing components. Taking MTS400 multi sensor board of Crossbow Technology, Inc. [9] as an example, it can sense temperature, humidity, barometric pressure, and ambient light. When we consider a single sensing component, for example, the temperature, if it rises above some predefined threshold, an *atomic event* is detected. A *composite event* is a combination of several *atomic events*. For example, consider a fire-detection application. A *composite event* fire might be defined as a combination of the *atomic events* temperature $> th_1$, light $> th_2$, and smoke $> th_3$, where "th" denotes a threshold for the corresponding attribute. That is $fire = (temperature > th_1) \wedge (light > th_2) \wedge (smoke > th_3)$. It is more accurate to report the fire when all these atomic events occur, instead of the case when only one attribute is above the threshold.

Let us consider that M atomic events $x_1, x_2, ..., x_M$ form the composite event. Sensors are equipped with single or multiple sensing components. Fig. 1 shows an example with $M = 3$. For example, x_1, x_2, and x_3 are temperature, light, and smoke respectively. For a sensor which has only the temperature and light sensing components, we use the set $\{x_1, x_2\}$ to denote its sensing ability.

Sensor nodes may be equipped with different numbers and types of sensing components due to the following reasons [5]: they might be manufactured with different sensing capabilities, a sensor node might be unable to use some of its sensing components due to the lack of memory for storing data, or some sensor components might fail over time. A sensor can be equipped with at most one sensing component of each type. All of a sensor's sensing components turn on or off simultaneously. To achieve a reliable surveillance, an event is required to be

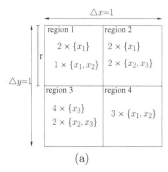

Fig. 1. An example. (a)Initial network deployment. (b)Network deployment after sensor relocation.

observed by more than one sensor. We define the k-watched atomic/composite event [6]:

Definition 1 (k-watched atomic event). *An atomic event is k-watched by a set of sensors if at any time this event occurs at any point within the interested area, at least k sensors in the network can detect this occurrence.*

Definition 2 (k-watched composite event). *A composite event is k-watched by a set of sensors if every atomic event part of the composite event is k-watched by the set of sensors.*

In this paper, the objective is that the composite event is k-watched by the sensors of each region. Due to a random initial deployment of the WSN, some regions will not provide the k-watching property. We define the *breach* of a region as the maximum gap in achieving the k-watching of an atomic event.

$n_i^{x_j}$ denotes the total number of sensing components x_j in region i. The *breach* of the region i is defined as:

$$breach_i = \max(0, k - n_i^{x_1}, k - n_i^{x_2}, ..., k - n_i^{x_M}) \tag{1}$$

To achieve a good quality in monitoring the composite event, the objective is to minimize the maximum breach for all the regions in the monitored area. In the initial deployment, some regions might have a higher breach, while others might have additional sensors. We propose to use sensor movement to relocate sensors such that to minimize the maximum breach in the network.

Definition 3 (Movement-assisted sensor Deployment for Composite Event Detection in wireless sensor networks - **MDCED** problem). *Given a WSN with N sensors randomly deployed in a square area which is partitioned into $r \times r$ grids, and given the maximum sensor moving distance d_{max}, design a sensor moving strategy such that to minimize the maximum breach for all the regions in the network, that is $MAX_{i=1..R}breach_i = MINIMUM$.*

Fig. 1 shows an example with $k = 2$, $M = 3$, and $d_{max} = 1$. This means that each of the three atomic events has to be 2-watched in each region and the maximum moving distance of a sensor is 1 (each sensor can only move to a neighboring region).

In this example, the monitored area is divided into four regions and there are four sensing combinations $\{x_1\}, \{x_1, x_2\}, \{x_2, x_3\}, \{x_3\}$. Fig. 1a shows the initial sensor deployment. Region 1 has two sensors $\{x_1\}$ and one sensor $\{x_1, x_2\}$, region 2 has two sensors $\{x_1\}$ and two sensors $\{x_2, x_3\}$, region 3 has four sensors $\{x_3\}$ and two sensors $\{x_2, x_3\}$, and region 4 has three sensors $\{x_1, x_2\}$. The maximum breach in the initial deployment is 2, occurring in the regions 1 (no sensing component x_3), 3 (no sensing component x_1), and 4 (no sensing component x_3).

Our goal is to relocate sensors such that to minimize the maximum breach for all regions. A possible deployment after sensor repositioning is shown in Fig. 1b. The moving strategy is: two sensors $\{x_2, x_3\}$ move from region 3 to region 1, one sensor $\{x_1, x_2\}$ moves from region 1 to region 3, two sensors $\{x_3\}$ move from region 3 to region 4, and one sensor $\{x_1, x_2\}$ moves from region 4 to region 3. The total number of sensor movements is 6 and every region has breach 0 (or no breach) after sensors relocation.

4   Solutions for the MDCED Problem

4.1   Centralized Integer-Programming Approach

We use P to denote the number of sensing combinations deployed, containing one or more sensing components which can watch atomic events of interest. In the worst case, $P = \binom{M}{0} + \binom{M}{1} + ... + \binom{M}{M} = 2^M$. However, in practice, a fewer number of combinations might be deployed. In our example in Fig. 1, there are $P = 4$ sensing combinations: $\{x_1\}, \{x_1, x_3\}, \{x_2, x_3\}$, and $\{x_3\}$ instead of $2^3 = 8$.

The objective is to compute the number of sensors with sensing combination l $(1 \leq l \leq P)$ which move from a region s to a region t, $X_{st}^l \in \{0, 1, ..., w_s^l\}$, when $d(s, t) \leq d_{max}$. If the Manhattan distance between the regions $d(s, t) > d_{max}$, then $X_{st}^l = 0$. Note that X_{ss}^l represents the number of sensors with sensing combination l which do not leave region s. We denote w_s^l the original number of sensors equipped with sensing combination l in region s. The optimal solution is modeled using the following IP formulation:

$$\text{Minimize} \underset{1 \leq i \leq R}{MAX} \; breach_i$$

$$\text{subject to} \sum_{t=1}^{R} X_{st}^l = w_s^l \text{ for } 1 \leq s \leq R, 1 \leq l \leq P$$

$$X_{st}^l = 0 \text{ for } d(s, t) > d_{max}, 1 \leq s, t \leq R, \\ \text{and } 1 \leq l \leq P$$

$$\text{where} \quad X_{st}^l \in \{0, 1, ..., w_s^l\} \text{ for all } 1 \leq s, t \leq R, \\ \text{and } 1 \leq l \leq P$$

Remarks:

- The objective function asks to minimize the maximum breach for all regions $i, 1 \leq i \leq R$.
- The first constraint requires that the number of sensors with sensing combination l that leave or stay in region s equals the total number of sensors with sensing combination l originally in region s, w_s^l.
- The second constraint ensures that no sensor moves from a region s to a region t if the Manhattan distance between them is greater than the maximum distance d_{max}. This constraint guarantees that the total movement distance of a sensor does not exceed d_{max}.

The value $breach_i$ in the IP objective function is computed using formula 2. It compares the number of each sensing component the region has with k to get the breach for each sensing component and then finds the maximum one as the breach of the region.

$$breach_i = \max(0, k - \sum_{x_1 \in l, l=1}^{P} \sum_{j=1}^{R} X_{ji}^l, \ldots, k - \sum_{x_M \in l, l=1}^{P} \sum_{j=1}^{R} X_{ji}^l) \qquad (2)$$

The updated values of the number of sensing components x_u in region i are computed as $n_i^{x_u} = \sum_{x_u \in l, l=1}^{P} \sum_{j=1}^{R} X_{ji}^l$.

X_{st}^l are the only variables in the IP formulation, thus the total number of variables is R^2P. We use CPLEX solver to implement the IP approach.

After getting the optimal maximum breach, we can use other integer programming formulations to optimize the number of movements and the moving distance. The objective function for optimizing the number of movements is $\sum_{l=1}^{P} \sum_{i=1}^{R} \sum_{\substack{j=1 \\ i \neq j}}^{R} X_{ij}^l$. For optimizing the moving distance, the objective is $\sum_{l=1}^{P} \sum_{i=1}^{R} \sum_{\substack{j=1 \\ i \neq j}}^{R} (d(i,j) \times X_{ij}^l)$. They have the same two constraints with the previous IP formulation and there is the third constraint, which is $breach_i \leq optBreach$ for $1 \leq i \leq R$, where $optBreach$ is the optimal maximum breach.

The IP algorithm is executed as follows. The representative of each region communicates with all the sensors in the region and transmits region location and w_i^l values to the sink. The sink uses an IP-solver to compute the sensors' movement plan, e.g. X_{st}^l values and then inform region representatives. The representatives coordinate sensors movement inside their regions.

4.2   Localized Algorithm

The localized solution is organized in rounds and incrementally reduces the maximum breach in the network. The algorithm runs $k + \sigma$ rounds, where $\sigma > 0$ is a tunable parameter. The regions that initiate the mechanism to reduce their breach in a round are called *initiator regions*, or simply *initiators*.

After the initial deployment, the maximum breach in the network is up to k. In the first round, the initiators are the regions with breach k. At the end of this round, depending on the network characteristics, there might be initiators

Algorithm 1. Localized Method - Initiator Region

1: Wait time T
2: Broadcast *Request* message using TTL to limit the number of hops
3: **if** *Reply* messages received **then**
4:    Decide which sensors to take
5:    Broadcast *ACK* message to candidate regions
6: **end if**
7: **if** receive sensors from candidate regions **then**
8:    Update the breach
9: **end if**

---

that could not decrease their breach. In the second round, the initiators are the regions with breach k or $k-1$. More generally, in the $h^{th}(h \leq k)$ round, the initiators are the regions with breaches greater than or equal to $k+1-h$. In the rounds $k+1 \dots k+\sigma$, the initiators are all the regions with breaches greater than 0. A higher priority is given in reducing higher breaches.

In general, there are two ways to reduce the breach of an initiator. When a region has transferable sensors, then it can directly assign sensors to the initiator. Otherwise, if no sensors can be moved but there are transferable sensing components, the region first tries to get transferable sensors by exchange and then assigns transferable sensors to initiators. The first method has higher priority since fewer sensor movements are involved.

In a round, each initiator has zero or more *candidate regions*. A candidate region must have the breach less than the initiator's breach and must satisfy condition 1 and one of the conditions 2 or 3:

1. Being located at a distance less than or equal to d_{max} from the initiator, since sensors' maximum moving distance is upper-bounded by d_{max}.
2. *First class candidate region*: have transferable sensors equipped with one or more of the initiator's *key sensing components* (sensing components with maximum breach in the initiator). A sensor is *transferable* if moving that sensor from the candidate region will keep the breach of the candidate region less than the initiator's breach. Our goal is to minimize the maximum breach in every round, and therefore sensor movements must not generate a new higher breach.
3. *Second class candidate region*: have one or more transferable key sensing components. The candidate may get transferable sensors through exchanging sensors with other regions. In this case, the breach of the candidate will not drop as result of the exchange.

In each round, the algorithm consists of a negotiation process between initiators and their candidates. The process is started by the initiators and after the negotiation process, sensors are moved. The main steps of a round in the algorithm are presented in Algorithms 1, 2, and 3.

In each round, initiators use controlled flooding to send *Request* messages, in an attempt to reduce their breaches. An initiator waits a time T before sending the request in order to reduce collisions, avoiding adjacent neighbors sending

---

Algorithm 2. Localized Method - Candidate Region

1: **if** first class candidate region **then**
2:     **if** *Request* message received **then**
3:         Decide the allotment
4:         Send back *Reply* message to the initiator
5:         **if** $TTL > 1$ **then**
6:             $TTL = TTL - 1$
7:             Forward the request message
8:         **end if**
9:     **end if**
10:    **if** *ACK* message received **then**
11:        Move required sensors to the initiator
12:    **end if**
13: **end if**
14: **if** second class candidate region **then**
15:    **if** *Request* message received **then**
16:        **if** $TTL > 1$ **then**
17:            Attach exchange information to the request message
18:            $TTL = TTL - 1$
19:            Forward the request message
20:        **end if**
21:    **end if**
22:    **if** *Reply* message received **then**
23:        Record the exchange region
24:        Send *Reply* message to the initiator
25:    **end if**
26:    **if** *ACK* message received **then**
27:        Exchange sensors and send the corresponding transferable sensors to the initiator
28:    **end if**
29: **end if**

---

requests at the same time. The value of T is computed based on the initiator's breach and a small random number. In general, the higher the breach is, the smaller the value of T is.

The request message generated by initiator i has the format: *Request* $(RID = i, n_i^{x_1}, n_i^{x_2}, ..., n_i^{x_M}, breach, TTL = d_{max})$. RID is the initiator's identifier. $\{n_i^{x_1}, n_i^{x_2}, ..., n_i^{x_M}\}$ are the numbers of each sensing component the initiator has and they also indicate which types of sensing components are needed. *breach* is the breach of the initiator and TTL (Time-To-Live) is used to control the number of hops the message is forwarded. Every intermediate region that receives the message for the first time decreases the TTL by 1 and forwards the message only if $TTL \geq 1$.

When a second class candidate receives the request, it asks for exchanging sensors. Consider the case when a request asks for the key sensing component $\{x_1\}$ and the candidate has a sensor $\{x_1, x_2\}$ which can not be directly assigned to the initiator since sensing component x_2 is still needed by the candidate. If the candidate region can exchange the sensor $\{x_1, x_2\}$ for one sensor

Algorithm 3. Localized Method - Non-candidate Region

```
1: if Request message received then
2:    Check the exchange information
3:    if can make the exchange then
4:       Send a Reply message to the candidate who asks for the exchange
5:       Remove exchange information from the request message
6:    end if
7:    if TTL > 1 then
8:       TTL = TTL − 1
9:       forward the request message
10:   end if
11: end if
```

$\{x_1\}$ and another sensor $\{x_2\}$, then it can give the initiator the transferable sensor $\{x_1\}$. The candidate region asks for an exchange by attaching the fields: $\{RID, keyComp, otherCompList, EXCHAGE\}$ to the end of the request message, where RID is the identifier of the exchange requestor, $keyComp$ is the key sensing component, and $otherCompList$ is the list of the other sensing components in the sensing combination and $EXCHAGE$ shows the type of the movement. The candidate region decreases TTL in the request by 1 and forwards the message if $TTL \geq 1$.

When a first class candidate receives a request message, it follows the following steps to decide whether it will give one or more sensors to the initiators.

1. A region may receive more than one request messages. The candidate region i computes a priority for each request it receives and sorts them in decreasing order, assigning first sensors to the initiators with higher priorities. For a request from the initiator region j, the priority is the initiator's breach value, taken from the request message. The Manhattan distance between these two regions, which can be computed from the TTL value in the request message, is used to be the second criterion to break the tie. A shorter distance has higher priority.

2. The contribution $\varphi_i = \frac{hf_i}{sc_i}$ of each transferable sensor i is computed, where hf_i is the number of helpful sensing components in the transferable sensor i and sc_i is the total number of sensing components sensor i has. Note that the transferable sensor must contain at least one key sensing component of the initiator. Otherwise, it can not reduce the breach of the initiator. For example, if the initiator's request message has breaches for the sensing components x_1 and x_2, then the contribution of a sensor $\{x_1, x_3\}$ is $\frac{1}{2}$, since only $\{x_1\}$ is helpful for this request and the sensor has 2 sensing components in total. The contribution of a sensor $\{x_1\}$ is 1.

3. A candidate region addresses the requests in the sorted order. It computes the contribution of each transferable sensor, sorts them in decreasing order and assigns the first $\lfloor \delta \cdot N_{transfer} \rfloor$ sensors to the request. δ is an input parameter and $N_{transfer}$ is the number of transferable sensors.

4. After having made the decision, the candidate sends back *Reply* messages to the initiators to whom sensors have been assigned. A reply message has

the form $Reply$ (RID_1, RID_2, $sensorList$, $breach'$, $dist$, $GIVE$), where RID_1 is the candidate region identifier and RID_2 is the initiator's identifier. $sensorList$ is the list of sensors which can be assigned to the initiator. The breach of the candidate may change due to the assignment. $breach'$ is the new breach and $dist$ is the distance between the candidate region and the initiator region. $GIVE$ means the sensors come from a first class candidate. The reply is a unicast message sent along the reverse path established when the request message was sent.

5. If the TTL in the received request message is greater than 1, it decrements the TTL by 1 and forwards it. If the received request message contains an exchange request whose requested sensing components have been assigned by the candidate region, then the exchange information is removed from the request message.

When an intermediate region which is not a candidate (Non-candidate Region) receives a request message, it checks the attached exchange information if there is any. If it can make the exchange, it sends back a $Reply$ message to the exchange requestor. The message has the form $Reply$ (RID_1, RID_2, $keyComp$, $otherCompList$, $EXCHAGE$), where RID_1 is the identifier of the region sensing the reply message, RID_2 is the identifier of the exchange requestor, $keyComp$ and $otherCompList$ are the sensing components that can be exchanged. Then the request message is updated (TTL is decremented by 1 and the exchange information is removed) and forwarded if $TTL \geq 1$.

When the exchange requestor receives the reply message, it updates the reply message with its own transferable sensor information and forwards it to the corresponding initiator.

An initiator may receive multiple reply messages from several candidate regions. It follows the following steps to decide which sensors to take from the first class candidates and then, if the breach is still greater than 0, the initiator considers taking sensors from second class candidates.

1. It computes the contribution $\varphi_i = \frac{hf_i}{sc_i}$ for each sensor i in the $sensorList$ of the message.
2. The initiator considers sensors from $sensorList$ of the candidates in increasing order of the $breach'$ values first and then in the decreasing order of the sensor's contribution to break the tie.
3. The initiator considers taking sensors as long as its breach can be decreased and is greater than 0.
4. The initiator sends one ACK message indicating the movement plan (number and types of sensors it will take from each candidate). The ACK message is sent using localized flooding with TTL equal to the distance between the initiator and the farthest candidate with sensors in the movement plan. The sensor reservation made by other candidates will expire if they are not included in an ACK message.

When first class regions receive ACK messages, sensors are actually moved to the initiator. When second class regions receive ACK messages, they first exchange sensors and then move the corresponding transferable sensors to the initiator.

5   Simulations

Simulation environment: Metrics in the simulations include the breach, which is computed according to formula 1 in the localized algorithm and formula 2 in IP approach, the total moving distance and the total number of movements, which are metrics to measure the energy consumption in moving.

We conduct the simulations on a custom discrete event simulator, which generates a random initial sensor deployment. All the tests are repeated 50 times and the results are averaged. In the simulations, there are 6×6 grids in the monitored area and $M = 3$, $k = 3$.

Simulation results: In Fig. 2, $d_{max} = 3$, and $\sigma = 2$, which means that the localized approach runs 5 rounds. Fig. 2a measures the maximum breach among all regions after applying integer programming and localized approaches. It shows that the localized algorithm gets close results with the IP approach, and they improve the initial deployment in terms of the maximum breach. In Fig. 2b and Fig. 2c, the curves for the integer programming are both optimal results using integer programming formulations discussed in section 4.1. When there are 150 sensors in the network, the number of movements and moving distance of the localized method is the highest. It is because when there are only 100 sensors, the density is too low to decrease the breach, and in this case, there are

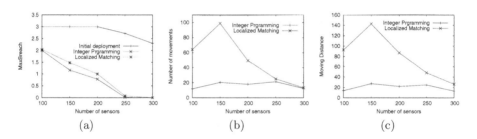

Fig. 2. Comparisons between two algorithms (a)Maximum breaches. (b)The total number of movements. (c)The total moving distance.

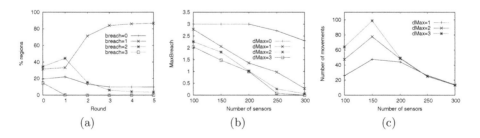

Fig. 3. Localized approach (a)Maximum breaches in every round. (b)Maximum breaches using different d_{Max}. (c)The total number of movements using different d_{Max}.

fewer movements and shorter moving distance. When the density is high enough, sensors do not have to move much to achieve the lower breach.

In Fig. 3, we study the localized method. Fig. 3a shows the percentage of regions with each breach value for each round. Round 0 shows the initial deployment. With running of the algorithm, the number of regions with breach 3 decreases. No region has breach 3 starting with the second round. In the end, most regions have breach 1 and there are a small number of regions having breach 2. In Fig. 3b and Fig. 3c, d_{max} varies from 1 to 3. In Fig. 3b, the curve, $d_{max} = 0$, shows the maximum breaches in the initial deployment. When $d_{max} = 3$, it has the lowest maximum breach. When $d_{max} = 1$, it achieves the highest maximum breaches, however, it still improves the initial deployment. When the density is low, $d_{max} = 3$ can achieve lower breach and consequently, the number of movements is larger. When the density is high, e.g., 250 and 300, $d_{max} = 3$ moves less compared with other two cases.

6   Conclusions and Future Work

In this paper, we focus on the Movement-assisted sensor Deployment for Composite Event Detection in wireless sensor networks (MDCED) problem. The integer programming approach and localized method are proposed. Simulation results show that the localized method gets close maximum breach results with the integer programming approach. In our future work, we will continue to study additional methods for the MDCED problem.

References

1. Akyildiz, I., Su, W., Sankarasubramaniam, Y., Cayirci, E.: Wireless sensor networks: a survey. Computer Networks 38(4), 393–422 (2002)
2. Chellappan, S., Bai, X., Ma, B., Xuan, D., Xu, C.: Mobility limited flip-based sensor networks deployment. IEEE Transactions of Parallel and Distributed Systems 18(2), 199–211 (2007)
3. Dantu, K., Rahimi, M.H., Shah, H., Babel, S., Dhariwal, A., Sukhatme, G.S.: Robomote: enabling mobility in sensor networks. In: IPSN 2005, pp. 404–409 (2005)
4. Lee, U., Magistretti, E.O., Zhou, B.O., Gerla, M., Bellavista, P., Corradi, A.: Efficient data harvesting in mobile sensor platforms. In: PerCom Workshops, pp. 352–356 (2006)
5. Kumar, A.V.U.P., Reddy, A.M.V., Janakiram, D.: Distributed collaboration for event detection in wireless sensor networks. In: MPAC 2005 (2005)
6. Vu, C.T., Beyah, R.A., Li, Y.: Composite event detection in wireless sensor networks. In: 26th IEEE IPCCC (2007)
7. Wang, G., Cao, G., LaPorta, T.F.: Movement-assisted sensor deployment. IEEE Transactions on Mobile Computing 5(6), 640–652 (2006)
8. Wu, J., Yang, S.: SMART: a scan-based movement-assisted sensor deployment method in wireless sensor networks. IEEE INFOCOM, 2313–2324 (2005)
9. http://www.xbow.com/Home/HomePage.aspx
10. Yang, S., Wu, J., Dai, F.: Localized movement-assisted sensor deployment in wireless sensor networks. In: (WiMa) (in conjunction with IEEE MASS 2006) (2006)

Reliable and Fast Detection of Gradual Events in Wireless Sensor Networks

Liping Peng, Hong Gao, Jianzhong Li, Shengfei Shi, and Boduo Li

Harbin Institute of Technology, China
{lppeng,honggao,lijzh,shengfei,boduo}@hit.edu.cn

Abstract. Event detection is among the most important applications of wireless sensor networks. Due to the fact that sensor readings do not always represent the true attribute values, previous literatures suggested threshold-based voting mechanism which involves collecting votes of all neighbors to disambiguate node failures from events, instead of reporting an event directly based on the judgement of single sensor node. Although such mechanism significantly reduces false positives, it inevitably introduces false negatives which lead to a detection delay under the scenario of gradual events. In this paper, we propose a new detection method – the bit-string match voting (BMV), which provides a response time close to that of the direct reporting method and a false positive rate even lower than that of the threshold-based voting method. Furthermore, BMV is able to avoid repeated and redundant reports of the same event, thus prolongs the life of the network. Extensive simulations are given to demonstrate and verify the advantages of BMV.

1 Introduction

Wireless sensor networks (WSN) are of great significance in resolving many real-world problems, and have attracted increasing research interests in recent years. One of the most important applications of WSN is the detection of events, most of which in the real-world have the property of gradualness – we call them *gradual events*, such as fire and gas leakage[1]. The range of a gradual event changes slowly and the effect of a gradual event attenuates gradually as the distance from the event increases. It is very challenging to achieve a gradual-event-oriented detection with both short response time and high report reliability due to the node failures and the reading errors. In this paper, we focus on the reliable and fast detection of gradual events defined by thresholds, meanwhile guarantee a low energy cost by proposing an in-network method.

There are two existing methods to detect threshold-based events. The first one is a natural yet naive method – a sensor node directly reports an event whenever its reading exceeds the threshold[5]. We name it as *direct reporting* (DR) mechanism. Although this method can detect events in a short response time, it lacks a high report reliability since sensor readings do not always reveal the genuine attribute values due to the node failure and reading error caused by the intrinsic hardware constraints. For example, when a sensor node is damaged

Y. Li et al. (Eds.): WASA 2008, LNCS 5258, pp. 261–273, 2008.

or energy-exhausted, the sensor readings are likely to be constantly high[2] and may exceed the threshold upon which certain event is defined. If a node directly reports an event when its readings exceeds the threshold, the network, as a consequence, intends to report fake events, which is referred as *false positive*.

The second method is a *threshold-based voting* (TV) mechanism[1] proposed in [4]. Considering the fact that faulty nodes are likely to be uncorrelated, while environmental conditions are spatially correlated, TV mechanism disambiguates node failures and reading errors by examining the readings of nearby nodes to reduce false positives and thus to enhance the reliability of event detection. However, it causes the report of true events delayed or even missed inevitably under the scenario of a gradual event (we will formally describe the characteristics of gradual events in detail in Sect. 3.1). Name a node which is the first to detect an event and asks its neighbor nodes to vote for this event as a *reporting node*. Since its neighbors are farther away from the event and thus their readings may not reach the threshold, they will likely give negative votes. As a result, this event will not be reported to the base station until it has escalated to a certain scale, making at least half of neighbors' readings reach the threshold. This is referred as *false negative* in the event detection. As we can see, the false negatives lead to a delay in the detection of events, which need to be maximally eliminated.

Contour map matching is recently introduced to detect events with complex tempo-spatial patterns[1], which are quite different from the threshold-based events. However, it involves matching between globally constructed snapshots of a contour map and a user-specified event pattern, and thus consumes much energy. Actually, the detection of gradual events defined by thresholds can be accomplished locally.

In this paper, we propose a novel detection method for gradual events – *Bit-string Match Voting* (BMV). The intuition is that although readings of a certain node may not be dramatically affected by a gradual event to reach the threshold, there must be a trend in its recent readings. We use bit-strings to record trends and each neighbor of the reporting node votes by matching its own bit-string with that of the reporting node.

The contributions of this paper include:

- To the best of our knowledge, this is the first work to specifically put forward the concept of the gradual event.
- We propose a novel in-network detection method: Bit-string Match Voting (BMV), to quickly and reliably detect gradual events with little energy consumption. It provides a short response time close to that of the DR method and a report reliability which is even higher than that of the TV method.
- Extensive simulations are conducted, which validate the effectiveness of BMV.

The rest of the paper is organized as follows. Section 2 discusses related work. Section 3 presents the framework of Bit-string Match Voting method, whose efficiency and reliability are corroborated by extensive simulative evaluations in Sect. 4. We conclude the paper in Sect. 5.

---

[1] This mechanism is named as Optimal Threshold Decision Scheme in [4].

2   Related Work

The definitions of events in previous literature fall into two categories: threshold-based[5,4,3] and non-threshold-based[1,6], the methods of which are discussed in the following two paragraphs correspondingly.

Events are defined as complex filters in [5], each of which can be considered as a special form of the threshold, then expressed as a table of conditions, which can be distributed throughout the network. Once a tuple is satisfied, a report is returned. [3] develops a local event detection method – exponentially weighted moving average(EWMA) without collecting neighbors' readings, while still maintaining certain reliability in the presence of reading errors. It calculates short-term and long-term moving averages with different gain parameters and compares the ratio of the short-term average to the long-term average with a pre-defined threshold to decide whether an event has occurred. However, the value of the ratio threshold is less intuitive compared with the straightforward attribute threshold, thus it needs more prior knowledge to set the threshold. Furthermore, false positives caused by sensor failures cannot be tackled by EWMA. [4] defines event directly upon attribute thresholds, and introduces Optimal Threshold Decision Scheme. The detection method involves the collection of 0/1 judge predicates provided by neighbors according to whether their readings exceed the threshold. However, within the context of gradual events, when the reading of the sensor node which is the nearest to the event exceeds the threshold, the readings on most of its neighbors may remain below the threshold, as a gradual event expands slowly and its impact on sensor readings attenuates with distance. Thus, the voting inclines to reject the event report when a gradual event just appears until the event has grown to certain scale. Although the event will finally be reported, the delay may be intolerable as such events may cause tremendous loss and become more uncontrollable every minute.

[1] defines event as time series with each element of the series representing a user-specified partial contour map of certain attribute, which is able to characterize the spatial-temporal patterns of event, and converts the event detection problem into a pattern matching one. The network builds or updates contour maps bottom-up at each time stamp and the matching between this globally constructed contour map and a predefined event is carried out at the base station. Since the method is not localized and the messages transmitted between two nodes are complicated, the cost of this method is higher compared with TV method proposed in [4]. [7,6] try to discover homogeneous regions to estimate the event boundary (which splits the whole region into event area and non-event area) to indirectly detect events. Our work differs with [7,6] since we focus on the direct detection and we adopt threshold-based definition of events.

3   Bit-String Match Voting

In this section, we discuss the problem of detecting gradual events and present the bit-string match voting (BMV) method. The goal is to report as soon as possible when an event occurs and avoid reporting fake events caused by the inaccuracy of sensor readings. We assume that we have a reliable network layer for safe data transmission.

3.1 Preliminaries

Suppose that the surveillance area is a 2-dimensional space $\mathcal{R}$. The actual value of some attribute for a point $p \in \mathcal{R}$ at a time stamp t is $A(p, t)$.

For any t, $A(p, t)$ is spatially continuous. For ease of discussion in later parts, we introduce the symbol $\mathcal{D}(k, t)$ as the *k-region at time t*, which is defined as

$$\mathcal{D}(k, t) = \{p : A(p, t) \geq k\},$$

and the notation $|\mathcal{D}(k, t)|$ as the area of region $\mathcal{D}(k, t)$.

Definition 1 (Event). *Given an attribute value λ_e as a priori, if $\exists p \in \mathcal{R}$ such that $A(p, t) \geq \lambda_e$, we say an event exists at time t. We call λ_e the event value and $\mathcal{D}(\lambda_e, t)$ the event region at time t.*

λ_e is the character attribute value of an event and is obtained from natural observations. For example, $\lambda_e = 800K$ in a fire event means that the fire flame temperature is 800K.

Events can be divided into two categories: the *upgrowth event* whose event value is greater than the normal attribute values, and the *downgrowth event* whose event value is less than the normal attribute values. Considering that these two cases are theoretically equivalent, we only discuss the upgrowth events in this paper without losing generality. The downgrowth events can be handled in the similar way.

In real applications, in order to detect events earlier and at the same time avoid false positives, the judgement of the occurrence of events is usually based on another attribute value λ_r which lies between λ_e and the normal attribute value when no event appears, rather than λ_e itself. For example, the temperature of a fire event is usually 600-1000K[8], the temperature under normal situations is 250-310K, and the threshold of reporting a fire event can be set to 380K.

Definition 2 (Report Region). *Given a predetermined threshold λ_r, $\mathcal{D}(\lambda_r, t)$ is called the report region at time t.*

In this paper, we focus on the detection of gradual events, which keep growing in a certain duration of time rather than disappear immediately after they happen. Now we describe the *gradual event* by listing its properties. Some properties of gradual events are widely used, but never clearly defined. A gradual event is an event that has the following two properties.

Property 1 (Spatial Gradualness). There exists a positive number α, $\forall p_1, p_2 \in \mathcal{R} - \mathcal{D}(\lambda_e, t)$, $|A(p_1, t) - A(p_2, t)| \leq \alpha \cdot ||p_1 - p_2||$, where $||p_1 - p_2||$ is the euclidian distance between p_1 and p_2.

α limits the geographical change of attribute values. Property 1 indicates the spatial correlation of attribute values. Generally, the effect on attribute values brought by an event is proportional to d^{-2} [9], where d is the distance from the event.

Property 2 (Temporal Gradualness). $\forall t$ when an event exists, $\mathcal{D}(\lambda_e, t) \subset \mathcal{D}(\lambda_e, t+1)$, and $E(|\mathcal{D}(\lambda_e, t+1) - \mathcal{D}(\lambda_e, t)|) = V_e \cdot f(\mathcal{D}(\lambda_e, t))$, with E representing the expectation and f representing a function that always returns a positive number. Different functions stand for different event models(will be further discussed soon). V_e is a positive number used to limit the growing speed.

Property 2 describes that an event keeps growing, which is quite common for physical events(e.g. fires). As most physical events grow irregularly, we use the expectation to describe the growing in Property 2, where V_e is the *growing speed* and f is the *growing model*. However, V_e can not be arbitrarily small – it has to grow apparently faster than the change of the natural environment.

As the first attempt to put forward the concept of the gradual event, we further introduce three basic growing models that we observe in the real world.

- *Linearly Growing Model*
  In this type, $f(\mathcal{D}(\lambda_e, t)) = 1$. Therefore $|\mathcal{D}(\lambda_e, t)|$ can be approximately considered as an arithmetic progression. A typical example is the gas leakage. At the very beginning of a gas leakage event, the source of the leakage uniformly emits gas, making the leakage area grows linearly.
- *Exponentially Growing Model*
  In this type, $f(\mathcal{D}(\lambda_e, t)) = |\mathcal{D}(\lambda_e, t)|$. Therefore $|\mathcal{D}(\lambda_e, t)|$ can be approximately considered as a geometric progression. A typical example is the eutrophication, a process where water bodies receive excess nutrients that stimulate excessive and exponential propagation of floating algae [10].
- *Boundary Growing Model*
  In this type, $f(\mathcal{D}(\lambda_e, t)) = |\mathcal{B}(\mathcal{D}(\lambda_e, t))|$, where $\mathcal{B}(\mathcal{D}(\lambda_e, t))$ is the boundary of region $\mathcal{D}(\lambda_e, t)$ and $|\mathcal{B}(\mathcal{D}(\lambda_e, t))|$ is its length. A typical example is the fire, where the flame at the boundary spreads and ignites the adjacent region.

The intuitive meaning of V_e differs for different models. For example, $V_e = 10$ for the first model means that the event extends 10 units of area per sample period; $V_e = 0.3$ for the second model means that the event extends 30% of current size in the next sample period, and for the third model means that the event extends 30% of the neighbor area of the current boundary.

In real applications, the readings of a sensor node may not accurately tell the actual attribute values mainly in two aspects. First, a sensor node may fail and keep reporting readings nowhere near the actual attribute values. Besides, even if a sensor node is properly working, its reading may still contain errors, though typically not far away from the actual attribute values. Let $A'(p, t)$ denotes a sensor reading at the position p and time stamp t, so the error is $A'(p, t) - A(p, t)$.

Since the inaccuracy of sensor readings may lead to both false positives and false negatives in the event detection, the immediate question is how to make the network reliable and at the same time responsive. We present BMV, which leverages the special properties of gradual events together with the voting mechanism, as a solution in Sect. 3.2.

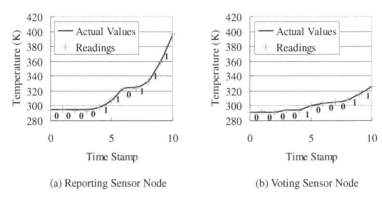

(a) Reporting Sensor Node   (b) Voting Sensor Node

Fig. 1. Example of pattern encoding

3.2 Voting Strategy

We design a new strategy to give votes more accurately, rather than simply voting according to the event threshold. According to Property 1, when a node calls its neighbors to vote, although the readings of a neighbor node may not exceed the threshold, its recent sample readings should follow a similar pattern with that of the node that starts the voting, if both nodes are working properly. Since the communication in WSN is very costly, we encode the pattern into a bit-string on the basis of Property 2 to save the communication cost.

In our approach, each sensor node periodically samples the attribute values. A buffer is set on each node to keep several latest sample readings. When the current reading on a sensor node exceeds the event threshold (thus it becomes a *reporting node*), it encodes its buffered readings into a bit-string which records the growing pattern of these latest readings. Then this node calls for a voting process by sending its bit-string to its neighbors. If a neighbor's reading at current time stamp reaches the threshold, it returns a positive vote. If not, it encodes its buffered readings into a bit-string, and tries to match the two bit-strings by our matching method, which will be introduced later. If the matching succeeds, the neighbor node gives a positive vote. After the reporting node collects all votes from its neighbors, it reports the event to the base station only if positive voting rate exceeds an *voting percent q*. We name our method as Bit-string Match Voting (BMV). We first introduce the pattern encoding and bit-string matching method, then give the detailed voting process.

Pattern Encoding. Intuitively, if the values of two adjacent readings on a node differ significantly, it means the scale of the event has been escalated, which is called a *jump*. If such a *jump* can also be captured and verified by its nearby sensor nodes, then it is evidence that the reporting sensor node is working properly, and the event should be reported. Based on this intuition, we propose the encoding scenario as follows:

If a node's local buffer contains $n + 1$ readings $A'(p, t - n)$, $A'(p, t - n + 1)$, $\ldots$, $A'(p, t)$, then we can get an n-bit string $(b_0, b_1, \ldots, b_{n-1})$, where

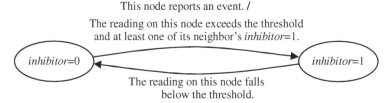

Fig. 2. Status transformation of inhibitor

$$b_i = \begin{cases} 1 & \text{if } A'(p, t - n + i + 1) - A'(p, t - n + i) > \delta \\ 0 & \text{otherwise} \end{cases}.$$

δ is a positive number which should be determined according to the distribution of the reading error, and is typically set to be β times of the standard deviation of reading error's distribution. Correspondingly, we call δ the *encoding distance* and β the *relative encoding distance*. Recall that here what we consider is upgrowth events, therefore we do not record any decreasing trend.

Example 1. If a sensor node buffers the latest 11 temperature readings (294, 295, 293.4, 292.9, 297.8, 308.1, 322.7, 322.9, 332.3, 359.1, 396.3), as shown in Fig. 1 (a), the corresponding bit-string is 0000110111 for $\delta = 5$.

Bit-string Matching. We define two functions $AND(\omega_1, \omega_2)$ and $COUNT(\omega)$ where ω_1, ω_2 and ω are all bit-strings, and the length of ω_1 equals to that of ω_2. $AND(\omega_1, \omega_2)$ returns the bit-string which is the logic AND of ω_1 and ω_2. $COUNT(\omega)$ returns the number of 1's in ω.

When a voting node performs the bit-string matching, it should have already received a bit-string ω_r from the reporting node. To match ω_r with locally buffered readings, the voting node encodes its own readings to ω_v by the same pattern encoding methods. ω_r matches with the pattern on the voting node if and only if

$$AND(\omega_r, \omega_v) = \omega_v \text{ and } COUNT(\omega_v) > 0.$$

Example 2. If the reporting node is the same as in Example 1, and the buffered readings of a voting node is (291.1, 292.7, 290.9, 293.6, 293.8, 299.5, 304.3, 304.7, 308, 315.7, 325.9), thus ω_r is 0000110111 and ω_v is 0000100011 for $\delta = 5$. So ω_r matches the pattern on this voting node.

Voting Process. The voting process has been briefly introduced at the beginning of Sect. 3.2. But one event may be reported repeatedly for quite a long period, which will reduce the lifetime of the network. To solve this problem, we set a bit flag called *inhibitor* on each node, initialized as 0. The status of *inhibitor* is maintained according to Fig. 2. A nodes p's *inhibitor* is 1 at time t means that, $p \in \mathcal{D}(\lambda_r, t)$ and there exists a node $p' \in \mathcal{D}(\lambda_r, t)$ where p' satisfies:

1. p' reported an event before t.
2. There exists a multi-hop communication path $p' \to p$ such that all the nodes on the path are in $\mathcal{D}(\lambda_r, t)$.

Algorithm 1. ExceedThreshold()

Input: encoding distance δ, bit-string length n, voting percent q, locally buffered
readings $readings[\,]$
1: **if** $inhibitor = 0$ **then**
2:    $neighInhibitors[\,] = $ CollectNeighborInhibitor();
3:    **for all** i is a neighbor **do**
4:       **if** $neighInhibitors[i] = 1$ **then**
5:          $inhibitor = 1$;
6:    **if** $inhibitor = 0$ **then**
7:       $bitString = $ Encode(δ, n, $readings[\,]$);
8:       $voteResult = $ RequestVoting($bitString$);
9:       **if** $voteResult$.positiveVotePercent$\geq q$ **then**
10:          ReportEvent();
11:          $inhibitor = 1$;

Algorithm 2. ReceiveVotingRequest()

Input: the bit-string received from the reporting sensor node $bitString$, threshold λ_r,
encoding distance δ, bit-string length n, locally buffered readings $readings[\,]$
1: **if** $readings[\,]$.mostRecentReading$\geq \lambda_r$ **then**
2:    ReturnVote(POSITIVE);
3: **else**
4:    $localString = $ Encode(δ, n, $readings[\,]$);
5:    $match = $ Match($localString$, $bitString$);
6:    **if** $match = $TRUE **then**
7:       ReturnVote(POSITIVE);
8:    **else**
9:       ReturnVote(NEGATIVE);

Intuitively, if a node's *inhibitor* is 1, at least one node in the same connected
subregion of the report region has already reported the event. Therefore, another
report is unnecessary.

The detailed voting process is described in Algorithm 1 and 2. The procedure
ExceedThreshold() is called on a node whenever its latest reading exceeds λ_r.
Line 2 collects all its neighbor nodes' *inhibitors*. Line 8 starts a voting, and
broadcasts the bit-string to all neighbors. Line 10 reports an event to the base
station. The procedure ReceiveVotingRequest() runs on a node whenever it
receives the request for voting from its neighbor. Line 2, 7 and 9 send its vote
to the reporting node.

4   Simulations

In this section we present simulative study of our approach compared with DR
and TV. The response time and reliability of the three approaches are tested
respectively.

4.1   Simulation Setup

We perform all simulations with C++ codes and some interface functions provided by MATLAB C Math Library. Each of our simulation results represents an average summary of 100 runs.

Event. Based on Sect. 3.1, we simulate a fire event whose event value λ_e is 800K. It firstly occurs at a random point in the network and then gradually grows at a velocity of V_e. At any time stamp t, the attribute value $A(p,t)$ is λ_e if p is inside the event area $\mathcal{D}(\lambda_e, t)$. If p is outside the event area,

$$A(p,t) = \lambda_e \cdot \left(1 + \frac{d(p)}{\sqrt{\frac{|\mathcal{D}(\lambda_e, t)|}{\pi}}} \right)^{-2}$$

where $d(p)$ represents the euclidean distance between p and $\mathcal{B}(\mathcal{D}(\lambda_e, t))$.

Network. In our simulation, 100 sensor nodes are uniformly distributed in a square area of 100×100 m^2. The communication radius is 20m. The readings of a normally working node fluctuate around the actual attribute values at corresponding time stamps due to the existence of errors, which are independent and obey the normal distribution $N(0, \sigma^2)$. Based on our data set collected from real sensor nodes as well as the Intel Lab Data[2], the readings of a failed node slowly and linearly grow until one reading meets the physical limitation of the sensor, and then the constant high readings are given out. The growing speed is much slower than an event. For our temperature data set, it is about 1-2K per minute, and we adopt this real phenomenon in the simulation.

Table 1. System Parameters

Parameter	Default Value
Growing speed	0.3
Error's standard deviation	2K
Event threshold	380K
Voting percent	50%
Encoding length	7
Relative encoding distance	2

Parameters and Metrics. We simulate two scenarios: one is that a fire event exists in the network, and the other is that there are some failed sensor nodes in the network but no event actually exists. The former scenario is used to demonstrate the response time of DR method, TV method and BMV method, whereas the latter one is to exhibit the report reliability of the TV method and BMV method.

In the first scenario, we test the response time (from the occurrence of an event till the reporting node sends the report to the base station) of the three approaches with respect to several parameters, including the growing speed V_e, the error's standard deviation σ, the event threshold λ_r, the encoding length n, the relative encoding distance β and the voting percent q. The first three parameters impact the sensor readings and therefore they affect the response time of all the three methods. On the contrary, the other three parameters are the input of the BMV method, so they only influence the response time of the BMV method. In the second scenario, the only parameter that we care about is the percentage of the failed nodes in the network, and the metric is the report reliability. The default values are listed in Table 1 and in each simulation we examine only one parameter.

4.2   Response Time

Growing Speed. In this set of experiments, we test the three typical models of events discussed in Sect. 3.1 in order to exhibit the suitability of BMV under different growing models. The results are depicted in Fig. 3 (a)-(c). It can be observed that BMV's response time is quite close to DR's and better than TV's in all cases. This observation validates the effectiveness of our method. Figure 3 also shows that, as the growing speed increases, all three methods can detect events in less time, but the difference between BMV and TV are decreasing. This phenomenon indicates that although BMV always outperforms TV, it benefits more to use BMV in the scenario of gradual events.

Error's Standard Deviation. We incrementally change the error's standard deviation σ and Fig. 4 (a) shows the effect of changing σ on DR, TV and BMV. The result reveals that the increase of σ does not affect DR and TV much yet raises the response time of BMV. The reason behind this phenomenon is the principles of the three methods. DR and TV just care about whether the absolute reading exceeds the threshold, therefore the error's standard deviation has less to do with these two methods. However, for BMV, since we fix the relative encoding distance as 2 (Table 1), the absolute encoding distance increases at a two times speed of the increasing of σ. Therefore, it is more possible for sensor nodes to generate all-zero bit-strings when the error's standard deviation is high, which will then result in the "dis-match" and finally lead to a slow response. However, thanks to current hardware design techniques, our test dataset well covers the possible values of the error's standard deviation of temperature sensors in real applications. As can be observed in Fig. 4 (a), our method outperforms TV significantly in all cases.

Event Threshold. In this simulation, we alter the event threshold from 350K to 750K in steps of 50K and Fig. 4 (b) displays the effects on the response time of the three methods brought by the threshold. As expected, a lower threshold brings a faster response. Again, the result suggests that BMV is much more efficient than TV in all cases.

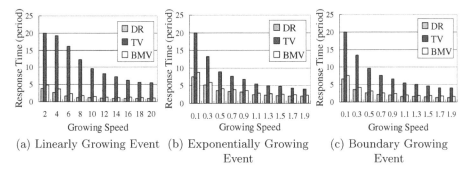

(a) Linearly Growing Event (b) Exponentially Growing   (c) Boundary Growing
                                      Event   Event

Fig. 3. Response time v.s. growing speed for three event models

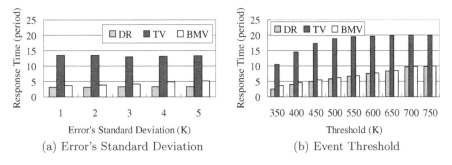

(a) Error's Standard Deviation   (b) Event Threshold

Fig. 4. Response time w.r.t. error's standard deviation, event threshold

Voting Percent. As an input parameter for BMV, in this simulation, we vary the voting percent from 10% to 100% to see its effect on BMV's response time. Fig. 5 (a) shows the result. As expected, a higher voting percent brings a slower response.

Relative Encoding Distance and Encoding Length. These two parameters influence the response time of BMV by determining the bit-strings generated by sensor nodes. Figure 5 (b)-(c) shows the impact of relative encoding distance and encoding length on BMV's response time. In both figures, the response time first decreases and then increases. The reason behind this trend is as follows: It is likely to have the "inverse bit" between two bit-strings given a small value of relative encoding distance because it will easily consider the fluctuation brought by the reading error as a jump, but the reading error is independent. And a big value of relative encoding distance will likely lead to the all-zero bit-string; Quite similarly, a small value of encoding length is more likely to generate all-zero bit-strings while a big one is more likely to result in the "inverse bit" between two bit-strings. According to Sect. 3.2, both "inverse bit" and all-zero bit-strings will bring the "dis-match" and thus a slow response.

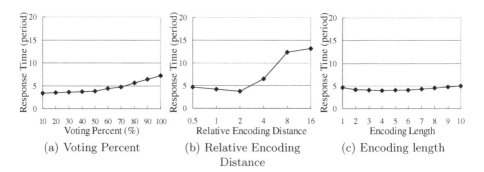

Fig. 5. Response time w.r.t. voting percent, relative encoding distance, encoding length

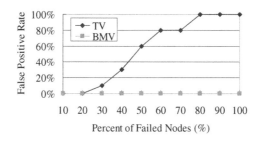

Fig. 6. False Positive Rate w.r.t. Failure Probability

4.3   Report Reliability

Fig. 6 shows that BMV never pass a fake report and the false positive rate of TV increases with the increasing of the percentage of failed nodes. Since the failed nodes always give out high readings above the threshold according to our data set collected by real nodes and the Intel Lab Data[2], the bit-strings generated by failed neighbor nodes are "all-zero", as a consequence, no neighbor will give a positive vote. On the contrary, as for the TV method, the failed neighbors are likely to wrongly pass the fake report due to the threshold-based judgement.

In summary, the BMV method on one hand provides a short response time close to that of the DR method, and on the other hand has a report reliability even higher than that of the TV method.

5   Conclusions

In this paper, we put forward the concept of the gradual event and design a new reliable and fast event detection method – the Bit-string Match Voting (BMV), which first encodes the readings in each sensor node's buffer into bit-strings and then determines whether to support a report by matching the bit-string of the reporting node with that of its neighbor nodes. This method on one hand maximally eliminates false negatives introduced by the threshold-based voting (TV) method under the scenario of gradual events, thus provides a short response time close to that of the direct reporting (DR) method. On the other hand, considering the failed sensor nodes intend to present fixed reading pattern, the BMV method can avoid false positives as well even all neighbors of a failed reporting node are failed, thus provides the report reliability even higher than that of the TV method. Furthermore, BMV is able to avoid frequent requests for the voting process as well as the repeated and redundant reports of the same event, and thus prolong the life of the network.

Acknowledgements

This work is supported by the National Grand Fundamental Research 973 Program of China under Grant No. 2006CB303000, the Key Program of the National Natural Science Foundation of China under Grant No. 60533110, and the Program for New Century Excellent Talents in University under Grant No. NCET-05-0333.

References

1. Xue, W., Luo, Q., Chen, L., Liu, Y.: Contour map matching for event detection in sensor networks. SIGMOD (2006)
2. Intel Lab Data: `http://berkeley.intel-research.net/labdata/`
3. Werner-Allen, G., Johnson, J., Ruiz, M., Lees, J., Welsh, M.: Monitoring volcanic eruptions with a wireless sensor network. EWSN (2005)
4. Krishnamachari, B., Sitharama, I.: Distributed bayesian algorithms for fault-tolerant event region detection in wireless sensor network. IEEE Transactions on Computers (2004)
5. Abadi, D., Madden, S., Lindner, W.: Reed: Robust, efficient filtering and event detection in sensor networks. VLDB (2005)
6. Subramaniam, S., Kalogeraki, V., Palpanas, T.: Distributed real-time detection and tracking of homogeneous regions in sensor networks. RTSS (2006)
7. Nowak, R., Mitra, U.: Boundary estimation in sensor networks: Theory and methods. In: Zhao, F., Guibas, L.J. (eds.) IPSN 2003. LNCS, vol. 2634, Springer, Heidelberg (2003)
8. Lim, A., Chin Liew, S., Lim, K., Kwoh, L.: Retrieval of subpixel fire temperature and fire area in moderate resolution imaging spectrometer. IGARSS (2002)
9. Yu, X., Niyogi, K., Mehrotra, S., Venkatasubramanian, N.: Adaptive target tracking in sensor networks. CNDS (2004)
10. Eutrophication, `http://toxics.usgs.gov/definitions/eutrophication.html`

Mobility Model and Relay Management for Disaster Area Wireless Networks

Wenxuan Guo and Xinming Huang

Department of Electrical and Computer Engineering
Worcester Polytechnic Institute, 100 Institute Road, Worcester, MA 01609
{wxguo,xhuang}@wpi.edu

Abstract. This paper investigates the disaster area communication system using relay-assisted wireless networks. At first, a novel mobility model is proposed to describe the movement pattern of the first responders as Mobile Nodes (MNs) within a large disaster area. Secondly, we study the relay management of placing a fixed number of Relay Nodes (RNs) to cover as many MNs as possible within the disaster area. We first formulate the Mobile Node Association (MNA) problem, and propose a Bipartite-graph based Approach (BA). Afterwards, a Relay Node Placement (RNP) problem is formulated and two different algorithms, including the Constrained Exhaustive Search (CES) algorithm as the optimal solution and the Bipartite graph based Incremental Greedy (BIG) algorithm. Simulation results are presented to compare the performance of two algorithms, which show that the BIG algorithm can produce near-optimal solutions but with significantly reduced computational complexity.

1 Introduction

First responders require robust communication systems in catastrophe situations, thus a rapidly deployable replacement network is needed due to probable collapse of primary communication infrastructure over the disaster area. Such a communication system features: no restrictions of wires or to a fixed connection, quick and effortless installation, and most importantly, mobile nodes (MNs), instantiated by transceivers carried by first responders, need to be connected to the backbone networks and eventually reach some command center. The properties of wireless network, such as easiness to deploy, freedom to connect, and communicating through radio waves instead of data cables, guarantee wireless network technology to be a perfect candidate for disaster area communication. When establishing such a Disaster Area Wireless Network (DAWN), we need to understand the mobility model of MNs as well as calculate positions for placing Relay Nodes (RNs) such that all the MNs can be connected to the backbone network.

When maintaining the functionality of DAWN, understanding the mobility model of the MNs is an important task because the network topology highly depends on the model used. Traditional assumptions are: MNs are allowed to move over the whole disaster area; MNs are connected to the backbone network all the time. However, such assumptions do not always apply in reality. First of all, the assumption that MNs can choose any destination within the disaster area is not valid. For instance, a firefighter walking across a burning forest would endanger his life. Then, does it always apply

Y. Li et al. (Eds.): WASA 2008, LNCS 5258, pp. 274–285, 2008.

that the MNs can connect to the backbone network? Again, the answer would be negative in most occasions because MNs have limited transmission range. As rescue teams are moving further away from the access point, they risk losing connection with the backbone network. Therefore, we have to build a practical mobility model for first responders within the disaster area with all the above-mentioned essentials taken into account.

Connectivity is of the greatest importance to MNs in DAWN. The frequently lost connection to the backbone network could decrease disaster relief efficiency, disorder rescue efforts and even jeopardize first responders' lives. We ought to place RNs near the MNs to establish the backbone network. Due to the abundance of available bandwidth in disaster area, we assume that each RN can set its bands at unused frequencies, so that they do not interfere with each other.

In this paper, we mainly fulfill two tasks:

– *proposing a novel and practical mobility model for MNs in disaster area*: we describe typical movement pattern of first responders in a disaster area.
– *placing fixed number of RNs such that maximal number of MNs can access the backbone network*: based on the mobility model, we first discretize the planar space and formulate the Relay Node Placement (RNP) problem. Then we propose two algorithms: the Constrained Exhaustive Search (CES) algorithm and Bipartite graph based Incremental Greedy (BIG) algorithm to solve the RNP algorithm.

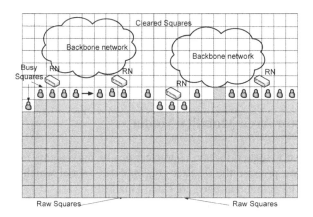

Fig. 1. A realistic scenario of DAWN in the middle of the disaster area relief process. The squares with head portraits denote busy squares. White squares denote cleared squares. Shaded squares denote raw squares yet to clear.

The rest of this paper is organized as follows. In Section 2, related work on disaster area networks and mobility model are presented; In Section 3, we describe the mobility model of MNs within the disaster area; Section 4 formulates the MNA and RNP problem, followed by the bipartite graph based approach presented in Section 5 and BIG and CES algorithms are presented in Section 6. Simulation results are given in 8 followed by conclusions in Section 9.

2   Related Work

Research efforts focusing on disaster area networks begin to increase in recent years due to frequent happening of natural and man-made disasters. In [8], a hybrid system model of wireless data networks for emergency communications in disaster area is proposed. The system modelling incorporates network-controlled handover, resource allocation, and admission control. In [9], a data collection framework for disaster mitigation and rescue operation in addition to a wireless sensor network protocol is proposed. There are also research efforts focusing on first responder networks. [6] examines two hierarchical network solutions which allow the delivery of mission-critical multimedia data between rescue teams and headquarters over extremely long distances using a combination of wireless network technologies and multimedia software applications to meet the requirements of disaster rescue communication scenarios. In [3], an empirical long-time measurement of a single first responder channel is presented, and data analysis is then performed to generate a realistic model of synthetical push-to-talk voice traffic for network simulation in disaster area network studies.

In recent years a lot of different mobility models have been proposed and used for performance evaluation of networks. Models like the abstract Random-Waypoint-Mobility-Model [4] or Gauss-Markov-Mobility-Model [5] describe random-based movement and distribute the nodes over the complete simulation area. However, a distribution and movement of the nodes over the complete simulation area does not fit into the characteristics of a disaster area. [10] investigated a collaboration scheme for rescue robots for reliable and effective operation of rescue systems using robots, which focused on the collaborative movement of robots to maintain their wireless network. Furthermore, there are two approaches [2,7] that describe two event-driven role-based mobility model for disaster area relief applications. However, these two models only apply in small area with specific disaster sites.

3   The Disaster Area Mobility Model

In this section we first describe the characteristics of movements in a large disaster area. Secondly, we propose the disaster area mobility model which represents these characteristics. The notation utilized are listed in table 2.

3.1   Movements Within a Large Disaster Area

We first discretize the whole disaster area into small squares, each square with a CI value to show how severe the disaster is in it. The squares that have never been relieved are called raw squares. When there are MNs in one square, its CI value decreases linearly with time multiplied by the number of MNs, as in Eq. (1). Such squares are named as busy squares. Obviously, raw squares and busy squares are uncleared squares. A square is said to be cleared if the CI value is reduced to zero. It is thus called as a cleared square. Each first responder does not stop working in the square until it is cleared. When first responders finish clearing one square, they split up and enter the adjacent uncleared squares. Specifically, the larger number of first responders working in the square and less the CI value of the square is, the fewer first responders are entering that square. In this way, from several beginning squares, the first responders can finally clear the whole disaster area as they go deeper and wider.

$$CI_{t+1,i,j} = \begin{cases} CI_{t,i,j} - \xi MN_{t,i,j} & : & CI_{t,i,j} > \xi MN_{t,i,j} \\ 0 & : & CI_{t,i,j} \leq \xi MN_{t,i,j} \end{cases} \qquad (1)$$

Now we understand the square-based movement pattern for the MNs, then what about their mobility pattern within each square? As we are unknown about the differences between the situations in each square, we presume first responders are moving according to the Waypoint model [4] for simplicity concerns: each picks up a random destination within the square and then heads for it. The proposition of MNs' random movement within a small square would render this mobility model easily extended to other kinds of disaster area scenarios.

3.2 Mobility Model for First Responders

In section 3.1 we discussed the movements of first responders to relieve a large scale disaster area and provide intuition behind. In this section we formalize the mobility model of MNs as in table 1.

Table 1. Mobility Model for MNs

1   Divide disaster area into squares;
2   **while** $CI_t \neq zero$ /∗ Uncleared square(s) still exist∗/
3   $\triangle \leftarrow 0$;
4   **for** each busy square $s_{i,j}$
5   **if** $CI_{i,j,t} > \xi MN_{i,j,t}$ /∗ $s_{i,j}$ can not be cleared now∗/
6         $CI_{i,j,t+1}=CI_{i,j,t}-\xi MN_{i,j,t}$;
7   **else**
8         $\triangle = Regroup(\triangle, MN_t, s_{i,j}, CI_t)$;
/ ∗ $MN_{i,j,t}$ split up and enter into neighbors of $s_{i,j}$ ∗/
9         $CI_{i,j,t+1}=0$;
10   **end if**
11   **end for**
12   $MN_{t+1} = MN_t + \triangle$;
13   $t=t+1$;
14 **end while**

From table 1,the function $Regroup$ is adopted to compute how the MNs split up and enter different adjacent squares when they clear one square. The procedure of the function $Regroup$ goes as follows: First obtain the CI values and number of MNs of the 3 squares adjacent to $s_{i,j}$, which are $CI_{i,(j-1),t}, CI_{i,(j+1),t}, CI_{i+1,j,t}$ and $MN_{i,j-1,t}$, $MN_{i,j+1,t}$, $MN_{i+1,j,t}$.(without loss of generality, we assume that the MNs enter the disaster area from the top boundary and explore downward, leftward and rightward). The number of MNs moving towards an square plus the number of MNs in that destination square should be in inverse proportion to the CI value of the square, such that

Table 2. Notation Utilized in Mobility Model

$Symbol$	$Definitions$
t	Time counter to record the current time
CI_t	CI values of squares within the disaster area at time t;
MN_t	Distribution of MNs over the disaster area at time t
$\triangle$	Change of MNs over the disaster area at the next time unit;
$s_{i,j}$	Square of the ith row and jth column
$MN_{i,j,t}$	Number of MNs in $s_{i,j}$ at time t
$CI_{i,j,t}$	The CI value of $s_{i,j}$ at time t
ξ	Time needed for one MN to reduce one unit of CI
$MN_{i,j,t}^d$	Number of MNs move downward at time t from $s_{i,j}$
$MN_{i,j,t}^l$	Number of MNs move leftward at time t from $s_{i,j}$
$MN_{i,j,t}^r$	Number of MNs move rightward at time t from $s_{i,j}$

the three adjacent neighboring squares can be cleared at the same time, illustrated as Eq. (2). In this case, the time required to clear the 3 adjacent squares would be as (3). Then we compute the change of the number of MNs in these squares after the $Regroup$ function is executed at $s_{i,j}$, and add the change into the record matrix $\triangle$.

$$\frac{CI_{i,j+1,t}}{MN_{i,j+1,t}+MN_{i,j,t}^r} = \frac{CI_{i,j+1,t}}{MN_{i,j-1,t}+MN_{i,j,t}^l} = \frac{CI_{i+1,j,t}}{MN_{i+1,j,t}+MN_{i,j,t}^d} \qquad (2)$$

$$T = \frac{CI_{i,j+1,t}+CI_{i,j-1,t}+CI_{i+1,j,t}}{\xi*(MN_{i,j+1,t}+MN_{i,j-1,t}+MN_{i+1,j,t}+MN_{i,j,t})} \qquad (3)$$

4   System Modelling and Problem Formulation

4.1   Network Modelling

We consider a set of MNs moving within the disaster area following the above mentioned mobility model and assume that a fixed number of RNs have to be deployed near MNs to keep all the MNs connected with the backbone network. We assume that all the MNs have small transmission range r, while the transmission range of RNs is large, and they can communicate with each other wherever their positions are. The transmission range of one MN is defined as the area of all points having a distance no larger than r with the MN. An MN n_i can communicate bi-directionally with a RN r_j if the distance between them $d(n_i, r_j) \leq r$. In other words, the MN n_i is said to be "covered" by r_j if r_j is within the transmission range of n_i. RNs are able to communicate with each other without distance constraints and they form the backbone network. We define the number of users each RN can support as the capacity of the RN, denoted as C. We assume that each RN's channel frequencies are different, thus no interference issues are considered in our network model.

4.2   Problem Formulation

As an ultimate goal, RNs should be placed at positions to maximize the number of MNs which can connect to RNs. As MNs are randomly moving within each busy square, it is impossible to get their exact position. Thus we need to cover the busy squares in order to get MNs connected.

Then we begin to present definition 1 before we start to formulate our problem.

Definition 1. *Denote the feasible circle area of busy square s_j is f_j. Assume f_{i_1}, $f_{i_2},....,f_{i_l}$ have some area overlap, then the shared area is defined as a circle region that only MNs within squares $s_{i_k},(1 \le k \le l)$ can access, denoted as $CR(f_{i_1}, f_{i_2}, ..., f_{i_l})$.*

Then the MNA problem is formulated as: At any time, MNs are distributed within a set of busy squares. The feasible circles of these busy squares intersect and yield a set of circle regions $\mathcal{CR} = \{CR(f_{i_1}, f_{i_2}, ..., f_{i_l}), 1 \le i \le |\mathcal{CR}|\}$, where $|\mathcal{CR}|$ denotes the cardinality of the set $\mathcal{CR}$. A fixed number of RNs $\{r_1, r_2, ..., r_M\}$ are deployed at $CR(f_{j_1}, f_{j_2}, ..., f_{j_l}), 1 \le j \le M$. Each RN can support at most C MNs to access in the squares covered by the RN.

$$
\begin{aligned}
max \quad & \sum_{i=1}^{N} \sum_{j=1}^{M} x_{ij} \\
s.t. \quad & x_{ij} \in \{0,1\}; \\
& \sum_{j=1}^{M} x_{ij} = 1; \\
& \sum_{i=1}^{N} x_{ij} \le C;
\end{aligned}
\tag{4}
$$

where $x_{ij} = 1$ denotes n_i is connected with r_j and 0 otherwise. The second constraint denotes that each MN can at most connect to one RN. The third constraint shows that at most C MNs can connect to one RN.

The RNP problem is formulated as: Given a set of busy squares, a number of MNs, with a transmission range r, distributed and moving randomly within these squares and a fixed number of RNs with a capacity of C, find the optimal position for the RNs, such that the most number of MNs can connect to RNs.

5   Optimal Association between MNs and RNs

In this section, we will describe a Bipartite graph-based Approach (BA) to find the optimal association between MNs and RNs. BA first transforms the MNA problem into a max-matching problem within a bipartite graph, and use a sparse matrix-based approach to find the maximum-size matching between the MNs and RNs. We first show how we transform the MNA problem into a max-matching problem within a bipartite graph.

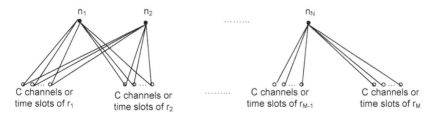

Fig. 2. The bipartite graph example showing the association relationship between MNs and RNs

Table 3. ACR

ACR($\mathcal{CR}$)
1   $\bar{\mathcal{CR}} \leftarrow CR_1$;
2   **for** i=2 to $|\mathcal{CR}|$
3   sign=0;
4   **for** j=1 to $|\bar{\mathcal{CR}}|$
5   **if** CR_j belongs to CR_i
6   remove CR_j from $\bar{\mathcal{CR}}$;
7   sign=1;
8   **end if**;
9   **if** CR_i belongs to CR_j
10   sign=2;
11   break;
12   **end if**;
13   **end for**;
14   **if** sign==0 or sign==1
15   add CR_i to $\bar{\mathcal{CR}}$;
16   **end if**;
17   **end for**;
18   **return** $\bar{\mathcal{CR}}$;

Given MNs placed within busy squares, and RNs deployed in some circle regions, the bipartite graph can be generated as Figure 2, where n_i denotes the ith MN, and N denotes the number of MNs.

In this paper, we use a sparse matrix-based approach presented in the paper [1] to find the maximal matching between MNs and channels of RNs or time slots for each RN. This approach yields the optimal solution. The complexity of finding the maximal matching within a bipartite graph is $O(M \times N)$.

6   Placing RNs for RNP Problem

In this section, we will introduce two algorithms: BIG algorithm and CES algorithm to find the optimal placements of RNs in circle regions, such that the maximal number of MNs can connect to RNs based on the method presented in section 5. Before introducing these two algorithms, I would like to present an approach, Aggregating Circle Regions (ACR), to decrease the complexities of the two algorithms.

6.1   ACR

The ACR algorithm aims to reduce the cardinality of the set of circle regions, thus greatly diminishes the solution space. Given a set of circle regions $\mathcal{CR}$, the ACR algorithm proceeds as in table 3. We assume CR($f_{i_1}, f_{i_2}, ..., f_{i_l}$) belongs to $CR(f_{j_1}, f_{j_2}, ..., f_{j_k})$ if $\{i_1, i_2, ..., i_l\} \subset \{j_1, j_2, ..., j_k\}$. Let $\mathcal{CR}$ and $\bar{\mathcal{CR}}$ denote the set of all circle regions and reduced set circle regions respectively. $|\mathcal{CR}|$ denotes the cardinality of the set $\mathcal{CR}$. CR_i denotes the ith circle region. f_i denotes the feasible circle of the ith square.

6.2 BIG

After executing the ACR algorithm to obtain a much smaller set of circle regions, we will describe our BIG algorithm to place RNs. The BIG algorithm is based on the following simple idea. Although it is not computationally feasible to perform an exhaustive search for placing M RNs simultaneously, it is possible to choose an optimal position to place one RN at a time. When the RN is placed at each circle region, the maximal matching between RNs and MNs can be obtained by utilizing BA. The best circle region for placing one node can be found by exhaustively searching all circle regions in $\mathcal{CR}$. Once the location for this RN is fixed, we can place the next RN following by exhaustively searching all circle regions again. However, it should be noted that when placing next RN, those previously placed RNs should be jointly considered to yield the maximum matching between RNs and MNs by utilizing the BA. Under this approach, the RNs are placed one by one until all M potential RNs are placed in the set of circle regions $\mathcal{CR}$. **BA**$(\tilde{CR})$ denotes the calculated optimal maximal matching when each element as a circle region in $\tilde{CR}$ contains one RN. The detailed algorithm is shown as in table 4.

Table 4. BIG

BIG$(\mathcal{CR})$
1   $\hat{CR} \leftarrow \emptyset$;
2   **for** i=1 to M
3   **for** j=1 to $|\mathcal{CR}|$
4       $\tilde{CR} \leftarrow \hat{CR} + \mathcal{CR}_j$
5       $value_j \leftarrow$ **BA**$(\tilde{CR})$
6   **end for**;
7   [maximum, index]=**Max**(value);
8     $\hat{CR} \leftarrow \hat{CR} + \mathcal{CR}_{index}$;
9   **end for**;
10 **return** $\hat{CR}$;

6.3 CES

In this section, we will introduce our CES algorithm. In order to obtain the optimal solution as a benchmark for our BIG algorithm, we try to search all the possible combinations of the circle regions. However, even after employing the ACR algorithm to reduce the size of solution space, the complexity for searching the optimal solution could still be as high as $\bar{\mathcal{CR}}^M$. Therefore, we resort to devising the CES algorithm to further reduce the solution space by adding more constraints to the combinations of circle regions. The constraint is that when playing RNs into circle regions, we try to avoid placing too many RNs within one circle region that some RNs have no MNs to support while there are MNs unable to access to any RNs within their vicinity. In particular, the number of RNs placed in one circle region times the number of MNs each RN can support should not exceed the sum of number of MNs in those busy squares that are covered by the RNs by more than C, as shown in Eq (5). Let $CR_i = CR(i_1, i_2, ..., i_l)$,

Num_i denotes the number RNs placed at CR_i, C denotes the number of MNs each RN can support.

$$Num_i \times C \leq \sum_{k=1}^{l} MN_{i_k} + C \tag{5}$$

7 Performance Evaluation

We first discuss the complexity of the ACR algorithm. Based on table 3, the procedure between line 5 to line 12 is iterated $(|\mathcal{CR}| - 1) \times |\mathcal{CR}|$ times, and the procedure between line 14 to line 16 is iterated $—\mathcal{CR}—$ times. The complexity for the ACR algorithm is $(|\mathcal{CR}| - 1) \times |\bar{\mathcal{CR}}| + |\mathcal{CR}| \times OM \times N$. Thus the final complexity of the ACR algorithm is $O(M \times N \times |\mathcal{CR}| \times |\bar{\mathcal{CR}}|)$.

Secondly, we will analyze the complexity of the BIG algorithm. Based on table 4, as the procedure on line 4 to 5 is iterated $M \times |\bar{\mathcal{CR}}|$ times, the complexity of the BIG algorithm is $O(M^2 \times N \times |\bar{\mathcal{CR}}|)$, where M denotes the number of RNs to be placed.

Thirdly, with respect to the CES algorithm, the complexity analysis is more complicated. According to the constraint in Eq. 5, each circle region can not host more than a limited number of RNs, thus by extending the list of circle regions a limited number (denoted as ϵ on average) of times, then we only need to pick up non-repeated M circle regions from the extended list to place the M RNs. Therefore, based on combinatorial theory, the complexity for the CES algorithm is $\frac{M \times N \times (\epsilon \times |\bar{\mathcal{CR}}|)!}{((\epsilon \times |\bar{\mathcal{CR}}|) - M)! \times M!}$, where ϵ denotes the average times each circle region is extended.

8 Numerical Investigation

We first establish a large 20*20 square disaster area. There are 100 first responders staying at $s_{1,1}$ and another 100 at $s_{1,2}$. The CI values are all set to be 10 at first. $\xi = 1$ means unit time is needed for one first responder to ease one unit of CI.

We set the number of RN to be 5, the transmission range of MNs to be 2, and the number of users each RN can support to be 40. The reduced set of circle regions after utilizing the ACR algorithm is shown in table 5. The deployment results yielded by the BIG and CES algorithm are shown in table 6.

Figure 3(a) shows the number of circle regions when the transmission range of MNs change. The cardinality of the original generated set of circle regions increases greatly as the transmission range of MNs increases from 1.5 to 2.75. The reason is that the

Table 5. Reduced set of circle regions

$CR(s_{12,10}, s_{13,9})$	$CR(s_{13,9}, s_{14,8})$	$CR(s_{1,14}, s_{2,14}, s_{3,14})$
$CR(s_{2,14}, s_{3,14}, s_{4,13})$	$CR(s_{3,14}, s_{4,13}, s_{5,14})$	$CR(s_{4,13}, s_{5,14}, s_{6,14})$
$CR(s_{5,14}, s_{6,14}, s_{7,11})$	$CR(s_{7,11}, s_{7,13}, s_{8,12})$	$CR(s_{7,11}, s_{8,12}, s_{9,11})$
$CR(s_{8,12}, s_{9,11}, s_{10,11})$	$CR(s_{9,11}, s_{10,11}, s_{11,11})$	$CR(s_{10,11}, s_{11,11}, s_{12,10})$
$CR(s_{14,8}, s_{15,6}, s_{15,7})$	$CR(s_{15,1}, s_{15,2}, s_{15,3})$	$CR(s_{15,2}, s_{15,3}, s_{15,4})$
$CR(s_{15,3}, s_{15,4}, s_{15,5})$	$CR(s_{15,4}, s_{15,5}, s_{15,6})$	$CR(s_{15,5}, s_{15,6}, s_{15,7})$

Table 6. Deployment results for RNs for both BIG and CES algorithm

BIG	CES
$CR(s_{12,10}, s_{13,9})$	$CR(s_{12,10}, s_{13,9})$
$CR(s_{13,9}, s_{14,8})$	$CR(s_{1,14}, s_{2,14}, s_{3,14})$
$CR(s_{8,12}, s_{9,11}, s_{10,11})$	$CR(s_{10,11}, s_{11,11}, s_{12,10})$
$CR(s_{15,1}, s_{15,2}, s_{15,3})$	$CR(s_{14,8}, s_{15,6}, s_{15,7})$
$CR(s_{15,5}, s_{15,6}, s_{15,7})$	$CR(s_{15,1}, s_{15,2}, s_{15,3})$

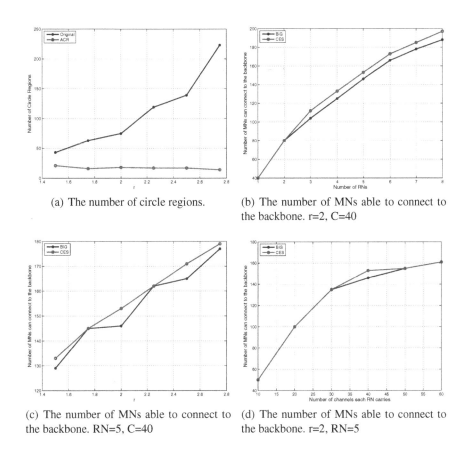

(a) The number of circle regions.

(b) The number of MNs able to connect to the backbone. r=2, C=40

(c) The number of MNs able to connect to the backbone. RN=5, C=40

(d) The number of MNs able to connect to the backbone. r=2, RN=5

Fig. 3. Simulation results based on the scenario at time 20

increased transmission range of MNs could yield larger feasible circle for each busy square, and thus more potential intersection between them. Using the ACR algorithm, we can greatly reduces the cardinality of the set of circle regions without losing any critical points. As can be seen from Figure 3(a), the increased transmission range of MNs does not have an obvious impact on the cardinality of reduced set of circle regions. This is because although the number of circle regions increases as a result of increased transmission range of MNs, many of them could be contained by a few circle regions, which are demarcated by a large number of feasible circles of busy squares.

Figure 3(b) shows the number of MNs that are able to connect to RNs when the number RNs increases from 1 to 8. It is straightforward to see the increase in the number of MNs able to connect to RNs, because more RNs provides more channels or time slots for MNs to access. It can also be seen that our proposed BIG algorithm yields close-to-optimal solution even when the number of RNs is large.

Figure 3(c) shows the number of MNs that are supported by RNs to connect to the backbone as the transmission range of MNs changes from 1.5 to 2.75. The main trend is that as the transmission range of MNs increase, more MNs can connect to RNs. This phenomenon can be explained by the fact that the MNs can have more chance to connect to the backbone by finding farther RNs that have available channels or time slots to access with a larger transmission range, therefore the negative impact caused by spatial limitations could be lessened. Again, as can be seen from Figure 3(c)our proposed BIG algorithm approximates to the optimal solution at different transmission ranges.

Figure 3(d) shows the number of MNs that can access the backbone as the capacity of each RN changes from 10 to 60. It is clear from the figure that as RNs' capacity becomes larger, more MNs are able to access the backbone, and the increase margin of MNs that are able to connect to RNs, however, becomes less. The reason behind is that as the capacity of RNs increases, the number of MNs that can not access to RNs becomes less, thus the increased part of capacity at each RN can only satisfy less number of unconnected MNs due to their distribution among spatially diverse squares. In this case, the BIG algorithm performs optimally except only a small disadvantage when each RN carries 40 channels or has 40 time slots.

9   Conclusion

In this paper, we study the topology control of DAWN to facilitate MNs' communication by deploying a fixed number of RNs dynamically. We first put forward a novel mobility model that describes the movement of first responders within a large disaster area. Secondly, we formulate the MNA and RNP problem and propose the BA approach to solve the MNA problem, the BIG and SEC algorithm to solve the RNP problem. The BA approach transforms the MNA problem into a maximum matching problem within a bipartite graph, and yields the optimal solution. Simulation results demonstrate that based on our proposed mobility model, first responders can eventually clear the disaster area within a short period of time, and at each time, RNs only have to cover a small number of busy squares. We also investigate carefully into the performance comparison between the BIG and SEC algorithm. As the optimal benchmark approach, the CES algorithm yields the deployment of RNs that can support the most number of MNs, with a complexity of $\frac{M \times N \times (\epsilon \times |\mathcal{C}\bar{\mathcal{R}}|)!}{((\epsilon \times |\mathcal{C}\bar{\mathcal{R}}|) - M)! \times M!}$. The BIG algorithm produces results that are close to the optimal, with a complexity of $O(M^2 \times N \times |\mathcal{C}\bar{\mathcal{R}}|)$. As $\epsilon \times |\mathcal{C}\bar{\mathcal{R}}|$ is a lot larger than M, the complexity for the BIG algorithm is much smaller than that of the CES algorithm.

References

1. Pothen, A., Fan, C.: Computing the block triangular form of a sparse matrix. ACM Transactions on Mathematical Software 16(4), 303–324 (1990)
2. Aschenbruck, N., Gerhards-Padilla, E., Gerharz, M., Frank, M., Martini, P.: Modelling mobility in disaster area scenarios. In: MSWIM 2007 (October 2007)
3. Aschenbruck, N., Martini, P., Gerharz, M.: Characterisation and modelling of voice traffic in first responder networks. In: LCN 2007 (October 2007)
4. Johnson, D., Maltz, D.: Dynamic Source Routing in Ad Hoc Wireless Networks, Mobile Computing. Kluwer Academic Publishers, Dordrecht (1996)
5. Liang, B., Haas, Z.: Predictive distance-based mobility management for PCS networks. In: IEEE Infocom 1999 (1999)
6. Lu, W., Seah, W., Peh, E., Ge, Y.: Communications support for disaster recovery operations using hybrid mobile ad-hoc networks. In: LCN 2007 (October 2007)
7. Nelson, S., Harris, A., Kravets, R.: Event–driven, role–based mobility in disaster recovery networks. In: CHANTS 2007 (September 2007)
8. Nguyen, J., Gyoda, K., Okada, K., Takizawa, O.: On the performance of a hybrid wireless network for emergency communications in disaster areas. In: ICSN 2007 (2007)
9. Saha, S., Matsumoto, M.: A framework for disaster management system and wsn protocol for rescue operation. In: TENCON 2007 (2007)
10. Sugiyama, H., Tsujioka, T., Murata, M.: Collaborative movement of rescue robots for reliable and effective networking in disaster area. In: COLCOM 2005 (December 2005)

Relay Nodes in Wireless Sensor Networks

Gruia Călinescu* and Sutep Tongngam**

Illinois Institute of Technology, Chicago, IL 60616
calinescu@iit.edu, tongsut@iit.edu

Abstract. Motivated by application to wireless sensor networks, we study the following problem. We are given a set S of wireless sensor nodes, given as a set of points in the two-dimensional plane, and real numbers $0 < r \leq R$. We must place a minimum-size set Q of wireless relay nodes in the two dimensional plane to connect S, where connectivity is explained formally next. The nodes of S can communicate to nodes within distance r, and the relay nodes of Q can communicate within distance R. Once the nodes of Q are placed, they together with S *induce* an undirected graph $G = (V, E)$ defined as follows: $V = S \cup Q$, and $E = \{uv | u, v \in Q$ and $||u, v|| \leq R\} \cup \{xu | x \in S$ and $u \in (Q \cup S)$ and $||u, x|| \leq r\}$, where $||u, v||$ denotes the Euclidean distance from u to v. G must be connected.

It was shown in [1] that an algorithm based on Minimum Spanning Tree achieves approximation ratio 7. We improve the analysis of this algorithm to 6, and propose a post-processing heuristic called *Post-Order Greedy* to practically improve the performance of the approximation algorithms. Experiments on random instances give Post-Order Greedy applied after Minimum Spanning Tree an average improvement of up to 23%. Applying Post-Order Greedy after an optimum Steiner Tree algorithm results in another circa 6% improvement considering the same instances.

1 Introduction

A wireless sensor network is composed of a large number of sensors, which can be densely deployed to monitor the targeted environment. Some of the most important application areas of sensor networks include military, natural calamities such as forest fire detection and tornado motion, and different sorts of surveillance. When compared to traditional ad hoc networks, the most noticeable point about sensor networks is that they are limited in power, computational capacities, and memory.

Sensors may have a short transmission range since long transmission consumes more energy, and the sensors normally have limited power. Therefore, network partitions may occur or more sensors must be placed to maintain connectivity. In some case, simple sensors may not be able to do more complex work such as data aggregation and storage. Obviously, in the latter case, deploying more sensors is not the solution. As mentioned earlier, the number of sensors distributed in the area is usually large, hence placing sophisticated wireless nodes instead is costly. In order to solve these problems, one may

* Research supported in part by NSF grant CCF-0515088.
** Research supported in part by The Royal Thai Government.

Y. Li et al. (Eds.): WASA 2008, LNCS 5258, pp. 286–297, 2008.
© Springer-Verlag Berlin Heidelberg 2008

consider placing higher capability (and of higher cost) relay nodes. Due to the higher cost of relay nodes, the minimum number of relay nodes is aimed while maintaining network connectivity and functionality.

As explained in [2], an example of the scenario using this network model is in desertification monitoring. Many types of sensors are placed in the predefined sites of the desert assumably 2-dimensional plane. The transmission ranges of sensors are fixed according to their limited capabilities. Since the area is large and the transmission range of the sensors is limited, information from each sensor is delivered to a sink in the multihop manner. Also network partitions may occur as a result of the mentioned limitations. In this situation, relay nodes may take important roles in both processing and forwarding information, and in maintaining network connectivity.

1.1 Problem Definition

We study the so-called SINGLE-TIERED RELAY NODE PLACEMENT problem, where sensors can communicate with other nodes within distance r and relay nodes can communicate with other nodes within distance R, $R \geq r$ and $r > 0$. In this problem, we are given a set of sensors and asked to put the minimum number of relay nodes such that all sensors are connected. The formal problem definition is:

We are given a set S of wireless sensor nodes, given as a set of points in the two-dimensional plane, and real numbers $0 < r \leq R$. We must place a minimum-size set Q of wireless relay nodes in the two dimensional plane to connect S, where connectivity is explained formally next. The nodes of S can communicate to nodes within distance r, and the relay nodes of Q can communicate within distance R. Once the nodes of Q are placed, they together with S *induce* an undirected graph $G = (V, E)$ defined as follows: $V = S \cup Q$, and $E = \{uv | u, v \in Q$ and $||u, v|| \leq R\} \cup \{xu | x \in S$ and $u \in (Q \cup S)$ and $||u, x|| \leq r\}$, where $||u, v||$ denotes the Euclidean distance from u to v. G must be connected.

Note that in the SINGLE-TIERED RELAY NODE PLACEMENT problem sensor nodes can directly communicate with each other. A related problem is the TWO-TIERED RELAY NODE PLACEMENT problem, where sensors cannot communicate with each other, only with relay nodes.

1.2 Previous Work

Lloyd and Xue [1], among other results, propose a Minimum Spanning Tree based approximation algorithm for SINGLE-TIERED RELAY NODE PLACEMENT problem. The algorithm yields 7 approximation ratio, and works as follows: it first constructs an undirected edge-weighted complete graph of the set of sensors, where the edge weight is the Euclidean distance between two sensors. Then it computes a minimum spanning tree of that graph. Finally, if the length of an edge, d, is greater than sensor's transmission range, r, but less than or equal to $2r$, the algorithm places a relay node on the middle of the edge. Otherwise, it places two relay nodes at the points, the distance of which is r from each end-point of the edge, and another $\lceil \frac{d-2r}{R} \rceil - 1$ relay nodes on the rest of the edge, keeping the same distance between any two consecutive relay nodes on this edge. One can easily check this distance is at most R.

1.3 New Results

Our improved analysis shows that the approximation ratio of the algorithm in [1] is, in fact, 6. In the following we use MST to refer to the Minimum Spanning Tree and SMT to refer to a Minimum Steiner Tree (a tree of minimum total length that connects the nodes of S but can use additional Steiner nodes).

We also propose a post-processing heuristic called *Post-Order Greedy* to practically improve the performance of the approximation algorithms. Experiments on random instances give Post-Order Greedy applied after MST an average improvement of up to 23%. Applying Post-Order Greedy after an optimum Steiner Tree algorithm results in another circa 6% improvement. Note that this last heuristic is based on finding an optimum Euclidean Steiner tree - an NP-Hard problem - and therefore we cannot solve very large instances.

1.4 Related Work

An important case is when the transmission range of relay nodes is equal to the one of sensors' ($R = r$). This is also called Steiner Minimum Tree with Minimum number of Steiner Points and bounded edge length (SMT-MSP) [3], and is NP-Hard.

> In the SMT-MSP problem, we are given a set of terminals V in the plane and a constant R. The problem asks to find a Steiner tree spanning V with minimum number of Steiner points such that every edge in the tree has length at most R.

Modeling the SINGLE-TIERED RELAY NODE PLACEMENT problem as SMT-MSP, D. Chen et. al [4] present a 3-approximation algorithm for SMT-MSP. Later, X. Cheng et. al [2] improve the running time of the algorithms found in [4] while the approximation ratio is unchanged. They also present a randomized algorithm with approximation ratio 2.5 for the same problem.

Also for SMT-MSP, Măndoiu and Zelikovsky [5] give a tight analysis of the MST heuristic introduced by G. Lin and G. Xue in [3]. The analysis of [5] has shown that the approximation ratio of the heuristic is actually 4 in the Euclidean plane. D. Chen et. al also prove in [4] the same ratio but with a different approach.

In [6], J. Tang et. al present a 4.5-approximation algorithm for SINGLE-TIERED RELAY NODE PLACEMENT and its version where two connectivity is required. However, they assume that the transmission range of relay nodes is at least four times more than the sensors' communication range ($R \geq 4r$), and that the sensors are uniformly distributed.

For the TWO-TIERED RELAY NODE PLACEMENT problem, H. Liu et. al propose in [7] a $(6 + \epsilon)$ approximation algorithm for connectivity, and $(24 + \epsilon)$ and $(\frac{6}{T} + 12 + \epsilon)$ approximation algorithms for two-connectivity, with the assumption that the transmission range of the relay nodes is equal to that of the sensor ($R = r$). Lloyd and Xue [1] improved the approximation ratio for TWO-TIERED RELAY NODE PLACEMENT to $(5 + \epsilon)$, also allowing $R > r$. Works by Q. Wang et. al include a base station in the sensor network model and include in [8] and [9] traffic allocation and relay node placement algorithms, respectively.

A. Kashyap et. al [10] prove that an approximation algorithm based on the Khuller and Raghavachari [11] algorithm for Minimum-Weight Two-Connected Sub-graph has

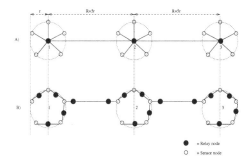

Fig. 1. A) is an optimal solution B) is an output from the MST-based algorithm

an approximation ratio of at most 10 for the the two connectivity variant of SINGLE-TIERED RELAY NODE PLACEMENT with $R = r$. With $R > r$, W. Zhang et. [12] present a 14 approximation algorithm. They also consider SINGLE-TIERED RELAY NODE PLACEMENT problem, where a base station is included and two connectivity is required. For this variant, they obtain a 16-approximation algorithm. In [13], X. Han et. al study SINGLE-TIERED RELAY NODE PLACEMENT problem, where the sensors have different radii while all relay nodes have the same radius.

This paper is organized as follows: In the next section, we present our analysis of the MST-based algorithm. Section 3 presents our new *Post-Order Greedy* heuristic and its experimental results showing an advantage on previously proposed MST-based algorithm. Section 4 concludes our work.

2 Analysis of the MST-Based Algorithm

E. L. Lloyd and G. Xue [1] give examples that the approximation ratio of MST-based algorithm is at least 6. We include such examples for completeness [See Figure 1]: if optimum uses j relay nodes (in the figure, $j = 3$), the MST-based algorithm uses $6j - 2$ relay nodes.

Many ideas in this section come from [5]. Call a feasible solution Q of the RELAY NODE PLACEMENT problem a *bead-solution* if the induced graph $G = G(Q)$ contains a spanning tree T where each node from Q has degree exactly two. The MST-based algorithm produces a bead solution - see for example Figure 1, B. In a bead-solution, we may call the relay nodes *beads*.

For $x, y \in S$, define

$$w(x, y) = \begin{cases} 0 & \text{if } ||x, y|| \leq r \\ 1 + \lceil \frac{||u,v||-2r}{R} \rceil & \text{if } r < ||x, y|| \end{cases}$$

One can easily verify that $w(x, y)$ is the minimum number of relay nodes required to connect x and y, and that $w(x, y)$ is an increasing function of $||x, y||$. Moreover, if one is to construct a bead-solution, then only the spanning tree T matters, and we may as well directly construct a spanning tree with minimum number of beads - that is a tree T' spanning S with minimum $\sum_{xy \in E(T')} w(x, y)$.

We now notice that the MST-based algorithm also constructs a tree spanning S with minimum number of beads - as indeed Kruskal's algorithm gives the same result whether we use the weight w or Euclidean distance to measure the weight of each edge: the permutation of the edges is the same.

Lemma 1. *Given Q a solution to the* RELAY NODE PLACEMENT *problem with input S, we can construct a bead-solution Q' for S with $|Q'| \leq 6|Q|$.*

Proof. Let G be the connected graph induced by Q and the input S, and T be a minimum spanning tree in G where the edge weights are the Euclidean distance, and ties are broken such as edges between two nodes of S are lighter than edges with only one end-point in S.

Partition Q into A and B: the nodes of A have a neighbor from S in T, and the nodes of B do not. So a node of B has, in T, only neighbors from Q. The fact that T has minimum Euclidean length among the sub-graphs of G implies from a standard argument [3] that each node of B has at most 6 neighbors from Q. (One can improve this number to 5 [3,5], but it does not help our proof). Our proof, like [3,5], is based on replicating nodes of Q, which means replacing a node by a number of beads placed in the same position.

Take a maximal set X of B which is connected in T. X together with the nodes of A adjacent to it induces a sub-tree T_X of T (this is akin to the Steiner component used for the Steiner tree problem [14,15]). We use the standard argument of doubling each edge of T_X, and doing an Eulerian tour of T_X starting from a node of A. Each node of A other than the start appears once in this tour, and each node of B exactly as many times as its degree in T_X, that is, at most 6 times. Replicate each node of B according to its degree, and replace T_X by the Eulerian tour above minus the last edge of the tour. Do this for all such X and obtain a new tree T' with node set $S \cup A \cup B'$, where B' are the nodes obtained by replicating nodes of B, and such that T' is spanning and each node of B' has degree at most two, i.e., is a bead. Note that $|B'| \leq 6|B|$.

Repeatedly remove nodes of $A \cup B'$ if they have degree one, resulting in a spanning tree T'' with node set $S \cup A' \cup B''$, where B'' and A' respectively, are those nodes of B' and A respectively, not removed. Thus in T'' all the leafs are from S, and all the nodes of B'' have degree exactly two and neighbors only in $A' \cup B''$.

Root T'' at an arbitrary leaf, and then execute a post-order traversal of T'', processing each node of $a \in A'$ as described below. While doing this we construct a new tree T_3. Node a must have, in T'', at least one neighbor in S - and in fact, since the neighbors of a from S in T'' are exactly neighbors of a from S in T, we can derive that a has at most five neighbors from S in T''. This is the standard argument, which we repeat for the sake of completeness: if a has six or more neighbors in T from S, then a has two neighbors $x, y \in S$ with the angle $\widehat{xay} \leq \pi/3$, resulting in the edge xy being no longer than at least one of ax and ay. Replace in T the longer of ax and ay by xy, and we obtain a lighter tree - recall that we broke ties in favor of edges with both end-points in S. This makes T a non-minimum spanning tree, a contradiction.

During the post-order traversal, we maintain the following invariant: each node of $a \in A'$ ready to be processed (that is, with all its descendants in A' already processed) has between one and five children, and all are from S. Also, except for a, all its

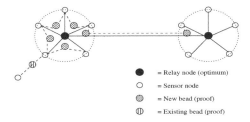

●	= Relay node (optimum)
○	= Sensor node
⊛	= New bead (proof)
⏚	= Existing bead (proof)

Fig. 2. Illustration of the first sub-case

descendants are nodes from S or beads. In addition, at all times, nodes from B'' remain beads with neighbors only from B'' or A' or beads newly introduced.

Note that this invariant holds for nodes from A' which do not have proper descendants from A': such a node a' must have descendants or it would have been removed, and if a' has a child b from B'', then b must be on path to a node s from S (or all the sub-tree rooted at b would have been removed, starting with the leafs). Now, on the path from b to s there must be a node from A' - since nodes of B'' are not adjacent in T'' to nodes of S. Thus if b is a child of a', we obtain that a' has proper descendants from A' - a contradiction.

Now we describe how a node a from A' is processed: let $s_1, s_2, \ldots, s_k$ be its children; recall that all belong to S and that $1 \le k \le 5$. If the parent of a in T_3 is a node s from S, replicate a k times connecting, by paths of length two with the middle node a bead, s_1 to s_2, s_2 to s_3, and so on until s_k is connected to s.

If the parent of a in T_3 is not from S, then there is a path P from a to an ancestor node $a' \in A'$ with all the intermediate nodes from B'' - this is since the root is from S and nodes in B'' are never adjacent in T_3 with nodes from S. Let s' be some node of S adjacent to a'. For ease of presentation, we consider two sub-cases: P has two nodes or more.

In the first sub-case, a is the child of a'. Replicate a k times into beads $a_1, a_2, \ldots, a_k$, and add a new bead, called a'', connecting by beads $s_1 - a_1 - s_2 - a_2 \ldots a_{k-1} - s_k - a_k - a'' - s'$. This is possible by placing a'' at the same position as a'. If a' is left without children, remove it from T_3. Otherwise a' stays in T_3, with one less neighbor (a is gone, and the new nodes are not adjacent directly to a'), until all its descendants are processed. See Figure 2 for an illustration. The result is that all the nodes of the sub-tree rooted at a go in a sub-tree rooted at s', and this sub-tree consists only of nodes of S and beads. In total, instead of a, we introduced up to $k + 1 \le 6$ beads.

In the second sub-case, let x be the second node of P and y be the next to last node of P; note that $x, y \in B''$, and it is possible $x = y$. Replicate a k times, connecting by paths of length two with the middle node a bead: s_1 and s_2, etc, s_{k-1} to s_k, and s_k to x. Also, add another bead a'' connecting y to s' by a path of length two. This is possible with a'' being a bead in the same position as a'. If a' is left without children, remove it from T_3. Otherwise a' stays in T_3, with one less neighbor (y is not adjacent to a' anymore, and the new nodes are not adjacent directly to a'), until all its descendants are processed. See Figure 3 for an illustration. As before, the result is that all the nodes in the sub-tree rooted at y go in a sub-tree rooted at s', and this sub-tree consists only of nodes of S and beads. In total, instead of a, we introduced up to $k + 1 \le 6$ beads.

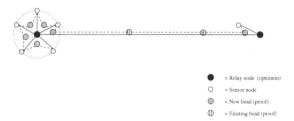

Fig. 3. Illustration of the second sub-case

Note that in no case a node of A' maintains children from $A' \cup B''$ when it is time to be processed - such children are now adjacent to some newly introduced bead a'', and a'' is adjacent to some node in S. Thus the invariant is maintained, each node of A' is replaced by six beads, and by the time we finish this post-order processing T_3 consists of beads only, with the number of new beads being at most $6|A'|$.

We conclude that the final T_3 has only nodes of S and beads, and the number of beads does not exceed $|B''| + 6|A'| \leq |B'| + 6|A| \leq 6|B| + 6|A| = 6|Q|$. ∎

The approximation ratio of the MST-based algorithm comes immediately from the above lemma and the discussion preceding it: if we let Q be an optimum solution to the RELAY NODE PLACEMENT problem on input S, then there exist a bead-solution Q' for S with $|Q'| \leq 6|Q|$, and the MST-based algorithm will find such a solution.

3   The Post-Order Greedy Heuristic and Experimental Results

In this section, we present our heuristic, named *Post-Order Greedy*. It takes advantage of the longer transmission of relay nodes by utilizing the connection between relay nodes and possibly connecting sensors to only one relay node. Our experimental results have shown that our idea improves the results up to 23% and 29% on given MST-tree and SMT-tree, respectively.

3.1   The Post-Order Greedy Heuristic

The main idea of this algorithm is that we try to put the relay nodes such that each sensor will communicate with a minimum number of relay nodes while maintaining connectivity by taking advantage of the longer communication range of relay nodes, i.e., $R > r$. The larger R is compared to r, the larger the possibility of the algorithm saving relay nodes. Figure 4 shows a simple example where our algorithm can save one relay node over the MST-based algorithm and the connectivity is still guaranteed. When applied on SMT-tree, the algorithm may relocate the Steiner nodes and the number of relay nodes will be a number of Steiner nodes plus a number of relay nodes added by the algorithm.

Post-Order Greedy has as input a tree T such that $S \subseteq V(T)$. Our *Post-Order Greedy* algorithm begins with picking a leaf node of a given tree as the root of the tree. Then, from all edges toward the root, put relay nodes as needed for connectivity. A critical

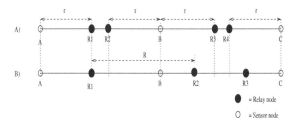

Fig. 4. A) is an output from MST-based algorithm B) is an output from Post-Order Greedy algorithm

part of the algorithm is that if a sensor needs to directly communicate with only one relay node in order to communicate with other nodes, we will put only a needed relay node and let that relay node communicate with other nodes. We take advantage of the relay node because it has a longer transmission range than a sensor's. Again, Figure 4 shows how our algorithm can decrease the number of relay nodes compared to the number given by the MST-based algorithm.

The *Post-Order Greedy* consists of two parts. Algorithm 1 sets up and processes all leaf nodes. The second part, Algorithm 2, is for all parent nodes including the *root*. Once all nodes are *processed*, the algorithm is done.

Post-Order Greedy heuristic runs in $O(|S| + |Q|)$ time. Recall that S is the set of sensor nodes and Q is the set of relay nodes. We can see from the algorithm shown in algorithm 1 and 2 that the algorithm will process each node only once. The algorithm calculates the distance either to place a new relay node or , in case the input is SMT-trees, to move the current relay node to on the edge where the node belongs. Then the algorithm moves on along that edge to the other end of the edge. Given a tree, the number of sensor nodes equals the number of $|S|$, all relay nodes placed on all edges are equal to $|Q|$, and the time to calculate the position to put the relay node is constant, therefore, the running time of the algorithm is $O(|S| + |Q|)$. In case of SMT-trees, all Steiner nodes obtained from SMT solution are input and included in $|Q|$ which, as explained above, are processed only once.

3.2   Experimental Results

We consider networks of sensors randomly distributed over 50×50, 100×100, 500×500, and 1000×1000. areas. The number of sensors is varied to 10, 20, and 50, the transmission range of sensors, r, is set to 1, and the transmission range of relay nodes, R, is 3. We apply our algorithm on both MST-trees and SMT-trees. We randomly generate 20 instances for each network size and the output shown in all tables is the average for those 20 instances.

Tables 1 - 4 show that our algorithm applied on MST-trees and SMT-trees beats the MST-based algorithm on every number of input sensors. When applied on MST-trees, the improvement is up to 23%, while when applied on SMT-trees, the improvement is up to 29% (see Table 5).

Algorithm 1. Post-Order Algorithm

Input: Given a tree T having k sensors and m relay nodes
Output: A tree T' having k sensors and m' relay nodes
 1: Pick a sensor, leaf in T, to be a root of T
 2: $m' = m$
 3: Process in post-order each edge $\overrightarrow{ij}$, where $\overrightarrow{ij}$ has end-points v_i and v_j, v_j being the parent
 4: **for** (each leaf node v_i (of edge $\overrightarrow{ij}$)) **do**
 5:     $u = v_i$; mark v_i *processed*
 6:     $distance$ = EuclideanDistance(i, j)
 7:     **while** $(distance > 0)$ **do**
 8:         **if** (u is a sensor) **then**
 9:             **if** $(distance > r)$ **then**
10:                 $m' + +$
11:                 Add $v_{k+m'}$ on $\overrightarrow{ij}$ at distance r from u ; mark $v_{k+m'}$ *processed*
12:                 $distance = distance - r$
13:                 $u = v_{k+m'}$
14:             **else**
15:                 $distance = 0$
16:             **end if**
17:         **else**
18:             **if** $(distance > R)$ **then**
19:                 $m' + +$
20:                 Add $v_{k+m'}$ on $\overrightarrow{ij}$ at distance R from u ; mark $v_{k+m'}$ *processed*
21:                 $distance = distance - R$
22:                 $u = v_{k+m'}$
23:             **else**
24:                 $distance = 0$
25:             **end if**
26:         **end if**
27:     **end while**
28: **end for**
29: Do Algorithm 2

Table 1. Average decrease in the number of relay nodes on a 50×50 area

Number of sensors	MST-based	Post-Order on MST	Post-Order on SMT
10	39.8	3.8	5
20	66	11.4	14.4
50	119.2	28	34.4

It is worth observing that our heuristic gives better outcomes when applied on SMT-trees. This is because the total edge length of the Steiner tree is significantly less than that of the MST-tree. The reduced length has a bigger effect than the extra relay nodes placed in or around the Steiner points. So adding Steiner nodes yields more savings, but there is a trade-off with running time since finding SMT-trees is NP-hard.

When applying the heuristic on MST-trees under various areas, the decrease in the number of relay nodes does not vary significantly (See Table 1, 2, 3, and 4). It instead

Algorithm 2. Algorithm on parent nodes

1: **for** (each parent node v_i whose all children are *processed*) **do**
2:    $distance$ = EuclideanDistance(i, j) ; $u = v_i$; mark v_i *processed*
3:    ds = max(Euclidean distance between v_i and its relay node children)
4:    **if** (u is a sensor) **then**
5:       **if** ($ds \leq r$) **then**
6:          **if** (u is not the *root*) **then**
7:             m'++
8:             **if** (all children of v_i are sensors) **then**
9:                Add $v_{k+m'}$ at r from u ; mark $v_{k+m'}$ *processed* ; $distance = distance - r$
10:            **else**
11:               Add $v_{k+m'}$ at $R - d$ from u ; mark $v_{k+m'}$ *processed*
12:               $distance = distance - (R - ds)$
13:            **end if**
14:            $u = v_{k+m'}$
15:         **end if**
16:      **else**
17:         **if** (u is the *root*) **then**
18:            m'++ ; Add $v_{k+m'}$ at the same position of u ; mark $v_{k+m'}$ *processed*
19:            $u = v_{k+m'}$; $distance = distance - (R - ds)$
20:         **else**
21:            **if** ($R - ds > r$) **then**
22:               m'++ ; Add $v_{k+m'}$ at $R - ds$ from u ; mark $v_{k+m'}$ *processed*
23:               $u = v_{k+m'}$; $distance = distance - (R - ds)$
24:            **else**
25:               m'++ ; Add $v_{k+m'}$ at r from u ; mark $v_{k+m'}$ *processed*
26:               $u = v_{k+m'}$; $distance = distance - r$
27:            **end if**
28:         **end if**
29:      **end if**
30:   **else**
31:      /* v_i is a relay node */
32:      **if** (a child of v_i is a sensor) **then**
33:         Relocate v_i to the point on $\overrightarrow{ij}$ that makes the distance between v_i and its child $= r$
34:      **else**
35:         Relocate v_i to the point on $\overrightarrow{ij}$ that makes $ds = R$
36:      **end if**
37:      $distance$ = EuclideanDistance(i, j)
38:   **end if**
39:   **while** ($distance > 0$) **do**
40:      **if** ($distance > R$) **then**
41:         m'++ ; Add $v_{k+m'}$ at R from u ; mark $v_{k+m'}$ *processed*
42:         $u = v_{k+m'}$; $distance = distance - R$
43:      **else**
44:         $distance = 0$
45:      **end if**
46:   **end while**
47: **end for**

Table 2. Average decrease in the number of relay nodes on a 100×100 area

Number of sensors	MST-based	Post-Order on MST	Post-Order on SMT
10	79	4.2	6.4
20	120.4	10.6	14
50	199	30.8	36.8

Table 3. Average decrease in the number of relay nodes on a 500×500 area

Number of sensors	MST-based	Post-Order on MST	Post-Order on SMT
10	392.7	6.4	16
20	473	13	25.3
50	856	31.7	60

Table 4. Average decrease in the number of relay nodes on a 1000×1000 area

Number of sensors	MST-based	Post-Order on MST	Post-Order on SMT
10	769	5.7	28.3
20	1034.7	12	35.4
50	1609	32.7	64.7

Table 5. Improvement (%) over MST-based algorithm

Area	Number of sensors	MST-base	Post-Order on MST	Post-Order on SMT
50×50	10	100	9.55	12.56
50×50	20	100	17.27	21.82
50×50	50	100	23.49	28.86
100×100	10	100	5.32	8.1
100×100	20	100	8.8	11.63
100×100	50	100	15.48	18.49
Average			13.32	16.91

relates to the number of sensors. This is because, as shown in Figure 4, the relay nodes eliminated by the heuristic are normally around the sensors. In the MST-based algorithm, a sensor connects to all of its neighbors with respect to the tree paths. In our heuristic, on the other hand, by arranging the position of the relay nodes, a sensor connects to only some of its neighbors if that still makes the sensor connect to the rest of the network.

4   Conclusion

Our analysis shows that the approximation algorithm given by E. L. Lloyd and G. Xue in [1] for the SINGLE-TIERED RELAY NODE PLACEMENT problem (where sensors can communicate with other nodes within distance r and relay nodes can communicate with other nodes within distance R, $R \geq r > 0$) has in fact approximation ratio 6.

We also propose a heuristic, called *Post-Order Greedy*, applied on MST-trees and SMT-trees, which experimentally improves over the previously proposed MST-based algorithm by up to 23% and 29%, respectively.

References

1. Lloyd, E.L., Xue, G.: Relay node placement in wireless sensor networks. IEEE Transactions on Computers 56(1), 134–138 (2007)
2. Cheng, X., Du, D.Z., Wang, L., Xu, B.: Relay sensor placement in wireless sensor networks. ACM Wireless Networks (January 2007)
3. Lin, G., Xue, G.: Steiner tree problem with minimum number of steiner points and bounded edge-length. Information Processing Letters 69, 53–57 (1999)
4. Chen, D., Du, D.Z., Hu, X., Lin, G., Wang, L., Xu, G.: Approximation for steiner trees with minimum number of steiner points. Journal of Global Optimization 18, 17–33 (2000)
5. Măndoiu, I.I., Zelikovsky, A.Z.: A note on the mst heuristic for bounded edge-length steiner trees with minimum number of steiner points. Inf. Process. Lett. 75(4), 165–167 (2000)
6. Tang, J., Hao, B., Sen, A.: Relay node placement in large scale wireless sensor networks. Computer Communications 29, 490–501 (2006)
7. Liu, H., Wan, P.J., Jia, X.: Fault tolerant relay node placement in wireless sensor networks. In: Wang, L. (ed.) COCOON 2005. LNCS, vol. 3595, Springer, Heidelberg (2005)
8. Wang, Q., Takahara, G., Hassanein, H., Xu, K.: On relay node placement and locally optimal traffic allocation in heterogeneous wireless sensor networks. In: IEEE Conference on Local Computer Networks (LCN 2005) (2005)
9. Wang, Q., Xu, K., Takahara, G., Hassanein, H.: Locally optimally relay node placement in heterogeneous wireless sensor networks. IEEE GlobeCom, 3549–3553 (2005)
10. Kashyap, A., Khuller, S., Shayman, M.: Relay placement for higher order connectivity in wireless sensor networks. In: INFOCOM 2006. 25th IEEE International Conference on Computer Communications. Proceedings, pp. 1–12 (April 2006)
11. Khuller, S., Raghavachari, B.: Improved approximation algorithms for uniform connectivity problems. Journal of Algorithms 21, 433–450 (1996)
12. Zhang, W., Xue, G., Misra, S.: Fault-tolerant relay node placement in wireless sensor networks: Problems and algorithms. In: INFOCOM 2007. 26th IEEE International Conference on Computer Communications. Proceedings, pp. 1649–1657 (May 2007)
13. Han, X., Cao, X., Lloyd, E., Shen, C.C.: Fault-tolerant relay node placement in heterogeneous wireless sensor networks. In: INFOCOM 2007. 26th IEEE International Conference on Computer Communications. Proceedings, pp. 1667–1675 (May 2007)
14. Zelikovsky, A.: An 11/6-approximation algorithm for the network Steiner problem. Algorithmica 9, 463–470 (1993)
15. Borchers, A., Du, D.Z.: The k-steiner ratio in graphs. SIAM Journal on Computing 26(3), 857–869 (1997)

Transmission Scheduling for CBR Traffic in Multihop Wireless Networks

Maggie X. Cheng[1], Xuan Gong[1], Lin Cai[2], and Ahmad Abdullah[2]

[1] Department of Computer Science, Missouri University of Science and Technology,
Rolla, MO 65401
{chengm,xgwt2}@mst.edu
[2] Department of Electrical and Computer Engineering, University of Victoria,
Victoria, BC V8W 3P6, Canada
{cai,abdullah}@ece.uvic.ca

Abstract. In multihop wireless ad hoc networks, interference from transmissions on nearby links makes it difficult to predict available bandwidth and reserve bandwidth for Constant Bit Rate traffic. In this paper, we present a MAC layer scheme that supports constant bit rate traffic through transmission scheduling. The paper details the sufficient condition on bandwidth requirement, and presents a time slot assignment algorithm that assigns each link a number of slots proportional to the traffic load on itself. The theoretical analysis proves that the sufficient condition is indeed sufficient to provide a network-wide collision-free transmission schedule, and the time slot assignment algorithm can completely avoid the hidden and exposed terminal problems. Through extensive simulations, we verified that a TDMA scheme serves much better than a random, contention-based scheme in the context of maximizing network throughput and providing guaranteed end-to-end data rate.

1 Introduction

To carry multimedia traffic over wireless links is challenging due to the impairments and low capacity of the radio channel. To communicate multimedia data over multihop wireless networks is more so because of the self-contention among links on the same path, and moreover, the interference from different flows. In multihop wireless networks, to deliver Constant Bit Rate (CBR) traffic at a high data rate is among the most difficult. Solutions to address this problem are sought at different layers in the past few years. In this paper, we present a MAC layer solution, as part of the cross layer design between the routing and MAC layer.

The challenge arises from the difficulty to reserve channel resource to support CBR traffic. In wired networks, guaranteed data rates can be provided by reserving channel bandwidth. However, in wireless networks, not only that the link capacity is more limited, but also that the remaining capacity cannot be easily determined after reserving a portion of channel bandwidth. This is because in wireless communication with omnidirectional antenna, the collision domain is complicated. It is not simply defined as a one-hop or two-hop neighborhood, it is rather specific to the source and destination pairs.

Y. Li et al. (Eds.): WASA 2008, LNCS 5258, pp. 298–309, 2008.
© Springer-Verlag Berlin Heidelberg 2008

Fig. 1. After reserving 1/3 of the link bandwidth B, the remaining available bandwidth is zero

In wired networks, to reserve u bps from a link with bandwidth B bps, the remaining bandwidth can be easily determined to be $B - u$. However, to send u bps through a wireless link with bandwidth B, the remaining capacity is not always $B - u$ bps. Figure 1 shows that after reserving $B/3$ bps through the 3-hop path with link bandwidth B bps, the collision domain of node i is saturated and it cannot send anything else.

The objective of this paper is to provide guaranteed end-to-end data rate for CBR traffic and at the same time to maximize network throughput through MAC layer transmission scheduling. A random MAC scheme such as IEEE 802.11 DCF won't be a good fit for CBR traffic because of its inefficiency and unfairness among wireless transmitters. A deterministic scheme such as TDMA gives better promise because it provides guaranteed channel access time.

Traditional TDMA approach either assigns each node a distinct slot, or allow some nodes to use the same slot if they are sufficiently apart. Channel reuse can improve channel efficiency, for which vertex coloring is usually used as a theoretical basis to minimize the number of slots being used. However, this is only good when each node carries the same traffic load. In multihop wireless networks, the truth is, even each node has the same amount of source data to send, as a result of multihop routing some node needs to use the channel for a longer period of time than others. As shown in Figure 1, if each node sends one unit of source data, node j actually needs to send three units of data. The problem becomes more complicated when multiple routing paths share a single relay node. If we assign each node one slot, the nodes in "hot-spot" (i.e., at the intersection of multiple paths) will accumulate a large number of packets in its queue and eventually start to drop packets.

Therefore in this paper, we use variable-length TDMA. Specifically, instead of assigning each node one slot, we assign each *link* a number of slots, with the number of slots proportional to the data rate carried on the link. The contribution of this paper is summarized as follows: (1) we designed a TDMA scheme that provides guaranteed end-to-end data rate, and completely solved the hidden and exposed terminal problems; (2) we pointed out the sufficient condition to provide guaranteed data rate in a multihop wireless network; (3) we formulated the optimization problem that addresses the cross layer design of routing and transmission scheduling for maximum throughput with guaranteed data rate.

The rest of the paper is organized as follows: Section 2 briefly surveys previous work related to cross layer design of routing and Multiple Access Control; Section 3 presents the sufficient condition for throughput guarantee and formulates the maximum throughput optimization problem; Section 4 presents the time slot assignment algorithm with theoretical analysis; Section 5 provides numerical

Fig. 2. Conflicting transmissions in a collision domain

simulation results that show the comparison of our TDMA scheme with 802.11 MAC; Section 6 concludes the article with directions for future research.

2   Related Work

Bandwidth resource is scarce in wireless networks. How to improve the performance of multihop wireless networks, especially to maximize network throughput, has been a very active research area. Some researchers resort to routing schemes to find high-throughput paths ([1,2]); more others turn to cross-layer design and address it as an optimization problem.

Optimization problems in multihop wireless networks are naturally cross-layer problems ([3,4]). It involves PHY layer coding, modulation and error control, MAC/link layer resource (both bandwidth and power) management, network layer routing, and transport layer flow and congestion control. Many of the related work in cross-layer design focused on how to minimize energy consumption under various constraints [5,6,7,8]. Reference [5] proposed to adjust the transmission powers of nodes in a multihop wireless network to create a desired topology, aimed to minimize power used while maintaining network connectivity. Cruz and Santhanam studied the problem of joint routing, link scheduling and power control to support high data rates for broadband wireless multihop networks in [6]. The main objective is still to minimize the total average transmission power. Since most cross-layer optimization problems are too complex to solve, distributed algorithms with suboptimal (and potentially distributed) scheduling component were studied in [3,7].

Fairness is another issue that is difficult to address and needs special attention in multihop wireless environment. In [9, 10, 11], packet scheduling, end-to-end congestion control and antenna technology were adopted to achieve fairness in multihop networks.

To the best of our knowledge, how to maximize network throughput with fairness and provide guaranteed data rate for CBR traffic is still an open issue in multihop wireless networks, which is the main focus of this paper.

3   Preliminaries

3.1   Collision Domain

The purpose of having a TDMA scheme rather than a random access scheme is to avoid the waste of channel resource due to collisions and unnecessary idle time. We first identify that the transmissions shown in Figure 2 cannot be assigned to the same time slots.

Without knowing the specific data rate on each link, a scheduler would assign each link in the same collision domain a different time slot. However, when the data rate on each wireless link is different, simply assigning each link a different slot is not enough, because some links require more slots than others. How do we know if there is enough channel bandwidth to accommodate every active link? The following section discusses a sufficient condition that guarantees the given link data rates can be accommodated.

3.2 Sufficient Condition

Let R_{ij} denote the data rate from node i to node j. Let B be the channel bandwidth in bits per second. Let N_i denote the one-hop neighbors of node i excluding i itself. To avoid collisions, if node i is sending, it cannot be receiving; if it is receiving, it cannot be sending, and none of the neighbors except its sender should be sending. The above observations lead to the following necessary conditions for node i's receiving to be conflict-free:

1. $\sum_{j \in N_i} (R_{ij} + R_{ji}) \leq B$

2. $\sum_{j \in N_i} R_{ji} + \max_{j \in N_i} \left(\sum_{k \in N_j, \, k \neq i} R_{jk} \right) \leq B$.

However, this is a local condition and it only guarantees that in i's collision domain, transmissions from node i itself as well as other neighbors will not interfere with i's receiving; The inequality ensures at node i, the required bandwidth for i's sending and receiving can be satisfied. Other than that, we have no way of knowing whether other transmissions on links (j, k), $j \in N_i, k \in N_j$ can be assigned to the same slot or not. If they cannot, condition (2) is not sufficient to guarantee a global conflict-free transmission schedule. In fact, it is very likely that the transmission on (j_1, k_1) conflicts with the transmission on (j_2, k_2) if they are in a close neighborhood.

To find the sufficient condition, we assume the worse case—i.e., assume all other transmissions on $\{(j, k) | j \in N_i, \, k \in N_j, k \neq i\}$ cannot be scheduled at the same time. This leads to the following sufficient condition:

$$\sum_{j \in N_i} R_{ij} + f_i \cdot \sum_{j \in N_i} \sum_{k \in N_j} R_{jk} \leq B, \quad \forall i$$

Where f_i indicates whether node i is a receiver: when $\sum_{j \in N_i} R_{ji} > 0$, $f_i = 1$; otherwise $f_i = 0$.

The above sufficient condition may demand more bandwidth than it actually needs, but it is sufficient to provide a network-wide conflict-free transmission schedule with guaranteed end-to-end data rate.

In section 3, we propose a time slot assignment algorithm based on the given transmission data rates on all links, which presumably satisfy the above sufficient condition. If the link rates are not given, but instead the relay nodes are given, we can get the link rate on each link (i,j) by solving the following linear program. Let R_i be the source rate, R_L and R_H are the predetermined lower and upper bounds of source rates. The objective is to maximize the MAC layer throughput.

maximize
$$\sum_i R_i \tag{1}$$

subject to

$$\sum_{j \in N_i} (R_{ij} - R_{ji}) = R_i, \qquad \forall i \tag{2a}$$

$$\sum_{j \in N_i} R_{ij} + f_i \cdot \sum_{j \in N_i} \sum_{k \in N_j} R_{jk} \leq B, \qquad \forall i \tag{2b}$$

$$R_L \leq R_i \leq R_H, \qquad \forall i \tag{2c}$$

$$0 \leq R_{ij} \leq B, \qquad \forall i, \forall j \tag{2d}$$

4   Slot Assignment Algorithm

In this section, we present a time slot assignment algorithm that allows each wireless link to have different transmission rate. Link data rates $R = \{R_{ij} | \forall i, \forall j\}$ are given and satisfy the sufficient condition in section 3.

SLOTASSIGNMENT$(G(V,E), R)$

1   Scale the link rates R_{ij} to integers.
2   Find the most bandwidth-contentious node v according to inequality (2b), and compute the required bandwidth B_v at node v's collision domain:
$$v = argmax_{i \in V} \left(\sum_{j \in N_i} R_{ij} + f_i \cdot \sum_{j \in N_i} \sum_{k \in N_j} R_{jk} \right)$$
$$B_v = \sum_{j \in N_v} R_{vj} + f_v \cdot \sum_{j \in N_v} \sum_{k \in N_j} R_{jk}$$
3   Let slot size $\tau = 1$.
4   Let frame size $T = B_v$. Number the slots from 1 to T.
5   Generate a table of size $2 \times T$ associated with each node's sending and receiving schedules. (Use S row for sending and R row for receiving)
6   Let $L = V$. Repeat the following until $L = \phi$:
   (a) Randomly pick a node i from L;
   (b) For each node $j \in N_i$, if $R_{ij} > 0$, assign R_{ij} slots to link (i,j), starting from the smallest available slot; a slot is available if it is available in both the S row of table[i] and the R row of table[j];
   Mark those slots unavailable in the S row of table[j];
   For each $k \in N_j$, if $k \neq i$, mark those slots unavailable in the S row of table[k];
   (c) Mark those slots unavailable in the R row of table[i];
   (d) For each node $j \in N_i$, mark those slots unavailable in the R row of table[j], if they are not assigned yet;
   (e) Remove i from L.
7   Update frame size T to be the largest slot number used.

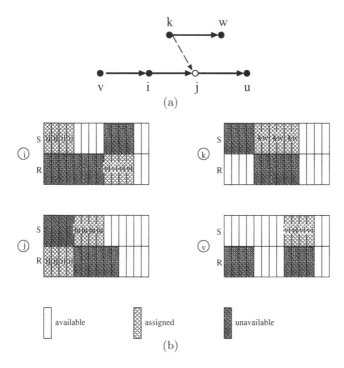

Fig. 3. A walk-through example for the `SlotAssignment` algorithm. (a) the network topology; (b) suppose $R_{vi} = R_{ij} = R_{ju} = 4$, $R_{kw} = 6$, so node j is the most bandwidth-contentious node; frame size T=14 slots; the order that nodes are randomly picked at step 6 is i, j, k, v.

In Figure 3, the sufficient condition requires T=14 slots, but actually it only needs 12 slots by allowing the transmissions on (k, w) and (j, u) to occur at the same time. The sloppiness in the sufficient condition guarantees no matter whether there is a link between (j, w) or not, there are always sufficient slots to use regardless of the order that nodes are picked. This property makes it easy to implement the algorithm in a localized and distributed manner.

Lemma 1. *The* `SlotAssignment` *algorithm generates a collision-free transmission schedule.*

Proof: Lemma 1 is interpreted as the following:

1. There are always sufficient number of slots to use, i.e., at step 6(b), the number of available slots $\geq$ the number of slots needed for any node i being considered, and
2. The resulting schedule is collision-free.

The second statement is obvious because all conflicting transmissions are scheduled at different time— when i is sending to j, j is not sending, and other neighbors of j are not sending, so there is no collision at j according to step 6(b);

i is not receiving according to 6(c) so there is no collision at i; other neighbors of i are not receiving according to 6(d) so there is no collision at i's neighbors.

The first statement is proved as follows. Let N_1 be the total number of slots that are needed for sending when a random node i is picked at step 6(a), so $N_1 = \sum_{j \in N_i} R_{ij}$, and let N_2 be the number of slots that are still available for sending at this time.

- Case (1), when i is not a receiver ($f_i = 0$): the only reason that i's S row is marked unavailable is when a neighbor l is receiving from another node k (Fig. 4.(a)). Let $C = \{(k,l)\}$ be the maximum set of such conflicting transmissions, so the total unavailable slots in i's S row is $\sum_{(k,l) \in C} R_{kl}$. Similarly, for each receiver node j of i, the only reason that the R row of j is marked unavailable is because j's neighbor u is transmitting. Transmissions on (k,l) and (u,v), if non-conflicting, can be arranged at the same slot. Therefore, as long as the condition (2b) holds at both l and j with $f_l = 1$ for l and $f_j = 1$ for j, the number of available slots N_2 for i's transmission is still $\geq \sum_{j \in N_i} R_{ij}$. Therefore, $N_2 \geq N_1$ is held.

- Case (2), when i is a receiver ($f_i = 1$): from case (1) to case (2), there will be $\sum_{l \in N_i} R_{li}$ additional slots marked unavailable in the S row of i, according to step 6(b); others remain unchanged. As long as the condition (2b) holds at node i with $f_i = 1$, the number of available slots N_2 for i's transmission is still $\geq \sum_{j \in N_i} R_{ij}$. Therefore $N_2 \geq N_1$ is held. Because during the iteration in step 6, $T = \max_i \{ \sum_{j \in N_i} R_{ij} + f_i \cdot \sum_{j \in N_i} \sum_{k \in N_j} R_{jk} \}$, so N_2 is sufficient for any node i.

Lemma 2. *The* `SlotAssignment` *algorithm can completely avoid the exposed terminal problem.*

Proof:
Even though the sloppiness of the sufficient condition requires more slots than necessary, the `SlotAssignment` algorithm itself does not prevent non-conflicting transmissions from happening at the same time.

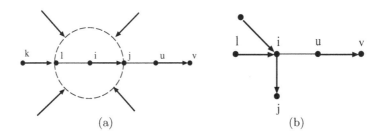

(a)   (b)

Fig. 4. (a) $f_i = 0$; (b)$f_i = 1$

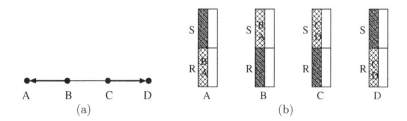

Fig. 5. (a) Exposed terminal problem: $C \to D$ are not allowed to occur at the same time as $B \to A$; (b) The `SlotAssignment` algorithm would allow $C \to D$ and $A \to B$ to occur at the same time

In figure 5.(b), the transmissions on (C, D) and (B, A) can be scheduled in the same slot because B's transmission in slot 1 only marked the R row of C unavailable, the S row is still available.

Theorem 1. *The following condition is sufficient for a TDMA schedule that completely avoids collision and the exposed terminal problem in a multihop wireless networks with omnidirectional antenna:*

$$\sum_{j \in N_i} R_{ij} + f_i \cdot \sum_{j \in N_i} \sum_{k \in N_j} R_{jk} \leq B, \ \forall i$$

Proof. By constructive proof, using the `SlotAssignment` algorithm described above, we can always find a TDMA schedule that completely avoids collision and the exposed terminal problem, as long as the given input R_{ij} satisfies $\sum_{j \in N_i} R_{ij} + f_i \cdot \sum_{j \in N_i} \sum_{k \in N_j} R_{jk} \leq B$ at any node i.

5   Simulation

5.1   Simulation I

In this simulation, we try to compare IEEE 802.11 MAC (RTS-CTS-DATA-ACK scheme) and our TDMA scheme on two metrics: channel efficiency and fairness. In the simple network as in Figure 6.(a), assuming sending one unit of data needs one slot, if A, B, C, and D each need to send one unit of data and then stop, 802.11 would need four slots to finish, because none of the transmissions can be paralleled with another; but our TDMA scheme only needs two slots. Figure 6.(b) shows how the slots are arranged. Such time slot assignment guarantees there is no collision, and there are no hidden and exposed terminal problems. But when each source has an infinite number of packets to send, channel resource may not be equally allocated to each of them using 802.11 MAC. When the source rates of the competing flows exceed certain threshold, simulation results reveal not only its inefficiency but also its severe unfairness problem, as shown in Figure

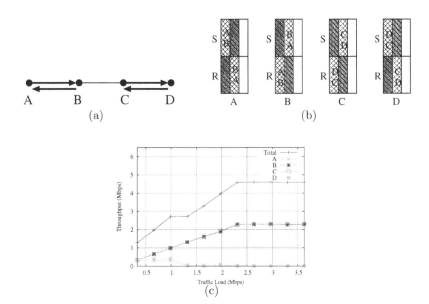

Fig. 6. (a) If A, B, C, D each sends one unit of data, 802.11 MAC would need 4 slots; (b) our TDMA scheme only needs 2 slots; (c) ns2 simulation results show the inefficiency and unfairness of 802.11 MAC

6.(c). With wireless link data rate 11 Mbps, the highest per flow throughput is only 2.3 Mbps and the lowest is dropped to close to zero. Figure 6.(c) shows as the applied traffic load on each node increases from 0.33 Mbps to 3.63 Mbps, nodes A and D can hardly send anything after a certain point (at 1.32 Mbps) because their destinations are exposed to the transmissions of control packets or data packets by the hidden terminals, but nodes B and C can still send because their destinations are not interfered by other transmissions. When the network is saturated, B and C share the channel equally with a throughput of 2.3 Mbps each. Further increasing the source rate will not gain higher throughput. The maximum network throughput is 4.6 Mbps. The throughput result reported here is the payload throughput, i.e., how many bits of the applied traffic can be put through, which is obtained after we take into consideration the PHY/MAC layer overhead occurred in 802.11 standard. The overhead is estimated to be 16.6% for the 11 Mbps channel with a packet size of 1500 bytes.

Our TDMA scheme, on the other hand, can achieve much higher throughput. If we assume the same PHY/MAC overhead, the channel efficiency $\eta = 83.4\%$, our TDMA scheme can achieve a per flow throughput of $0.5*(11*83.4\%) = 4.59$ Mbps after the initial setup phase, because each sender can use half of the time to send its packets without collision. If we compare the total network throughput, 802.11 MAC can only achieve 4.6 Mbps, while our TDMA scheme achieves $4*4.59 = 18.36$ Mbps after the initial setup phase. The network throughput is nearly four times that of 802.11 MAC.

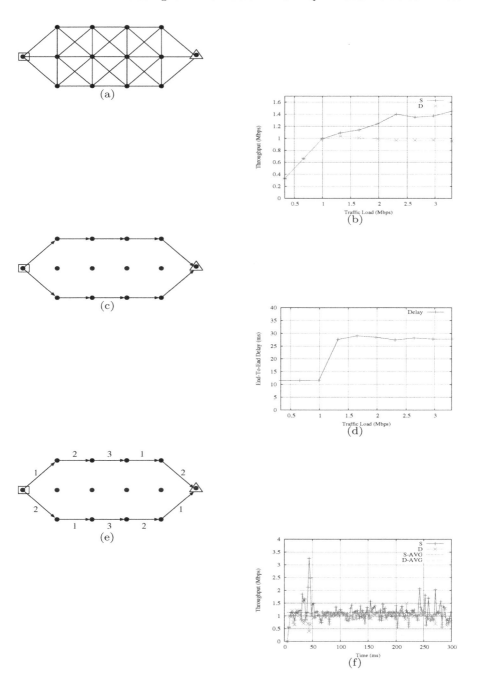

Fig. 7. (a) The network topology; (b) throughput results as traffic load increases; (c) the routing scheme used by our scheme; (d) delay as traffic load increases; (e) time slot assignment by our TDMA scheme; labels on each link are slot numbers; (f) throughput fluctuation over time

5.2 Simulation II

In this simulation, we try to observe how transmissions in the same collision domain influence each other. We use the network topology in Figure 7.(a) with a single source node and a sink node. We chose the AODV protocol for routing and IEEE 802.11 DCF for Multiple Access Control in ns2. The AODV routing scheme would use any 5-hop path, because from the routing's point of view, all shortest paths are equally good. Figure 7.(b) and (c) show the evolution of throughput and delay as traffic load increases. Average results for 34 runs are plotted. Each time the AODV routing scheme randomly picks a shortest path. When the traffic load is low, throughput increases with applied traffic load until the network is saturated. Further increase the traffic load will only increase the packet drop ratio, but the achievable end-to-end throughput will not increase. A maximum throughput of 1.035 Mbps is achieved at input rate 1.32 Mbps. After this threshold, the end-to-end delay soars and the end-to-end throughput stops increasing and then starts decreasing.

The randomness of the 802.11 MAC also causes throughput fluctuation. As shown in Figure 7.(e), even with only one flow with source rate 3.3 Mbps, due to the contention among transmissions on different links along the path, the end-to-end throughput still fluctuates over time; and the received data at the sink is still 13% less than the data sent by the source due to packet loss.

In comparison, using the routing scheme shown in Figure 7.(c) and the time slot assignment in Figure 7.(e), the performance can be much better w.r.t. all three metrics: throughput, delay and instantaneous throughput, which is important for CBR traffic. The slot assignment scheme shows in each cycle, each link on the routing paths can use up to one third of the channel bandwidth, therefore can support a constant data rate of 11/3 Mbps. From the time slot assignment, we can derive that the throughput curve will be increasing with the traffic load until 7.3η Mbps and then stabilize at 7.3η Mbps, and the instantaneous throughput is constant with a maximum achievable throughput 7.3η Mbps. Since there is no contention among nodes, there is no collision and backoff etc., so the MAC layer access delay is zero after the initial setup phase.

6   Conclusion and Future Work

This paper addresses the problem of how to provide guaranteed data rate for CBR traffic in wireless networks through MAC layer transmission scheduling. It provides a time slot assignment algorithm that is proved to be free of the hidden and exposed terminal problems. Moreover, this paper contributed a generic result that can be used for other TDMA schemes or FDMA schemes— the sufficient condition on whether the required data rate can be support by a given wireless network. Simulation results show that a deterministic scheme as such can perform much better than a random, contention-based scheme in terms of providing guaranteed data rate and improving channel efficiency.

The proposed time slot algorithm can be easily implemented in a local and distributed manner as it only requires communication within a two-hop neighborhood.

In the future, we will implement it in a distributed environment and complete the communication protocol. Furthermore, the optimization model presented in this paper can also be extended to support traffic of different priority by manipulating the lower bound of the data rate.

Acknowledgement

Cheng and Gong are supported in part by National Science Foundation under grant CCF-0514940 and UTC grant; Cai is supported in part by Natural Sciences and Engineering Research Council of Canada under grant STPSC 356682.

References

1. Draves, R., Padhye, J., Zil, B.: Comparison of routing metrics for static multi-hop wireless networks. ACM SIGCOMM Computer Communication Review 34(4), 133–144 (2004)
2. Couto1, D.S.J.D., Aguayo1, D., Bicket1, J., Morris, R.: A high-throughput path metric for multi-hop wireless routing. Springer Wireless Networks 11(4), 1022–1038 (2005)
3. Lin, X., Shroff, N.B., Srikant, R.: A tutorial on cross-layer optimization in wireless networks. IEEE JSAC 24(8), 1452–1463 (2006)
4. Toumpis, S., Goldsmith, A.J.: Performance, optimization, and cross-layer design of media access protocols for wireless ad hoc networks. In: IEEE ICC 2003, vol. 3, pp. 2234–2240 (2003)
5. Ramanathan, R., Rosales-Hain, R.: Topology control of multihop wireless networks using transmit poweradjustment. In: IEEE Infocom 2000, vol. 2, pp. 404–413 (2000)
6. Cruz, R.L., Santhanam, A.V.: Optimal routing, link scheduling and power control in multihop wireless networks. In: IEEE Infocom 2003, vol. 1, pp. 702–711 (March/April 2003)
7. Lin, X., Shroff, N.B.: The impact of imperfect scheduling on cross-layer rate control in wireless networks. In: IEEE Infocom 2005, vol. 3, pp. 1804–1814 (March 2005)
8. Cui, S., Madan, R., Goldsmith, A., Lall, S.: Joint routing, MAC, and link layer optimization in sensor networks with energy constraints. In: IEEE ICC 2005, vol. 2, pp. 725–729 (May 2005)
9. Luo, H., Lu, S., Bharghavan, V.: A new model for packet scheduling in multihop wireless networks. In: ACM Mobicom 2000, pp. 76–86 (2000)
10. Gambiroza, V., Sadeghi, B., Knightly, E.W.: End-to-end performance and fairness in multihop wireless backhaul networks. In: ACM Mobicom 2004, (2–4), pp. 287–301 (2004)
11. Johansson, M., Xiao, L.: Scheduling, routing and power allocation for fairness in wireless networks. In: IEEE VTC 2004-Spring, vol. 3, pp. 1355–1360 (May 2004)

Leader Election Algorithms for Multi-channel Wireless Networks

Tarun Bansal, Neeraj Mittal, and S. Venkatesan

Department of Computer Science
The University of Texas at Dallas
Richardson, TX 75080, USA
tarun@student.utdallas.edu, {neerajm,venky}@utdallas.edu

Abstract. We study the leader election problem in single-hop multi-channel wireless networks with single-antenna radio nodes. The objective is to elect leaders for all channels on which one or more nodes in the network can operate. We assume that nodes do not have collision detection capability. In this paper, we propose three algorithms for leader election: one deterministic and two randomized. The deterministic algorithm executes for at most $2N + M\lceil \log M \rceil$ time slots and guarantees leader election for all the channels, where M is the size of the universal channel set available to the nodes and N is the size of the label space used to assign unique labels to the nodes. The randomized algorithms guarantee that a leader is elected for all the channels with probability at least $1 - 1/f$ within $O(M \log^2(n_{\max}) + M \log^2(Mf))$ and $O(M \log(n_{\max}) \log(Mf))$ time slots, respectively, where $n_{\max}$ is the maximum number of nodes operating on any channel in the network. To the best of our knowledge, this is the first work on leader election in single-antenna multi-channel radio networks.

Keywords: wireless networks, cognitive radios, multiple channels, leader election.

1 Introduction

Currently, the wireless channels are allocated using the fixed spectrum allocation policy in which the spectrum is assigned by a central authority to various services. However some frequencies are much more in demand than other owing to their lower energy requirements, low error rate and higher transmission range. As a result, a large portion of the spectrum is sporadically used whereas in some portions the usage is a lot more concentrated [1]. In order to allocate channels efficiently so as to avoid spectrum holes, the use of *cognitive radios* has been recommended [1,2].

Cognitive radios (CRs) are able to change their transmission and reception parameters to communicate efficiently avoiding interference with other users by sensing the spectrum. This adjustment can be done dynamically and can include changes in communication frequency, encoding, link layer parameters etc.

Y. Li et al. (Eds.): WASA 2008, LNCS 5258, pp. 310–321, 2008.

Even though cognitive radios are equipped with only a single antenna, still this dynamic adjustment allows them to operate on multiple channels.

While availability of multiple channels allow better network throughput potentially, but it also makes the setting up of the network much more difficult. This is because different nodes may have different capabilities. For example, a node R_1 may be able to communicate on channel C_5, but a neighboring node R_2 may not be able to communicate on that channel because of different hardware capability or spatial variance of the channel availability set [1]. This makes it a lot more difficult to solve traditional problems for multi-channel radio networks. Leader election is one such fundamental problem. It involves selecting a *distinguished* node in the network. In wireless networks, leader election has been used to solve many other problems like routing [3], key distribution [4], coordination in sensor networks [5], neighbor discovery [6,7] and so on.

For multi-channel networks, a leader can be elected in two different ways: (*i*) one leader for all the channels, or (*ii*) one leader on each channel with possibly different leaders for different channels. Having one leader for all the channels is not feasible if no node in the network has the capability to communicate on all the channels. Therefore, to ensure that every node in the network can communicate with a leader of a channel in a single step, we have to ensure that there is a leader for every channel on which one or more nodes in the network can operate.

In this paper, we propose several leader election algorithms (one deterministic and two randomized) for single-hop multi-channel networks (like cognitive radio networks). The deterministic algorithm guarantees that a leader is elected for all channels using at most $2N + M\lceil \log M \rceil$ time slots, where M is the size of the universal channel set available to the nodes and N is the size of the label space used to assign unique labels to the nodes. Note that the time complexity of our deterministic algorithm is much lower than that of the naïve algorithm, which uses MN time slots. The randomized algorithms guarantee that a leader is elected for all the channels with probability at least $1 - \frac{1}{f}$ within $O(M \log^2(n_{\max}) + M \log^2(Mf))$ and $O(M \log(n_{\max}) \log(Mf))$ time slots, respectively, where $n_{\max}$ is the maximum number of nodes operating on any channel in the network. Both randomized algorithms work without assuming the knowledge of $n_{\max}$ or N. As it can be observed, the time complexity of both randomized algorithms is asymptotically much lower than that of the deterministic algorithm when $N \gg M \log^2(n_{\max}) + M \log^2(Mf)$.

The rest of the paper is organized as follows. In section 2, we discuss the previous work conducted on leader election in single channel networks. We describe our system model in section 3. In section 4 we describe a deterministic algorithm for leader election. In section 5, we describe two randomized algorithms for leader election. Finally we conclude the paper in section 6. Due to space constraints, some of the proofs have been omitted and can be found elsewhere [8].

2   Related Work

Depending on radio transceiver's capability to detect collision, two radio models have been used in literature [9] for developing wireless algorithms viz. "Strong Radio model" and "Weak Radio Model". In the weak radio model, nodes cannot distinguish between "no transmission" and "multiple transmissions". This is also known as *Radio Network with no Collision Detection* (no-CD RN). Moreover, the transmitting nodes are not capable of monitoring the state of the channel simultaneously while transmitting. In strong radio model, nodes have collision detection capability which allows them to differentiate between "no transmission" and "multiple transmissions". Strong radio model also allows transmitting nodes to detect collision by simultaneously allowing them to monitor the channel state. As pointed out by the authors [9], only the weak radio model is consistent with the IEEE 802.11 standards and current WLAN standards.

For deterministic leader election algorithms for single channel weak radio networks, Jurdzinski et al. [10] have proved that the lower bound on time requirements for such algorithms is $N - 1$ time slots. Nakano et al. [11] have given one such time optimal and energy efficient deterministic algorithm which terminates in optimal number of time slots.

A trivial way to design deterministic algorithm for leader election for multiple channels could be to run M instances of Nakano's [11] algorithm on each channel. However, in that case the time complexity of the protocol would become $O(NM)$. In this paper, we present a deterministic algorithm for leader election which makes use of FDMA to achieve a much lower time complexity of $O(N+M \log M)$.

Different randomized algorithms for leader election have been proposed in the literature for different radio models. The leader election algorithms proposed in [10], [12], [13], [14] are based on strong radio model. They either assume that the nodes have collision detection capability or that the nodes can monitor the state of the channel at the same time while transmitting. In this paper, we consider only those algorithms that assume weak radio model.

Metcalfe et al. [15] have proposed algorithms for leader election which assumes the knowledge of the number of nodes present in the network. However for multi-channel networks, it is possible that the number of nodes present on different channels differ vastly. This may be due to different hardware capabilities of the devices or because of the spatial variance of the channel availability set [1]. For example, a higher percentage of nodes may be able to communicate on channels which have low energy requirements, low error rate etc. as compared to channels which do not exhibit these properties. This makes it very difficult to predict the number of nodes on each channel as required by their algorithm.

Hayashi et al. [16] have given a randomized algorithm for leader election for the weak radio model with unknown number of nodes present on the channel, which terminates in $O(\log^2 n)$ broadcast rounds with probability exceeding $1 - 1/n$ where n is the actual number of nodes present on the channel. Their algorithm proceeds in multiple rounds and each round is further divided into time slots. The number of time slots in a round increase with the round number. The ith round of execution is divided into i time slots. At the beginning of each round, nodes set the probability of transmission as $1/2$ and with each time slot in that round, the probability of transmission is reduced by half. The algorithm terminates as soon as a time slot occurs in which exactly a single node transmits.

For the networks where the number of radio nodes present is not known, Nakano et al. [11] have also proposed three different algorithms for leader election. The first algorithm proposed by them terminates with probability exceeding $1 - 1/f$ in $O((\log^2 n) + (\log^2 f))$ time slots. One of our randomized leader election algorithm is derived from this algorithm.

3   System Model

We consider leader election problem for one hop radio network with weak radio model. We term the set of all the channels as universal channel set, A_{univ}. The nodes can communicate on only a subset of the channels of the global channel set. So two nodes R_i and R_j would be termed as neighbors only if there exists some channel C_k such that both R_i and R_j can communicate on C_k. We assume that the nodes have been assigned unique labels from the set: $\{1, 2, 3, ..., N\}$. In this paper we give a deterministic and a randomized algorithm for leader election in multi channel networks. Unless otherwise stated, we assume that all nodes are aware of the global channel set and the size of the label space. We use the following notation to describe our algorithms:

- M = Number of channels in the universal channel set
- A_{univ} = Universal channel set
- N = Size of the label space assigned to the nodes
- C_i = Channel i from the universal channel set A_{univ}
- R_i = Radio node with label i
- A_i = Set of channels available to node R_i, if R_i is present in the network
- n_{max} = Maximum number of nodes present on any channel

Observe that N acts as an upper bound on n_{max}. However, in practice, n_{max} may be much smaller than N. Also, observe that there may be one or more channels on which no node can operate. Clearly, a leader cannot be elected for such channels. Therefore we call a channel *relevant* if there are one or more nodes in the network that can operate on that channel.

4   Deterministic Algorithm for Leader Election

In this section, we propose a deterministic leader election algorithm which runs in multiple phases. With each phase, on each channel, we reduce the label space of the competing nodes by a factor of 2. Initially, the label space of the nodes competing to become leader is N for each channel. When $\log N$ phases have completed execution, the label space is reduced to a unit size for each channel. Also, we ensure that for every channel, there is exactly one node with that label in the entire network. This unique node is then elected as the leader of the corresponding channel.

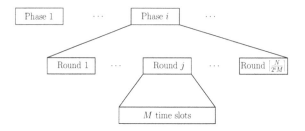

Fig. 1. Phases and rounds

Figure 1 gives the high level overview of the working of the algorithm. The execution of the algorithm is divided into $\log N$ phases and each phase is further divided into k rounds where k depends on the label space size at the beginning of the round. Further, each round takes M time slots to complete.

Working within a phase: Let us assume that at the beginning of the phase, the size of the label space of the competing nodes is X. So we divide this label space into groups of size $2M$. There are $\lceil \frac{X}{2M} \rceil$ such groups. We then further divide the execution of the phase into $\lceil \frac{X}{2M} \rceil$ rounds.

In each round, the algorithm handles one block of label space of size $2M$. In each round, we reduce the size of label space of competing nodes from $2M$ to M. So if at the start of the round, all the label space was occupied by nodes such that there were up to $2M$ nodes competing to become leader, we ensure that when the execution of the round terminates, out of the $2M$ nodes at most M nodes are still qualified for being elected as leaders. Thereafter, only these M nodes, get the chance to participate in the leader election process in the next phase. The remaining M nodes are no longer eligible for leader election on that channel.

However, if at the beginning of the phase, number of competing nodes is less than $2M$, then the phase would complete in a single round. Note that in this case as well, the algorithm would be able to reduce the label space size by a factor of 2.

Working of a round: At the beginning of each round, we group the $2M$ nodes into pairs of two and then these M node-pairs can resolve priority between themselves on all the channels in M time slots. Only the node with the higher prioirty, gets the chance to compete for leader election on that channel in the next round.

Table 1 shows the working of the protocol within each round. We make use of FDMA so as to reduce the number of time slots required to complete the execution of one round. This helps us reduce the time complexity of the algorithm. Also, note that the schedule is designed in such a way that all the M node-pairs get the chance to decide priority between themselves on every channel. The table is shown for the case when the range of labels of the nodes in the group is from 1

Table 1. Shows the execution of the algorithm within a round when label space of participating nodes is $\{1, 2, ..., 2M\}$. The addition is done modulo M. In case there are some labels with no nodes, then the time slots corresponding to those labels remain blank.

Channel / Time Slot	C_1	C_2	...	C_j	...	C_{M-1}	C_M
1	$1, 2$	$3, 4$		$2j - 1, 2j$		$2M - 3, 2M - 2$	$2M - 1, 2M$
2	$2M - 1, 2M$	$1, 2$		$2j - 3, 2j - 2$		$2M - 5, 2M - 4$	$2M - 3, 2M - 2$
i	$2M - 2i + 3, 2M - 2i + 4$	$2M - 2i + 5, 2M - 2i + 6$		$2M - 2i + 2j + 1, 2M - 2i + 2j + 2$		$2M - 2i - 1, 2M - 2i$	$2M - 2i + 1, 2M - 2i + 2$
$M - 1$	$5, 6$	$7, 8$		$2j + 3, 2j + 4$		$1, 2$	$3, 4$
M	$3, 4$	$5, 6$		$2j + 1, 2j + 2$		$2M - 1, 2M$	$1, 2$

to $2M$. However, if the participating nodes have labels in a different range (say $x + 1$ to $x + 2M$), then in order to figure out the transmission schedule for them, we first need to change their range temporarily from 1 to $2M$. This can be done trivially by subtracting a suitable number (x in this case) from all the labels.

So from the table we can see that for example in slot 1, nodes belonging to pair 1, *viz.* nodes 1 and 2, decide priority between themselves on channel C_1. Also at the same time the nodes belonging to pair 2, *viz.* nodes 3 and 4, decide priority on channel C_2.

However, if at the beginning of the round, the number of nodes competing to become leader on the channel is less than $2M$, the time taken to run the round is still M time slots.

To decide priority between two nodes (R_i and R_j) in a single time slot on some channel (C_k), we use the short routine given in Algorithm 1. The node which has higher priority moves to the next phase on channel C_k. Note that if there is no node with either of the labels, then the time slot goes empty and none of them is able to move to the next phase.

Also the nodes which move to next phase reduce their *label* by a factor of 2 and if it comes out to be fractional it is rounded up. This helps us to reduce the size of the label space by 2 with each phase. Note that the way node-pairs are formed, it is guaranteed that on any channel, two nodes with same label will never compete to become the leader. Since the size of the label space would be smaller in next phase, the number of rounds in the next phase would also reduce by a factor of 2. (Since number of rounds in a phase is proportional to the size of the label space at the beginning of the phase). However this trend continues only as longs as the number of competing nodes is more than $2M$. After that, each phase contains exactly one round. We will now prove the correctness of the algorithm.

Algorithm 1. decide_priority

---
if $R_i.exists$ and $C_k \in A_i$ **then**

    R_i sends beacon on C_k, R_i knows it has higher priority between R_i and R_j.

    if $R_j.exists$ and $C_k \in A_j$ **then**

        R_j receives beacon from R_i. R_j knows R_i has higher priority.

    end if

else if $(\neg R_i.exists$ or $C_k \notin A_i)$ and $(R_j.exists$ and $C_k \in A_j)$ **then**

    R_j does not receive any beacon, then R_j has higher priority between R_i and R_j

else if $(\neg R_i.exist$ or $C_k \notin A_i)$ and $(\neg R_j.exists$ or $C_k \notin A_j)$ **then**

    None of the nodes can communicate on C_k. So none of them move to the next phase.

end if

Lemma 1. *On any channel, no two nodes which are competing to become leader on that channel can have the same label.*

Lemma 2. *Leader is elected for all the channels wherever possible.*

Lemma 3. *For each channel, at most one leader is elected.*

Lemma 4. *The number of rounds in phase i is $\lceil \frac{N}{2^i \times M} \rceil$.*

Theorem 1. *The deterministic algorithm takes at most $2N + M\lceil \log M \rceil$ time slots for completion.*

Proof. Phase i has $\lceil \frac{N}{2^i \times M} \rceil$ rounds and each round takes M time slots for execution. Therefore the time required for completing Phase i would be $\lceil \frac{N}{2^i \times M} \rceil \times M$. Hence, total time required would be:

$$\sum_{i=1}^{X} \left\lceil \frac{N}{2^i \times M} \right\rceil \times M \qquad (1)$$

where X is the number of phases in the execution. For values of N of the form $M \times 2^t$ (where $t \in \mathbb{N}$), $X = t + \lceil \log M \rceil$. The first t phases reduce the label space size from N to M and the remaining $\lceil \log M \rceil$ phases reduce the label space size from M to 1. It can be verified that this summation evaluates to $N - M + M\lceil \log M \rceil$. For general values of N with $N > M$ which are not of this form, we pick the smallest integer N' of the form $M \times 2^t$ (where $t \in \mathbb{N}$) that is at least N. This new integer N' is then considered as the new N. The time required for completion would be $N' - M + M\lceil \log M \rceil$ time slots. Since $N' \leq 2N$, the execution of the deterministic protocol takes at most $2N - M + M\lceil \log M \rceil$ time slots.

    Finally, for values of N and M such that $N \leq M$, it can be shown that summation simplifies to $M\lceil \log N \rceil$, which is at most $M\lceil \log M \rceil$. ☐

Table 2. Description of the execution of the protocol over the multiple phases. Column 2 shows the range of original labels possible for the nodes having the corresponding labels in Column 1 during the particular phase. (a) Phase 1 execution: Six labels (or 3 rows of the table) are processed in 1st round of execution. Only 4 labels are processed in the 2nd round. (b) Phase 2 execution, (c) Phase 3 execution, and (d) Phase 4 execution.

Label	Original Label	C_1	C_2	C_3
1 & 2	1 - 2	1		
3 & 4	3 - 4	3	3	
5 & 6	5 - 6		6	
7 & 8	7 - 8			7
9 & 10	9 - 10			9

(a)

Label	Original Label	C_1	C_2	C_3
1 & 2	1 - 4	1	3	
3 & 4	5 - 8		6	7
5	9 - 10			9

(b)

Label	Original Label	C_1	C_2	C_3
1 & 2	1 - 8	1	3	7
3	9 - 10			9

(c)

Label	Original Label	C_1	C_2	C_3
1 & 2	1 - 10	1	3	7

(d)

Example: We now show the working of the deterministic algorithm through an example. Let us assume that there are 3 channels and 5 nodes in the network. The initial size of label space is 10. The channel availability set of the nodes is: $A_1 = \{C_1\}$, $A_3 = \{C_1, C_2\}$, $A_6 = \{C_2\}$, $A_7 = \{C_3\}$, $A_9 = \{C_3\}$.

During the first phase, we group the label space into two groups of size 6 and 4 respectively. The transmissions during phase 1 have been given in Table 2(a). This phase takes 2 rounds to complete. We have shown the execution during both the rounds of Phase 1. Since during the phase 1, labels of the nodes are same as their original labels, therefore the values in column 1 and 2 are same. The values in the cells are the original labels of the node which had higher priority during the execution of *decide_priority()* on that channel. For example, R_1 can communicate on channel 1, therefore it has higher priority over R_2 (which does not exist in this case) on this channel.

Similarly, when the second phase terminates, the label space size would reduce to 3 (see Table 2(b)). This time the phase execution would complete in a single round. Since the node labels have now reduced by a factor of 2, therefore a node which has label 2 would actually have its original label as 3 or 4. Also note that even though both the nodes R_1 and R_3 were able to move to Phase 2 on channel 1, still only R_1 would move to Phase 3 as given by *decide_priority()*.

In the 3rd phase, the label space size would reduce to 2. This time also the phase execution would complete in a single round. (see Table 2(c)). On termination of the 4th phase, the label space size would reduce to 1. The execution proceeds in a single round as shown in Table 2(d).

Total rounds required for the execution (over all the phases) $= 2 + 1 + 1 + 1 = 5$. Each round takes 3 time slots to complete. Hence total execution time is

15 time slots. Note that if we had elected leaders the trivial way, the total time slots required would have been $NM = 10 * 3 = 30$ time slots.

5   Randomized Algorithms for Leader Election

In this section, we propose two different randomized algorithms for leader election. Both the algorithms work even when an upper bound on the number of nodes in the network is *not known*. We refer to the first algorithm as *Rand-Elect* and to the second as *Fast-Rand-Elect*.

5.1   Algorithm *Rand-Elect*

This algorithm for multi-channel leader election uses the algorithm proposed by Nakano and Olariu in [11] as a subroutine. Readers are referred to [11] for a detailed description. Here, we present a short overview of their algorithm. Their algorithm proceeds in multiple phases. At the beginning of each phase, nodes start with probability of transmission as $1/2$, and with each slot within the phase, the probability of transmission is reduced by a factor of 2. The number of time slots in a phase are gradually incremented by one. Therefore, phase i consists of i time slots. And, in time slot j of phase i, nodes transmit with probability $1/2^j$ (and listen with probability $1 - 1/2^j$). At the beginning of next phase, the probability of transmission is again reset to $1/2$. This pattern is continued until some time slot occurs in which *exactly one* node transmits and all other nodes listen. As soon as that happens, the unique node that transmitted in this time slot is elected as the leader of the network. Nakano and Olariu's algorithm gurantees that a leader is elected with probability at least $1 - \frac{1}{f}$ within $O(\log^2 n + \log^2 f)$ time slots, where n is the actual number of nodes present in the network [11].

To solve the leader election problem for multiple channels, we propose to run M instances of their algorithm on each of the M channels *concurrently*. The multi-channel leader election algorithm executes in rounds. Each round consists of M time slots. In the ith time slot of every round, we simulate a single step of the ith instance of the algorithm, which is running on channel C_i. Observe that only nodes with channel C_i in their channel availability set participate in the ith instance of the algorithm.

Theorem 2. *Let $n_{\max}$ denote the maximum number of nodes that can be present on any channel in the network. Then Rand-Elect elects leader for all relevant channels within $O(M \log^2(n_{\max}) + M \log^2(Mf))$ time slots with probability at least $1 - \frac{1}{f}$.*

Proof. Since $(1 - \frac{1}{Mf})^M \geq 1 - \frac{1}{f}$, therefore in order to elect leaders for all relevant channels with probability exceeding $1 - \frac{1}{f}$, it is sufficient to ensure that the probability of leader election on individual channels exceeds $1 - \frac{1}{Mf}$. Now, the ith instance of Nakano and Olariu's algorithm guarantees leader election on channel C_i with probability at least $1 - \frac{1}{Mf}$ within $O(\log^2(n_i) + \log^2(Mf))$ steps, where n_i is the number of nodes that can operate on channel C_i. Since one round simulates one step of each instance of Nakano and Olariu's algorithm, *Rand-Elect* guarantees leader election for all relevant channels with probability at least $1 - \frac{1}{f}$ within $O(M \log^2(n_{\max}) + M \log^2(Mf))$ time slots. Hence the result.   □

5.2 Algorithm *Fast-Rand-Elect*

We now present another randomized leader election algorithm, which we call as *Fast-Rand-Elect*, that is faster than *Rand-Elect* in many cases. Before we describe the working of the new algorithm, we first describe a leader election algorithm (*Alg-Known-Size*) for single channel networks when the number of nodes present is known beforehand. The pseudo code for *Alg-Known-Size* is given in Algorithm 2 where S is the number of nodes present in the network and T is the maximum number of time slots for which the algorithm can run. In the pseudo-code, t denotes the sequence number of the current time slot.

Algorithm 2. *Alg-Known-Size(S, T)*

$t \leftarrow 1$
repeat
    transmit with probability $\frac{1}{S}$
    $t \leftarrow t + 1$
until exactly one node transmits or $t > T$

It can be shown that *Alg-Known-Size* guarantees leader election with probability at least $1 - \frac{1}{e^{T/4}}$ [15], [16], [11]. Now, suppose we wish to elect a leader for all relevant channels in a multi-channel network with probability at least $1 - \frac{1}{f}$. Clearly, it is sufficient to ensure that a leader is elected for each relevant channel with probability at least $1 - \frac{1}{Mf}$ because $(1 - \frac{1}{Mf})^M \geq 1 - \frac{1}{f}$.

To elect leaders for all relevant channels in a multi-channel network when the network size (or even an upper bound on network size) is *not known*, we run multiple instances of *Alg-Known-Size* on each of the channels one-by-one with geometrically increasing values of network size. The pseudo-code of the algorithm *Fast-Rand-Elect* is given in Algorithm 3. Specifically, the execution of *Fast-Rand-Elect* is divided into multiple rounds. In round x, we run an instance of *Alg-Known-Size* on each of the channels one-by-one using an estimate of 2^x for network size. Again, as before, only those nodes in the network that can operate on channel C_i participate in the instance of *Alg-Known-Size* running on channel C_i. In the pseudo-code, i denotes the channel number and x denotes the current round number.

We now prove the correctness of the algorithm.

Lemma 5. *Let n_i denote the number of nodes in the network that can operate on channel C_i with $n_i \geq 1$. Then, by the end of $\lceil \log(n_i) \rceil$ rounds, Fast-Rand-Elect elects a leader on channel C_i with probability exceeding $1 - \frac{1}{Mf}$.*

Algorithm 3. *Fast-Rand-Elect* for multi-channel networks

$x \leftarrow 1$
loop
    for $i = 1$ to M **do**
        run an instance of *Alg-Known-Size*$(2^x, 8\ln(Mf))$ on channel C_i
    end for
    $x \leftarrow x + 1$
end loop

Theorem 3. *Let $n_{\max}$ denote the maximum number of nodes present on any channel in the network. Then Fast-Rand-Elect elects a leader on all relevant channels with probability exceeding $1 - \frac{1}{f}$ within $O(M \log(n_{\max}) \log(Mf))$ time slots.*

Proof. From Lemma 5, *Fast-Rand-Elect* elects a leader on a relevant channel with probability at least $1 - \frac{1}{Mf}$ within $O(\log(n_{\max}))$ rounds. Each round consists of $O(M \log(Mf))$ time slots. Therefore *Fast-Rand-Elect* elects a leader on a relevant channel with probability at least $1 - \frac{1}{Mf}$ within $O(M \log(n_{\max}) \log(Mf))$ time slots. This, in turn, implies that *Fast-Rand-Elect* elects a leader on *all* relevant channels with probability at least $1 - \frac{1}{f}$ within $O(M \log(n_{\max}) \log(Mf))$ time slots.   □

Observe that *Fast-Rand-Elect* has better asymptotic time complexity than *Rand-Elect* if $\log(n_{\max})$ is either $o(\log(Mf))$ or $\omega(\log(Mf))$. In other words, $\log(n_{\max}) \notin \Theta(\log(Mf))$. In case $\log(n_{\max}) = \Theta(\log(Mf))$, the two algorithms have the same asymptotic time complexity. On the other hand, *Fast-Rand-Elect* requires a user to fix the success probability (given by $1 - 1/f$) a priori.

6   Conclusion

In this paper, we have presented three leader election algorithms for multi chan-nel radio networks with no collision detection. The deterministic algorithm guar-antees leader election for all relevant channels (available to one or more nodes in the network) and takes at most $2N + M\lceil \log M \rceil$ time slots, which is a considerable improvement over the trivial algorithm which takes NM time slots for comple-tion. The two randomized algorithms guarantee leader election for all relevant channels with probability at least $1 - \frac{1}{f}$ within $O(M \log^2(n_{\max}) + M \log^2(Mf))$ and $O(M \log(n_{\max}) \log(Mf))$ time slots, respectively.

Note that, when $n_{\max} = \Theta(M)$, the deterministic algorithm has time-complexity of $O(M \log M)$, which is asymptotically better than that of the ran-domized algorithms. Moreover, with a randomized algorithm, there is always a non-zero probability that a leader may not be elected for one or more of the rel-evant channels. However, the deterministic algorithm guarantees that a leader is elected for all the relevant channels with 100% confidence.

References

1. Akyildiz, I.F., Lee, W.Y., Vuran, M.C., Mohanty, S.: Next generation/dynamic spectrum access/cognitive radio wireless networks: A survey. Computer Networks 50(13), 2127–2159 (2006)
2. Mitola, J.: Cognitive radio: An Integrated Agent Architecture for Software Defined Radio. PhD thesis, Royal Institute of Technology (2000)
3. Perkins, C.E., Belding-Royer, E.M.: Ad-hoc on-demand distance vector routing. In: Proceedings of the 2nd Workshop on Mobile Computing Systems and Applications (WMCSA), pp. 90–100. IEEE Computer Society, Los Alamitos (1999)
4. DeCleene, B., Dondeti, L., Griffin, S., Hardjono, T., Kiwior, D., Kurose, J., Towsley, D., Vasudevan, S., Zhang, C.: Secure group communication for wireless networks. In: Proceedings of the IEEE Military Communications Conference (MILCOM), pp. 113–117 (2001)
5. Heinzelman, W.R., Chandrakasan, A., Balakrishnan, H.: Energy-efficient communication protocol for wireless microsensor networks. In: Proceedings of the Annual Hawaii International Conference on System Sciences (HICSS) (2000)
6. Mittal, N., Krishnamurthy, S., Chandrasekaran, R., Venkatesan, S.: A Fast Deterministic Algorithm for Neighbor Discovery in Multi-Channel Cognitive Radio Networks. Technical Report UTDCS-14-07, The University of Texas at Dallas (2007)
7. Krishnamurthy, S., Thoppian, M.R., Kuppa, S., Chandrasekaran, R., Mittal, N., Venkatesan, S., Prakash, R.: Time-efficient distributed layer-2 auto-configuration for cognitive radio networks. Computer Networks 52(4), 831–849 (2008)
8. Bansal, T., Mittal, N., Venkatesan, S.: Leader Election Algorithms for Multi-Channel Wireless Networks. Technical Report UTDCS-19-08, The University of Texas at Dallas (2008)
9. Jurdzinski, T., Kutylowski, M., Zatopianski, J.: Weak communication in single-hop radio networks: Adjusting algorithms to industrial standards. Concurrency and Computation: Practice and Experience 15(11-12), 1117–1131 (2003)
10. Jurdzinski, T., Kutylowski, M., Zatopianski, J.: Efficient algorithms for leader election in radio networks. In: Proceedings of the 21st ACM Symposium on Principles of Distributed Computing (PODC), pp. 51–57 (2002)
11. Nakano, K., Olariu, S.: Randomized leader election protocols in radio networks with no collision detection. In: Lee, D.T., Teng, S.-H. (eds.) ISAAC 2000. LNCS, vol. 1969, pp. 362–373. Springer, Heidelberg (2000)
12. Nakano, K., Olariu, S.: Uniform leader election protocols for radio networks. IEEE Trans. Parallel Distrib. Syst. 13(5), 516–526 (2002)
13. Bordim, J.L., Ito, Y., Nakano, K.: An energy efficient leader election protocol for radio network with a single transceiver. IEICE Transactions 89-A(5), 1355–1361 (2006)
14. Nakano, K., Olariu, S.: A survey on leader election protocols for radio networks. In: Proceedings of the International Symposium on Parallel Architectures, Algorithms and Networks (ISPAN), pp. 63–68. IEEE Computer Society, Los Alamitos (2002)
15. Metcalfe, R., Boggs, D.: Ethernet: Distributed packet switching for local computer networks. Commun. ACM 19(7), 395–404 (1976)
16. Hayashi, T., Nakano, K., Olariu, S.: Randomized initialization protocols for packet radio networks. In: Proceedings of the 13th International Parallel and Processing Symposium (IPPS), pp. 544–548. IEEE Computer Society, Los Alamitos (1999)

Clock Offset Estimation in Wireless Sensor Networks Using Bootstrap Bias Correction

Jaehan Lee, Jangsub Kim, and Erchin Serpedin

Department of Electrical and Computer Engineering,
Texas A&M University,
College Station, Texas 77843-3128
{jhlee,serpedin}@ece.tamu.edu
jsk615@gmail.com

Abstract. Wireless sensor networks have become an important and promising research area during the last recent years. Clock synchronization is one of the areas that play a crucial role in the design, implementation, and operation of wireless sensor networks. Under the assumption that there is no clock skew between sensor nodes, the Maximum Likelihood Estimate (MLE) of clock offset was proved by [1] for clock synchronization protocols that assume exponential random delays and a two-way message exchange mechanism such as TPSN (Timing-sync Protocol for Sensor Networks [2]). This MLE is asymptotically unbiased. However, the estimator is biased in the presence of a finite number of samples and much more biased in asymmetric random delay models, where the upstream delay characteristics are different from the downstream delay characteristics, and thus its performance is deteriorated. This paper proposes clock offset estimators based on the bootstrap bias correction approach, which estimates and corrects the bias of the MLE in the exponential delay model, and hence it results in better performances in mean squared error (MSE).

Keywords: Clock Synchronization, Wireless Sensor Networks, Bias Correction, Bootstrap.

1 Introduction

Recent advances in micro electro-mechanical systems (MEMS) technology, in digital circuits design, integration and packaging, and in wireless communications have led to smaller, cheaper and low-power devices capable of carrying out onboard sensing, computing and communication tasks. Wireless sensor networks (WSNs) are composed of a large number of tiny devices, which are networked in an ad-hoc manner without any common infrastructure [3]. The constraints of the sensor devices create WSNs with peculiar characteristics such as cheap, unreliable and unattended sensor nodes, limited bandwidth and limited energy resources. However, WSNs have received an increased attention due to a wide range of applications in various areas such as detection of enemies' attacks, traffic

Y. Li et al. (Eds.): WASA 2008, LNCS 5258, pp. 322–329, 2008.
© Springer-Verlag Berlin Heidelberg 2008

monitoring, surveillance, human physiological monitoring, acoustic and seismic detection, environmental monitoring, etc.

Time synchronization is critical to WSNs at many layers of their design. It enables better duty cycling of the radio, accurate localization, beamforming, data fusion, and other collaborative signal processing. The time synchronization problem has been addressed thoroughly on the Internet and local-area-networks (LANs). Many existing algorithms depend on time information from GPS. However, GPS has weaknesses: it is not available ubiquitously and requires a relatively high-power receiver, which is almost impossible on tiny and cheap sensor devices. In addition, the sensor nodes may be left unattended for a considerable period of time, e.g., on the ocean floor or in wild habitats. Moreover, the constraints [4] of WSNs make it infeasible to apply the traditional network synchronization protocols to WSNs. Therefore, time synchronization protocols specifically satisfying the constrains of WSNs are necessary.

In general, there are two stages involved in the time synchronization mechanism of WSNs. The first step is to synchronize the sensor nodes in WSNs to one common absolute time which is achieved by adjusting the clock offset among the nodes. The next step is to correct the clock skew relative to a certain standard frequency. The imperfections in the quartz crystal and the environmental conditions make clocks in sensor nodes run at different frequencies, which necessitates the second step. In fact, clock offsets keep drifting away due to the effect of clock skew. Therefore, by correcting each node's clock skew, it is possible to improve the long-term reliability of clock synchronization, and thus reduce energy consumption among the sensor nodes in WSNs. Developing long-term and energy-efficient clock synchronization protocols play a crucial role in deploying successfully long-lasting WSNs. In this paper, clock offset estimators based on the bootstrap bias correction approach are proposed, which estimates and corrects the bias of the MLE in the exponential delay model, and hence it results in better performances in mean squared error (MSE).

2   Problem Modeling

The two-way timing message exchange scheme between two nodes is shown in Fig. 1. *Node A* sends the synchronization message to *Node B* with its current timestamp $T_{1,i}$ (although it is not required, timestamping in the MAC layer increases the accuracy, as suggested by [2]). *Node B* records its current time $T_{2,i}$ at the reception of this message, and then sends at time $T_{3,i}$ a synchronization message to *Node A* containing $T_{2,i}$ and $T_{3,i}$. *Node A* timestamps the reception time of the message sent by *Node B* as $T_{4,i}$ (see Fig. 1). Hence, *Node A* has a set of timestamps $\{T_{1,i}, T_{2,i}, T_{3,i}, T_{4,i}\}$, $i = 1, \ldots, N$, at the end of N rounds of message exchanges. Note that $T_{1,1}$ is considered to be the reference time, and hence every reading $\{T_{1,i}, T_{2,i}, T_{3,i}, T_{4,i}\}$ is actually the difference between the recorded time and $T_{1,1}$.

Modeling of network delays in WSN seems to be a challenging task [7]. Several probability distribution function (pdf) models for random queuing delays have

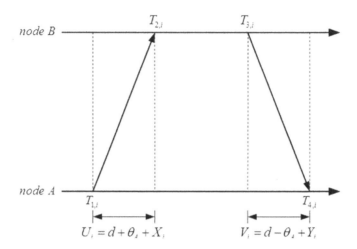

Fig. 1. Two-way timing message exchange model with clock offset (θ_A : clock offset, d : propagation delay, X_i, Y_i : random delays)

been proposed so far, the most widely used being exponential, gamma, Weibull, and log-normal distributions [8]-[9]. Amongst them, the exponential distribution is suited well for several applications [10]. Also, a single-server M/M/1 queue can fittingly represent the cumulative link delay for point-to-point Hypothetical Reference Connection, where the random delays are independently modeled as exponential random variables [5]. Moreover, [6] experimentally demonstrated the superiority of the MnLD (Minimum Link Delay) algorithm among the various algorithms proposed by [5], which was mathematically proved by [1] assuming exponential delays, thus confirming that the exponential delay assumption fits well the experimental observations. The reason for adopting the Gaussian model is due to the Central Limit Theorem (CLT), which asserts that the pdf of the sum of a large number of independent and identically distributed (iid) approaches that of a Gaussian RV. This model is proper if the delays are thought to be the addition of numerous independent random processes. The Gaussian distribution for the clock offset errors was also reported by a few authors, such as [6], based on laboratory tests.

Next, it is assumed that there is no clock skew in the two-way timing message exchange model. The ith up and down link delay observations corresponding to the ith timing message exchange are given by $U_i = T_{2,i} - T_{1,i} = d + \theta_A + X_i$ and $V_i = T_{4,i} - T_{3,i} = d - \theta_A + Y_i$, respectively. The fixed value θ_A, d, X_i and Y_i denote the clock offset between the two nodes, the propagation delay, and variable portions of delays, respectively. In general, the delay distribution in the upstream, F_X is not equal to that in the downstream, F_Y, because the $node A \rightarrow node B$ and $node B \rightarrow node A$ transmission paths through the network typically have different traffic characteristics, and thus the network delays in each path are potentially different. Hence, it is important to estimate the clock offset more accurately in the asymmetric delay models.

In the symmetric exponential delay model, the MLE of θ_A exists and is given by

$$\hat{\theta}_A = \frac{\min\limits_{1 \leq i \leq N} U_i - \min\limits_{1 \leq i \leq N} V_i}{2} \tag{1}$$

where N denotes the number of observations of delay measurements [1].

3   The Method

If this MLE is used in the asymmetric exponential delay model, there will be a bias in the clock offset. Therefore, it is necessary to achieve a more accurate estimate of the clock offset by using an alternate approach. In this paper, bootstrap techniques are applied to estimating the clock offset in the asymmetric delay models. Bias-corrected estimators through non-parametric and parametric bootstrap are suggested. The procedures of bootstrap bias correction are as follows [11][12].

3.1   The Nonparametric Bootstrap

Step 0. Conduct the experiment to obtain the random sample $X = \{X_1, X_2, \ldots, X_n\}$ and calculate the estimate $\hat{\theta}$ from the sample X.

Step 1. Construct the empirical distribution $\hat{F}$, which puts equal mass $1/n$ at each observation $X_1 = x_1, X_2 = x_2, \ldots, X_n = x_n$

Step 2. From $\hat{F}$, draw a sample $X^* = \{X_1^*, X_2^*, \ldots, X_n^*\}$, called the bootstrap resample.

Step 3. Approximate the distribution of $\hat{\theta}$ by the distribution of $\hat{\theta}^*$ derived from the bootstrap resample X^*.

3.2   The Parametric Bootstrap

Suppose that one has some partial information about F. For example, F is known to be the exponential distribution but with unknown mean μ. This suggests that we should draw a resample of size n from the exponential distribution with mean $\hat{\mu}$ where $\hat{\mu}$ is estimated from X rather than from a non-parametric estimate $\hat{F}$ of F. We use the exponential distribution in the suggested bias correction through parametric bootstrapping. The parametric bootstrap principle is almost the same as the above non-parametric bootstrap principle, except some steps.

3.3   The Bootstrap Estimate of Bias

Let us suppose that an unknown probability distribution F assumes the data $\mathbf{x} = (x_1, x_2, \ldots, x_n)$ by random sampling, $F \to x$. We want to estimate a real-valued parameter $\theta = t(F)$. For now we will assume the estimator to be any statistic $\hat{\theta} = s(\mathbf{x})$. The *bias* of $\hat{\theta} = s(\mathbf{x})$ as an estimate of θ is defined to be the difference between the expectation of $\hat{\theta}$ and the value of the parameter θ,

$$bias_F = bias_F(\hat{\theta}, \theta) = E_F[s(\mathbf{x})] - t(F) \tag{2}$$

A large bias is usually an undesirable aspect of an estimator's performance. We can use the bootstrap to assess the bias of any estimator $\hat{\theta} = s(\mathbf{x})$. The *bootstrap estimate of bias* is defined to be the estimate $bias_{\hat{F}}$ obtained by substituting $\hat{F}$ for F,

$$bias_{\hat{F}} = E_F[s(\mathbf{x}^*)] - t(\hat{F}). \tag{3}$$

For most statistics that arise in practice, the ideal bootstrap estimate $bias_{\hat{F}}$ must be approximated by Monte Carlo simulations. We generate independent bootstrap samples $\mathbf{x}^{*1}, \mathbf{x}^{*2}, \ldots, \mathbf{x}^{*B}$, evaluate the boostrap replications $\hat{\theta}^*(b) = s(\mathbf{x}^{*b})$, and approximate the bootstrap expectation $E_{\hat{F}}[s(\mathbf{x}^*)]$ by the average

$$\hat{\theta}^*(\cdot) = \sum_{b=1}^{B} \hat{\theta}^*(b)/B = \sum_{b=1}^{B} s(\mathbf{x}^{*b})/B. \tag{4}$$

The bootstrap estimate of bias based on the B replications $\hat{bias}_B$, is (2) with $\hat{\theta}^*(\cdot)$ substituted for $E_{\hat{F}}[s(\mathbf{x}^*)]$,

$$\hat{bias}_B = \hat{\theta}^*(\cdot) - t(\hat{F}). \tag{5}$$

3.4 Bias Correction

The usual reason why we want to estimate the bias of $\hat{\theta}$ is to correct $\hat{\theta}$ so that it becomes less biased. If $\hat{bias}$ is an estimate of $bias_F(\hat{\theta}, \theta)$, then the obvious *bias-corrected estimator* is

$$\bar{\theta} = \hat{\theta} - \hat{bias} \tag{6}$$

Taking $\hat{bias}$ equal to $\hat{bias}_B = \hat{\theta}^*(\cdot) - \hat{\theta}$ gives

$$\bar{\theta} = 2\hat{\theta} - \hat{\theta}^*(\cdot). \tag{7}$$

4 Performance Analysis

We simulated the performances of the MLE and the estimators based on bootstrap bias correction for asymmetric exponential, gamma, and Weibull delays, respectively. Fig. 2 - 5 show the MSEs in environments where the distributions of the network delays are exponential, gamma, and Weibull. In Fig. 2 and Fig. 3, μ_1 and μ_2 denote the exponential delay parameters for the uplink and the downlink delay distributions, respectively. For the gamma delay model, the shape parameters (α_1 and α_2) were chosen to be two, and the scale parameters (β_1 and β_2) taken to be one and two for the uplink delay and the downlink delay, respectively.

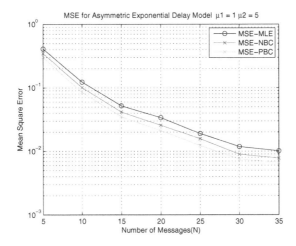

Fig. 2. MSEs of clock offset estimators for asymmetric exponential delays ($\mu_1 = 1$, $\mu_2 = 5$)

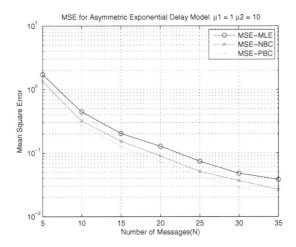

Fig. 3. MSEs of clock offset estimators for asymmetric exponential delays ($\mu_1 = 1$, $\mu_2 = 10$)

In the Weibull case, the shape parameters (β_1 and β_2) were set to be two, and the scale parameters (α_1 and α_2) chosen to be two and six for the uplink delay and the downlink delay, respectively. In the following figures, MSE-MLE, MSE-NBC, and MSE-PBC denote the mean squared error of estimate (1) which is the MLE in symmetric exponential delay model, that of the bias-corrected estimator through nonparametric bootstrapping, and that of the bias-corrected estimator through parametric bootstrapping, respectively. It is clear that the performance

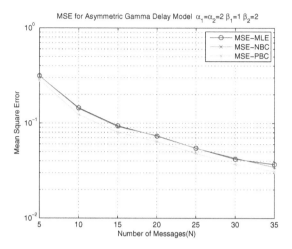

Fig. 4. MSEs of clock offset estimators for asymmetric gamma delays ($\alpha_1 = \alpha_2 = 2, \beta_1 = 1, \beta_2 = 2$)

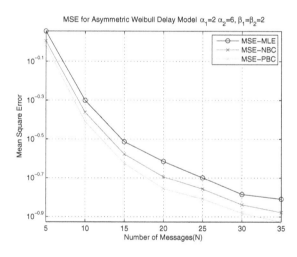

Fig. 5. MSEs of clock offset estimators for asymmetric Weibull delays ($\alpha_1 = 2, \alpha_2 = 6, \beta_1 = \beta_2 = 2$)

of the bias-corrected estimators are improved in several asymmetric delay models and the bias corrected estimator through parametric bootstrapping method has the best performance for the asymmetric exponential, gamma, and Weibull delay distributions. In Fig. 2 and 3, we also notice that as the asymmetry of the downlink and the uplink increases, the MSE vaules are affected and increased by the variance of observations.

5   Conclusion

We proposed clock offset estimators based on the bootstrap bias correction method in a clock synchronization protocol involving a two-way message exchange mechanism. We also illustrated that bootstrap bias-corrected clock offset estimators present smaller MSEs under several exponential families for network delays than the MLE in the exponential delay model. Moreover, the bootstrap bias-corrected estimator through parametric bootstrapping produces the best performance in terms of MSEs. In the future, we are looking forward to extend and apply these estimators to other time synchronization protocols.

References

1. Jeske, D.R.: On the Maximum Likelihood Estimation of Clock Offset. IEEE Trans. Commun. 53(1), 53–54 (2005)
2. Ganeriwal, S., Kumar, R., Srivastava, M.B.: Timing Synch Protocol for Sensor Networks. In: Proceedings of 1st International Conference on Embedded Network Sensor Systems 2003, pp. 138–149. ACM Press, New York (2003)
3. Akyildiz, I.F., Su, W., Sankarasubramaniam, Y., Cayirci, E.: Wireless sensor networks: a survey. Computer Networks 38(4), 393–422 (2002)
4. Sundararaman, B., Buy, U., Kshemkalyani, A.D.: Clock synchronization for wireless sensor networks: a survey. Ad-Hoc Networks 3(3), 281–323 (2005)
5. Abdel-Ghaffar, H.S.: Analysis of synchronization algorithm with time-out control over networks with exponentially symmetric delays. IEEE Trans. Commun. 50, 1652–1661 (2002)
6. Paxson, V.: On calibrating measurements of packet transit times. In: Proc. 7th ACM Sigmetrics Conf., vol. 26, pp. 11–21 (June 1998)
7. Narasimhan, S., Kunniyur, S.S.: Effect of network parameters on delay in wireless ad-hoc netwoks. University of Pennsylvania Technical Report (June 2004)
8. Papoulis, A.: Probability, Random Variables and Stochastic Processes, 3rd edn. McGraw-Hill, New York (1991)
9. Bovy, C., Mertodimedjo, H., Hooghiemstra, G., Uijterwaal, H., Mieghem, P.: Analysis of end-to-end delay measurements in Internet. In: Passive and Active Measurements Workshop, Fort Collins, CO (March 2002)
10. Moon, S., Skelley, P., Towsley, D.: Estimation and removal of clock skew from network delay measurements. In: Proceddings of the IEEE INFOCOM Conference on Computer Communications, New York (March 1999)
11. Efron, B., Tibshirani, R.J.: An Introduction to the Bootstrap. Chapman & Hall, Boca Raton (1993)
12. Zoubir, A.M., Iskander, D.R.: Bootstrap Techniques for Signal Processing, Cambridge (2004)

Correlation Analysis for Spreading Codewords in Quasi-synchronous CDMA Communication

Sujit Jos

Dept. of Electronics and Electrical Communication Engineering
Indian Institute of Technology, Kharagpur
sujit@gssst.iitkgp.ernet.in

Abstract. Spreading codes are designed to have good autocorrelation and crosscorrelation properties. Perfect synchronization is necessary to maintain the correlation properties to achieve the desired performance. But, due to imperfect synchronization in practical scenario, the correlation properties differ from the desired value. Individual codewords within a codeset behave differently due to difference in their autocorrelation and crosscorrelation properties. In this work, analysis of autocorrelation and crosscorrelation function is presented for fractional chip delays. Based on the analysis, a new performance metric is proposed to successfully rate the individual codewords in terms of their BER performance in quasi-synchronous scenario. Monte-Carlo simulation has been carried out to verify the analysis.

1 Introduction

Direct Sequence Code Division multiple access (DS-CDMA) has been considered as an attractive candidate for next generation cellular applications. The performance of DS-CDMA system is optimal if the users are perfectly aligned in time. Orthogonal codes are the obvious choice when perfect synchronization is maintained. However, this could never be guaranteed as a result of different channel profiles experienced by different users. When the synchronization error present in the system is less than a chip period, the DS-CDMA system is usually referred to as Quasi-Synchronous CDMA or QS-CDMA system [1].

The performance of QS-CDMA system relies largely on the correlation properties of the codewords employed for spreading the user signal. Numerous literatures have dealt with the correlation properties of different codesets employed in a DS-CDMA system [2]-[4]. Though these literatures give good insight into the properties which helps in the selection of a specific codeset, they have not adequately addressed the issue of performance of individual codewords in presence of access timing errors. In [5], the issue of sequence selection in QS-CDMA system is addressed by considering the effect of Multi access interference (MAI) alone.

In this work, expressions for correlation functions have been derived in terms of hamming distances for delays limited to chip duration. The delay of single chip duration is justified because the present day communication systems can synchronize the reception within fraction of a chip. The analysis gives insight into the performance of individual codewords in a codeset. Based on the analysis, a new performance metric

Y. Li et al. (Eds.): WASA 2008, LNCS 5258, pp. 330–337, 2008.

is formulated for Individual codewords. The performance metric also accounts for the loss in autocorrelation value due to lack of synchronization. The performance metric allows us to rate the individual codewords in terms of their BER performance. Monte-Carlo simulation has been carried out to validate the analysis.

In the next section, system model of QS-CDMA with BPSK signalling is presented. In section 3, expressions for autocorrelation and crosscorrelation function are derived. Performance metric for individual codewords is formulated in section 4. Numerical and simulation results are presented in section 5 followed by the conclusion.

2   System Model for QS-CDMA with BPSK

The basic Introduction to the system is referred from [6]. The system consists of K different users simultaneously signalling over a common transmission   channel. With BPSK transmission, the signal of k 'th user can be written as

$$u_k(t) = A_k \sum_{l=-\infty}^{\infty} b_k^l s_k(t - lT_b), k = 0, \ldots, K-1 \tag{1}$$

with amplitude A_k, symbol duration T_b, $b_k^l \in \{-1, 1\}$ and spreading codeword $s_k(t)$, which is given by

$$s_k(t) = \sum_{j=0}^{N-1} s_k^j p_c(t - jT_c) \tag{2}$$

with $T_b = NT_c$ and $s_k^j = \pm 1$ the elements of the k 'th codeword with chip duration T_c and length N. The function $p_c(t) = 1$ if $0 < t < T_c$, and $p_c(t) = 0$ otherwise. The received signal $r(t)$ is given by

$$r(t) = \sum_{k=0}^{K-1} u_k(t - \tau_k) + n(t) \tag{3}$$

where $\tau_k \in [-T_c, T_c]$ is the time shift between the transmitted and the received signal of user k and $n(t)$ is the additive white Gaussian noise process with two sided power spectral density $\dfrac{N_0}{2}$. If a correlator is used to detect the desired symbol b_n^i, we have the receiver output as

$$b_i^{\tilde{} n} = \frac{1}{T_b} \int_0^{T_b} s_i(t) r(t + nT_b) dt + z \tag{4}$$

Where,

$$z = \frac{1}{T_b} \int_0^{T_b} s_i(t) n(t) dt \tag{5}$$

Substituting (3) in (4), $b_i^{\tilde{} n}$ can be expanded into

$$b_i^{\sim n} = \frac{1}{T_b} \int_0^{T_b} s_i(t) \left[\sum_{k=0}^{K-1} A_k \sum_{l=-\infty}^{\infty} b_k^l s_k(t + (n-l)T_b - \tau_k) \right] dt + z \tag{6}$$

Following the assumptions in [7], the above equation may be approximated by:

$$b_i^{\sim n} = \frac{1}{T_b} \int_0^{T_b} s_i(t) \left[\sum_{k=0}^{K-1} A_k b_k^n s_k(t - \tau_k) \right] dt + z$$

$$= A_i b_i^n \varphi_{ii}(\tau_i) + \sum_{k=0,k\neq i}^{K-1} A_k b_k^n \varphi_{ik}(\tau_k) + z \tag{7}$$

Where,

$$\varphi_{ik}(\tau_k) = \frac{1}{NT_c} \int_0^{NT_c} s_i(t) s_k(t - \tau_k) dt \tag{8}$$

is the correlation between codeword $s_i(t)$ and codeword $s_k(t)$ delayed by τ_k. From (7), we observe that the amplitude of the desired user is degraded by the autocorrelation coefficient which is unity in case of perfect synchronization. The nonunity autocorrelation coefficient results in reduced signal strength in the despreaded signal. Synchronization errors generally result in increased MAI because of the higher value of crosscorrelation compared to the zero phase crosscorrelation. Irrespective of the polarity of data symbol b_i^n, the detection is error free if

$$A_i \varphi_{ii}(\tau_i) \pm \sum_{k=0,k\neq i}^{K-1} A_k \varphi_{ik}(\tau_k) + z > 0 \tag{9}$$

The above inequality may be rewritten as

$$A_i \varphi_{ii}(\tau_i) + I_i > 0 \tag{10}$$

where

$$I_i = z + MAI_i \tag{11}$$

In the above expression MAI_i is the multi access interference for the i'th user given by

$$MAI_i = \pm \sum_{k=0,k\neq i}^{K-1} A_k \varphi_{ik}(\tau_k) \tag{12}$$

An error is made in the detection process of b_i^n when I_i exceeds $A_i \varphi_{ii}(\tau_i)$. To determine the probability of symbol error we need the distribution of MAI_i which depends on the crosscorrelation between the codewords. Since, we assume that data symbols are equiprobable, MAI_i approaches a Gaussian random variable as the number of interferers increases. Under the Gaussian approximation of MAI_i, we can model the interference noise I_i as Gaussian. With the Gaussian approximation the probability of error or BER of i'th user is given by

$$BER_i = \frac{1}{\sqrt{2\pi}\sigma} \int_{A_i\varphi_{ii}(\tau_i)}^{\infty} e^{-I_i^2/2\sigma^2} \, dI_i \tag{13}$$

Let

$$x = \frac{I_i}{\sqrt{2}\sigma} \tag{14}$$

Equation (13) then takes the form

$$BER_i = \sqrt{2}\sigma \times \frac{1}{\sqrt{2\pi}\sigma} \int_{\frac{A_i\varphi_{ii}(\tau_i)}{\sqrt{2}\sigma}}^{\infty} e^{-x^2} \, dx \tag{15}$$

$$= \frac{1}{2} erfc\left(\frac{A_i\varphi_{ii}(\tau_i)}{\sqrt{2}\sigma} \right) \tag{16}$$

$$= Q\left(\sqrt{\frac{A_i^2\varphi_{ii}^2(\tau_i)}{\sigma^2}} \right) \tag{17}$$

where

$$\sigma^2 = \sigma_z^2 + \sigma_{MAI_i}^2 \tag{18}$$

Here, $\sigma_z^2 = \dfrac{N_0}{2}$ and the variance of MAI, $\sigma_{MAI_i}^2$ can be calculated as

$$\sigma_{MAI_i}^2 = E\{MAI_i\}$$

$$= \sum_{k=0,k\neq i}^{K-1} A_k^2\varphi_{ik}^2(\tau_k) \tag{19}$$

From (17) and (19), we have the final equation for the BER of i'th user as

$$BER_i = Q\left(\sqrt{\frac{A_i^2\varphi_{ii}^2(\tau_i)}{\frac{N_0}{2} + \sum_{k=0,k\neq i}^{K-1} A_k^2\varphi_{ik}^2(\tau_k)}} \right) \tag{20}$$

From (20), it is evident that codewords which maintain higher values of autocorrelation and lower values of crosscorrelation with other codewords perform better in presence of timing error. The following section derives the expressions for correlation functions for fractional chip delays. Based on these expressions, we will formulate a performance metric which could successfully rate the individual codewords in terms of their BER performance.

3   Analysis of Correlation Functions for Fractional Chip Delays

A. *Analysis of Crosscorrelation function*
The crosscorrelation expression in previous section is reproduced here for continuity.

$$\varphi_{ik}(\tau_k) = \frac{1}{NT_c} \int_0^{NT_c} s_i(t)s_k(t-\tau_k)dt \quad , \ \tau_k < T_c$$

The value of zero phase crosscorrelation $\varphi_{ik}(0)$ is given by

$$\varphi_{ik}(0) = \frac{1}{NT_c} \int_0^{NT_c} s_i(t)s_k(t)dt \tag{21}$$

But when $\tau_k \neq 0$, there is a loss/gain in crosscorrelation with respect to the zero phase crosscorrelation which is given by

$$\frac{1}{NT_c}\int_0^{NT_c} s_i(t)s_k(t)dt - \frac{1}{NT_c}\int_0^{NT_c} s_i(t)s_k(t-\tau_k)dt = \left(\frac{N'-2z_{ik}}{NT_c}\right)\tau_k \tag{22}$$

Where,

$$N' = (1+\varphi_{ik}(0))N \quad \text{and} \quad z_{ik} = N - w_{ik'} \tag{23}$$

Here, $z_{ik} = N - w_{ik'}$, where $w_{ik'}$ is the hamming distance between codeword $s_i(t)$ and unit chip delayed replica of codeword $s_k(t)$. Equation (22) could be equivalently written as,

$$\varphi_{ik}(\tau_k) = \varphi_{ik}(0) - \left(\frac{N'-2z_{ik}}{NT_c}\right)\tau_k \tag{24}$$

Substituting $\tau_k = T_c$ in (24), we have

$$-\left(\frac{N'-2z_{ik}}{NT_c}\right) = \left(\frac{\varphi_{ik}(T_c)-\varphi_{ik}(0)}{T_c-0}\right) \tag{25}$$

From (24) and (25), we have

$$\varphi_{ik}(\tau_k) = \varphi_{ik}(0) + \left(\frac{\varphi(T_c)-\varphi(0)}{T_c-0}\right)\tau_k \tag{26}$$

As shown by equation (26), for any codeword with rectangular pulse shape the crosscorrelation function follows the generic relationship given by (26) which resembles the equation of the straight line given by the equation

$$y = mx + c \tag{27}$$

Here, y is a function of x, m is slope of the line and c is the intercept made by the function on y-axis.

Comparing equation (26) and (27), we have

$$m = \frac{\varphi_{ik}(T_c) - \varphi_{ik}(0)}{T_c - 0} \quad \text{and} \quad c = \varphi_{ik}(0) \tag{28}$$

Hence, equation (26) proves the linearity property of correlation function within a delay of chip duration.

B. Analysis of Autocorrelation function

When $s_i(t) = s_k(t)$, (8) can be written as

$$\varphi_{ii}(\tau_i) = \frac{1}{NT_c} \int_0^{NT_c} s_i(t) s_i(t - \tau_i) dt \quad , \quad \tau_i < T_c \tag{29}$$

and $\varphi_{ii}(0) = 1$ so that $N' = 2N$

Therefore, the autocorrelation function for the code $s_i(t)$ can be written as

$$\varphi_{ii}(\tau) = \varphi_{ii}(0) - 2\left(\frac{N - z_{ii}}{NT_c}\right)\tau_i \tag{30}$$

The equations (24) and (30) give the value of crosscorrelation and autocorrelation function at any fractional chip delay. It is observed from equations (24) and (30) that the crosscorrelation and autocorrelation value at any time delay depends on z_{ik} apart from N which is constant for a given codeset. The above expressions have been verified by numerical computation.

4   Formulation of Performance Metric

As indicated by (20), for the codeword $s_i(t)$ to perform better in quasi-synchronous environment, it should have higher value of autocorrelation and lower values of crosscorrelation with other codewords in the codeset. For meeting the above said requirements, a codeword should have high value of ' z_{ii} ' in the autocorrelation expression and low values of ' z_{ik} ' for all k 's in the crosscorrelation expression. Therefore, we can define a performance metric ' d^i_{corr} ' for the i 'th codeword $s_i(t)$ as

$$d^i_{corr} = z_{ii} - \frac{1}{K-1} \sum_{k=0,k\neq i}^{K-1} z_{ik} \tag{31}$$

The parameter ' d^i_{corr} ' decides the BER performance of the i 'th codeword $s_i(t)$. Higher the value of d^i_{corr}, better will be the BER performance of $s_i(t)$.

5 Numerical and Simulation Results

The codewords from Walsh Hadamard matrix of order 8 have been arranged in the decreasing order of 'd^i_{corr}'. The value of 'd^i_{corr}' is given in the descending order along with the respective codeword indices in table 1. Monte-Carlo simulations were also carried out to show the BER performance of respective codewords.

Table 1. Values of d^i_{corr} for different codewords from Walsh Hadamard matrix of order 8

d^i_{corr}	INDEX
4.0000	1
1.7143	5,7
0.5714	4
-0.5714	3
-1.7143	6,8
-4.0000	2

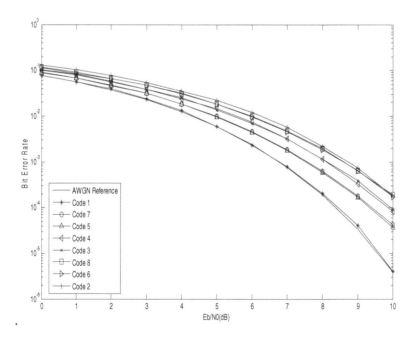

Fig. 1. BER Performance of individual codewords from Walsh Hadamard Matrix of order 8 at synchronization error of 0.1Tc

Fig. 1 shows BER performance of individual codewords from Walsh Hadamard matrix of order 8 in presence of constant synchronization error of 0.1Tc. Synchronization error of 0.1Tc means that all codewords are at a synchronization error of 0.1Tc at the receiver including the desired user i. Theoretical BPSK curve under perfect synchronization (AWGN Reference) is also shown.

From Fig. 1, we can see that 1st codeword gives the best BER performance as indicated by its highest value of d^i_{corr}. It is followed by 5th and 7th codewords which gives the same BER performance because of their identical value of d^i_{corr}. It is followed by 4th and 3rd codeword. Then next best performance is given by the 6th and 8th codeword which perform identically. Finally, the worst performance is given by 2nd codeword which has the least value of d^i_{corr}.

It is observed from the figure that the codewords perform in the exact order of 'd^i_{corr}' as given in Table 1.Therefore, it is well understood that the proposed performance metric could successfully predict the relative performance of Individual codewords from a given codeset.

6   Conclusion

Analysis of autocorrelation and crosscorrelation functions is presented for delays limited to chip duration. A new performance metric for individual codewords is formulated based on the analysis. Individual codewords in the codeset are rated based on their autocorrelation and crosscorrelation properties to perform best in quasi-synchronous environment. Numerical computations and Monte-Carlo simulation have been carried out to verify the analytical results.

References

1. Lin, X.D., Kyung, H.C.: Optimal PN sequence design for quasi-synchronous CDMA communication systems. IEEE Trans. Commn. 45, 221–226 (1997)
2. Karkkainen, K.H.A.: Mean-Square Cross-Correlation as a Performance Measure for Department of Spreading Code Families. In: Proceedings of ISSSTA 1992, pp. 147–150 (1992)
3. Kuramoto, A.S.R., Abrao, T., Jeszensky, P.J.: Spreading sequences comparison for DS-CDMA systems. In: Proceedings of ISSSTA 2004, pp. 350–354 (2004)
4. Matolak, D.W., Manchiraju, D.: Evaluation of pseudorandom sequences for third generation spread spectrum systems. In: Proceedings of Southeastern Symposium on system theory 2003, pp. 288–290 (2003)
5. Jeszensky, P.J., Junior, J.R.F.: Sequences selection for quasi-synchronous CDMA systems. In: Proceedings of ISSSTA 1998, pp. 706–708 (1998)
6. Houtum, W.J.V.: Quasi-synchronous codeword-division multiple access with high-order modulation. IEEE Trans. Commn. 49, 1240–1249 (2001)
7. Dasilva, V.M., Sousa, E.S.: Multicarrier Orthogonal CDMA signals for quasi-synchronous communication systems. IEEE JSAC 12, 842–852 (1994)

Energy Consumption Reduction of a WSN Node Using 4-bit ADPCM

Mohammed Billoo and Carl Sable

SProCom²
Dept. of Electrical Engineering
The Cooper Union for the Advancement of Science and Art
New York, NY 1003

Abstract. A 4-bit adaptive differential pulse-code modulation (AD-PCM) scheme applied to the sensor data of a Zigbee based wireless sensor network node is shown to decrease the energy consumption of the analog front-end of the node by 58%. Simulation results from an energy model of an 802.15.4 based analog front-end show that the energy consumed by the network node is inversely proportional to the number of bits used to encode the digital data. The quantization error of a 4-bit ADPCM scheme is on average -14 dB for low frequency data and only 3 dB higher than a traditional 8-bit PCM scheme. By modifying the modulation scheme in the software with no modification of the hardware, the lifetime of the node can be increased significantly with minimal modifications.

1 Introduction

A Wireless Sensor Network (WSN) is an ad-hoc network of nodes, where each node acquires data from the physical world. The sensors themselves then transmit the data to a base station, either through single or multiple hops. The challenges in designing a WSN mainly revolve around developing a protocol to route data that ensures minimum energy consumption, availability, and reliability of the data itself. While availability and reliability address node failure, which force the nodes to update routes, power and energy consumption is a critical metric as well. This is due to the fact that inserting human personnel to either replace entire nodes or simply replenish the energy source is financially significant. Hence, money can be saved by reducing the energy consumption of a WSN node and in turn increasing the lifetime of the node. Also, replacement of traditional energy sources in the node by renewable energy sources requires that the node be optimized for energy consumption to take full advantage of such resources.

Previous methods in reducing the power consumption of a WSN node have been done at the data link layer [1]. The IEEE 802.15.4 standard, which is employed by most WSN nodes and serves as a foundation for the ZigBee protocol, includes a few methods to reduce the energy consumption of the radio module in a WSN node. For example, the standard has developed a new frame structure

Y. Li et al. (Eds.): WASA 2008, LNCS 5258, pp. 338–348, 2008.

called a superframe. Each superframe has an active and an inactive period [1]. The node can only transmit during the active period, and must remain idle for the inactive period to conserve energy. The time division between the active and inactive period is usually controlled by a network coordinator, which may be the base station of a network. By increasing the inactive period in the superframe, the node can conserve an increased amount of energy but there will be a delay in its reception of messages.

Another energy reduction technique offered by 802.15.4 is the use of indirect transmissions. In an indirect transmission, a special frame is dedicated within the active period of the superframe in which the network coordinator holds the messages of a particular node. Pending messages are stored in the coordinator's frame, and in its own active period, the client polls the coordinator's indirect transmission queue; this communication requires relatively little power [1]. If a message does exist for the client, a more power intensive communication is done to transfer the message. Our procedure involves using 4-bit adaptive pulse code modulation (ADPCM) to modulate the data instead of the conventional 8-bit PCM technique used in 802.15.4. It has been noted that the majority of the energy in a wireless node is consumed by the analog front-end [2]. There have been efforts to optimize the hardware design of WSN front-ends [3]-[5]. However, constant hardware optimizations require extensive resources. In contrast, our method attempts to reduce the energy consumption of the hardware by making modifications in the software. In other words, changes we make to how the DSP handles the data reduce the energy consumed by the front-end. Thus, it is important to develop a power model to simulate the interface between the DSP and the front-end and use the results of the simulations to conclude that reducing the resolution of the digital data at the output of the DSP reduces the energy consumed by the analog front-end.

A 4-bit ADPCM scheme has been used to offer a balance between a reduction in energy consumption and quantization error. This methodology has two significant advantages. First, by using an adaptive modulation scheme to represent the data with fewer bits, energy consumption of the wireless node is reduced as shown in the simulation results. Second, and more importantly, our technique optimizes energy consumption at a higher level than current research and is not specific to a specific hardware. Section 2 provides a theoretical basis for the rest of the paper, including discussions on power consumption and ADPCM. Section 3 discusses the experimental setup, including the power simulator and the method used to calculate quantization error. Simulation results are presented in Section 4 and concluding remarks are made in Section 5.

2   Theoretical Framework

2.1   Power Consumption

In any CMOS circuit, there are two components that contribute to power dissipation: static dissipation due to leakage current or current drawn continuously from the power supply and dynamic dissipation due to switching current and the charging/discharging of capacitors [1]. Only dynamic power dissipation is considered since energy dissipated due to switching is more dominant than static dissipation. For a digital CMOS circuit, the average dynamic dissipated power, P_d, is given by [1]:

$$P_d = \frac{1}{t_p} \int_0^{\frac{t_p}{2}} i_n(t)V_{in}dt + \frac{1}{t_p} \int_{\frac{t_p}{2}}^{t_p} i_p(V_{DD} - V_{in})dt \qquad (1)$$

where i_n and i_p are the transient currents for the n-type and p-type devices, respectively, V_{DD} is the supply voltage, V_{in} is the input waveform, and t_p is the period of the waveform. If a capacitive load is assumed to exist at the output such that:

$$i_n(t) = C_L \frac{dV_{out}}{dt} \qquad (2)$$

$$i_p(t) = C_L \frac{dV_{DD} - V_{in}}{dt} \qquad (3)$$

where C_L is the load capacitance and V_{out} is the output voltage, then the dissipated dynamic power, and in turn, the total dissipated power of a CMOS circuit can be expressed as:

$$P_d = C_L V_{DD}^2 f_p \qquad (4)$$

where f_p is the clock frequency of the digital circuit. Thus, in a traditional digital CMOS circuit, the dissipated power increases with the frequency of the pulses. However, in the case of a typical WSN node framework, these calculations provide little insight into reducing the power consumed by a node. In a WSN node, the analog front-end consumes most of the power and is independent of the clock frequency of the digital portion of the node. Indeed, varying the clock frequency of the digital portion of the node will change the power consumed by the node, but it will have minimal impact on the overall power consumed by the node. Instead, a power model is developed in this paper for the analog front-end that is used to determine the impact of digital parameters such as modulation scheme and data resolution on the analog portion.

2.2 Adaptive Differential Pulse Code Modulation (ADPCM)

Adaptive differential pulse code modulation (ADPCM) was initially designed to encode speech data, noting that there is a high correlation between consecutive speech samples [6]. Due to the high correlation between the samples, ADPCM is used to encode the difference between a future predicted sample and the current sample. For certain signals, ADPCM provides a highly efficient compression scheme without sacrificing signal quality. Figure 1 shows the block diagrams for the ADPCM encoder and decoder, which is based on the ITU G.721 ADPCM algorithm [6]. The predicted sample, s_p, is subtracted from the current input sample, s_i, to generate a difference, d. The difference is quantized resulting in a

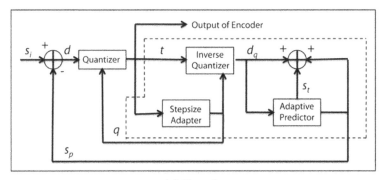

(a) Encoder

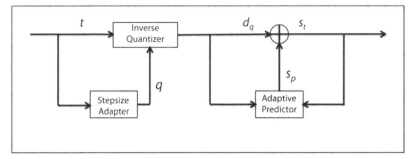

(b) Decoder

Fig. 1. ADPCM [6]

4-bit ADPCM value, t. The adaptive predictor of the encoder adjusts based on the value of the input sample, a weighted average of the past six differences and past two predicted values. The decoder in Figure 1(b) uses the APDCM value to update the inverse quantizer, to produce the difference, d_q [6]. The difference is added to the predicted sample to generate the output sample. The encoding and decoding algorithms are discussed in additional detail in [6].

ADPCM has been studied quite extensively. For example, Liu and Goldstein in [7] analyze the quantization error of ADPCM as a function of frequency. They take RC-filtered Gaussian random signals as their input, quantize the signal using ADPCM, and compare the spectrum of the reconstructed ADPCM signal with the original. Their results indicate that the quantization error is relatively low for signals with a normalized frequency less than 0.2 but becomes significant at higher frequencies. Quantization error due to ADPCM has also been studied in significant detail by Liu and Goldstein in [8] and [9]. In [8], a zero-mean unit-variance first-order Markov sequence is chosen as the input to the system, and a method is devised for computing the exact joint probability distribution function of quantization error and step-size for an ADPCM system. It is shown that the system quantization error and adaptive step-size in this particular scenario form a two-dimensionsal vector-Markov process. The Markov process is analyzed to generate the steady-state joint probability distribution function of the quantization error and step-size in ADPCM. There is a very high agreement between empirical distributions obtained from simulations and the theoretical results.

Whereas [8] illustrates a theoretical analysis of the quantization error in AD-PCM for a specific input, [9] presents a set of more general expressions describing the quantization noise in ADPCM. Not only are these expressions substantiated with simulation results, but the different forms of quantization error due to an ADPCM scheme are also presented. There are three main types of quantization noise: granularity, slope overload, and quantizer saturation. Granular noise is caused by the fact that the adaptive quantizer only has a finite number of steps to represent the input data. Slope overload occurs as the input signal increases at a faster rate than the system can follow [9]. Quantizer saturation is due to the fact that the step-size drifts to a small enough value so that the input frequently overloads the adaptive quantizer itself [9]. The expressions for each of these different noise types are given as:

$$N_g = \frac{2}{3} \frac{b_0}{f_0^2} \frac{1}{4^{b-1}c^2} \frac{1}{F_s^3} \tag{5}$$

$$N_s = \frac{8}{3} \frac{b_0}{f_0^2} \frac{\gamma^2 - 1}{c^2} \frac{1}{F_s^3} P_0 \tag{6}$$

$$N_0 = \frac{24.2}{\beta^5} \left(\frac{b_0^2}{b_2}\right) e^{-\frac{\beta^2}{2}} A(X) \frac{2f(\alpha)}{[1 + \frac{\alpha}{\beta}^2]^5} \tag{7}$$

The key parameters in the above expressions are f_0, the signal bandwidth and $F_s = \frac{f_s}{f_0}$, which is the sampling frequency-to-signal bandwidth ratio. Granularity is the dominant form of quantization noise in an ADPCM system, with quantizer saturation occurring infrequently, and with slope overload being almost negligible. Another important result from these expressions is that quantization noise due to granularity and saturation becomes significant at higher frequencies, with a set sampling frequency. By modeling the sensor input from a WSN node as a band limited Gaussian signal, this paper shows that quantization noise due to an ADPCM scheme is relatively low for low frequency signals and increases for high frequency signals. However, there are significant energy savings in using a 4-bit ADPCM scheme compared to an 8-bit PCM scheme. Also, there is significant error reduction in using a 4-bit ADPCM scheme compared to a 4-bit PCM scheme; tests conducted in this paper show that overflow always occurred when trying to quantize data with 4-bit PCM. Thus, for WSN applications where there is little variation in the environment, a 4-bit ADPCM scheme offers significant energy reductions compared to a traditional 8-bit PCM scheme with comparable quantization error.

3   Test Setup

In this section, the experimental setup is described. First, the power simulator that is developed and used to correlate parameters on the DSP portion of

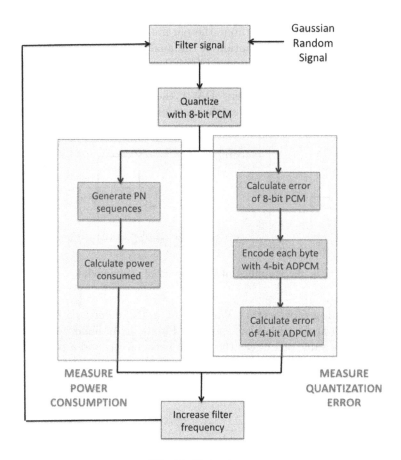

Fig. 2. Test setup

the WSN to power consumed by the analog front-end is described. Second, the method to compare the quantization error between a 4-bit ADPCM scheme and an 8-bit PCM scheme is also described.

Figure 2 shows a block diagram of the experimental method that is used. First, a Gaussian random signal is input to the system where it is low pass filtered by a filter with a varying cutoff frequency. The resulting data is then sampled and quantized with the traditional 8-bit PCM scheme. Then the simulations are broken into two sections. On the left, each 8-bit quantized data is mapped to a pseudo random number (PN) sequence and the power consumed by the analog front-end is calculated for the particular set of PN sequences. On the right, the quantization error of each 8-bit piece of quantized data is calculated, the data is encoded using a 4-bit ADPCM scheme, and the error of the resulting 4-bit encoded data is calculated. The frequency of the low pass filter is then increased and the simulation is run again. The frequency of the filter was swept from DC to the Nyquist rate.

3.1 Power Simulator

A power model is used to determine the parameters that have the most significant impact on energy consumption of the analog front-end. Figure 3 shows a simplified block diagram of a Chipcon CC2420 module, which supports 802.15.4. The main components of the module that are incorporated into the power model are the digital-to-analog converters (DAC), the low-pass filters (LPF), and the frequency synthesizer, which is modeled as a phase-locked loop.

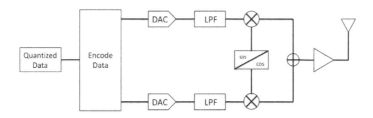

Fig. 3. Simplified block diagram of radio module

Digital to Analog Converter. Wang, *et al.* in [10] describe a power model of a DAC based on an R-2R ladder, shown in Figure 4. As binary data enters the resistor ladder, a value of 1 closes the switch between V_{dd} and a pair of resistors. A value of 0 leaves the pair resistors connected to ground [10]. A voltage is present at V_{out} based on the binary data on the input. If d_i is the individual bit for resistor rung i, then the power dissipated by the R-2R ladder can be computed by:

$$P = \sum_{i=1}^{n} d_i I_i V_{dd} \qquad (8)$$

where I_i is given by:

$$I_i = \frac{d_i V_{dd} - V_{out} + R \sum_{k=1}^{i=1}(i - k)I_k}{2R} \qquad (9)$$

$$V_{out} = \frac{D}{2^n} V_{dd} \qquad (10)$$

and V_{dd} is the DAC reference voltage, and D is the input number.

Low Pass Filter. Lawuers and Gielen present a method to estimate the power consumption of an analog filter [11]. Their method involves developing an expression to fit empirical data. Their expression for the power consumed by a low pass filter is described by:

$$P_{est} = \frac{order^{-1}}{10^{\frac{K - \frac{DR}{V_{dd}}}{20}}} \qquad (11)$$

Additional details regarding this equation can be found in [11].

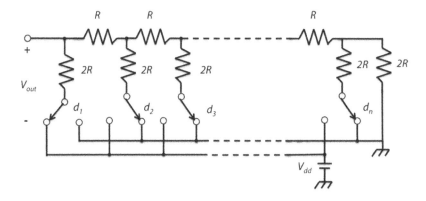

Fig. 4. DAC model

PLL. A phase-locked loop (PLL) is used to describe the frequency synthesizer. Duarte in [12] presents a power model for the PLL in both the acquisition and lock stages. His model takes into account component level parameters such as gate capacitance and transistor width. It is assumed in this case that the acquisition and lock times are equal. Additional details regarding the derivations of the expressions for the power consumption can be found in [12].

4   Simulation Results

It is important to compare the quantization error of ADPCM to traditional PCM to determine the effectiveness of such a modulation scheme. However, first, it is vital to determine whether even reducing the number of bits to represent the digital information results in any energy savings. To determine energy savings, the power simulator is tested with band-limited Gaussian sensor input.

Figure 5 shows the results of the power simulator with band-limited Gaussian sensor input that is modulated with 8-bit PCM. The figure indicates that power consumption of the analog portion of the node remains constant, on average, with increasing sensor data frequency. The reason for constant power consumption is that only the value of the binary number at the input of the DAC contributes significantly to the power consumed by the front-end, regardless of the frequency of the actual data itself. If a binary 1 is input to a resistor rung, then power is dissipated and if a binary 0 is input to the resistor rung, there is no power dissipated. Since the PN sequences that are input to the DAC are generated by the same algorithm, the number of binary 1's and binary 0's in a PN sequence are statistically similar, and thus maintain a constant power consumed by the DAC. However, there are minute oscillations in Figure 5 of approximately 0.2 mW. These oscillations can be attributed to the fact that the PN sequences are indeed different and have different number of binary 1's and binary 0's even though they are statistically similar, making the power dissipated different for each PN sequence. Thus, two techniques can be utilized to reduce the power

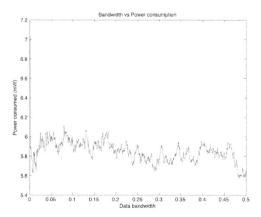

Fig. 5. Power dissipation

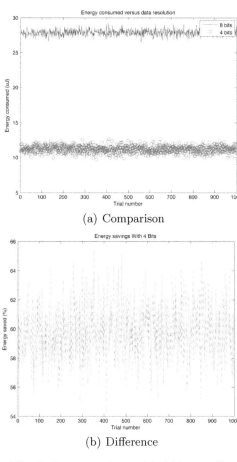

(a) Comparison

(b) Difference

Fig. 6. Energy savings with 4-bit encoding

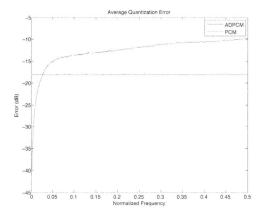

Fig. 7. Error comparison between 4-bit ADPCM and 8-bit PCM

consumed by the analog front-end. First, the PN sequence can be modified to reduce the power consumption. However, this change will impact the robustness of the overall communication system and requires a significant analysis to rectify. Instead, by representing the actual data with fewer bits before it is mapped to a PN sequence, energy can be saved. Thus, by reducing the number of bits used to quantized the sensor data, energy is reduced in the WSN node.

In 802.15.4, sensor data is first sampled, and quantized with 8-bit PCM. The resulting 8-bit wide sample is split into two 4-bit words and mapped to a set of 16 PN sequences [1]. With our method, by reducing the resolution of the sensor information from 8-bits to 4-bits, the same amount of information is transmitted in less time, resulting in energy savings. The energy consumed by the node is calculated by multiplying the power consumed by the node with the time it takes to transmit the information. Figure 6a shows the savings in using a 4-bit encoding scheme compared to an 8-bit scheme performed for 1000 trials. Figure 6b shows that for the same 1000 trials, there is an average energy saving of 58%.

By using 4-bit ADPCM to represent the information, a tradeoff exists between high energy consumption (such as in 8-bit PCM) and high quantization error (as in 4-bit PCM). When band limited Gaussian input is modulated with 4-bit PCM, overflow occurs because there is not enough resolution to represent the data, making such a modulation scheme infeasible. Figure 7 shows the error comparison between a 4-bit ADPCM scheme and an 8-bit PCM scheme. The figure illustrates that at frequencies of 0.1 and 0.2, which are assumed to be frequencies of the sensor data of a WSN node, the difference in quantization error between the 8-bit PCM and the 4-bit ADPCM schemes is only 3 dB. At higher frequencies, the error of the 4-bit ADPCM scheme becomes significant compared to the 8-bit PCM scheme and cannot be used.

5   Conclusion

It is shown that by using a 4-bit ADPCM scheme to quantize the sensor data of a WSN node, an energy savings of 58% is achieved. By quantizing low frequency sensor data, which is representative of the type of data encountered by a WSN node, with a 4-bit ADPCM scheme, there is only a 3 dB difference in quantization error between the 4-bit ADPCM scheme and the traditional 8-bit scheme. Thus, by using a 4-bit ADPCM scheme to represent sensor data within the digital portion of the WSN node, a significant amount of energy can be conserved by the WSN as a whole and used to increase the battery of life of a node. An increase in battery life equates to less resources used to deploy personnel to replenish energy sources. Also, by using a software based approach to reduce energy consumed by the node compared to a hardware based approach, significant resources do not need to be used to redesign WSN nodes.

References

1. IEEE Standard for Information technology - Telecommunications and information exchange between systems - Local and metropolitan area networks - Specific requirements, Part 15.4: Wireless Medium Access Control (MAC) and Physical Layer (PHY) Specifications for Low-Rate Wireless Personal Area Networks (WPANS)
2. Wang, Q., Hempstead, M., Yang, W.: A Realistic Power Consumption Model for Wireless Sensor Network Devices. IEEE Comm. Society on Sensor and Ad Hoc Comm. and Networks 1, 286–295 (2006)
3. Li, Y., Bakkaloglu, B., Chakrabarti, C.: A Comprehensive Model and Energy-Quality Evaluation of Wireless Transceiver Front-Ends. In: Proc. of IEEE Workshop on SIPS, pp. 262–267 (November 2005)
4. Wang, Q., Wooward, Y.: Energy Consumption for Power Management in Wireless Sensor Networks. In: 4th Annual IEEE Comm. Soc. Conf. on SECON 2007, pp. 142–151 (June 2007)
5. Kan, B., Cai, L., Zhao, L., Xu, Y.: Energy Efficient Design of WSN Based on An Accurate Power Consumption Model. In: Int. Conf. on WiCOM 2007, pp. 2751–2754 (September 2007)
6. Richey, R.: Adaptive Differential Pulse Code Modulation Using PICMicro Microcontrollers. Microchip Application note AN643 (1997)
7. Liu, B., Goldstein, L.: Power Spectra of ADPCM. IEEE Trans. Acoust., Speech, and Signal Processing ASSP-25(1), 56–62 (1977)
8. Goldstein, L., Liu, B.: Quantization Error and Step-Size Distributions in ADPCM. IEEE Trans. on Information Theory IT-23(2), 216–223 (1977)
9. Goldstein, L., Liu, B.: Quantization Noise in ADPCM Systems. IEEE Trans. on Communications COM-25(2), 227–238 (1977)
10. Wang, L., Fukatsu, Y., Watanabe, K.: Characterization of Current-Mode CMOS R-2R Ladder Digital-to-Analog Converters. IEEE Trans. on Instrumentation and Measurement 56(2), 1781–1786 (2001)
11. Lawuers, E., Gielen: High-level Power Estimator for Analog Filters. In: IEEE/ProRISC 1999, pp. 255–260 (October 1999)
12. Duarte, E.: Clock Network and Phase-Locked Loop Power Estimation and Experimentation, Ph.D. dissertation, Pennsylvania State University, PA, USA, pp. 36–57 (May 2002)

Minimizing Transferred Data for Code Update on Wireless Sensor Network*

Jingtong Hu[1], Chun Jason Xue[2], Meikang Qiu[3], Wei-Che Tseng[1],
Cathy Qun Xu[1], Lei Zhang[1], and Edwin H.-M. Sha[1]

[1] Department of Computer Science
University of Texas at Dallas
Richardson, Texas 75083, USA
{jxh068100,wxt043000,cathyxu,lxz076000,edsha}@utdallas.edu
[2] Department of Computer Science
City University of Hong Kong
Tat Chee Ave, Kowloon, Hong Kong
jasonxue@cityu.edu.hku
[3] Department of Electrical Engineering
University of New Orleans
2000 Lakeshore Dr., New Orleans, LA 70148, USA
mqiu@uno.edu

Abstract. In Wireless Sensor Networks, the preloaded program code and data on sensor nodes often need to be updated due to changes in user requirements or environmental conditions. Sensor nodes are severely restricted by energy constraints. It is especially energy consuming for sensor nodes to update code through radio packages. To efficiently update code through radio, we propose an algorithm, *Minimum Data trasferred by Copying and Downloading* (MDCD), to find the optimum combination of copying from the old code image and downloading from the host machine to minimize the number of bytes needed to be transferred from the host machine to the sensor node. Our experiments show that, for small code modifications, MDCD reduces the number of bytes transferred by 92.77% over the existing Rsync-based algorithm. For normal code changes, MDCD shows an improvement of 46.03% in average.

1 Introduction

A Wireless Sensor Network(WSN) is a network that consists of many low-cost, battery-powered sensor nodes which are preloaded with application code and data. It is usually deployed into a field to track events of interest. Since sensor nodes are usually left unattended after deployment, they are severely constrained by energy.

Due to the changes of user requirements and environmental conditions, the preloaded program code and data on wireless sensors often need to be updated.

---

* This work is partially supported by TI University Program, NSF CCR-0309461, NSF IIS-0513669, HK CERG B-Q60B and NSFC 60728206.

Y. Li et al. (Eds.): WASA 2008, LNCS 5258, pp. 349–360, 2008.

For example, a WSN may be deployed in unfamiliar territory. Using the information gathered, the code may need to be updated to find more interesting information. Reprogramming sensor nodes is more economical and practical than deploying new sensor nodes [1].

To disseminate new code through radio is energy intensive. Sending a single bit of data consumes about the same energy as executing 1000 instructions [2]. Thus, reducing data sent over radio extends the lifetime of sensor nodes. In this paper, we present the Minimum Data transferred by Copying and Downloading (MDCD) algorithm to minimize the bytes transferred from the host machine to the sensor nodes to save power for the sensor nodes.

In general, network programming is processed in three steps: (1) encoding, (2) dissemination and (3) decoding. In the first step, a host program reads the application program code and prepares code packets to send. In the second step, the host program sends the code packets to sensor nodes. In the last step, the sensor nodes rebuild the program code.

A simple way to update code in a sensor node is to send all of the new code image to the sensor node like XNP. This is inefficient because there are usually many common segments between the old program image and the new program image. We can take advantage of this to reduce the number of bytes transferred.

Fixed-block comparison[3] was proposed to find common blocks between the old program image and the new program image. The host machine can send a small message to tell the sensor node to copy from old code image stored in its own memory to the new code image for each common block. This method needs less bytes to be sent than XNP, but it is not efficient when there is some shift in the code image. Jaein[4], tuned the Rsync algorithm[5], which was originally made for computationally powerful machines to update binary files over a low-bandwidth communication link. It can achieve some savings for minor changes in the source code, but for major code changes, it will not work effectively.

Li et al[6] considered the updating problem from the compiler's perspective of view. When compiling new code for sensor nodes, the compiler will, as much as possible, keep the new code the same as the old code. This approach can be combined with our algorithm to reduce the data transferred.

In this paper, we propose the MDCD algorithm to find common segments between the old code image and the new code image and compute the least number of bytes needed to be sent to sensor node to construct the new code image.

Our paper is organized in following way: In Section 2, we present two motivational examples. The MDCD algorithm and its correctness are presented in Section 3. Experimental results are provided in Section 4.

2   Motivational Example

When updating the code of sensor nodes, we want to reduce the number of bytes transferred. Comparison-based algorithms are proposed to reduce number of bytes transferred to sensor nodes. Comparison-based algorithms compare the code of successive versions and find similarities and differences between the old code image and the new code image in the host machine. Then the host machine tells sensor nodes to either copy parts of the new code image from the old code image with a *copy message* or write parts explicitly with a *download message*. With the addition of the MDCD algorithm, there are three comparison-based algorithms based on code comparison.

1. The first algorithm is a fixed-block comparison(FBC) algorithm [3]. It divides the code images to blocks and then compare each corresponding block. If there is a matching block, it will send a copy message for the matching block. Otherwise, it will send the whole block via a download message.
2. The second algorithm is also a block-based algorithm[4]. It is based on the Rsync algorithm[5]. We call it the $Rsync_{berkeley}$ algorithm. It divides the old code image into blocks. It has a window with the same size as a block. This window goes through the new code image from the beginning, comparing the window with every block in the old code image. Whenever a match is found, a copy message is sent, and the window moves forwards a block. If a window does not match any blocks, then the window moves forward one byte, marking that byte as a non-matching byte. Once another match is found, it will send the non-matching bytes in a download message.
3. In the MDCD algorithm, we use a byte-oriented approach to find all common blocks between the old code image and the new code image. Common blocks in the MDCD algorithm are not of fixed-lengths. After we find all the common blocks between the old code image and the new code image, we use a dynamic programming approach to find the least number of bytes to be sent from the host machine to sensor nodes.

In this section, we provide two motivational examples to show that existing methods are not good enough in finding common blocks between the old code image and the new code image, and that we can do a better job in reducing the number of bytes transferred.

In our first example, which is shown in Figure 1 (A), our code images have four blocks. One new byte is inserted into the second block of the old code image. The following code image shifts forward one byte, and the last byte is truncated.

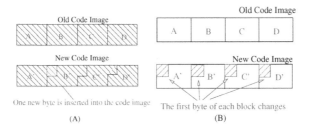

Fig. 1. (A) : One new byte is inserted into the code image (B): The first byte of each block changes

We assume that a copy message takes 12 bytes and a download message takes the same number of bytes as bytes that need to be transferred. Furthermore, we assume that, in block-based algorithms, each block is 256 bytes.

Here are the results of the different algorithms running this example:

1. The FBC algorithm can find that block A and A' are common block, but the rest of these blocks will be sent via download messages explicitly. It sends one copy message and three download messages, totalling up to 780 bytes.
2. $Rsync_{Berkeley}$ can find that blocks A, B, and C are the same as blocks A', B', and C'. It sends three copy messages for the common blocks and one download message for the last block, totalling up to 292 bytes.
3. Our algorithm can do a better job. MDCD can find that block D' is the same as the first 255 bytes of block D. It sends one copy message for block A, one download message for the inserted byte, and one more copy message for the rest of the code image. (Note that, since MDCD is not block-based, it can copy a block of any length with one copy message.) It sends two copy messages and one 1-byte download message, totalling up to 25 bytes.

In the second example, shown in Figure 1 (B), the first byte of each block changes. The results of different algorithms running this example are as follows:

1. The FBC algorithm cannot find any common blocks. It sends the whole new code image to the sensor nodes via download messages. It sends a total of 1024 bytes.
2. $Rsync_{berkeley}$ cannot find any common blocks either. It will also send total of 1024 bytes.
3. Since each block is the same as the old code image with the exception of the first byte, MDCD can find four common blocks. It sends a copy message for each of these blocks, and the four bytes in a download message. It sends a total of 52 bytes.

Table 1 summarizes the results of our examples.

Table 1. Example Results

	FBC	$Rsync_{berkeley}$	MDCD
Example 1	780	292	25
Example 2	1024	1024	52

3   MDCD Algorithm and Its Correctness

In this section we first describe the communication model under which our algorithm works. We then present our algorithm in detail, illustrating it with an example. Then we show the correctness and complexity of our algorithm. We prove that our algorithm minimizes the number of bytes to be transferred under the communication model.

3.1   Communication Model

We have an old code image X that sensor nodes need to update a new code image Y. Before the update, X is already on the sensor nodes, and host machine has both X and Y. The host machine wants to send the minimum number of bytes to the sensor nodes such that the sensor nodes can construct Y.

The host machine can send two types of messages: copy messages and download messages. Each copy message, consisting of the beginning address in X, the beginning address in Y, and the length of the segment to be copied, instructs the sensor node to copy a segment of X to Y. A download message is a segment of data that the sensor node writes into Y. With these two types of messages, sensor nodes can construct Y by copying of it from X, and downloading the remaining parts from the host machine.

The communication model between host machine and sensor nodes are described as follows:

First, the host machine tells sensor nodes the number of copy messages it will send and the length of Y. Sensor nodes allocate memory for Y. Then the host machine tells sensor nodes that it will begin sending copy messages.

As the host machine sends copy messages, sensor nodes constructs parts of Y by copying a segment from X for each copy message.

After sending all the copy messages, the host machine then sends all the remaining bytes to the sensor nodes sequentially. The sensor nodes go back and fill in all the blanks not filled in by copy messages.

In our model, each copy message will cost β number of bytes, and the cost of download messages will be the number of bytes sent.

3.2   Minimum Data Transferred by Copying and Downloading (MDCD)

Our algorithm is called *Minimum Data transferred by Copying and Downloading (MDCD)*. The MDCD algorithm, as shown in Algorithm 3.1, consists of three phases: Phase 1 finds all the common segments. Phase 2 finds the optimal combination of common segments to copy. Phase 3 generates the copy and download messages.

We use an example to illustrate our algorithm throughout this section. MDCD operates on two binary files, and in this example, we use the alphabet to represent binary code. Each character represents one byte of binary code.

$X = \langle A, B, C, D, E, F, G, H, I, J, K, L, M, N \rangle.$
$Y = \langle B, C, D, E, F, D, E, F, G, H, O, H, I, J \rangle.$

Phase 1: Find Common Segments Algorithm 3.3 takes array X, array Y, length of array X, length of array Y as inputs. The outputs are the common segments between X and Y which are represented by an array CS[ ] of quadruples $(Starting_X, Ending_X, Starting_Y, Ending_Y)$. Algorithm 3.3 has two nested FOR loops to go through every combination of i and j. For every combination of

---

Algorithm 3.1. Overall MDCD Algorithm

Require: Array of binary bytes of old code image X and array of binary bytes of new
code image Y, X = $\langle x_1, x_2, ..., x_m \rangle$ and Y = $\langle y_1, y_2, .., y_m \rangle$
Ensure: Copy messages and download messages to be sent to the sensor nodes
1. Find Common Segments
2. Find Optimal Combination of Copy and Download Messages
3. Construct Messages

Algorithm 3.2. *Search_Segment*

Require: Array X, Array Y, Position i in X, Position j in Y
Ensure: Starting position and ending position of common segment
    if $i = 0$ or $j = 0$ **then**
        return i+1, j+1 ;
    end if
    if $X[i] = Y[j]$ and T[i,j] $\neq$ NULL **then**
        $T[i,j] \leftarrow$ NULL; Search_Segment $(X, Y, i - 1, j - 1)$;
    else
        return i+1, j+1 ;
    end if

---

i and j, it calls procedure *Search_Segment*, shown in Figure 3.2, with parameters
i and j. If there is a common segment ending at i in X and j in Y , the function
returns the starting positions of that common segment and mark the combinations of i and j so that the same common segment is not be output twice. In our
example, *Search_Segment*(5, 6) outputs (1,2). *Search_Segment*(10,8) outputs
(6,4). *Search_Segment*(14, 10) outputs (12, 8).

After executing algorithm 3.3, we obtain array CS[ ] which records common
segments between the old code image and the new code image. The result of
algorithm 3.3 applied to our example is shown below.
    CS[ ] = ((2, 6, 1, 5), (4, 8, 6 ,10), (8, 10, 12, 14)).

Phase 2: Find Optimal Combination of Copy and Download Messages
After obtaining array CS[ ], which records the common segments between X and
Y, we begin to decide which segments are to be copied, and which segments are
to be downloaded. We use (m, n) to represent a common segment whose starting
address in Y is m, and ending address in Y is n. If a segment is transferred by a
download message, we say it is a *downloaded segment*. If a segment is transferred
by a copy message, we say it is a *copied segment*.

We refer to our example to illustrate the complications caused by the overlap
of common segments. In our example, $\beta = 3$. There are three common segments
after phase 2. The first segment is (2, 6), the second is (4, 8) and the third is
(8, 10).

Common segments are overlapping in Y, shown in Figure 2. Such overlaps
happen frequently when X and Y are large. If we copy all segments, we will
waste resources. In our example, if we copy all common segments, bytes 4, 5, 6,

Algorithm 3.3. *Find Common Segments*

Require: Array X, Array Y, Length of array X, Length of array Y
Ensure: *Array CS of ($Starting_X$, $Ending_X$, $Starting_Y$, $Ending_Y$)* quadruples. *$Starting_X$, $Ending_X$ is starting and ending positions in X respectively, $Starting_Y$, $Ending_Y$ is starting and ending positions in Y respectively.*
  for $i = length[X]$ to 1 **do**
    for $j = length[Y]$ to 1 **do**
      $Ending_X \leftarrow i$;
      $Ending_Y \leftarrow j$;
      $Starting_X, Starting_Y \leftarrow Search\_Segment(X, Y, i, j)$;
      if $Starting_X \geq Ending_X$ **then**
        $CS[k++] \leftarrow (Starting_X, Starting_Y, Ending_X, Ending_Y)$;
      end if
    end for
  end for

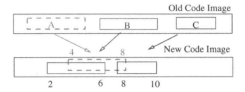

Fig. 2. Example of overlapping segments

and 8 will be copied twice. Actually, we can copy from the segments 2 to 6 and 8 to 10. We can just send byte 7 as a download message instead of copying 4 to 8. We need an algorithm to find the best combination of copy and download messages.

Given a set of common segments, Algorithm 3.4 finds the minimum number of bytes transferred such that sensor nodes can construct the new code image Y.

Let *local_optimum*[i] be the minimum number of bytes transferred to tell sensor nodes how to construct Y up to and including the *i*th byte of Y.

Let $j(i) = \min\{ m \mid \exists$ *a common segment*$(m, n), m \leq i \leq n\}$ where m and n are positions in Y. If such a common segment does not exist, we let $j(i) = \infty$. Our recursive formulation is:

$$local\_optimum[i] = \begin{cases} 0 & \text{if } i = 0 \\ local\_optimum[i-1]+1 & \text{if } j(i) = \infty \\ \min(\min_{j(i)-1 \leq k < i}\{local\_optimum[k]+\beta\}, \\ local\_optimum[i-1]+1) & \text{if } j(i) \leq i \end{cases} \quad (1)$$

We also need two arrays $s[\ ]$ and $Message[\ ]$ to keep track of the information we need to construct copy and download messages. $s[i]$ stores the size of subproblem that has been solved, and $Message[i]$ stores the action to take to construct the last part of the new code image.

Algorithm 3.4. Find Optimal Combination of Copy and Download Messages

---

Require: Common segments array CS from algorithm 3.3, Size of New code image
   N, Array Y
Ensure: Array s, Array Message, Array local_optimum
   $local\_optimum[0] \leftarrow 0$;
   for $i \leftarrow 0$ to N **do**
      $local\_optimum[i] \leftarrow local\_optimum[i-1] + 1$;
      s[i] = i-1 ;
      Message[i] = Y[i] ;
      for $k \leftarrow j(i)$ - 1 to i-1 **do**
         if $local\_optimum[i] \geq local\_optimum[k] + \beta$ **then**
            $local\_optimum[i] \leftarrow local\_optimum[k] + \beta$;
            Find corresponding address of k+1 in old code image from array CS, say l ;
            s[i] = k ;
            Message[i] = "Copy , $Starting_X = l$, $Starting_Y = $ k+1, $length = $ (i - k)";
         end if
      end for
   end for

Algorithm 3.4 first sets $local\_optimum[0]$ to be 0. Then it has a for loop to go
from the first to the last byte of Y. For each byte i, it computes $local\_optimum[i]$.
First, it sets $local\_optimum[i] = local\_optimum[i-1] + 1$ for the case when we
download this byte. Then, it finds a common segment that intersects with i. If
it will cost fewer number of bytes to send this byte with a copy message, it will
set $local\_optimum[i] = \min_{j(i)-1 \leq k < i} \{ local\_optimum[k] + \beta \}$.

Phase 3: Construct Messages. After arrays s and $Message$ are obtained, we
begin to construct the copy and download messages. The inputs to this phase are
the arrays s and $Message$, and the output are the copy and download messages.
The initial invocation is $Construct\_Messages($ length of Y $)$.

Algorithm 3.5. $Construct\_Messages$

Require: Arrays s and Message
Ensure: Instructions for constructing copy and download messages
   if $i = 0$ **then**
      return ;
   else
      $Construct\_Messages(s[i])$;
      Output Message[i];
   end if

The host machine constructs all the final copy messages to be sent to the
sensor nodes. In our example, there are two copy messages, $(1, 2, 5)$ and $(12, 8, 3)$.
After all the copy messages are done, the host machine concatenates all the
download messages together. In our example, the final download message is
(AGKLMN). The host machine sends all the copy messages first, followed by
the concatenated download message.

3.3   Correctness of the Algorithm

Lemma 1. *(Correctness of optimal substructure)*
Let $(Message_{n_1}, Message_{n_2}, ..., Message_{n_i})$ be an optimal combination of copy and download messages that requires the least number of bytes to be transferred from the host machine to sensor nodes to construct the new code image up to and including the n_ith byte of the new code image. Then, $(Message_{n_1}, Message_{n_2}, ..., Message_{n_{i-1}})$ is an optimal combination of copy and download messages to construct the new code image up to the n_{i-1}th byte in the new code image.

Proof. We can prove this with the cut-and-paste argument. If there exists a combination of copy and download messages $(M'_{n_1}, M'_{n_2}, ..., M'_{n_{i-1}})$ that requires fewer number of bytes to be transferred to construct the new code image up to the $n_{i-1}th$ byte in the new code image, we can have a new combination of copy and download messages $(M'_{n_1}, M'_{n_2}, ..., M'_{n_{i-1}}, M_{n_i})$ that requires fewer number of bytes to be transferred to construct the new code image up to and including the n_ith byte of the new code image. This is a contradiction to "$(M_{n_1}, M_{n_2}, ..., M_{n_i})$ is an optimal combination of copy and download messages". Thus, $(M_{n_1}, M_{n_2}, ..., M_{n_{i-1}})$ is an optimal combination of download and copy messages to construct the new code image up to and including the n_{i-1} th byte of the new code image.

Lemma 2. *The following recursive formulation is correct.*

$$local\_optimum[i] = \begin{cases} 0 & \text{if } i = 0 \\ local\_optimum[i-1] + 1 & \text{if } j(i) = \infty \\ \min(\min_{j(i)-1 \leq k < i}\{local\_optimum[k] + \beta\}, & \\ local\_optimum[i-1] + 1) & \text{if } j(i) \leq i \end{cases} \quad (2)$$

Proof. We prove this lemma by induction on i, the index of the bytes in the new code image.

Base case: When $i = 0$, there is no new code image, thus, $local\_optimum[0] = 0$.

Induction Step: Let the Induction Hypothesis(I.H.) [$local\_optimum[i]$ is the minimum number of bytes transferred to tell sensor nodes how to construct the new code image up to and including the ith byte of the new code image] be true for all values of i up to some $I \geq 0$. When we come to $I + 1$, we know that byte $I + 1$ is sent to the sensor nodes either with a copy or a download message, depending on which way requires fewer number of bytes.

If it is sent with a download message, then according to I.H., $local\_optimum[I + 1] = local\_optimum[I] + 1$.

If byte $I + 1$ is sent via a copy message, then the copy message used to construct the new code image up to the $I + 1$th byte is to construct from some position k to $I + 1$ in the new code image($k \leq I$). Then according to Lemma 1 and I.H., $local\_optimum[I+1] = local\_optimum[k] + \beta$. But here, we assume we know k, which we do not. Since, there are only $(I+1-j(I+1))$ possibilities for k, $local\_optimum[I+1] = \min\limits_{j(I+1)-1 \leq k < I+1} \{local\_optimum[k] + \beta\}$.

We compare the cost of sending this byte as a download message versus a copy message to get the smaller one. Note that if $j(I+1) = \infty$, it means we can not construct byte $I+1$ via a copy message, so we will send it with a download message. So $local\_optimum[I+1]$ equals $local\_optimum[I]+1$, if j(i) $= \infty$, and equals $\min(\min\limits_{j(I+1)-1 \leq k < I+1} \{local\_optimum[k] + \beta\}, local\_optimum[I]+1)$ if j(i) $\leq$ i.

Theorem 1. *Algorithm 3.4 finds the best combination of copy and download messages which requires the least number of bytes to be transferred from the host machine to sensor nodes to construct the new code image.*

Proof. Algorithm 3.4 first sets $local\_optimum[0]$ to be 0. Then for each byte i from the first to the last byte of the new code image, algorithm 3.4 first sets $local\_optimum[i]$ to be $local\_optimum[i-1]+1$. Then it checks to see if the host machine can send this byte with a copy message with fewer bytes. Algorithm 3.4 sets $local\_optimum[i]$ be the least number of bytes. Hence, it implements the recursive function proved by Lemma 2. Thus, the MDCD algorithm finds the best combination of copy and download messages requiring the least number of bytes to be transferred from the host machine to sensor nodes to construct the new code image.

3.4   Time Complexity of MDCD Algorithm

Let n be the size of the code image. Since algorithm 3.3 only visits each entry in table T once, and procedure *Search_Segment* in Algorithm 3.2 will only visit each entry in table T at most twice, the time complexity of algorithm 3.3 is $\Theta(n^2)$. The complexity of algorithm 3.4 is $\Theta(n^2)$. Hence, the complexity of the MDCD algorithm is $\Theta(n^2)$.

4   Experiments

4.1   Experiment Setup

To evaluate the performance of our algorithm, we compare the number of bytes transferred by MDCD with the number of bytes transferred by $Rsync_{berkeley}$. We use the source code of the dijkstra algorithm in the network package of Mibench[7] as the code we are going to update.

Assumptions. For MDCD, we assume a copy message needs 4 bytes for the starting position in the old code image, 4 bytes for the starting position in the new code image, and 4 bytes for the length of the common segment. A download message costs the number of bytes to be sent to sensor nodes explicitly.

Table 2. Experiment test cases

	Description	Binary File size(After compilation)
Case1	Change one constant	9328B
Case2	Add a counter	9340B
Case3	Change type of five variables	9404B
Case4	Add a variable	9460B
Case5	Change declaration of an array	9284B
Case6	Add a few lines of source code	9428B
Case7	Delete a few lines of source code	8960B
Case8	Comment a few lines of source code	9156B
Case9	Relocate a block of source code	9332B
Case10	Two totally different files	17020B

Table 3. Experiment result for $Rysnc_{berkeley}$ algorithm

	Case1	Case2	Case3	Case4	Case5	Case6	Case7	Case8	Case9	Case10
Original File Size	9328B	9340B	9404B	9460B	9284B	9428B	8960B	9156B	9332B	17020B
Copied Bytes	8448B	1536B	1536B	1536B	768B	1536B	512B	512B	4352B	256B
Ratio	90.57%	16.45%	16.33%	16.24%	8.27%	16.29%	5.71%	5.59%	46.64%	1.50%
Total Bytes	1066B	7854B	7918B	7974B	8551B	7942B	8467B	8669B	5115B	16654B

Table 4. Experiment result for our algorithm

	Case1	Case2	Case3	Case4	Case5	Case6	Case7	Case8	Case9	Case10
Original File Size	9328B	9340B	9404B	9460B	9284B	9428B	8960B	9156B	9332B	17020B
Copied Bytes	9321B	8813B	8349B	8598B	8277B	8665B	7707B	8129B	9290B	5865B
Ratio	99.92%	94.36%	88.78%	90.89%	89.15%	91.91%	86.02%	88.78%	99.55%	34.46%
Total Bytes	77B	4157B	4720B	4752B	5042B	4428B	5273B	5057B	1767B	15075B

For $Rsyc_{berkeley}$, we assume a copy message needs 4 bytes to indicate the sequence number of the block in the old code image. A download message will cost the number of bytes to be sent to sensor nodes explicitly. We assume one block contains 256 bytes.

Test Cases. The test cases are shown in Table 2.

4.2 Results

Table 3 shows the experiment results for $Rysnc_{berkeley}$ while Table 4 shows the experiment results for MDCD. The first row shows the original file size. The second row shows how many bytes of the new code image is copied. The third row shows the ratio of copied bytes to the file size of the new code image. The forth row shows, totally, how many bytes are sent from the host machine to sensor nodes.

Table 5. Comparison

	Case1	Case2	Case3	Case4	Case5	Case6	Case7	Case8	Case9	Case10
Use $Rsync_{berkeley}$	1066B	7854B	7918B	7974B	8551B	7942B	8467B	8669B	5115B	16654B
MDCD Algorithm	77B	4157B	4720B	4752B	5042B	4428B	5273B	5057B	1767B	15075B
Improvement	92.77%	47.07%	40.39%	40.41%	41.04%	44.25%	37.72%	41.67%	65.45%	9.48%

To evaluate the performance of our algorithm, we compare the total bytes transferred using $Rsync_{berkeley}$ and total bytes transferred using MDCD. The results are shown in Table 5.

The results show that when there are small changes in the source code, we can reduce the number of bytes transferred by 92.77%. In average, we can reduce the number of bytes transferred by 46.03%.

References

1. Levis, P., Culler, D.: Mate: A tiny virtual machine for sensor networks. In: International Conference on Architectural Support for Programming Languages and Operating Systems (ASPLOS) (2007)
2. Reijers, N., Langendoen, K.: Efficient code distribution in wireless sensor networks. In: International Workshop on Wireless Sensor Network Architecture, pp. 60–67 (2003)
3. Jeong, J.: Node-level representation and system support for network programming, p. 109 (December 2003)
4. Jeong, J., Culler, D.: Incremental network programming for wireless sensors. In: IEEE SECON, p. 109 (October 2004)
5. Tridgll, A.: Efficient Algorithms for Sorting and Synchronization, Ph.D. thesis, Australian National University (1999)
6. Li, W., Zhang, Y., Yang, J., Zheng, J.: Ucc:update-conscious compilation for energy efficiency in wireless sensor networks. In: PLDI 2007, pp. 104–109 (June 2007)
7. Ernst, D., Austin, T.M., Mudge, T., Brown, R.B., Guthaus, M.R., Ringenberg, J.S.: Mibench: A free, commercially representative embedded benchmark suite. In: IEEE 4th Annual Workshop on Workload Characterization (December 2001)

Opportunistic Cooperation with Receiver-Based Ratio Combining Strategy

Qian Wang[1], Kui Ren[1], Yanchao Zhang[2], and Bo Zhu[3]

[1] Illinois Institute of Technology, Chicago, IL 60616, USA
{kren,qwang}@ece.iit.edu
[2] New Jersey Institute of Technology, Newark, NJ 07102, USA
yczhang@njit.edu
[3] Concordia University, MontreaH3G 1M8, Canadal, QC
zhubo@ciise.concordia.ca

Abstract. In cooperative wireless communication systems, many combining techniques could be employed at the receiver, such as maximal ratio combining (MRC), equal gain combining (EGC), etc. To address the effect of receiver diversity combining on optimum energy allocation, we analyze the problem of minimizing average total transmit energy under a SNR constraint when different ratio combining methods are utilized at destination. For maximal ratio combining (MRC), based on the explicit analytical solution an asymptotic solution for normalized optimum total energy in terms of μ and η was derived in the high-SNR scenario. For fixed ratio combining (FRC), we find that there does not exist an explicit analytical solution to the optimum energy allocation problem. However, the convexity proof for the energy function provides a way of using numerical convex optimization methods to find the unique solution. Our results also show that, while direct transmission ($\mathcal{E}_r^* = 0$) is optimum for certain channel states when the destination uses MRC, the relay should always transmit, i.e. $\mathcal{E}_r^* > 0$ for all channel states, when the combining ratio β is a fixed number.

-

1 Introduction

In cooperative wireless communication, each user is assumed to transmit data as well as act as a cooperative agent for another user. The transmitters or receivers can collectively act as an antenna array and create a virtual or distributed multiple-input multiple-output (MIMO) system. The basic ideas behind cooperative communication can be traced back to the work of Cover and El Gamal on the information theoretic properties of the relay channel [1]. However, the earliest work specifically on user cooperation is due to Sedonaris et al. in [2]-[3] for cellular networks and Laneman et al. in [4]-[5] for *ad hoc* networks.

It has been shown that the cooperative transmission strategy provides powerful benefits of multi-antenna systems without the need for physical arrays, e.g. an increased capacity, a robustness to fading and reduced outage probability. Recent results in implementation of different cooperative signaling methods such

Y. Li et al. (Eds.): WASA 2008, LNCS 5258, pp. 361–372, 2008.
© Springer-Verlag Berlin Heidelberg 2008

as amplify-and-forward [4] and decode-and-forward [6]-[7], indicate that cooperative communication has a promising future. These results also demonstrated that while knowledge of channel state information at the transmitters (CSIT) is beneficial, it is not necessary to achieve significant gains in energy efficiency with respect to direct (non-cooperative) transmission.

While recent work in this area has focused on the goal of minimizing BER, minimizing total power to a rate constraint, minimizing total power subject to fixed SNR and outage probability constraints, the problem of how the diversity combining methods affect the optimum energy allocation has not been fully investigated.

In this paper, we consider the problem of optimum energy allocation and weighted total energy minimization under SNR constraint in two scenarios: (i) $\beta = \beta_{\mathsf{mrc}}$, i.e. maximal ratio combining (MRC) is used at the receiver and (ii) β is a fixed number, i.e. fixed ratio combining (FRC) is used at the receiver. In both cases, we derive the optimum opportunistic energy allocation strategies and explicitly describe the set of channel conditions under which the objective can be realized. Our analysis shows that, when MRC is utilized at destination, cooperative transmission is more energy efficient than direct transmission except when the relay-destination channel is not advantaged. The asymptotic solution we derived for the high-SNR scenario can best illustrate this. We also show that, while direct transmission ($\mathcal{E}_r^* = 0$) is optimum for certain channel states when the destination uses MRC, the relay should always transmit when fixed ratio combining (FRC) is utilized at destination, i.e. $\mathcal{E}_r^* > 0$ for all channel states. The impact of channel state information on AF cooperative transmission using MRC and EGC has been studied in [8] and [9], respectively, the intuitive results in this paper could be regarded as an extension of prior works.

2   System Model

To facilitate analysis, we consider the same system model as in [8] (Figure 1). In the network, each source is both a user and a relay, one source communicates directly to a destination and another source acts as a relay under certain channel conditions. The channels in the system are all assumed to be frequency non-selective and the channel magnitudes $|g_s|$, $|g_r|$, and $|h|$ are assumed to be independent Rayleigh distributed random variables. We also assume the channels stay roughly constant for several timeslots, i.e., in the process of cooperation.

In this paper, we use Amplify-and-forward as our signaling method in cooperative communication sytem. Amplify-and-forward is a simple method that lends itself to analysis, and thus has been very useful in furthering our understanding of cooperative communication systems. This method was proposed and analyzed by Laneman et al. [4]. It has been shown that for the two-source case, this method achieves diversity order of two, which is the best possible outcome at high SNR. In AF, each source receives a noisy version of the signal transmitted by its partner (relay). The relay then amplifies and retransmits this noisy

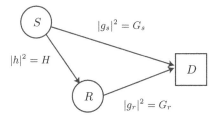

Fig. 1. System model

version. The destination combines the information sent by the source and relay, and makes a final decision on the transmitted bit.

- In the first timeslot, the source transmits the symbol x to the destination. The signals received by the destination and relay in this timeslot are as follows

$$y_{sd} = |g_s|a_s x + w_{sd}$$
$$y_{sr} = |h|a_s x + w_{sr},$$

where a_s is the amplitude of the source's transmission and w_{sd} and w_{sr} are additive white Gaussian noise at the receivers of the destination and relay , respectively.
- In the second timeslot, the relay retransmits the signal that it observed in the first timeslot to the destination. The signal received by the destination in this slot is

$$y_{rd} = |g_r|a_r y_{sr} + w_{rd}$$
$$= |g_r|a_r|h|a_s x + |g_r|a_r w_{sr} + w_{rd}$$

where a_r is the amplitude of the relay's transmission and w_{rd} denotes the receiver noise at the destination in the second timeslot.
- The destination makes a final decision on x based on the observations in the two timeslots

$$y_d = \beta_1 y_{sd} + \beta_2 y_{rd}$$

where β_1 and β_2 are nonnegative combining ratios.

3   SNR Analysis

We model AWGN as independent normal random variables with zero mean and unit variance. The instantaneous SNR of the final decision can be written as

$$\text{SNR}(\beta_1, \beta_2) = \frac{\left(\beta_1|g_s| + \beta_2|g_r|a_r|h|\right)^2 a_s^2 \text{E}[x^H x]}{\beta_1^2 + \beta_2^2\left(|g_r|^2 a_r^2 + 1\right)} \tag{1}$$

By setting $\beta = \beta_1/\beta_2$ and plugging $G_s = |g_s|^2$, $G_r = |g_r|^2$, $H = |h|^2$, (1) can be rewritten as

$$\text{SNR} = \frac{\beta^2 G_s \mathcal{E}_s(H\mathcal{E}_s + 1) + G_r \mathcal{E}_r H\mathcal{E}_s + 2\beta\mathcal{E}_s\sqrt{G_r\mathcal{E}_r G_s H(H\mathcal{E}_s + 1)}}{G_r\mathcal{E}_r + (\beta^2 + 1)(H\mathcal{E}_s + 1)} \quad (2)$$

where $\mathcal{E}_s = a_s^2 \mathrm{E}[x^H x]$ and $\mathcal{E}_r = a_r^2(H\mathcal{E}_s + 1)$.

Note that the relay transmission energy is conditioned on $H\mathcal{E}_s$ and includes both a signal component and a noise component. The noise component is a consequence of the fact that the relay transmission is simply an amplified copy of the noisy signal received in the first timeslot.

When the destination has full access to the channel state information (CSI) and transmit energies, maximal ratio combining (MRC) can be used to maximize the SNR of the decision statistic. The resulting instantaneous SNR at the destination, after MRC, can be expressed as [8]

$$\text{SNR}_{\text{mrc}} = G_s \mathcal{E}_s + \frac{G_r \mathcal{E}_r H\mathcal{E}_s}{G_r\mathcal{E}_r + H\mathcal{E}_s + 1}. \quad (3)$$

where

$$\beta_{\text{mrc}}^2 = \frac{G_s\left((H\mathcal{E}_s + 1) + G_r\mathcal{E}_r\right)^2}{G_r H\mathcal{E}_r(H\mathcal{E}_s + 1)}.$$

Note that the first part of (3) is the SNR of direct transmission.

When the destination does not have access to the channel state, equal gain combining (EGC) can be used (i.e. $\beta_{\text{egc}} = 1$). The resulting instantaneous SNR at the destination, after EGC, can be expressed as [9]

$$\text{SNR}_{\text{egc}} = \frac{G_s\mathcal{E}_s}{2} + \frac{G_r\mathcal{E}_r\mathcal{E}_s(H - G_s/2) + 2\mathcal{E}_s\sqrt{G_r\mathcal{E}_r G_s H(H\mathcal{E}_s + 1)}}{G_r\mathcal{E}_r + 2(H\mathcal{E}_s + 1)}. \quad (4)$$

In this paper, to establish a framework for optimum energy allocation, we define

$$\mathcal{E}_{\text{tot}} = \mathcal{E}_s + \alpha\mathcal{E}_r \quad (5)$$

as the *weighted total transmission energy* used in the cooperative transmission interval. The parameter $\alpha \geq 0$ allows for a weighting of the cost of the relay's energy relative to the cost of the source's energy. The following sections derive the optimum energy allocation strategies for an AF cooperative transmission under MRC and FRC using the weighted total transmission energy metric (5).

4   Optimum Energy Allocation

In this section, for a given channel state $\mathbf{s} = \{G_s, G_r, H\}$, we consider the problem finding the optimum energy allocation $\{\mathcal{E}_s^*, \mathcal{E}_r^*\}$ that minimizes the weighted total energy under a minimum SNR constraint ρ, i.e.,

$$\mathcal{E}_{\text{tot}}^* = \min_{\{\mathcal{E}_s, \mathcal{E}_r\} \in \mathcal{B}} \mathcal{E}_{\text{tot}} \quad (6)$$

where $\mathcal{B}$ is the set of energy allocations satisfying $\mathcal{E}_s \geq 0$, $\mathcal{E}_r \geq 0$, and the SNR constraint $\mathsf{SNR}(\mathbf{s}, \beta, \mathcal{E}_s, \mathcal{E}_r) \geq \rho$.

The SNR of the sources' information at the destination is determined not only by the channel states and the transmission energies but also by how the destination forms its decision statistic from the received source and relay transmissions. In the following sections, we first analyze the energy minimization problem when MRC technique is utilized at the destination, where the destination has full access to the channel states and transmit energies of both sources in both timeslots. In this case, β is a function of channel states and transmit power. In the second part of this section, we will discuss another situation, when fixed ratio combining (FRC) is utilized at the destination, i.e., β is a fixed number.

4.1   Maximal Ratio Combining

To facilitate analysis of (6) in the case of a destination using MRC, we define two non-negative quantities

$$\mu := \frac{\alpha G_s}{G_r} \left(1 + \frac{G_s}{H\rho} \right) \tag{7}$$

and

$$\eta := \frac{H}{H + G_s}. \tag{8}$$

The explicit solution to the total energy minimization problem for a destination using MRC is given in the following proposition.

Proposition 1. *When* $\beta = \beta_{\mathsf{mrc}}$, *the normalized minimum weighted total energy* $\frac{\mathcal{E}_{\mathsf{tot}}^*}{\rho G_s^{-1}}$ *can be expressed as*

$$\begin{cases} \dfrac{\left(\sqrt{\rho G_s (G_r(G_s+H) - \alpha G_s H)} + \sqrt{\alpha G_s H(G_s+H+\rho H)} \right)^2 - \alpha G_s (G_s+H)^2}{\rho G_r (G_s+H)^2} & 0 \leq \mu < 1, \\ 1 & \mu \geq 1. \end{cases} \tag{9}$$

The proof of Proposition 1 is provided in Appendix A.

We note that when the SNR constraint $\rho \to \infty$, $\mu \approx \alpha G_s / G_r$ can be considered an indicator of source or relay channel advantage, i.e. $\mu > 1$ indicates that the source has an advantaged channel to the destination and $\mu < 1$ indicates that the relay is advantaged. Similarly, η can be considered an indicator of source-relay or source advantage. When H is large with respect to G_s, the quantity $\eta \approx 1$, which means the source and relay are much closer in proximity than the source and destination.

Without loss of generality, we consider the problem in high-SNR scenario. When $\rho \to \infty$, the normalized minimum weighted total energy can be expressed in terms of μ and η as

$$\mathcal{E}_{tot}^*/\rho G_s^{-1} = \begin{cases} \left((\eta^2\mu)^{\frac{1}{2}} + [(1-\eta)(1-\eta\mu)]^{\frac{1}{2}} \right)^2 & \text{when } 0 \le \mu < 1, \\ 1 & \text{when } \mu \ge 1. \end{cases} \quad (10)$$

We can also define the total energy gain of optimum cooperative transmission as the ratio of the $\mathcal{E}_{tot}$ achieved with direct transmission, i.e. $\frac{\rho}{G_s}$ to the $\mathcal{E}_{tot}^*$ achieved with optimum AF cooperative transmission.

Similarly, we can show that the asymptotic solution for normalized optimum source energy in the high-SNR scenario can be expressed as

$$\mathcal{E}_s^*/\mathcal{E}_{tot}^* = \begin{cases} (\frac{1-\eta}{1-\eta\mu})^{\frac{1}{2}} \left((\eta^2\mu)^{\frac{1}{2}} + [(1-\eta)(1-\eta\mu)]^{\frac{1}{2}} \right)^{-1} & \text{when } 0 \le \mu < 1, \\ 1 & \text{when } \mu \ge 1. \end{cases}$$

$$(11)$$

4.2   Fixed Ratio Combining

This section analyzes the scenario when FRC is used at the destination (β is a fixed number), i.e. it is not dependent on the channel states and transmit power. Note that equal gain combining (EGC) can be considered as a special case of FRC where $\beta_{egc} = 1$.

The relay node energy $\mathcal{E}_r$ can be written as a function of ρ and $\mathcal{E}_s$ by solving (2) for $\mathcal{E}_r$ when $\mathsf{SNR}(\beta) = \rho$. The solution yields two roots for $\mathcal{E}_r$. When $\mathcal{E}_r = 0$, by solving the equation $\mathsf{SNR}(\beta) = \rho$ we have $\mathcal{E}_s = \frac{(\beta^2+1)\rho}{\beta^2 G_s}$. The correct root should satisfy this condition and can be written as

$$\mathcal{E}_r = \frac{(H\mathcal{E}_s + 1)(\beta^2 G_s H\mathcal{E}_s^2 + (\beta^2+1)\rho H\mathcal{E}_s + \beta^2 G_s \mathcal{E}_s \rho - (\beta^2+1)\rho^2)}{G_r(\rho - H\mathcal{E}_s)^2}$$
$$- \frac{2\beta\mathcal{E}_s\sqrt{G_s H\rho[(\beta^2+1)H\mathcal{E}_s + \beta^2 G_s \mathcal{E}_s - (\beta^2+1)\rho]}}{G_r(\rho - H\mathcal{E}_s)^2} \quad (12)$$

The admissible range of instantaneous energy allocations that satisfy $\mathsf{SNR}(\beta) = \rho$ can be described as the region in $\mathbb{R}^2$ where $\mathcal{E}_r \ge 0$ and $\frac{(\beta^2+1)\rho}{(\beta^2+1)H+\beta^2 G_s} \le \mathcal{E}_s \le \frac{(\beta^2+1)\rho}{\beta^2 G_s}$. The case $\mathcal{E}_r = 0$ establishes the upper limit on the interval of admissible solutions for $\mathcal{E}_s$. The lower limit on the interval is established by the requirement for total energy to be a real-valued quantity. The square root in the numerator of (12) reveals that $\mathcal{E}_r \in \mathbb{R}$ only if $\mathcal{E}_s \ge \frac{(\beta^2+1)\rho}{(\beta^2+1)H+\beta^2 G_s}$.

Denote the admissible range $[\frac{(\beta^2+1)\rho}{(\beta^2+1)H+\beta^2 G_s}, \frac{(\beta^2+1)\rho}{\beta^2 G_s}]$ of $\mathcal{E}_s$ as $\mathcal{A}$. Given ρ and the squared channel amplitudes G_s, G_r, and H, (12) implies that $\mathcal{E}_r$ is dependent on $\mathcal{E}_s$. It can be shown that it is hard to find an explicit analytical solution to (6). Numerical solutions to (6), however, are aided by the following result.

Proposition 2. *When FRC is used at the destination, the total energy* $\mathcal{E}_{\text{tot}}$ *is still a convex function of* $\mathcal{E}_s$ *on* $\mathcal{A}$.

The proof of Proposition 2 is provided in Appendix B.

Proposition 2 implies that standard numerical convex optimization methods can be used to find the unique solution to (6).

Denote $\mathcal{E}_s^*$ as the value of $\mathcal{E}_s$ that attains the minimum in (6) and note that $\mathcal{E}_r^*$ is implied by (12). Given the convexity of $\mathcal{E}_{\text{tot}}$ on $\mathcal{A}$, we can determine whether the unique minimum of $\mathcal{E}_{\text{tot}}$ on $\mathcal{A}$ occurs at the point $\mathcal{E}_s = \frac{(\beta^2+1)\rho}{\beta^2 G_s}$ by evaluating $\frac{\partial \mathcal{E}_{\text{tot}}}{\partial \mathcal{E}_s}$ at this point. If $\frac{\partial \mathcal{E}_{\text{tot}}}{\partial \mathcal{E}_s} > 0$ at $\mathcal{E}_s = \frac{(\beta^2+1)\rho}{\beta^2 G_s}$, then the minimum of $\mathcal{E}_{\text{tot}}$ on $\mathcal{A}$ must occur at $\mathcal{E}_s < \frac{(\beta^2+1)\rho}{\beta^2 G_s}$ (corresponding to $\mathcal{E}_r^* > 0$), otherwise the minimum occurs at $\mathcal{E}_s = \frac{(\beta^2+1)\rho}{\beta^2 G_s}$ (corresponding to $\mathcal{E}_r^* = 0$). It can be shown that

$$\left. \frac{\partial \mathcal{E}_{\text{tot}}}{\partial \mathcal{E}_s} \right|_{\mathcal{E}_s = \frac{(\beta^2+1)\rho}{\beta^2 G_s}} = 1 > 0,$$

hence the unique minimum of $\mathcal{E}_{\text{tot}}$ on $\mathcal{A}$ must occur at $\mathcal{E}_s < \frac{(\beta^2+1)\rho}{\beta^2 G_s}$. This implies that $\mathcal{E}_r^* > 0$ for all G_s, G_r, H, ρ. Thus in the case of FRC, the relay should always transmit, i.e. $\mathcal{E}_r^* > 0$ for all channel states. This is in contrast to the result in Section 4.1 showing that direct transmission ($\mathcal{E}_r^* = 0$) is optimum for certain channel states when the destination uses MRC.

5   Simulation Results

In this section, we present the performance of the optimum energy allocation scheme and show how the optimum total energy gain are affected by this scheme.

Proposition 1 implies when the relay does not have an advantaged channel to the destination, the total energy is minimized when all of the transmission energy is allocated to the source and the relay does not transmit. Figure 2 shows the total energy gain of optimum AF cooperative transmission when $\rho \to \infty$. Similarly, the largest gains occur when $\mu \ll 1$, which corresponds to the case where the relay has a advantaged channel to the destination and $\eta \to 1$, which corresponds to the case where the source and relay are much closer in proximity than the source and destination.

In figure 3, it can be shown that $\frac{\mathcal{E}_s^*}{\mathcal{E}_{\text{tot}}^*} = 1$ when $\mu \geq 1$, i.e. the relay does not have an advantaged channel to the destination, all of the transmission energy is allocated to the source. Only when $0 \leq \mu < 1$, i.e. the relay has an advantaged channel that the total energy could be minimized through cooperation transmission. As expected, for a fixed μ, $\frac{\mathcal{E}_s^*}{\mathcal{E}_{\text{tot}}^*}$ decreases when η increases, which corresponds to the case when the source-relay channel are more favorable, more transmission energy is allocated to the relay. Note that for a fixed η, when $\mu \to 0$, i.e. the relay has a much advantaged channel to the destination, the relay only needs a small amount of transmission energy to satisfy the SNR requirement, thus $\frac{\mathcal{E}_s^*}{\mathcal{E}_{\text{tot}}^*}$ becomes larger.

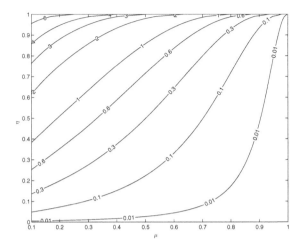

Fig. 2. $\mathcal{E}_{tot}$ gain, in dB with respect to direct transmission, of AF cooperative transmission with optimum energy allocation $\{\mathcal{E}_s^*, \mathcal{E}_r^*\}$ as a function of the parameters μ and η

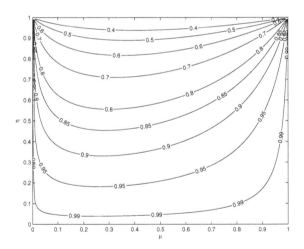

Fig. 3. Normalized optimum source energy allocation $\mathcal{E}_s^*/\mathcal{E}_{\text{tot}}^*$ as a function of the parameters μ and η

6   Conclusion

This paper examines optimum energy allocation for amplify-and-forward cooperation with the goal of minimizing average total transmit energy under a SNR constraint in two scenarios: i) maximal ratio combining (MRC) and (ii) fixed ratio combining (FRC). For MRC, based on the explicit analytical solution an asymptotic solution for normalized optimum total energy in terms of μ and η

was derived in the high-SNR scenario. For FRC, we find that though it is hard to find an explicit analytical solution, standard numerical convex optimization methods can be used to find the unique solution to the problem. Based on these analysis, we explicitly describe the set of channel conditions under which the optimum energy allocation strategy can be realized.

Acknowledgement

This research is supported in part by ERIF, IIT, National Science Foundation Grant CNS-0716302, and National Sciences and Engineering Research Council of Canada (NSERC).

References

1. Cover, T.M., Gamal, A.A.E.: Capacity Theorems for the Relay Channel. IEEE Trans. Info. Theory 25(5), 572–584 (1979)
2. Sendonaris, A., Erkip, E., Aazhang, B.: User cooperation diversity — part i: System description. IEEE Trans. Commun. 51(11), 1927–1938 (2003)
3. Sendonaris, A., Erkip, E., Aazhang, B.: User cooperation diversity — part ii: Implementation aspects and performance analysis. IEEE Trans. Commun. 51(11), 1939–1948 (2003)
4. Laneman, J.N., Wornell, G.W., Tse, D.N.C.: An Efficient Protocol for Realizing Cooperative Diversity in Wireless Networks. In: Proc. IEEE ISIT, Washington, DC, June 2001, p. 294 (2001)
5. Scaglione, A., Goeckel, D.L., Laneman, J.N.: Cooperative communications in mobile ad hoc networks. IEEE Signal Processing Magazine 23(5), 18–29 (2006)
6. Hunter, T.E., Nosratinia, A.: Cooperative Diversity through Coding. In: Proc. IEEE ISIT, Laussane, Switzerland, July 2002, p. 220 (2002)
7. Hunter, T.E., Nosratinia, A.: Diversity through Coded Cooperation. IEEE Transactions on Wireless Communications 5(2), 283–289 (2006)
8. Yang, J., Brown III, D.R.: The effect of channel state information on optimum energy allocation and energy efficiency of cooperative wireless transmission systems. In: Conference on Info. Sciences and Systems (CISS), pp. 1044–1049 (2006)
9. Yang, J., Brown III, D.R.: The Effect of Receiver Diversity Combining on Optimum Energy Allocation and Energy Efficiency of Cooperative Wireless Transmission Systems. In: Conference on Acoustics, Speech and Signal Processing (ICASSP), vol. 3, pp. III-493-III-496

A   Proof of Proposition 1

Proof. Before deriving the minimum weighted total energy under a minimum SNR constraint, we first determine the conditions for direct transmission and cooperative transmission. From (3), we note that the space of admissible energy allocations satisfying $\mathsf{SNR}_{\mathsf{mrc}} = \rho$ can be described as the region in $\mathbb{R}^2$ where $\mathcal{E}_r \geq 0$ and $\frac{\rho}{H+G_s} < \mathcal{E}_s \leq \frac{\rho}{G_s}$, where the upper limit to $\mathcal{E}_s$ corresponds to the case when $\mathcal{E}_r = 0$ and the lower limit corresponds to the case when $\mathcal{E}_r \to \infty$.

Using (3), the total energy required to satisfy the constraint $\mathsf{SNR}_{\mathrm{mrc}} = \rho$ can be written as

$$\mathcal{E}_{\mathrm{tot}} := \mathcal{E}_s + \alpha \mathcal{E}_r = \mathcal{E}_s + \alpha \frac{H\mathcal{E}_s^2 G_s + (G_s - H\rho)\mathcal{E}_s - \rho}{G_r(\rho - (H + G_s)\mathcal{E}_s)}. \tag{13}$$

Define the interval $\mathcal{A} = \left(\frac{\rho}{H+G_s}, \frac{\rho}{G_s} \right]$. If

$$\mathcal{E}_{\mathrm{tot}}^* = \arg \min_{\mathcal{E}_s \in \mathcal{A}} \mathcal{E}_{\mathrm{tot}} = \frac{\rho}{G_s}$$

then $\mathcal{E}_r = 0$ and $\mathcal{E}_{\mathrm{tot}}$ is minimized with direct transmission. Otherwise, $\mathcal{E}_r > 0$ and cooperative transmission minimizes $\mathcal{E}_{\mathrm{tot}}$.

In order to determine if the minimum of (13) on $\mathcal{A}$ occurs at the point $\mathcal{E}_s = \frac{\rho}{G_s}$, we first establish that (13) can have only one minimum on $\mathcal{A}$ by proving that (13) is a strictly convex function of $\mathcal{E}_s$ on $\mathcal{A}$. The second derivative of (13) with respect to $\mathcal{E}_s$ can be written as

$$\mathcal{E}_{\mathrm{tot}}'' := \frac{\partial^2}{\partial \mathcal{E}_s^2} \mathcal{E}_{\mathrm{tot}} = \alpha \frac{-2H\rho[(\rho + 1)H + G_s]}{G_r(\rho - (H + G_s)\mathcal{E}_s)^3} \tag{14}$$

Note that the numerator of (14) is a negative quantity not dependent on $\mathcal{E}_s$. Since $\mathcal{E}_s(H + G_s) > \rho$ and $G_r > 0$, the denominator of (14) is also negative on the interval $\mathcal{E}_s \in \mathcal{A}$, hence $\mathcal{E}_{\mathrm{tot}}''$ is always positive on $\mathcal{A}$. This implies that $\mathcal{E}_{\mathrm{tot}}$ is a strictly convex function of $\mathcal{E}_s$ on $\mathcal{A}$.

Given the convexity of $\mathcal{E}_{\mathrm{tot}}$ on $\mathcal{A}$, we can determine whether the unique minimum of (13) on $\mathcal{A}$ occurs at the point $\mathcal{E}_s = \frac{\rho}{G_s}$ by evaluating the first derivative of (13) at this point. If the first derivative is positive, then the minimum of (13) on $\mathcal{A}$ must occur at $\mathcal{E}_s < \frac{\rho}{G_s}$ (corresponding to cooperative transmission), otherwise the minimum occurs at $\mathcal{E}_s = \frac{\rho}{G_s}$ (corresponding to direct transmission). The first derivative of (13) evaluated at $\mathcal{E}_s = \frac{\rho}{G_s}$ can be written as

$$\mathcal{E}_{\mathrm{tot}}'\left(\frac{\rho}{G_s} \right) := \frac{\partial}{\partial \mathcal{E}_s} \mathcal{E}_{\mathrm{tot}}\left(\frac{\rho}{G_s} \right) = 1 - \alpha \frac{G_s(H\rho + G_s)}{G_r H\rho} \tag{15}$$

This quantity is positive if and only if the condition of $\frac{\alpha G_s}{G_r}\left(1 + \frac{G_s}{H\rho} \right) < 1$ are satisfied, i.e. $\mu < 1$, hence the unique minimum of (13) on $\mathcal{A}$ must occur at $\mathcal{E}_s < \frac{\rho}{G_s}$ when $0 \leq \mu < 1$. Otherwise, when $\mu \geq 1$ the minimum of (13) on $\mathcal{A}$ must occur at $\mathcal{E}_s = \frac{\rho}{G_s}$ and direct transmission is optimum.

We now derive the explicit solution to the total energy minimization problem. The optimal source energy allocation can be found by solving $\frac{\partial}{\partial \mathcal{E}_s} \mathcal{E}_{\mathrm{tot}} = 0$. Computation of the partial derivative and algebraic simplification yields

$$1 + \frac{\alpha(H(2G_s\mathcal{E}_s - \rho) + G_s)}{G_r(\rho - (H + G_s)\mathcal{E}_s)} + \frac{\alpha(G_s\mathcal{E}_s(1 + H) - \rho(1 + H\mathcal{E}_s))}{G_r(\rho - (H + G_s)\mathcal{E}_s)^2} = 0 \tag{16}$$

By solving this equation for $\mathcal{E}_s$, the correct root which satisfies $\frac{\partial^2}{\partial \mathcal{E}_s^2} \mathcal{E}_{\mathrm{tot}}(\mathcal{E}_s) \geq 0$ is

$$\mathcal{E}_s = \frac{\rho}{H + G_s} + \frac{\sqrt{\alpha \rho H (G_s + (1 + \rho)H)}}{(H + G_s)\sqrt{H(G_r - \alpha G_s) + G_s G_r}} \tag{17}$$

In the case $0 \leq \mu < 1$, the total energy can be minimized through cooperative transmission. By plugging $\mathcal{E}_s^*$ into (14), the minimized total energy can be expressed as

$$\mathcal{E}_{\text{tot}}^* = \frac{\left(\sqrt{\rho(G_r(G_s + H) - \alpha G_s H)} + \sqrt{\alpha H(G_s + H + \rho H)}\right)^2 - \alpha(G_s + H)^2}{G_r(G_s + H)^2}$$

B   Proof of Proposition 2

Proof. To prove $\mathcal{E}_{\text{tot}}$ is convex, and hence has a unique minimum on $\mathcal{A} = [\frac{(\beta^2+1)\rho}{(\beta^2+1)H+\beta^2 G_s}, \frac{(\beta^2+1)\rho}{\beta^2 G_s}]$, we will show that $\frac{\partial^2 \mathcal{E}_{\text{tot}}}{\partial \mathcal{E}_s^2} > 0$ a.s. Here, $\frac{\partial^2 \mathcal{E}_{\text{tot}}}{\partial \mathcal{E}_s^2}$ is a function of $\mathcal{E}_s$. Substitute $\mathcal{E}_s$ with y, we have

$$\frac{\partial^2 \mathcal{E}_{\text{tot}}}{\partial \mathcal{E}_s^2} = F(y)G(y). \tag{18}$$

The function

$$
\begin{aligned}
F(y) =\ & \beta y^4 + 4\beta^2 G_s \rho y^3 - (6(\beta^3 + \beta)\rho^2 G_s H + 3\beta^3 \rho G_s^2 + 3(\beta^3 + \beta)\rho G_s H)y^2 \\
& + (4(\beta^2 + 1)^2 \rho^3 H^2 G_s + 4(\beta^4 + \beta^2)\rho^2 H G_s^2 + 4(\beta^2 + 1)^2 \rho^2 H^2 G_s)y \quad (19) \\
& + (\beta^5 + 2\beta^3 + \beta)G_s^2 H^2 \rho^4 + (\beta^5 + \beta^3)G_s^3 H \rho^3 + (\beta^5 + 2\beta^3 + \beta)H^2 G_s^2 \rho^3.
\end{aligned}
$$

and

$$G(y) = \frac{\alpha \rho^2 G_s^2 H(\beta^2 G_s + \beta^2 H + H)^2}{2G_r(y + \beta \rho G_s)^4 y^3} \tag{20}$$

where $y := \sqrt{G_s H \rho((\beta^2 + 1)H\mathcal{E}_s + \beta^2 G_s \mathcal{E}_s - (\beta^2 + 1)\rho)}$.

Note that the squared channel amplitudes G_s, G_r and H are exponentially distributed, thus $\lim_{\epsilon \to 0} P\{X \leq 0\} = 0$, where X denotes the squared channel amplitudes. Thus $G(y) > 0$ a.s. on $\mathcal{A}$ (Note that $y \neq 0$). Hence, the condition $\frac{\partial^2 \mathcal{E}_{\text{tot}}}{\partial \mathcal{E}_s^2} > 0$ a.s. on $\mathcal{A} \Leftrightarrow F(y) > 0$ a.s. on $\mathcal{C}$, where $\mathcal{C} = \left[0, \frac{(\beta^2+1)\rho H}{\beta}\right]$. Observe that only the y^2 term has negative coefficient. The function $F(y)$ can be written as

$$F(y) = R(y) + S(y) + T(y), \tag{21}$$

where

$$
\begin{aligned}
R(y) &= -(3\beta^3 \rho G_s^2 + 3(\beta^3 + \beta)\rho G_s H)y^2 + (4(\beta^4 + \beta^2)\rho^2 H G_s^2 + 4(\beta^2 + 1)^2 \rho^2 H^2 G_s)y \\
S(y) &= 4\beta^2 G_s \rho y^3 - 6(\beta^3 + \beta)\rho^2 G_s H y^2 + 4(\beta^2 + 1)^2 \rho^3 H^2 G_s y \\
T(y) &= \beta y^4 + (\beta^5 + 2\beta^3 + \beta)G_s^2 H^2 \rho^4 + (\beta^5 + \beta^3)G_s^3 H \rho^3 + (\beta^5 + 2\beta^3 + \beta)H^2 G_s^2 \rho^3.
\end{aligned}
$$

Note that $T(y) \geq 0$ for $\left[0, \frac{(\beta^2+1)\rho H}{\beta}\right]$. We will consider the behavior of $R(y)$ and $S(y)$ in following claims.

Claim 1: $R(y) > 0$ a.s. on $\mathcal{C}$.

proof: Observe that $R(y)$ is a quadratic equation of one variable. It can be written as

$$R(y) = yr(y), \tag{22}$$

where

$$r(y) = -(3\beta^3 \rho G_s^2 + 3(\beta^3 + \beta)\rho G_s H)y + 4(\beta^4 + \beta^2)\rho^2 HG_s^2 + 4(\beta^2 + 1)^2 \rho^2 H^2 G_s.$$

First, we consider the case when $\beta > 0$. Observe that $y > 0$ and $r(\frac{(\beta^2+1)\rho H}{\beta}) = (\beta^4 + \beta^2)\rho^2 HG_s^2 + (\beta^2 + 1)^2 \rho^2 H^2 G_s > 0$ a.s. Thus, to prove $R(y) > 0$ a.s. on $\mathcal{C}$, it is only necessary to prove that $r(y)$ is decreasing on $\mathcal{C}$. It can be shown that

$$\frac{\partial r(y)}{\partial y} = -3\beta^3 \rho G_s^2 - 3(\beta^3 + \beta)\rho G_s H < 0 \quad a.s. \tag{23}$$

Thus, $r(y) > 0$ a.s. on $\mathcal{C}$, this result implies $R(y) > 0$ a.s. on $\mathcal{C}$. When $\beta = 0$, $R(y) = 4y\rho^2 H^2 G_s > 0$ a.s. on $\mathcal{C}$.

Claim 2: $S(y) > 0$ a.s. on $\mathcal{C}$.

proof: Observe that $S(y)$ is a cubic equation of one variable. It can be written as

$$S(y) = ys(y), \tag{24}$$

where

$$s(y) = 4\beta^2 G_s \rho y^2 - 6(\beta^3 + \beta)\rho^2 G_s Hy + 4(\beta^2 + 1)^2 \rho^3 H^2 G_s.$$

First, we consider the case when $\beta > 0$. Observe that $y > 0$ and $s(y)$ is a quadratic equation. To prove that $S(y) > 0$ a.s. on $\mathcal{C}$, it is only necessary to prove that $s(y) > 0$ a.s. on $\mathcal{C}$. It can be shown that $\frac{\partial^2 s(y)}{\partial y^2} = 4\beta^2 G_s \rho > 0$ a.s., hence $s(y)$ is convex on $\mathcal{C}$. Thus, to prove $s(y) > 0$ a.s. on $\mathcal{C}$, it is only necessary to prove that $s(y)$ has no real root a.s. It can be shown

$$[6(\beta^3 + \beta)\rho^2 G_s H]^2 - 4(4\beta^2 G_s \rho)[4(\beta^2 + 1)^2 \rho^3 H^2 G_s] = -28\beta^2(\beta^2 + 1)^2 \rho^4 G_s^2 H^2 < 0 \quad a.s.$$

This implies that $s(y) > 0$ a.s. on $\mathcal{C}$, which implies $S(y) > 0$ a.s. on $\mathcal{C}$. When $\beta = 0$, $S(y) = 4y\rho^3 H^2 G_s > 0$ a.s. on $\mathcal{C}$.

Message-Driven Frequency Hopping
— Design and Analysis

Qi Ling, Jian Ren, and Tongtong Li

Michigan State University, East Landing, MI 48864-1226, USA
{lingqi,renjian,tongli}@egr.msu.edu

Abstract. Originally developed for secure communications in military applications, frequency hopping systems possess anti-jamming and anti-interception features by exploiting time-frequency diversity over large spectrum. However, the spectral efficiency of existing FH systems is very low due to inappropriate use of the total available bandwidth. To improve the system capacity, in this paper, we propose an innovative message-driven frequency hopping (MDFH) scheme. Unlike in traditional FH systems where the hopping pattern of each user is determined by a pre-assigned pseudo-random (PN) sequence, in MDFH, part of the message stream will be acting as the the PN sequence for hopping frequency selection. Essentially, transmission of information through hopping frequency control introduces another dimension to the signal space, and the corresponding coding gain increases system efficiency by multiple times. The MDFH scheme can be further enhanced by allowing simultaneous transmissions over multiple frequency bands. Including both MDFH and OFDM as special cases, the enhanced MDFH scheme, named E-MDFH, can achieve higher spectral efficiency while providing excellent design flexibility. E-MDFH can readily be extended to a FH-based collision-free multiple access scheme.

Keywords: frequency hopping, spectral efficiency, secure communication.

1 Introduction

Relying on time-frequency diversity over large bandwidth, the frequency hopping scheme was originally designed to be inherently secure and reliable under adverse battle conditions for military purpose [1,2,3]. In traditional FH systems, the transmitter hops in a pseudo-random manner among available frequencies according to a pre-specified algorithm, the receiver then operates in strict synchronization with the transmitter and remains tuned to the same center frequency. Relying on random hopping over large spectrum, FH systems are robust against hostile jamming, interception and detection.

There are two major limitations with the conventional FH systems: (i) *Strong requirement on frequency acquisition.* In the current FH system, exact frequency synchronization has to be kept between transmitter and receiver. The strict requirement on synchronization directly influences the complexity, design and performance of the system [4], and turns out to be a significant challenge in

Y. Li et al. (Eds.): WASA 2008, LNCS 5258, pp. 373–384, 2008.

fast hopping system design. (ii) *Low spectral efficiency over large bandwidth.*
Typically, FH systems require large bandwidth, which is proportional to the
product of the hopping rate and the total number of all the available channels.
In multiple access FH systems, each user hops independently based on its own PN
sequence, collisions occur whenever there are two users transmit over the same
frequency band. Mainly limited by the collision effect, the spectral efficiency
of conventional FH systems is very low. In literature, considerable efforts have
been devoted to increasing the spectral efficiency of FH systems by applying
high-dimensional modulation schemes [5,6,7,8,9,10,11]. However, existing work
is far from adequate to address the ever increasing demand on inherently secure
high speed wireless communication.

In this paper, we propose an innovative message-driven frequency hopping
(MDFH) scheme. The basic idea is that part of the message will be acting as the
PN sequence for carrier frequency selection at the transmitter. In other words,
selection of carrier frequencies is directly controlled by the (encrypted) message
stream rather than by a predetermined pseudo-random sequence as in the conventional FH systems. Taking the original modulation technique used in the FH
systems (such as FSK or PSK) into consideration, transmission of information
through frequency control in fact adds another dimension to existing constella-
tions and the resulting coding gain increases the spectral efficiency by multiple
times. At the receiver, the transmitting frequency is captured using a filter bank
as in the FSK receiver rather than using the frequency synthesizer. As a result,
frequency synchronization is no longer required at the receiver, and the carrier frequency (hence the information embedded in frequency selection) can be blindly
detected at each hop. Potentially, MDFH makes it possible for faster frequency
hopping in wide band systems. It also reinforces the jamming resistance of the
FH system since the message-driven hopping pattern is totally unpredictable.

To further increase the spectral efficiency, we propose an enhanced MDFH
(E-MDFH) which enables simultaneous transmissions on multiple channels at
each hop. Including both MDFH and OFDM as special cases, this enhanced
transmission scheme provides better design flexibility, and high spectral efficiency through a careful design of the hopping process. The E-MDFH system
can easily be extended to a collision-free multiple access FH system. Quantitative analysis on BER and spectral efficiency will be provided to demonstrate the
superior performance of the proposed schemes.

2   The Concept of Message-Driven Frequency Hopping

2.1   Transmitter Design

Let N_c be the total number of available channels, with $\{f_1, f_2, \cdots, f_{N_c}\}$ being the
set of all available carrier frequencies. Ideally all the available channels should
be involved in the hop selection, as is required by current frequency hopping
specifications (e.g., Bluetooth). The number of bits required to specify each
individual channel is $B_c = \lfloor \log_2 N_c \rfloor$, where $\lfloor x \rfloor$ denotes that largest integer less
than or equal to x. If N_c is a power of 2, then each channel can be uniquely

represented by B_c bits. Otherwise, for $i = 1, \cdots, N_c$, the ith channel will be associated with the binary representation of the modulated channel index, $[(i-1) \bmod 2^{B_c}] + 1$. That is, when N_c is not a power of 2, we will allow some B_c-bit strings to be mapped to more than one channels. In the following, for simplicity of notation, we assume that $N_c = 2^{B_c}$.

Let Ω be the selected constellation that contains M symbols, each symbol in the constellation represents $B_s = \log_2 M$ bits. Let T_s and T_h denote the symbol period and the hop duration, respectively, then the number of hops per symbol period is given by $N_h \triangleq \frac{T_s}{T_h}$. We assume that N_h is an integer larger or equal to 1. In other words, we focus on fast hopping systems.

We start by dividing the data stream into blocks of length $L \triangleq N_h B_c + B_s$. Each block consists of $N_h B_c$ *carrier bits* and B_s *ordinary bits*. The *carrier bits* are used to determine the hopping frequencies, and the *ordinary bits* are mapped to a symbol which is transmitted through the selected N_h channels successively. Note that the number of the carrier bits is determined by B_c (the number of bits used to specify one hopping frequency) and N_h (the number of hops within one symbol period). The number of ordinary bits is exactly the number of bits represented by one individual symbol in constellation Ω. Denote the nth block by X_n, we intend to transmit X_n within one symbol period. The carrier bits in block X_n are further grouped into N_h vectors of length B_c, denoted by $[X_{n,1}, \cdots, X_{n,N_h}]$. The bit vector composed of B_s ordinary bits is denoted by Y_n, as shown in Fig. 1.

The transmitter block diagram of the proposed MDFH scheme is illustrated in Fig. 2. Each input data block, X_n, is fed into a serial-to-parallel (S/P) converter, where the carrier bits and the ordinary bits are split into two parallel data streams. The selected carrier frequencies corresponding to the nth block are denoted by $\{f_{n,1}, \cdots, f_{n,N_h}\}$, where each $f_{n,i} \in \{f_1, f_2, \cdots, f_{N_c}\}, \forall i \in [1, N_h]$. Assume Y_n is mapped to symbol A_n, we denote the baseband signal generated from A_n by $m(t)$.

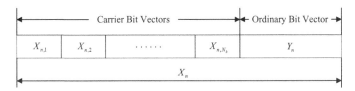

Fig. 1. The nth block of the information data

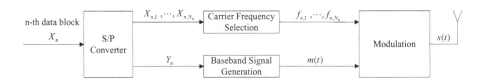

Fig. 2. Block diagram of the transmitter design

If PAM (pulse amplitude modulation) is adopted for baseband signal generation, then

$$m(t) = \sum_{n=-\infty}^{\infty} \sum_{i=1}^{N_h} A_n\, g(t - nT_s - (i-1)T_h), \tag{1}$$

where $g(t)$ is the pulse-shaping filter. Define $m_{n,i}(t) \overset{\Delta}{=} A_n\, g(t - nT_s - (i-1)T_h)$, then $m(t) = \sum_{n=-\infty}^{\infty} \sum_{i=1}^{N_h} m_{n,i}(t)$. The corresponding passband waveform can be obtained as:

$$s(t) = \sqrt{\frac{2}{T_h}} Re\{ \sum_{n=-\infty}^{\infty} \sum_{i=1}^{N_h} m_{n,i}(t) e^{j2\pi f_{n,i} t} \chi_{n,i}(t)\}, \tag{2}$$

where

$$\chi_{n,i}(t) = \begin{cases} 1, t \in [nT_s + (i-1)T_h, nT_s + iT_h], \\ 0, otherwise. \end{cases} \tag{3}$$

If MFSK is utilized for baseband modulation, then

$$s(t) = \sqrt{\frac{2}{T_h}} \sum_{n=-\infty}^{\infty} \sum_{i=1}^{N_h} cos2\pi[f_{n,i}t + K_f \int_{-\infty}^{t} m_{n,i}(\tau)d\tau]\chi_{n,i}(t). \tag{4}$$

where K_f is a preselected constant.

2.2   Receiver Design

The structure of the receiver is shown in Fig. 3. Recall that $\{f_1, f_2, \cdots, f_{N_c}\}$ is the set of all available carrier frequencies. To detect the active frequency band, a bank of N_c bandpass filters (BPF), each centered at f_i ($i = 1, 2, \cdots, N_c$), and with the same channel bandwidth as the transmitter, is deployed simultaneously at the receiver's front end. Since only one frequency band is occupied at any given moment, we simply measure the outputs of bandpass filters at each possible signaling frequency. The actual carrier frequency at a certain hopping period can be detected by selecting the one that captures the strongest signal. As a result, blind detection of the carrier frequency is achieved at the receiver.

Next, the estimated hopping frequencies $\{\hat{f}_{n,1}, \cdots, \hat{f}_{n,N_h}\}$ are used for extraction of the input signal. The ordinary bit-vector, Y_n, is first estimated independently for each hop, then bit-wise majority voting is applied for all the N_h estimates to make the final decision on each ordinary bit in Y_n. We denote the estimated ordinary bit-vector as $\hat{Y}_n$. At the same time, $\{\hat{f}_{n,1}, \cdots, \hat{f}_{n,N_h}\}$ are mapped back to B_c-bit strings to recover the carrier bits. Denote the estimated carrier bit-vectors as $\{\hat{X}_{n,1}, \cdots, \hat{X}_{n,N_h}\}$, it then follows that the estimate of the nth block X_n can be obtained as: $\hat{X}_n = [\hat{X}_{n,1}, \cdots, \hat{X}_{n,N_h}, \hat{Y}_n]$.

It is interesting to note that in [12], the message is used to select the spreading code in CDMA and therefore increases the system capacity.

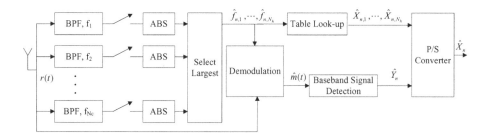

Fig. 3. Block diagram of the receiver design, where ABS means taking the absolute value

Remark 1. Design of the MDFH receiver leads to a security observation: if such a filter bank is available to a malicious user, then both the conventional FH signals and the MDFH signals can largely be intercepted by an unauthorized party. This implies that to prevent unauthorized interception, information has to be encrypted before being transmitted over an FH system.

3   Efficiency Enhanced MDFH

To further improve the spectral efficiency and the design flexibility, in this section, we refine the transceiver design of the MDFH system. And the modified scheme is referred to as enhanced MDFH (E-MDFH).

3.1   Modified Carrier Frequency Selection

Recall that $N_c = 2^{B_c}$ is the number of all available carriers. We split the N_c carriers into N_g non-overlapping groups $\{C_l\}_{l=1}^{N_g}$, with $N_g = 2^{B_g}$, then each group has $N_f \triangleq N_c/N_g = 2^{B_c - B_g}$ carriers. Specifically, $C_1 = \{f_1, \cdots, f_{N_f}\}, C_2 = \{f_{N_f+1}, \cdots, f_{2N_f}\}, \cdots, C_{N_g} = \{f_{N_c-N_f+1}, \cdots, f_{N_c}\}$. Now we consider to modify the transmitter design in MDFH, such that simultaneous multiple transmissions can be achieved at each hop. An intuitive method is to employ an independent MDFH scheme within each C_l for $l = 1, \cdots, N_g$. In this case, the frequency hopping processing is limited to N_f ($<< N_c$) successive carriers, leading to insufficient randomness and therefore inadequate jamming resistance.

To maximize the randomness, here we present an alternative approach. We divide the incoming data stream into blocks of length $[N_h(B_c - B_g) + B_s]N_g$. Denote the nth block by X_n. X_n is further divided into N_g vectors: $X_n = [Z_{n,1}, \cdots, Z_{n,N_g}]$. For $m = 1, \cdots, N_g$, each $Z_{n,m}$ contains $N_h(B_c - B_g) + B_s$ bits. Write $Z_{n,m} = [D_{n,m}^1, \cdots, D_{n,m}^{N_h}, Y_{n,m}]$, where each $D_{n,m}^i$ is a bit-vector consisting of $(B_c - B_g)$ carrier bits, and bit-vector $Y_{n,m}$ consists of B_s ordinary bits. We adopt the notation used in Matlab "bin2dec" to denote the operation of converting a binary vector to a decimal number, and "dec2bin" the reverse operation. For $m = 1, \cdots, N_g, i = 1, \cdots, N_h$, we define $d_{n,m}^i \triangleq \text{bin2dec}(D_{n,m}^i) + 1$.

Recall that there are N_h hops in one symbol period, at each hop, the signal will be transmitted through N_g carriers simultaneously. For $i = 1, \cdots, N_h$, the frequency index for the mth carrier at the ith hop is defined as:

$$
\begin{aligned}
I_{n,1}^i &= d_{n,1}^i, & \text{when } m = 1 \\
I_{n,m}^i &= I_{n,m-1}^i + d_{n,m}^i, & \text{when } m = 2, \cdots, N_g.
\end{aligned}
\tag{5}
$$

This carrier selection procedure is designed to ensure that: (i) All the available carriers are involved in the hop selection process; (ii) The hopping frequencies have no collision with each other at any given moment. In fact, at each hop, $I_{n,1}^i < I_{n,2}^i < \cdots < I_{n,N_g}^i$, since $I_{n,1}^i \in [1, N_f], I_{n,2}^i \in [I_{n,1}^i + 1, 2N_f], \cdots, I_{n,N_g}^i \in [I_{n,N_g-1}^i + 1, N_c]$. After the hopping frequencies are determined for all the N_g carriers, each $Y_{n,m}$ ($m = 1, \cdots, N_g$) is mapped to a symbol in constellation Ω and then transmitted through the mth carrier, which hops through frequencies $f_{I_{n,m}^1}, \cdots, f_{I_{n,m}^{N_h}}$. As the result, X_n is now transmitted in one symbol period over multiple carriers under the message-driven frequency hopping framework.

3.2   Signal Detection

As in MDFH, the receiver in E-MDFH also consists of a bank of N_c bandpass filters. However, the signal detection procedure needs to be modified. Take the extraction of X_n as an example. At the ith hop, instead of searching for the bandpass filter which captures the strongest output as in MDFH, we now identify N_g filters which deliver the largest N_g outputs. The indices of these N_g bandpass filters are sorted in ascending order, to obtain the estimated indices for $I_{n,m}^i$, that is, $\hat{I}_{n,1}^i < \hat{I}_{n,2}^i < \cdots < \hat{I}_{n,N_g}^i$. Now the carrier-bit vectors can be estimated as:

$$
\begin{aligned}
\hat{D}_{n,1}^i &= \mathrm{dec2bin}(\hat{I}_{n,1}^i - 1), & \text{when } m = 1 \\
\hat{D}_{n,m}^i &= \mathrm{dec2bin}(\hat{I}_{n,m}^i - \hat{I}_{n,m-1}^i - 1), & \text{when } m \in [2, N_g].
\end{aligned}
$$

At the same time, each ordinary bit-vector $Y_{n,m}$ is estimated from the received signal corresponding to the mth carrier based on majority voting, similar to that in MDFH (please see Section 2.2).

Remark 2. Taking the carrier usage into consideration, the modified design structure includes MDFH and OFDM as special cases. In fact, if $N_g = 1$, then E-MDFH is reduced to MDFH. Likewise, if $N_g = N_c$, then E-MDFH can readily be implemented through an OFDM system, and be extended to an FH based collision-free multiple access system.

4   Performance Analysis of E-MDFH

In this section, we will analyze the bit error probability and the spectral efficiency of E-MDFH through both theoretical derivation and simulation results.

4.1 BER Analysis

It is interesting to note that *non-uniformity* exists between the carrier bits and the ordinary bits, in the sense that they have different BER performances.

BER of the carrier bits. Based on the receiver design in E-MDFH, BER analysis of the carrier bits is analogous to that of non-coherent FSK demodulation. For non-coherent detection of M_F-ary FSK signals, *the probability of symbol error* is given by

$$P_{s,FSK}\left(\frac{E_b}{N_0}\right) = \sum_{m=1}^{M_F-1}\binom{M_F-1}{m}\frac{(-1)^{m+1}}{m+1}e^{-\frac{m\log_2 M_F}{(m+1)}\frac{E_b}{N_0}}, \tag{6}$$

where $\frac{E_b}{N_0}$ is the bit-level SNR. Let $k_F = \log_2 M_F$, then *the probability of bit error*, $P_{e,FSK}$, can be written as

$$P_{e,FSK}\left(\frac{E_b}{N_0}\right) = \frac{2^{(k_F-1)}}{2^{k_F}-1}P_{s,FSK}\left(\frac{E_b}{N_0}\right). \tag{7}$$

For an E-MDFH system with N_c channels, $M_F = N_c$, and $k_F = B_c$. Let $\frac{E_b^{(c)}}{N_0}$ and $\frac{E_b^{(o)}}{N_0}$ denote the effective bit-level SNR corresponding to the carrier bits and the ordinary bits, respectively, and $\frac{E_b}{N_0}$ the average bit-level SNR for the E-MDFH system. Recall that in the E-MDFH scheme, the length of each block is $L = [N_h(B_c - B_g) + B_s]2^{B_g}$, out of which there are $B_s 2^{B_g}$ ordinary bits and $N_h(B_c - B_g)2^{B_g}$ carrier bits. Note that in E-MDFH, the carrier bits are embedded in the carrier selection process and do not consume additional transmit power, the average bit-level SNR $\frac{E_b}{N_0}$ is

$$\frac{E_b}{N_0} = \frac{N_h N_g \bar{E}_s}{N_0[N_h(B_c - B_g) + B_s]2^{B_g}}, \tag{8}$$

where $\bar{E}_s$ is the average symbol energy per baseband symbol. The effective bit-level SNR corresponding to the carrier bits and the ordinary bits can be calculated as:

$$\frac{E_b^{(c)}}{N_0} = \frac{\bar{E}_s}{N_0 B_c}, \quad \frac{E_b^{(o)}}{N_0} = \frac{\bar{E}_s}{N_0 B_s}, \tag{9}$$

respectively, since each frequency is uniquely identified by B_c bits, and each symbol respresents B_s bits. Substituting (8) into (9), it yields that $\frac{E_b^{(c)}}{N_0} = \frac{[N_h(B_c-B_g)+B_s]}{N_h B_c}\frac{E_b}{N_0}, \frac{E_b^{(o)}}{N_0} = \frac{[N_h(B_c-B_g)+B_s]}{N_h B_s}\frac{E_b}{N_0}.$

In the particular case when $N_g = 1$, E-MDFH is reduced to MDFH. Following (6), the BER for the carrier bits in MDFH can be obtained as:

$$P_{e,MDFH}^{(c)}\left(\frac{E_b}{N_0}\right) = \frac{2^{(B_c-1)}}{2^{B_c}-1}\sum_{m=1}^{N_c-1}\binom{N_c-1}{m}\frac{(-1)^{m+1}}{m+1}e^{-\frac{km}{(m+1)}\frac{E_i}{E_s}\frac{E_b^{(c)}}{N_0}}. \tag{10}$$

Let $P_{s,MDFH}^{(c)}$ denote the probability of carrier frequency detection error (corresponding to the symbol error in FSK) in MDFH, then we have

$$P_{s,MDFH}^{(c)} \left(\frac{E_b}{N_0} \right) = \frac{2^{B_c} - 1}{2^{(B_c-1)}} P_{e,MDFH}^{(c)} \left(\frac{E_b}{N_0} \right). \tag{11}$$

In the more general case when $N_g \neq 1$, detection of the carrier bits in E-MDFH is similar to that of differential encoding (please refer to Section 3.2). Estimation error in one carrier index may cause detection errors in two neighboring carrier bit blocks. Denote the probability of carrier frequency detection error in E-MDFH as $P_{E-MDFH}^{(c)} \left(\frac{E_b}{N_0} \right)$. It follows from (6) that

$$P_{E-MDFH}^{(c)} \left(\frac{E_b}{N_0} \right) = \sum_{i=1}^{N_t} p_i \sum_{m=1}^{N_c-1} \binom{N_c - 1}{m} \frac{(-1)^{m+1}}{m + 1} e^{-\frac{m B_c}{(m+1)} \frac{E_i}{E_s} \frac{E_b^{(c)}}{N_0}}. \tag{12}$$

Recall that for $i = 1, \cdots, N_h, m = 1, \cdots, N_g$, $I_{n,m}^i$ denotes the frequency index for the mth carrier at the ith hop. At each hop, $I_{n,m}^i$ should satisfy $I_{n,1}^i < I_{n,2}^i < \cdots < I_{n,N_g}^i$. For signal detection, after each individual carrier index is estimated, they are then sorted in ascending order to recover $I_{n,m}^i$. An error in the carrier index estimation may further introduce errors in the sorting process, and hence has negative impact on the index estimation for more than one $I_{n,m}^i$. Therefore, if $P_{E-MDFH}^{(I)} \left(\frac{E_b}{N_0} \right)$ denotes the average probability that an index $I_{n,m}^i$ is incorrectly estimated, then we have $P_{E-MDFH}^{(I)} \left(\frac{E_b}{N_0} \right) \geq P_{E-MDFH}^{(c)} \left(\frac{E_b}{N_0} \right)$.

The lower and upper bounds of the BER for the carrier bits can be obtained as (13) and (14), respectively:

$$P_{e,E-MDFH}^{(c),L} \left(\frac{E_b}{N_0} \right) = \frac{2^{(B_c-B_g-1)}}{2^{(B_c-B_g)} - 1} \left\{ \frac{1}{N_g} P_{E-MDFH}^{(c)} \left(\frac{E_b}{N_0} \right) + \right.$$
$$\left. \frac{N_g - 1}{N_g} \left\{ 1 - \left[1 - P_{E-MDFH}^{(c)} \left(\frac{E_b}{N_0} \right) \right]^2 \right\} \right\}. \tag{13}$$

$$P_{e,E-MDFH}^{(c),U} \left(\frac{E_b}{N_0} \right) = \frac{2^{(B_c-B_g-1)}}{2^{(B_c-B_g)} - 1} \left\{ 1 - \left[1 - P_{E-MDFH}^{(c)} \left(\frac{E_b}{N_0} \right) \right]^{N_g} \right\}. \tag{14}$$

BER of the ordinary bits. BER of the ordinary bits is determined by the modulation scheme used in the system. If FSK is utilized, then the BER can be calculated in a similar manner as that of the carrier bits. In the following, we consider the case of transmitting the ordinary bits through M-ary QAM. We start with MDFH, which is easier to analyze, then extend the results to E-MDFH.

In MDFH, each QAM symbol undergoes N_h hops (we assume that N_h is odd). For signal detection, we first estimate the QAM symbol independently for each hop, and then apply *bit-wise majority voting* for the N_h estimates to make the final decision. Accordingly, the BER of the ordinary bits, $P_{e,MDFH}^{(o)}$, can be calculated as follows:

1. *BER analysis at each individual hop.* At each hop, the bit error can be classified as two groups. *Type I error: bit is in error given that the carrier frequency is correctly detected.* When the carrier frequency is detected correctly, for which the probability is $\left(1 - P_{s,MDFH}^{(c)}\left(\frac{E_b}{N_0}\right)\right)$, the probability of bit error can be calculated based on the BER of coherently detected M-ary QAM, given by
$$P_{e1} \triangleq P_{e,MQAM}\left(\frac{E_b^{(o)}}{N_0}\right).$$

Type II error: bit is in error when the carrier frequency is not correctly detected. When the carrier frequency is not correctly detected, for which the probability is $P_{s,MDFH}^{(c)}\left(\frac{E_b}{N_0}\right)$, it is reasonable to assume that probability of bit error is $P_{e2} \triangleq \frac{1}{2}$.

Following (8) and (9), since the carrier bits do not consume additional power,
$$\frac{E_b}{N_0} = \frac{N_h B_s}{N_h B_c + B_s}\frac{E_b^{(o)}}{N_0}.$$

2. *Average BER calculation based on majority voting.* In MDFH, each QAM symbol is transmitted through N_h hops. As a result, an error in a particular bit location is caused by at least $\lceil\frac{N_h}{2}\rceil$ unsuccessful recovery, where $\lceil x \rceil$ denotes the smallest integer greater than or equal to x. Let $P_{e,i}$, $i = 0, 1, \cdots, N_h$, be the conditional probability of bit error given that i out of N_h carrier frequencies are not correctly detected (i.e, $N_h - i$ carrier frequencies are correctly detected). If j denotes the number of unsuccessful bit recovery, then $P_{e,i}$ can easily be calculated as

$$P_{e,i}\left(\frac{E_b}{N_0}\right) = \sum_{j=\lceil\frac{N_h}{2}\rceil}^{N_h} \sum_{k=0}^{j} \binom{N_h - i}{k} (P_{e1})^k (1 - P_{e1})^{N_h - i - k} \binom{i}{j - k} (P_{e2})^{j-k}(1 - P_{e2})^{i - j + k}.$$

Here we adopt the convention $\binom{n}{m} = 0$ when $n < m$. Taking the effect of the majority voting into consideration, the error probability for the ordinary bits, $P_{e,MDFH}^{(o)}$, is given by (15).

The lower and upper bounds of the probability of bit error for the ordinary bits can be obtained by substituting $P_{s,E-MDFH}^{(c),L}\left(\frac{E_b}{N_0}\right)$ and $P_{s,E-MDFH}^{(c),U}\left(\frac{E_b}{N_0}\right)$ for $P_{s,MDFH}^{(c)}\left(\frac{E_b}{N_0}\right)$ in (15), respectively.

$$P_{e,MDFH}^{(o)}\left(\frac{E_b}{N_0}\right) = \sum_{i=0}^{N_h}\binom{N_h}{i}\left[P_{s,MDFH}^{(c)}\left(\frac{E_b}{N_0}\right)\right]^i$$
$$\times \left[1 - P_{s,MDFH}^{(c)}\left(\frac{E_b}{N_0}\right)\right]^{N_h - i} P_{e,i}\left(\frac{E_b}{N_0}\right). \quad (15)$$

Overall BER for E-MDFH. The overall BER of the E-MDFH scheme is calculated as the linear combination of $P_{e,E-MDFH}^{(c)}$ and $P_{e,E-MDFH}^{(o)}$ based on the number of carrier bits and the number of ordinary bits in each block,

$$P_{e,E-MDFH}\left(\frac{E_b}{N_0}\right) = \frac{N_h(B_c-B_g)}{N_h(B_c-B_g)+B_s}P_{e,E-MDFH}^{(c)}\left(\frac{E_b}{N_0}\right)$$
$$+ \frac{B_s}{N_h(B_c-B_g)+B_s}P_{e,E-MDFH}^{(o)}\left(\frac{E_b}{N_0}\right). \quad (16)$$

Simulation Example 1: BER Performance of E-MDFH. Assume the number of available carriers $N_c = 64$, and 16-QAM is adopted for baseband modulation in an E-MDFH system. Each 16-QAM symbol is transmitted via three hops. Four carriers are simultaneously used at each hop. In other words, $B_c = 6$, $B_s = 4$, $N_h = 3$, $B_g = 2$. The BEE performance of the system is presented in Fig. 4.

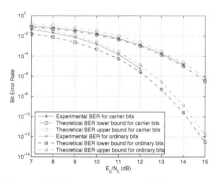

Fig. 4. BER comparison of the carrier bits and the ordinary bits in E-MDFH: $N_h = 3$, $B_c = 6$, $B_s = 4$, $B_g = 2$

4.2   Spectral Efficiency Analysis

Next, we compare the spectral efficiency of the proposed E-MDFH scheme with that of the conventional FH scheme. For fair comparison, we assume that both systems have the same symbol period T_s, the same number of hops per symbol, N_h, and use the same constellation of size M, i.e., the number of bits per symbol is $B_s = \log_2 M$. Let $R_s \triangleq 1/T_s$ be the symbol rate. Accordingly, in the single user case, the bit rate of conventional FH can be expressed as:

$$R_{b,FH} = B_s R_s \text{ bits/second} \quad (17)$$

Recall that the data rate of E-MDFH $R_{b,E-MDFH}$ is $[N_h(B_c - B_g) + B_s]2^{B_g}$ bits every symbol period. That is,

$$R_{b,E-MDFH} = [N_h(B_c - B_g) + B_s]2^{B_g}R_s \text{ bits/second.} \quad (18)$$

Given N_h, B_c, B_s, an interesting question is to find the optimal B_g that maximizes $R_{b,E-MDFH}$. By solving $\frac{dR_{b,E-MDFH}}{dB_g} = 0$, we have $B_g = B_c + \frac{B_s}{N_h} - \frac{1}{\ln 2}$. Note that B_g must be an integer and $B_g \in [0, B_c]$, we have the following results:

Proposition 1. *Let* $B_g^\perp \triangleq \max\{0, \lfloor B_c + \frac{B_s}{N_h} - \frac{1}{\ln 2} \rfloor\}$ *and* $B_g^\top \triangleq \min\{B_c, \lceil B_c + \frac{B_s}{N_h} - \frac{1}{\ln 2} \rceil\}$, *where* $\lfloor x \rfloor$ *denotes the largest integer less than or equal to* x *and* $\lceil x \rceil$ *the smallest integer greater than or equal to* x. *The optimal value of* B_g, *denoted by* B_g^*, *that maximizes the throughput of the E-MDFH is given by*

$$B_g^* = \begin{cases} B_g^\perp, & if \ \frac{[N_h(B_c-B_g^\perp)+B_s]2^{B_g^\perp}}{[N_h(B_c-B_g^\top)+B_s]2^{B_g^\top}} > 1, \\ B_g^\top, & otherwise. \end{cases} \quad (19)$$

□

Given that the total bandwidth $W_B = c_0 \frac{N_c}{T_h}$, where c_0 is a constant, the spectral efficiency (in bits/second/Hz) of the conventional fast FH and E-MDFH are given by

$$\eta_{FH} = \frac{R_{b,FH}}{W_B} = \frac{B_s}{c_0 N_c N_h}, \tag{20}$$

$$\eta_{E-MDFH} = \frac{R_{b,E-MDFH}}{W_B} = \frac{[N_h(B_c - B_g^*) + B_s]2^{B_g^*}}{c_0 N_c N_h}. \tag{21}$$

It is obvious that we always have $\eta_{E-MDFH} > \eta_{FH}$. That is, E-MDFH is always much more efficient than the conventional fast FH scheme.

In the more general case where there are *multiple users* in both systems, we compare the total information bits allowed to be transmitted under the same BER and bandwidth requirements (i.e., the same hopping rate). As it is not easy to derive an explicit expression of the date rate in terms of BER for both conventional FH and E-MDFH systems, we illustrate the system performance through the following numerical example.

Simulation Example 2: Assume $N_c = 64$ (i.e., $B_c = 6$), $N_h = 5$, $B_s = 4$, $B_g = 2$, and the required BER is 10^{-4}. Consider the transmission over one symbol period.

From Fig. 5(a), the E-MDFH scheme can achieve the desired BER at $\frac{E_b}{N_0} = 13.6$dB. During one symbol period, the total number of transmitted information bits in E-MDFH is $[N_h(B_c - B_g) + B_s]2^{B_g} = 4(5 \cdot 4 + 4) = 96$. Fig. 5(b) depicts the BER as a function of $\frac{E_b}{N_0}$ for $N_u = 2, \cdots, 7$. It can be observed that the conventional fast FH system can only accommodate up to 5 users at $\frac{E_b}{N_0} = 13.6$dB, in order to achieve BER $= 10^{-4}$. Therefore, during one symbol period, the FH system can transmit at most $N_u B_c = 5 \cdot 6 = 30$ bits. By comparison, the E-MDFH scheme achieves an increase of 220% in spectral efficiency.

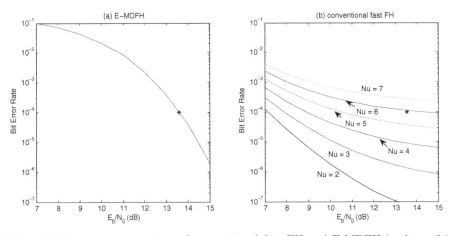

Fig. 5. Performance comparison of conventional fast FH and E-MDFH in the multi-user case: $N_c = 64$, $N_h = 5$, $B_s = 4$, $B_g = 2$

5 Conclusion

In this paper, we proposed a highly efficient spread spectrum scheme — message-driven frequency hopping. By transmitting a large portion of the information through message-driven hopping frequency control, spectral efficiency of the FH systems can be significantly improved. The efficiency of MDFH can be further enhanced by allowing simultaneous transmission over multiple channels. Quantitative performance analysis and simulation examples were provided to demonstrate the superior performance of the proposed schemes.

References

1. Viterbi, A.: A processing-satellite transponder for multlple access by low rate mobile users. In: Proc. Digital Satellite Commun. Conf., Montreal, Canada, October 1978, pp. 166–174 (1978)
2. Geraniotis, E.: Multiple-access capability of frequency-hopped spread-spectrum revisited: An analysis of the effect of unequal power levels. IEEE Trans. Commun. 38, 1066–1077 (1990)
3. Tsai, Y., Chang, J.: Using frequency hopping spread spectrum technique to combat multipath interference in a multiaccessing environment. IEEE Trans. Veh. Technol. 43, 211–222 (1994)
4. Dominique, F., Reed, J.: Robust frequency hop synchronisation algorithm. Electronics Letters 32, 1450–1451 (1996)
5. Simon, M., Huth, G., Polydoros, A.: Differentially coherent detection of QASK for frequency-hopping systems–part i: Performance in the presence of a gaussian noise environment. IEEE Trans. Commun. 30, 158–164 (1982)
6. Lam, Y., Wittke, P.: Frequency-hopped spread-spectrum transmission with band-efficient modulations and simplified noncoherent sequence estimation. IEEE Trans. Commun. 38, 2184–2196 (1990)
7. Cho, J., Kim, Y., Cheun, K.: A novel FHSS multiple-access network using M-ary orthogonal Walsh modulation. In: Proc. 52nd IEEE Veh. Technol. Conf., September 2000, vol. 3, pp. 1134–1141 (2000)
8. Glisic, S., Nikolic, Z., Milosevic, N., Pouttu, A.: Advanced frequency hopping modulation for spread spectrum WLAN. IEEE J. Sel. Areas Commun. 18, 16–29 (2000)
9. Choi, K., Cheun, K.: Maximum throughput of FHSS multiple-access networks using MFSK modulation. IEEE Trans. Commun. 52, 426–434 (2004)
10. Peng, K.-C., Huang, C.-H., Li, C.-J., Horng, T.-S.: High-performance frequency-hopping transmitters using two-point delta-sigma modulation. IEEE Trans. Microw. Theory Tech. 52, 2529–2535 (2004)
11. Choi, K., Cheun, K.: Optimum parameters for maximum throughput of FHMA system with multilevel FSK. IEEE Trans. Veh. Technol. 55, 1485–1492 (2006)
12. Fitzek, F.: The medium is the message. In: Proc. IEEE Intl. Conf. Commun., June 2006, vol. 11, pp. 5016–5021 (2006)

Toward a Real and Remote Wireless Sensor Network Testbed*

Shu Chen, Yan Huang, and Chengyang Zhang

Department of Computer Science & Engineering
University of North Texas
Denton, TX 76207, USA
{shuchen,huangyan,chengyang}@unt.edu

Abstract. A real outdoor wireless sensor network (WSN) testbed will face challenges not seen in indoor environment, including remote OAP (over-the-air-programming) and efficient energy use. In this paper, we propose to build a real remote WSN testbed that allows reprogramming of the whole network over-the-air with reasonable energy cost. Our system provides a user-friendly web interface to allow developers upload their application codes and test their algorithms or protocols. In order to support repeated reprogramming requests, we present a novel protocol named VMOAP(Versatile Multi-hop Over-the-Air Programming). Unlike traditional OAP protocols, VMOAP provides an arbitrary way to support the testing of low level protocols(such as routing protocols), while maintaining system's fundamental capability to accept future OAP reprogramming requests. VMOAP is implemented in a MICAz-motes-based sensor network. We test our approach in a small real network, and in Tossim simulator with a larger network size. We also perform simulations to evaluate our system's energy cost using our Micaz energy model. The results indicate that our system is suitable for large WSNs, and can be fully supported by one Silicon 16530 solar panel (small), and can also survive up to 113 hours at standby state powered solely by two AA batteries.

Keywords: wireless sensor network, over-the-air reprogramming, testbed, energy simulation.

1 Introduction

Wireless sensor networks (WSN) have shown great potential in providing extensive, unobtrusive and fine spatial/temporal level environmental monitoring in a wide range of applications [1]. These applications often require the network to operate for a long time, and dynamically adjust behaviors to accommodate

---

* This work is supported in part by NSF under Grants OCI-0636421, CNS-0709285, and by Texas Advanced Research Program under Grant 003594-0010-2006.

Y. Li et al. (Eds.): WASA 2008, LNCS 5258, pp. 385–396, 2008.

changing environments. Therefore it is often important to allow the reprogramming of WSN nodes. For WSN developers and researchers, it is also useful to build a real testbed in a typical area of the targeted application domain, and allow them to test their algorithms or protocols remotely.

Existing testbeds such as Motelab [2] and Kansei [3] allow users to create and schedule experiments on their indoor systems. However, a real outdoor wireless sensor network (WSN) testbed will face challenges not seen in indoor environment, including remote OAP(Over-the-Air-Programming) and efficient energy use. MOAP (Multi-hop Over-the-Air Programming) protocol is very useful in connecting and reprogramming sensor motes over the air in outdoor environments. Previous approaches such as Deluge [4] and MOAP [5] have utilized and implemented the MOAP protocol. Unfortunately, these approaches need to use their own protocols (e.g. Ripple dissemination protocol for MOAP) to implement code dissemination, which may conflict with testing codes, especially with those involving routing or MAC layer protocols. Energy cost is another important issue for outdoor systems in order to support long term running networks without direct AC power support.

In this paper, we propose to build a real remote WSN testbed that allows reprogramming of the whole network over-the-air with reasonable energy cost. By implementing above functions, our system has made following contributions:

- In order to support repeated reprogramming requests, we present a novel protocol named VMOAP(Versatile Multi-hop Over-the-Air Programming). Unlike traditional OAP protocols, VMOAP is capable of testing low level protocols by removing the process of OAP code dissemination. It keeps one extra image of traditional MOAP in the external flash of sensor nodes, and uses timer or active messages to roll back to the MOAP image. The roll-backed state called standby state can accept future OAP reprogramming requests after one testing cycle.
- VMOAP is implemented in a MICAz-motes-based sensor network. The experimental results show that 100% of the motes are sucessfully reprogrammed within reasonable amount of time.
- Our system provides a user-friendly web interface to allow developers upload their application codes and test their algorithms or protocols.
- We also perform simulations to evaluate our system's energy cost using our Micaz based energy model. The results indicate that our system can be fully supported by a small Silicon 16530 solar panel, and can also survive up to 113 hours at standby state powered solely by two AA batteries.

The rest of the paper is organized as follows. Section 2 introduces related work. Section 3 gives an overview of our system. Detailed VMOAP protocol design and implementation are discussed in Section 4. This section also compares the experimental results of VMOAP with Deluge. In Section 5, a MICAz energy model is used to perform energy simulation of the VMOAP system. Finally Section 6 concludes the paper and presents our future work.

2   Related Work

2.1   Testbed

Some indoor testbeds, such as MoteLab [2] and Kansei [3], have been developed to support the research and application of wireless sensor networks. MoteLab is an ethernet-connected sensor network testbed with a set of permanently deployed nodes. It provides a web interface for users to directly interact with individual nodes. Kansei is another indoor testbed with heterogeneous nodes in a large scale. It can also be used in conjunction with model composition and hybrid simulation tools to perform large-scale sensing experiments with high fidelity. However, none of these testbeds are suitable for outdoor environments. By contrast, our system will be deployed in a real outdoor environment (Greenbelt Corridor Park, Denton, TX), with limited access. Therefore remote over-the-air reprogramming is more desirable. Energy saving also becomes an important issue in such an environment.

2.2   Network Reprogramming

Crossbow provides MoteWorks (a series of Windows GUI utility based on XNP) [6] to perform over-the-air programming. However, it only supports single-hop protocols, which requires all nodes within the bidirectional communication range of the source node. MOAP[5] is a more comprehensive network reprogramming approach. It supports multi-hop programming for reliable dissemination of large volume data in resource constrained motes. Deluge [4] further provides some useful capacities such as automatic system voltage checking, hardware write protection, and rollback mechanism in case of failure. Reijers *et al.* [7] proposes a protocol to support updates of binary code images at instruction level. Kapur *et al.* [8] further extends the work to support incremental network programming.

   However, to the best of our knowledge, none of these systems allow arbitrarily deploying new protocols(e.g. routing protocols) of WSN through network reprograming, while still maintaining the fundamental over-the-air reprogramming capability to support future network reprogramming requests.

2.3   Energy Simulation

Existing measurements on Micaz motes can be found in [9] and [10]. The difference between our work and [9] is that the energy consumption of EEPROM is included in our model. Our measurements have some differences from those described in [10]. Aeon [11] and Powertossim [12] support energy simulation by using analysis model and the states given out by emulators (Avrora and Tossim). We use a similar approach in our simulation. The main difference between [11],[12] and ours is that their power simulations are based on Mica2 motes, but our simulations are based on Micaz motes.

3   System Overview

At current stage, our system is deployed at our CSE lab. In the near future, we will migrate the system into Greenbelt Corridor Park near Denton, TX. We aim at providing a real outdoor environmental monitoring sensor network testbed, which allows developers and researchers to test their protocols and algorithms in such an outdoor environment. In satisfying this need, we have mainly tackled two challenges, namely, the support of remote over-the-air reprogramming and outdoor energy harvesting.

As shown in Figure 1, our system consists of following components:

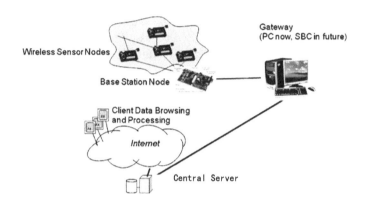

Fig. 1. System Structure

- *Wireless Sensor Nodes.* Our system uses Crossbow MicaZ motes, with one base station directly connected to an MIB510 interface board to communicate with the gateway machine. Each mote is pre-installed with MOAP code in one volume of its external flash to provide the capability of over-the-air reprogramming. The motes are powered by regular rechargeable AA batteries in the lab and will be powered by solar panels and the batteries in the field.
- *Base Station Node.* A base activity node is deployed to be continuously running. It serves as a server in the sensor network to provide data logging, relaying and events signaling.
- *Gateway.* Gateway is a Linux-OS based computer in charge of sending commands to motes, and gathering data from motes through the base station. The gateway is a normal linux machine in the lab and will be replaced by a Debian-OS single board computer(SBC) in the field. Data collected from sensor motes are first stored in the MySQL database on the Gateway before sent back to the database server.
- *Central Server.* Central server handles the following tasks: scheduling, queuing reprogramming requests, and fetching data from the gateway.
- *User Interface.* Authorized users can access our system by using a web-based interface(http://groucho.csci.unt.edu:8080/system/upload) to upload their

codes, schedule tasks, and download data. For now we have provided one sample program package for users to test the functionality. Once the program is uploaded, it will be scheduled and pushed into program execution task queue of the database. The user will receive an email notification once the program starts to run. The gateway server communicates with the web server and executes assigned tasks. When a program package arrives, the server will uncompress the program and append relevant head files and libraries. Then the program starts collecting data using the wireless sensor networks. When the program finishes, the user will receive another email notification containing the web address to download the data file collected.

Fig. 2. Greenbelt Weather Station

Figure 2 shows our existing weather station system deployed in Greenbelt Corridor Park near Denton, Texas. Our system's final deployment will add several features to this station or in another similar station. First, we will provide energy kits to support individual motes with solar cells and overcharge protection chips to recharge the battery. Second, an SBC (Single Board Computer) will act as the Gateway to save overall energy cost. Third, a GPRS Modem will be used to communicate with the database server because wired network is not supported in the field.

4   VMOAP System Design and Evaluation

As shown in Figure 3, in traditional OAP, the application code to be tested is first encoded and disseminated through radio packets, and then stored in the external flash of the mote. This code is further decoded and transferred to the programming flash through RAM by the boot loader. The new code will overwrite the existing system code, then the mote will reboot with the new code.

However, once the reprogramming system code is overwritten, the mote also loses the capability to perform over-the-air programming because this system functionality is no longer supported by the application code. In order to satisfy repeated remote OAP requests, our VMOAP system separates the storage of user's code from the system standby code, which is attentive to OAP requests.

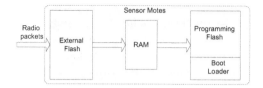

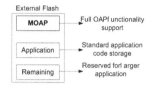

Fig. 3. Process of Network Programming   **Fig. 4.** Illustration of VMOAP

The system will rollback to the standby state when the life cycle of the application code ends. We will first introduces how this feature is designed in VMOAP system, and then describe the implementation of VMOAP as well as present the experimental evaluation results.

4.1   Code Storage Design

In VMOAP, we use two contiguous memory chunks in the external flash to store both the original over-the-air reprogramming system codes(MOAP) for the standby state and new application codes, as shown in Figure 4. The MOAP block is protected by software to ensure that it will not be modified by application programs. The application code to be distributed is stored next to the MOAP system code. The remaining section in the flash is reserved to accommodate larger application code or used for data storage.

4.2   Rollback Mechanism Design

Two mechanisms are designed in VMOAP to allow the system to automatically rollback to the standby state when the life cycle of application code ends: timer based triggers and active message based triggers. Rolling back to a standby state after the execution of an arbitrary program will ensure the mote to support arbitrary application codes without interfering with over-the-air programming functionalities.

Rollback Using Timer. Timer is a very useful utility in TinyOS. In VMOAP system, user can specify the total running time of the application code. When the time specified has passed, the timer will trigger the boot loader to perform rollback operation using the MOAP code in the storage.

1. First, the timer automatically triggers an event to call boot loader(stored in a special location in the programming flash, and is added to application code by VMOAP).
2. After testing the accessibility of the protected block in the external flash, the boot loader will access the system code (MOAP).
3. The MOAP will be copied from external flash to the programming flash controlled by mote's programming micro-controller.
4. The mote will reboot and rollback to the standby state.

Rollback Using Active Message. Alternatively, VMAOP adds a message function to the application code. The Central Server can send an active message through the network at any time. The VMOAP inside each mote will then trigger the similar rollback process as above. Active message is especially useful when application running time is not predefined, or the user wish to adjust running time dynamically.

4.3   Implementation of VMOAP

A mote only runs one TinyOS image at a time, which consists of the components needed for a single application. Therefore addressing functions are necessary to locate the pre-injected code and use it to roll back the system to standby state. TinyOS has two types of components, namely configurations and modules. Configurations describe how the modules (or other configurations) are wired(i.e. connected) together, while modules implement program logic and contain executable code.

Figure 5 and 6 show VMOAP wiring structures. The boxes with double border lines denote configurations, and the boxes with single border lines indicate modules. Dashed border lines indicate that the component is generic (which can be instantiated within a configuration), and solid lines indicate that the component is a singleton (which can not be instantiated). Shaded ovals denote wireable interfaces. The direction of the arrows shows the sequence of wiring with labeled interfaces and parameters. A more detailed description on nesC graph can be found in [13].

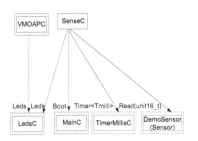

Fig. 5. Top Architecture

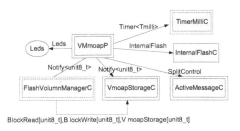

Fig. 6. Detailed Architecture

Figure 5 gives a top layer wiring structure example based on a small sensor application. It periodically samples the default sensor and displays the bottom bits of the readings on the leds of the node. A top level configuration VmoapAppC contains both the Vmoap component and a singleton module SenseC. SenseC can be replaced by any application code. It wires to several components: MainC, Leds (to give out current state), TimerMilliC (to schedule tasks) and DemoSensor (to execute sensing tasks).

A more detailed structure of VMOAP component is given in Figure 6. It eliminates the dissemination part in order to avoid possible deep conflicts between

VMOAP module and user's application, as well as save the transmission cost. We uses VmoapStorageC to provide interfaces (such as BlockRead, BlockWrite) to support operations on external flash and software level storage protection on the pre-installed image. FlashVolumeManagerC manages different volumes injected. InternalFlashC is in charge of reprogramming motes by calling a bootloader. ActiveMessageC will wait for messages to perform reprogramming. A timer is used to support timer based reprogramming. Leds interface is used to show current state of the motes, and will not be included during the deployment.

4.4 Experimental Results

We have implemented both VMOAP and Deluge in MicaZ motes. A MicaZ mote has 128Kb programming flash, 512Kb external flash, and 4Kb EEPROM. Our preliminary goal is to test the effectiveness of VMAOP in a small testbed consisting of one base station and 15 MicaZ motes. Figure 7 shows the deployment of our testbed(a grid based network with 15 nodes). The experimental results show that, 100% of the motes are successful reprogrammed and rolled back.

To compare the efficiency of our approach with the original Deluge, we measured the completion time w.r.t. different number of nodes in Figure 9. Average

Fig. 7. Nodes Deployment

Fig. 8. Silicon 16530

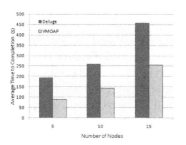

Fig. 9. Completion Time

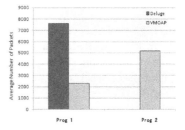

Fig. 10. Average Number of Packets

number of packets (with each packet having fixed size) received by individual nodes are recorded in two scenarios. Program 1 uses a simple blink application, and program 2 uses a routing protocol called parrot that is not supported by Deluge, as shown in Figure 10. Each experiment was repeated for three times and the results were averaged. We are also planning to measure more metrics like delay or packet loss ratio in our future experiments after our system is actually deployed.

5   Energy Model and Power Simulation

5.1   MICAz Energy Model

Energy consumption is an important issue in outdoor environments. In order to evaluate MOAP system's energy cost before real deployment, we investigate MICAz energy model in VMOAP, and performed extensive simulation. To the best of our knowledge, although some measurements and analysis have been made, most of existing models cannot be directly applied to our system to give an energy outline.

Our system is based on Crossbow MicaZ mote, which features an 8-bit Atmel microcontroller with RISC architecture, clocked at 7.3728 MHz, with 4KB internal SRAM, 4KB data EEPROM and 128KB internal flash memory. The ZigBee-compliant wireless transceiver chip operates at data rates of up to 250 Kb/s. A 512KB flash memory can be accessed via two SRAM page buffers of 264 bytes each. Three LEDs can be used to show the operational status of the device and each node is equipped with a serial-number chip that gives a node its unique ID. The MicaZ has a 51-pin expansion connector as an interface to any sensors. The architecture of Micaz mote is shown in Figure 11.

The energy consumption of the serial-number chip is negligible (less than 0.1mA). We ignore serial-number chip part in our energy model, and a state model is given in Table 1 with four main components (ATMega, Transceiver, Leds and EEPROM). Some data come from Crossbow datasheet and some are from actual measurements by our Agilent 34401A multimeter. In our model, the micro controller ATMege has 7 states, and the energy consumption may change when the ATMege speed goes down in active state. The transceiver has 5 states

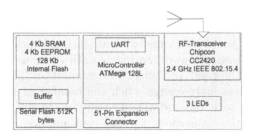

Fig. 11. Architecture of Micaz

Table 1. Micaz Energy Model

Component	Mode	Current	Component	Mode	Current
ATMege	Active	8.6mA	**Tranceiver**	Idle	0mA
	Idle	3.2mA		Off	0mA
	ADCMode	1.3mA		Listen	22.9mA
	Power down	0mA		Receive	20.1mA
	Power save	0mA		Send	17.1mA
	Standby	1.2mA	**EEPROM**	Read	4.1mA
	Extended Standby	0.1mA		Write	15.2mA
Leds	LedsOn	2.4mA			
	LedsOff	0mA			

(idle, off, listen, receive and send), and has 31 different speed levels. We give one typical speed level(15) that is used in our system(Tx15 in the figure).

To analyze the energy cost and give an outline of life time of our system, we also give a simple equation 1 to calculate the total energy consumed by the specified task. In Equation 1, P is the power consumed at any state, t is the time spent at this state. P can be simply calculated from measured current. We will give our simulation results in thenext section.

$$E = \sum_{t_{ATMega}} P_{S_{ATMega}} \times t_{ATMega} + \sum_{t_{Trans}} P_{S_{Trans}} \times t_{Trans}$$

$$+ \sum_{t_{EEPROM}} P_{S_{EEPROM}} \times t_{EEPROM} + P_{LedsOn} \times t_{LedsOn} \qquad (1)$$

5.2   Power Simulation

In order to fit outside environment with no direct AC power support, we simulate Deluge dissemination to roll back to standby state using TOSSIM with slight changes of code to fit the simulation environment. An outside analysis module calculates the energy cost of both individual nodes and the whole network. While TOSSIM does not imitate Micaz platform precisely, the purpose of these experiments is to estimate the daily power consumption to further adjust solar panel and external capacitor support.

In Figure 12, the simulation runs twice for each network size. It starts from one source in grid based network, and runs until every node receives all code pages. We also give the result of Deluge as a comparison. The results show that our approach can save more energy when the number of nodes increase. The saving is about 10% with 100 nodes, and reaches up to 30% with 400 nodes.

Figure 13 shows the simulation of power comsumption at constant standby state for individual nodes during 18 hours. To validate our simulation results, we also perform experiments by using a multimeter to measure the instant current of Micaz motes at standby state. The instant current we measured is around

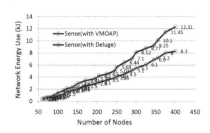

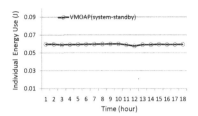

Fig. 12. Network Dissemination Power Cost

Fig. 13. Power Consumption at Standby State

22 mA, which shows that although our results are not very accurate, they are still reasonable (assuming voltage is around 2.4 V). The solar panel we choose is Silicon 16530 with 4 voltage and 0.4 watt output (Figure 8). To take into consideration of the vegetation cover in our real environment, we assume the possible energy income is 10% of its full output, which can support nearly 100mA constant current. In case of bad weather, fully charged 2500mA AA batteries can also support standby state for more than 113 hours. We keep monitoring 3 Micaz motes with MTS310. One dies in 109 hours and the other two in 103 hours and 101 hours respectively. The experiment results achieved in our CSE lab show that a single node can survive for at least 100 hours.

6   Conclusion and Future Work

In this paper, we have presented our prototype system toward a real remote wireless sensor network testbed system. We compared our VMOAP protocol with Deluge system and performed energy simulation in the lab. Our system will soon be deployed in a real outdoor environment inside the Greenbelt Corridor Park (near Denton, TX), and another station with similar environment. We are currently working on testing the scalability of the system by running over 100 motes. The energy simulation model will also be improved by real observation data in the future.

Acknowledgments. We thank the group members of the TEO project for valuable discussions and feedbacks.

References

1. Cerpa, A., Busek, N., Estrin, D.: SCALE: A Tool for Simple Connectivity Assessment in Lossy Environments. In: Cerpa, A., Busek, N., Estrin, D. (eds.) SCALE: A tool for simple connectivity assessment in lossy environments. Technical Report 0021, UCLA (2003)
2. motelab: Harvard sensor network testbed. web,
   http://motelab.eecs.harvard.edu

3. Ertin, E., Arora, A., Ramnath, R., Naik, V., Bapat, S., Kulathumani, V., Sridharan, M., Zhang, H., Cao, H., Nesterenko, M.: Kansei: a testbed for sensing at scale. In: IPSN 2006. Proceedings of the fifth international conference on Information processing in sensor networks, pp. 399–406. ACM, New York (2006)
4. Hui, J.W., Culler, D.: The dynamic behavior of a data dissemination protocol for network programming at scale. In: Proceedings of the 2nd international conference on Embedded networked sensor systems, pp. 81–94. ACM Press, New York (2004)
5. Stathopoulos, T., Heidemann, J., Estrin, D.: A remote code update mechanism for wireless sensor networks. In: Stathopoulos, T., Heidemann, J., Estrin, D. (eds.) A remote code update mechanism for wireless sensor networks. Technical Report CENS Technical Report 30 (2004)
6. Technology, C.: Mote In Network Programming User Reference. Technical report, TinyOS document
7. Reijers, N., Langendoen, K.: Efficient code distribution in wireless sensor networks. In: WSNA 2003. Proceedings of the 2nd ACM international conference on Wireless sensor networks and applications, pp. 60–67. ACM, New York (2003)
8. Rahul Kapur, T.Y., Lahoti, U.: Differential Wireless Reprogramming of Sensor Networks. Technical report, UCLA (2003)
9. Krämer, M., Geraldy, A.: Energy measurements for micaz node. In: 5. GI/ITG KuVS Fachgespräch Drahtlose Sensornetze, Institut für Parallele und Verteilte Systeme, pp. 61–68 (July 2006)
10. Crossbow: Micaz Energy Datasheet. Technical report, Crossbow Inc.
11. Landsiedel, O., Wehrle, K., Gotz, S.: Accurate prediction of power consumption in sensor networks. In: Proceedings of The Second IEEE Workshop on Embedded Networked Sensors (EmNetS-II) (2005)
12. Shnayder, V., Hempstead, M., Rong Chen, B., Allen, G.W., Welsh, M.: Simulating the power consumption of large-scale sensor network applications. In: SenSys 2004. Proceedings of the 2nd international conference on Embedded networked sensor systems, pp. 188–200. ACM, New York (2004)
13. Levis, P.: TinyOS Programming. Technical report, Stanford University (2006)

An Optimal Algorithm for Minimizing Cluster Overlap of ACE

Qiang Hu^{1,*}, Qiaoliang Li^{1,3}, Xiaoming Wang^{2,3}, Naixue Xiong^3, and Yi Pan^3

^{1} School of Computer Science and Communication, Hunan University,
Changsha 410082, China
^{2} School of Computer Science, Shanxi Normal University, Xi'an 710062, China
^{3} Department of Computer Science, Georgia State University, Atlanta 30319, USA
xiaoqiang_hd2000@yahoo.com.cn, lqlbox@163.com, wangxmsnnu@hotmail.com,
nxiong@cs.gsu.edu, pan@cs.gsu.edu

Abstract. In order to reduce channel contention, support scalability and prolong the lifetime of the sensor networks, sensor nodes are often grouped into clusters. Algorithm for Cluster Establishment (ACE) is a clustering algorithm for sensor networks that uses three rounds of feedback to induce the formation of a highly efficient cover of uniform clusters over the network. In this paper, we present an optimizing algorithm for minimizing the cluster overlap of ACE. Simulation shows the proposed algorithm can efficiently eliminate the redundant cluster heads and minimize the cluster overlap.

Keywords: clustering, ACE algorithm, sensor networks.

1 Introduction

Wireless Sensor networks appear in a variety applications, including military battle-field, disaster relief, sensing and monitoring. One of the advantages of wireless sensor networks (WSNs) is the ability to operate unattended in harsh environment. Therefore, sensors are expected to be deployed randomly in the area of interest by relative uncontrolled means, which makes it difficult or impossible to recharge or replace their batteries. Therefore, designing energy-aware algorithms becomes an important factor for extending the lifetime of sensor networks.

Network lifetime can be defined as the time elapsed until the first node (or the last node) in the network depletes its energy (dies). The lifetime of a sensor is critical for maximum field coverage. Several protocols have been proposed to prolong the lifetime of sensor networks. Clustering techniques can aid in reducing useful energy consumption[1].

Clustering has been extensively studied in the data processing and wired network literatures. Conventional algorithms that use centralized and global properties of the network cannot be applied directly to WSNs due to the unique

---

* Supported by National Natural Science Foundation of China (NSFC) under Grant No.60773224, 10571052, the Key Research Project of Ministry of Education of China under Grant No.107106, and the 111 Project of China under Grant No.111-2-14.

Y. Li et al. (Eds.): WASA 2008, LNCS 5258, pp. 397–408, 2008.

deployment and operational characteristics of sensor networks. Specially, WSNs are deployed in ad hoc manner and have a large number of nodes. The nodes are typically unaware of their locations. Hence, distributed clustering protocols that rely only on neighborhood information are preferred for WSNs (however, most studies in this area still assume that the network topology is known to a centralized controller). Furthermore, nodes in WSNs operate on battery power with limited energy. Hence the clustering algorithms must have low message overhead.

Conventional algorithms that use centralized and global properties of the sensor network have inherent difficulties in the properties of scalability and robustness. As an alternative to the centralized algorithms, localized algorithms reduced the amount of central coordination necessary and only require each node to interact with its local neighbors while sometimes harder to design, these algorithms do not have the limitations of centralized algorithms and are often highly scalable.

Emergent algorithm is a special class of localized algorithms. This class of algorithm has the additional characteristic that the individual agents only encode simple local behaviors and do not explicitly coordinate on a global scale. Through repeated interaction and feedback at the individual level, global properties emerge in the system as a whole. Recently, H. Chan and A. Perrig [2] proposed a new emergent protocol for node clustering called ACE (Algorithm for Cluster Establishment). ACE is scale independent (it completes in constant time regardless of the size of the network) and operates without needing geographic knowledge. ACE clusters the sensor network within a constant number of iterations using the node degree as the main parameter. Some of the weaknesses of ACE are: First, ACE randomly selects candidate node in each iteration which creates different results each time on the same sensor network. Second, spawning threshold function is used in ACE to control the formation of new cluster by using two manually adjusted according to the size and shape of a sensor network.

In this paper, we propose an optimizing algorithm for ACE that can efficiently eliminate redundant cluster headers and minimize the cluster overlap. The rest of the paper is organized as followers. In section 2, we present related works and in section 3, we overview the ACE. The proposed optimization algorithm is illustrated in section 4. Experimental results are presented in section 5. Finally we conclude the paper in section 6.

2   Related Works

LEACH (Low Energy Adaptive Clustering Hierarchy)[3] is the first clustering protocol proposed for periodical data gathering in WSNs. This approach relies on the following two main assumptions (1) there exists a unique base-station with which all the sensors want to communicate (2) all the sensors have the ability to communicate directly with the base station. In order to save energy, the LEACH protocol selects a fraction p of the sensors to serve as cluster-heads, where p is a design parameter that must be engineered off-line. Cluster heads communicate directly with the base station whereas other nodes forward their data through the cluster heads (typically, the one closet to them). In order to share the energy load, the LEACH protocol implements a load balancing procedure that allows different nodes to become cluster heads at different times. Other work related to LEACH include the PEGASIS [4], Sensitive Energy Efficient sensor network protocol (TEEN)[5], Hybrid Energy Efficient Distributed clustering (HEED)[6], Lower Energy Adaptive Clustering Hierarchy with Deterministic cluster-head (LEACH-D)[7] and so on.

Algorithm for Cluster Establishment (ACE) employs an emergent algorithm to cluster nodes in sensor network. ACE has two logical parts: the spawning process of the new clusters and the migration of the existing clusters. In the spawning process, an unclustered node counts the number l of its potential loyal followers. A loyal follower is a follower of only one cluster. If $l \geq f_{min}(t)$ ($f_{min}(t)$ is the spawning threshold function), the node declares itself a cluster header. In the migration process, a cluster-head polls all of its neighbors to find the best candidate for the new cluster-head. The best candidate is the node which has the largest number of nodes in its neighbor set which are either unclustered or loyal followers of the cluster-head. If the cluster head finds the best candidate, it migrates the cluster onto the candidate node. ACE clusters the sensor network in 3 iterations and uses only intra-cluster communications.

Some of weakness of ACE are: First, ACE randomly selects candidate node in each iteration which creates different results each time on the same sensor network. Second, spawning threshold function is used in ACE to control the formation of new cluster by using two mutually adjusted parameters. ACE relies on these parameters which are mutually adjusted according to the size and shape of a sensor network. Realizing these weakness, K. Shin, A. Abraham and S. Y. Han [8] proposed some new algorithms that does not require manually adjusted parameters which could also provide identical results in each test on the same sensor network to overcome the weakness of ACE. Other work to improve ACE can be seen in [9][10]

3   Overview of ACE

Clustering problem can be defined as following. Assume that nodes are randomly dispersed in a field. At the clustering process, each node belongs to one cluster exactly and be able to communicate with the cluster head directly via a single hop. Each cluster consists of a single cluster head and a bunch of followers. The purpose of clustering algorithm is to form the smallest number of clusters that makes all nodes of network to belong to the clusters. Minimizing the number of cluster heads would not only provide an efficient cover of the whole network but also minimizes the cluster overlaps. This reduces the amount of channel contention between clusters, and also improves the efficiency of the algorithms that executes at the level of the cluster heads.

ACE has two logical parts: the spawning of new clusters and the migration of existing clusters. New clusters are spawned in a self-elective process. When a node decides to become a cluster head, it will broadcast a recruit message to its neighbors, who will become followers of the new cluster. A node can be a follower of more than one cluster while the protocol is running (it picks a single cluster for membership only at the end of the protocol). Migration of an existing cluster is controlled by the cluster head. Each cluster head will periodically poll all its followers to determine which is the best candidate to become the new leader of the cluster. The best candidate is the node which, if it were to become cluster head, it will promote the best candidate as the new cluster head and abdicate its position as the old cluster head. Thus, the position of the cluster head will appear to migrate in the direction of the new cluster head as some of the former followers of the old cluster head are no longer part of the cluster, while some new nodes near the new cluster head become new followers of the cluster.

In the spawning process of ACE, an unclustered node declares itself a cluster head if the number of loyal followers $l \geq f_{min}(t)$, where $f_{min}(t)$ is the spawning threshold function:

$$f_{min} = (e^{-k_1 \frac{t}{cI}} - k_2)d \tag{1}$$

In this formula, t is the time passed since the protocol began, c is the desired average number of iterations, I is the expected length of the iteration interval, d is the estimated average degree (number of neighbors) of a node in the network, k_1 and k_2 are chosen constants. In the case of $k_1 = 2.3$ and $k_2 = 0.1$, $f_{min}(t)$ starts at $0.9d$ at the beginning and reduces to 0 at the last. So in the final iteration of ACE, some unclustered nodes whose loyal followers are very few declare itself the cluster head, and around these cluster heads, the cluster overlap is very high. This increases communication cost and the probability of channel contention.

4   Optimized ACE

In this section, we present the algorithm for optimizing the clustered result of ACE. The algorithm consists of two optimizing processes: unclustered node merging and cluster merging.

4.1   Unclustered Node Merging Process

At the end of ACE, there may exist a small number of unclustered nodes that can not be covered by any cluster. In ACE, these nodes simply pick a clustered neighbor to join the neighboring cluster and become two-hop followers. Instead of simply joining neighboring cluster, unclustered node merging process is for merging these unclustered nodes to reduce the cluster overlap and communication cost.

When an unclustered node (for example, node D in figure 1(a)), is triggered by its timer to run the merging process, it sends a merge investigation message which contains its node id to the cluster headers of its neighbor clusters. When a cluster header (node B) receives the investigation message, it broadcasts a

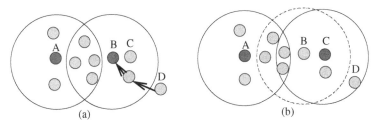

Fig. 1. Example of Unclustered Node Merging Process

candidate message which contains its cluster member table and node D's ID to all of its neighbors to find the best candidate. Each item of the cluster member table contains the members id and a flag indicating whether the member is a loyal follower. The best candidate is the node which has all of the loyal followers and node D in its neighbor sets, and within its one hop radius, the number of cluster members is the largest. If node B fails to find a candidate, then B does nothing. Otherwise, node B will send a reply which contains B's ID and the ID of B' s candidate to node D. Node D then choose a cluster header and sends a Merge-Request to the chosen cluster header. After receiving the Merge-Request, the cluster header migrates the cluster onto the new cluster head (node C in figure 1(a))as ACE. In figure 1(b), we can see that after unclustered node merging process, the cluster overlap is lower than before.

In the proposed optimizing algorithm, unclustered node merging process should be executed twice. For the first time, we execute the merging process after the sensor network is divided into disjoint clusters by ACE and for the second time, the merging process is executed after the cluster merging process which we will describe below.

4.2   Cluster Merging Process

When a cluster header (for example, node B in figure 2(a)) is triggered by its local timer to run the cluster merging process, it counts the number l of its loyal followers. If B doesn't have a loyal member ($l = 0$), it checks whether there exists a cluster header in its neighbor sets. If there exists a cluster header within B's communication range, B simply issues an ABDICATE message to its neighbors as in ACE to tell them to exit its cluster, and becomes a member of the neighboring cluster header. If l is greater than zero and $l \leq L_{avg}$ (L_{avg} is the average number of loyal followers, the choosing of L_{avg} will describe later), node B sends a Merge investigation message which contains its loyal member list to the header nodes of its neighboring clusters. The loyal member list contains the IDs of all the loyal member of node B. When a header node (node A or node C in figure 2(a)) receives this message, node A broadcasts a candidate message which contains the A's cluster member table and node B's loyal member list to its neighbors to find a best candidate. A's members, which have all of A's loyal members in their neighbor sets, reply to A with a list which contains B's loyal

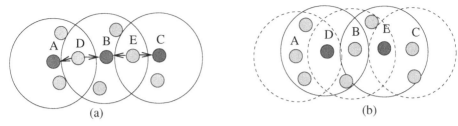

Fig. 2. Example of Cluster Merging Process

followers they can reach. The best candidate is the node which has all of A's loyal members in its neighbor set, and within its one hop radius, the number of B's loyal member is the largest. Then A sends a reply which contains the candidate's id and a list of B's loyal member that the neighbors can reach to node B. After node B has received replies from all its neighboring clusters, it checks the replies to find whether there exists a candidate that can reach all its loyal members, If it fails, it will try to find whether there exist several candidates, and the union of the loyal members of those candidates can reach contains all of B's loyal members (for example, node D and E in figure 2(a)). If node B find one or several candidates, it will then issue an ABDICATE message to its neighbors as ACE to tell them to exit its cluster, then it sends a merge request message to the cluster headers of the candidates. When the cluster header receives the merge-request, it migrates the cluster onto the best candidate as ACE. Figure 2(b) shows the result to cluster merging.

In cluster merging process, there is no need for every cluster header to send the merge investigation, A cluster header will send merge investigation if the number l of its loyal members is less than or equal to L_{avg}. We simulate ACE in 600×600 rectangle area with a uniform random distribution of 3600 nodes, and the node degree d is adjusted from 4 to 80. Figure 3 shows the average number of loyal followers as a fraction of d of various node degree ($k_1 = 2.3$ and $k_2 = 0.1$). Based on the results, we choose the value of L_{avg} as follows:

$$L_{avg} = \begin{cases} 0.5d, \, d \le 10 \\ 0.4d, \, d > 10 \end{cases} \qquad (2)$$

We also simulated the cluster merging process after sensor network is divided into disjoint clusters by ACE. Results for the simulation with $D = 20$ are shown in figure 4. We note that increasing the number of iterations above 3 yielded only very slight improvement in minimizing the cluster overlap and reducing the number of cluster headers. So we choose to run three iterations of cluster merging process.

4.3   Avoid Collision

There may exist collision in unclustered node merging process and cluster merging process. For example,if two neighboring clusters receive merge requests

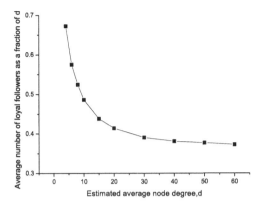

Fig. 3. Average number of loyal followers as a fraction of d of various node degrees

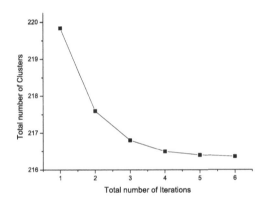

Fig. 4. Performance results of various maximum iterations, d=20

simultaneously, then after cluster migration, some nodes laying in the overlap of the two neighboring clusters can not covered by any cluster.

We could set the timer of sensor node to avoid collision. We assume every node in the network has a unique node ID, and every cluster header can generate a unique cluster ID during the clustering. So we could use the unique node ID or cluster ID to set the timer.

As we have described above, when a cluster header receives a merge investigation message, it broadcasts a candidate message to its neighbors to find a best candidate. If a member node receives a candidate message, it schedules a timer with a fixed interval and stores the ID of the cluster header which sends the message. When the node is triggered by the timer next time, it deletes the stored ID. If the node receives another candidate message within the interval, it replies a retry message to that cluster header to avoid collision. When the cluster header receives the retry message, it relays the message to the node which sends the merge investigation message. After receiving this message, the node reschedules a timer to run the merging process.

The detailed optimizing algorithm are listed below.

Algorithm 1. Pseudo codes of optimization algorithm

Procedure Unclustered node merge()
if MyState=UNCLUSTERED **then**
    send Merge Investigation {myID} to the cluster headers of neighboring clusters
    wait for replies
else
    if reply is Retry **then**
        reschedule timer to rerun the process
    else
        choose a cluster header from replies and send Merge-Request to the chosen
        cluster header
    end if
end if
if myState= CLUSTER-HEAD **then**
    wait for message
    if message is Merge investigation **then**
        send Candidate {cluster members table, ID of the unclustered node } to its
        neighbors
        wait for replies
        if reply is Retry **then**
            send Retry to the unclustered node
        else
            check the replies form its neighbors and find a best candidate send a reply {
            myID, Candidate ID } to the unclustered node
        end if
    else
        if message is Merge-Request **then**
            migrates the cluster onto the new cluster head
        end if
    end if
end if
if myState= CLUSTERED **then**
    wait for Candidate message
    if the unclustered node's ID in candidate is not equal to the ID stored in cache
    then
        send Retry to the cluster header
    else
        store the id of the unclustered node and schedule a timer to delete it
        if all of loyal members and the unclustered node in its neighbor sets **then**
            send reply { List of loyal members that it can reach} to its cluster header
        end if
    end if
end if
end procedure

Procedure Cluster merge()
if myState= CLUSTER-HEAD then
    Count the number L of loyal members
    if $L \leq L_{avg}$ then
        if $L = 0$ and there exist a neighboring cluster header then
            Broadcast an ABDICATE message to its neighbors
            Become a member of the neighboring cluster header
        else
            Send a Merge Investigation { Loyal members list } to the header nodes of
            neighboring clusters
            Wait for replies
            if reply is Retry then
                reschedule timer to rerun the process
            else
                try to find one or several candidates that can reach all of its loyal members

                if find an or several candidates then
                    send Merge-Request to the cluster headers of the candidates
                end if
            end if
        end if
    else
        wait for Merge Investigation
        send a Candidate {Loyal members table, list of loyal members of the node which
        sends the investigation } to its neighbors
        wait for replies
        if reply is Retry then
            send Retry to the cluster node which sends the investigation
        else
            check the replies form its neighbors and find a best candidate
            send a reply {myID, Candidate ID, list of loyal members which the candidate
            can reach} to the cluster node which sends the investigation
        end if
    end if
else
    if myState= CLUSTERED then
        wait for candidate message
        if the unclustered node's id in Candidate is not equal to the ID stored in cache
        then
            send Retry to the cluster header
        else
            store the ID of the unclustered node and schedule a timer to delete it
            if the node has all of loyal members of its cluster head in its neighbor sets
            then
                send a reply { List of loyal members that it can reach} to its
                cluster header
            end if
        end if
    end if
end if
end procedure

---

5   Simulation and Results

To evaluate the effectiveness of the proposed algorithm. We simulated ACE ($k_1 = 2.3, k_2 = 0.1$) and the optimizing algorithm in 600×600 rectangle area with an uniform random distribution of 3600 nodes, and we set the average node degree as 4, 10, 20, 30 ,40, 50 and 60. ACE and the optimizing algorithm were run 2500 times and the average value is calculated. As shown in Table 1, the optimizing algorithm could reduce the number of clusters by about 9.33% for 3600 nodes when compared to the ACE. And we also compare the improvement of our algorithm to OSOS (Optimized Self Organized Sensor Networks). Figure 5 shows the improvements of the two algorithms, it is noticed that the performance of the proposed algorithm is better than OSOS. From Figure 6 and Figure 7, we can see by optimization of ACE, the average number of clusters with $L \leq L_{avg}$ reduces and the average number of loyal followers increases. As we know, the larger the average number of loyal followers, the lower the cluster overlap is. So the proposed optimization algorithm can efficiently reduce the clustering overlap.

Table 1. Clustering results of various node degrees

Node degree	Average Number of Clusters		Improvement
	ACE	By Optimization	
4	804.73	758.1	5.79%
10	432.58	395.23	8.63%
20	244.07	218.06	10.66%
30	169.59	152.43	10.12%
40	130.14	116.33	10.16%
50	104.59	94.23	9.91%
60	88.26	79.81	9.57%
Avg			9.33%

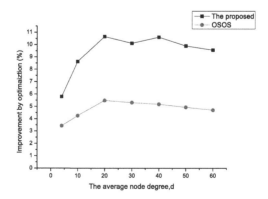

Fig. 5. Improvement of the two optimization algorithm

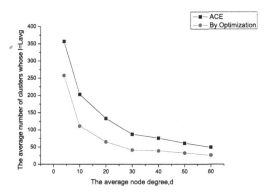

Fig. 6. Average number of clusters whose $l \leq Lavg$ of various node degrees

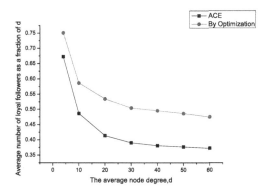

Fig. 7. Average number of loyal followers as a fraction of d

6   Concluding Remarks

In this paper, we proposed an optimizing algorithm for eliminating the redundant cluster header and minimizing the cluster overlap of ACE. The proposed algorithm contains two processes: unclustered node merging process and cluster merging process. We also introduced some methods to avoid collision. Experimental results clearly show that the optimizing could minimizing the cluster overlap efficiently.

References

1. Heinzelman, W.R., Chandrakkasan, A.: An application-specific protocol architecture for wireless microsensor networks. IEEE Transactions on wireless communications 1(4), 660–670 (2002)
2. Chan, H., Perrig, A.: ACE: An Emergent Algorithm for Highly Uniform Cluster Formation. In: Karl, H., Wolisz, A., Willig, A. (eds.) EWSN 2004. LNCS, vol. 2920, pp. 154–171. Springer, Heidelberg (2004)

3. Heinzelman, W., Chandrakasan, A., Balakrishnan, H.: Energy- efficint communication protocol for wireless micro sensor networks. In: Proceedings of the Hawaiian International Conference on Systems Science, pp. 1–10. IEEE Communication Society, Stockholm (2000)

4. Lindsey, S., Raghavenda, C.S.: PEGSIS: Power efficient GAthering in sensor Information Systems. In: Proceedings of IEEE Aerospace Conference, pp. 3-1125-3-1130. IEEE Communications Society, Stockholm (2002)

5. Manjeshwar, A., Agrawal, D.P.: TEEN: a routing protocol for enhanced efficiency in wireless sensor networks. In: 1st International Workshop on Parallel and Distributed Computing Issues in Wireless Networks and Mobile Computing, pp. 2009–2015. IEEE Computer Society, San Francisco (2001)

6. Younis, O., Fahmy, S.: Heed: A Hybrid, Energy-Efficient, Distributed Clustering Approach for Ad Hoc Sensor Networks. IEEE Trans on Mobile Computing 3(4), 366–379 (2004)

7. Handy, M.J., Hasse, M., Timmermann, D.: Lower energy adaptive clustering hierarchy with deterministic cluster-head selection. In: 4th International Workshop on Mobile and Wireless Communications Network, pp. 368–372. IEEE Communications Society, Stockholm (2002)

8. Shin, K., Abraham, A., Han, S.Y.: Self organizing sensor networks using intelligent clustering. In: Gavrilova, M.L., Gervasi, O., Kumar, V., Tan, C.J.K., Taniar, D., Laganá, A., Mun, Y., Choo, H. (eds.) ICCSA 2006. LNCS, vol. 3983, pp. 40–49. Springer, Heidelberg (2006)

9. Park, S., Shin, K., Abraham, A., Han, S.: Optimized self organized sensor networks. Sensors 7, 730–742 (2007)

10. Chan, H., Luk, M., Perrig, A.: Using clustering information for sensor network localization. In: Prasanna, V.K., Iyengar, S.S., Spirakis, P.G., Welsh, M. (eds.) DCOSS 2005. LNCS, vol. 3560, pp. 109–125. Springer, Heidelberg (2005)

11. Lin, C.R., Gerla, M.: Adaptive clustering for mobile wireless networks. IEEE J. Selected Areas Commun. 15(7), 1265–1275 (1997)

Supporting IPv6 Interaction with Wireless Sensor Networks Using NP++

Matthew Jakeman[1], Danny Hughes[1], Geoff Coulson[1], Gordon Blair[1], Steve Pink[1], and Kevin Lee[2]

[1] Computing Department, InfoLab 21, Lancaster University, Lancaster, UK. LA1 4WA
m.jakeman@lancaster.ac.uk,
{danny,geoff,gordon,pink}@comp.lancs.ac.uk
[2] School of Computer Science, University of Manchester, Manchester, UK. M13 9PL
klee@cs.man.ac.uk

Abstract. There is growing interest in exploiting standard Internet protocols such as IPv6 in wireless sensor networks. Support for IPv6 has the potential to facilitate application development, increase the flexibility of sensor node interaction, and better integrate sensor nodes into the 'Internet of things'. Unfortunately, IPv6 is poorly suited for resource-constrained environments and is particularly wasteful for typical wireless sensor network data flows. This paper presents NP++, a flexible network protocol that provides efficient mapping of IPv6 onto heterogeneous physical networks. The performance of NP++ is evaluated in the context of a deployed WSN-based flood monitoring and warning system.

Keywords: Wireless Sensor Networks, IPv6, IPHC, TSMP.

1 Introduction

The vision of nodes in wireless sensor networks (WSNs) as first class Internet entities - a part of the 'Internet of things' [1] - holds significant promise in terms of facilitating access to WSN data, facilitating the development of WSN applications, and supporting tighter integration between modeling/control facilities and WSN deployments.

In order to realize this vision, sensor nodes must interoperate with IPv6 [2]. Unfortunately, IPv6 is poorly suited to resource-constrained environments such as wireless sensor networks, where power, bandwidth and computational resources are extremely scarce. Specifically IPv6 is poorly suited for supporting typical WSN data flows as it introduces significant overhead due to its large packet headers. Existing gateway-based approaches to WSN/Internet integration limit the flexibility of interaction with sensor nodes via the Internet and increase the burden on developers who must develop using both WSN-specific protocols as well as standard IP-based protocols. NP++ addresses these problems using a layer of indirection which allows developers to write applications using a standard IPv6 *logical specification*, which is transparently mapped onto optimised *physical specifications* tailored to suit different network media and environments.

This paper introduces NP++, a flexible network protocol that uses a layer of indirection to efficiently map IPv6 onto heterogeneous network media, while offering a

Y. Li et al. (Eds.): WASA 2008, LNCS 5258, pp. 409–419, 2008.

consistent representation of IPv6 to the upper layers of the network stack and allowing WSN motes to be addressed as standard IPv6 nodes. In the paper we evaluate
NP++ in the context of a multi-network flood modeling and warning scenario [3]. In
this scenario, which is currently deployed and operational, NP++ allows direct IPv6
interaction with sensor nodes, while optimizing the protocol's performance to suit
each of the three network media employed. In a general sense, this illustrates the
power of NP++ for integrating diverse network technologies while offering a common
interface to application developers.

The remainder of this paper is structured as follows: Section 2 describes our 'Grid-
Stix' flood monitoring platform and deployment environment. Section 3 introduces
the NP++ protocol. Section 4 describes the physical specifications that are used to
optimize NP++ for the different media types used in this scenario. Section 5 provides
an initial evaluation. Section 6 places NP++ in the context of related work. Finally,
Section 7 discusses avenues of future research and concludes.

2   GridStix Flood Monitoring Platform

Each GridStix node is based on the Gumstix [4] embedded computing platform, so
named as each device is roughly the same size as a pack of gum. Despite their small-
size, each of these devices is equipped with a
400 MHz Intel XScale PXA255 CPU, 64Mb of
RAM and 16MB of flash memory. These
hardware resources support the execution of a
standard Linux kernel and Java Virtual Machine along with our Open Overlays WSN
middleware [15]. In the field, each GridStix is
connected to a variety of sensors including
pressure-based depth sensors to monitor water
levels, conductivity sensors to monitor pollution, and digital cameras which are used to
support image-based flow measurement [16].
In terms of networking, each device is
equipped with a Dust Networks mote [12],
which acts as a low-power 802.15.4 time synchronized network interface. Furthermore, a
small number of the devices are equipped with
a GPRS uplink and DVB satellite downlink for

Fig. 1. A Deployed GridStix

transmitting and receiving data from off-site. The devices are powered by solar arrays
of four $15CM^2$ 2.5W solar panels in combination with a 12V 7AH battery, which
ensures reliable operation even during the dark British winter months. To minimize
the effects of harsh weather, flooding, vandalism etc., the devices are housed in dura-
ble, water-tight containers, and all external wiring is enclosed in resilient piping. A
first-generation GridStix node is shown in Figure 1 (current versions have a larger
solar array and more resilient cable-housing).

Between 2005 and 2007, a network of 15 GridStix was deployed along a 3KM stretch of the River Ribble in North West England, and a similar deployment is currently being rolled out on the River Dee in North Wales.

3 NP++

The problem of integrating networked embedded devices, such as the nodes in a wireless sensor network, with the Internet has typically been tackled through the use of specialized gateways, as in the Arch Rock Primer Pack [14]. A gateway-based approach supports the external addressing of sensor nodes, while allowing nodes within the sensor network to use specialized protocols [13], [5] that are specifically designed for dynamic and resource constrained WSN environments. Unfortunately, a gateway-based approach has two major disadvantages. Firstly, it reduces the flexibility of interaction between sensor nodes and other Internet devices. Secondly, it increases the burden on developers of end-to-end WSN systems, who must develop using both WSN-specific protocols as well as standard IP-based protocols.

NP++ addresses these problems by using a layer of indirection which separates the *logical specification* of a network protocol, as seen by developers, from the underlying *physical specification* which defines the control information and data that are actually transmitted on the media. This approach reduces the burden on developers, who may develop applications using a single logical specification, while the underlying physical specification is transparently modified to suit different network environments. This transformation is accomplished through a *mapping function*, which translates the logical specification into one of a larger number of physical specifications. In this paper, we specifically focus on the ability of NP++ to facilitate the interoperation of WSNs with the Internet by offering a common logical specification (IPv6) to developers while at the same time tailoring the performance of this protocol to suit the underlying network using per-media physical specifications.

The physical specifications which are presented and evaluated in this paper represent just a few examples of how the use of different physical mappings can optimize NP++ for different network media. Additional examples include providing support for label switching, field ordering and error detection. In all cases, NP++ offers developers a consistent logical specification.

3.1 Naming, Addressing and Routing

NP++ uses IPv6 as its logical specification as well as its default physical specification. As naming, addressing and routing functionality are inherited from IPv6, each NP++ node has an IPv6 address along with addresses for each physical specification that requires one (e.g. the 8 bit address used in TSMP [13]). For each node in its routing table, NP++ maintains addresses for all physical specifications along with the node's logical address. When required to route a message to a given logical address, NP++ scans its routing table for a match and then uses the associated physical address to create and forward a packet using the appropriate physical specification.

3.2   Physical Mappings and Conflict Resolution

Each NP++ node maintains a list of available physical mappings, which are associated with links in order of priority. When a node joins a network, the node negotiates with its neighbours on which mapping to use. This negotiation is performed on a per-link basis and the highest priority mapping known to both nodes is selected as the physical specification. This priority-based mechanism allows the choice of just one mapping per link and thus avoids the conflicts that can arise in IP (e.g. attempting to use Network Address Translation (NAT) on an encrypted header). In order to ensure that NP++ nodes can always communicate, NP++ requires that each node also implement the default IPv6 physical specification.

In our GridStix scenario, three physical mappings are used to optimize the performance of IPv6 for each of the network media used in the scenario: the GSM uplink, DVB satellite downlink and low power on-site TSMP networking. The physical specifications used to achieve this are described in section 4.

4   Physical Specifications

As described, distinct physical specifications are used to optimize NP++ for each of the 3 network media used in our scenario. The mappings are as follows:

GSM Uplink: For this bandwidth-constrained link type, NP++ uses IP Header Compression (IPHC) [5] as its physical specification. This is capable of compressing both IPv4 and IPv6 headers. IPHC on average reduces an IPv6 packet header from 40 bytes to just 4 bytes. This leads to significant bandwidth savings and also reduces packet loss (as packet loss tends to increase as a function of packet size [6]). While the use of IPHC does not allow for enhanced IPv6 features such as extensions headers and security, the highly resource constrained nature of the GSM uplink renders these features infeasible costly.

DVB Satellite Downlink: For this high performance satellite downlink NP++ uses the default IPv6 physical mapping. This allows the features of IPv6 such as optional extensions headers, support for mobility and enhanced security to be fully exploited. Furthermore, as the satellite downlink offers relatively high throughput and low loss the overhead incurred by running IPv6 is quite acceptable.

On-site TSMP Network: In the case of the on-site 802.15.4 network, NP++ maps onto a specially developed protocol known as Peer-to-peer Time Synchronized Mesh Protocol (P-TSMP). P-TSMP builds on the core TSMP protocol [13], which is a commercial time-synchronized protocol for WSNs implemented by the Dust Networks motes [12] used in our scenario. While TSMP is efficient and has very low power requirements, it only supports the transmission of messages between motes and a centralised manager. P-TSMP extends this by adding support for peer-to-peer messaging between motes, and for network-wide broadcast. To support these features, simple routing functionality has been added to the Dust manager, and the Dust packet format has been extended as shown in Figure 2.

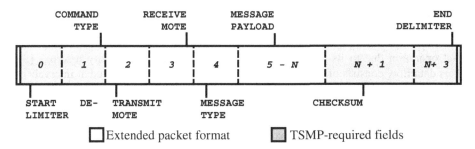

Fig. 2. P-TSMP Packet Structure

Of those fields not required by the Dust mote's implementation of TSMP, the P-TSMP packet structure is as follows:

- *Byte 2* - Address of the originating Dust mote.
- *Byte 3* - Address of the destination Dust mote.
- *Byte 4* - Message type: The extended packet format supports four message types: reliable/unreliable mote-mote messaging and reliable/unreliable broadcast.

P-TSMP thus provides flexible and low power mote-to-mote messaging with an overhead of just 8 bytes per packet. This reduction in packet size compared to IPv6 is expected to have a number of benefits including better compatibility with the smaller frame sizes of 802.15.4, increased throughput, and reduced packet loss. Furthermore, while it may appear that IPHC (described in section 4.1) has even lower packet overhead, the underlying TSMP implementation offered by the Dust motes results in an additional overhead of 5 bytes per packet (as shown in figure 2). Thus, running IPHC over TSMP would result in an overhead of 9 bytes while offering neither broadcast nor reliable routing. As with the GSM connection, the use of a low overhead physical mapping prevents use of enhanced IPv6 features, though the small frame size of the TSMP network makes this highly infeasible.

5 Evaluation

The below evaluation was performed using the GridStix implementation of NP++ at the gateway of our flood monitoring WSN. As described previously, the gateway node is connected to a GSM uplink and a DVB satellite downlink [3] as well as the on-site TSMP network. The below experiments were conducted under 'typical' gateway conditions, with satellite signal strength at 'good', GSM signal strength at 67%, and in fair weather. The on-site TSMP network was configured with its default settings: 31.25ms time-slots and a frame length of 200 slots.

Section 5.1 evaluates the extent to which NP++ can optimize IPv6 for the GSM link by reducing packet size and hence loss; Section 5.2 investigates how NP++ can optimize IPv6 for the on-site TSMP network; and Section 5.3 discusses the benefits of a unified logical specification. Throughout, optimized physical mappings are compared to the IPv6 physical specification which is used on the higher performance DVB satellite downlink.

5.1 Optimizing NP++ for GSM Using an IPHC Physical Mapping

The flood monitoring system generates a predictable upstream data flow during normal operation due to its periodic reporting of depth and conductivity readings [3]. This data flow consists of 100 bytes of data per node and is transmitted at intervals of 1 minute. When NP++ is configured to use the IPHC [5] physical mapping, the header size for TCP traffic such as sensor readings is reduced from 40 bytes to just 4 bytes - a reduction of 90%.

As the packet payloads generated during the reporting of sensor readings are relatively small (100 bytes), the IPHC physical specification results in a significant reduction in total packet size: from 140 bytes using an IPv6 physical mapping to just 104 bytes using an IPHC physical mapping (the effects of this reduction on packet loss and power consumption are explored in section 5.2 and 5.3 respectively).

In the context of the DVB satellite down-link, such optimisations are unnecessary due to the higher bandwidth and better quality of service offered by this link. Furthermore, the use of an IPv6 physical mapping allows the full flexibility of IPv6 networking to be exploited.

Research has shown that packet loss on radio links is strongly correlated with packet size [6]. We therefore specifically analyzed the relationship between packet size and loss on our GSM uplink and DVB downlink using iPerf [7]. iPerf was configured to send long sequences of UDP datagrams in sizes ranging from 10bytes to 160bytes (at intervals of 10 bytes) and the rate of packet loss was recorded. Each

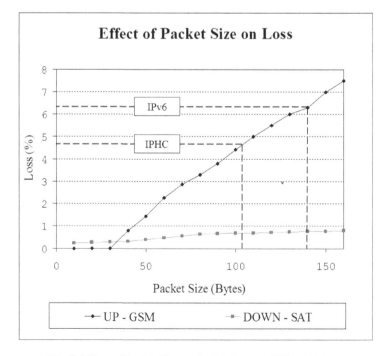

Fig. 3. Effect of Packet Size on Packet Loss on GSM uplink

experiment was repeated 10 times and the results logged. As can be seen from figure 3, there is indeed a strong correlation between packet size and packet loss.

Considering the reduction in packet size achieved using IPHC on the GSM up-link (from 140 bytes for IPv6 to 104 bytes for IPHC), we would expect packet loss to be significantly reduced: from 6.4% using IPv6 to 4.7% using IPHC - a net reduction of in packet loss of 27%. Conversely on the DVB satellite downlink, packet size has a relatively low impact on packet loss and thus the rich features of the IPv6 physical mapping may be exploited at minimal cost (Reducing packet loss also has significant implications for power consumption on the GSM connection, as discussed in Section 5.1.1).

5.1.1 Implications for Power Consumption

Power consumption is a critical factor in any WSN application and the IPHC physical mapping is expected to have a significant impact on the power consumption of the GSM connection (as the lower volume of data being transmitted means that networking hardware is not active for as long). The GSM uplink and Satellite downlink may remain physically switched on, but they will use less power as they are not active. Average power consumption figures for the GSM uplink and the DVB satellite downlink are provided in Table 1 below.

As can be seen from the table, the GSM uplink consumes significantly less power when the connection is inactive compared to when the connection is active (under 250mA compared to over 400mA). Reducing the volume of data that must be transmitted, and in turn the time period that the GSM connection is active, thus leads to significant power savings. In addition, as fewer packets are lost using the IPHC physical mapping (see section 5.2), power consumption due to packet retransmission is also minimized.

Table 1. Power Consumption

	GSM	SAT
Inactive	248 mA	806 mA
TX / RX	424 / 416 mA	849 mA

In the case of the DVB satellite downlink, there is little difference in power consumption whether the link is inactive or receiving (806mA v 849mA). This further supports our argument that an IPv6 physical mapping can be used to provide rich networking support on the satellite downlink at minimal cost in terms of packet loss, or power consumption.

5.2 Optimizing NP++ for 802.15.4 Using a TSMP Physical Mapping

Section 5.1 highlighted the benefits of using an IPHC header to reduce loss on the GSM uplink of the site gateway. This section will now investigate the benefits of using a P-TSMP mapping to minimize the number of packets transmitted via the on-site 802.15.4 network.

Each TSMP node [13] is allocated a *time-slot* (31.25ms) for packet transmission. A complete sequence of time-slots is referred to as a *frame*. By default each TSMP frame contains 200 time-slots (giving a frame length of 6,250ms). While strict scheduling makes TSMP extremely power-efficient, it results in high latency, as in the default configuration, motes transmit only one packet in each network frame. Thus, it is particularly critical that packet overhead be minimized to prevent the transmission of unnecessary packets, each of which has a high lag due to the wait for an available time-slot.

Consider the encapsulation and transmission of 100 byte sensor readings over TSMP using IPv6. TSMP packets have a maximum size of 80 bytes, of which the IPv6 header consumes 40 bytes. Thus the transmission of 100 bytes of sensor data using IPv6 requires the transmission of three IPv6 encapsulated packets over TSMP. In comparison, encapsulating sensor data using our P-TSMP packet format consumes just 3 additional bytes per packet, and thus the same 100 bytes of sensor data can be transmitted using two P-TSMP packets. This significantly reduces the latency of data transmission, from 18,750ms .to 12,500ms – a reduction of 6,250ms or 33%.

While this latency improvement derives from the data-flow pattern of this specific application, these results serve to illustrate the importance of reducing packet overhead in networks with small frame sizes or high lag. As with the IPHC physical mapping, which is used for the GSM uplink, reduction in packet size is expected to result in a significant reduction in power consumption. This is discussed in section 5.2.1.

5.2.1 Implications for Power Consumption

As previously discussed, power consumption is a critical factor in all WSN applications, and the reduction in packet transmissions that can be achieved using P-TSMP will lead to significant power savings for any application (as radios are activated less frequently). Power consumption data for the Dust motes is shown in Table 2 below [12].

Table 2. Power Consumption of Dust Motes

	Average	Maximum
Transmit	50mA	90mA
Receive	22mA	30mA
Sleep	10μA	15μA

As described in the previous section, based on the data distribution requirements of this application, transmitting sensor data using our P–TSMP physical mapping, reduces the number of packets that are transmitted during each reporting period by one third. Assuming the maximum power consumption for each state enumerated in Table 2, the default IPv6 physical mapping will result in an average power draw of 3mA, while the using the P-TSMP physical mapping results in a power draw of 2.1mA. Thus the use of the P-TSMP physical mapping is expected to increase battery life by approximately 30%.

5.3 Benefits of a Unified Logical Representation

Sections 5.1 and 5.2 have shown that through the use of specific physical mappings it is possible to optimize NP++ for various network media. In the case of our GSM uplink, the use of an IPHC physical mapping significantly reduces average packet sizes and thus loss. In the case of the on-site 802.15.4 network, the use of a P-TSMP physical mapping significantly reduces the number of transmissions and therefore power consumption.

Perhaps an even greater advantage is that, when using NP++, the developer is shielded from the complexity inherent in using multiple network protocols tailored for different environments. The application developer simply addresses nodes using standard IPv6, and NP++ efficiently maps this onto the underlying network.

By separating the physical and logical representations of a network protocol, NP++ allows the most recent advances in network protocols and network media to be exploited with no effort from application developers. Moreover, as protocol developers are expected to develop physical mappings, systems built using NP++ are expected to be of higher quality than those where application developers must also be concerned with the low-level details of different protocol implementations.

6   Related Work

The Flexible Interconnecting Protocol (FLIP) [8] provides support for heterogeneous devices and network links using a 'meta-header' which defines the fields present in the packet header. While this design is somewhat flexible, it is limited to field suppression and thus, unlike NP++, it is unable to provide additional features such as label switching, field ordering or error detection.

Braden et al [9] introduce a Role-Based Architecture (RBA) which does not use the OSI network stack. Instead, the system uses a 'heap' of role headers which interact based upon defined rules. These headers are also persistent, such that down-stream nodes are aware of previous packet treatment. While this allows for a comparable level of flexibility to NP++, it does so at the cost of considerable overhead, making it unsuitable for resource-constrained environments such as WSNs.

Pv6 over Low Power Wireless Personal Area Networks (6LowPAN) [10] allows IPv6 to be supported on highly resource-constrained networks. Specifically, 6LowPAN allows IPv6 to be supported on 802.15.4 frames which have a maximum transmission unit of just 127 octets. 6LowPAN also implements header compression, including compression of node addresses. While this approach allows easy interoperation between WSN and Internet devices, the approach is not as flexible as NP++, essentially offering a single physical mapping optimised for 802.15.4.

7   Conclusions and Future Research

The 'real-world' evaluation presented in this paper suggests that significant benefits may be achieved by using different physical specifications to tailor the performance of a unified network protocol to fit the requirements of heterogeneous data flows and network media. For example: in the case of our GSM uplink, the IPHC physical specification provides significant bandwidth and power savings while reducing packet loss. Conversely, in the case of the DVB satellite downlink the more flexible IPv6 physical specification can be used while incurring minimal cost in terms of power consumption and packet loss.

Our future research will focus on deploying our flood monitoring network as a new and larger site on the River Dee. Once operational, this will enable a more complete evaluation of our proposed NP++-based approach to WSN networking. For example, we plan to log network performance and power consumption over periods of days in order to take into account varying environmental conditions. We will also investigate the benefits of NP++ in terms of providing rich networking support between WSN monitoring facilities and off-site modeling and control facilities. Finally, we intend to investigate the potential of integrating NP++ with our Open Overlays [11] WSN middleware platform.

References

[1] The International Telecommunication Union, Internet Report: The Internet of Things, http://www.itu.int/dms_pub/itu-s/opb/pol/S-POL-IR.IT-2005-SUM-PDF-E.pdf

[2] The Internet Society Network Working Group, RFC 2460 - Internet Protocol, Version 6 (IPv6) specification, http://www.faqs.org/rfcs/rfc2460.html

[3] Hughes, D., Greenwood, P., Coulson, G., Blair, G., Pappenberger, F., Smith, P., Beven, K.: An Intelligent and Adaptable Flood Monitoring and Warning System. In: The proceedings of the 5th UK E-Science All Hands Meeting (AHM 2006), Nottingham, UK (September 2006)

[4] GumStix Embedded Computing Platform (February 2008), http://gumstix.com/

[5] Degermark, M., Nordgren, B., Pink, S.: RFC 2507 - IP Header Compression (IPHC) RFC, http://www.ietf.org/rfc/rfc2507.txt

[6] Korhonen, J., Wang, Y.: Effect of packet size on loss rate and delay in wireless links. In: The proceedings of the IEEE Wireless Communications and Networking Conference (WCNC 2005), New Orleans, USA, March 2005, vol. 3, pp. 1608–1613 (2005)

[7] NLANR/DAST, iPerf Network Measurement Tool, http://sourceforge.net/projects/iperf

[8] Solis, I., Obraczka, K., Marcos, J.: FLIP: a flexible protocol for efficient communication between heterogeneous devices. In: ISCC, pp. 100–106. IEEE Computer Society, Los Alamitos (2001)

[9] Braden, R., Faber, T., Handley, M.: From Protocol Stack to Protocol Heap: Role-Based Architecture. Computer Communication Review 33(1), 17–22 (2003)

[10] Montenegro, G., Kushalnagar, N., Hui, J., Culler, D.: RFC 4944 - IPv6 over Low Power Wireless Personal Area Networks (6LowPAN) RFC, http://www.ietf.org/rfc/rfc4944.txt

[11] Grace, P., Hughes, D., Porter, B., Blair, G., Coulson, G., Taiani, F.: Experiences with Open Overlays: A Middleware Approach to Network Heterogeneity. In: The proceedings of the European Conference on Computer Systems (EuroSys 2008), Glasgow, UK (March 2008)

[12] Dust Networks, SmartMesh XT 2135 Mote Data Sheet, http://www.dustnetworks.com/docs/M2135.pdf

[13] Dust Networks, Technical Overview of TSMP, white paper,
     http://www.dustnetworks.com/docs/TSMP_Whitepaper.pdf
[14] Rock, A.: Primer Pack:
     http://www.archrock.com/products/primer_pack_ip.php
[15] Grace, P., Hughes, D., Porter, B., Blair, G., Coulson, G., Taiani, F.: Experiences with
     Open Overlays: A Middleware Approach to Network Heterogeneity. In: The proceedings
     of the European Conference on Computer Systems (EuroSys 2008) (March 2008)
[16] Creutin, J.D., Muste, M., Bradley, A.A., Kim, S.C.: River Gauging using PIV Tech-
     niques: A Proof of Concept on The Iowa River. Kruger, A. (ed.) Journal of Hydrology,
     277, 182–194 (2003)

The Effect of Re-sampling on Incremental Nelder-Mead Simplex Algorithm: Distributed Regression in Wireless Sensor Networks

Parisa Jalili Marandi, Muharram Mansooriazdeh, and Nasrollah Moghadam Charkari

Parallel Processing Lab, Computer and Electrical Engineering Department,
Faculty of Engineering, Tarbiat Modares University, Tehran, Iran
{parisa.jalili,mansoorm,charkari}@modares.ac.ir

Abstract. Wireless sensor networks (WSNs) have been of great interest among academia and industry, due to their diverse applications in recent years. The main goal of a WSN is data collection. As the amount of the collected data increases, it would be essential to develop some techniques to analyze them. In this paper, we propose an in-network optimization algorithm based on Nelder-Mead simplex (NM simplex) to incrementally do regression analysis over distributed data. Then improve the regression accuracy by the use of re-sampling in each node. Simulation results show that the proposed algorithm not only increases the accuracy to more than that of the centralized approach, but is also more efficient in terms of communication compared to its counterparts.

Keywords: Distributed Optimization, Regression, Nelder-Mead Simplex, Re-sampling, Wireless Sensor Networks.

1 Introduction

A wireless sensor network (WSN) comprises a group of sensors with restricted capabilities. Sensors usually have low power supply, limited computational capacity and memory. The main use of WSNs is for data collection. As the amount of the collected data increases, some methods to analyze them are required [1, 2]. Machine learning approaches are good solutions, in this regard. Transmitting all the collected data to a fusion center for centrally analyzing the behavior of data and modeling it leads to a high accuracy in the final result. But, since communication capabilities of sensors are limited, this central approach significantly drains the energy of each node and decreases the life time of the network as a whole. In order to deviate with this problem, in-network approach is adapted which eliminates the need for transmitting data to the fusion center [3]. In-network processing increases local computation to prevent energy wasting through a large amount of communications required in central approach due to data collection. Based on [3] a learning problem can be converted into one of optimization which is much easier to be dealt with. Accordingly, we aim to propose an incremental optimization algorithm to do regression analysis over distributed data which should also adapt to the limitations of WSNs. Distributed optimization for WSNs based on gradient optimization has been previously studied in [1,4-5]. For the algorithm proposed in [1] a Hamiltonian cycle is set on sensors, prior to distributed

Y. Li et al. (Eds.): WASA 2008, LNCS 5258, pp. 420–431, 2008.
© Springer-Verlag Berlin Heidelberg 2008

optimization. Then, the estimate for parameter vector is transmitted from one neighboring sensor to the other and each sensor, using incremental sub-gradient optimization, adjusts the parameters. The algorithm in [4] shows that clustering the network and setting a Hamiltonian cycle within each cluster not only increases the accuracy of final parameters but also makes the algorithm more robust to failures compared to the algorithm proposed in [1]. According to this approach, parameter estimation process starts simultaneously in all the clusters, and at the end of each Hamiltonian cycle, the parameter vector is transmitted to the fusion center. Fusion center averages out received parameters and announces the final parameter vector to the user. While [4] sets a Hamiltonian cycle among nodes of each cluster, [5] sets a Hamiltonian cycle among cluster heads and adapts an approach for each sensor to transmit compressed data to the head of the cluster to which it belongs. This algorithm is much more efficient in terms of accuracy, communication cost, and network latency compared to the previously proposed gradient based algorithms. In optimization community, when the form of the objective function is known and it is differentiable, the best decision is to use first order class of optimization algorithms, where incremental sub-gradient is one of them. However, we have some reasons to apply NM simplex method to optimization problem in WSNs which has not been studied previously in the field. In this paper we first, develop an incremental version of NM simplex algorithm for WSNs, and later improve the results by the use of local re-sampling. Simulation results show that local re-sampling does really improve the accuracy of final regressor, while minimizing the communication. *Thus the main contributions of this paper are: a) to apply NM simplex rather than gradient based optimization and b) to improve the regression accuracy by local re-sampling in the context of WSNs.* The rest of this paper is organized as follows. Section 2 provides an overview of supervised learning and its application to WSNs and some basics about NM simplex optimization are also reviewed in this section. In section 3, assumptions and problem statement are stated. The motivations to use NM simplex are discussed in section 4. In section 5, we present proposed algorithm and describe its properties. Simulation results are presented in section 6. Finally, in section 7 we conclude the paper and state some of future works.

2 Preliminaries

In this section basic knowledge required to understand the proposed algorithm are provided.

2.1 Supervised Learning and Its Application to WSNs

According to [6], Supervised, Semi-supervised and Unsupervised are three types of learning. Supervised learning, being the least intelligent, requires a labeled data set indicated as Eq. (1).

$$GD = \{(a_1, b_1), \dots, (a_N, b_N)\}$$

$$, \tag{1}$$

where $A = \{a_k\}_{k=1}^N$ and $B = \{b_k\}_{k=1}^N$ are feature and label sets, respectively. Features describe data and labels indicate the class to which data belongs. The goal of supervised learning is to map A to B by a function like $f : A \rightarrow B$ such that $b = f(a)$. In other words, this type of learning aims to learn f using labeled data set, where a_k is usually a vector by itself. This means that instead of one feature, a set of features describes data. There are several algorithms for supervised learning one of which is regression, which fits a model to existing data. For further information about regression refer to [7]. Sensors collect lots of data spatially and temporally. In order to gain benefit of the collected data, there must be some analyzing methods. If we consider these data as a kind of labeled data then supervised learning can easily be applied. Throughout this paper, we will consider a network of sensors distributed in an environment which can measure temperature temporally and localize themselves using an existing efficient localization algorithm such as [8]. Here the labeled dataset includes time and location as features and temperature as the label. Thus supervised learning has to discover the function which given the time and the location will predict the temperature with least possible error.

2.2 Nelder-Mead Simplex

NM simplex which was first proposed in 1965 [9] is a local optimization algorithm. There are some works done to free NM simplex from local optima such as [10]. NM simplex employs a regular pattern of points in the search space sequentially to obtain the optimizer. Computationally it is relatively uncomplicated, hence easy to implement and quick to debug [11]. One of the major drawbacks of NM simplex is the lack of convergence proof. Further research, study and experimental results are expected to help understand its behavior. Details of NM simplex algorithm implemented in the experiments of this study are the same as [12] where for termination criterion the approach proposed in [13] is employed.

3 Assumptions and Problem Statement

This section introduces the assumptions and outlines the problem more precisely.

3.1 Assumptions

The following assumptions are considered throughout the paper:

1. There are n sensors as $S = \{s_1, \dots, s_n\}$, each of which has collected m data.
2. i, j indices are used to refer to i^{th} sensor and j^{th} data in an arbitrary sensor, respectively ($i \in \{1, \dots, n\}$, $j \in \{1, \dots, m\}$). Thus (a_{ij}, b_{ij}) indicates j^{th} data from i^{th} sensor.
3. Sensors are distributed in a bi-dimensional area. Coordinates of s_i are indicated by x_i, y_i.

4. Three features and one label are chosen for describing data such that $a_{i,j} = [x_i, y_i, time_{i,j}]$ and $b_{i,j} = temperature_{i,j}$, where $time_{i,j}$ and $temperature_{i,j}$ indicate the time of jth measurement and j^{th} temperature in s_i, respectively.

5. Local dataset of s_i is indicated by LD_i, where $|LD_i| = m$.

6. Global dataset, which is the dataset that could be obtained if transmission over long distances was possible, is denoted by GD, where $GD = \cup_{i=1}^{n}(LD_i)$ and $|GD| = N$, where $N = n \times m$.

7. A Hamiltonian path is set among nodes (a distributed algorithm to set a Hamiltonian cycle is described in [14]). This is the routing scheme used in [1]. We selected it because of its simplicity and ability to clarify the main points of the proposed algorithm. Fig. 1 depicts this path. Here we have set a Hamiltonian path rather than a Hamiltonian cycle over the nodes. As every such a cycle can be converted to a Hamiltonian path by removing one of its edges, so the algorithm in [14] is applicable.

8. We assume that s_1 and s_n are the head and the tail nodes of the Hamiltonian path, respectively.

9. As NM simplex is a heuristic method [11], it builds several simplexes to reach the optimizer. The number of local simplexes formed in s_i, which might be different from one sensor to another, and depends on LD_i is denoted by c_i.

10. Before learning starts, a query dissemination process distributes to all the sensors in the network the user's desired model to fit data. We have followed [15] in fitting a model to data, which suggests some polynomial models among which we chose 'Linear space and quadratic time' which will be called 'quadratic' in the remaining of the paper.

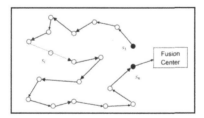

Fig. 1. A Hamiltonian path over the network nodes

3.2 Problem Statement

The goal of the proposed algorithm is to incrementally fit a model to the collected data. Considering the quadratic modeling of data from section 3.1-Assumption 10, where temperature is to be stated in terms of location and time of measurements, the model is as Eq. (2)

$$F(x, y, time) = R[1] \times (x) + R[2] \times (y) + R[3] \times (time)^2 + R[4] \times (time) + R[5] \quad (2)$$

in which R is a vector of unknown constants. Given a set of basis functions as $(1, time, time^2, x, y)$ the algorithm aims to estimate their coefficients such that the final model fits data with less possible error (Similar to the approach used in [15]). Based on [1, 3], the learning problem of F can be converted to an optimization problem to compute R, such that applying least-square error Eq. (3) is minimized:

$$G(R) = \frac{1}{n}\sum_{i=1}^{n}\frac{1}{m}\sum_{j=1}^{m}\left(R[1] \times (x_i) + R[2] \times (y_i) + R[3] \times (time_{i,j})^2 + R[4] \times (time_{i,j}) + R[5] - temperature_{i,j}\right)^2 \tag{3}$$

That is to say, we would like to determine R in a way that the final model fits all the data with the least possible error. Here, optimization is the same as minimization. So, for quadratic modeling the problem of learning is converted into a minimization problem with five parameters. Although least-square error is used, other error functions which are less sensitive to noise might be applied. As mentioned previously in section 1, it is impossible or at least difficult to centrally compute G, as Eq. (3) is highly dependent on individual data and their transmission to fusion center is energy-consuming. So, it is not feasible to have this formula centrally, but distributed. In fact, there are n sub formulas in the form of Eq. (4):

$$g_i(R) = \frac{1}{m}\sum_{j=1}^{m}\left(R[1] \times (x_i) + R[2] \times (y_i) + R[3] \times (time_{i,j})^2 + R[4] \times (time_{i,j}) + R[5] - temperature_{i,j}\right)^2 \tag{4}$$

which when added up give the central formula of Eq. (3). Following this consideration, Eq. (3) is rewritten as Eq. (5):

$$G(R) = \frac{1}{n}\sum_{i=1}^{n}g_i(R) \tag{5}$$

where $g_i : \mathfrak{R}^L \to \mathfrak{R}$, $G : \mathfrak{R}^L \to \mathfrak{R}$ and L, the length of R, is the number of parameters to be estimated (for quadratic modeling $L = 5$). So, the goal of the proposed algorithm is to do the regression analysis by fitting a pre-specified model to the existing data in a distributed manner and to compute the final parameters as a vector R_G $(|R|_G = L)$.

4   The Motivation for the Proposed Algorithm

The reason to use gradient methods in the previous works, as mentioned in section 1, was the fact that when objective function is in hand, having the formula of its first derivative is inevitable. Thus, there is a compelling reason to apply gradient-based optimization. But, examining the previous works revealed some deficiencies that made us to apply another optimization algorithm to overcome those defects. Here we have listed the shortcomings encountered:

1. For the incremental sub-gradient method to work, there must be an estimate of Θ, a non-empty, closed, and convex subset of $\Re^L$ in which optimizer is expected to exist [1, 4]. Determining such a subset prior to algorithm execution seems to be a difficult job and distributed nature of data makes it even worse.
2. If in any stage of the algorithm execution in any sensor, the estimate falls out of Θ, a projection must be done to keep the value in the boundary. The experiments done in this study showed that the final results highly depend on the projection procedure.
3. In incremental gradient method, each sensor modifies parameters received from its neighbor, and thus, at the end of cycle, parameters suffer from an error. Experiments show that the obtained accuracy for our objective function is far from the central results. It must be stated that the behavior of optimization methods depends on the objective function and hence, inaccurate results of one method over a special function does not label it as a non-efficient method.
4. When the objective function is quadratic, [1] estimates that often one cycle suffices to find the optimizer with a low error. However, their experiments showed that, in one special function, 45 cycles led to the answer, which means large energy consumption.

Based on the deficiencies mentioned, it is desired to propose an algorithm which reduces the final error and frees the user or programmer from specifying Θ as well as the projection procedure. Reduction of communication in the expense of computation increase is another goal followed. NM simplex is selected to fulfill these desires. One of the reasons for applying NM simplex rather than any other optimization method was its popularity among practitioners, despite the absence of any general proof for its convergence. So, further experiments and mathematical analyses will be helpful to discover the nature of NM simplex method more than the current status. The other main reason to choose NM simplex was its computationally light procedure as stated in section 2.2, which is consistent with sensors limited computational capacity.

5 Proposed Algorithm

Based on fundamentals of NM simplex optimization described in section 2.2 and the motivations of section 4, in this section we describe the proposed algorithm.

5.1 IS: Incremental NM Simplex

Incremental NM Simplex algorithm, IS henceforth, is illustrated in Fig. 2. Starting from the first sensor on the path, each sensor runs a NM simplex algorithm on the local data and sends the computed parameters to the neighboring sensor. The neighboring sensor uses received parameters as the start point for its local simplex execution. In step II of Fig. 2 the notion of R_{i,c_i} indicates the coefficients of the final local regressor in s_i. As mentioned in section 3.1-Assumption 9, there are c_i locally built simplexes in s_i numbered through 1 to c_i, where c_i^{th} simplex leads to the final local optimizer. At the end of the algorithm, s_n includes $R_G = R_{n,c_n}$.

```
procedure IS

For i = 1, ..., n: sᵢ does the followings:

    I.     Computes gᵢ , the same as Eq. (4), based on LDᵢ .
    II.    Runs a local NM simplex, the same as section 2.2, over LDᵢ ,
           where gᵢ is the local objective function. (Starting point for sᵢ's
           local simplex algorithm is Rᵢ,₀ = Rᵢ₋₁,cᵢ₋₁ , which indicates
           coefficients of the final regressor in sᵢ₋₁ , and R₁,₀ = R₀, is any
           arbitrary vector in ℜ ).
           If (i ≠ n)
    III.   Transmits Rᵢ,cᵢ to sᵢ₊₁ .

end procedure.
```

Fig. 2. Steps of Incremental NM Simplex (IS) algorithm

5.2 'IS with Re-sampling': Incremental NM Simplex Based on Re-sampling

In the IS algorithm of section 5.1, a sensor has no access to previous nodes datasets. The only information conveyed from previous nodes is reflected on the finally

```
procedure IS + Re-Sampling

For i = 1, ..., n: sᵢ does the followings:

           If (i ≠ 1)
    I.     Generates m more data based on:
               1.   Rᵢ₋₁,cᵢ₋₁,
               2.   timeⱼ(jϵ{1, ..., m}),
               3.   (xᵢ₋₁, yᵢ₋₁).
           , and appends them to LDᵢ . The new local dataset is called (RS + LD)ᵢ ,
           where |(RS + LD)ᵢ| = 2m.
    II.    Computes gᵢ, the same as Eq. (4), based on
               1.   LDᵢ if (i = 1)
               2.   (RS + LD)ᵢ if (i > 1)
    III.   Runs a local NM simplex the same as section 2.2 over local dataset.
           (Starting point for sᵢ's local simplex algorithm is Rᵢ,₀ = Rᵢ₋₁,cᵢ₋₁ , which
           indicates coefficients of the final regressor in sᵢ₋₁ , and R₁,₀ = R₀ is
           any arbitrary vector in ℜ ).

           If (i ≠ 1)

    IV.    Transmits Rᵢ,cᵢ as well as (xᵢ, yᵢ) to sᵢ₊₁ .

end procedure
```

Fig. 3. Steps of IS with Re-Sampling (the proposed algorithm)

calculated coefficients of immediate previous sensor's regressor, which is used as the starting point for local simplex in the current node. On the other hand central approach is believed to be more accurate in terms of globally computed regressor in that, the dataset it operates on is more integrated and diverse. Therefore one reason that makes incrementally computed regressors, as that of section 5.1 and also those gradient based counterparts, to suffer from error is the small local dataset of individual nodes. Accordingly if each sensor could have a more perfect dataset, then the computed final local regressors and also the final global regressor would be more accurate. However certain limitations specific to WSNs do not allow for transmission of data. Thus another approach is adapted here which simulates this transmission. This approach is re-sampling. In this approach, current sensor will re generate the previous sensors datasets based on the coefficients received from the immediate previous sensor on the path. Receiver sensor, using its own time epochs and previous sensor's location and regressor, $B_{i-1}c_{i-1}$, generates m additional data and appends them to its own local dataset. In exception to the s_1, all the nodes apply re-sampling, until s_n includes $2m$ data which is actually a brief representation of CD. The proposed algorithm based on re-sampling is depicted in Fig. 3 more precisely. The procedure is the same as IS except for the addition of re-sampling step. Although the idea is simple, it leads in good results as explained in section 6.

6   Experiments

We used the publically available Intel Lab dataset which contains data collected from 54 sensors deployed in the Intel Berkley Research Lab. Mica2Dot sensors with weather boards has collected time stamped topology information, along with humidity, temperature, light and voltage values once every 31 seconds [16]. Fig 4 depicts relation between temperature and time epochs for an arbitrary sensor. All the sensors in the network show the same behavior. It is evident from the figure that except some noisy measurements, a polynomial model, repeated over time intervals, relates temperature to time epochs. Here we evaluate algorithms over such an interval which is randomly selected.   The simulation was run over some distinct intervals and the

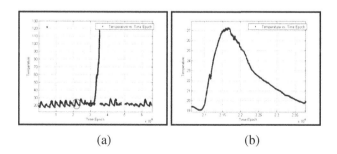

(a)   (b)

Fig. 4. (a) Illustration of temperature variation over time for a randomly selected sensor. (b) Illustration of temperature readings over a randomly selected time interval which is also shown by an oval in (a).

results were almost similar, leading to the same conclusions. $n = 48$ sensors which contained uniformly distributed measurements over the interval were selected. For each sensor $m = 20$ data were selected over the interval. Obviously a single sensor's measured temperatures are constantly related to its location. But for multiple sensors distributed over an area, temperature varies with changes in location. Thus the intended model is comprised of some basis functions as $(1, time, time^2, x, y)$ which is also shown in Eq. 2 of section 3.2. Additional basis functions such as $time^3, time^4 \ldots$ might improve the regression accuracy. But the important is the relative accuracy of different algorithms, which is independent of the fitting model and depends on the nature of the algorithms applied.

6.1 Accuracy

Fig. 5 (a) depicts Root Mean Square error (RMS) of regressors obtained from IS, 'IS with Re-Sampling', Incremental Gradient and Centralized approach. Results shown for Incremental Gradient are for one pass over the network. As it was repeated for more passes, minor improvements were achieved in contrast to consumed energy. A better accuracy was achieved for 36 more passes over the network, and improved very little after that, which was yet far from that of the others. As it is evident from the figures 'IS with Re-Sampling' is superior to its counterparts in terms of accuracy. Fig. 5 (b) depicts the accuracy of IS with Re-Sampling and Centralized algorithm. As it is expected in both methods, except in some sensors, the overall RMS is decreasing as parameters reach the last sensor, which means that dataset is growing and more data is included.

When the dataset of abnormally behaving sensors were examined closely, it was realized that for these sensors, measurements distribution over the time interval was not as uniform as the others (due to missing data). Application of local re-sampling the way explained in section 5.2 causes the final regressor's RMS to fall even below

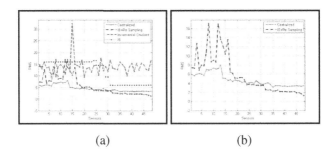

(a)   (b)

Fig. 5. (a) Depicts RMS of the final regressor for Incremental Gradient, Centralized approach, IS, and 'IS with Re-Sampling', As it is evident from the curves 'IS with Re-Sampling' has the least RMS compared to its counterparts. (b) Depicts RMS of the 'IS with Re-Sampling' and the Centralized approach. For the Centralized curve, RMS in s_i is calculated for the regressor trained over $\bigcup_{k=1}^{i} LD_k$.

that of the Centralized approach. Theoretically, following motives go in prove of the observed increase in final accuracy: 1) Regenerating data according to the previous sensor's regressor, rather than considering actual data. 2) Elimination of "new-old data interference" phenomenon [17]. It appears when a sequential training is in progress and the model changes it's parameters in the favor of the new data. But if we could make it possible for all the data to be present at the same time, the problem would be solved. Thanks to local re-sampling a somehow similar condition is provided here. The curve of IS in Fig. 5 (a) is also more stable than that of the Incremental Gradient.

6.2 Communication Requirements

There is one parameter transmitted among nodes in IS: Coefficients of a locally obtained regressor which is a vector of size L. And there are two parameters transmitted among nodes in 'IS with Re-Sampling': 1) Coefficients of a locally obtained regressor, which is a vector of size L. 2) Sensor location, which includes two doubles as x, y. Hence L parameters in IS and $L + 2$ parameters in 'IS with Re-Sampling' are transmitted between two adjacent nodes. And there is one parameter transmitted in Incremental Gradient: Coefficients of a locally obtained regressor, which is a vector of size L. Also at the end of each of the mentioned algorithms there is a transmission for the final regressor from s_n to the fusion center which is a vector of size L. Let's denote the number of passes over the network for Incremental Gradient algorithm by P. In the central approach there are N vectors transmitted from sensors to the fusion center each of which has a size of 3 for assumed labeled dataset as mentioned in section 2.1. Following [18] and considering the case where n nodes are uniformly distributed in a unit square, the average distance between two successive nodes over a Hamiltonian path is: $O(\sqrt{\log n/n})$ Whereas in the Centralized approach the average distance between a sensor and the fusion center is 1 over the unite square. Based on these considerations Table 1 shows communication order of the four algorithms. If $P \gg 1$ and $L \gg 1$ then $P \times L \geq (L + 2) \gg L$, thus IS and 'IS with Re-Sampling' are

Table 1. Communication order of Centralized approach, Incremental Gradient (IG), IS, IS with Re-Sampling. P is the number of passes in incremental gradient algorithm to reach an optimal solution.

Algorithm	Communication Cost
Centralized Approach	$O(3nn) = O(nn)$
Incremental Gradient	$O\left(P \times L \times \sqrt{\log^2 n/n}\right)$
Incremental NM Simplex	$O\left((L) \times \sqrt{\log^2 n/n}\right)$
Incremental NM Simplex + Re-Sampling	$O\left((L + 2) \times \sqrt{\log^2 n/n}\right)$

more efficient in terms of communication than Incremental Gradient. And as usually $l \ll m$, IS, 'IS with Re-Sampling' and Incremental Gradient are much more efficient than the Centralized approach.

7 Conclusions

In this paper we proposed an in-network optimization technique for distributed regression in wireless sensor networks. To overcome deficiencies of incremental gradient optimization, NM simplex algorithm was applied and an incremental version of it was developed. Although, the accuracy of Incremental NM simplex algorithm was higher than that of the incremental gradient, yet improvements were needed. Hence local re-sampling was applied, and the global accuracy did really improve. Experiments also illustrated the actual effect of re-sampling in improving the accuracy. Efficiency of proposed algorithm has also been analyzed from the point of communication. The conclusion is that, the proposed algorithm is more efficient in terms of accuracy and communication cost compared to its gradient based predecessors and also central approach. We have used the least-square error for converting regression to optimization problem; other error functions which are more robust to noise might be applied. Clustering the network should also improve the results. Other optimization algorithms rather than simplex should be considered, as well. Examining the evolutionary algorithms and comparing their performance with that of this paper is left for a later time.

Acknowledgements. The authors wish to thank Iran Telecommunication Research center (ITRC) for partial funding of this research and Intel researchers for their hard effort in data collection.

References

1. Rabbat, M., Nowak, R.: Distributed optimization in sensor networks. In: International Symposium on information processing in sensor networks. ACM Press, Berkley (2004)
2. Wang, B., He, Z.: Distributed Optimization over Wireless Sensor Networks using Swarm Intelligence. In: IEEE International Symposium on Circuits and Systems, pp. 2502–2505 (2005)
3. Predd, J.B., Kulkarni, S.R., Poor, H.V.: Distributed Learning in Wireless Sensor Networks. J. Signal Processing 23, 56–69 (2006)
4. Son, S.H., Chiang, M., Kulkarni, S.R., Schwartz, S.C.: The value of clustering in distributed estimation for sensor networks. In: Proceedings of International Conference on Wireless Networks, Communications and Mobile Computing, vol. 2, pp. 969–974. IEEE, Maui (2005)
5. Charkari, N.M., Marandi, P.J.: Distributed Regression based on gradient optimization in Wireless sensor networks. In: Proceedings of first Iranian Data Mining Conference, Tehran, Iran (2007)
6. Chapelle, O., Scholkopf, B., Zien, A.: Semi Supervised Learning. MIT Press, Cambridge (2006)
7. Draper, N.R., Smith, H.: Applied Regression Analysis. Wiley Press, Chichester (1998)

8. Langendoen, K., Reijers, N.: Distributed localization in wireless sensor networks: a quantitative comparison. J. Computer and Telecommunications Networking, vol. 43, pp. 499–518 (2003)

9. Nelder, J.A., Mead, R.: A simplex method for function minimization. J. Computer 7, 308–313 (1965)

10. Pedroso, J.P.: Simple Metaheuristics Using the Simplex Algorithm for Non-linear Programming. In: Stützle, T., Birattari, M., H. Hoos, H. (eds.) SLS 2007. LNCS, vol. 4638, pp. 217–221. Springer, Heidelberg (2007)

11. Reklaitis, G.V., Ravindran, A., Ragsdell, K.M.: Engineering Optimization: Methods and Applications. John Wiley Press, Chichester (1983)

12. Lagarias, J.C., Reeds, J.A., Wright, M.H., Wright, P.E.: Convergence properties of the Nelder-Mead simplex method in low dimensions. SIAM J. Optima 9, 112–147 (1998)

13. Padmanabhan, V., Rhinehart, R.R.: A Novel Termination Criterion for Optimization. In: Proceedings of the Americal Control Conference, Portland, OR, USA, vol. 4, pp. 2281–2286 (2005)

14. Petit, J.: Hamiltonian cycles in faulty random geometric networks. In: Proceedings of International Workshop on Approximation and Randomization Algorithms in Communication Networks, BRICS Aarhus, Denmark (2001)

15. Guestrin, C., Bodi, P., Thibau, R., Paskin, M., Madde, S.: Distributed regression: An efficient framework for modeling sensor network data. In: Proceedings of third international symposium on Information processing in sensor networks, pp. 1–10. ACM Press, Berkeley (2004)

16. http://berkeley.intel-research.net/labdata/

17. Schaal, S.: Nonparametric Regression for Learning. In: Proceedings of the Conference on Prerational Intelligence- Adaptive and Learning Behavior, Bielefeld, Germany (1994)

18. Rabbat, M., Nowak, R.: Quantized Incremental Algorithms for Distributed Optimization. IEEE J. Sel Areas Commun. 23(4), 798–808 (2005)

C-kNN Query Processing in Object Tracking Sensor Networks

Jinghua Zhu[*], Jianzhong Li, Jizhou Luo, Wei Zhang, and Hongzhi Wang

School of Computer Science & Technology
Harbin Institute of Technology, 150001, Harbin, China
{zhujinghua,lijzh,luojizhou,weizhang,hongzhi}@hit.edu.cn

Abstract. Wireless sensor networks (WSNs) are being developed for a variety of applications. Continuous k nearest neighbors (C-kNN) query is an essential class of spatial query in object tracking applications. Due to the limited power of individual node, energy is the most critical resource in sensor networks. In order to always report the up-to-date results, a centralized solution requires the transmission of a large number of location update messages. Intuitively, current information is necessary only for objects that may influence some query results. Motivated by this observation, we propose a threshold-based C-kNN search algorithm with the minimal message transmissions. The key idea is to set thresholds for moving objects corresponding to each query so that only the location updates which affect the final results are transmitted. The proposed method can be used with multiple, static or moving queries. The experiments results show the effectiveness and efficiency of our approach in terms of energy and latency.

Keywords: Wireless sensor networks, Moving object tracking, C-kNN query processing, Localized algorithm.

1 Introduction

With the recent advancements in micro-electromechanical-systems (MEMS) related technology, it has now become feasible to manufacture low power sensors that integrate detection of infrared radiation, heat, sound, vibration, and magnetism together with on-chip intelligence and wireless communication [1]. Progress in this area is significant for the wide use of sensor networks in applications such as environmental and habitat monitoring, civil engineering and moving object tracking [2] etc.

K-nearest neighbor (k-NN) query is one of the fundamental kinds of queries in spatial-temporal databases. A k-NN query finds the k neighbors that are nearest to the query location. A continuous k-NN (C-kNN) query over a set of moving objects is a k-NN query that runs continuously and updates the query result whenever the movement

---

[*] This work is partly supported by the National Grand Fundamental Research 973 Program of China under Grant No. 2006CB303000,the Key Program of the National Natural Science Foundation of China under Grant No.60533110,and No.60473075, Program for New Century Excellent Talents in University under Grant NCET-05-0333, Heilongjiang Province Fund For Young Scholars under Grant QC06C033.

Y. Li et al. (Eds.): WASA 2008, LNCS 5258, pp. 432–443, 2008.

of the objects causes a change to the query's result. C-kNN query has many interesting applications such as surrounding monitoring, object tracking and location-based services. In this paper we focus on efficient monitoring for C-kNN queries in object tracking sensor networks.

In the context of database system, there has already been an extensive work on efficient execution of C-kNN query. Most of these work focus on various index structures based on R-tree. However, these centralized methods can not be directly used in sensor networks due to the followings: 1) sensor networks have strict resources constraints (CPU, memory, energy, bandwidth), centralized methods are not suitable for sensor networks due to their larger computational and communication requirements. 2) in sensor network, any node should be able to inject a query to the system. 3) sensor networks are deployed in a large adverse condition, it is not feasible for a human to set up and maintain the network. To sum up, decentralized version of spatial query processing method is needed for sensor network which would be possible to contact only the relevant nodes for the execution of a spatial query and hence achieve minimal energy consumption.

In this paper, we propose a threshold-based algorithm that can efficiently monitor C-kNN query in-network. Nodes in sensor network are organized into grid cells. Index node (I-Node) in each cell is used to store/index object locations and queries information. Such localized schema avoids transmitting large location information by multi-hop to the base station. The processing of a C-kNN query can be divided into two phases: initial processing and continuous update. Initial processing takes the query as a snapshot kNN query and finds its initial kNN result. Then in the continuous update phase, the query's result is updated whenever the moving objects' location update messages cause a change to its result. Intuitively, although in practical applications there exist numerous objects that move with arbitrary velocities toward arbitrary directions, we only care about the ones that may influence some query (i.e., they may be included in the nearest neighbor set of some queries). For the rest of the objects, we do not need up-to-date information. Motivated by this, we propose a threshold-based algorithm to incrementally maintain the query results. The algorithm set up thresholds for objects in the initial kNN result corresponding to each query. The kNN result do not need to be updated unless some object's new location violate its thresholds. Such method can reduce a lot of unnecessary message transmission and thus prolong network lifetime. Since both the objects and the queries may move during the query period, we also consider how to update the kNN result when query move. We conduct a series of experiments to evaluate the performance of our algorithm and the results show that our method is effective and efficient in terms of energy saving and query respond time.

2 Related Works

Answering k nearest neighbor queries is a classical database problem. Most methods use indices built on the data to assist the kNN search. Perhaps the most widely used algorithm is the branch-and-bound algorithm based on R-tree. Recently, a number of studies have explored in-network kNN query processing techniques for sensor networks. M. Demirbas et al. [3] proposed a decentralized R-tree index structure called peer-tree and a kNN query processing algorithm that can minimize the total energy consumption and response time based on the peer tree. KPT [4] is proposed to handle the kNN query without fixed indexing. J. Winter *et al.* [5] proposed two in-network kNN query processing algorithm called GRT and KBT suitable for static and dynamic network respectively. Lee *et al.* [6] proposed an algorithm to solve the same problem. Wu *et al.* [7] proposed a maintenance-fee, itinerary-based approach called DIKNN for locating the k nearest sensor nodes in mobile sensor networks where the locations of sensor nodes usually change over time.

Recently, some grid-based methods are explored in continuous monitoring of kNN queries. Examples include YPK-CNN [8] and CPM [9]. These methods assume that there is a centralized repository to store all object locations and all location updates are simply reported to the centralized repository.

3   Preliminaries

3.1   Problem Statement

Given a query q on a set of moving objects O, the task is to ensure that the query's result set O', which is a subset of O, always satisfies the following conditions with minimal energy consumption:

$$|O'| = k \text{ and } \forall o \in (O\text{-}O'), \text{dist}(q,o) \geq \text{Max } \{\text{dist}(q,o')|o' \in O'\}$$

The first condition ensures that query's result set contains k objects, and the second condition ensures that these $k$objects are the $k$nearest ones to q.

3.2   System Assumption

We assume sensor network is deployed in a two-dimensional region and mobile objects freely move in and out of the region. The node density is high enough to grantee the connectivity. Each sensor node not only is location-aware through GPS or other localization algorithms, but also aware of the locations of its neighbors through message exchange. Sensor nodes can detect moving objects within their sensing range and sample their locations periodically. Objects being tracked are identifiable. Instead of sending all collected location data to a central repository, we propose to store them locally at the detecting nodes. A continuous kNN query can be issued by any sensor node which is called the query initial node (Q-node) instead of by one or more stationary access points in the networks.

To support energy efficient C-kNN query processing over moving objects in wireless sensor network, the grid structure has been adopted in this paper. The whole sensor network is divided into a number of grid cells. As shown in Figure 1, each grid cell is a square of size $\alpha \times \alpha$. The sensor node closest to the centroid of a grid cell is called a *grid index node* (*I-node*). Moving objects are indexed in the corresponding *I-node* according to their locations. Each *I-node* has an object list that contains the objects information that fall in this cell. It is also responsible for receiving query and/or sending result message from *Q-node* and the other *I-nodes*, broadcasting probe location update message to those nodes belonging to it and collecting these location updates.

When *Q-node* gets a new *C-kNN* query, the query is first processed as a snapshot query, then its result is continuously updated based on the location update messages from *I-node*. These two steps are called initial *k*NN query processing and continuous maintenance. The objective of the first step is to find the initial *k* nearest neighbors for this query. The next section will introduce the initial query process in detail. Since communication energy consumption dominates the whole sensor network energy consumption, an efficient *C-kNN* query algorithm should minimize the total amount of data transmitted. We propose a threshold-based algorithm which avoids unnecessary and redundant searching when updating a query's result in section 4.

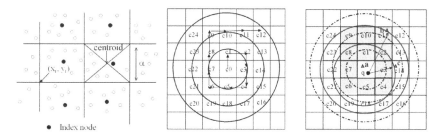

Fig. 1. Grid Structure   **Fig. 2.** Circle Search Method   **Fig. 3.** Initial *k*NN search

3.3   Initial kNN Query Processing

The task of initial processing of a *C-kNN* query is to find the query's initial *k*NN set. It proceeds in two phases: (i) *coarse search* and (ii) *refined search*. The purpose of coarse search is to find *boundary object* and define the search space.

boundary object: Let O be the set of objects detected by coarse search and $|O| \geq k$. *The boundary object* o_b *is the object that satisfying:*
$$\{o_b \in O \mid o' \in O - o_b, dist(o_b, q) \geq dist(o', q)\}.$$

search space: A circle centered at query point with radius of $dist(o_b, q)$.

In coarse search, the query message is routed from *Q-node* to the nearest *I-node* denoted as I_0 by routing protocol, then those *I-nodes* surrounding I_0 are visited by message passing until at least *k* objects are collected. A search space is defined based on the location of the boundary object to guarantee that it includes all sensor nodes possibly detecting an object closer to the query point than the boundary object. During the refined search, the *I-nodes* in the search space that are not yet visited in the coarse search are visited to locate the *k* nearest objects. Finally, the query result is routed back to *Q-node*.

Now, we discuss the coarse search and the refined search in detail.

Coarse Search. The search is divided into rounds. In each round i, the unvisited grid cells intersecting with the circle centered at the centroid of I_0 and with a radius of $i \cdot \alpha$ are visited in clockwise order (see Figure 2). This is done by sequentially passing a message from the grid index node of one cell to that of another, e.g. c0→c1→c2→c3...→c8. The message contains the query ID, location, number of nearest neighbors the query wants to find, and the time period during which the query should be continuously running. Note that given the location of the query, each *I-node* can determine autonomously which grid cell to visit next. The coarse search completes when the number of collected objects is no less than k. Among these objects, the kth object closest to the query point q is chosen as the boundary object. The search space is then defined as a circle centered at q and with a radius of the distance between the boundary object and q.

Algorithm 1: Coarse Search

Input: (1) query ID q_{id}, (2) query location q_{loc}, and (3) number of
       nearest neighbors k
Output: The set of k nearest moving objects
1: $i = 0, RSet = NULL, NUM = 0$
2: **while** $NUM < k$ **do**
3:     $R = i \cdot \alpha$
4:     Find the nearest cell I_0 to q
5:     $SearchList = Cells\ intersect\ with\ or\ in\ Circle(I_0, R)$
6:     **while** $NUM < k \& SearchList \neq NULL$ **do**
7:        Check a cell c from SearchList
8:        **if** Find an object o in cell c **then**
9:           $NUM = NUM + 1;$
10:          Put o into RSet;
11:        **if** $NUM = k$ **then**
12:          Return RSet;
13:        SearchList = SearchList - c
14:        **if** $SearchList = NULL$ **then**
15:          i=i+1

Refined Search. In refined search, a *search list* is given by all grid cells within or intersecting with the search circle, excluding those already visited in the coarse search. The query message passed among the grid cells in the refined search contains the search list, the locations of the k recorded objects, and the query point q. When a grid cell c receives the query message, it first removes c from the search list. After sending a probe message and collecting object locations from the other sensor nodes in c, one of the following three cases can occur: (i) no object is detected by any sensor node in c; (ii) all objects detected are further away from the query point q than the boundary object; (iii) at least one object detected is closer to q than the boundary object. In cases (i) and (ii), the search list and the objects recorded in the message do not change. In case (iii), the detected objects nearer to q than the boundary object are used to update the k nearest objects recorded in the message. Meanwhile, the boundary object is updated as the new kth nearest object and the search circle is shrunk accordingly. The search list is then updated by removing all grid cells outside the new search circle. On finishing with a grid cell c, the query message is routed to the cell on the search list that is closest to c. The refined search continues until the search list becomes empty. On completion of the refined search, the message is routed to I_0 and the locations of k recorded objects are returned to the user as the query result.

Figure 3 shows an example of 2NN query processing. The grid cells in shadow are visited in the coarse search. Suppose the boundary object b is found in grid cell c_{11}. Object b determines the search circle (shown by the outer solid circle in Figure 3) and derives the set of grid cells in the search list including: c12-c24, c32-c35, and c37-c40. The query message is passed among the *I*-nodes of grid cells in the search list, and the object locations are collected. Suppose that at cell c14, a nearer boundary object c□is found. Then, the search circle is shrunk accordingly. The circle centered at q and with radius d_{qc} in Figure 3 is the new search circle. The grid cells c15, c17, c18 are now the only three unvisited grid cells left in the revised search list. The refined search completes when the search list becomes empty. The final result of 2NN are {a,c}.

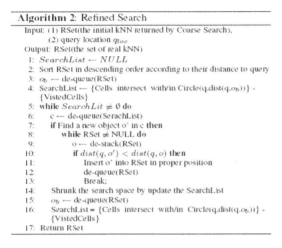

```
Algorithm 2: Refined Search

Input: (1) RSet(the initial kNN returned by Coarse Search),
       (2) query location q_loc
Output: RSet(the set of real kNN)
1:  SearchList ← NULL
2:  Sort RSet in descending order according to their distance to query
3:  o_b ← de-queue(RSet)
4:  SearchList ← {Cells intersect with/in Circle(q,dist(q,o_b))} -
    {VistedCells}
5:  while SearchLit ≠ ∅ do
6:      c ← de-queue(SerachList)
7:      if Find a new object o' in c then
8:          while RSet ≠ NULL do
9:              o ← de-stack(RSet)
10:             if dist(q,o') < dist(q,o) then
11:                 Insert o' into RSet in proper position
12:                 de-queue(RSet)
13:                 Break;
14:         Shrunk the search space by update the SearchList
15:         o_b ← de-queue(RSet)
16:         SearchList = {Cells intersect with/in Circle(q,dist(q,o_b))} -
            {VistedCells}
17: Return RSet
```

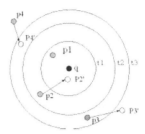

Fig. 4. Threshold for 3NN monitoring

4   Continuous kNN Queries

After the initial process, the set of *k*NN is returned to the user through *Q-node*. Since both the objects and the user query may move during the query period, the *k*NN set should be continuously updated over time. The naive method to report the *k*NN result up-to-date is to call the initial query processing repeatedly every time interval *dt* which would incur a lot of waste of energy. In fact, only those location updates that may potentially affect the *k*NN result are needed to be transmitted. Motivated by this, we propose a threshold-based algorithm to efficiently monitor *C-k*NN result. The key idea of the threshold-based algorithm is to set up *k* thresholds based on the distance between the query and the *k* nearest neighbors. When visit the grid cell, the *I-node* send a probe message including the query ID, query location and thresholds of this query to all nodes in this cell. Then the sensor node detecting objects location violation will report the new location to the *Q-node*. For simplicity, we first consider the single static query, then extend the algorithm to multiple moving query.

4.1   Single Static Query

For ease of presentation, we first describe our methodology for the continuous monitoring of a single static query before covering multiple moving queries. Starting with a single static query q in Fig.4, assume that we want to continuously monitor the 3-NNs (the initial NNs are p1, p2, p3). Fig. 4 contains three thresholds t1, t2, t3 which define a range for each object, such that if its distance from q lies within the range, the result of the query is guaranteed to remain unchanged. We initially set $t_i = (d_i+d_{i+1})/2$, i.e., in the middle of the distances of the two consecutive NNs (for the first NN, $t_0=0$). The grid cells intersecting with the circle centered at q and with a radius of t_i are monitoring cells. The index nodes of these monitoring cells locally keep the position of the query, the position of the relevant object, and the relevant thresholds. The index nodes of these monitoring cells broadcast a probe message including the information stored in it for data collection. All sensor nodes in the grid cell can receive the probe message and they will start reporting the location updates to the index node from the following sampling interval. When some sensor node in these monitoring cells detects an object violates its threshold(s), it sends the new location message to its index node and then the index node send the same information to the query node.

Once a query q arrives at a sensor node, the sensor node first transmits the query message to the nearest index node I_0 who will retrieve the initial set of k-NNs using the method described in section 3.2. After the initial computation, I_0 gets the ID and positions of the initial k-NNs and set up the thresholds for each NN. I_0 broadcast the information to the corresponding grid cells. After the initial computation, I_0 has to continuously monitor the result and report changes.

Let I and O be the sets of *incoming* (e.g., outer objects that come within distance t_k from q) and *outgoing* objects (e.g., inner objects that move out of t_k). Let V be the set of all objects that incur violations at some timestamp, i.e., $V=I \cup O \cup$ {inner objects that violate their thresholds but not t_k }. If $V \neq \varnothing$, I_0 needs to assign new thresholds for each object. Due to the limited pages, the detail of thresholds assignment is omitted here. If the set of NNs (or their order) changes, the new result is transmitted to the user. In addition, the new thresholds are sent to the corresponding grid cells. The monitoring circles are updated according to the new thresholds.

If $|I| < |O|$, the above process will not produce a sufficient number k of neighbors. We need to search more objects outside the circle centered at q and with a radius of d_k. This is equivalent to the initial search of kNN described in section 3.2.

Algorithm 3: Threshold-based Continuous Monitoring

Input: (1) q_{id}, (2) query location q_{loc}, and
      (3) number of nearest neighbors k
Output: The set of k nearest moving objects

1: Call Coarse Search and Refined Search to get the initial kNN;
2: for i =1 to k do
3:     Assign thresholds t_i for each objects o_i in kNN
4:     $AC = AC \cup \{Cells\ intersect\ with\ Circle(q, t_i)\}$
5:     Each I-node in AC send a probe message to collect the location update in these cell
6:     $V = I \cup O \cup \{objects\ that\ violate\ thresholds\ but\ not\ t_k\}$
7:     while $V \neq \emptyset$ do
8:         if $|I| \geq |O|$ then
9:             Sort objects in ascending order and keep the nearest k object
10:         if $|I| < |O|$ then
11:             Expand Search in Circle(q, dist(q.o_k))
12:         update the thresholds for the new kNN
13:     If there are changes in kNN, inform the user

4.2   Cost Analyze

The cost of a C-kNN query include three parts:1) query request; 2) initial kNN search; 3) incremental maintain results. The first two parts are supposed to be fix and we only care about the last part, the overhead of message from the *I*-node to *Q*-node for tracking the change of kNN results. We focus on three different location update strategies.

Upper Bound
The upper bound corresponds to the naive policy, where *Q*-node issues the same initial kNN search repeatedly at each interval. Assuming that the period of the query *T* and the time interval for *Q*-node to update the kNN results is *dt*, the cost for the initial kNN search is $C_{initial}$, so the cost of each query is:

$$Cost_{UB} = (T / dt) \cdot C_{initial}.$$

Lower Bound
The lower bound for the communication cost may be computed by only considering the number of NN changes at each interval. Let C_{up} is the communication cost of location updates from *I*-node to *Q*-node and C_{down} is the message cost of threshold updates from *Q*-node to *I*-node. For instance, in Fig. 5 the (formerly outer) object o_6 overpasses o_5 to become the new fifth NN. Thus, the positions of o_6 and o_5 are essential for determining the change. On the other hand, the updates of o_2, o_3, and o_4 are not required because their relative order in the result remains the same despite the violations. Similarly, in Fig. 6, we only need the current locations of o_4, o_2 to determine the new result. In general, the set *S* of objects that need to issue updates contains:1) inner objects involved in a NN order change; 2) outer objects become part of the result; 3) inner objects no longer belong to the result.

The lower bound of cost is the following: $Cost_{LB} = |S| \cdot C_{up}$

Here |S| is the cardinality of *S*. The maximum value of $Cost_{LB}$ is $2kC_{up}$, and occurs when all *k* NNs are replaced by outer objects.

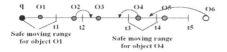 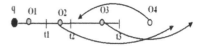

Fig. 5. Incoming objects more than outgoings   **Fig. 6.** Outgoing objects more than incomings

Threshold-based
Threshold-based strategy corresponds to our approach and aims at minimizing the message overhead. In order to obtain its cost, we distinguish the two cases of Section 4.1. The first one refers to the situation where $|I| \geq |O|$, and incurs cost:

$$Cost_{TB1} = (|V| + |U|) \cdot C_{up} + (|V| + 2|U|) \cdot C_{down}.$$

Here *V* is the set of objects that violate the thresholds assigned to them and *U* is the set of objects that have to report their locations to *Q*-node although they have not incurred violations. The objects in *V* have violated their distance range, so sensor nodes detecting this violation must report the new location of these objects to Q-node, and meanwhile, in order to update the thresholds , Q-node needs to get some other objects' new location, for instance the objects in set U. Hence the location update cost is $(|V|+|U|) \cdot C_{up}$, and the threshold update cost is $(|V|+2|U|) \cdot C_{down}$. The total cost of the first situation is the above formula.

In the case of $|O| > |I|$, an extra range query has to be performed to get enough k nearest neighbors. The cost is: $Cost_{TB} = Cost_{TB1} + C_{initial}$. We expect that for most practical scenarios, $Cost_{LB} < Cost_{TB} \ll Cost_{UB}$, but the exact value depends on the specific parameters, such as object moving speed, query rate and query period.

5   Experimental Evaluations

In this section, we conduct a wide range of experiments to evaluate the performance of our threshold-based C-kNN processing algorithm in terms of energy and latency and compare it with the baseline algorithm. The baseline algorithm update kNN results by calling the initial kNN search every time interval dt during the query period. We first study the performance metrics by varying the value of the application parameter k. We then investigate the impact of varying system parameters such as number of objects, rate of queries, period of query and mobility of objects for the purpose to test the performance of our threshold-based algorithm to these factors. Table 1 summarizes the system parameters and their settings.

Table 1. System Parameters

Parameters	Description	Default value
N	number of sensor nodes	10^3
R	communication range	125m
$s \times s$	size of network	$1000m^2$
$\alpha \times \alpha$	size of grid cells	$125m^2$
n	number of objects	200
v	velocity of objects	10m/s
k	number of neighbors	4-64
q	query rate	0-100/s

5.1   Effect of k

Both the query processing time and the number of message transmission increase with k, but our threshold-based method increases slower, as shown in figure 7 and figure 8. In figure 7, the almost linear increasing of processing time is quite natural because when k increases, we need to find more neighbors and it is more likely a query's result will change. When k increases, the gap between threshold-based method and naive method gets larger because the query's search space increases with k, thus more communication is saved by threshold-based method with bigger k.

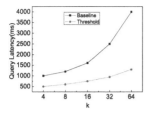

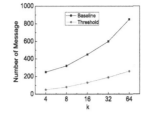

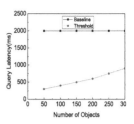

Fig. 7. k VS query latency   **Fig. 8.** k VS number of mes-   **Fig. 9.** Number of Obj. VS
                                   sage   query latency

5.2 Effect of Number of Objects

Figure 9 compares the baseline method and the threshold method with different numbers of objects when k = 8. It is seen that the query latency of the threshold method is much fewer than that of the baseline method. This because in order to get the up-to-date kNN result, the baseline method needs to execute the initial kNN search repeatedly, the threshold method only need to monitor the small number of kNN result calculated before.

It also can be seen from Figure 10 that the average energy consumption of the threshold method is much smaller than that of the baseline method due to fewer location updates. The performance of the baseline method degrades rapidly with increasing number of objects due to the fact that more location updates are sent to the query node with more objects in the network.

5.3 Effect of Query

Figure 11 shows the performance results for different query periods. The results indicate that the overall message complexity increases with query period for both methods. Due to the incremental maintenance of kNN in threshold method, the number of query processing messages is much smaller than baseline method. Figure 12 shows the message for different query rate. The number of location update messages is independent of the query rate for both methods. The number of query processing messages increases with query rate, leading to an increase in the overall message complexity. Threshold method outperforms Baseline method over a wide range of query rates. In general, the improvement of our method over baseline method is larger for larger query rate.

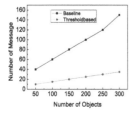

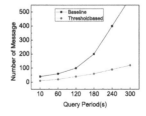

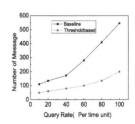

Fig. 10. Object Number VS   **Fig. 11.** Query Period VS   **Fig. 12.** Query rate VS
Query Cost   Message   Message

5.4 Effect of Moving Speed of Objects

Figure 13 shows the performance results for different $P_{violate}$ values. It is intuitive that the objects move faster and hence incur more location threshold violation at larger $P_{violate}$ values. Since the number of location update messages in threshold method is much lower than the number of query processing messages, the total number of messages in threshold method is not significantly affected by the increase in $P_{violate}$. The overall message complexity of Baseline, on the other hand, substantially increases with $P_{violate}$. This is because the total number of messages in Baseline is dominated by that of query processing messages. As shown in Figure 13, threshold method considerably outperforms Baseline over a wide range of $P_{violate}$ values.

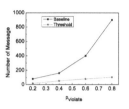 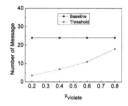 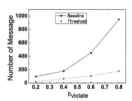

Fig. 13(a). Location Message VS p_violate

Fig. 13(b). Query Message VS p_violate

Fig. 13(c). Total Message VS p_violate

6 Conclusions

This paper introduces and solves the problem of continuous k-NN monitoring over moving objects in wireless sensor networks. In order to reduce the amount of transmissions of location updates, we propose a grid structure to index the objects and a threshold-based algorithm to incrementally update the kNN result over time. Experiments results show that the in-network processing schema and the threshold-based monitoring method can achieve low energy consumption compared with the naive method.

References

1. Akyildiz, I.F., et al.: Wireless sensor networks: A survey. Computer Networks 38(4), 392–422 (2002)
2. Kim, W., Mechitov, K., Choi, J.-Y., Ham, S.: On target tracking with binary proximity sensors. In: Proc. IPSN (2005)
3. Demirbas, M., Ferhatosmanoglus, H.: Peer-to-peer spatial queries in sensor networks. In: Proceedings of the 3rd IEEE International Conference on Peer-to-Peer Computing, Linkoping, Sweden (2003)
4. Winter, J., Lee, W.-C.: KPT: A dynamic KNN query processing algorithm for location-aware sensor networks. In: The 1st VLDB Workshop DMSN 2004, Toronto, Canada (2004)

5. Winter, J., Xu, Y., Lee, W.: Energy efficient processing of k nearest neighbor queries in location-aware sensor networks. In: Proceedings of MobiQuitous (2005)
6. Xu, Y., Lee, W., Xu, J., Mitchell, G.: Processing window queries in wireless sensor networks. In: Proceedings of International Conference on Data Engineering (2006)
7. Wu, S.-H., Chuang, K.-T., Chen, C.-M., Chen, M.-S.: DIKNN: An Itinerary-based KNN Query Processing Algorithm for Mobile Sensor Networks. In: Proceedings of the 23rd IEEE International Conference on Data Engineering (ICDE 2007), April 16-20 (2007)
8. Yu, X., Pu, K., Koudas, N.: Monitoring k-nearest neighbor queries over moving objects. In: Proceedings of ICDE 2005 (2005)
9. Mouratidis, K., Hadjieleftheriou, M., Papadias, D.: Conceptual partitioning: An efficient method for continous nearest neighbor monitoring. In: Proceedings SIGMOD 2005 (2005)
10. Prabhakar, S., Xia, Y., Kalashnikov, D., Aref, W., Hambrusch, S.: Query Indexing and Velocity Constrained Indexing: Scalable Techniques for Continuous Queries on Moving Objects. IEEE Trans. Computers 51(10), 1124–1140 (2002)

Power-Efficient Data Exchanging Algorithm in Wireless Mesh Networks[*]

Jinbao Li, Peng Wang, and Qianqian Ren

School of Computer Science and Technology, Heilongjiang University,
150080, Harbin, China
Jbli@hlju.edu.cn, Qqren@hit.edu.cn

Abstract. Energy efficiency is a key problem in wireless mesh network. In this paper, we propose an energy efficient data exchanging algorithm in wireless mesh networks. From the perspective of the energy consumption needed by exchanging data in the node, we first investigate the state and size of the data being cached, and then select candidate data to exchange considering its energy consumption, to reduce the amount of data exchanging. The analytical and experimental results demonstrate that our algorithm can save the energy cost of data exchanging efficiently with guarantee of hit ratio, thus extend the life of the network.

Keywords: wireless mesh network; data caching; data exchanging.

1 Introduction

Wireless mesh networks is a kind of networks that in-network nodes are deployed discretionarily, and inter-connected with its neighbors. It consists of two types of nodes: mesh router and mesh client. The former has routing and transmitting functionality with which can be used as a gateway or an access point toward other networks. It's usually stationary and has stable power. The latter such as laptops, phones, PDAs, etc has some relaying functionality but no gateway functionality. It's usually equipped with a battery. Wireless mesh networks has three types of architectures: hybrid, backbone and client wireless mesh networks. Hybrid architecture is the most common one.

Recent years, wireless mesh networks related technologies are gaining more attentions. On going with the development of wireless network technologies, data caching problem in wireless mesh networks has becoming a researching hotspot. In wireless mesh networks, it's often to find out that required data is not locally, and need to be downloaded from other nodes or server through wireless networks. In case data is required frequently, the bandwidth will be consumed greatly and the network will be exhausted easily. If employ data caching technologies in wireless mesh networks, we

---

[*] This paper has been supported by the Natural Science Foundation of Heilongjiang Province of China under Grant No.ZJG03-05 and No.QC04C40; the Innovation Foundation of Education Department of Heilongjiang Province of China under Grant No.1055G032; the Science Foundation of Education Department of Heilongjiang Province of China under Grant No.11531276.

Y. Li et al. (Eds.): WASA 2008, LNCS 5258, pp. 444–453, 2008.

may download data from remote server and cache it in local node or related nodes, thus reduce requiring and communicational hops, save the limited communication bandwidth of network and depress the energy consumption through wireless transmission. In consideration of the communication cost and energy efficiency, to exploit data caching technologies will result better effect. Data caching technologies consists of many problems such as caching node routing and caching management, data exchanging, etc. Among which, data exchanging problem has direct influence to data accessing hit ratio, energy consumption and bandwidth utilities.

Recently, most data exchanging algorithms are based on sequential, random or hash exchange methods, the main drawback is that they didn't consider the essentiality of caching data, thus result in continually exchanging data in nodes. Subsequently, a data access rate based data exchanging method had been proposed for the sake of reducing the times of exchanging. However, these existing methods did not analyze exchanging operation from the energy consumption point of view. The nodes in wireless mesh networks have larger storage as well as different node stores variety size of data. Since the size of data stored in the node is not the same, exchanging different data will consume different energy. Some larger data may be exchanged out of buffer due to low access rate, when user requires it again, it consumes more energy during download it from remote site. Based on this characteristic of data storing in wireless mesh networks, if one can compute the energy consumption of each data exchanging by analyzing its state and size, then make exchange decision according to their different energy consumptions, thus reserve energy during data exchanging.

This paper proposed an energy efficient data exchanging algorithm from the perspective of the energy consumed in data exchanging operation. Through compute the consumption by analyzing the state and size of each data, and choose exchanging data according to its energy consumption, it can reserve energy consumption and extend nodes' lifetime.

2   Related Work

Recently, the research on data caching technologies in wireless network is mostly focus on data consistency and cooperative caching, and they mainly investigate the problem of caching efficiency and hit ratio.

Zheng et al. proposed a distributed dynamic adaptive replica allocation algorithm [1,2]. Replica node collects access request information of replicas from its neighbors, and decides whether extend the replica to its neighbor or remove it from local storage. Adapt allocating replica to the changing topology and access request dynamically.

Takahiro et al. proposed three replica-allocating methods [3, 4]. The first method considered accessing data by local node only. The second method considered accessing data by both local node and its one-hop-neighbors, remove redundant replicas inter-neighbors according to access request information. The third method divides nodes into stable groups, which avoids in-net work data redundancy when placing replicas. The second and third methods aim to avoid redundancy of replica allocation and try to replicate more types of data, but each node need to broadcast its data access request information to all in-network nodes, thus the nodes can have the topology information and then select some cooperative nodes to allocate replicas. These two methods consume great energies, especially the latter.

Wang et al. proposed a routing-aware dynamic caching algorithm [5, 6]. It mainly address on how to transfer the data to the caching node. However, it need to compute many times when choosing route path, therefore it consumes large bandwidth and energies.

Shen et al. proposed two strategies to cache data and route path [7]. The advantage of these strategies is that they reduced the consumption of bandwidth and save the energy during query execution. However, they did not take data consistency in to account and increase local energy consumption while saving others.

Data exchanging is a key issue in data caching technology, it affects caching efficiency, utility of nodes and network bandwidth directly. A good data exchange algorithm can reduce the bandwidth consume between nodes and fully explore the caching resource. So far, much work has been done for data exchanging in wireless environment, but they mostly focus on making exchange decision by the data arriving time and data-accessing ratio. Nodes in wireless mesh networks equipped with transceivers powered by limited battery. Therefore, it is not sufficient only analyze caching time and access ratio when considering data exchange. The energy is also a key factor. To illustrate this, imaging a big volume data is caching in one node and its access ratio may be low. Thus, when the exchange process is setup, it can be removed due to its low access rate. When the data is requested again, it will spend large bandwidth and energy to download. For saving unnecessary bandwidth and prolong node lifetime, we investigate data exchange in way of energy consumption.

3 *PDEA* : Power-Efficient Data Exchange Algorithm

In this section, we will give the implementation of the power efficient data exchange algorithm.

3.1 The Implementation of *PDEA*

Generally, there are three state of caching data: certain, uncertain and invalid. Certain state means neither received invalid information nor disconnection and dormancy have occurred during caching, and when the data is request, it can be access directly. The state becomes uncertain when disconnection or dormancy occurs, and before access uncertain data, check validity process should be taken. When node receives invalid information of one data, the data's state become invalid and it would be removed. It will be downloaded again next time when be requested. During the data request, different state has different energy cost. When deciding which data item should be removed, make decision from energy of view is necessary.

Fig. 1 illustrates the conversion among each state. Uncertain state can be changed into invalidated state (circs 1) or certain state (circs 2) after been certified. During caching, certain state data may experience three circs. First is keep certain (circs 5), second is turn to invalidated after receiving invalid information, third is turn to uncertain due to disconnection or dormancy occurs. Process different state consumes different energy, we farther discussing energy consumption in each conversion step.

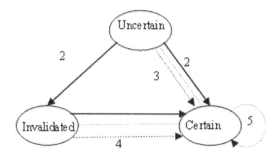

Fig. 1. The figure of three states transformation

1.   Uncertain state data

Uncertain state data d_i comes forth two possible states during cached in node. One is having not received any invalid information so still uncertain. The other is it received an invalid information and turns to invalidated state. If d_i is requested, the node should first send an *upm* (uplink message) to server to check state. After compare with the local data, the server sends back a *dwn* (download message) if the data is valid, as shows in circs 2 of Fig. 1; or send the new d_i to the node directly, as shows in circs 1of Fig. 1. For the possible cases of an uncertain data, the energy consumption of it is follow formula 1:

$$E_u=P_{i1}(E(upm)+E(dwn))+P_{i2}(E(upm)+E(s_i)) \qquad (1)$$

E_u represents the energy consumption derived by the possible changes of an uncertain data. P_{i1} represents the probability of the first case happening, and P_{i2} represents the probability of the second case happening, $P_{i1}+P_{i2}=1$. $E(upm)$ represents the energy consumed by sending a *upm*. $E(dwm)$ represents the energy consumed by sending a *dwm*. s_i represents the size of d_i. $E(s_i)$ represents the energy consumption of download d_i.

2.   Certain state data

Certain state data d_i comes forth three possible states. The first one is not receiving invalid information and still being certain. The second one is becoming uncertain after node disconnection or dormancy. The third one is receiving invalid information and becoming invalid. For the first case, d_i will be sent to request node directly. For the second case, it first sends an *upm* to server, then receives a *dwn* if d_i is valid, other-wise a new d_i is received, as show in circs 3 and 4 of Fig. 1 respectively. For the possible cases of a certain state data, the energy consumption is shown in formula 2:

$$E_c=P_{i2}(E(upm)+E(dwn))+P_{i3}(E(upm)+E(s_i)) \qquad (2)$$

E_c represents the energy consumption derived by the possible changes of a certain data. P_{i1}, P_{i2} and P_{i3} represents the probability of the first case, second case and third case happening respectively, where $P_{i1}+P_{i2}+P_{i3}=1$.

We define unit energy consumption of different state through their total energy consumption as:

$$U_u=E_u/s_i$$
$$=(P_{i1}(E(upm)+E(dwn))+P_{i2}(E(upm)+E(s_i)))/s_i \quad (3)$$

Where U_u represents the energy consumption of one unit of uncertain data. U_c represents the energy consumption of one unit certain data.

$$U_c=E_c/s_i$$
$$=(P_{i2}(E(upm)+E(dwn))+P_{i3}(E(upm)+E(s_i)))/s_i \quad (4)$$

Where U_u equals to U_c no matter how large the data size is. Therefore, we use E_c and E_u to represent the energy consumed during data exchanging. E_c and E_u will be large if the data have a large size. Thus, we add the consideration of energy consumption factor when processing data exchange.

We assume each case of caching data has same probability. Formulas 1to4 can be rewritten as:

$$E_u=1/2(2E(upm)+E(dwn)+E(s_i)) \quad (5)$$

$$E_c=1/3(2E(upm)+E(dwn)+E(s_i)) \quad (6)$$

$$U_u=E_u/s_i=(1/2(2E(upm)+E(dwn)+E(s_i)))/s_i \quad (7)$$

$$U_c=E_c/s_i=(1/3(2E(upm)+E(dwn)+E(s_i)))/s_i \quad (8)$$

According to above analysis, we are clear about different energy consumptions derived by different state of data. To reduce energy consumption during data exchanging, we go through steps listed below.

For clear description, we introduce some parameters at first. H is the set of datum in buffer; u_i is the cost parameter of exchange d_i, this parameter is related to data size and access radio; Min is the minimal cost in the buffer.

When data request arrives, one of following three cases will happen:

Case 1. d_i is in the buffer and is certain, send it to the request node.
Case 2. d_i is in the buffer but is uncertain, send a check message upm to server.
Case 3. d_i is not in the buffer, send a miss hit message to server.

In case 2 and 3, as soon as receiving the server response, the following work will be done:

1. If the sever has confirmed that d_i is valid, then it sets its state as *certain* state and send d_i to request nodes, evaluates its cost.
2. If the sever sends a new d_i, it means that the old d_i is invalid. Then it checks whether the buffer is full. If it is, it searches for the data item with minimal cost and removes it, meanwhile adds new d_i into buffer, sends it to request nodes and evaluates its cost.

3.2 Algorithm *PDEA*

The power-efficient data exchanging algorithm is described as follows, the variable in the algorithm is given in table 1.

Table 1. Details of variable in algorithm 1

Variable	meaning
H	set of datum in buffer
u_i	the cost parameter of exchange
min	the minimal cost in the buffer
M_i	message of request data item d_i

Algorithm1: *PDEA*
Set *min*=0 and assume a request message M_i
1   receive a request message of data item d_i
2   *if* data item d_i is in buffer
3   *if* data item d_i is certain
4          $u_i = E_c$
5   send d_i to request node
6   *else if* data item d_i is uncertain
7   send upm to server
8   *if* data item d_i is not in local buffer
9   send a miss data message to server
10   wait server response
11   receive message M_i from server
12   *if* M_i is a confirm message
13   convert d_i to certain state
14      $u_i = E_u$
15   send d_i to request node
16   *if* M_i contains d_i
17   *if* is download item
18   *while* insufficient place for cache d_i
19            $min = MIN(u_j)$ $(d_j \in H)$
20   remove d_j from buffer
21   *end while*
22   flush exchanging buffer place
23   download d_i to buffer
24         $u_i = E_u$
25   send d_i to request node
26   *else* drop M_i

Power-efficient data exchanging algorithm mainly solve how to reduce the energy consumption during the process of data exchanging. To settle this, the algorithm first analyzes the energy consumed by process necessary operation. For certain data and uncertain data, the energy consumption is derived by sending and receiving messages and downloading data when process check data validity. The algorithm also analyzes the energy consumption derived by each possible cases of checking data validity. For one exchanging data item, its energy consumption is formed by two parts: One is derived by checking the data validity, the other is derived by downloading the item from server. That's if a data with a large size is considered to be exchange, not only use its arriving time or access ratio to make the decision, but also take the energy consumption of its downloading into account. By computing the energy consumption of each data item in the buffer, the minimal cost item can be chosen and be removed during data exchanging. Thus through analyzing the energy consumption of each operation in data exchanging, the algorithm provides a power-efficient caching method, obtains save energy during data exchanging.

4   Experiments and Performance Analysis

We compared our *PDEA* algorithm with *FIFO* and *RDC* exchange algorithm by simulating experiment. *FIFO* algorithm exchanges selects exchanging data item by its arriving time, while *RDC* selects exchanging data item randomly till it is satisfied the download size request.

We randomly place 40 nodes in a 500×500 network environment. The radius of each node is 50, and the transfer bandwidth is 36Mbit/s. Each store unit is 1Kbit.

Fig. 2 shows the results of how the buffer size affects the energy consumption of data exchange. The test environment set as:

1) The buffer size increases from 1000 store units to 5000 store units, each step increases 1000;
2) The test data is generated randomly and 100 simulate data items are generated each time, during which different data item rate is 20%;
3) Each data item size ranges from 50 store units to 350 store units;
4) U_c consumption is one energy unit, U_u consumption is 2 energy units;
5) We test each buffer size 10 times and obtain the average results.

As shown in Fig. 2, the exchanging energy consumption decrease on going with the increasing of buffer size. But the power-efficient exchange algorithm consumption is lower than *FIFO* and *RDC* algorithms obviously. And the decrease trend of power-efficient algorithm is faster than the other two. The reason is that along with increasing buffer size, caching data amount is increasing, so does the energy consumption search space. Thus, power-efficient algorithm has energy consumption during data exchanging decreasing faster.

Fig. 3 shows the result of how does the different data item rate affects energy consumption during data exchanging, in case when the buffer size is 3000 store units. Test environment set as:

1) buffer size is fixed;
2) The test data is generated randomly and 100 simulate data items are generated each time, the different data item rate is from 20% to 60%;
3) Each data item size ranges from 50 store units to 350 store units;
4) U_c consumption is 1 energy unit, U_u consumption is 2 energy units;
5) We test each buffer size 10 times and obtain the average results.

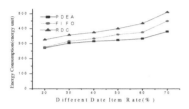

Fig. 2. the influence of buffer size on energy consumption

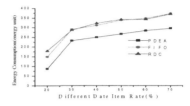

Fig. 3. The energy consumption when buffer size is 3000

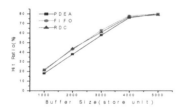

Fig. 4. The energy consumption when buffer size is 2000

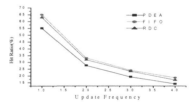

Fig. 5. The energy consumption when buffer size is 4000

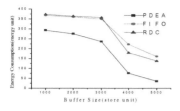

Fig. 6. The comparison of hit ratio

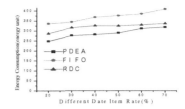

Fig. 7. The influence of update frequency on data hit ratio

As shown in Fig. 3, in case buffer size is 3000, three algorithms' energy consumptions are all increasing along with the increasing of different data item rate. But *FIFO* and *RDC* algorithm is increasing faster than power-efficient algorithm markedly. The main reason is that when the buffer size is 3000 and the different rate is low, data exchanging frequency is low. However, as increasing the different data item rate, the hit ratio is reducing, which results in *FIFO* and *RDC* algorithms' energy consumption increasing evidently.

Fig. 4 and 5 show the results of how does the different data item rate affects energy consumption during data exchanging when the buffer size is 2000 and 4000.

As shown in Fig. 4, when the buffer size is low as set to 2000, and different data item rate is high, *FIFO* and *RDC* algorithms' energy consumption widely increased, but the trend of power-efficient algorithm is gent. This is because the buffer size is small and different data item rate is high, so hit rate is low and data exchanging frequently. For the algorithm does not consider the energy consumption like *FIFO* and *RDC*, the energy consumption is going higher. As shown in Fig. 5, when the buffer is large as the size is 4000, and the different data item rate is low, all three algorithms' energy consumption increased widely. The most conceivable reason is that in case the buffer size is large with low different data item rate, hit ratio is high, thus few data exchanging, the energy consumption is also low. As the different data item rate heightening, the hit rate falls, thus data exchanging frequently and energy consumption heightening. But from the result,, we can see that for the purpose of reduce energy consumption, our power-efficient algorithm is still perform better than *FIFO* and *RDC* algorithms obviously.

Fig.6 is the result of how does the buffer size affects data hit ratio. We investigated how does the power-efficient algorithm performs on data hit ratio. Data hit ratio is a key factor that affects network communication, the higher hit ratio, the lower network transmission load. The test environment set as:

1) The buffer size increases from 1000 store units to 5000 store units;
2) The test data is generated randomly and 100 simulate data items are generated each time, during which different data item rate is 20%;
3) Each data item size ranges from 50 store units to 350 store units;
4) We test each buffer size 10 times and obtain the average results.

As shown in Fig. 6, as the buffer size enlarges, the hit ratio of three algorithms all increased, and about the same. This illustrate that our power-efficient algorithm do not bring in extend network transmission load.

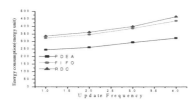

Fig. 8. The influence of update frequency on energy consumption

Fig. 7 is the result of how does the update frequency affects data hit ratio. Test environment set as: 1) buffer size is 3000; 2) test data generated randomly, each time generates 100 simulate data items, different data item rate is from 20% to 60%; 3) each data item size is range from 50 store units to 350 store units; 4) update frequency increase from 1 to 4 during data accessing.

As shown in Fig. 7, as the update frequency increase, all algorithms' hit ratio is fall, the power-efficient algorithm is little lower than the others. This is because the power-efficient algorithm makes exchange decision by the energy consumption angle. Thus, data with low energy consumption but high access frequency may be removed out of buffer. And lead to lower hit ratio. But we can see from the experimental result that, the hit ratio of power-efficient algorithm does not fall much.

Fig. 8 is the result of how does the update frequency affects energy consumption. Test environment set as: 1) buffer size is 3000; 2) test data generated randomly, each time generates 100 simulate data items, different data item rate is from 20% to 60%; 3) each data item size is range from 50 store units to 350 store units; 4) update frequency increase from 1 to 4 during data accessing.

As shown in Fig. 8, from the comparison of energy consumption of three algorithms, we can find out that the energy consumption increase on going with the update frequency increasing. Nevertheless, power-efficient algorithm is much better than *FIFO* and *RDC* algorithms. Through the experimental result of Fig. 6, 7 and 8, we educe that our power-efficient algorithm can reduce the energy consumption during data exchanging, meanwhile guarantee the hit ratio, and achieve the energy efficient goal.

5 Conclusions

To investigate the issue of energy consumption during data exchanging and data caching, this paper propose a power-efficient algorithm. By taking full advantage of the data size and state, the algorithm computes the energy consumption of a unit data under different states firstly, and then measures the energy consumption of each exchanging data item combining with data size. When data exchanging is needed, the algorithm searches for the buffer, finds out the data item with minimal energy consumption cost and achieves reducing energy consumption during data exchanging.

References

1. Zheng, J., Lu, X.C., Wang, Y.J.: A clustering-Based Data Replication Algorithm in Mobile Ad Hoc Networks for Improving Data Availability. Journal of Software 16(8), 1474–1483 (2005)
2. Zheng, J., Wang, Y.J., Lu, X.C.: A Dynamic Adaptive Replica Allocation algorithm in Mobile Ad Hoc Networks. In: Proceedings of the Second IEEE Annual Conference on Pervasive Computing and Communications Workshops (PERCOMW 2004). IEEE Computer Society, Los Alamitos (2004)
3. Takahiro, H.: Strategies for Data Location Management in Mobile Ad Hoc Networks. In: Proc. IEEE ICPADS 2005, pp. 147–153 (2005)
4. Takahiro, H.: Data Replication for Improving Data Accessibility in Ad Hoc Networks. IEEE Transactions on Publication 5(11), 1515–1532 (2006)
5. Wang, Y.H., Chen, J.H., Chao, C.F., Lee, C.M.: A Transparent Cache-Based Mechanism for Mobile Ad Hoc Networks. In: Third International Conference on Information Technology and Applications (ICITA 2005), pp. 305–310 (2005)
6. Wang, Y.H., Chao, C.F., Lin, S.W., Chen, J.H.: A Distributed Data Caching Framework for Mobile Ad Hoc Networks. In: Proceedings of IWCMC 2006, Vancouver, British Columbia, Canada, pp. 1357–1362 (2006)
7. Shen, H., Sajal, K., Kumar, M., Wang, Z.J.: Cooperative Caching with Optimal Radius in Hybrid Wireless Networks. In: Mitrou, N.M., Kontovasilis, K., Rouskas, G.N., Iliadis, I., Merakos, L. (eds.) NETWORKING 2004. LNCS, vol. 3042, pp. 841–853. Springer, Heidelberg (2004)

Composite Spatio-Temporal Co-occurrence Pattern Mining

Zhongnan Zhang and Weili Wu

Department of Computer Science, The University of Texas at Dallas,
Richardson TX 75080, USA
{znzhang,weiliwu}@utdallas.edu

Abstract. Spatio-temporal co-occurrence patterns (STCOPs) represent subsets of features that are located together in space and time. Mining such patterns is important for many spatio-temporal application domains. However, a co-occurrence analysis across multiple spatio-temporal datasets is computationally expensive when the dimension of the time series and number of locations in the spaces are large. In this paper, we first defined STCOPs and the STCOPs mining problem. We proposed a monotonic composite measure, which is the composition of the spatial prevalence and temporal prevalence measures. A novel and computationally efficient algorithm, $\textsc{Costcop}^+$, is presented by applying the composite measure. We proved that the proposed algorithm is correct and complete in finding STCOPs. Using a real dataset, the experiments illustrate that the algorithm is efficient.

1 Introduction

A spatial framework [1] consists a collection of locations and a neighbor relationship. A temporal dataset is a sequence of observations for a feature taken sequentially in time [2]. A spatio-temporal datasets is a collection of temporal dataset, each referencing a different location in a common spatial framework. Spatio-temporal co-occurrence patterns (STCOPs) represent subsets of features that are located together in space and time. Mining such patterns is important for many spatio-temporal application domains, including the military (battlefield planning and strategy), ecology (tracking species and pollutant movements), homeland security (looking for significant "events"), and transportation (road and network planning) [3,4].

Co-occurrence analysis is to identify potentially interacting pairs of features across spatial time series datasets. A strongly co-occurrence pairs of features indicates one feature's potential movement in time series accompanied with some other features' movement in the same time. For example, El Nino, the anomalous warming of the eastern tropical region of the Pacific, has been linked to climate phenomena such as droughts in Australia and heavy rainfall along the Western coast of South America.

However, a co-occurrence analysis across multiple spatio-temporal datasets is computationally expensive when the dimension of the time series and number

Y. Li et al. (Eds.): WASA 2008, LNCS 5258, pp. 454–465, 2008.

of locations in the spaces are large. The computational cost can be reduced by reducing time series dimensionality or reducing the number of spatial co-location subsets to be tested, or both.

In this paper, a new monotonic composite interest measure and a novel and computationally efficient mining algorithm was proposed to discover STCOPs. The organization of the rest paper is as follows. We discuss some related works in Section 2. In Section 3, the basic concepts related to co-location patterns are provided. The problem definition is formally given in Section 4. In Section 5, we propose CostCop$^+$ algorithm for STCOPs' mining. Section 6 presents our experiment with the algorithm on a real-life dataset. Finally, we discuss the related future work and conclude with summary.

2   Related Works

Approaches to discover co-occurrence patterns in the literature can be categorized into two classes, namely spatial statistics and association rules. Spatial statistics-based [5] approaches use measures of spatial correlation to characterize the relationship between different types of spatial features. Measures of spatial correlation include chi-square tests, correlation coefficients, and regression models as well as their generalizations using spatial neighborhood relationships. Computing spatial correlation measures for all possible co-occurrence patterns can be computationally expensive due to the exponential number of candidates given a large collection of spatial boolean features.

Previous studies for mining spatio-temporal co-occurrence patterns can also be classified into two categories, namely, mining of uniform groups of features (e.g., flock patterns [6]) and mining of mixed groups of features (e.g., moving clusters [7]). Our problem belongs to the latter one. A flock pattern is a moving group of the same kind of feature, such as a sheep flock or a bird flock. Gudmundsson et al. proposed algorithms for detection of the flock pattern in spatio-temporal datasets [6]. Since our problem is to mine groups of different features, the proposed algorithms by Gudmundsson et al. to discover flock patterns may not be applicable to our problem. Kalnis et al. defined the problem of discovering moving clusters and proposed clustering-based methods to mine such patterns [7]. In their approach, if there is a large enough number of common features between clusters in consecutive time slots, such clusters are called moving clusters. Moving cluster patterns can be either uniform or a group of different features [7]. However if there is no overlap between the clusters in consecutive time slots, their proposed algorithms for mining moving clusters will fail to discover STCOPs. Celik et al. defined the problem of mining mixed-drove spatio-temporal co-occurrence patterns and proposed a distance based algorithm for discovery in [8]. Using the similar method, Celik et al. defined the problem of sustained emerging spatio-temporal co-occurrence patterns and proposed another distance based algorithm for discover in [9]. However for both of these two problems, the authors considered the effect of spatial prevalence and temporal prevalence separately. On the contrary, our algorithm combines the two

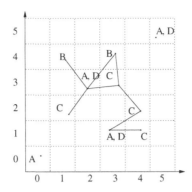

Fig. 1. Spatial dataset to illustrate co-location model

prevalence measures together and applies it into the process of discovery. This improvement will make the results include some patterns which represent bursting but short-term or undominant but long-lasting group of features.

3   Basic Concepts

Given the difficulty in creating explicit disjoint correlations from continuous spatial data, this section defines approaches to model co-location patterns. Figure 1 [10] is used as an example spatial dataset to illustrate the relationship.

Definition 1. *A* ***co-location*** *is a subset of boolean spatial features* [10].

Definition 2. *A* ***space*** *is the set of universal locations* $S = \{l_1, l_2, \ldots, l_m\}$. *S is predefined by the application.*

From the example in Figure 1, there are four boolean spatial features: A, B, C, and D. Therefore $\{A, B\}$ is a *co-location*. The *space* is a six by six grid. Each *cell* has a (x, y) address. Multiple features can be located in one same cell. However each feature can only have at most one instance for one cell. For each instance of a spatial feature, this address is an important attribute to distinguish it from other instances of the same spatial feature.

Definition 3. *A* ***neighbor relation*** $\mathcal{R}$ *is a reflexive and symmetric relation.* $a\mathcal{R}b$ *means location b is a neighbor of location a. For any one spatial location* $l \in S$, $l\mathcal{R}l$ *satisfies. For two spatial locations* $l \in S$ *and* $l' \in S$, *if* $l\mathcal{R}l'$ *satisfies, so does* $l'\mathcal{R}l$.

Definition 4. *The* ***neighborhood*** *of the location l is a set of locations* $L = \{l_1, l_2, \ldots, l_k\}$ *such that* $l\mathcal{R}l_i$ *($\forall i \in 1 \ldots k$). We use* $\odot$ *to represent the neighborhood operation, so that* $\odot l = L$.

The definition of neighbor relation $\mathcal{R}$ is an input and is based on the semantics of application domains. It may be defined using topological relationships (e.g. connected, adjacent), metric relationships (e.g. Euclidean distance) or a combination (e.g. shortest-path distance in a graph such as road-map). In general there are infinite neighborhoods over continuous space and it may not be possible to materialize all of them. But we are only interested in the locations where instances of spatial feature types occurs. Even confined to these locations, enumerating all the neighborhoods incurs substantial computational cost because support-based pruning cannot be carried out before the enumeration of all the neighborhoods is complete and the total number of neighborhoods is obtained. Here, we use the rectangular lattice as the topology of neighborhood.

Definition 5. *The **instances** of a co-location $C = \{f_1, f_2, \ldots, f_k\}$ is $I_C = \{i_{a,b}|a \in C, b \in S\}$. Therefore, the **neighborhoods of instances** I_C can be generated by the self-join of I_C on the relation $\mathcal{R}$:*

$$\Box I_C = \overset{k}{\underset{x=2}{\cup}} \Box I_C^{(x)} \tag{1}$$

where

$$\Box I_C^{(k)} = \begin{cases} I_C \bowtie_{\mathcal{R}} I_C & k = 2 \\ \overset{k}{\underset{x=1}{\cup}} (\Box I_{C-\{f_x\}}^{(k-1)} \bowtie_{\mathcal{R}} I_{\{f_x\}}) & k > 2 \end{cases} \tag{2}$$

$$I_C \bowtie_{\mathcal{R}} I_C = \{\{i_{a,\alpha}, i_{b,\beta}\}|a, b \in C, \alpha, \beta \in S, a \neq b, \alpha \mathcal{R} \beta\} \tag{3}$$

$$\Box I_{C-\{f_x\}}^{(k-1)} \bowtie_{\mathcal{R}} I_{\{f_x\}} = \{\{i_{f_1,l_1}, i_{f_2,l_2}, \ldots, i_{f_x,l_x}, \ldots, i_{f_k,l_k}\}|f_1, \ldots, f_k \in C,$$
$$l_1, \ldots, l_k \in S, f_1 \neq \ldots \neq f_x \neq \ldots \neq f_k, l_1 \mathcal{R} l_x, \ldots, l_k \mathcal{R} l_x, i_{f_x,l_x} \in I_{\{f_x\}},$$
$$\{i_{f_1,l_1}, \ldots, i_{f_{x-1},l_{x-1}}, i_{f_{x+1},l_{x+1}} \ldots, i_{f_k,l_k}\} \in \Box I_{C-\{f_x\}}^{(k-1)}\} \tag{4}$$

The neighborhoods of instances of a size k co-location are a combination of all possible and valid neighborhoods with size from two to k, which is represented in Equation 1. How to generate all size k neighborhoods? We use a recursive definition to express the process. A size k neighborhood is generated from a size $k - 1$ neighborhood by adding a new spatial feature instance. This new added instance must be a neighbor of all the instances included in the $k - 1$ neighborhood. Since this new added instance can be the instance of any of the k spatial features, the result would be a combination of all the possibilities.

Using the example in Figure 1, for co-location $\{A, B\}$, we can get that $I_{\{A,B\}} = \{i_{A,(0,0)}, i_{B,(1,4)}, i_{A,(2,3)}, i_{A,(3,1)}, i_{B,(3,4)}, i_{A,(5,5)}\}$. Therefore, $\Box I_{\{A,B\}}$ includes $\{i_{A,(2,3)}, i_{B,(1,4)}\}$ and $\{i_{A,(2,3)}, i_{B,(3,4)}\}$, supposing we use a 8-way neighborhood.

Definition 6. *The **participation ratio** $pr(C, f_x)$ for feature type f_x of a co-location $C = \{f_1, f_2, \ldots, f_k\}$ is the fraction of distinct instances of f_x which participate in any neighborhood of co-location C. It can be formally defined as:*

$$pr(C, f_x) = \frac{|\{i_{f_x,l_x}|\forall\{i_{f_1,l_1}, \ldots, i_{f_x,l_x}, \ldots, i_{f_k,l_k}\} \in \Box I_C^{(k)}\}|}{|I_{\{f_x\}}|} \tag{5}$$

Continuing to consider the above example, we can get that only one instance of spatial feature A at location (2,3) participates in co-location $\{A, B\}$. The total number of the instances of feature A in the space is four. So $pr(\{A, B\}, A)$ is $\frac{1}{4}$.

Definition 7. *The **participation index** of a co-location $C = \{f_1, f_2, \ldots, f_k\}$ is* [11]:

$$pi(C) = \min_{1 \leq i \leq k} pr(C, f_i) \tag{6}$$

From above, the participation ratio $pr(\{A, B\}, A)$ of feature A in co-location $\{A, B\}$ is 0.25. Similarly $pr(\{A, B\}, B)$ is 1.0. Therefore, the participation index for co-location $\{A, B\}$ is $\min\{0.25, 1.0\} = 0.25$.

4   Formal Model

Given a set of spatio-temporal features and a set of their instances with a neighbor relationship $\mathcal{R}$, a spatio-temporal co-occurrence pattern is a subset of spatio-temporal features whose instances are neighbors in space and time. The following are definitions used to measure the prevalence of a pattern.

Definition 8. *Given a spatio-temporal pattern C_i and a set of L time slots, $\mathcal{T} = \{t_1, t_2, \ldots, t_L\}$, the temporal prevalence measure of the pattern is the fraction of time slots where the pattern occurs over the total number of time slots and it's represented as $tp(C_i)$.*

Definition 9. *Given a sptaio-temporal pattern, a spatial framework $\mathcal{S}$, and a neighbor relationship $\mathcal{R}$, the spatial prevalence measure of the pattern is the participation index value of the pattern.*

Definition 10. *Given a spatio-temporal dataset $\mathcal{P}$ and two thresholds, θ_s and θ_t, a spatio-temporal co-occurrence pattern's prevalence measure satisfies the following:*

$$\sum_{t=1}^{L} pi(C_i)_t \geq (L \times \theta_t) \times \theta_s \tag{7}$$

where $pi(C_i)_t$ represents the participation index value of the pattern C_i for time slot t, θ_t is the temporal prevalence threshold, and θ_s is the spatial prevalence threshold.

The composite spatio-temporal co-occurrence pattern mining problem can be formalized as follows:

Given:
  - A set of K boolean spatio-temporal features $\mathcal{F} = \{f_1, f_2, \ldots, f_K\}$.
  - A spatial framework $\mathcal{S}$.
  - A set of L time slots, $\mathcal{T} = \{t_1, t_2, \ldots, t_L\}$.
  - A set of N instances $\mathcal{P} = \{p_1, p_2, \ldots, p_N\}$. Each $p_i \in \mathcal{P}$ is a vector $\langle i, f_{p_i}, (x, y), t_{p_i} \rangle$, where $f_{p_i} \in \mathcal{F}$, $(x, y) \in \mathcal{S}$, and $t_{p_i} \in \mathcal{T}$.

- A neighbor relationship $\mathcal{R}$ over locations in $\mathcal{S}$.
- A spatial prevalence threshold θ_s and a temporal prevalence threshold θ_t.

Find: All spatio-temporal co-occurrence patterns $c_i \subseteq \mathcal{F}$.

Objective:

- Completeness: All spatio-temporal patterns satisfy Equation 7 will be found.
- Correctness: Any found out patterns satisfy Equation 7.

Constraints:

1. $K \ll N$.
2. $0 \leq \theta_s \leq 1$ and $0 \leq \theta_t \leq 1$.

5   COmposite Spatio-Temporal Co-Occurrence Pattern (COSTCOP$^+$) Mining Algorithm

In this section, we first discuss a naïve approach and then propose our novel COSTCOP$^+$ mining algorithm to mine STCOPs.

A naïve approach can use a spatial co-location mining algorithm for each time slot to find spatial prevalent co-locations. It will generate size $k+1$ candidate co-locations for each time slot using spatial prevalent size k subclasses until there are no more candidate spatial co-locations. After finding all size spatial prevalent co-locations in each time slot, a post-processing step can be used to discover STCOPs by pruning out time non-prevalent co-locations. Even though this approach will prune out spatial non-prevalent co-locations early, it will not prune out time non-prevalent co-locations that are spatial prevalent before the post-processing step. This leads to unnecessary computational cost.

5.1   Lower Bound

From the Equation 7, we know the lower bound of the prevalence measure for a qualified candidate spatio-temporal co-occurrence pattern. Using this lower bound, we can also get the lower bound of the spatial prevalence measure and the temporal prevalence measure for the pattern.

From the following equation:

$$\max_{1 \leq t \leq L} (pi(c_i)_t) \times L \geq \sum_{t=1}^{L} pi(c_i)_t \geq (L \times \theta_t) \times \theta_s \tag{8}$$

we can get the relation:

$$\max_{1 \leq t \leq L} (pi(c_i)_t) \geq \theta_t \times \theta_s \tag{9}$$

This relation suggests that for all the L time slots, there must exist one time slot such that for this time slot the participate index value of a qualified candidate pattern c_i must be greater than or equal to $\theta_t \times \theta_s$.

From another equation:

$$tp(c_i) \times L \times 1 \geq \sum_{t=1}^{L} pi(c_i)_t \geq (L \times \theta_t) \times \theta_s \qquad (10)$$

we can get the relation:

$$tp(C_i) \geq \theta_t \times \theta_s \qquad (11)$$

This relation suggests that the temporal prevalence measure of a qualified candidate pattern must be greater than or equal to $\theta_t \times \theta_s$.

If we let θ_{st} as $\theta_s \times \theta_t$, we can rewrite the two relations as:

$$\max_{1 \leq t \leq L} (pi(c_i)_t) \geq \theta_{st}$$
$$tp(c_i) \geq \theta_{st} \qquad (12)$$

5.2   COSTCOP$^+$ Algorithm

We propose COSTCOP$^+$ mining algorithm to discover STCOPs by incorporating a composite prevalence based filtering step in each iteration of the algorithm. The first part of the algorithm is the initialization of the parameters. The second part is a loop to generate size k prevalence STCOPs using size $k-1$ composite prevalence STCOPs from k is 2. If there's no more pattern can be generated after running the loop, the loop will stop and the algorithm continues to the next part. The last part is to get a union of the result for each operation of the loop. In general, the loop part of the COSTCOP$^+$ algorithm consists of the following three stages:

Stage I: Calculating spatial prevalence

1. Use ST_{k-1} to generate all the candidate patterns with size k, $C_k = \{c_{k_1}, \ldots, c_{k_n}\}$ [12].
2. Calculate the pi (participation index) values for each of these patterns for all the L time slots.
3. We can group the patterns by the results:
   (a) C_{k_1}: the pattern c_{k_i} in this group satisfies that for every time slot c_{k_i} appears, $pi(c_{k_i}) \geq \theta_s$.
   (b) C_{k_2}: the pattern c_{k_i} in this group satisfies that for every time slot c_{k_i} appears, there exist at least one time slot a such that $pi(c_{k_i})_a > \theta_s$ and at least one slot b such that $pi(c_{k_i})_b < \theta_s$.
   (c) C_{k_3}: the pattern c_{k_i} in this group satisfies that for every time slot c_{k_i} appears, $pi(c_{k_i}) \leq \theta_s$ and there exist at least one time slot a such that $pi(c_{k_i})_a < \theta_s$ and at least one slot b such that $pi(c_{k_i})_b \geq \theta_{st}$.
   (d) C_{k_4}: the pattern c_{k_i} in this group satisfies that for every time slot c_{k_i} appears, $pi(c_{k_i}) < \theta_{st}$.

Stage II: Calculating temporal prevalence

1. Calculate the tp (time prevalence) values for all the candidate patterns in C_k.
2. We can group the patterns by the results:
   (a) C_{k_5}: the pattern c_{k_i} in this group satisfies that $tp(c_{k_i}) > \theta_t$.
   (b) C_{k_6}: the pattern c_{k_i} in this group satisfies that $tp(c_{k_i}) = \theta_t$.
   (c) C_{k_7}: the pattern c_{k_i} in this group satisfies that $\theta_{st} \le tp(c_{k_i}) < \theta_t$.
   (d) C_{k_8}: the pattern c_{k_i} in this group satisfies that $tp(c_{k_i}) < \theta_{st}$.

Stage III: Pruning

1. Let C_{k_F} be $(C_{k_3} \cap (C_{k_6} \cup C_{k_7})) \cup C_{k_4} \cup C_{k_8}$ and let C_{k_S} be $C_{k_1} \cap (C_{k_5} \cup C_{k_6})$.
2. Add all patterns in C_{k_S} into ST_k.
3. For all other candidate patterns c_{k_i} in $(C_k - (C_{k_F} \cup C_{k_S}))$, if $\sum_{t=1}^{L} pi(c_{k_i})_t \ge (L \times \theta_t) \times \theta_s$, add it to ST_k.

From the description of the algorithm, we can get the following lemmas:

Lemma 1. $C_k = \bigcup_{1 \le i \le 4} C_{k_i}$ and $\forall_{1 \le i < j \le 4}(C_{k_i} \cap C_{k_j}) = \varnothing$

Lemma 2. $C_k = \bigcup_{5 \le i \le 8} C_{k_i}$ and $\forall_{5 \le i < j \le 8}(C_{k_i} \cap C_{k_j}) = \varnothing$

Lemma 3. $C_{k_F} \cap C_{k_S} = \varnothing$

Based on the request that is set up in Equation 7 and 12, we can see that:

1. For a candidate pattern, if it cannot satisfy either requirement of the lower bound, it is definitely unqualified.
2. For a candidate pattern, when all of its participate index values are not greater than the threshold θ_s, one value is less than the threshold, and one value is less than the lower bound θ_{st}, if it appears in more than $\theta_t \times L$ time slots, it may be qualified. Otherwise, it will be definitely unqualified.
3. For a candidate pattern, when all of its participate index values are not less than the threshold θ_s, if it appears in at least $\theta_t \times L$ time slots, it will be definitely qualified.

Using these three basic observations to define the subset C_{k_F} and C_{k_S}, we can decrease the number of candidates that needs further check in Stage III.

6   Experimental Evaluation

In this section, we present our experimental evaluations of several design decisions and workload parameters of our COSTCOP$^+$ algorithm. The real data used are satellite images captured by GOES-E. For each image, we treat it as one time slot. Each image is divided into 12×9 blocks. Therefore, the *space* is a twelve by nine grid. We start the address from $(0, 0)$ to $(11, 9)$. So each *cell*, or *block*, has

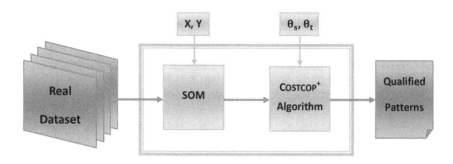

Fig. 2. The analyzing model

a unique address. For each *cell*, we use Self-Organizing Map (SOM) to get an feature ID (an SOM feature map address). Since each address can only have one *cell*, any address in the *space* will only have one spatial feature. We evaluated the behavior of the COSTCOP$^+$ algorithm by changing the number of time slots (the number of images), the number of features (the size of a SOM map), and the spatial prevalence threshold and temporal prevalence threshold. Figure 2 shows the whole structure of the experiments. Experiments were conducted on a computer with an Intel Pentium IV 3.80GHz CPU and 1GB of RAM.

There're six different configurations for the number of time slots: 8, 16, 24, 32, 48, 64. There're also six different configurations for the number of features: 4, 6, 9, 12, 16, 20. In Figure 2, the SOM has two inputs, X and Y. Therefore, the size of feature map that generated by SOM is determined by $X \times Y$. If X is 3 and Y is 4, the size of the map is 12, which also means there will be 12 different features in the input data. For the temporal prevalence threshold θ_t, there're five different configurations as: .2, .4, .6, .8, 1. So does the spatial prevalence threshold θ_s, which has .2, .3, .4, .5, and .6 as its configurations.

Using different configurations for different parameters, we generate the following experiments.

6.1   Effect of the Number of Time Slots

In the first experiment, we evaluate the effect of the number of time slots on the running time for three different configurations of the number of features (Figure 3). The value of θ_s and θ_t are fixed with 0.2 and 0.4. From the result, we can get that when the number of time slots increases, the total running time is also increasing. For a small number of features, this increase is not obvious. However, for a large number of features, this increase is remarkable. But it still approximates to a linear increase.

6.2   Effect of the Number of Features

In the second experiment, we evaluate the effect of the number of features on the execution time for three different configurations of the number of time slots

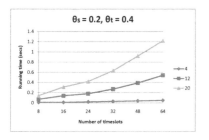

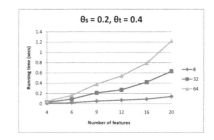

Fig. 3. Effective of number of time slots

Fig. 4. Effective of number of features

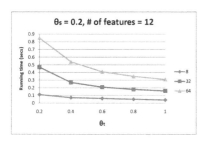

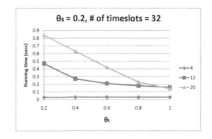

Fig. 5. Effective of the temporal prevalence threshold with the number of features fixed

Fig. 6. Effective of the temporal prevalence threshold with the number of timeslots fixed

(Figure 4). The value of θ_s and θ_t are still fixed with 0.2 and 0.4. From the result, we can see that the total running time is increasing with the increase of the number of features. The increasing speed is almost in proportion to the square of the increase of the number of features. This is easy for understanding since when the number of features doubles, the total number of candidate patterns will have a four times increase.

6.3   Effect of the Temporal Prevalence Threshold

In the third experiment, we evaluate the effect of the temporal prevalence threshold. This experiment has two parts: $(1)\theta_s$ and the number of features are fixed and the number of time slots is configured with three different values; $(2)\theta_s$ and the number of time slots are fixed and the number of features is configured with three different values; Figure 5 illustrates the result for part (1) and Figure 6 shows the result for part (2).

In both of cases, with the increase of θ_t, the total running time is decreasing, since for each "step" of candidate generation, we will have less number of qualified patterns to use. When the value of θ_t was increased to 1, most of candidate patterns will be pruned for the first a few "steps". Therefore, the process will stop much earlier. However, the decreasing speeds are not very same for these two parts. Considering the situations we have already analyzed above, we can get

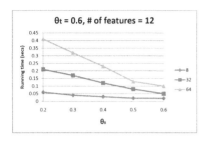
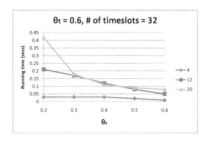

Fig. 7. Effective of the spatial prevalence threshold with the number of features fixed

Fig. 8. Effective of the spatial prevalence threshold with the number of timeslots fixed

that the change of the number of features should have a more remarkable impact on the total running time. So the second part has a more sharper decrease than the first one.

6.4   Effect of the Spatial Prevalence Threshold

In the fourth experiment, we evaluate the effect of the spatial prevalence threshold. This experiment also has two parts: $(1)\theta_t$ and the number of features are fixed and the number of time slots is configured with three different values; $(2)\theta_t$ and the number of time slots are fixed and the number of features is configured with three different values; Figure 7 illustrates the result for part (1) and Figure 8 shows the result for part (2).

The results are in a very similar situation with the third experiment and the reasons are almost the same.

7   Conclusion

In this paper, we defined spatio-temporal co-occurrence patterns (STCOPs) and the spatio-temporal co-occurrence pattern mining problem. We also proposed a new monotonic composite measure in Equation 7, which is the composition of the spatial prevalence and temporal prevalence measures. Later, we presented a novel and computationally efficient algorithm, COSTCOP+. We proved that the proposed algorithm is correct and complete in finding spatio-temporal co-occurrence patterns. The algorithm is also proved to be efficient compared with the naïve approach. Using a real dataset, the experiments provide further evidence of the viability of the proposed algorithm.

One of the future works of this problem is to utilize another measure to justify whether a candidate pattern is qualified or not. In [13], the authors proposed a method to calculate the correlation by using cone concepts. However, the efficiency of this method is restricted with low dimensional data. Therefore, for high dimensional data, this method needs to be improved.

Another future work is about the method to generate candidate patterns. Our algorithm uses a self-join operation to generate candidate patterns. Yoo et al. proposed a join-less approach for mining spatial co-location patterns [14]. However, this method is a distance-based but not a grid-based approach. Therefore, some accommodations need to be applied on this approach.

References

1. Worboys, M.: GIS: A Computing Perspective. Taylor & Francis, London (1995)
2. Box, G.E.P., Jenkins, G.M., Reinsel, G.C.: Time Series Analysis: Forcasting and Control, 3rd edn. Prentice-Hall, Englewood Cliffs (1994)
3. Güting, R.H., Schneider, M.: Moving Object Databases. Morgan Kaufmann, San Francisco (2005)
4. Koubarakis, M., Sellis, T., Frank, A.U., Grumbach, S., Güting, R.H., Jensen, C.S., Lorentzos, N., Manolopoulos, Y., Nardelli, E., Pernici, B., Schek, H.J., Scholl, M., Theodoulidis, B., Tryfona, N.: Spatio-Temporal Databases. LNCS, vol. 2520. Springer, Heidelberg (2003)
5. Cressie, N.A.C.: Statistics for spatial data. Wiley, New York (1993)
6. Gudmundsson, J., van Kreveld, M.J., Speckmann, B.: Efficient detection of motion patterns in spatio-temporal data sets. In: Pfoser, D., Cruz, I.F., Ronthaler, M. (eds.) 12th ACM International Workshop on Geographic Information Systems, ACM-GIS 2004, Washington, D.C., pp. 250–257 (2004)
7. Kalnis, P., Mamoulis, N., Bakiras, S.: On discovering moving clusters in spatio-temporal data. In: Bauzer Medeiros, C., Egenhofer, M.J., Bertino, E. (eds.) SSTD 2005. LNCS, vol. 3633, pp. 364–381. Springer, Heidelberg (2005)
8. Celik, M., Shekhar, S., Rogers, J.P., Shine, J.A., Yoo, J.S.: Mixed-drove spatio-temporal co-occurence pattern mining: A summary of results. In: ICDM 2006, pp. 119–128. IEEE Computer Society, Los Alamitos (2006)
9. Celik, M., Shekhar, S., Rogers, J.P., Shine, J.A.: Sustained emerging spatio-temporal co-occurrence pattern mining: A summary of results. In: Proceedings of the 18th International Conference on Tools with Artificial Intelligence (ICTAI 2006), pp. 106–115. IEEE Computer Society, Los Alamitos (2006)
10. Shekhar, S., Huang, Y.: Discovering spatial co-location patterns: A summary of results. In: Jensen, C.S., Schneider, M., Seeger, B., Tsotras, V.J. (eds.) SSTD 2001. LNCS, vol. 2121, pp. 236–256. Springer, Heidelberg (2001)
11. Huang, Y., Shekhar, S., Xiong, H.: Discovering colocation patterns from spatial data sets: A general approach. IEEE Transactions on Knowledge and Data Engineering 16(12), 1472–1485 (2004)
12. Han, J., Kamber, M.: Data Mining: Concepts and Techniques. Morgan Kaufmann, San Francisco (2000)
13. Zhang, P., Huang, Y., Shekhar, S., Kumar, V.: Correlation analysis of spatial time series datasets: A filter-and-refine approach. In: Whang, K.-Y., Jeon, J., Shim, K., Srivastava, J. (eds.) PAKDD 2003. LNCS (LNAI), vol. 2637, pp. 532–544. Springer, Heidelberg (2003)
14. Yoo, J.S., Shekhar, S.: A joinless approach for mining spatial colocation patterns. IEEE Transactions on Knowledge and Data Engineering 18(10), 1323–1337 (2006)

Belief Propagation in Wireless Sensor Networks - A Practical Approach

Tal Anker[1,2], Danny Dolev[1], and Bracha Hod[1]

[1] The Hebrew University of Jerusalem, Israel
{anker,dolev,hodb}@cs.huji.ac.il
[2] Marvell Semiconductor, CA, USA
tala@marvell.com

Abstract. Distributed inference schemes for detection, estimation and learning comprise an attractive approach to Wireless Sensor Networks (WSNs), because of properties such as asynchronous operation and robustness in the face of failures.

Belief Propagation (BP) is a method for distributed inference which provides accurate results with rapid convergence properties. However, applying a BP algorithm to WSN is challenging. Many papers that proposed using BP for WSNs do not consider all of the constraints which these networks impose.

This paper presents a framework that implements both localized and data-centric approaches to improve the effectiveness and the robustness of this algorithm in the WSN environment. The proposed solution is empirically evaluated, as applied to the clustering problem, and it can be easily extended to suit many other applications that use BP as an underlying algorithm.

Keywords: Belief Propagation, Wireless Sensor Networks.

1 Introduction

It is generally believed that Wireless Sensor Networks (WSNs) will be ubiquitously accepted as an infrastructure for applications in areas as diverse as environmental monitoring, health-care applications, and home automation. Data fusion and processing will be the core information gathering activities performed by the sensor nodes. Consequently, inference methods, which are important means of performing data fusion, have become an increasing research interest in the field of WSNs.

The goal of distributed inference in WSNs can be achieved using several methods that were originally developed for graphical models [1], such as Belief Propagation (BP) [2]. BP is an iterative algorithm for computing maximal or marginal posterior probability, by means of local message-passing. BP is presented in the literature as an effective and useful inference method for a wide range of communication applications and network topologies, including WSNs [3], [4].

The adoption of an inference algorithm such as BP for WSNs presents a great opportunity, because learning techniques which fully utilize the available

Y. Li et al. (Eds.): WASA 2008, LNCS 5258, pp. 466–479, 2008.

information can achieve nearly optimal results. However, it is also a formidable challenge, due to the distinctive characteristics of these networks: Energy efficiency is a major design goal in WSNs because the nodes have limited power sources and restricted computational capacities. The wireless medium imposes many other constraints, such as collisions and errors. Other properties of this medium, such as interferences and poor link quality, result in changes to the topology of the network, which, together with the fact that the network is self-organizing, create a unique and challenging network dynamic. WSNs are also likely to have a large number of nodes which may result in potentially drastic scaling problems.

The significance of this paper is twofold:

Firstly, our research provides important insights regarding real-world challenges in WSNs, which may significantly affect the inference quality. These insights are relevant to many WSN inference schemes, and are addressed in this paper in a broader manner than has been previously presented (such as in [3], [4], [5] and [6], which either posit impractical assumptions about network topology, or otherwise neglect issues such as the overhead of communication or scalability of the solution).

Secondly, driven by the need for a practical solution, we propose a general BP framework that takes both localized [7] and data-centric [8] approaches. Using simulations, we demonstrate and analyze the properties of the scheme within the context of a solution to the clustering problem. The entire framework is fully distributed and localized, and presents an excellent approximation to the optimal inference solution. Moreover, it is shown to be asynchronous and robust, and to introduce only a minor and consistent cost in communication and overhead, regardless of the size of the network.

In contrast with previous work in this area [9], this paper focuses on the general construction and properties of the BP framework in the WSN, rather than on the application itself. The goal of this paper is to understand the general characteristics of the BP framework, which has not been presented to date. Introduction of new concepts about the clustering task is beyond the scope of the paper.

The rest of the paper is organized as follows. Section 2 briefly describes the related work in this area. A short background is provided in Section 3. The practical issues involved in WSNs are described in Section 4. An efficient BP scheme for distributed inference is presented in Section 5. Section 6 includes an analysis of this method using simulations. Section 7 concludes the paper with a summary.

2   Related Work

A graphical-model-oriented perspective of distributed data fusion in WSNs is presented in [10]. The paper provides a bridge between the field of graphical models to the data fusion in WSNs, discusses the tradeoffs between approximation and energy conservation and presents message censoring as an approach for solving the problem. The paper concludes that the results are far from complete and that the mapping between the two domains is still an area for research.

A general and robust architecture for distributed inference in sensor networks is proposed in [5]. The architecture presented in that paper considers practical issues and provides an analysis using a real deployment of WSNs. The method is based on a junction tree for message-passing, and as such has two main drawbacks: First, construction and maintenance of the tree require a large amount of communication and processing overhead, as well as usage of reliable mechanisms. Moreover, exact inference in large networks becomes unrealistic since the method scales exponentially with the number of nodes, because of the complexity of the junction tree.

Loopy belief propagation (LBP) [11] is presented in [3] as an attractive method for use with WSNs, due to its distributed nature and its robustness in environments with asynchronous communication, noise and failures. However, the paper in question does not deal with practical issues, such as energy consumption or topology changes. Furthermore, the LBP was proven to be effective mainly in decoding applications, when the graph has long cycles. This is not the situation in WSNs, which contain many short cycles.

Nonparametric belief propagation is proposed in [4] for solving the localization problem. That paper is the first to present the broadcast variation of BP and it refers to many of the communication constraints that might appear in sensor networks. While that paper uses the LBP, our alternative approach of operating on trees can suit other applications. Additionally, some realistic issues, such as the effect of topology changes, are beyond the scope of that paper.

Reweighted belief propagation, implemented by [6], simulates a running of the basic algorithm of BP multiple times on different spanning trees, using different weights each time, to overcome the convergence problem of LBP and to find a fixed point. As presented in [10], the amount of communication required for the Tree Reweighted Max Product method is significantly larger than the basic max product algorithm.

3   Background

Graphical models [1] play an important role in machine learning algorithms that deal with uncertainty and complexity. They involve a mixture of probability theory and graph theory and are based on the basic idea of modularity, thus allowing a complex system to be viewed as a combination of many simpler pieces connected by probability theory. The graph theoretical aspects of the models provide a methodology to understand and formulate the system.

In a probabilistic graphical model, an undirected graph $G = (V, E)$ is a set of nodes V and arcs E, which represent dependencies among random variables. We denote by x_i the variable representing the set of possible states of a node i. $\psi_i(x_i)$ represents a local (previously known) distribution function of node i and $\psi_{ij}(x_i, x_j)$ refers to a joint function of two connected nodes i and j. These functions are also called potential functions.

In the BP method [12], [13], the inference is carried out in a local and distributed manner by each node, using a message-passing technique. $m_{ij}(x_j)$ is a

The idea behind the BP algorithm is that the marginal or posterior probabilities can be efficiently computed in a distributed manner, using Bayes' theorem and by means of local message-passing. Consider, for instance, the four events as illustrated. It is possible to globally compute the probability of event D, using 8−sum calculation:

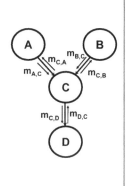

$$p(x_D) = \sum_{x_C, x_B, x_A} p(x_D, x_C, x_B, x_A) \ .$$

Alternatively, by a local computation, only 6−sum calculation is required:

$$p(x_C) = \sum_{x_B, x_A} p(x_C | x_B, x_A) p(x_B) p(x_A) \ .$$

$$p(x_D) = \sum_{x_C} p(x_C) \ .$$

Fig. 1. Intuition to the BP method

message from node i to node j regarding the next state of node j. Node i calculates the message using previous messages it receives from its adjacent neighbors $N(i)$. The message update rule performed by a node i in round t is:

$$m_{ij}(x_j)^t = \sum_{x_i} \psi_i(x_i) \psi_{ij}(x_i, x_j) \prod_{k \in N(i) \backslash j} m_{ki}(x_i)^{t-1} \ .$$

The update rule being calculated by node i to determine the preferred state x_j of node j is a sum of all the possible states x_i of node i, assuming that j is in state x_j. Three elements are incorporated to each state: previously known information about the local node $\psi_i(x_i)$, the joint function $\psi_{ij}(x_i, x_j)$ and the information about the immediately adjacent neighbors $m_{ki}(x_i)^{t-1}$.

Upon termination, after round $\bar{t}$, the belief at a node i (the marginal of the variable) is the product of the local evidence together with all the incoming messages and a normalization constant α:

$$b_i(x_i) = \alpha \psi_i(x_i) \prod_{k \in N(i)} m_{ki}(x_i)^{\bar{t}} \ .$$

The BP algorithm for trees is an exact inference algorithm, which means that the belief converges to the correct marginal values in a finite number of iterations equal to the diameter of the tree.

A traditional BP algorithm massively uses floating point computations, which are expensive. We propose to use the Min-Sum algorithm [14], which is a variant of the BP algorithm, applied in the log-probability domain. The Min-Sum algorithm requires only addition and substraction operations and works well with integer values. The goal of the algorithm is to minimize the overall cost over all the nodes in the network, based on the local cost functions and the constraints among the nodes. The reader is referred to [9] for further details about the Min-Sum algorithm and its broadcast implementation.

4   Practical Issues

WSNs operate under a set of unique constraints and requirements that demand significant improvements and modifications to traditional algorithms. In particular, the BP algorithm cannot be embedded into WSNs in its original form. Several issues should be addressed to enable its efficiency in WSNs.

4.1   Mapping WSN to Graphical Model

Mapping of a WSN into the graphical model appears to be the most challenging task in the realization of this goal. The mapping of the network can be either to a tree or to a cyclic network.

Several papers, such as [3], have shown good results of the LBP in practical applications, mainly decoding. [15] discusses the convergence of the BP algorithm in general networks with single or multiple loops. The LBP worked well in these cases mostly because the cycles in the graph were large, so the effects of the cycles faded after only a few iterations. WSNs are associated with short cycles made by the broadcast range, so LBP is not an appropriate method for many applications in such networks. The use of the Min-Sum algorithm for energy efficiency also implies some limitations upon operating in a cyclic network. The convergence problem of the Min-Sum algorithm is similar to the convergence of the distance-vector routing protocol [16] and it is guaranteed only in acyclic networks. The split horizon rule cannot be applied in a BP algorithm, because of the algorithm structure.

Alternative methods remove the loops by replacing the cyclic network with trees. The junction tree is the most common such method and it is based on two properties: (1) every clique of the original graph is contained in some clique of the junction tree; and (2) for each node of the original graph, the cliques and all the edges containing it form a connected subtree of the junction tree.

Paskin and Guestrin in [5], argue about the need for a special architecture for distributed inference. Their major claim is that an optimized junction tree may reduce the overall communication cost. Additionally, the junction tree is more stable, flexible and does not depend on the network layer. The key disadvantage of the junction tree method is the large communication overhead it requires. Construction and maintenance of such a tree, when the network is continuously changing, incurs considerable overhead by the nodes.

4.2   Robustness against Failures

BP has a rapid convergence property, but when too many errors are involved, it is likely that the convergence will be slower and the nodes will converge to an incorrect value. WSNs are exposed to a fairly large amount of communication and node failures. Apart from the ordinary failures in WSNs, such as packet errors and loss due to interferences and poor link quality, BP is especially vulnerable to broadcast message-passing, synchronization problems and topology changes during the message transmission.

Broadcast Communication. The wireless medium allows transmission of a single one-to-many message instead of multiple one-to-one messages. However at the same time, it imposes larger constraints on the shared medium, such as collisions and contention.

Message transmission in a broadcast manner reduces the communication volume, but at the same time it is much more sensitive to synchronization problems and is more error-prone than the original algorithm. Instead of receiving a unicast message $m_{ji}(x_i)^t$ from node j, node i is required to extract the relevant information from the broadcast message, by a subtraction of its own information from the previous round's, and by calculating it on its own [9]:

$$m_{ji}(x_i)^t = \min_{x_j}\{\psi_{ij}(x_i, x_j) + m_{j*}(x_j)^t - m_{ij}(x_j)^{t-1}\} \ .$$

The separation of a single update rule into two rules performed by different nodes, increases the potential errors and the synchronization issues that are involved with this method. Consider a situation where node j sends a message $m_{j*}(x_j)^t$. Upon reception of this message by node i, it subtracts its last message $m_{ij}(x_j)^{t-1}$, assuming that it was included in node j's message. In the event of message loss, when $m_{i*}(x_i)^{t-1}$ was not received by node j and was not included in its broadcast message, node i's belief will be wrong and this error may be propagated through the network to other nodes. The nodes may ultimately converge to a common belief, but there is no guarantee that they will converge to the correct value. In the original protocol such a scenario will not occur, since the entire calculation is an atomic operation by a single node. In case of message loss, the nodes may synchronize in a subsequent iteration.

Synchronization. Perfect synchronization among the nodes in WSNs is difficult to achieve in practice, because of clock drifts. Therefore, message-passing would be better off if performed asynchronously, upon message reception from other nodes or upon external events.

The nodes' duty cycle is another factor to consider in the context of asynchronous operation; the message-passing algorithm should take into account cases where nodes wake up only in the middle of a process.

The general BP algorithm enforces some message ordering in each of the message-passing iterations. In the asynchronous method, there are no sequencing constraints and the messages may be transmitted arbitrarily during an iteration. Every node stores the received messages and computes them at the end of the iteration. The lack of synchronization thus introduces the additional cost of storage, and adds even further cost because some messages may be recomputed and retransmitted several times.

Topology Changes. WSNs are usually defined as semi-static networks because the nodes are not mobile in the sense of mobile networks. However, the nodes may nevertheless be repositioned by external factors, such as wind. Most commonly, the topology might change because the wireless links are not stable and sensor nodes are prone to failure. Therefore, the message-passing algorithm must not assume static topology during its invocation, and scenarios such as link break must be taken into consideration during the message-passing. A link break between some key node and its descendant may harm the convergence of the entire network, as the connectivity may be broken into separate components. Even when the message-passing tree is re-constructed, the synchronization between the nodes may not be restored. Therefore, it is very important to build a stable tree to minimize the effect of topology changes on the message-passing process, while managing such common scenarios.

4.3   Scalability

Since scalability is a main concern in WSNs, localized algorithms [7] are used as the building blocks in these networks. These localized algorithms are distributed and only a subset of the nodes participate. The nodes interact with each other only in a restricted vicinity, thus using only a limited amount of communication, computation, and storage resources - all crucial for energy efficiency in WSNs. While this approach seems to promise scalability, the design of such algorithms under the constraints of WSNs is not a trivial undertaking. Following this paradigm and the self-organization property of WSNs [17], the key challenge is to find localized behavior rules that may lead to the desired global property or at least approximate it, when applied by all the nodes.

Although BP is based on local message-passing, it is not inherently limited to a small region, and most of the proposed inference approaches based on BP are not localized. Localizing BP means that the algorithm is required to involve only part of the network and have a constant number of iterations, independent of the network diameter. Consequently, this decreases the number of transmitted messages and the time to deliver them, as well as resulting in low latency, regardless of the size of the network.

5   Efficient BP Framework for WSN

In light of the challenges presented in the previous section, this section describes the BP scheme for distributed inference in WSN.

5.1   Mapping WSN to Graphical Model

Our scheme maps a WSN into a graphical model by constructing multiple trees, where each tree combines the properties of the routing tree (such as hop count and link quality) together with clique properties. Thus, nodes that exist in the same clique in the graph are likely to be in the same message-passing tree. The cliques in the graph may be generated according to some metric, depending on the application, and/or according to the physical layout. The spatial locality property of WSNs means that nodes which are physically close are likely to maintain relevant information, so it is common to have trees which were developed as a function both of their physical properties (e.g. a routing tree) and of the information which they contain.

The requirement for associating a clique to the tree, in addition to the routing requirements, can be understood from two different points of view. From the perspective of the graphical model, the ideal mapping of the network to a tree is to apply methods (such as the junction tree) which preserve the clique structure of the original graph. Construction of a tree, based on partial knowledge of the cliques in the graph results in a closer approximation of the actual junction tree, implying an improved result.

The second viewpoint is based on the data-centric approach to WSNs. Data centricity [7], [8] is a basic term in WSNs, which refers to the greater reliance upon the information content than on the geography or the identity of the nodes in the network. Concentration of the data content enables design of a more robust application, and outperforms idealized traditional schemes.

We improve our message-passing tree by considering the information that the nodes hold, similarly to the concept presented in the Directed Diffusion method [18]. Every tree is created on-the-fly using a single message that contains routing information, including parent and hop count, in addition to application-specific information. The fact that the tree is dynamically and locally created without any maintenance requirements, means that it scales and is efficient. The node that starts the inference process (i.e. with no prior information from its neighbors) operates as a root, by setting its hop count to zero. The nodes that receive the message can either select the sender as a parent, or wait a random short period (limited by a timer) in search of a better candidate. To be selected, a parent must fulfill the routing requirements and reside in the same clique in the graph. If a node does not find any parent after a given period, it operates as a root.

Each time the node selects a parent, it increments its hop count, This mechanism is used to detect and break cycles in the graph. Once every node is either designated as a root or has a parent, the trees are defined and it is now possible to perform the entire Min-Sum algorithm.

5.2   Robustness

The overall robustness of the algorithm has been presented. It should be noted that it is not possible to totally overcome the algorithm's sensitivity to failures, such as malformed messages and message loss. However, it is possible to reduce the occurrence of failures by using several heuristics:

1. The asynchronous nature of the sensors can be overcome by means of a "round" field in each message. This field designates the time interval in which messages are grouped together. Messages that arrive too early can be stored in a buffer and messages that arrive too late can be ignored.

Tree Construction:

(1) Upon a triggering event or a timer:

    (1.1) If no BP messages with positive *propagationLimit* have been received, start the process as a root by setting *hop* to zero and the localized predefined value of *propagationLimit*;

    (1.2) Otherwise, select the best possible parent and start the process with the parent's *propagationLimit* decreased by one; The parent is defined as "final" if it meets all the requirements;

(2) Upon reception of a first-round BP message from other nodes:

    (2.1) If already in the message-passing process:

        (2.1.1) If the current parent meets both the routing tree requirement and the clique requirement → process the message if it originates from this node's parent or descendant;

        (2.1.2) If the current parent is not final: if the message's sender meets the requirements and also has a positive *propagationLimit*, then replace the parent with the message sender and process its message;

    (2.2) If not in the message-passing process:

        (2.2.1) If the message's sender meets all the requirements, and also has a positive *propagationLimit*, select that node as a parent and start the process with the given *propagationLimit* decreased by one;

        (2.2.2) Otherwise, set a timer to start the process in a later time.

Fig. 2. Sketch of the Tree Formation

2. The "round" field in each message can also be used for detection and reproduction of message loss. Reproduction of the last message is performed by processing the last message that was received by this node, as if it had been received in the current round. Reproduction of the message keeps the nodes synchronized and enables convergence in later iterations.

3. The Min-Sum algorithm computes cost information by subtracting previous messages, under the assumption that the cost cannot decrease from one round to another. We use a broadcast version of this algorithm, which can cause errors in the subtraction operation, in that a value greater than the current value may be subtracted, resulting in an (incorrect) negative value. Some of these errors may be detected, because the application assumes that these values fall within some range, so that any deviation from this range will signify an error. The wrong information is ignored in this case.

4. Link breaks between neighbors that are not mapped in the graphical model as a parent and its descendant, do not affect the message-passing process. When the link break affects the graphical model, a node may either select a new parent and try to synchronize with it, or it may become a root.

5.3 Scalability

The BP algorithm is not inherently localized and requires global processing of all the groups of nodes in order to achieve a global optimum. Construction of a fully localized algorithm is similar to the general scheme with a few salient differences: (1) The localized algorithm operates locally, and therefore tends to create multiple trees, instead of a single global tree. (2) Flooding control is managed by a "propagation limit" field in each message, which determines the diameter of the message-passing tree. This field may be set to any desired small value, so only nodes within this vicinity are able to participate in the message-passing process. (3) Scalability is also achieved by defining, a priori, the number of rounds until termination, resulting in a constant message and time overhead, regardless of the size of the network. This limit is necessary not only for reducing the processing and the communication overhead, but also to ensure the termination of the process. This is due to the fact that convergence is not guaranteed in an asynchronous environment with failures and errors.

6   Empirical Evaluation

6.1   Case Study: Clustering

In this section, we analyze the BP framework that was constructed above, by applying it to an implementation of the clustering problem. The implementation provides us with a way to confirm the quality of the inference in the constructed framework.

The only aspect of this application which is implementation-specific is the content of the BP packets, and not the construction of the trees for the message-passing. Therefore we can derive conclusions from our analysis which are also applicable to other applications.

We model the sensor network as a directed graph G = (V,E), where V is a set of nodes, where each node is assigned a local unique identifier. E is a set of wireless links connecting two adjacent nodes. Nodes are defined as adjacent if and only if they are within transmission range of each other.

The key challenge that we address here regarding clustering schemes in multi-hop WSNs is how to efficiently form a connected disjointed group of nodes in a local and distributed manner. Each group contains a single leader and several ordinary nodes. An efficient scheme is used to select cluster heads (CHs) that: (1) minimize the total transmission power aggregated over all nodes in the selected path; (2) balance the load among the nodes to prolong the network lifetime.

Optimal cluster selection is equivalent to the minimum dominating set problem, which is an NP-complete problem. Using the BP method, it is possible to achieve a good approximation in polynomial time, since the computation is dispersed and divided among all the nodes,

Following the graphical model definitions and the cost functions as presented in [9], the clustering problem can be formulated as follows: x_i is defined to be a CH candidate of node i and $\psi_i(x_i)$ defines a local cost function of connecting node i to x_i. $\psi_{ij}(x_i, x_j)$ represents the constraints between two neighbors i and j to prevent improper assignment of CH association. The constraints are: (1) two neighbors cannot both be CHs; (2) a node can select another node to be its CH only if that node announces that it is a CH. If one of the constraints is true, the function approaches infinity; otherwise the function approaches zero.

Broadcasting a message as part of the Min-Sum algorithm incurs a cost. Accordingly, each message stores cost information of two types: (1) The individual cost of a node to become a cluster head, independent of the other nodes. (2) The cost of connecting to other nodes, which is a function of the link between the nodes as well as other information. The information regarding these costs is updated based on the information received from the parent and the descendants in the tree structure, according to the Min-Sum algorithm. The final goal of the nodes is to select CHs that minimize the overall cost, over the whole network, based on the cost values and the constraints between the nodes [9]. In this application, two connected nodes in the graph are considered to be in the same clique if they have some predefined number of common neighbors.

6.2   Simulation Framework

TOSSIM, TinyOS simulator [19], was used for performance analysis of the clustering algorithm. The simulator provides an environment which is close to reality and includes realistic properties of a network, such as interferences, asymmetric links, changes in link quality, node death, failure, etc. Link Estimation and Parent Selection [20] was used as the routing protocol in the multihop network.

Every plot was taken as an average of 20 different runs and over five different time slots, to verify the behavior in different topologies of the network. The duration between two consecutive time slots was large enough for topology changes to take place and for different routing trees to be constructed, but obviously the changes are not too radical, reflecting a common trait of WSNs.

In all the simulations, the localized algorithm operates in a vicinity of two hops, with the constant number of rounds equal to eight. This number of rounds was set to guarantee convergence in an asynchronous environment when taking into account the fact that the number of rounds necessary until convergence of the clustering application is larger than the size of the tree diameter. This is because the decision about the CH candidates is done after observing the nodes in the subtree, which in itself takes several rounds. Two nodes are considered to be in the same clique when at least half of their neighbors are common.

6.3   Simulation Results

We determine the quality of the inference scheme by examining the number of clusters that are constructed in the network. The optimal number of clusters in WSNs depends upon network dynamics - such as connectivity and density - which change over time. Using the setup of TOSSIM (which supports at most 16 neighbors and a density of around 14 in practice), we conclude that the optimal number of clusters is about four clusters for each group of 50 nodes.

Figure 3 shows the number of CHs achieved by the localized scheme in networks with 50 to 250 nodes. As shown, the algorithm's approximation is very close to the optimal solution, which is evidence of the ability of the constructed scheme to achieve a good approximation in an inference problem.

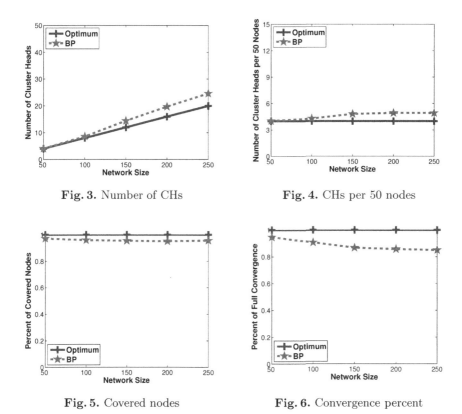

Fig. 3. Number of CHs

Fig. 4. CHs per 50 nodes

Fig. 5. Covered nodes

Fig. 6. Convergence percent

While it is hard to conclude the scalability of the solution from Figure 3, Figure 4 shows that the algorithm reaches a constant competitive ratio of about five cluster heads for each group of 50 nodes - as opposed to four, in medium to large groups. We chose to use a simulator that fully simulates the sensor behavior, instead of using a rough estimate given by the Matlab simulator, whose scalability constraints do not allow us to feasibly simulate networks of more than 250 sensors. However, the competitive ratio remains constant as we approach the 250-node limit. This implies that the quality of the solution will remain constant even for larger networks. The conclusion that the solution is scalable is further supported by the localized properties of the scheme, which operates in a constant vicinity with a constant number of rounds.

The convergence of the nodes into a common value, as shown in Figure 6, is inversely proportional to the number of clusters that were selected in the network. Figure 6 presents the high convergence of the algorithm, which varies between 95 to 85 percent using eight rounds. Figure 8 and Figure 7 demonstrate the average number of lost messages in the network and for each message-passing tree. It appears that large networks suffer from more errors than small networks, due to the fact that more packets are routed in these networks. These errors, in turn, slow down the convergence. When simulating networks with 200 nodes over

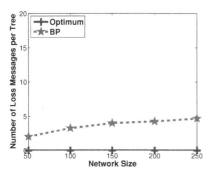

Fig. 7. Loss messages per tree

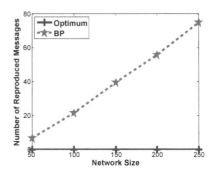

Fig. 8. Total loss messages

ten rounds instead of eight, the convergence increases from around 85 percent to about 90 percent.

To verify the effect of dynamic topology, we simulated, in networks with 250 nodes, more rapid changes in the link quality than the usual, resulting in an average of 20 significant changes during the message-passing. As can be concluded from Figure 6 and Figure 7, the scheme is robust, even in adverse network conditions, such as variable link quality.

Even in the absence of a perfect convergence, once the decision about the CHs is made, the majority of the nodes find a suitable CH in the area, as shown Figure 5. This means that the quality of the inference is very high because the clusters are spread over all the networks, and even if some rounds are missed, thus delaying the convergence at some nodes, the general inference nevertheless succeeds.

This success is due to the general inference of a value which is close to the convergence point, even in the absence of complete convergence of the nodes. The full convergence can be deduced within a few more rounds. Therefore, the final belief is almost perfect, in that it is close to that of nodes which have already converged.

7   Summary

This paper introduces and analyzes an efficient and practical BP framework for distributed inference. Using localized and data-centric approaches, our scheme takes into account the special characteristics and constraints of the WSN environment and consequently it provides better scaling and robustness than other approaches. With a small constant overhead, the scheme achieves outstanding results when compared to the optimal solution. The construction of the scheme is application-independent, and therefore suitable for a large variety of applications that require inference.

Acknowledgment. We would like to thank Danny Bickson and Amy Fredj for many valuable comments.

References

1. Jordan, M.: Learning in Graphical Models. Kluwer Academic Publishers, Dordrecht (1998)
2. Pearl, J.: Probabilistic Reasoning in Intelligent Systems: Networks of Plausible Inference. Morgan Kaufmann, San Francisco (1988)
3. Crick, C., Pfeffer, A.: Loopy belief propagation as a basis for communication in sensor networks. In: UAI (2003)
4. Ihler, A.T., Fisher III, J.W., Moses, R.L., Willsky, A.S.: Nonparametric belief propagation for self-calibration in sensor networks. IEEE Journal of Selected Areas in Communication (2005)
5. Paskin, M.A., Guestrin, C., McFadden, J.: A robust architecture for distributed inference in sensor networks. In: IPSN (2005)
6. Schiff, J., Antonelli, D., Dimakis, A.G., Chu, D., Wainwright, M.J.: Robust message-passing for statistical inference in sensor networks. In: IPSN (2007)
7. Estrin, D., Govindan, R., Heidemann, J., Kumar, S.: Next century challenges: scalable coordination in sensor networks. In: MobiCom. (1999)
8. Krishnamachari, B., Estrin, D., Wicker, S.: Modelling Data-Centric Routing in Wireless Sensor Networks. IEEE INFOCOM (2002)
9. Anker, T., Bickson, D., Dolev, D., Hod, B.: Efficient clustering for improving network performance in wireless sensor networks. In: Verdone, R. (ed.) EWSN 2008. LNCS, vol. 4913. Springer, Heidelberg (2008)
10. Cetin, M., Chen, L., Fisher, J., Ihler, A., Moses, R., Wainwright, M., Willsky, A.: Distributed fusion in sensor networks: A graphical models perspective. IEEE Signal Processing Magazine 23(4) (2006)
11. Murphy, K.P., Weiss, Y., Jordan, M.I.: Loopy belief propagation for approximate inference: An empirical study. In: UAI (1999)
12. Yedidia, J.S., Freeman, W.T., Weiss, Y.: Understanding belief propagation and its generalizations. Technical Report TR-2001-22, MERL (2002)
13. Jordan, M.I., Weiss, Y.: Probabilistic inference in graphical models. In: The Handbook of Brain Theory and Neural Networks. MIT Press, Cambridge (2002)
14. Wiberg, N.: Codes and Decoding on General Graphs. PhD thesis, Dept. of Electrical Engineering, Linköping, Sweden (1996)
15. Weiss, Y.: Correctness of local probability propagation in graphical models with loops. Neural Comput. 12(1) (2000)
16. Chiang, M., Bambos, N.: Distributed network control through sum product algorithm on graphs. In: GLOBECOM (2002)
17. Prehofer, C., Bettstetter, C.: Self-organization in communication networks: principles and design paradigms. IEEE Communications Magazine 43(7) (2005)
18. Intanagonwiwat, C., Govindan, R., Estrin, D.: Directed diffusion: A scalable and robust communication paradigm for sensor networks. MobiCom (2000)
19. TinyOs: http://www.tinyos.net/
20. Woo, A., Tong, T., Culler, D.: Taming the underlying challenges of reliable multi-hop routing in sensor networks. In: SenSys. (2003)

A Random Key Management Scheme for Wireless Sensor Networks

Qing Yang[1,*], QiaoLiang Li[1,3], Xiaoming Wang[2,3], Naixue Xiong[3], and Yi Pan[3]

[1] School of Computer Science and Communication, Hunan University,
Changsha 410082, China
[2] School of Computer Science, Shanxi Normal University, Xi'an 710062, China
[3] Department of Computer Science, Georgia State University, Atlanta 30319, USA
sinis@tom.com.cn, lqlbox@163.com, wangxmsnnu@hotmail.com,
nxiong@cs.gsu.edu, pan@cs.gsu.edu

Abstract. The establishment of shared keys between communicating neighbor nodes in wireless sensor networks is a challenge due to resource-constrained sensor networks. Several key pre-distribution schemes have been proposed in literatures to establish pairwise keys between sensor nodes. However, many of them are either too complicated to fit for wireless sensor networks or insecure for some common aggressions. In this paper, we propose a random key management scheme based on random key pre-distribution for wireless sensor networks. To achieve better performance and security, the proposed scheme employs two different phases to establish enhanced pairwise keys between neighboring nodes. Compared with other existing random key pre-distribution schemes, our scheme has better resilience against node capture and also performs better in terms of network connectivity and scalability with appropriate memory, computation and communication overheads.

Keywords: Security, Wireless sensor networks, Key management, Key pre-distribution, Pairwise Key.

1 Introduction

Advances in communication and electronics have enabled the development of low-cost, low-power, multifunctional sensor nodes. The manufacturing of sensors has become technically and economically feasible. In typical application scenarios, these sensor nodes, which consisting of sensing, computation, and wireless communication modules, are spread randomly over the deployment region, and can be networked in many applications that require unattended operations [5]. Generally, a wireless sensor network (WSN) is composed of a large number of tiny sensor nodes, and presents solutions to some of our challenging problems. For example, military sensing and tracking, data collecting, environmental monitoring and traffic flows measuring.

* Supported by National Natural Science Foundation of China (NSFC) under Grant No.60773224,and 10571052, the Key Research Project of Ministry of Education of China under Grant No.107106, and the 111 Project of China under Grant No.111-2-14.

Y. Li et al. (Eds.): WASA 2008, LNCS 5258, pp. 480–490, 2008.

When WSNs are deployed in a hostile environment, security becomes extremely important. To enhance the security, communications between sensor nodes should be encrypted. It is vital to set up secret keys among communicating nodes. Hence, key management is proposed for secure communication in WSNs.

Since WSNs suffer from many limitations, such as the use of insecure wireless communication channels, resource constraints on sensor nodes and uncontrolled environments where these nodes are left unattended, WSNs are more vulnerable to attacks than wired ones. All these limitations greatly affect on the implementation of key management schemes in WSNs. Although the results from recent studies [7][11] show that publi-key cryptography might be possible in WSNs, it remains complexity and infeasibility for most part in WSNs. Thus the key management scheme based on symmetric key cryptography is preferred to WSN due to its efficiency.

Generally, WSNs have various general security requirements such as integrity, availability, authentication, confidentiality, survivability and degradation of security services; the following parameters are used as metrics throughout the paper to evaluate key management schemes:

- Connectivity: probability that two (or more) sensor nodes store the same key or keying material. Enough connectivity must be provided for a WSN to perform its intended functionality.
- Overheads: amount of memory required storing security materials (memory overhead), amount of processor cycles required to establish a key (computation overhead) and the number of messages exchanging during a key generation process (communication overhead) should be considered due to the resouces constrained sensor nodes.
- Scalability: ability to support larger networks. Key distribution scheme should support large networks, and must be flexible against substantial increase in the size of the network even after deployment.
- Resilience: resistance against node capture. Compromise of security materials, which are stored on a sensor node or exchanged over radio links, should not reveal information store on a non-compromised node.

We propose a new efficient pairwise key management scheme for WSNs. In our scheme, the establishment of pairwise key includes two phases, keys pre-loading phase and pairwise key generation phase, which are used to ensure the perfect network connectivity and generate distinct pairwise keys between any neighboring nodes respectively.

The remainder of this paper is organized as follows: Related work is sketched in section 2. The preliminaries, assumptions and detailed introduction of the proposed scheme are presented in section 3. Section 4 gives analysis and evaluation of our scheme. Finally, we conclude our work in section 5.

2 Related Work

A number of key management schemes have been investigated in literatures. Eschenauer and Gligor [4] first proposed basic random key pre-distribution scheme. The basic idea of their scheme is randomly selecting a subset of communication keys from a very large size key pool, and storing into each wireless sensor node's memory before it is deployed. Chan et al presented q-composite scheme to enhance the security and resilience of the network [2]. The q-composite scheme also uses the key pool but a pair of sensor nodes are required to compute a pairwise key at least q shared pre-distribution keys. Pietro et al proposed the cooperative pairwise key establishment protocol [10]. In cooperative protocol, a set of cooperative nodes are chosen by a pair of nodes to help establish the reinforced pairwise key. The cooperative protocol in general increases processing and communication overheads, but provides good resilience in the sense that a compromised key-chain does not directly affect on security of any links in the WSN. Liu et al. [9] and Du et al. [3] further extended the basic random key pre-distribution scheme to pairwise key pre-distribution scheme in which the shared key between any two sensor nodes is unique so that the resilience against node capture is significantly improved. All above mentioned schemes assume that do not know any network pre-deployment knowledge. In case that certain pre-deployment knowledge is available [6][8], the performance of the key pre-distribution can be improved by exploiting such knowledge.

In this paper, we focus on the random key pre-distribution schemes [2][4] without network pre-deployment knowledge. One drawback of them is that [2] and [4] are not suitable for large-scale networks as they required each node to load a large number of keys. Another weakness of these schemes is key reuse, which means some nodes' capture may compromise the communication between other non-compromised nodes. Compared with existing random key pre-distribution schemes [2][4], our scheme can provide the complete network connectivity, large network size supporting and better resilience against node capture attack with appropriate memory, computation and communication overheads.

3 Proposed Scheme

3.1 Preliminaries

Eschenauer and Gligor first proposed a random key pre-distribution scheme. The basic idea of their scheme as follows. Before sensor nodes are deployed, a large key pool P with $|P|$ keys is generated. For each sensor, $|R|$ keys are randomly drawn from the key-pool P without replacement. Thus, any two nodes will share at least one key with some probability. However, we notice that when $|P|$ becomes small, where $|R|<|P|<2|R|$, then any two nodes would share at least one key inevitably. According to Pigeonhole principle, we describe the lemma which is employed as follows:

Lemma. Given $|P|$ and $|R|$ the size of key pool P and key ring R respectively, For each sensor, $|R|$ keys are uniformly randomly drawn from the key-pool P. $|R|<|P|<2|R|$ such that any pair of nodes share at least one key and at most $|R|$ keys.

This key distribution approach can provide perfect network connectivity but poor resilience. Adversary may compromise other nodes or even the entire network through the compromised keys or secret materials. To address the problems of connectivity and resilience, two kinds of methods are considered in our proposed scheme. One is the improved key pre-distribution, which is used to ensure the perfect network connectivity. The other is the enhanced pairwise key, which is established by two communication parties under certain rules. Each pairwise key is distinct to others, any compromised sensor can not compromise non-captured nodes' pairwise key.

3.2 Assumptions

We assume a large number of homogeneous sensors are randomly distributed over the unattended deployment region, sensor nodes are not tamper resistant and adversary can capture node randomly. However, sensors deployed in a hostile environment must be designed to survive at least a short interval longer than the pairwise key establishment procedure when captured by an adversary; otherwise, the whole network can be easily taken over by the adversary [1].

3.3 Two Phases of Our Scheme

In our scheme, pairwise key is established through two phases, keys pre-loading phase and pairwise key generation phase. In this work, a WSN is administrated by an off-line authority called key server (KS). KS is responsible for node initialization and deployment. Before the network deployment, KS assigns a unique identifier to each sensor node. KS also generates a set $P_s = \{P_1, P_2, ..., P_L\}$ consisting of a series of key pools. Each element of P_s has equivalent number of keys and $P_i \cap P_j = \phi$ for $i, j = 1, ..., L$ and $i \neq j$. Each sensor node is also pre-loaded a cryptographically secure one-way hash function $y = \mathbf{WH}(x, k)$ [12], which has the following property: (1) given x, it is computationally infeasible to find y without knowing the value of k; (2) given y and k, it is computationally infeasible to find x.

Where $y = \mathbf{WH}(x, k)$ is a class of universal hash functions proposed for sensor nodes with 2^{-w} collision probability, where w is the length of input message block, each input message such as x or k can be split into blocks of w bits [12]. This hash function is highly power efficient. The implementation of $\mathbf{WH}$ shows that it consumes only 11.6μW at 500 kHz [12]. Hence we use $\mathbf{WH}$ in our pairwise key generation phase to ensure that it is computationally infeasible to compromise pairwise key between any pair of nodes with the knowledge of either input of $\mathbf{WH}$.More detail of $\mathbf{WH}$ can be referred in [12].

3.3.1 Keys Pre-loading Phase
In this phase, KS selects a series of keys from the set P_s. To ensure any two nodes sharing at least a common keys after deployment, KS pre-loads these keys and other security materials.

First, KS generates a key pool set $P_s = \{P_1, P_2, ..., P_L\}$ containing L key pools where each key pool consists of M keys. Second, KS randomly selects $\lceil (L+1)/2 \rceil$ key pools from P_s, there are $\binom{L}{\lceil (L+1)/2 \rceil}$ distinct ways of picking $\lceil (L+1)/2 \rceil$ keys from L key pools in set P_s. For the selected $\lceil (L+1)/2 \rceil$ key pools, KS randomly chooses $\lceil (M+1)/2 \rceil$ keys from each selected key pool, there are aggregately

$\left(\begin{array}{c} M \\ \lceil (M+1)/2\rceil \end{array}\right)$ different ways of choosing $\lceil (M+1)/2\rceil$ from a selected key pool. Hence, there are aggregately $\lceil (L+1)/2\rceil * \lceil (M+1)/2\rceil$ keys storing in each sensor node and $\left(\begin{array}{c} L \\ \lceil (L+1)/2\rceil \end{array}\right) * \left(\begin{array}{c} M \\ \lceil (M+1)/2\rceil \end{array}\right)$ ways of picking these keys from P_s. Since any pair of nodes have at least a shared key from a common key pool, our scheme can guarantee that a secure link can be established between any two sensor nodes. There-fore, the proposed scheme can provide full connectivity no matter how and where the sensors are deployed lately, which releases the assumption of prior knowledge of sensor deployment location. Fig.1 shows an example of the key rings pre-loaded in node a and b by KS respectively, where $L = 5$ and $M = 5$. It is easy to see that node a and b have a shared common key K_{33}.

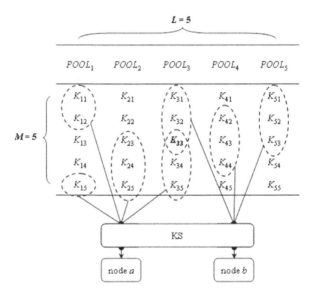

Fig. 1. For L = 5, M = 5, the key rings stored in nodes a and b are illustrated respectively

3.3.2 Pairwise Key Generation Phase

A pairwise key is required to be generated between any two neighboring sensors in this phase. In order to do that, each node needs to find the shared keys with its neighbors firstly. After deployment, nodes carry out the shared common key discov-ery at once and then broadcast the discovery messages with tiny random delay in order to avoid collisions of messages between neighboring nodes.

Assuming sensor a and b are two neighboring nodes, node a firstly broadcasts a message {id_a, $nonce_a$, List(C_a, $E(C_a, K_{ax})$, x=1, ..., $|R|$)} to its one-hop neighbors. Where id_a is the identifier of node a, $nonce_a$ is a one-time used random bit-string which is generated by node a (Nonce is used to prevent the adversary deriving the pairwise key directly from a lately compromised key ring). List(...) is a Merkle puzzle, which is used for discovering all common keys between a pair of nodes, C_a is a challenge generated by node a randomly, $E(C_a, K_{ax})$ denotes that C_a is encrypted with x-th key K_{ax} of node a.

Similarly, node b broadcasts a message $\{id_b, nonce_b, \text{List}(C_b, E(C_b, K_{bx}), x=1, ..., |R|)\}$ to its neighbors also. After exchanging the broadcasting information, node a obtains id_b, $nonce_b$ and List(...) from node b. For $x =1, ..., |R|$, node a can find the shared keys with node b according to the decryption of $E(C_b, K_{bx})$ with proper key. In the same way, node b can get the corresponding information from node a and discover the shared common keys between them. Once the process of exchanging the key information is finished, the pairwise key between node a and b can be calculated by Equation (1).

$$PK_{a,b} = \mathbf{WH}(K_{a,b}, nonce_a \oplus nonce_b) . \tag{1}$$

Where " $\oplus$ " is the exclusive-or operator, $PK_{a,b}$ denotes the pairwise key between nodes a and b, $K_{a,b}$ denotes that the result of all the shared common keys between a and b being XOR-ed together (e.g., if the shared common key between node a and b are K_1, K_2 and K_3, then $K_{a,b} = K_1 \oplus K_2 \oplus K_3$). $K_{a,b}$ and $nonce_a \oplus nonce_b$ are two input messages of $\mathbf{WH}$.

Once pairwise key generation phase finished, each sensor erases all generated and received nonces and pre-loaded security materials such as key ring R from its memory to prevent the possible compromise in the future. By randomly pre-distributing keys to node with our proposed rule, any pair of sensors can share at least a common key, which means, a secure link between any two sensors within their radio transmission range can be directly established without the third node's involvement. In addition, each side of the communication parties generates a random nonce to participate the pairwise key generation procedure. This can prevents the adversary from calculating the established pairwise key lately, even compromising the stored key rings in sensors.

4   Analysis and Evaluation

We analyze and evaluate the proposed scheme by comparing it with random key predistribution scheme (RPKS) [2][4], which are related work to ours.

4.1 Connectivity

Since the low connectivity will incur significant communication overhead, enough connectivity must be provided for a WSN to perform its intended functionality. Based on the random graph theory, RPKS only provides probabilistic connectivity of a network. In other words, RPKS can not guarantee the connectivity between any two nodes. It is quite possible that some nodes or some portions of a network could be isolated from the rest of the network when there are no common keys between them.

Our scheme can guarantee the full secure connectivity of the entire network. Since each pair of nodes has at least one shared key from a common key pool, our scheme ensures any pair of nodes sharing at least a pre-loaded keys. Therefore, a unique pairwise key can be established between any pair of sensors within the radio transmission range.

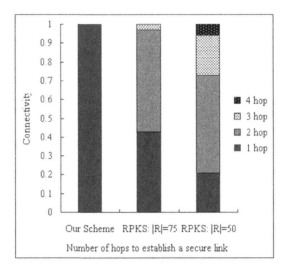

Fig. 2. Compared with RPKS with key ring |R| = 75 and |R| = 50, our scheme can perform a completely connected network by exchanging one-hop neighbors' key information

We use the metrics in [4] for conveniences with |R| is 50 and 75. Fig.2 shows that our scheme performs a completely connected network exchanging only one-hop neighbors' key information. But in [4], RPKS with |R| = 75 and |R| = 50 can only ensure that two nodes set up a pairwise key within one hop with the probability of approximately 0.44 and 0.23 respectively. If a pair of neighboring nodes cannot be reached via their shared key, then two or more hops information need to be exchanged in order to set up a pairwise key between them. Actually, establishment of pairwise key via multi-hops not only reduce security of the related pairwise key, but also involve more communication and computation overheads such as finding the disjoint paths and transmitting the generated key. Therefore, our scheme performs superior capabilities by using only one hop pairwise key.

4.2   Overheads

We assume that the number of keys stored in a node is denoted by |R|. As described in Section 2.2.1, primary memory overhead can be calculated by Equation (2):

$$|R| = \lceil (L+1)/2 \rceil * \lceil (M+1)/2 \rceil. \tag{2}$$

Where L denotes the number of key pools in P_s, M denotes the number of keys in each key pool.

After deployment, sensors will exchange the broadcasting information to discover shared keys between its one-hop neighbors. The communication overhead in our scheme is mainly determined by the size of broadcasting information. Assume that d denotes the average degree of network and each entry in broadcasting information occupies an equal memory unit, the broadcasting information will occupy $O(|R|)$ units, there are d neighbors of the sender side will receive the broadcasting information.

Therefore, the communication overhead for every node is $O(d|R|)$ on the receiver side and $O(|R|)$ on the sender side.

The computational overhead of a sensor node consists of two parts. First, since we use the Merkle puzzle to find shared keys between nodes. As described in section 3.3.2, to generate a Merkle puzzle, each node encrypts a randomly generated plain text by $|R|$ keys respectively and broadcasts the message to its neighbors. The neighbors received the message will use its $|R|$ keys to decrypt the Merkle puzzle, for one received Merkle pizzle, a node will perform $|R|^2$ at the worst case. Then the key discovery procedure requires $|R|$ encryptions on the sender side and $d|R|^2$ decryptions on the receiver side. Second, node would generate pairwise key with its neighbors after shared key discovery. A node would perform $d|R|$ XOR operations (There are $|R|$ shared common keys in the most extreme case, a node will execute XOR operation $|R|$ times to obtain $K_{a,b}$ and $nonce_a \oplus nonce_b$) and d **WH** operations (A node will calculate d distinct keys with its d neighbors by performing **WH** operation d times).

Table 1. Overheads of a sensor in our scheme

Memory overhead	Communication overhead	Computation overhead
$O(|R|)$	$O(d|R|)$ received $O(|R|)$ send	$|R|$ encryptions $d|R|^2$ decryptions $d|R|$ XOR operations d **WH** operations

For a given network degree d, it is obvious that the primary influencing factor of communication and computation overheads in our scheme is memory space $|R|$ of each node.

4.3 Scalability

Let us consider the network size supported by our scheme. Although memory space is a very scarce resource for the current generation of sensor nodes (4 KB RAM in a Berkeley Mica Mote), but storage is not an issue in our scheme.

For $|R| = \lceil (L+1)/2 \rceil * \lceil (M+1)/2 \rceil$ and $i = 1, \ldots, |R|$, any pair of nodes will have i shared common keys to a certainty, there are $\binom{|R|}{i}$ ways to pick the i shared common key out of key ring R to generate a pairwise key and form a link between them. Hence, there are $\sum_{i=1}^{|R|} \binom{|R|}{i} = 2^{|R|}$ links supported by $|R|$ keys aggregately. Consider a network consists of N nodes, there at most exsit $N(N-1)/2 \approx N^2/2$ links in entire network.. From $N^2/2 = 2^{|R|}$, we can deduce the maximum supported network size $N = 2^{|R|/2}$.

Compared with RPKS[2][3], which provides the network size are linearly increasing as $|R|$ increases. It is easy to see that the network size of our proposed scheme provides an exponential increasing network size when the key ring size $|R|$ increases.

4.4 Resilience

Resilience against node capture is one of the main indicators of the key pre-distribution security in sensor networks. The higher the resilience, the more difficulty of the attackers making use of the security materials, which are stored in the captured nodes to attack the other parts of networks.

We assume the strong node-compromise attack model adopted by the previously scheme [2][4]. In RPKS, each sensor has knowledge of $|R|$ keys, the probability of total number of compromised keys is $1-(1-(|R|/|P|)^x)$, where x is the number of sensors compromised [2]. Hence, any node's capture could compromise other non-captured nodes' pairwise key, which is defined as the network resilience. But in our scheme, each side of the communication parties generates a random nonce to participate the pairwise key generation, and we use **WH** to ensure that it is computationally infeasible to compromise pairwise key between any pair of nodes with the knowledge of either input of **WH**. This measure prevents the adversary from composing the established pairwise key between non-compromised nodes lately.

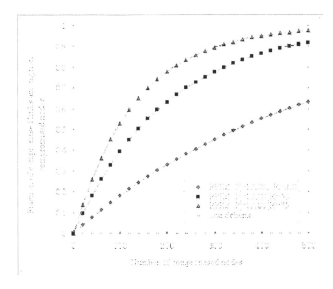

Fig. 3. Probability of a random communication link between two random non-compromised nodes a, b being decrypted by the adversary, who has compromised some nodes exclude a or b

Fig.3 shows the relationship between the number of compromised nodes and the fraction of compromised links among non-compromised nodes. Given RPKS with parameters $|P|$=10000, $|R|$=50 and $|P|$=10000, $|R|$=75. When only 100 nodes are captured, approximately 40% and 54% of the communication links among the non-compromised nodes could be compromised respectively. When $|P|$=100000, $|R|$=200, the network resilience is improved by reducing the proportion of $|R|$ to $|P|$ in keys number, and less than 20% links between non-compromised nodes could be compromised when 100 nodes are compromised. In our proposed scheme, each pair of neighboring nodes has a distinct pairwise key that is distinct to others. An adversary cannot derive the pairwise key between non-compromised nodes by the captured nodes. Compared with RPKS with $|P|=100000$, $|R|=200$, we can see that when 500 nodes are captured, above 60% of the communication between non-compromised nodes are compromised. Nevertheless, in our proposed scheme, no communication between non-compromised nodes will be compromised no matter how many nodes are captured by the adversary.

For the purpose of security, compromised keys must be removed from the network instantly. In our proposed scheme, each node has the knowledge of its neighbor's identifier and shares a distinct pairwise key with its one-hop neighbors. Once a misbehaving node is detected (If the device of malicious node detection is used), only its one-hop neighbors need to remove the corresponding pairwise key and the identifier from their memory. No other nodes need to be involved in this compromised key revocation procedure.

Similarly, node replication attack can also be completely avoided in our scheme. Due to the distinct pairwise key between any one-hop neighbors and the knowledge of the neighbors' id, each node only communicates with its one-hop neighbors after the network initialization phase. Without the proper pairwise key's authentication and neighborhood identification, any stranger's communication request will be ignored, which can prevent the node from replication attack in the network.

5 Conclusion

In this paper, we propose a random key management scheme for wireless sensor networks based on random key pre-distribution. The proposed scheme which is scalable and feasible shows many advantages. Compared with previous random key predistribution schemes, our scheme can provide favorable performances such as full connectivity between any pair of nodes, larger maximum supported network size, appropriate energy consumption and perfect resilience.

Acknowledgments. Supported by National Natural Science Foundation of China (NSFC) under Grant No.60773224,and 10571052, the Key Research Project of Ministry of Education of China under Grant No.107106, and the 111 Project of China under Grant No.111-2-14.

References

1. Anderson, R.J., Chan, H., Perrig, A.: Key Infection: Smart Trust for Smart Dust. In: Proceedings of the 12th IEEE International Conference on Network Protocols (ICNP), pp. 206–215 (2004)
2. Chan, H., Perrig, A., Song, D.: Random key predistribution schemes for sensor networks. In: Proceedings of the 24th IEEE Symposium on Security and Privacy, pp. 197–215 (2003)
3. Du, W., Deng, J., Han, Y.S., Varshney, P.: A pairwise key predistribution scheme for wireless sensor networks. In: Proceedings of the 10th ACM Conference on Computer and Communications Security (2003)

4. Eschenauer, L., Gligor, V.D.: A key-management scheme for distributed sensor networks. In: Proceedings of the 9th ACM Conference on Computer and Communications Security (CCS) (2002)

5. Estrin, D., Girod, L., Pottie, G., Srivastava, M.: Instrumenting the World with Wireless Sensor Networks. In: Proceedings of the 1st IEEE international Conference on Acoustics, Speech, and Signal Processing (ICASSP) (2001)

6. Fang, L., Jose, R., Xiuzhen, C.: Location-aware Key Establishment in Wireless Sensor Networks. In: Proceedings of the International Conference on Communications and Mobile Computing, Computer and Network Security Symposium (IWCMC), pp. 21–26 (2006)

7. Gura, N., Patel, A., Arvinderpal, W., Eberle, H., Sheueling, C.S.: Comparing Elliptic Curve Cryptography and RSA on 8-bit CPUs. In: Proceedings of the Workshop on Cryptographic Hardware and Embedded Systems (CHES) (2004)

8. Liu, D., Ning, P.: Location-based pairwise key establishments for relatively static Sensor networks. In: Proceedings of ACM Workshop on Security of Ad Hoc and Sensor Networks (SASN) (2003)

9. Liu, D., Ning, P.: Establishing pairwise keys in distributed sensor networks. In: Proceedings of the 10th ACM Conference on Computer and Communications Security (CCS) (2003)

10. Pietro, R., Mancini, L., Mei, A.: Random key assignment secure wireless sensor networks. In: Proceedings of the 1st ACM workshop on Security of Ad Hoc and Sensor Networks (2003)

11. Wander, A.S., Gura, N., Eberle, H., Gupta, V., Shantz, S.C.: Energy Analysis of Public-Key Cryptography for Wireless Sensor Networks. In: Proceedings of the 3rd IEEE international Conference on International Pervasive Computing and Communications (PerCom), pp. 324–328 (2005)

12. Yuksel, K., Kaps, J.P., Sunar, B.: Universal hash functions for emerging ultra-low-power networks. In: The Communications Networks and Distributed Systems Modeling and Simulation Conference (WMC) (2004)

WORMEROS: A New Framework for Defending against Wormhole Attacks on Wireless Ad Hoc Networks

Hai Vu, Ajay Kulkarni, Kamil Sarac, and Neeraj Mittal

Department of Computer Science
The University of Texas at Dallas
Richardson, TX 75080, USA

Abstract. Wormhole attack is a type of replay attack in wireless networks that has serious consequences and is hard to defend against. This is because the attacker does not need to modify packets or compromise wireless nodes. This paper introduces Wormeros, a new framework to detect wormhole attacks in wireless networks. The framework contains two phases namely suspicion and confirmation. Our solution does not require any special hardware (such as GPS) or expensive mechanisms (such as time synchronization) added to the wireless nodes. Using analysis and simulation, we show that our solution is effective in detecting and defending against wormhole attacks.

1 Introduction

Wireless ad hoc networks consist of wireless devices that do not require an infrastructure to operate on. Such networks are vulnerable to many security threats, as data is broadcasted over a shared channel. We focus on wormhole attacks, wherein an attacker captures data in one region of the network, tunnels it to another region (possibly using higher transmission power or an out-of-band channel), and injects it back into the network. We illustrate a wormhole attack in ad hoc networks (see Figure 1) below.

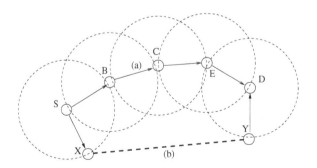

Fig. 1. A wormhole attack in ad hoc networks: (a) Normal link, (b) Wormhole link

In the ad hoc network in Figure 1, assume that S, B, C, D, E are legitimate nodes and S can communicate with D using the path $S - B - C - E - D$. An attacker

Y. Li et al. (Eds.): WASA 2008, LNCS 5258, pp. 491–502, 2008.

places two nodes in the network, X and Y, which are close to S and D, respectively. The attacker can make S and D think that they are neighbors by having X capture the packets sent by S, tunnel the packets to Y, which replays the packets to D. From then on, S and D use the erroneous direct link for communication. Thus, the attacker has successfully mounted the wormhole attack. He now controls the link and can mount further attacks such as flow analysis, blackhole attack, etc [1].

The attacker can initiate a wormhole attack in a passive mode without modifying any packet and thus neither needs to break the authentication scheme nor needs to have the knowledge of encryption keys that are used between the two nodes in the network. As a result, the attacker does not need to compromise a node in the network to success-fully launch the wormhole attack. Hence, a solution that depends only on cryptographic techniques is clearly not effective enough to defend against wormhole attacks.

In this paper we present a novel framework that combines multiple simple techniques which help detect wormhole attacks on wireless ad-hoc networks. Our main contribu-tion is to show how simple protocols can be jointly applied to first suspect a link and then challenge the link to confirm this suspicion. The specific techniques we present in the paper are just examples of how to employ different protocols in each phase of our framework.

The rest of the paper is structured as follows. In Section 2, we describe the previous work in wormhole detection. In Section 3, we describe our ideas and how our solution differs from other solutions. In Section 4, we present Wormeros framework in details. Security analysis and experiment results of our framework are presented in Section 5 and Section 6, respectively. We conclude the paper in Section 7.

2   Related Work

Packet Leashes [1] is among the first work in defending against wormhole attacks. The authors introduce two solutions: *Geographical Leashes* and *Temporal Leashes*. In the first one, location information (e.g. from GPS devices), included in the packets, is used to detect the presence of wormhole link. In the latter, nodes are tightly time synchronized and the packet being transmitted between a source node and a destination node contains the time at which it is sent. The destination node will not accept if the packet is expired.

Hu and Evans [2] use directional antennas (introduced in [3]) to detect wormhole attacks while SECTOR [4] uses another type of special hardware and depends on the fact that the distance between two nodes can be measured accurately based on the speed of data transmitted between them.

TrueLink [5] depends on the RTS-CTS-Data-ACK mechanism of IEEE 802.11 MAC protocol to defend against wormhole attacks. In this solution the nodes have a time constraint to authenticate each other and thus wormhole attacks are prevented.

LITEWORP [6] introduces a notion of *guard node*, which is a common neighbor of two nodes to detect a legitimate link between them. The guard node can detect the wormhole if one of its neighbor is behaving maliciously. In a sparse network, however, it is not always possible to find a guard node for a particular link.

Maheswari et al. [7] propose a different approach to detect wormhole attacks. Their idea is to look for some *forbidden substructures* in the connectivity graph that should not exist in a network that has no wormhole.

The authors in [8,9] use RTT (round-trip-time) to detect wormhole attacks. Chiu et al. [8] measure the delay per hop in the whole path while Tran et al. [9] measure the RTT for each successive links in the whole path. If this measurement is higher than some threshold value, then the alarm is raised. These solutions, however, require the cooperation of all nodes in the path.

3   Wormeros Framework

Our main work in the paper is to introduce and analyze Wormeros(the name is inspired from Kerberos), a framework that consists of two phases to detect wormhole attacks. The first phase applies inexpensive techniques and utilizes local information that is available during the normal operation of wireless nodes. Advanced techniques in the second phase are applied only when a wormhole attack is suspected. Thus, in case there are no wormholes in the network, the wireless nodes do not need to waste computation and communication resources.

Following are two phases of Wormeros:

- **Phase I - Suspicion**: We use two techniques to examine the existence of the wormhole attack in the network. First, we measure the RTT between a node S and all of its immediate neighbors. If RTT(S, D), where D is one of S's neighbors, is abnormally higher than the average RTT of all links from S to its neighbors, then there might be a wormhole between S and D. This technique is different from work in [8,9] in that we do not require the cooperation of all nodes in the path between S and D. Second, we use an observation that in a dense network, two neighbors S and D are likely to share some common neighbors. This technique is similar to work in [6,7] but we only use local information instead of global information. If any of the techniques in the Suspicion phase detects the existence of a suspicious link, then we move to the second phase of Wormeros to confirm the wormhole.
- **Phase II - Confirmation**: Having suspected a possible wormhole link in the network, Wormeros launches a series of challenges to make sure that the wormhole is correctly identified. In this phase, the two legitimate nodes being attacked by the wormhole link collaborate to challenge the attacker. We propose to use frequency hopping for this purpose. TrueLink [5] can also be used in this phase.

To the best of our knowledge, this paper is the first to introduce a framework consisting of more than one techniques to defend against wormhole attacks. Our solution differs from work of [1,2,4] in that we do not require additional hardware devices or expensive time synchronization. Work in [6,7] are not efficient in sparse networks, but in the Suspicion phase of our solution we overcome this by adding techniques based on RTT measurements which work well in sparse networks. TrueLink [5] is efficient but expensive if applied all the time. In our framework, expensive techniques such as TrueLink are only used in the second phase where a link is suspected and this helps reduce overhead for the wireless nodes in the network.

4   Details of Wormeros Framework

4.1   System Model and Notation

We consider a wireless ad hoc network with no centralized server. We assume that none of the nodes in the network is compromised. The links are assumed to be bidirectional and all nodes use the same transmission power. We assume that the topology does not change rapidly and there is at least one RTS/CTS/Data/Ack period of time that a pair of nodes can communicate. We further assume that any pair of nodes in the network share two cryptographic keys K_1 and K_2. This assumption is common in the area and can be achieved by applying a key exchange scheme like Diffie-Hellman or a scheme by Eschenauer and Gligor [10].

In the remaining sections of the paper, we use the following notations:

- p: the propagation delay of a legitimate link
- $RTT_{(S,D)}$: RTT between node S and node D
- $RTT_{wormhole}$: RTT of a link under wormhole attack
- Avg_{All}^S: the average RTT of all links from S to its neighbors
- w: the time to tunnel a packet between two wormhole ends
- d: the number of neighbors of a node
- E(K, M): the message M is encrypted using secret key K
- HMAC(K, M): the message digest of M, using a secure hash function with secret key K

4.2   Suspicion Phase

In this phase, we use simple triggers to find out if a link should be suspected and challenged. One of the simplest triggers is based on the round trip delay of a link. Let a node S communicate with a neighbor node D. During peace time, the RTT between S and D is $2p$. If the direct link (S, D) is formed as a result of a wormhole attack, then the round trip time would be $RTT_{wormhole} = 2(p + w + p) = 2(2p + w)$. Thus we believe the RTT of the wormhole link should be at least two times the RTT of a normal link, even though w can be smaller than p. In Section 6 we conduct experiments to confirm this fact.

We develop a simple scheme for wormhole suspicion based on RTT in Algorithm 1 as illustrated in Figure 2. Let node S communicate with node D through a wormhole link XY. Node S knows that A, B, C, D, E are its neighbors and S can measure the RTT with all of the links $(S, A), (S, B), (S, C), (S, D)$ and (S, E). If the $RTT_{(S,D)}$ is at least k times the average RTT between S and all its neighboring nodes, then the link (S, D) may be a wormhole. The value of k is the system parameter which depends on d and w. In Section 5.1 we explain how the value of k is determined. Algorithm 1 is similar to the scheme proposed in [9] which detects the presence of wormhole by measuring the RTT during route discovery. However, the difference is that we define deterministic threshold value while the scheme in [9] decides the threshold value based on simulations.

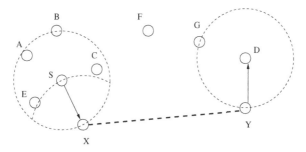

Fig. 2. Probing neighbors to find out suspicious link

Algorithm 1. RTTDetection(S, D)

1: S calculates the average RTT of each link, based on n (system parameter) samples
2: S calculates the average RTT of all d neighbors, Avg^S_{All}
3: **if** $RTT_{(S,D)} \geq k * Avg^S_{All}$ **then**
4:    Confirm the link (S, D) is suspicious and execute Challenge phase.
5: **end if**

Other techniques can also be applied simultaneously to Algorithm 1 in Suspicion phase. For example, Algorithm 2 uses the neighbor information available at each node to detect a suspicious link. The idea of Algorithm 2 is that if S and D are far away, then it is very likely that D will not be in the neighbor list of any of S's neighbors. In Figure 2, S's neighbors are A, B, C and E; none of these nodes have D as their neighbor. By applying Algorithm 2, S will find the link (S, D) suspicious.

Algorithm 2. NeighborDetection(S, D)

1: S collects identity of its one-hop and two-hop neighbors and creates the Neighborhood Set.
2: S checks the Neighborhood Set to see if D belongs to the set.
3: **if** D is not an element of the set **then**
4:    Confirm the link (S, D) is suspicious and execute the Challenge phase.
5: **end if**

Note that the more techniques we apply in the Suspicion phase, the more accurate it is to detect wormhole attacks. This is because each technique is applied independently and thus the wormhole links that are bypassed by one technique are likely to be detected by another technique. However, there is a trade-off to consider: the higher number of techniques is applied, the higher cost it is. Therefore, we suggest to use a small number of techniques in the Suspicion phase.

4.3 Confirmation Phase

In this phase we use frequency hopping for confirming the existence of a wormhole. The pseudo-code is presented in Algorithm 3.

Algorithm 3. FrequencyHoppingChallenge(S, D)

1: S sends an encrypted message to D requesting to challenge the link (S, D). The message is transmitted using frequency f_1.
2: D replies with an encrypted message accepting the challenge, and specifies a random frequency f_2. The message is transmitted in frequency f_1.
3: D switches its receiver to f_2 and waits for $2 * RTT_{(S,D)}$ time.
4: After receiving the reply message, S transmits a message in frequency f_2 and starts waiting for acknowledgment in f_2.
5: **if** S does not receive an acknowledgment from D in frequency f_2 within a duration of $2 * RTT_{(S,D)}$ time, **then**
6:     Confirm link (S, D) is a wormhole link
7: **end if**

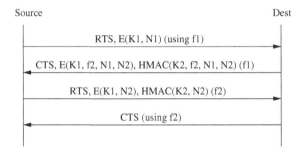

Fig. 3. Frequency hopping challenge

We illustrate the implementation of Algorithm 3 using RTS/CTS mechanism of IEEE 802.11b standards in Figure 3. In the first message, S sends RTS and a nonce N_1 (encrypted using K_1) to D using a frequency f_1 being used for communication between them. Upon receiving this message from S, D replies in frequency f_1 with a CTS message that contains the frequency f_2 (picked from the set of common frequencies shared by S and D), the nonce N_1 received previously and a new nonce N_2, also encrypted with K_1. To protect the integrity of the packet, D can optionally compute a message digest using HMAC function with key K_2.

After replying to S with CTS packet, D switches its receiver to frequency f_2 and starts waiting for a packet from S. Here we assume the CTS always gets through if the environment conditions are stable. Later in the analysis section we discuss this assumption in depth. Immediately after receiving CTS, S switches its transmitter to frequency f_2 and sends a new RTS message to D that contains N_2 for the sake of authentication. Finally D replies with a CTS packet to finish the challenge.

If S and D are far away and become direct neighbors due to the wormhole, then by switching to the new frequency they will not be able to receive messages from each other. This is because the attacker does not know the new frequency and thus cannot forward the messages between S and D.

The use of nonces N_1 and N_2 is to avoid the replay attacks. Without the nonces, the attacker can launch the attack as follows. Suppose that the attacker has captured a

CTS packet which contains an encrypted frequency f_2 that he does not know. He can store the message and try to scan all the frequencies to find out the one in which S and D are communicating. On correctly identifying the frequency, he can replay the same message for any new challenge between the same pair S and D, thus effectively breaking the solution. This attack is not possible if we use nonces because they can help detect replayed messages. We can further improve the security for these messages by including the expiry time for each message (for example, each message is expired after 10 seconds).

5   Security Analysis

5.1   Analysis of Suspicion Phase

In Algorithm 1 we require that $RTT_{(S,D)}$ be at least k times Avg_{All}^S so that S can start suspecting the link (S, D) to be a wormhole. Now we show how each node can determine the value of k. Let d be the number of neighbors a node has and assume that among d neighbors there exists at most m ($m < d$) wormhole link. We have:

$$RTT_{(S,D)} = 2(2p + w)$$
$$Avg_{All}^S = \frac{(d - m)2p + 2(2p + w)m}{d}$$
$$Test = \frac{RTT_{(S,D)}}{Avg_{All}^S} = \frac{2(2p + w)d}{(d - m)2p + 2(2p + w)m} \geq k$$

Observe that $Test$ increases when w increases. Thus, to avoid detection, the attacker should try to decrease the value of $Test$ by decreasing w. However, w is always greater than 0. Thus, if we set the threshold value k for $w = 0$ then the attacker will very likely be detected. In that case, $k = \dfrac{2d}{d + 2m}$ and can easily be computed by each wireless node. For example, if $d = 6$ and $m = 1$, then the threshold value k will be $12/7 = 1.7$. This is a deterministic value, contradicting with the one in [9], where the threshold value varies in different networks.

5.2   Analysis of Confirmation Phase

802.11 RTS-CTS Mechanism. The wireless channel is unreliable and nodes use the CSMA/CA mechanism protocol for transmitting. The unreliability is caused by two factors: noise and collisions. We assume that during one execution of RTS-CTS-Data-ACK the environment is stable, thus loss of packets due to noise spike can be ignored. Hence, if the sender has successfully sent the RTS to the receiver, all of its neighbors would have received the RTS and would not contend for the channel. Therefore, the CTS will be received correctly at the sender.

Attacking the Confirmation Phase. The attacker has two options to respond to the challenge: either to drop the RTS packet or to allow the packet to pass through to D. We now show that using any of these options is not helpful to the wormhole attack and it will eventually be discovered.

a) Dropping the RTS Packet

In our solution if S does not get the CTS reply in a finite amount of time it will timeout and resend the RTS. In 802.11 mechanism each node retries r times (typically $r = 7$) before declaring a transmission failure. If a transmission failure occurs our solution considers that to be a missed challenge. If a link has M such continuous missed challenges, our solution declares that link to be malicious.

If node S is sending an RTS frame then the probability that collisions occurs is given by:

$$P[\text{collision}] = 1 - (1 - \tau)^{d-1}$$

where τ is the probability of transmission at a moment t of each node and d is the number of neighbors of a node. If S does not get the CTS reply within a finite amount of time it times out and resends the RTS frame. If all these r RTS frames were to collide with transmissions from other node then the probability of that happening is:

$$P[\text{Losing r RTS}] = [1 - (1 - \tau)^{d-1}]^r$$

The probability of failing M challenges due to wireless issues rather than wormhole is:

$$P[\text{Failing M challenges}] = [1 - (1 - \tau)^{d-1}]^{rM}$$

Using $M = 5, r = 7, d = 10$ and $\tau = 0.1$ we get

$$P[\text{Failing M challenges}] = 5.3 * 10^{-8}.$$

This probability of failing M challenges without the existence of wormhole is thus negligible. Hence the strategy of dropping RTS packets is not in the interest of the wormhole.

b) Allowing the RTS Packet Through

The other option for the wormhole is to allow the RTS to go through. We assume that (i) it is too expensive for the attacker to listen on all the available channels and (ii) it is computationally infeasible for the attacker to break the encryption to obtain f_2 in a short duration. Therefore, by allowing the RTS get through the attacker has to guess the frequency f_2, because the content of the message is encrypted and integrity protected.

The probability of correctly guessing the right frequency is $1/N$, where N is the number of channels. If we further force each node to pass the challenge for δ times this probability of guessing the correct frequency every time is reduced to $1/N^\delta$. Using appropriate values of δ and N this probability can be made very small. For example if $N = 11$ (802.11b network) and $\delta = 2$ the probability is less than 1%. The wormhole thus is unlikely to pass the Confirmation phase.

6   Performance Evaluation

First, we conduct experiments to study the impact of wormhole links on the RTT values. In the first set of experiments, we verify if the RTT of a wormhole link is twice as much

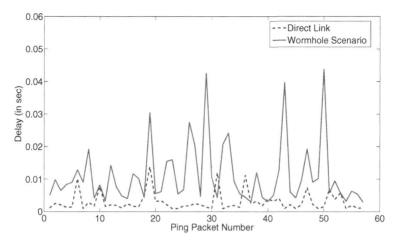

Fig. 4. Round trip time (wormhole link and normal link)

as that of a normal link. We set up a simple ad hoc network consisting of two PDAs running in ad hoc mode. We measure the average RTT when sending an ICMP ping packet from one PDA to another and receive an acknowledgment back for the same packet. In the second set of experiments, we mimic a wormhole attack where a packet sent from one PDA is captured at the first laptop, tunneled to the second laptop, and replayed at the second PDA. The rationale behind using a laptops is to mimic the high resource capability of a wormhole node.

We conduct both experiments for two minutes continuously and take the average of the results. Figure 4 show that the round trip time when the wormhole existed is much higher than that in normal case. The average RTT of sending a packet through wormhole link and a legitimate link was observed to be 11.09msec and 4.9msec, respectively. Thus the node can use the delay as an indicator to suspect any link.

Next, we use ns-2 [11] simulator to implement two algorithms in Suspicion phase. For Algrithm 1 we create a network topology and randomly pick a node S. We then create a wormhole link between S and a distant node D. Repeating the experiment many times we can select S with varying degree of neighbors. We then measure the RTT between the neighbors of S and calculate k (threshold) as described in Section 5.1. Comparison of the simulated values to the analytical value is shown in Figure 5. We observe that the ratio of the wormhole RTT to average RTT is always above the calculated threshold and hence we conclude that the threshold value we suggested is effective.

As for Algorithm 2, we design two tests to evaluate its performance:

– Test 1: The percentage of wormhole detection. Specifically, for all the wormhole links, how many of them will be detected by Algorithm 2. Note that if q is the percentage of wormhole links being detected then $1 - q$ is the percentage of false negative, i.e. number of links that escaped an algorithm.
– Test 2: The percentage of false positive, i.e. the percentage of direct links which are falsely detected as wormhole link.

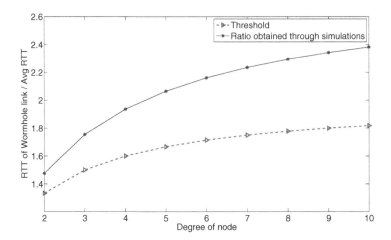

Fig. 5. Round trip time (simulated and analytical comparison)

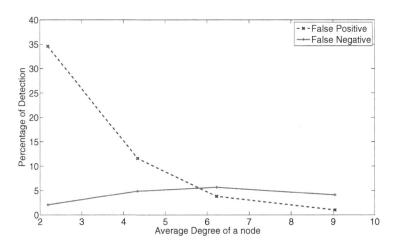

Fig. 6. Results of NeighborDetection algorithm

We set up a fixed network area of 2000m x 2000m with the transmission range of a node set to 250m. We conduct experiments by varying network density from 50 to 200 nodes. For Test 1, we randomly create a number of wormhole links in the network and apply Algorithm 2 to detect wormhole links. For Test 2, we pick a pair of directed neighbors (which is not under a wormhole attack) and apply Algorithm 2.

For each of the network size, we conduct multiple runs and take the average of the results. The final result is shown in Figure 6. The results show that in a dense network (200 nodes of 9.044 average degree), the chances of detecting wormhole is very high (92.92%) while the ratio of false positive is reduced closely to 1%. Our results in Figure 6 also show that Algorithm 2 has a high percentage of detecting wormhole links in

Test 1. These links will then be used in the Confirmation phase. While for Test 2 we observe a low result, which means that if a link is a real direct link, the algorithm is not likely to falsely interpret as a wormhole link. This would help in minimizing the resource (e.g. energy) consumption for communicating in the Confirmation phase.

Let the set of wormhole links that fail to be detected by Algorithm 1 and Algorithm 2 be $Fail_{Alg1}$ and $Fail_{Alg2}$, respectively. Since we move to Confirmation phase if either of the algorithms in Suspicion phase suspect a link, the set of false negative links of the whole Suspicion phase, i.e. the wormhole links that escape all algorithms, $Fail_{Suspicion}$, can be computed as:

- If $Fail_{Alg1}$ and $Fail_{Alg2}$ are mutually disjoint, then for the whole Suspicion phase, none of the wormhole links will be missed. Thus, $Fail_{Suspicion}$ will be empty.
- If $Fail_{Alg1}$ and $Fail_{Alg2}$ overlap, then some of wormhole links are missed by both algorithms. In this case, $Fail_{Suspicion}$ will be $Fail_{Alg1} \cap Fail_{Alg2}$. In the worst case, Sizeof($Fail_{Suspicion}$) = Min{Sizeof($Fail_{Alg1}$), Sizeof($Fail_{Alg2}$)}.

Given that one detection algorithm may work better than another in different situations, with the introduction of Wormeros, only a small fraction of wormhole will be able to escape all techniques applied in Suspicion phase. This is because, as we already show, Sizeof($Fail_{Suspicion}$) = Min{Sizeof($Fail_{Alg1}$), Sizeof($Fail_{Alg2}$), ..., Sizeof($Fail_{AlgN}$)} where N is the number of techniques.

As for false positive, if one of the techniques wrongly concludes that a normal link is suspicious, we move to Confirmation phase. Thus, the probability of false positive of the whole phase will be the sum of that of each technique. This is the trade-off of Detection phase in Wormeros: minimizing the probability of false negative while accepting higher probability of false positive.

Let us consider the performance of the whole framework. Let p_i be the probability of false positive for phase i ($i \in \{1, 2\}$). Similarly, let q_i be the probability of false negative for phase i ($i \in \{1, 2\}$). Then we have:

$$P[\text{fp}] = P[\text{false positive for framework}] = p_1 * p_2$$
$$P[\text{fn}] = P[\text{false nagative for framework}] = q_1 + (1 - q_1) * q_2$$

Interestingly enough, the probability of false positive is reduced significantly when combining two phases of Wormeros while the probability of false negative is almost the same as that in the first phase, because as analyzed the probability of false negative in the second phase is negligible. For example, let $p_1 = 0.1, p_2 = 0.01, q_1 = 0.03$ and $q_2 = 0.01$, then $\Pr[\text{fp}] = 0.001$ and $\Pr[\text{fn}] = 0.0397$. We can conclude that Wormeros handles very well both false negative and false positive.

7   Conclusions

The wormhole attack is considered to be a difficult attack to defend against. We propose Wormeros, a framework that uses simple techniques to identify the wormhole and then perform proper actions to confirm the existence of the attack. Through experiment and simulation, we make a compelling argument showing the ability of Wormeros to detect the wormhole attack. Our analysis further confirms the effectiveness of our framework.

References

1. Hu, Y.C., Perrig, A., Johnson, D.B.: Packet Leashes: A Defense against Wormhole Attacks in Wireless Networks. In: Proceedings of IEEE InfoCom. (April 2003)
2. Hu, L., Evans, D.: Using Directional Antennas to Prevent Wormhole Attacks. In: Network and Distributed System Security Symposium (February 2003)
3. Ko, Y.B., Shankarkumar, V., Vaidya, N.: Medium access control protocols using directional antennas in ad hoc networks. In: Proceedings of IEEE InfoCom., pp. 13–21 (March 2000)
4. Čapkun, S., Buttyán, L., Hubaux, J.P.: SECTOR: secure tracking of node encounters in multi-hop wireless networks. In: Proceedings of the 1st ACM workshop on Security of ad hoc and sensor networks, pp. 21–32 (October 2003)
5. Eriksson, J., Krishnamurthy, S.V., Faloutsos, M.: Truelink: A practical countermeasure to the wormhole attack in wireless networks. In: Proceedings of IEEE ICNP, pp. 75–84 (November 2006)
6. Khalil, I.: LITEWORP: A Lightweight Countermeasure for the Wormhole Attack in Multi-hop Wireless Networks. In: Proceedings of IEEE DSN, pp. 612–621 (June 2005)
7. Maheshwari, R., Gao, J., Das, S.R.: Detecting Wormhole Attacks in Wireless Networks Using Connectivity Information. In: Proceedings of IEEE InfoCom. (May 2007)
8. Chiu, H.S., Lui, K.S.: DelPHI: wormhole detection mechanism for ad hoc wireless networks. In: 1st International Symposium on Wireless Pervasive Computing (January 2006)
9. Tran, P.V., Hung, L.X., Lee, Y.K., Lee, S., Lee, H.: TTM: An Efficient Mechanism to Detect Wormhole Attacks in Wireless Ad-hoc Networks. In: 4th IEEE Consumer Communications and Networking Conference (January 2007)
10. Eschenauer, L., Gligor, V.D.: A key-management scheme for distributed sensor networks. In: Proceedings of ACM CCS, pp. 41–47 (November 2002)
11. The Network Simulator - ns-2, http://www.isi.edu/nsnam/ns/

Designing Secure Protocols for Wireless Sensor Networks

A. Selcuk Uluagac[1], Christopher P. Lee[1], Raheem A. Beyah[2],
and John A. Copeland[1]

[1] Communications Systems Center, School of Electrical and Computer Engineering
Georgia Institute of Tehnology, Atlanta, Georgia 30332, USA
[2] Communications Assurance and Performance Group, Georgia State University
34 Peachtree Street, Atlanta, Georgia 30303, USA
{selcuk,chris,jcopeland}@ece.gatech.edu, rbeyah@cs.gsu.edu

Abstract. Over the years, a myriad of protocols have been proposed
for resource-limited Wireless Sensor Networks (WSNs). Similarly, security research for WSNs has also evolved over the years. Although fundamental notions of WSN research are well established, optimization of the
limited resources has motivated new research directions in the field. In
this paper, we seek to present general principles to aid in the design of secure WSN protocols. Therefore, building upon both the established and
the new concepts, envisioned applications, and the experience garnered
from the WSNs research, we first review the desired security services (i.e.,
confidentiality, authentication, integrity, access control, availability, and
nonrepudiation) from WSNs perspective. Then, we question which services would be necessary for resource-constrained WSNs and when it
would be most reasonable to implement them for a WSN application.

Keywords: Wireless Sensor Networks, Security in Wireless Sensor Networks, Security Services for Wireless Sensor Networks.

1 Introduction

Throughout the last decade, the introduction of WSNs to the networking field
has gathered the attention of academia and industry. Today, WSNs are no longer
a nascent technology and future advances in technology will bring more sensor
applications into our daily lives as well as into many diverse and challenging application scenarios. For example, WSNs would be very instrumental in applications from real-time target tracking, homeland security, battlefield surveillance,
surveillance of territorial waters, to biological and chemical attack detection [1].

In this regard, designing secure protocols for wireless sensor networks is vital.
However, designing secure protocols for WSNs requires first the detailed understanding of the WSN technology and its relevant security aspects. Compared to
other wireless networking technologies, WSNs have unique characteristics that
need to be taken into account when building protocols. Among many factors, the
available resources (i.e., power, computational capacities, and memory) onboard

Y. Li et al. (Eds.): WASA 2008, LNCS 5258, pp. 503–514, 2008.

the sensor nodes are severely limited. For instance, a typical sensor [2] operates at the frequency of 2.4 GHz, has a data rate of 250Kbps, 128KB of program flash memory, 512KB of memory for measurements, transmit power between 100μW and 1mW, and 30m to 100m of communications range. Thus, the most important design parameter for WSN protocols is to be energy efficient. This fundamental fact heavily influences protocols that are designed for the WSN.

Although, over the years, a myriad of protocols have been proposed for WSNs and fundamental notions have been established well, trying to be energy efficient and optimize the limited resources available in WSN protocols have further brought new notions and directions in the WSN research. Some of these notions are directly in contrast to what have been considered and studied as reasonable for other types of wireless networks. For instance, today, it is believed that not all the communication layers from the protocol stack are needed to be implemented in the sensors [3]. This is reasonable as it both saves space from the implementation and reduces complexity. Thus, this work constitutes a bridge between salient features of the WSN protocols, applications and their security aspects by addressing the desired security services for WSNs.

The main goal of this work is to provide a basin of concepts for protocol designers to consider before attempting to build secure WSN protocols. Specifically, building upon the established concepts and the experience garnered from the previous research efforts in the literature, we sift through all the security services (confidentiality, authentication, integrity, access control, availability, and nonrepudiation). First, what a particular security service means from the WSN's perspective is discussed. Second, how that service has been studied in the literature is briefly addressed. Finally, we present further suggestions by questioning the need of that service for WSNs. We believe further improvements can be accomplished by unbundling some of the unnecassray security services, which may be contrary to most of the established principles.

The paper proceeds as follows. Section 2 briefly gives the traditional communication and threat models for WSNs. We also introduce a new threat model, called Target-Based attacks as a complementary threat model to the current literature. Desired security services are explored in Section 3. Section 4 discusses which service should be provided for a particular scenario. Finally, section 5 concludes the paper.

2   The WSN Communication and Threat Models

In this section, we articulate the communication and the threat models for the WSN, which is significant to capture the security aspect of the problem. In WSNs, only sensor-to-sensor, sink-to-sensor, and sensor-to-sink communications can occur. In rare applications, where more than one sink is present, there may be a sink-to-sink communication as well. The possible communications are illustrated in Figure 1.

There are several threats to a WSN protocol. Conceptually, the threats could be listed from different perspectives. The previous research have listed threats

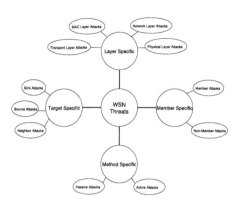

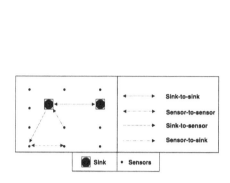

Fig. 1. WSNs communication model

Fig. 2. WSNs threat model including the new Target-Based Attacks

according to how attacks are accomplished (e.g., Passive-Active Attacks)[4], on which layer of the communication stack they are realized (e.g., Layered Attacks) [5], and finally whether the malicious node becomes a member of the network during the attack or not (e.g., Member and Non-Member Attacks) [6]. Essentially, current literature for threat models resemble the ones done for wireless networks in general, which is a legitimate starting point, because many of the attacks could be borrowed from the literature for wireless networks. However, given the unique nature of a WSN, threats can be studied from another perspective. For instance, different functionalities could have been implemented at different parts of the network in order to efficiently utilize the resources of the WSN. Thus, an attacker first identifies where the critical functionalities are implemented in the network and then perpetrates its malicious intent on those identified targets. Thus, motivated to define another proper threat model for WSNs, in this paper, we also introduce a new threat model, *Target-Based Threat Model*, which is distinguished according to where and on which networking components the attacks are targeted (i.e., Sink, Neighbor, and Source Attacks). Target-based model complements the previous research on the issue. In reality, there is no hard line between these attacking types. The threat model for the WSN is given in Figure 2.

3   Desired Security Services from the WSNs Perspective

Structured definition of desired security services and mechanisms for the interconnection of open systems have been developed as an international standard by the International Telecommunication Union (ITU) inside Recommendation X.800 [7], which is referred to as the Security Architecture for OSI. This security architecture has been a valuable guideline for many researchers and practitioners who aim to develop secure systems. Thus, in this section we look at this reference security architecture from the perspective of WSNs.

Inside X.800, there are five major service categories: *Authentication, Access Control, Data Confidentiality, Data Integrity,* and *Nonrepudiation.* Although *Availability* has not originally been considered as one of the security services in X.800, it is also included in our discussion below, as it pertains to desired security services for WSNs.

Similar to other WSNs protocols and applications, three performance metrics are pertinent when providing security services for WSNs. These performance metrics are independent of the chosen encryption mechanism. One is the *storage,* another is the *communication,* and the last is *computational* cost. For WSNs, the *communication cost* is the costliest among all the others and the chosen security mechanism implemented should try to use these scare resources efficiently.

These security services are studied below. Specifically, first, what the particular security service means in the WSN's domain is given; second, how that service has been addressed in the literature is articulated briefly.

3.1 Confidentiality

WSN Perspective Definition. Confidentiality refers to the protection of the exchanged content (e.g., gathered data, reports, commands) among the sink(s) and the sensors. An adversary which has the privilege to access the content, should not be able to decode the exchanged messages in the network.

Current Approaches. Providing a confidential service to WSN applications requires the usage of cryptographic measures like encryption techniques. In general, two distinct forms of encryption approaches are in common use: *symmetric* and *asymmetric* key based schemes. Symmetric key based encryption uses the same key at both ends of the communication to encrypt and decrypt the information from ciphertext to plaintext and vice verse. On the other hand, with asymmetric key based encryption, a different key (one private and one public) are utilized to convert and recover the information.

The general important observation about encryption mechanisms is that one cannot claim that one encryption method is superior to another as it is essentially a matter of the key size and the computational effort in breaking the encryption algorithm [4]. The second aspect to confidentiality research in WSNs entails designing efficient *key management* schemes because regardless of the encryption mechanism chosen for WSNs, the keys must be made available to the communicating nodes (e.g., sources, sink(s)) to maintain the privacy of the channels. The key management process involves two fundamental steps: generation (after an analysis) and distribution of keys; and it is triggered by keying events (e.g., due to node addition or an attack) in the network. Nonetheless, it is not an easy task and even in some applications it may be daunting to visit a large number of sensors and update their keys (e.g., for underwater sensor applications). Thus, intelligent key management schemes are necessary for WSN.

There are two further observations for confidentiality research in WSNs. First, the research mainly focuses on different keying mechanisms rather than on building efficient symmetric or asymmetric encryption algorithms. This is reasonable because it is not easy to devise a new encryption technique due to its complex and rigorous mathematical processes involved. Second, as for the keying mechanisms, it is seen that current research mainly revolves around the key distribution step because for the resource limited WSN, it is not efficient to repeat the analysis and key generation with every occurrence of a keying event.

The following list gives an overview of the research for both the encryption and key management mechanisms for WSNs.

- *Encryption mechanisms*: In recent works, the feasibility of two encryption techniques have been well scrutinized and understood for the WSN domain. With the current technological advances in the field of micro-electro-mechanical systems, symmetric encryption techniques is more tailored to WSNs. There are several reasons for this. First of all, using the same key at both ends saves the storage space. For instance in a simple worst case scenario assume that there are N number of nodes in the network. While for symmetric encryption, a given node must posses N-1 number of keys in order to communicate to the other N-1 nodes, for asymmetric encryption, the same node must have N keys, N-1 for others' public keys, one for its own private key. Considering the fact that the key sizes for symmetric algorithms (e.g., 128 bits for AES) are generally smaller than those of asymmetric ones (e.g., recommended 1024 bits for RSA and 160 bits for Elliptic Curve Cryptography (ECC) Based Public Key Scheme), one can conclude that depending on the specified key size of the particular algotrithm chosen, the symmetric encryption algorithms may help save from the per-node storage space. Secondly, the symmetric encryption algorithms have been known to utilize the resources more efficiently than their asymmetric counterparts as their cryptographic operations take lesser time and require much less energy consumption than that of asymmetric cryptographic ones [8]. This is primarily due to the fact that the symmetric encryption algorithms are faster in computation as they employ more primitive operations in their algorithms like substitution and permutation of symbols, which are implemented at the hardware level via shifts and XORs, rather than operations applying mathematical functions like modular arithmetic and exponentiation, which are the basis of public key encryption mechanisms. Lastly, the exchange of smaller size keys, when needed in a WSN application, consumes less communication resources, which favors symmetric schemes. A detailed discussion of key mechanisms are given below.
- *Key management mechanisms*: As mentioned above, there are two fundamental steps in the key management process: *generation* and *distribution* of keys. The *key generation* step deals with generation of the keys. Depending on the key type that is going to be deployed in the WSN, the keys can be generated once or multiple times during the lifetime of the WSN. The practical approach adopted so far in this avenue of research has been to generate one time different keys such as session, network-wise, master, and group-wise keys depending on the topology and on the application requirements of WSNs. While this helps decrease the computation cost for WSNs, it may

increase the storage over nodes depending on the key distribution scheme. The second step is the *distribution* of keys. The keys should be made available to the nodes without allowing others to see the keys. Traditionally, the keys have been exchanged between the end-points of the communication directly, or indirectly through trusted intermediaries (e.g., Key Distribution Center). The keys could be distributed to the sensors before the network is deployed or they could be re-distributed to nodes on demand as triggered by keying events. In the jargon of security research for WSNs, the former is phrased as *Static Key* management whereas the latter is as *Dynamic Key* management. For WSNs, the communication cost dominates other critical cost parameters, i.e., storage and computation [9]. Thus, the research for key distribution has focused more on static key management schemes. *Static key* management schemes perform key management functions statically prior to or shortly after network deployment. One famous pioneering work in this avenue is by Eschenauer and Gligor [9] [8], where each sensor in the WSN is pre-configured with a random subset of keys from a large key pool. To agree on a key for communication, two sensor nodes find one common key within their subsets and use this key as their shared secret key. On the other hand, *dynamic key* management schemes perform the key management steps either periodically or on demand due to keying events in the network. The leading approach in dynamic keying schemes involves exclusion-based systems [10], the basic notion of which requires each node to have k keys out of $k + m$ keys. m keys are disguised from the attackers and are used only when new keys need to be created once keying events are triggered in the network.

3.2 Authentication

WSN Perspective Definition. Authentication service involves genuineness of the communication. An authentication mechanism verifies if the exchanged information is emanating from the legitimate participant of the WSN because a malicious entity (e.g., a compromised node) may be able to inject counterfeit content or resend the same content into the network. Moreover, the X.800 specification recommends two sub-cases for authentication. The first involves the authentication of the peer entity and the second deals with the authentication of the origin of the data. For WSNs, the former means authentication of all the nodes that participate in the communication. Authentication can be done between two nodes communicating or one node (e.g., cluster head) and several other nodes around that node (i.e, broadcast authentication). The latter can be implemented at the sink or at an intermediary sensor node where data aggregation takes place.

Current Approaches. There are several traditional methods of authentication in the literature [4]. One is password based method depending on the premise of showing that one knows a secret. The node sends a password with its login information. The receiver verifies that the node is legitimate node by checking that the password is associated with the sender node.

The other one is cryptographic-based method, which is also called challenge-response. A classic technique to provide authentication would be to utilize Message Authentication Codes (MAC). The authenticated sensor node is required to provide the MAC code to be authenticated by the the authenticator sensor node. For MACs, hashes, symmetric key-based encryption, asymmetric key-based encryption methods may all be utilized. Thus, there are several practical ways of creating MACs, but simply creating a MAC involves possesing the same secret at both ends and either encrypting the hash of the content with that key or hashing both the key and the content together. However, as discussed in the confidentiality subsection above, the encryption mechanisms have their associated costs, thus they should be employed with caution.

The last authentication method is address-based or identy-based. For this, the authenticator sensor node can check the identity or the location of the sender node. The passwords is not sent across the network with these schemes. In comparison to the previous two mechanism, this method would be very practical for WSNs but would not provide a strong authentication mechanism because it is trivial to spoof a sensor ID.

Two of the former leading works include SPINS [11] and TinySec [12]. They both employ symmetric encryption algorithms and work at the link layer.

3.3   Integrity

WSN Perspective Definition. The recipients in the WSN should be able to detect if the exchanged content between the communicating participants of the WSN have been altered. Furthermore, for the WSN, the integrity service should also ensure that the exchanged content is not deleted, replication of old data, counterfeit, or stale.

Current Approaches. Integrity of the exchanged content is usually provided with the digest of the content appended to the content itself. When the recipient sensor node receives the message it checks to see if the digest of the content that it computes and the digest received equals each other. If they are, then it accepts it as a legitimate message.

Content digests in integrity are created with the usage of hashing algorithms. There are many hashing algorithms in use today. Usually, hashing algorithms do not require the presence of keys unless they are specifically designed to work with keys like keyed-hashing (e.g., HMAC, CMAC). Thus, their impact on a sensor node is only confined with their computational efficiencies. However, as for the keyed-hashing algorithms, previously discussed issues emanating from key generation, key storage, and key exchange are also pertinent here, hence the keyed-hashing techniques must utilize the resources (computation, communication, and storage) efficiently

Staleness of the data is of utmost significance in the integrity checking because decision processes of some applications may especially depend on if the data is recent or not. For example, in one very specific WSN application, a certain territory (e.g., territorial waters) could be protected with mines that are detonated by sinks. The freshness and the correct timing of the messages from the sensor nodes in this type of application is very important. A simple solution for these types of applications would be to use counters for the exchanged content. Lastly, another desired aspect of the integrity service may involve providing a recovery mechanism from the altered content.

3.4   Access Control

WSN Perspective Definition. With access control, unauthorized use of a resource is prevented in WSNs. It addresses which participant of the network reaches which content or service. For instance, sensor nodes should not be allowed to have the privileges of sinks such as changing network-wide parameters of the WSN protocols. Thus, limiting services or functionalities depending on the participant would be appropriate.

Current Approaches. One of the most challenging security services for WSNs is access control; hence, this is perhaps why access control for WSNs is one of the security services that have not been studied well in the literature [13]. We believe that part of this is because it is hard to formulate an access control scenario for WSNs. In practical implementations, normally there is one terminating point (i.e., sink) in the network where all the data collected from the network is collected. Thus, other sensors are not expected to access to any resource that may be hosted by other nodes. This is a reasonable expectation for WSN applications where sensors send their readings based on an event. However, there may be sensor applications where source sensor nodes are queried by other sensor nodes as well. For these circumstances, the access control policies can be used. An access control policy should prevent unauthorized nodes from accessing the important information.

Setting access policies may also be practical and instrumental for cluster-based or hierarchical sensor node implementations.

3.5   Nonrepudiation

WSN Perspective Definition. Nonrepudiation is service of ensuring that a sensor can not refute the reception of a message from the other involving party or the sent of a message to the other involving party in the communication. According to the X.800 recommendation, the former is the destination and the latter one is called the origin nonrepudiation.

Current Approaches. Similar to access control, nonrepudiation has not been formulated well in the WSNs domain. This could be attributed to the lack of need of such a service for WSNs. Or, it could have been thought inside integrity or authentication services implicitly.

Although the need for nonrepudiation service may not seem to be obvious, we think that it is an achievable important service to contemplate and that there are some practical advantageous in providing this service. A digital signature scheme (DSS) [4], which is based on utilizing encryption methods would also address nonrepudiation. Symmetric and asymmetric encryptions can be utilized for DSS. However, their viabilities should be explored in more detail for WSNs. For instance, on the one hand, using the same key both for signature and verification may be vulnerable to another sensor's impersonation of the original sensor's signature. On the other hand, however, employing asymmetric encryption based algorithms may be costly. Naturally, providing nonrepudiation service may facilitate the endorsement or proof by another entity for a sent or receipt message in WSN. Thus, alternatively, some other trusted node, either the sink or an aggregator node, in the network could provide this service.

3.6 Availability

WSN Perspective Definition. Due to threats to the WSN, some portion of the network or some of the functionalities or services provided by the network could be damaged and unavailable to the participants of the network. For instance, some sensors could die earlier than their expected lifetimes. Thus, availability service ensures that the necessary functionalities or the services provided by the WSN are always carried out, even in the case of attacks.

Current Approaches. Availability is a security service that has not been originally considered as one of the security services inside the X.800 recommendation. It may be claimed that it is independent of the security services. The outcome of the secure services provided by the network should guarantee the operations and functionalities aimed by the WSN application. Availability service for WSNs have been mostly studied from the perspective of Denial-of-Service type attacks [14] in the literature. One other pertinent study regarding availability has focused on the connectivity properties of WSNs [15].

4   When to Employ Specific Security Services

Sensor nodes are severely limited in their capabilities. There are three important design parameters for WSNs: communication, computation, and storage cost. The cost of communication dominates over those of the computation and storage. So, any security service designed for WSNs should always try to minimize the cost of these parameters. Thus, providing a security service comes with its associated costs naturally as it is an additional service on top of whatever is provided by the network.

When we look at the security services in general, we see that they are often provided as bundled services. Another observation from the literature is that in comparison to other security services, confidentiality has been explored more because it is fundamental to all of the other security services, except for availability. We believe that for resource constrained devices like sensor nodes in WSNs, there can be further minimization of the associated cost by just unbundling the unnecessary services. This would require the understanding of the needs of the network. Therefore, security services should be tailored to the applications, as it would be a waste of important resources in the network if all the security services are unnecessarily implemented. Looking at the security services and the improvements in the field, below is a discussion of how the security services should be analyzed for WSNs.

- Confidentiality of data should be always be questioned as the confidentiality will always be the most costly security service among all the security services. Unless it is utmost necessary for the WSN, it may not be employed. Integrity check on the data may suffice to determine the activity of a malicious entity in the WSN. Thus, confidentiality can be unbundled from the rest of the services and provided as an additional security service for the WSN and be addressed separately from the other services.
- Authentication service can be considered as a prevention mechanism for WSNs applications. This is reasonable because when authenticating a un-trusted sensor node, if that node is malicious one, it may have or not per-petrated its malicious intent yet. With authentication, the malicious node may be blocked from its activity. Thus, authentication may be used as a prevention mechanism. Furthermore, authentication may be necessary for aggregator sensor nodes, which collect the sensors' readings, where the agre-gator sensor nodes asks the source sensor nodes for their sensor readings. The source nodes may need to authenticate the aggregator node.
- Providing integrity definitely determines if a malicious activity exists in the network or not. It can be considered as a detection mechanism rather than a prevention mechanism like authentication. Specifically, integrity check for WSNs can be done either at every sensor node or at data-aggregating nodes or sink(s). Checking at every node increases the computation cost, but elim-inates the fake data immediately and prevents that data from propagating further. On the other hand, checking the integrity at aggregator nodes or sinks save from the computation, but not from the communication cost. This is an application specific parameter that should be considered when providing integrity for WSNs, which is a topic for further investigation.
- Intelligent bundling of the services is possible. For instance, the integrity can be embedded inside an authentication service. The nice thing about asym-metric systems is that they can be used for both authentication and integrity purposes. It is even possible to use an asymmetric encryption algorithm to provide authentication, integrity, and nonrepudiation. Although asymmetric encryption mechanisms are costlier than symmetric encryption mechanisms, further security services can be addressed in an all-in-one fashion. However, their applicability for WSNs needs further investigation.
- Access control comes naturally after authentication; thus, it may be bene-ficial to bundle these two. However, confidentiality and access control are separate issues that can be de-coupled and addressed separately.
- It is always cost effective for WSNs to employ security algorithms with smaller key sizes. Smaller key sizes will help save from the network stor-age, and further, if the keys are exchanged in the network, it will save from the communication as well because communication of smaller keys consumes

less communication overhead. Moreover, when smaller keys and asymmetric encryption is necessary, ECC based algorithms should be favored over the others as ECC based ones, have much better efficient utilization of the resources in place of others (e.g., RSA)

- Usage of different keys such as session, network-wise, master, and group-wise keys should be considered to isolate and to futher help counter malicious activities. Furthemore, albeit costlier than the static key management schemes, dynamic key management schemes is more tailored to WSN applications. There may be ways to generate keys dynamically without too much overhead. For instance, depending on something unique that a sensor posses, keys can be generated instead of being exchanged. For instance, the residual batter life or energy on a node [16] or identity of the node could be utilized for this. However, depending on the application type and the needs, if the lifetime of the network is more important than security, then static key management schemes may be preferred in place of dynamic.

- Due to the resource constrainted nature of WSNs, there have been new ideas that are shaping the future of WSNs. Some of the promising ones include collaboration of sensor for the distributed networking functionalities, and delayered of TCP/IP stack. There would be further savings from the scarce resources of WSNs, if these are considered when building secure WSN protocols. For instance, collaborative security, application-oriented security, and non-layered security approaches may be promising but they need further investigation.

- Availability should not be considered outside of security services, the network should have worst case secure data delivery scenarios in case of any security breach or malicious attack. However, this can be thought in a layered fashion. Unless there is a security problem in the network, the alternative availability mechanism may not be considered. However, this is again an application oriented issue for WSNs. For some applications, where the timely collection of data is utmost important, the availability should be considered at the same as security services.

- For application where different types of sensor nodes co-exist or a composite of events [17] occur in the same WSN application, it may be very important to provide an access control service. Similarly, having access policies may be instrumental for cluster-based or hierarchical sensor node implementations.

5 Conclusion

Both WSNs and the security for WSNs research fields have matured over the years. Furthermore, optimization of the limited resources has motivated new research directions in the field. In this work, considering the established concepts and new directions, we have discussed general principles for researchers who seek to design secure WSN protocols. Specifically, we have reviewed the desired security services, i.e., confidentiality, authentication, integrity, access control, availability, and nonrepudiation, and their necessity from the WSN perspective. We have determined and listed several valuable suggestions for protocols builders. The protocol designers should determine what is best for their WSN applications and needs.

References

[1] Akyildiz, I.F., Su, W., Sankarasubramaniam, Y., Cayirci, E.: Wireless sensor networks: A survey. Computer Networks (Elsevier) Journal 38(4), 393–422 (2002)

[2] Xbow, Crossbow technology (2008), http://www.xbow.com/

[3] Akyildiz, I.F., Vuran, M.C., Akan, O.B.: A cross layer protocol for wireless sensor networks. In: Proc. CISS 2006, Princeton, NJ (March 2006)

[4] Stallings, W.: Cryptography and Network Security: Principles and Practices, 3rd edn. Prentice Hall, Englewood Cliffs (2003)

[5] Roosta, T., Shieh, S., Sastry, S.: Taxonomy of security attacks in sensor networks. In: The First IEEE International Conference on System Integration and Reliability Improvements, Hanoi, Vietnam (December 2006)

[6] Shi, E., Perrig, A.: Designing secure sensor networks. IEEE Wireless Communications 11(6), 38–43 (2004)

[7] ITU. X. 800, Security architecture for open systems interconnection for ccitt applications (1991)

[8] Eschenauer, L., Gligor, V.D.: A key-management scheme for distributed sensor networks. In: Proceedings of the ACM CCS 2002, pp. 41–47 (2002)

[9] Law, Y.W., Doumen, J., Hartel, P.: Survey and benchmark of block ciphers for wireless sensor networks. ACM Trans. Sen. Netw. 2(1), 65–93 (2006)

[10] Eltoweissy, M., Moharrum, M., Mukkamala, R.: Dynamic key management in sensor networks. IEEE Communications Magazine 44(4), 122–130 (2006)

[11] Perrig, A., Szewczyk, R., Tygar, J.D., Wen, V., Culler, D.E.: Spins: security protocols for sensor networks. Wireles Networks 8(5), 521–534 (2002)

[12] Karlof, C., Sastry, N., Wagner, D.: Tinysec: A link layer security architecture for wireless sensor networks. In: ACM SenSys 2004 (November 2004)

[13] Zhou, Y., Zhang, Y., Fang, Y.: Access control in wireless sensor networks. Elsevier's AdHoc Networks Journal 5(1), 3–13 (2007)

[14] Wood, A.D., Stankovic, J.A.: Denial of service in sensor networks. IEEE Computer 35(10), 54–62 (2002)

[15] Pietro, R.D., Mancini, L., Mei, A., Panconesi, A., Radhakrishnan, J.: How to design connected sensor networks that are provably secure. Securecomm, 89–100 (2006)

[16] Hou, H., Corbett, C., Li, Y., Beyah, R.: Dynamic energy-based encoding and filtering in sensor networks. In: Proc. of the IEEE MILCOM (October 2007)

[17] Vu, C., Beyah, R., Li, Y.: A composite event detection in wireless sensor networks. In: Proc. of the IEEE IPCCC (April 2007)

Privacy-Preserving Communication Algorithms and Network Protocols

Jian Ren

Department of Electrical and Computer Engineering
Michigan State University
East Landing, MI 48864-1226, USA
renjian@egr.msu.edu

Abstract. Communication anonymity is becoming an increasingly important or even indispensable security requirement for critical information infrastructure protection and mission critical communications. Existing research in anonymous communications can largely be divided into two categories: mix-based systems and secure multiparty computation-based systems, originating from mixnet and DC-net respectively. However, all mix-based solutions require a trusted third party and cannot provide provable anonymity. While the secure multiparty computation-based approach suffers from transmission collusion problem that no practical solution exists to solve this problem. In this paper, we first propose a novel unconditionally secure source anonymous message (SAM) scheme that can be applied to any messages without relying on any trusted third parties. While ensuring message sender anonymity, the proposal scheme can also provide message content authenticity. We also propose a novel communication protocol that can hide both the senders and the recipients from each other and the network addresses of their end-to-end source and destination. The proposed protocols can be applied to both overlay networks as well as mobile ad hoc networks (MANETs). It can also be used for critical infrastructure protection and secure file sharing. The security analysis demonstrates that the proposed protocol is secure against various attacks. Our analysis also shows it is efficient and practical.

Keywords: Communication anonymity, unconditional security, sender anonymity, recipient anonymity, location privacy, content authenticity.

1 Introduction

The rapid growth of public acceptance of the Internet as a means of communication and information dissemination has made communication privacy, or communication anonymity, an increasingly important requirement for many network applications. While end-to-end encryption protects the data content of communications from adversarial access, it does not conceal all the relevant information that two users are communicating. Adversaries can still learn not only the network of the sender and receiver, but also the network addresses of its end-to-end source and destination.

Y. Li et al. (Eds.): WASA 2008, LNCS 5258, pp. 515–525, 2008.

In many situations, it is highly desirable or indispensable for users to be able to preserve the communications privacy. In other word, privacy-preserving is a fundamental security requirement for many applications.

Over the last years, overlay networks have evolved as a natural decentralized way to share data and services among a network of loosely connected components. The proliferation of overlay networks have also been propelled by popular applications, most notably secure file sharing and IP telephony (e.g., Gnutella, BitTorrent, Skype). People seeking for sensitive information have a strong desire to remain anonymous so as to avoid being stigmatized or even to avoid physical or social detriment by suppressors. The freedom of information exchange is another important issue that got increasing attention in the last years. Some organizations, such as governments or private companies, may regard a discussion topic or a report as inconvenient or even harmful. They may thus try to censor the exchange of undesired information by either suppressing resource providers, or if these are protected by anonymity, taking control of strategic regions of the network, such as gateways and proxies, and filtering the communication.

Without privacy protection, there are abundant opportunities for passive eavesdropping on data communications. The exposure of network addresses may result in a number of several consequences. Adversaries can easily overhear all the messages and perform traffic analysis. In a tactical military communication network, an abrupt change in traffic pattern may indicate some forthcoming activities. This could be extremely dangerous in that adversaries can easily identify critical network nodes and then launch directed attacks on them.

In the past two decades, originated largely from Chaum's mixnet [1] and DC-net [2], a number of anonymous communication protocols have been proposed. The mixnet family protocols use a set of "mix" servers that mix the received packets to make the communication path (including the sender and the recipient) ambiguous. They rely on the statistical properties of background traffic that is also referred to as the *cover traffic* to achieve the desired anonymity. The security of mixnet is based on the trust relationship of the mixers, and cannot provide provable anonymity. The DC-net family protocols (e.g., [2,3]) utilize secure multiparty computation techniques. They provide provable anonymity without relying on trusted third parties. However, they suffer from the transmission collision problem that does not have a practical solution.

As the computing, communicating, and cryptographic techniques progress rapidly, increasing emphasis has been placed on developing efficient and unconditionally secure anonymous communications schemes for overlay networks without relying on trusted third parties and free of collision.

In this paper, we first propose a novel unconditionally secure and efficient source private cryptographic algorithm for any messages without relying on any trusted third parties. While ensuring message sender anonymity, it can also provide message content authenticity. We then propose a novel communication protocol that can hide the senders and the receivers. The proposed protocols can be applied to both overlay networks as well as mobile ad hoc networks (MANETs) and can be used for secure file sharing.

2 Terminology and Preliminary

2.1 Terminology

Anonymity generally refers to the state of being not identifiable within a set of subjects. Full anonymity includes *sender anonymity, recipient anonymity* and *relationship anonymity* (the sender and the recipient are unlinkable, or cannot be identified as communicating with each other).

Definition 1 (SAM). *A* source anonymous message (SAM) *scheme consists of the following two algorithms:*

- generate $(m, y_1, \cdots, y_n)$: *Given a message m and the public keys* $y_1, \cdots, y_n$ *of the anonymity set (AS)* $S = \{A_1, \cdots, A_n\}$, *the actual message sender* $A_t, 1 \leq t \leq n$, *can produce an SAM* $S(m)$ *using her private key* x_t.
- verify $S(m)$: *Given a message m and a SAM* $S(m)$, *a verifier can determine whether* $S(m)$ *is a generated by a member in the AS.*

The security requirements for privacy-preserving schemes include:

- *Sender ambiguity*: The probability that a verifier successfully determines the real sender of a SAM is exactly $1/n$, where n is the total number of AS.
- *Unforgeability*: A SAM is unforgeable if no adversary, given the public keys of all members of the AS and the messages $m_1, m_2, \cdots, m_l$ adaptively chosen by the adversary, can produce in polynomial time a new valid SAM with non-negligible probability.

In this paper, the user ID and user public key will be used interchangeably without making any distinguish.

2.2 Modified ElGamal Signature Scheme (MES)

Definition 2 (MES). *The modified ElGamal signature scheme [4] consists of the following three algorithms:*

- Key generation algorithm: *The signer chooses a random large prime p and a generator g of* $\mathbb{Z}_p^*$. *Both p and g are made public. Then, for a random private key* $x \in \mathbb{Z}_p$, *the public key y is computed from* $y = g^x \bmod p$.
- Signature algorithm: *The MES has many variants. For the purpose of efficiency, we will use the* optimal scheme [5,6] *of the ElGamal signature. To sign a message m, one has to choose a random* $k \in \mathbb{Z}_{p-1}^*$, *then computes the exponentiation* $r = g^k \bmod p$ *and solve s from* $s = rxh(m, r) + k \bmod (p-1)$, *where h is a one-way hash function. The algorithm finally outputs the signature* (r, s) *of message m.*
- Verification algorithm: *The verifier checks whether the signature equation* $g^s = ry^{rh(m,r)} \bmod p$ *is true. If the equality holds true, then the verifier* "Accepts" *the signature and* "Rejects" *otherwise.*

2.3 Threat Model and Assumptions

We assume the participating network nodes voluntarily cooperate with each other to provide an anonymizing service. All nodes are potential message origina-tors of anonymous communications. The adversaries can collaborate to passively monitor and eavesdrop every network traffic. In addition, they may compromise any node in the target network to become an internal adversary, which could be the internal perpetrators. In this paper, we assume that passive adversaries can only compromise a fraction of nodes. We also assume that the adversaries are computationally bounded so that inverting and reading of encrypted messages are infeasible. Otherwise, it is believed that there is no workable cryptographic solution.

An agent of the adversary at a compromised node observes and collects all the information in the message, and thus reports the immediate predecessor and successor node for each message traversing the compromised node. Assume also that the adversary collects this information from all the compromised nodes, and uses it to derive the identity of the sender of a message. The sender has no information about the number or identity of nodes being compromised. The adversary collects all the information from the agents on the compromised nodes, and attempts to derive the true identity of the sender.

3 Unconditionally Secure Source Anonymous Message (SAM) Scheme

To transmit a message m, the message sender, or the sending node generates an unconditionally secure and efficient SAM for a message m. The generation is based on the MES scheme. Unlike ring signatures, which requires to com-pute a forgery signature for each member in the AS separately. In our scheme, the SAM generation requires only three steps. In addition, our design enables the SAM be verified through a single equation without individually verifying the signatures.

3.1 The Proposed Source Anonymous Message (SAM) Scheme

Suppose that the message sender (Alice) wishes to transmit a message m to any other node anonymously. The AS includes n members, $\mathcal{S} = \{A_1, \cdots, A_n\}$, where the actual message sender Alice is A_t, for some value $t, 1 \le t \le n$.

Let p be a large prime number and g be a primitive element of $\mathbb{Z}_p^*$. Both p and g are made public and shared by all members in $\mathcal{S}$. Each $A_i \in \mathcal{S}$ has a public key $y_i = g^{x_i} \bmod p$, where x_i is the randomly selected private key from $\mathbb{Z}_{p-1}^*$. We also write $\mathcal{S} = \{y_1, \cdots, y_n\}$.

To generate an efficient SAM for message m to be transmitted, Alice performs the following three steps:

1. Select a random and pairwise different k_i for each $1 \le i \le n, i \ne t$ and compute $r_i = g^{k_i} \bmod p$.

2. Choose a random $k \in \mathbb{Z}_p$ and compute $r_t = g^k \prod_{i \neq t} y_i^{-r_i h_i} \bmod p$ such that $r_t \neq 1$ and $r_t \neq r_i$ for any $i \neq t$, where $h_i = h(m, r_i)$.

3. Compute $s = k + \sum_{i \neq t} k_i + x_t r_t h_t \bmod (p - 1)$.

The SAM of the message m is defined as

$$S(m) = (m, S, r_1, \cdots, r_n, s), \tag{1}$$

where $g^s = r_1 \cdots r_n y_1^{r_1 h_1} \cdots y_n^{r_n h_n} \bmod p$, and $h_i = h(m, r_i)$.

3.2 Verification of SAM

A verifier can verify an alleged SAM

$$(m, S, r_1, \cdots, r_n, s)$$

for message m by verifying whether the following equation

$$g^s = r_1 \cdots r_n y_1^{r_1 h_1} \cdots y_n^{r_n h_n} \bmod p \tag{2}$$

holds. If equation (2) holds true, the verifier "Accepts" the SAM as a valid SAM for message m. Otherwise the verifier "Rejects" the SAM.

Theorem 1. *The proposed SAM can provide unconditional message sender anonymity.*

Theorem 2. *The proposed SAM is secure against adaptive chosen-message attack in the random oracle model.*

Due to page limitation, the readers are referred to the full paper for security proof of Theorems 1-7.

4   The Proposed Anonymous Communication Protocol

4.1   Network Model

In this paper, we adopt a structured overlay network topology used in many peer-to-peer systems such as KaZaa, Gnutella v0.6, Herbivore [3] and Chord [7] to organize the network. That is the participating nodes are divided into a set of small subgroups. The nodes in each subgroup are logically organized into an overlay shaped as a ring shown in Fig. 1. In each ring, there are n nodes, where n is a predefined security parameter. Each node/link can route message towards the *successor*, that is the next hop in the clockwise direction of the ring, referred as the *ring direction*. Our goal is to make the adversaries unable to distinguish the initiator traffic from the indirection traffic on an observable and open network. However, we know that no scheme can hide the fact that a node is participating. The best a scheme can do is to guarantee that no adversary can

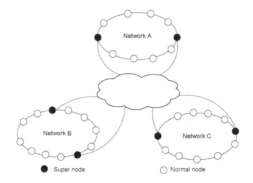

Fig. 1. Network topology of the proposed scheme

distinguish actively that a node initiates from mere participation in the protocol. In other words, a node can hide its own activities by handling traffic for other nodes.

We classify the network nodes into two categories, *normal nodes* and *super nodes*. A normal node is a network node that has no direct connection to the nodes in other networks. A super node can be a normal node that can also provide message forward services to other network nodes. It can also be a special node dedicated to providing message forward services to the other network nodes. Each network may have multiple super nodes as highlighted in Fig. 1.

Prior to network deployment, there should be an administrator. The administrator is responsible for selection of security parameters and a group-wise master key $s_G \in \mathbb{Z}_p^*$. The group master key should be well safeguarded from unauthorized access and never be disclosed to the ordinary group members. The administrator then chooses a collision-resistant cryptographic hash function h, mapping arbitrary inputs to fixed-length outputs on $\mathbb{Z}_p$, e.g., SHA-1 [8].

The administrator assigns each super node a sufficiently large set of collision-free pseudonyms that can be used to substitute the real IDs in communications to defend against passive attacks. If a super node uses one pseudonym continuously for some time, then it will not help to defend against possible attacks since the pseudonym can be analyzed the same way as its real ID. To solve this problem, each node should use dynamic pseudonyms instead. This requires each super node to sign up with the administrator, who will assign each super node a list of random and collision-resistant pseudonyms:

$$\mathscr{N}_A = \{\mathsf{id}_1^A, \cdots, \mathsf{id}_\tau^A\}.$$

In addition, each super node will also be assigned a corresponding *secret set*:

$$\mathscr{S}_s = \{g^{s_G h(\mathsf{id}_1^A)}, \cdots, g^{s_G h(\mathsf{id}_\tau^A)}\}.$$

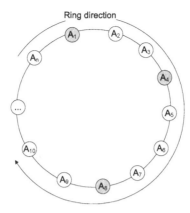

Fig. 2. Local ring

4.2   Anonymous Local Ring Communication

To realize anonymous network-layer communications, all of the information related to overlay addresses, including the destination ring where the recipient resides, should be embedded into the anonymizing message payload. Prior to network deployment, the administrator needs to select a set of security parameters for the entire system, including a large prime p, and a generator g of $\mathbb{Z}_p^*$. The network nodes $A_1, A_2, \cdots, A_n$ and the corresponding public keys $y_1, y_2, \cdots, y_n$ of the n participating network nodes, where $x_i \in \mathbb{Z}_p$, is a randomly selected private key of node A_i, and y_i is computed from $y_i = g^{x_i} \bmod p$. In each local ring, a normal node only has connection to other nodes in the same ring. The communication between two normal nodes in different rings has to be forwarded through the supper nodes in the respected local rings. Each network may have multiple super nodes as highlighted in Fig. 1.

Each message contains a nonce (N), a message flag (mF), a recipient flag (rF) and a secret key. The nonce is a random number that is used only once to prevent message replay attack. The message flag carries the priority of the message. The message flag value 0 means the transmitted message is a dummy message, or the cell is empty. The dummy message can be replaced if the current node has a message to transmit. The message flag 1 means the message is meaningful and should be transmitted. Priority can be defined for each message. The recipient flag enables the recipient to know whether he is the targeted receiver. The secret key is used to encrypt the subsequent block(s) using symmetric encryption algorithm.

Prior to data transmission, a super node needs to first initiate the data transmission in the local ring, which is a dummy message (the message flag is set to be 0) transmitted to the next super node following the ring direction in the local ring. When the packet reaches a normal node, if that node has data to transmit, it can replace the dummy data with its own message. However, to continue the message transmission and prevent the node from being identified as the receiver, the recipient node creates a new dummy message and send to the closest super node. Similarly, any node can substitute the dummy message with its own message. However, when a dummy message arrives at a super node, it needs to regenerate a dummy message and sends to the next super node so that this process can be continued.

At any time, multiple concurrent messages may be transmitted in the local ring. The number of such messages can be determined by the data transmission requirement as well as the node transmission capacity. The mix up of dummy information with the real messages makes the adversaries unable to detect the real message senders and the receivers. Since no single node will receive the same packet more than once, therefore, no single node is able to identify the real receiver of each message packet.

More specifically, for a node A_i to transmit a message m anonymously to a node A_j in the local ring, where $j > i$, node A_i generates a new message $\mathcal{M}(i, j)$ defined in equation (3) below:

$$
\begin{aligned}
\mathcal{M}(i,j) &= pk_{i+1}(N_{i+1}, mF_{i+1}, rF_{i+1}, sk_{i+1}) \| sk_{i+1}(\mathcal{M}(i+1,j)) \\
\mathcal{M}(i+1,j) &= pk_{i+2}(N_{i+2}, mF_{i+2}, rF_{i+2}, sk_{i+2}) \| sk_{i+2}(\mathcal{M}(i+2,j)) \\
&\vdots \\
\mathcal{M}(j-1,j) &= pk_j(N_j, mF_j, rF_j, sk_j) \| sk_j(\mathcal{S}(m)),
\end{aligned}
\tag{3}
$$

where for $l = i+1, \cdots, j$, N_l is a nonce, mF_l is a message flag, rF_l is a recipient flag, sk_l is the secret key used for one time message encryption, and $\|$ stands for message concatenation.

The message $\mathcal{M}(i, j)$ can be transmitted when a dummy message is received. The node substitutes the dummy message with $\mathcal{M}(i, j)$. The message will then be forwarded node to node to the successors nodes $A_{i+1}, A_{i+2}, \cdots, A_j$ until it reaches the message recipient in the ring direction, which is the clockwise direction.

When the node A_{i+1} receives the message packet, the node first verify the SAM to check the authenticity of the message. If the message check is successful according to equation (2), the recipient decrypts the first block of the received message using its private key corresponding to pk_{i+1}. After that, the node will get the recipient flag and message flag with the instruction for the following actions. If the check fails, then the recipient node should reset the message to dummy message so that effective communication can be continued.

The amount of traffic flow that a node creates as the initiator is concealed in the traffic that it forwards since the overall traffic that it receives is the same as the traffic that it forwards. In addition to the balanced traffic, the message is encrypted with the private key that only the recipient can recover. While the intermediate nodes can only view the instruction of the message allowed. As the sender's message is indistinguishable by other nodes, the sender and the recipient is thus hidden amongst the other nodes. *It is infeasible for the adversary to correlate messages using traffic analysis and timing analysis due to message encryption.* Therefore, perfect obscure of its own messages can be assured. Detailed security analysis will be presented later on.

Based on the measurement of dummy messages that it receives, the super nodes can determinate whether the volume of messages in concurrent transmission in the local ring should be increased, or decreased to optimize the overall system performance.

In the proposed protocol, a node's joining and leaving in the overlay ring is straightforward. When a node wishes to join a ring, it only needs to find two adjacent nodes where it would like to join the ring. For a node to leave the ring, the predecessor of the node should simply skip the current node and communicate directly to its successor as long as they each have the other node's necessary communication information.

4.3   Communications between Two Arbitrary Super Nodes

In the previous subsection, we present the mechanism that allows two arbitrary nodes to communicate anonymously in the same local ring. This includes communications between two super nodes in the same local ring. For two arbitrary super nodes in different rings to communicate anonymously, we will first introduce the concept of anonymous authentication, or secret handshake by Balfanz *et al.* [9]. Anonymous authentication allows two nodes in the same group to authenticate each other *secretly* in the sense that each party reveals its group membership to the other party only if the other party is also a group member. Non-members are not able to recognize group members. Secret handshake has been applied in anonymous routing in mobile ad hoc networks [10].

The scheme consists of a set of super nodes, an administrator who creates groups and enroll super nodes in groups. For this purpose, the administrator will assign each super node A a set of pseudonyms $\text{id}_1^A, \cdots, \text{id}_\tau^A$, where τ is a large security parameter. In addition, the administrator also calculates a corresponding *secret set* $\{g^{s_G h(\text{id}_1^A)} \bmod p, \cdots, g^{s_G h(\text{id}_\tau^A)} \bmod p\}$ for super node A, where s_G is the groups secret and h is a hash function. The pseudonyms will be dynamically selected and used to substitute the real IDs for each communications. This means that two super nodes A and B can know each other's group membership only if they belong to the same group.

When the super node A wants to authenticate to the super node B, the following secret handshake can be conducted:

1. $A \to B$: Super node A randomly selects an unused pseudonym id_i^A and a random nonce N_1, then sends id_i^A, N_1 to super node B.
2. $B \to A$: Super node B randomly selects an unused pseudonym id_i^B and a random nonce N_2, then sends $\text{id}_j^B, N_2, V_0 = h(K_{BA} \| \text{id}_i^A \| \text{id}_j^B \| N_1 \| N_2 \| 0)$ to super node A, where $K_{BA} = g^{s_G h(\text{id}_i^A) \cdot h(\text{id}_j^B)} \bmod p$.
3. $A \to B$: Super node A sends $V_1 = h(K_{AB} \| \text{id}_i^A \| \text{id}_j^B \| N_1 \| N_2 \| 1)$ to super node B, where $K_{AB} = g^{s_G h(\text{id}_j^B) \cdot h(\text{id}_i^A)} \bmod p$.

Since

$$K_{BA} = g^{s_G h(\text{id}_i^A) \cdot h(\text{id}_j^B)} = g^{s_G h(\text{id}_j^B) \cdot h(\text{id}_i^A)} = K_{AB} \bmod p,$$

A can verify V_0 by checking whether $V_0 \overset{?}{=} h(K_{AB}\|\text{id}_i^A\|\text{id}_j^B\|N_1\|N_2\|0)$. If the verification succeeds, then A knows that B is an authentic group peer. Similarly, B can verify A by checking whether $V_1 \overset{?}{=} h(K_{BA}\|\text{id}_i^A\|\text{id}_j^B\|N_1\|N_2\|1)$. If the verification succeeds, then B knows that A is also an authentic group peer. However, in this authentication process, neither super node A, nor super node B can get the real identity of the other node. In other words, the real identities of super node A and super node B remain anonymous after the authentication process.

4.4 Communications between Two Arbitrary Normal Nodes

Theorem 3. *It is computationally infeasible for an adversary to identify the message sender and recipient in the local ring. Therefore, the proposed anonymous communication protocol provides both sender and recipient anonymity in the local ring.*

Theorem 4. *The proposed communication protocol between two super nodes can provide both message sender and recipient anonymity.*

Corollary 1. *The proposed anonymous communication protocol can provide full anonymity for any sender and recipient in the overlay network ring(s).*

Theorem 5. *It is computationally infeasible for a PPT adversary $\mathcal{A}$ to impersonate as a super node.*

Theorem 6. *It is computationally infeasible for an adversary to successfully modify/reply an (honest) node's message.*

4.5 Efficiency and Performance Evaluation

Anonymity is achieved as a result of trade-off with efficiency and computational complexity. In our case, the transmission of dummy messages is required as a message carrier in the local ring. It thus increases the communication overhead and the average data latency. In terms of *communication complexity* (the messages transmitted in the network for every SAM), *time complexity* (time required to transmit a message) and *buffer complexity* (the buffer size required for each processor to the messages) [11], we have the following theorem.

Theorem 7. *In the proposed protocol, the communication complexity of the proposed protocol is $\mathcal{O}(n)$, time complexity is $\mathcal{O}(n)$, and buffer complexity is $\mathcal{O}(n)$.*

In addition, the proposed protocol also increases extra computational complexity of each node since it has to decrypt every received message and verify the message authentication code.

There is always a trade-off between time complexity and communication complexity. For example, to reduce the transmission latency, multiple messages can be transmitted in a ring currently. However, this will increase the computational complexity.

5   Conclusion

In this paper, we first propose a novel and efficient SAM that can be applied to any messages. While ensuring unconditional message sender anonymity, SMM can also provide message content authenticity. To provide provable anonymity without suffering from transmission collision problem, we then propose a novel anonymous communication protocol for both message sender and recipient. Security analysis shows that the proposed protocol is secure against various attacks. Our analysis also shows it is efficient and practical. The proposed protocol can be applied for secure file sharing.

References

1. Chaum, D.: Untraceable electronic mail, return addresses, and digital pseudonyms. Communications of the ACM 24, 84–88 (1981)
2. Chaum, D.: The dinning cryptographer problem: Unconditional sender and recipient untraceability. Journal of Cryptology 1(1), 65–75 (1988)
3. Goel, S., Robson, M., Polte, M., Sirer, E.G.: Herbivore: A Scalable and Efficient Protocol for Anonymous Communication. Tech. Rep. 2003-1890, Cornell University, Ithaca, NY (February 2003)
4. Pointcheval, D., Stern, J.: Security arguments for digital signatures and blind signatures. Journal of Cryptology 13(3), 361–396 (2000)
5. Harn, L., Xu, Y.: Design of generalized ElGamal type digital signature schemes based on discret logarithm. Electronics Letters 30(24), 2025–2026 (1994)
6. Nyberg, K., Rueppel, R.A.: Message recovery for signature schemes based on the discrete logarithm problem. In: Santis, A.D. (ed.) EUROCRYPT 1994. LNCS, vol. 950, pp. 182–193. Springer, Heidelberg (1995)
7. Reiter, M.K., Rubin, A.D.: Crowds: anonymity for web transaction. ACM Transactions on Information and System Security 1(1), 66–92 (1998)
8. F. P. 180-1, Secure hash standard (April 1995),
   http://itl.nist.gov/fipspubs/fips180-1.htm
9. Balfanz, D., Durfee, G., Shankar, N., Smetters, D., Staddon, J., Wong, H.C.: Secure handshakes from pairing-based key agreements. In: IEEE Symposium on Security & Privacy, Oakland, CA (May 2003)
10. Zhang, Y., Liu, W., Lou, W., Fang, Y.: MASK: Anonymous on-demand routing in mobile ad hoc networks. IEEE Transactions on Wireless Communications 5(9), 2376–2385 (2006)
11. Beimel, A., Dolev, S.: Buses for anonymous message delivery. J. Cryptology 16, 25–39 (2003)

Secure Multi-party Protocols for Privacy Preserving Data Mining

Qingkai Ma[1] and Ping Deng[2]

[1] Department of Economic Crime and Justice Studies,
Utica College, USA
qma@utica.edu
[2] Department of Computer Science,
University of Illinois at Springfield, USA
pdeng2@uis.edu

Abstract. People are more and more concerned with privacy protection while performing data mining. ID3 is a very popular decision tree building method in data mining. Entropy and Gini index are two different criteria used in ID3. While there is quite some work in privacy preserving ID3 using entropy, not much has been done for Gini index.

In this paper, we present protocols based on secure multiparty computation for privacy preserving ID3 using Gini index over both vertically and horizontally partitioned data. Our protocols don't require any third party server. However, some communication overhead is necessary so that the parties can carry out the secure protocols.

Keywords: privacy preserving data mining, secure multiparty computation.

1 Introduction

With the rapid growth of the amount of information, two or more organizations/parties often need to collaborate on data mining tasks nowadays. This leads to a lot of privacy concerns. The parties usually want to keep their own information private while still allowing certain data mining task performed on it. A lot of research has been done on privacy preserving data mining (PPDM) since the two cornerstone papers in 2000 [1,7]. A survey can be found in [9].

There are two types of PPDM. One is based on data perturbation and reconstruction. For this kind of approaches, data are perturbed and a special reconstruction procedure is designed for the perturbed data so that the original data privacy is preserved and accurate data mining models can be developed. The other type uses secure multiparty computation (SMC) protocols for PPDM. Since Yao first introduced the concept of SMC [11,12], many SMC protocols have been developed [2,4]. Researchers quickly found the connection between SMC and PPDM and applied SMC protocols for PPDM [3,7,8,9,10].

Classification is a very important problem in data mining. Decision tree is one of the most well known approaches for classification. ID3 is the most popular and

Y. Li et al. (Eds.): WASA 2008, LNCS 5258, pp. 526–537, 2008.

widely-used algorithm for the decision tree classifier. Entrophy and Gini index are two criteria commonly used for attribute selection in the ID3 algorithm. Although there has been quite some work on privacy preserving ID3 [3,7,8,10], not much work has been done on ID3 using Gini index.

In privacy preserving data mining, there are two types of data partitioning among the parties. For vertically partitioned data, each party holds the values of some attributes of all the data records in the dataset while for horizontally partitioned data, each party is assigned a subset of data records that contains all the attributes.

In this paper, we present protocols for privacy preserving decision tree building using Gini index over both vertically and horizontally partitioned data. We focus on the protocol for horizontally partitioned data as it is more challenging. For horizontally partitioned data, our protocol is based on some secure multiparty computation sub-protocols.

Same as most other research work, we assume a semi-honest adversary that follows the protocol as required, but may try to derive more information from all the knowledge it obtains from the protocol execution.

The rest of the paper is organized as follows. In Section 2, we discuss the background knowledge of the decision tree and Gini index. Related research work is given in Section 3. Then we present the privacy preserving approach for horizontally partitioned data in Section 4. Section 5 gives the protocols for vertically partitioned data. Section 6 summarizes the paper and identifies some future research directions.

2   Background

ID3 is the most commonly used algorithm for building decision trees. The algorithm works by keeping on splitting the leaf nodes according to some locally optimum criteria until all the data records in one leaf nodes belong to the same class. The most common criteria used are entrophy and Gini index.

The Gini index "measures the impurity of D, a data partition or a set of training tuples, as" [5]

$$Gini(D) = 1 - \sum_{i=1}^{k} p_i^2$$

p_i is the probability that a data record in D belongs to class i. Let's consider a split on D based on one of the attributes A. If the split partitions D into m partitions $D_1, D_2, \ldots, D_m$, the Gini index of the resulting partition is

$$Gini_A(D) = \frac{|D_1|}{|D|} Gini(D_1) + \cdots + \frac{|D_m|}{|D|} Gini(D_m)$$

The attribute that causes the maximum reduction of the Gini index value is chosen as the splitting attribute for the current node. When deciding the splitting attribute for the current node in the decision tree, $Gini(D)$ is fixed; so the attribute that leads to the minimum $Gini_A(D)$ is chosen.

3   Related Works

Some research work has been done to apply SMC protocols to privacy preserving decision tree building.

Pinkas and Lindell [7] propose a cryptographic technique involving two parties for the ID3 algorithm. More specifically, it is a SMC approach designed for horizontally partitioned data. Each node of the tree is privately computed. Entropy is used to choose the "best" predicting attribute at each step and oblivious polynomial evaluation (OPE) is used as the main building block of secure computation. The protocol for privately computing ID3 consists of a lot of invocations of smaller private computations. A secure protocol for the oblivious evaluation of $xlnx$ function is proposed to compute the information gain of each normal attribute.

Du and Zhan [3] study the process of building a decision tree classifier for a vertically distributed database and present a protocol built upon a secure scalar product protocol by using a third party which is a semi-trusted commodity server. The main building block used in the classification method is the two-party scalar product.

Vaidya and Clifton [8] introduce a protocol to construct a decision tree using the ID3 algorithm on vertically partitioned data. The developed method works for any number of parties. In addition, it works for the case where no party knows complete information for any instance and it can be easily extended to the case where all parties know the attributes. The proof of security is given and the complexity of the algorithm is analyzed.

Xiao etc. [10] propose several secure multiparty computation protocols to solve the problem of privacy preserving decision tree classification over horizontally partitioned data by applying the ID3 algorithm. The homomorphic encryption scheme is used in the proposed method. The solution is applicable to both the two-party case and the multi-party case.

4   Multiparty Computation Protocols over Horizontally Partitioned Data

To find the minimum $Gini_A(D)$, we give it a different expression.

$$Gini_A(D) = \sum_{i=1}^{m} \frac{|D_i|}{|D|} Gini(D_1)$$

$$= \sum_{i=1}^{m} \frac{|D_i|}{|D|} \left(1 - \sum_{j=1}^{k} \left(\frac{x_{ij}}{|D_i|} \right)^2 \right)$$

$$= \sum_{i=1}^{m} \frac{|D_i|}{|D|} \left(1 - \sum_{j=1}^{k} \left(\frac{x_{ij}}{x_{i0} + x_{i1} + \cdots x_{ik}} \right)^2 \right)$$

$$= 1 - \sum_{i=1}^{m} \frac{|D_i|}{|D|} \sum_{j=1}^{k} \left(\frac{x_{ij}}{x_{i0} + x_{i1} + \cdots x_{ik}} \right)^2$$

$$= 1 - \sum_{i=1}^{m} \frac{x_{i0}^2 + x_{i1}^2 + \cdots x_{ik}^2}{|D| \cdot (x_{i0} + x_{i1} + \cdots x_{ik})}$$

Here x_{ij} refers to the number of data records in D_i that belongs to class j. To find the minimum $Gini_A(D)$, we need to find the attribute split that achieve the maximum $\sum_{i=1}^{m} \frac{x_{i0}^2 + x_{i1}^2 + \cdots x_{ik}^2}{|D| \cdot (x_{i0} + x_{i1} + \cdots x_{ik})}$. Since $|D|$ is fixed, we need to find the attribute split that has the maximum $\sum_{i=1}^{m} \frac{x_{i0}^2 + x_{i1}^2 + \cdots x_{ik}^2}{(x_{i0} + x_{i1} + \cdots x_{ik})}$ (1)

As we can see, equation 1 is the sum of m numbers that are in the form of $\frac{y_1^2 + y_2^2 + \cdots + y_m^2}{y_1 + y_2 + \cdots + y_m}$ (2).

In order to calculate the value of equation 1, we just need to figure out the means to calculate equation 2.

Our privacy preserving approach is based on the secure multiparty computation protocols in the following sub-sections. In our scheme, a secret data d is partitioned into secret shares $d_0, d_1, \ldots, d_{n-1}$, where $d = \prod_{i=0}^{n-1} d_i$. The secret data here are the x_{ij}'s in equation 1. Note that the partitioning process is non-deterministic. The same number can be partitioned into totally different sets of secret shares. Also, it is not desirable to allow d_i to be a factor of d since, otherwise, it will be very easy to compromise d from an individual share d_i. If d is partitioned into real numbers, then there may be precision problem after several computations. Thus, we use a fraction to represent each d_i to avoid these problems. We have $d_i = s_i / t_i$, for some arbitrarily chosen s_i. The secret share d_i, or more specifically s_i and t_i, is sent to the host H_i. Only from all the secret shares can the original secret data d be reconstructed. For simplicity of presentation, we introduce the algorithms using d_i instead of s_i and t_i in some of the following subsections. The actual computation is performed on s_i and t_i correspondingly. Also, to avoid complicated expressions in indices, we assume that the "+" and "–" for index computation are modulo n operations (e.g., d_{i+1} is used to represent $d_{(i+1)mod n}$).

4.1 Multiplication/Division Computation

Consider two secret data d and d'. Let d_i, $i = 0, 1, \ldots, n-1$, be the secret shares of d and let d_i', $i = 0, 1, \ldots, n-1$, be the secret shares of d'. To compute $d \cdot d'$ (d/d'), each host H_i simply computes $d_i \cdot d_i'$ (d_i / d_i'). More specifically, H_i simply computes $s_i \cdot s_i'$ and $t_i \cdot t_i'$ $(s_i / s_i'$ and $t_i / t_i')$.

4.2 Testing Operation

Here, we show how to test a given data d and determine whether $d > 0$. To compare two secret data d and d', we can first compute $d - d'$ and then check whether $d - d' > 0$.

To determine whether $d > 0$, each host H_i first computes $sign(d_i)$, where

$$sign(x) = \begin{cases} 1, \ if \ x \ is \ positive \\ -1, \ otherwise \end{cases} .$$

For the comparison in ID3 using Gini index, when two attributes have the same Gini index value, it doesn't matter which attribute we choose. So we don't need a special handling of zero case. The party can choose to give 1 or –1 as the *sign* of its share. For consistency, we define the *sign* function returns –1 when the number is zero. This also has the benefit that no one except the party holding zero knows that d is equal to zero. Similar to the addition algorithm, a host H_x is chosen randomly to start the computation. Host H_x picks a random number α (which can be positive or negative) and computes $sign(\alpha \ d_i)$. Then, H_x sends $sign(\alpha \ d_i)$ to its neighbor $H_{(x+1)mod n}$.

Host H_i upon receiving data p from its neighbor executes the following code:

```
if (i ≠ x) then
compute p' = sign(d_i) × p;
send p' to H_(i+1)modn;
else
compute p' = sign(α) × p;
broadcast p' to all H_i, for all i;
endif;
```

After H_x obtains p', it broadcasts p' to all other hosts. Note that the final p' obtained by H_x is $sign(d)$. Thus, all hosts can make the same decision after the test based on the value p' ($= sign(d)$). A drawback of the test statement is that the sign information of the secret data d has to be revealed. It is an inevitable consequence for the test operation.

4.3   Aggregate Addition Computation

The aggregate addition computation is based on the addition operation. Detailed description of the single addition computation can be found in [6]. Here we focus on the aggregate addition as it is much more efficient communication-wise.

Protocol. Consider adding m secret data $d_0, d_1, \ldots, d_{m-1}$. Let d_{ki}, $i = 0, 1, \ldots, n-1$, be the secret shares of d_k for all $k \in [0, m-1]$. Let $d = \sum_{i=0}^{m-1} d_i$. To compute d, we can use

$$d = \sum_{i=0}^{m-1} d_i = \sum_{i=0}^{m-1} \prod_{j=0}^{n-1} d_{ij}$$

$$= \left(\prod_{i=0}^{n-1} d_{0i} \right) * \left(1 + \sum_{i=1}^{m-1} \prod_{j=0}^{n-1} (d_{ij}/d_{0j}) \right)$$

Same as in the addition computation, the computation of d_{ij}/d_{0j} is simple, but there is no easy way to compute $1 + \sum_{i=1}^{m-1} \prod_{j=0}^{n-1} (d_{ij}/d_{0j})$ autonomously. If a single host knows the value of $1+\sum_{i=1}^{m-1}\prod_{j=0}^{n-1}\left(d_{ij}/d_{0j}\right)$, then $\sum_{i=1}^{m-1}d_i/d_0$ will be revealed, then the host will know value of d / d_0. Thus, instead, we let the hosts compute $\lambda\cdot\left(1+\sum_{i=1}^{m-1}\prod_{j=0}^{n-1}\left(d_{ij}/d_{0j}\right)\right)$, i.e., $\lambda+\lambda\cdot\left(\sum_{i=1}^{m-1}\prod_{j=0}^{n-1}\left(d_{ij}/d_{0j}\right)\right)$, where λ is an arbitrary secret number. Note that λ has to remain secret during the computation. If we compute $\lambda\cdot\left(\sum_{i=1}^{m-1}\prod_{j=0}^{n-1}\left(d_{ij}/d_{0j}\right)\right)$ first and then add λ to it, it is similar to the computation of $1+\sum_{i=1}^{m-1}\prod_{j=0}^{n-1}\left(d_{ij}/d_{0j}\right)$, and we cannot find a good way to do the computation with the guarantee that a minority of compromised hosts cannot cooperate to know the value of λ and d /d'. To successfully compute $\lambda+\lambda\cdot\left(\sum_{i=1}^{m-1}\prod_{j=0}^{n-1}\left(d_{ij}/d_{0j}\right)\right)$ with guaranteed secrecy, we need to decompose λ in several different ways.

To facilitate the secret computation of $\lambda+\lambda\cdot\left(\sum_{i=1}^{m-1}\prod_{j=0}^{n-1}\left(d_{ij}/d_{0j}\right)\right)$, we first need to decompose λ into secret addition shares where $\lambda=\sum_{i=0}^{n-1}\beta_i$. In $\lambda\cdot\left(\sum_{i=1}^{m-1}\prod_{j=0}^{n-1}\left(d_{ij}/d_{0j}\right)\right)$, $\lambda\cdot\prod_{j=0}^{n-1}\left(d_{ij}/d_{0j}\right)$ has to be computed separately for each i. Also, $\lambda\cdot\prod_{j=0}^{n-1}\left(d_{ij}/d_{0j}\right)$ should be computed in a way such that each host gets a secret addition share of it, i.e., $\lambda\cdot\prod_{j=0}^{n-1}\left(d_{ij}/d_{0j}\right)=\sum_{k=0}^{n-1}\left(\rho_k\cdot\prod_{j=0}^{n-1}d_{ij}/d_{0j}\right)$ and host H_k gets share $\rho_k\cdot\prod_{j=0}^{n-1}d_{ij}/d_{0j}$ (how this term is computed will be addressed later). By doing so, each host, say host H_k, can easily compute $\beta_k+\rho_k\cdot\prod_{j=0}^{n-1}d_{ij}/d_{0j}$. To guarantee secrecy, we require $\beta_k\neq\rho_k$. However, host H_i still needs to obtain $\rho_k\cdot\prod_{j=0}^{n-1}d_{ij}/d_{0j}$ for $i=1, 2, \ldots, m-1$.

To compute $\rho_k\cdot\prod_{j=0}^{n-1}d_{ij}/d_{0j}$ for one specific i, H_k needs the cooperation of other hosts. Again, to guarantee secrecy, ρ_k is further decomposed into secret shares where $\rho_k=\prod_{j=0}^{n-1}\alpha_{i,j,k}$ and H_l holds $\alpha_{i,l,k}$. Thus, each host H_k can compute $\alpha_{i,l,k}\cdot d_j$ / d'_j and H_i can obtain $\rho_k\cdot\prod_{j=0}^{n-1}d_{ij}/d_{0j}$.

Note that after getting $\lambda\cdot\left(1+\sum_{i=1}^{m-1}\prod_{j=0}^{n-1}\left(d_{ij}/d_{0j}\right)\right)$, we need to divide it by λ to get $1+\sum_{i=1}^{m-1}\prod_{j=0}^{n-1}\left(d_{ij}/d_{0j}\right)$. Thus, we also need to decompose λ into secret shares where $\lambda=\prod_{i=0}^{n-1}\gamma_i$ and host H_i has the secret share γ_i.

In summary, for the aggregate addition operation, host H_i, $i=0, 1,\ldots, n-1$, has secret values $\alpha_{0,i,0}, \alpha_{0,i,1}, \ldots, \alpha_{0,i,n-1}, \alpha_{1,i,0}, \alpha_{1,i,1}, \ldots, \alpha_{1,i,n-1}, \ldots, \alpha_{m-1,i,0}, \alpha_{m-1,i,1}, \ldots, \alpha_{m-1,i,n-1}, \beta_i$ and γ_i that satisfy $\prod_{i=0}^{n-1}\gamma_i=\sum_{i=0}^{n-1}\beta_i=\sum_{i=0}^{n-1}\prod_{j=0}^{n-1}\alpha_{k,j,i}=\lambda$ for all $k\in[1, m-1]$ and $\beta_i\neq\prod_{j=0}^{n-1}\alpha_{k,j,i}$, for all i and all k.

These values are computed at the initialization time by a secure server. The secure server stores the secret numbers for one host in a file and sends one file to each host. The hosts read in one set of secret values for an aggregate addition operation, and for the next aggregate addition operation, it will use a different set of secret values to avoid information leakage.

From $\prod_{i=0}^{n-1} \gamma_i = \sum_{i=0}^{n-1} \beta_i = \sum_{i=0}^{n-1} \prod_{j=0}^{n-1} \alpha_{k,j,i} = \lambda$, we have

$$d = \sum_{i=0}^{m-1} d_i = \left(\prod_{i=0}^{n-1} d_{0i} \right) * \left(1 + \sum_{i=1}^{m-1} \prod_{j=0}^{n-1} (d_{ij}/d_{0j}) \right)$$

$$= \left(\prod_{i=0}^{n-1} d_{0i}/\gamma_i \right) * \left(\lambda + \lambda \cdot \sum_{i=1}^{m-1} \prod_{j=0}^{n-1} (d_{ij}/d_{0j}) \right)$$

Host H_i, $i = 0, 1, \ldots, n-1$, computes d_{0i}/γ_i locally. Each host computes a part of $\lambda + \lambda \cdot \sum_{i=1}^{m-1} \prod_{j=0}^{n-1} (d_{ij}/d_{0j})$ and sends the result to a chosen host H_x. H_x adds them up and multiplies the result with d'_x/γ_x to get its share of $d + d'$. Each host H_i, $i \neq x$, takes d'_i/γ_i as its share of $d + d'$. The pseudo-code for the aggregate addition operation is given in the following.

$\boldsymbol{H_i}$, ($\boldsymbol{i \neq x}$):
computes d_{0i}/γ_i and take it as its share of $d + d'$;
computes $\beta_i + \sum_{k=1}^{m-1} \prod_{j=0}^{n-1} \alpha_{k,j,i} \cdot d_{kj}/d_{0j}$ and send it to H_x;

$\boldsymbol{H_x}$:
computes d_{0x}/γ_x and $\mu = \beta_x + \sum_{k=1}^{m-1} \prod_{j=0}^{n-1} \alpha_{k,j,x} \cdot d_{kj}/d_{0j}$;

repeat
receive $\beta_i + \sum_{k=1}^{m-1} \prod_{j=0}^{n-1} \alpha_{k,j,i} \cdot d_{kj}/d_{0j}$ from H_i, for any i;
calculate

$$\mu = \mu + \left(\beta_i + \sum_{k=1}^{m-1} \prod_{j=0}^{n-1} \alpha_{k,j,i} \cdot d_{kj}/d_{0j} \right);$$

until received $\beta_i + \sum_{k=1}^{m-1} \prod_{j=0}^{n-1} \alpha_{k,j,i} \cdot d_{kj}/d_{0j}$, for all i;
compute $\mu \times d_{0x}/\gamma_x$ and take it as its share of $d + d'$.

Now let us look at the procedure for host H_i ($i = 0, 1, \ldots, n-1$) to compute $\beta_i + \sum_{k=1}^{m-1} \prod_{j=0}^{n-1} \alpha_{k,j,i} \cdot d_{kj}/d_{0j}$. H_i needs the cooperation of the other hosts for the computation. First, H_{i+1} computes all $\alpha_{k,i+1,i} \cdot d_{k(i+1)}/d_{0(i+1)}$ for all $k \in [1, m-1]$ and sends them in one message to H_{i+2}. H_{i+2} multiplies the all the data it receives by $\alpha_{k,i+2,i} \cdot d_{k(i+2)}/d_{0(i+2)}$ and sends the results in one message to H_{i+3}. The subsequent hosts do the same until the computation result gets to H_i. Finally, H_i multiplies all the data it receives by $\alpha_{k,i,i} \cdot d_{ki}/d_{0i}$ to get $\prod_{j=0}^{n-1} \alpha_{j,i} \cdot d_j/d'_j$ and then adds β_i to it to get $\beta_i + \prod_{j=0}^{n-1} \alpha_{j,i} \cdot d_j/d'_j$.

Secrecy. Host H_i holds share $d_{k,i}, i = 0, \ldots, m-1$ and secret numbers $\alpha_{0,i,0},$ $\alpha_{0,i,1}, \ldots, \alpha_{0,i,n-1}, \alpha_{1,i,0}, \ldots, \alpha_{1,i,n-1}, \ldots, \alpha_{m-1,i,0}, \ldots, \alpha_{m-1,i,n-1}, \beta_i,$ and γ_i.

During computation, it will get to know $\prod_{j=0}^{n-1} \alpha_{k,j,i} \cdot d_{kj}/d_{0j}$, $k = 0, 1, \ldots, m-1$ and $\prod_{j=m}^{i} \alpha_{k,j,m} \cdot d_{kj}/d_{0j}$, $m \neq i$, $k = 0, 1, \ldots, m-1$. From these data, H_i cannot get any critical information about other hosts' shares. Since each host H_i holds $d_{0,i}$ secretly and only provides $d_{k,i}/d_{0,i}$ multiplied by a secret number when needed, there is no way for the adversary to know the value of d_i for any i. What the adversary might get is the value of d_i/d_0 and d/d_0. However, from the analysis of the secret numbers we know that to know any of these values, the adversary needs to compromise all the hosts or know some specific secret values of all the hosts.

4.4   Aggregation of Consecutive Additions and a Test Statement

To aggregate consecutive additions and a test statement, we only need to make some small modifications to the protocol in Section 4.3. Host H_i includes the sign of d_{0i}/γ_i in the message when it sends $\beta_i + \sum_{k=1}^{m-1} \prod_{j=0}^{n-1} \alpha_{k,j,i} \cdot d_{kj}/d_{0j}$ to H_x. After computing the final $\mu \times d_{0x}/\gamma_x$, H_x compute the sign of $\sum_{i=0}^{m-1} d_i$ from the sign of $\mu \times d_{0x}/\gamma_x$ and all the signs it receives from other hosts. H_x then sends the sign to all the other hosts.

Secrecy. This protocol only extends the protocol in Section 4.3 by adding testing on the addition result; this testing won't reveal any additional information except the sign of the shares held by each host. From the proof in Section 4.3 we know the protocol preserves secrecy unless all the hosts are compromised.

4.5   Fraction Simplification

Unbounded growth in the size of the secret shares can be a potential problem in our approach due to the use of a nonlinear decomposition scheme (fraction representation). In most conventional multiparty computations, linear decomposition schemes are used. Therefore, it is straightforward to apply the modular arithmetic and the operations such as addition and multiplication can be defined in Z_n (where n is a large prime number) as modular n operations. Thus, all data from the computation are in a finite field Z_n and there is no unbounded growth problem (as long as the original computation does not overflow).

In our approach, we use fraction simplification technique to enforce bounds on the numerator and denominator values of each secret share. Two thresholds B_l and B_h are used, where B_h is the upper threshold and B_l is the lower threshold. For our protocol, if the maximum number that can be represented in a computer is z, we have $B_h \leq \sqrt{z}$. We also require $B_l \leq \sqrt{B_h}$. To guarantee the secrecy of the shares during fraction simplification, we impose some restrictions on the secret data d. We have $d = s/t$, where $s < B_l$ and $t < B_l$. All the intermediate results in the corresponding non-encrypted computation and secret numbers used for our intermediate computation should also satisfy this condition. When a value grows beyond B_h, fraction simplification is performed. Let v denote the value that grows beyond B_h. A factor from v is selected and sent out to one specific host H_x. H_x collects all such factors and computes their product r_1/r_2. From the constraint on the secret data and shares, we can see that the numerator (r_1) and denominator (r_2) definitely have common factors and can be canceled out. After the simplification of r_1/r_2, H_x will be able to decompose r_1/r_2 into $n+1$ shares and the numerator and denominator of each share are less than B_l. H_x then sends one share to each host.

After each aggregate addition or multiplication operation, all the hosts check their shares to see if there is a need for fraction simplification and broadcast their decision. If at least one host requires fraction simplification, then a host H_x is randomly chosen to coordinate the effort. For host H_i other than H_x, a new fraction number nu_i / de_i is chosen as H_i's temporary share with the requirement that both nu_i and de_i are less than B_l. H_i multiplies de_i / nu_i with its share, and sends the result to H_x. After H_x finishes its computation, it sends a new share ds_i / dt_i back to H_i, where both ds_i and dt_i are less than B_l. H_i then integrates the new factor into its own share. The code for H_i ($i \neq x$) is given in the following:

```
if fraction simplification is necessary then
choose nu_i and de_i s.t. nu_i < B_l and de_i < B_l,
send ( s_i / nu_i) / ( t_i / de_i) to H_x for fraction simplification ;
wait for share ds_i / dt_i from H_x;
compute new s_i = ds_i × nu_i;
compute new t_i = dt_i × de_i;
endif;
```

H_x collects all the factors sent from other hosts, multiplies them together with its own shares, and then decomposes the result it gets into $n+1$ shares where all the numbers in each share is less than B_l. H_x takes two such shares to derive its new secret share and sends one share to each of the other hosts. The code for host H_x is as follows:

```
if fraction simplification is necessary then
r_1 = s_x; r_2 = t_x;
while (have not received factor data sent from all other hosts)
wait for factor from other hosts;
if received factor (s_i/n_ui)/(t_i/d_ei) from H_i then
r_1 = r_1 × (s_i / n_ui); r_2 = r_2 × (t_i / d_ei);
endif
end while
decompose r_1 /r_2 into ( ds_0 / dt_0)× ( ds_1 / dt_1)×...× ( ds_n / dt_n) with the
requirement that ds_i < B_l and dt_i < B_l, i = 0, 1,..., n;
for all i ≠ x,send ( ds_i / dt_i) to H_i ;
compute new s_x = ds_x × ds_n;
compute new t_x = dt_x × dt_n;
endif;
```

Secrecy. As we discussed above, no secret data contains prime factor that is larger than B_l. So no one can tell whether the factors sent to and received from H_x are really a factor of the secret data. Also, host H_x have no way of knowing the factor of the secret data since host H_i, $i \neq x$, have flexibility in choosing n_{ui} and d_{ei}. It can choose n_{ui} to be a factor of s_i or a random number that is less than B_l, and similarly for d_{ei}. When H_x performs the decomposition, it has no way to decide whether any factor is part of the secret data. And no host can learn from its share any factor of the secret data because it doesn't know whether a factor of its share is a factor of the secret data or just generated during decomposition to protect the secret data from being cracked.

4.6   Gini Index Calculation

To use the protocols from Subsection 4.1 to 4.4 to calculate $\sum_{i=1}^{m} \frac{x_{i0}^2 + x_{i1}^2 + \cdots x_{ik}^2}{(x_{i0} + x_{i1} + \cdots x_{ik})}$, first each party j share x_{ij} in the way described at the beginning of Section 4. Then each party perform local operation to get a share of x_{ij}^2, then $2m$ aggregate addition protocols are executed to calculate all the $\frac{x_{i0}^2 + x_{i1}^2 + \cdots x_{ik}^2}{(x_{i0} + x_{i1} + \cdots x_{ik})}$. The next thing to do is to perform local division operation and another aggregate addition for each party to get a share of $\sum_{i=1}^{m} \frac{x_{i0}^2 + x_{i1}^2 + \cdots x_{ik}^2}{(x_{i0} + x_{i1} + \cdots x_{ik})}$.

To find the maximum $\sum_{i=1}^{m} \frac{x_{i0}^2 + x_{i1}^2 + \cdots x_{ik}^2}{(x_{i0} + x_{i1} + \cdots x_{ik})}$, $n - 1$ subtraction and testing protocols are needed. Subtraction can be performed using a slight modification of the addition protocol. Before the protocol execution, one party, say H_0, multiply its share of subtrahend by -1.

4.7   Performance Analysis and Discussion

We focus on the communication cost since it is a dominating factor. The multiplication and division operations are all performed at local hosts and no communication is involved. For each segment of computation (a sequence of arithmetic operations or a sequence of arithmetic operations with a test statement in the end), we only need one n-round message passing and a total of $n^2 - 1$ messages. This is much less than the conventional secure multiparty computation protocols.

In the case a secret data is zero, the owner of that secret data, when sending out the multiplicative shares of that secret data, will keep the zero to itself and send out random non-zero values to other parties.

In the aggregate addition operation, we need to make sure d_0 is not equal to zero; otherwise there will be a divide-by-zero error. This can be done with little release of information for achieving privacy preserving purpose. Since each secret data in the aggregate addition was held by one party before being shared, each party knows whether one of the secret data is zero. The parties perform a coin tossing one by one to decide whether it will broadcast if its secret data is not zero. The first one broadcasted not zero will be used as d_0 in the aggregate addition protocol.

5   Multiparty Protocol over Vertically Partitioned Data

In this case, as each party holds all the values for certain attributes, he/she can compute the Gini indexes for those attributes by himself/herself and find the minimum. The challenge lies in how to decide the minimum Gini index value of all parties without revealing any individual minimum Gini index value. Yao's protocol [11] can be used to achieve this purpose. The sub-protocols proposed in Section 4 can also be used here instead of Yao's protocol. More specifically, subtraction and testing protocols can be used to replace Yao's protocol.

When the minimum Gini index value $Gini_A(D)$ is found, the party that holds this value will perform partition of the current node according to the attribute A and send the partitioning result to all the other parties. Note that this party can give the partitioning result in an order that's different from the ascending/descending order of the attribute value for better privacy.

6   Summary and Future Research

We have presented protocols for privacy preserving ID3 using Gini index over vertically and horizontally partitioned data. For horizontally partitioned data, new protocols are designed so that the parties can collaboratively build the decision tree without any party being able to obtain the private information of other parties. The protocol for horizontally partitioned data is very efficient with regard to the communication cost. For vertically partitioned data, the protocol is based on Yao's secure multiparty computation protocol [11].

Our future research includes developing new PPDM protocols for other data mining algorithms and doing experimental study of the protocols.

References

1. Agrawal, R., Srikant, R.: Privacy-Preserving Data Mining. In: The 2000 ACM SIGMOD Conference on Management of Data, Dallas, TX, pp. 439–450 (2000)
2. Cramer, R.: Introduction to Secure Computation. In: Damgaard, I. (ed.) EEF School 1998. Springer LNCS Tutorial. LNCS, vol. 1561, pp. 16–62. Springer, Heidelberg (1999) (revised January 2000)
3. Du, W., Zhan, Z.: Building Decision Tree Classifier on Private Data. In: The 2002 IEEE International Conference on Privacy, Security and Data Mining, Australia, pp. 1–8 (2002)
4. Goldreich, O.: Secure multi-party computation. Foundations of Cryptography, vol. 2. Cambridge University Press, Cambridge (2004)
5. Han, J., Kamber, M.: Data Mining: Concepts and Techniques, 2nd edn. Morgan Kaufmann Publishers, San Francisco (2006)
6. Ma, Q., Hao, W., Yen, I., Bastani, F.: Multiparty Computation with Full Computation Power and Reduced Overhead. In: The 8th IEEE HASE, Tampa (2004)
7. Lindell, Y., Pinkas, B.: Privacy Preserving Data Mining. In: Bellare, M. (ed.) CRYPTO 2000. LNCS, vol. 1880, pp. 36–54. Springer, Heidelberg (2000)
8. Vaidya, J., Clifton, C.: Privacy-Preserving Decision Trees over Vertically Partitioned Data. In: Data and Application Security, pp. 139–152 (2005)

9. Verykios, V.S., Bertino, E., Fovino, I.N., Provenza, L.P., Saygin, Y., Theodoridis, Y.: State-of-the-art in privacy preserving data mining. ACM SIGMOD Record, 33(1), 50–57 (2004)
10. Xiao, M., Huang, L., Luo, Y., Shen, H.: Privacy Preserving ID3 Algorithm over Horizontally Partitioned Data. In: The 6th International Conference on Parallel and Distributed Computing, Applications and Technologies, pp. 239–243 (2005)
11. Yao, A.C.: Protocols for secure computations. In: Proc. 23rd FOCS, pp. 160–164 (1982)
12. Yao, A.C.: How to generate and exchange secrets. In: Proc. 27th FOCS, pp. 162–166 (1986)

Enhancing Software Product Line Maintenance with Source Code Mining

Michael Jiang[1], Jing Zhang[1], Hong Zhao[2], and Yuanyuan Zhou[3]

[1] Motorola Labs, Motorola, Schaumburg, IL 60196, USA
{michael.jiang,j.zhang}@motorola.com
[2] Mobile Devices, Motorola, Libertyville, IL 60048, USA
hzhao@motorola.com
[3] University of Illinois at Urbana-Champaign, Urbana, IL 61801, USA
yyzhou@cs.uiuc.edu

Abstract. Large-scale reuse and accelerated software development have been some of the key attractions behind software product lines. Various strategies and processes have been developed to facilitate product line development, maintenance, and evolution. However, experiences with software product lines also showed that it is a rather challenging task to maintain software product lines and families over a long period of time. The time and effort needed to manage and maintain product lines increase and quality degrades as product lines evolve. Without proper methods and tools to support the evolution, the cost can outweigh the benefits.

This paper describes an approach to simplifying the maintenance of software product lines and improving software quality by integrating traditional software maintenance practices with pattern-based source code mining for defect detection and correction. Our case studies were performed in an industrial setting where the evolution of multiple mobile phone models of a product line was investigated.

Keywords: Product Line, Software Maintenance, and Reuse.

1 Introduction

Software product lines have become a viable software design and development paradigm to improve productivity and quality through large-scale reuse [1]. Reports of industry practices showed 2-7X time-to-market improvement for various product lines [2]. To help promote software product line development, Software Engineering Institute pioneered many software product line practices. Various software product line architecture, tools, methods, and processes have been proposed and practiced.

Software product line development, on the other hand, also faces many difficult challenges [3,4]. These challenges can appear at the requirement, design, development, and maintenance phases. In theory, a well managed traceability mechanism between the phases needs to be in place to support product line evolution. In practice, however, it becomes very difficult to track and manage dependencies and variations over time, even though much effort is spent on maintaining the relationships

Y. Li et al. (Eds.): WASA 2008, LNCS 5258, pp. 538–547, 2008.

among all phases of the software development life cycle. In our mobile phone business, software products proliferate due to the need to produce many diverse types of phones and releases for incorporating new features and meeting the needs of different markets. The similarities among these many products and releases present a good opportunity to apply software product line development methods as well as opportunity for large-scale reuse. However, it becomes increasingly difficult to manage reuse and dependencies because of large number of features, components, and code modules. Product lines become more and more difficult to maintain and lead to gradual degradation of product quality as they evolve over a long period of time, in many cases over a decade.

This paper describes an integrated engineering approach to alleviate the maintenance of mobile phone product lines. In addition to the traditional engineering practices of maintaining traceability from feature and modification requests (requirements describing defects to be fixed, feature enhancement, or new features) down to source code changes, a data mining approach is done at the code level to help recover reuse modules and their linkages in related software products. A sequential pattern mining technique [5] was employed to facilitate the discovery of reuse and reuse with modification. By integrating with the software configuration management systems and defect tracking systems, reuse modules and modifications to reuse code can be traced. Our case studies showed that integrating this source code mining with the traditional software maintenance can further simplify the maintenance of mobile products and reduce the number of escaped defects from the software maintenance process.

2   Product Line Evolution for Wireless Phone Systems

In mobile phone business, the constant demand for new features and feature-rich applications leads to the proliferation of releases and models as shown in Fig. 1. New releases are created as new features are added. To meet the needs of different markets or deployment environment, such as CDMA and GSM, branches will be created and different models of phones with variations in features and capabilities will be produced.

The formation of a software product line presents opportunities for reuse, both in the large and in the small, as mobile phones share many common features and applications, such as phone books, cameras, voice recognition, etc. In some cases, an entire feature or an application can be reused with little modifications. For example, every mobile phone relies on RF-based communication protocols. In other cases, however, a feature has to be modified due to its interactions with new features added to newer releases or phone models. For instance, different phone models may require different features or capabilities of phone books.

The reuse of features and code modules across phone models also poses challenges to the development and maintenance. As the product line evolves, defect fixing, feature enhancement, and various software maintenance activities inevitably weaken the traceability of dependencies and reuse modules [3,6]. In

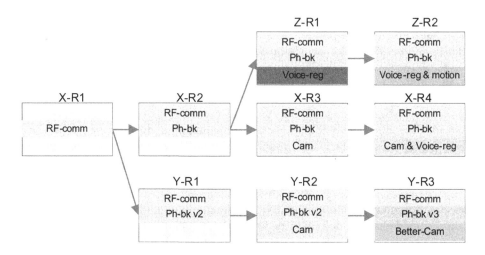

Fig. 1. A sample mobile phone product line

addition, the organizational structures and geographical distribution of development teams further hinder the maintenance of traceability.

Another challenging issue we experienced is that software maintenance tends to be code centric due to the urgency of defect fixing and the demand for very short turn-around time in the mobile phone business. Such software maintenance includes any activities from defect fixing, feature enhancement, to performance optimization. The code centric approach, however, tends to lose the big picture of reuse and dependencies. An enhancement or a defect fix in a release often fails to propagate to related releases in other phone models, as we found in industry practices.

As a remedy, one of the frequently used software engineering practices is to conduct cross-product reviews of all modification requests after each release of a product, in an effort to propagate any relevant modifications to other software products. This practice proves to be very effective in removing many software defects. The review process, however, is time consuming and requires much coordinated effort due to the involvement of many teams from related products. Due to the large number of modification requests and releases from multiple products, however, it is inevitable that many changes and enhancements escape the manual review process.

In the next section, we describe the integration of software clone detection [5,7] with our traditional software configuration management and defect tracking system to help recover and improve the traceability of reuse modules and coding changes across multiple phone models. As defects are fixed and features are enhanced, the source code of releases in other related products are searched, corresponding reuse modules (both with and without modifications) are detected, and recovered dependencies are presented to software maintenance engineers for review and modification.

3   Software Product Line Maintenance through Software Clone Detection and Configuration Management

Data mining and software clone detection techniques have been extensively studied and used to identify redundant (identical or similar) code in a program or a set of programs [7,8]. They have been shown to be very valuable in assisting source code refactoring and optimization, complementary to traditional compiler-based technologies and formal methods. Software Configuration Management (a.k.a., SCM) [9], on the other hand, is well-known for its popularity in the use for tracking and controlling changes in the software. In our approach, data mining technique is integrated with SCM to assist the evolution and maintenance of related software products.

3.1   Mining Source Code for Reuse Patterns

Software reuse ranges from the reuse of requirement, architecture elements, components, down to the lines of code. In this paper, our focus is on the source code level. A reuse pattern refers to a block of code that is reused within a program or among multiple programs. The block of reuse code can be identical or with some modifications to tailor its use in a different context. For a software product line, reuse patterns represent significant portion of the code due to the shared set of software assets within a collection of similar software systems.

Different techniques have been developed for identifying reuse patterns. A number of such tools are available for detecting reuse patterns and software plagiarism [7,8,10]. We used the CP-Miner tool [5] to perform source code mining for reuse patterns. CP-Miner uses data mining techniques to identify copy-pasted code in large software and detects copy-paste bugs. Here, "copy-pasted code" refers to duplicated code present in the software. The duplicated code may also contain some modifications and the extent of modifications can be set as thresholds for the tool to go beyond identical code modules. In our experiment, we only use the feature of detecting copy-paste patterns. Details of its detection method and other similar techniques can be found in [5,7,8,10].

We chose CP-Miner because its scanning is token-based, flexible to search textual patterns without depending on the complex build environment of the software product line. It is also efficient in extracting copy-paste patterns from large code base, another important factor due to the large code base of the mobile product line since scanning across multi-million lines of code for code patterns can be very time-consuming.

3.2   Identifying Defect-Related Dependencies for Software Maintenance

The reuse patterns in a product line provide opportunities to improve the software maintenance process. As a reuse pattern of a product goes through changes due to defect fix and enhancement, related reuse patterns in other products within the product line often need to be revised. By taking advantage of the relationship of products within the product line and discovering related reuse patterns, we can apply defect fix and enhancement across all the related products.

To identify defect-related patterns and dependencies, the CP-Miner tool needs to work with the SCM and the defect tracking system of the software product line. For any given release of a product, the defects fixed or feature enhancements can be queried from the defect tracking system. The corresponding source code changed by the release can be identified. By leveraging the version control system of SCM, we can retrieve the version trees of a product and extract any versions of code modules from the version control system. Then, we use CP-Miner to help identify copy-paste patterns related to the retrieved code module in other software products. As shown in Fig. 1, releases of various software products can be obtained from SCM. The detected copy-paste patterns and their dependencies from the SCM system allow software maintenance engineers to verify and fix defects in related releases and products. The same approach can also be applied for feature enhancement and performance optimization.

As discussed in [5], the CP-Miner tool can detect copy-paste patterns with modifications. And the percentage of modification can be configured. Allowing high percentage of modification, however, will lead to a considerably longer scanning process and higher false positive. On the other hand, a low modification threshold will result in higher false negative. To reduce the pattern scanning time, we applied domain knowledge from software designers to filter out unrelated products and releases that are not relevant or do not interest them. This can be easily accommodated by SCM and the defect tracking system.

3.3   Experimental Validation

To validate the approach, we experimented with 4 mobile phone models involving a number of product releases. Fig. 2 shows a simplified and partial representation of releases and relationship of the mobile phone products for this study. As shown in Fig. 2, all the four mobile phone models were originated from phone model PM1 (real model names are omitted due to the proprietary reasons). Model PM2 was formed by using PM1-R2 as its base. Similarly phone model PM3 was formed from PM2-R2 and PM4 from PM3-R2. To simplify our discussion, some of the common software assets shared by products are not shown in Fig. 2.

We first calculated the code reuse across all four models. Fig. 3 summarizes the results of our experiment across four product families, measured by using one phone model out of each family. For example, 72% of the code in phone model PM1 is reused in PM2 and the code size is increased by 13%. 48% of code in PM1 is reused in PM4 and the code size is almost doubled. The closer to the branching points in the product line evolution is, the higher the reuse of code. Column "Mined patterns" shows the percentage of reuse code discovered by CP-Miner that can not be detected based on traditional means of version control and SCM.

We further experimented with the traceability of defects across reuse modules. We used the defect fixing information from two releases of one mobile phone to

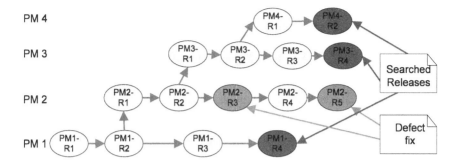

Fig. 2. Portion of a product line for experiment

	PM2			PM3			PM4		
	Size change	Reuse	Mined patterns	Size change	Reuse	Mined patterns	Size change	Reuse	Mined patterns
PM1	13%	72%	9%	80%	56%	22%	95%	48%	21%
PM2	-	-	-	60%	67%	18%	73%	61%	19%
PM3				-	-	-	8%	84%	12%

Fig. 3. Code reuse in a product line

detect related defect patterns in other three mobile phone models. The defect related information is kept in the defect tracking system. The phone model is named "PM-2" and the two releases are "R3" and "R5" as shown in Fig. 2. From these two releases, we collected information about the defect fixing and identified the corresponding code modules from our defect tracking system and SCM. We then used the CP-Miner tool to scan the other three phone models for code patterns matching the identified code modules from the release PM2-R3 and PM2-R5. The matched code patterns were presented to developers for review and validation.

We repeated the above process to search for reuse code modules using file comparison utilities available from SCM. Unlike the pattern mining method above, we had to rely on the file structures and version trees in the SCM system to identify files for comparison. If two identical files exist in two products, we compare the two files to see whether they both contain the defect-related code pattern. Finally we compared the results with those obtained from the data mining approach.

We scanned for code patterns in mobile phone model PM1, PM2, and PM4 based on three modification requests made to release PM2-R3 and two to release PM2-R5. We scanned the latest release for each of the three phone models using CP-Miner tool and the file comparison utilities in SCM. Fig. 4 shows the scanned results of where modification related code patterns were found in other three products. For MR (Modification Request) #1 in PM2-R3, the same defect was

PM	PM2 - R3									PM 2 - R5					
	MR #1			MR #2			MR #3			MR #1			MR #2		
	Status	SCM Utility	code mining	Status	SCM Utility	code mining	Status	SCM Utility	code mining	Status	SCM Utility	code mining	Status	SCM Utility	code mining
PM1-R4	Found, not fixed	Y	Y	Found, not fixed	Y	Y	Not found	N	N	Not found	N	N	Not found	N	N
PM3-R3	Found, not fixed	Y	Y	Fixed	Y	N	Not found	N	N	Found, not fixed	N	Y	Not found	N	N
PM4-R2	Found, not fixed	Y	Y	Fixed	Y	N	Not found	N	N	Found, not fixed	N	Y	Not found	N	N

Fig. 4. Defects across products

found in releases PM1-R4, PM3-R4, and PM4-R2 by both SCM utility and CP-Miner. For MR #2 in PM2-R3, the defect was present in PM1-R4 and detected by both SCM utility and CP-Miner. Only SCM utility was able to detect the defects fixed in PM3-R4 and PM4-R2. The changes made to the reused source code are beyond the threshold of the pattern matching set by CP-Miner.

No matched patterns were found in MR #3 of PM2-R3 and MR #2 of PM2-R5 by either SCM utility or CP-Miner. After examining the scan results with software developers, we realized that these modification requests are specific for features of mobile phone model PM2 only and hence no reuse patterns were found in other phone models by either tool.

4   Discussion

Our preliminary experiments proved that our approach can help recover some of the reuse dependencies across products within a product line. Although SCM tools have the capability to compute differences between different versions of files, it is more difficult to detect reuse patterns across related products if the file structures are not preserved. File structures and version trees may be reorganized across different products due to evolution, new features, and significant enhancements. In same cases, a block of code or a function is copied from one place to another, leading to code redundancy and making it untraceable from the SCM point of view.

The file comparison utility in SCM is much more efficient and accurate if the file structures and file contents are preserved across all products. Efficiency is achieved by localizing the search to relevant files only. It is also more accurate since the version trees preserve all the changes (delta) made to every version of a file.

Source coding mining, on the other hand, requires much longer scanning time due to the need to scan the entire code base of a release to identify reuse patterns. It also has both false positive and false negative due to the nature of pattern matching. The advantage of source coding mining lies in its ability to locate reuse patterns without depending on the file structures. Reuse code in multiple locations can be detected through pattern matching. It should be noted that source code mining cannot detect every reuse module depending on the percentage of changes in code involved. The revision history (based on the release trees

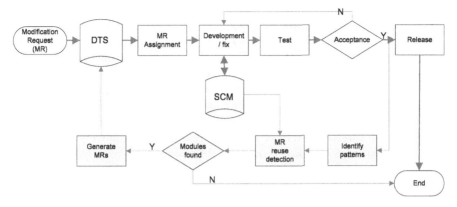

Fig. 5. An enhanced software maintenance process

in SCM) can assist in this process. However, there is still no guarantee of full coverage due to the nature of data mining approach we take.

Our experiment suggested that combining both approaches offers the potential to facilitate software maintenance across multiple related software products in a software product line. We proposed an enhanced software maintenance process with source code mining to facilitate the identification and correction of defects across products in a software product line as shown in Fig. 5. The traditional software maintenance starts from a Modification Request (MR) detailing the defect to be fixed. The MR is recorded in a defect tracking system and is assigned to developers for implementation. The implementation will go through review and testing before deployment. Finally the resolution is recorded in the defect tracking system. The enhancement to the software maintenance process (highlighted activities) is the mining of source code to identify potential defects in related software products when a defect is corrected in a product.

As illustrated in our experiment, both approaches complement each other in identifying reuse code across software products in a product line. In the traditional software maintenance process, traceability between feature / modification requests and source code is maintained to support software maintenance. Source code mining, on the other hand, recovers lost reuse patterns and missing traces such that enhancements and coding fix of one product can be propagated to related software products in a product line. Although our experiment is limited in scope, it has shown that both approaches are able to complement each other in identifying reuse code and facilitating defect correction.

5   Related Work

Extensive discussion on software maintenance process can be found from the IEEE software maintenance standard [11]. Majority of previous work, however, has been focused on forward engineering approach to product line maintenance, with emphasis on product line requirements, architectures, and management of variances. Much less work can be found on mining source code to support the maintenance of a software product line.

Authors in [3] proposed an architecture reconstruction method to maintain the architectural integrity of the platform and to support product line evolution.

A three-dimensional model [12] is employed to express the evolution of a software product line. The model and propagation graphs provide a means of traceability to facilitate reuse and maintenance within a product line. The asset mining for product lines is described in [13], with focus on architecture reconstruction which can be used, in return, to support product line evolution.

An integrated approach based on software reuse and SCM was proposed for supporting legacy software maintenance and evolution [14]. This approach, however, does not support product line maintenance.

Clone detection was applied in [15] as an effective means to manage product lines (e.g., to detect bugs in clones, or reveal design abstractions). This work is similar to ours in terms of the employment of data mining techniques to product line management. However, it lacks a systematic approach to integrate the mining technique with the traditional SCM systems to support product line maintenance.

In general, our work differs from previous work in several ways. Firstly, we attempt to complement the traditional software maintenance engineering with source code mining to recover reuse and dependencies lost due to product line evolution. Secondly, we integrate data mining techniques with SCM for product lines to enhance the detection of reuse patterns and code modules changed due to defect correction.

6   Conclusion

Software product lines have shown to be an effective approach to developing families of products by leveraging large-scale reuse. However, maintenance of software product lines can be very challenging as they evolve over a long period of time and the number of related product lines is large, as is the case in our mobile devices business. Information related to reuse and dependencies in a product line is difficult to maintain over time.

In this paper, we presented an enhanced approach to support the maintenance of a mobile phone product line. Data mining techniques are employed to detect code reuse and are integrated with SCM to recover dependencies for product line maintenance. Our approach was experimented on mobile phone software development to detect defect fixes and propagation of code changes within a product line. We believe this combined approach can be beneficial for the maintenance of large-scale and long-lasting product lines.

Our future work is to further automate the detection of reuse modules and integrate the source code mining approach into the traditional software maintenance process. One possible extension to the maintenance process is to automatically generate modification requests and feed into the defect tracking system when a defect is fixed in a product and related defects are discovered in other related products.

Acknowledgments. We thank Ling Li and Tony Hebert from the Mobile Devices business for support our experiment on several mobile phone models and software releases.

References

1. Software Engineering Institute (SEI): A Framework for Software Product Line Practice - Version 5.0. Carnegie Mellon University (2007)
2. Software Engineering Institute (SEI): Software Product Line Case Studies. Carnegie Mellon University,
   http://www.sei.cmu.edu/productlines/spl_case_studies.html
3. Riva, C., Del Rosso, C.: Experiences with Software Product Family Evolution. In: Proceedings of the Sixth International Workshop on Principles of Software Evolution (IWPSE 2003), Helsinki, Finland (2003)
4. Deng, G., Lenz, G., Schmidt, D.C.: Addressing Domain Evolution Challenges in Software Product Lines. In: Bruel, J.-M. (ed.) MoDELS 2005. LNCS, vol. 3844, pp. 247–261. Springer, Heidelberg (2006)
5. Li, Z., Lu, S., Myagmar, S., Zhou, Y.: CP-Miner: Finding Copy-paste and Related Bugs in Large-scale Software Code. IEEE Transactions on Software Engineering (2006)
6. Bergey, J., O'Brien, L., Smith, D.: Mining Existing Assets for Software Product Lines. Technical Note CMU/SEI-2000-TN-008. Carnegie Mellon University (2000)
7. Baker, B.S.: On Finding Duplication and Near Duplication in Large Software Systems. In: Proceeding of the 2nd Working Conference on Reverse Engineering, Toronto, Ontario, Canada (1995)
8. Kamiya, T., Kusumoto, S., Inoue, K.: CCFinder: a Multilinguistic Token-based Code Clone Detection System for Large Scale Source Code. IEEE Transaction on Software Engineering 28(7), 654–670 (2002)
9. Babich, W.A.: Software Configuration Management, Coordination for Team Productivity. Addison-Wesley, Reading (1986)
10. Prechelt, L., Malpohl, G., Philippsen, M.: Finding Plagiarisms among a Set of Programs with JPlag. Journal of Universal Computer Sciences 8(11) (2002)
11. IEEE Standard for Software Maintenance: IEEE Std 1219-1992 (1992)
12. Schach, S., Tomer, A.: Development/Maintenance/Reuse: Software Evolution in Product Lines. In: Proceedings of the First Software Product Line Conference (2000)
13. O'Brien, L., Hansen, F., Seacord, R., Smith, D.: Mining and Managing Software Assets. In: Proceedings of the 10th International Workshop on Software Technology and Engineering Practice (STEP 2002), Washington, DC (2002)
14. Kwon, O., Shin, G., Boldyreff, C., Munro, M.: Maintenance with Reuse: An Integrated Approach Based on Software Configuration Management. In: Proceedings of the Sixth Asia Pacific Software Engineering Conference (APSEC 1999), Takamatsu, Japan (1999)
15. Baxter, I., Churchett, D.: Using Clone Detection to Manage a Product Line. In: The 7th International Conference on Software Reuse (ICSR) Workshop on Industrial Experience with Product Line Approaches, Austin, TX (2002)

Software Fault Localization Using N-gram Analysis

Syeda Nessa, Muhammad Abedin, W. Eric Wong, Latifur Khan, and Yu Qi

Department of Computer Science
The University of Texas at Dallas
{skn051000,maa056000,ewong,lkhan,yxq014100}@utdallas.edu

Abstract. A major portion of software development effort is spent in testing and debugging. Execution sequence collected in the testing phase can be a rich source of information for locating the fault in the program, but the exact execution sequence of a program, i.e., the actual order of execution of the statements in the program, is seldom used due to the huge volume. In this study, we apply data mining techniques on this data to reduce the debugging time by narrowing down the possible location of the fault. Our method applies N-gram analysis to rank the executable statements of a software by level of suspicion. We conducted three case studies to demonstrate the effectiveness of our proposed method. We also present comparison with other approaches, and illustrate the potential of our method.

1 Introduction

Software fault localization is a long standing and very important problem in software engineering. Due to the human involvement in the software development process, it is virtually impossible to develop software free from any kind of fault (a.k.a. *bug* or *defect*). Once a fault is in a software, it is a tedious, time-consuming and difficult process to find its location in the source code as the developer may have to go through the entire code to find the fault. For this reason, research in automated fault localization techniques to indicate or point to possible fault locations is extremely valuable. A lot of research effort has gone into automating the process of discovering the fault location, or *Software fault localization* [1,2,3,4,5,6,7].

Usually fault localization utilizes test cases – sets of inputs with known expected outputs. If the actual output does not match the expected output, the test case has failed. Various information can be collected during the execution of the test cases for later analysis. This information may include statement coverage (the set of statements that were executed at least once during the execution), and exact execution sequence (the actual order in which the statements were executed during the test case executions). Since we will be working only with the exact execution sequence in this paper, we refer to it as *trace*. Usually, the usefulness of trace data is limited by the sheer volume. Data mining traditionally deals with large volumes of data, and in this research, we apply data mining techniques to process this trace data for fault localization.

Y. Li et al. (Eds.): WASA 2008, LNCS 5258, pp. 548–559, 2008.

From trace data, we generate N-grams, i.e., subsequences of length N. From these, we choose N-grams that appear more than a certain number of times in the failing traces. For these N-grams, we calculate the confidence – the conditional probability that a test case fails given that the N-gram appears in that test case's trace. We sort the N-grams in descending order of confidence and report the statements in the program in the order of their first occurrence in the sorted list. We have tested our method on the Siemens suite, the Space program and grep [8]. Our implementation have produced better results on these three suites than the most standard method Tarantula [1].

This paper is organized as follows. In Section 2, we discuss the related terminologies and ideas. In Section 3, we present the complete algorithm. In Section 4, we discuss the reults of applying our algorithm on Siemens suite, Space and grep. In Section 5, we discuss other relevant research. Finally, in Section 6, we present the conclusions from this study and discuss future directions of research.

2   Background

In this section, we discuss the concepts, ideas and definitions related to our method of solving the problem namely *execution sequences*, *N-gram analysis*, *linear execution blocks* and *association rule mining*.

2.1   Execution Sequence

Let P be a program with n lines of source code, labeled as $L = \{l_1, l_2, \ldots, l_n\}$. For example, in the sample program **mid** from [1] in Fig. 1(a), $L = \{4, 5, 6, 10, 11, 12, 13, 14, 15, 17, 18, 19, 20, 21, 24\}$ after excluding comments, blank lines and structural constructs like '}'. A *test case* is a set of input with known outputs. Let $T = \{t_1, t_2, \ldots, t_n\}$ be the n test cases for program P. Each test case $t_i = \langle I_i, X_i \rangle$ has the input I_i and expected output X_i. When program P is executed with input I_i, it produces actual output A_i. If $A_i = X_i$, then we say t_i is a passing test case, and if $A_i \neq X_i$ then we say t_i is a failing test case. For example, the 6 test cases for the program **mid** in [1], $T = \{t_1, t_2, \ldots, t_6\}$, are shown in Table 1. Let $Y = \langle y_1, y_2, \ldots, y_k \rangle, y_i \in L$ be the trace of program P when running test case T. Then, for **mid** the trace for the test case t_1 is $Y_1 = \langle 4, 4, 5, 10, 11, 12, 14, 15, 24, 6 \rangle$. We define two sets based on the outcome of the test cases – *passing traces* which is $Y_P = \{Y_i | t_i \text{ is a passing test case}\}$ and *failing traces* which is $Y_F = \{Y_i | t_i \text{ is a failing test case}\}$.

We define our problem as: *given program P with executable statements L, test cases T and actual outputs A, the problem is to rank the statements in L according to their probability of containing the fault*. To compare our method with other methods like [1], we report our results in terms of statements, but it can also work at function level.

Given an ordered list, an *N-gram* is any sub-list of N consecutive elements in the list. The elements of the N-gram must be in the same order as they were in the original list, and they must be consecutive. Given an execution trace Y,

Table 1. Test cases for program **mid** [1]

Test Case, t_i	Input I_i	Expected Output, X_i	Actual Output, A_i	Test case type	Trace
t_1	3, 3, 5	3	3	Passing	4,4,5,10,11,12,14,15,24,6
t_2	1, 2, 3	2	2	Passing	4,4,5,10,11,12,13,24,6
t_3	3, 2, 1	2	2	Passing	4,4,5,10,11,18,19,24,6
t_4	5, 5, 5	5	5	Passing	4,4,5,10,11,18,20,24,6
t_5	5, 3, 4	4	4	Passing	4,4,5,10,11,12,14,24,6
t_6	2, 1, 3	2	1	Failing	4,4,5,10,11,12,14,15,24,6

an N-gram $G_{Y,N,\alpha}$ is a contiguous subsequence $\langle y_\alpha, y_{\alpha+1}, y_{\alpha+2}, \ldots, y_{\alpha+N-1} \rangle$ of length N starting at position α. For a trace Y, the set of all line N-grams is $G_{Y,N} = \{G_{Y,N,1}, G_{Y,N,2}, \ldots, G_{Y,N,K-N+1}\}$.

2.2 Linear Execution Blocks

From the set of all traces, we identify the execution blocks, i.e., the code segments with a single point of entry and a single point of exit. For this, we construct the *Execution Sequence Graph* $XSG(P) = (V, E)$ where the set of vertices is $V \subseteq L$ such that for each $v_i \in V$, $v_i \in Y_k$ for some k. E is the set of edges such that for each edge $\langle v_i, v_j \rangle \in E$, we have $v_i, v_j \in Y_k$ for some k and that v_i and v_j are consecutive in Y_k. This is similar to a *Control Flow Graph*, but the vertices in an XSG represent statements rather than blocks. In this graph, there is an edge between two vertices only if they were executed in succession in at least one of

```
1   #include <stdio.h>
2   int main(){
3       int x, y, z, m;
4       scanf("%d_%d_%d,_"&x, &y, &z);
5       m = mid(x, y, z);
6       printf("%d",m);
7   }
8   int mid(int x, int y, int z){
9       int m;
10      m = z;
11      if (y<z){
12          if (x<y){
13              m = y;
14          }else if (x<z){
15              m = y;
16          }
17      }else{
18          if (x>y){
19              m = y;
20          }else if (x>z){
21              m = x;
22          }
23      }
24      return m;
25  }
```

Fig. 1. (a) Sample source code: mid.c, (b) execution sequence graph for program **mid**

the execution traces. The XSG for **mid** is given in Fig. 1(b), where we can see that the blocks of **mid** are $\{b_1, b_2, \ldots, b_{10}\} = \{$ $\langle 4 \rangle$, $\langle 5, 10, 11 \rangle$, $\langle 12 \rangle$, $\langle 18 \rangle$, $\langle 20 \rangle$, $\langle 19 \rangle$, $\langle 24, 6 \rangle$, $\langle 14 \rangle$, $\langle 13 \rangle$, $\langle 15 \rangle$ $\}$. Thus, trace of test case t_1 can be converted to block level trace by $\langle b_1, b_2, b_3, b_8, b_{10}, b_7 \rangle$.

It should be noted that our definition of blocks is different than the traditional blocks [9]. Since we identify blocks from traces, our blocks may include function or procedure entry points. For example, $\langle 5, 10, 11 \rangle$ will not be a single block by the traditional definition since it has a function started at line 10. Due to this difference, we name our blocks *Linear Execution Blocks*, defined as follows: *A Linear Execution Block $B = \langle v_i, v_{i+1}, \ldots, v_j \rangle$ is a directed path in XSG such that the indegree of each vertex $v_k \in B$ is 0 or 1*. Advantages of using block traces are: (a) it reduces the size of the traces, and, (b) in a block trace, each sequence of two blocks indicate one possible branch. Therefore, in N-gram analysis on block traces, each block N-gram represents $N - 1$ branches. This helps the choice of N for N-gram analysis, discussed in Section 3.1.

2.3   Association Rule Mining

Association Rule Mining searches for interesting relationships among items in a given data set [10]. It has the following two parts:

Frequent Itemset Generation. Search for sets of items occurring together frequently, called a *Frequent Itemset*, whose frequency in the data set, called *Support*, exceeds a predefined threshold, called *Minimum Support*.

Association Rule Generation. Look for association rules like $A \Rightarrow B$ among the elements of the frequent itemsets, meaning that the appearance of A in a set implies the appearance of B in the same set. The conditional probability $P(B|A)$ is called *Confidence*, which must be greater than a predefined *Minimum Confidence* for a rule to be considered. More details can be found in [10].

In our research, we model the blocks as items and the block traces as the transactions. For example, $Y_1 = \langle b_1, b_2, b_3, b_8, b_{10}, b_7 \rangle$ is a transaction for **mid** corresponding to the first test case, T_1. We generate frequent itemsets from the transactions with the additional constraint that the items in an itemset must be consecutive in the original transaction. To do this, we generate N-grams from the block traces, and from them, we choose the ones with at least the minimum support. For a block N-gram $G_{Y_i,N,p}$, support is the number of failing traces containing $G_{Y_i,N,p}$:

$$Support(G_{Y_i,N,p}) = |\{Y_j | G_{Y_i,N,p} \in Y_j \text{ and } Y_j \in Y_F\}| \tag{1}$$

For example, for **mid**, the support for $\langle b_2, b_3, b_8 \rangle$ is 1 since it occurs in one failing trace. We add the test case type to the itemset. For example, after adding the test case type to the itemset $\langle b_2, b_3, b_8 \rangle$, the itemset becomes $\langle b_2, b_3, b_8, passing \rangle$. Then, we try to discover association rules of the form $A \Rightarrow failing$ from these itemsets where the antecedent is a block N-gram and the consequent is *failing*. Therefore, the block N-grams that appear as antecedents in the association rules are most likely to have caused the failure of the test case. We sort these block N-grams in descending order of confidence. For a block N-gram $G_{Y_i,N,p}$, confidence is the conditional probability that the test case outcome is failure given that $G_{Y_i,N,p}$ appears in the trace of that test case. That is,

$$Confidence(G_{Y_i,N,p}) = \frac{Prob(G_{Y_i,N,p} \in Y_j \text{ and } t_j \text{ is a failing test case})}{Prob(G_{Y_i,N,p} \in Y_j)} \quad (2)$$

For example, the confidence the rule $\langle b_2, b_3, b_8 \rangle \Rightarrow failing$ has confidence 0.33. After sorting the block N-grams, we convert the blocks back to line numbers and report this sequence of lines to investigate to find the fault location.

3   Methodology

In this section, we present our methodology for localizing faults. As input we use the source code, the test case types and the traces for all the test cases, and produce as output an ordered list of statements, sorted in order of probability of containing the fault. We first convert the traces to block traces, and then apply N-gram analysis on these block traces to generate all possible unique N-grams for a given range of N. For each N-gram, we count its frequency in passing and failing traces. The set of N-grams and their frequencies are analyzed using the association rule mining technique described in Section 2.3.

The execution of the faulty statement may not always cause failure of the test case. There might be quite a number of test cases in which the faulty statement was executed but it did not cause a failure. In most cases, the failure is dependent on the sequence of execution. A specific sequence or path of execution will cause the program to fail, and this sequence will be very common in the failing traces but not so common in the passing traces. Therefore we can find these subsequences that are most likely to contain the fault by analyzing the traces during passing and failing test cases.

3.1   Parameters of Algorithm

There are two major parameters in the algorithm - the first one is $MinSup$, the minimum support for selecting the N-grams, and the second is N_{MAX}, the maximum value of N for generating the N-grams. Taking a low value of minimum support will result in the inclusion of irrelevant N-grams in consideration. Therefore, we should take minimum support at a high value. Our experience suggests that 90% is a good choice. However, choice of an appropriate N_{MAX} is harder. Two execution paths can differ because of conditional branches. Such differences can be detected by 2-grams. Again, the same function can be called from different functions, which can also be detected with 2-grams. Since we are using execution blocks, an N-gram can capture $(N-1)$ branches, and a choice of 2 or 3 for N_{MAX} should give good results in most cases. If we use higher N-grams, the algorithm will still be able to find the fault, but due to larger N-grams, we will have to examine more lines to find the fault.

Algorithm 1. Fault Localization using N-gram Analysis

1: **procedure** LOCALIZEFAULTS($Y, Y_F, K, MINSUP$)
2:     **for all** $Y_i \in Y$ **do**
3:         Convert Y_i to block trace
4:     **end for**
5:     $NG \leftarrow \phi$
6:     **for** $N = 1$ to N_{MAX} **do**
7:         $NG \leftarrow NG \cup GenerateNGrams(Y, N)$
8:     **end for**
9:     $L_{rel} \leftarrow \{n | n \in NG \text{ and } |n| = 1\}$
10:     **for all** $n \in L_{rel}$ **do**
11:         **if** $Support(n) \neq |Y_F|$ **then**
12:             Remove n from NG and L_{rel}
13:         **end if**
14:     **end for**
15:     $NG_1 \leftarrow \{n | n \in NG \text{ and for all } s \in L_{rel}, s \notin n\}$
16:     $NG \leftarrow NG - NG_1$
17:     **for all** $n \in NG$ **do**
18:         **if** $Support(n) < MINSUP$ **then**
19:             Remove n from NG
20:         **end if**
21:     **end for**
22:     **for all** $n \in NG$ **do**
23:         $NF \leftarrow | \{Y_k | Y_k \in Y_F \text{ and } n \in Y_k\} |$
24:         $NT \leftarrow | \{Y_k | Y_k \in Y \text{ and } n \in Y_k\} |$
25:         $n.confidence \leftarrow NF \div NT$
26:     **end for**
27:     Sort NG in descending order of confidence
28:     Convert the block numbers in the N-grams in NG to line numbers
29:     Report the line numbers in the order of their first appearance in NG
30: **end procedure**

3.2 Algorithm

In this section, the complete algorithm is presented in Algorithm 1. Following is a description of the steps in the algorithm.

L2B: Convert exact execution sequences to block traces. From the line level traces, we create the Execution Sequence Graph (XSG) as described in Section 2.1. From the XSG, we find the Linear Execution Blocks (LEB). Then we convert the traces into block traces in lines 2 to 4 of Algorithm 1.

GNG: Generate N-grams. In this step, we first generate all possible N-grams of lengths 1 to N_{MAX} from the block traces. The generation of all N-grams from a set of block traces for a given N is done in lines 1 to 7, and the generation and combination of all the N-grams are done in lines 5 to 8. Then, we find out how many passing and failing traces each N-gram occurs in.

Algorithm 2. N-gram generation

1: **function** GENERATENGRAMS(Y, N)
2:     $G \leftarrow \phi$
3:     **for** $Y_i \in Y$ **do**
4:         $G \leftarrow G \cup G_{Y_i,N}$
5:     **end for**
6:     **return** G
7: **end function**

FRB: Find Relevant Blocks. From 1-gram, we construct a set of relevant blocks, B_{rel} that contains only those blocks that have appeared in each of the failing traces in lines 10 to 14.

EIN: Eliminate Irrelevant N-grams. In lines 15 to 16, we discard those N-grams that do not contain any block from the relevant block set, B_{rel}.

FFN: Find Frequent N-grams. In lines 17 to 21, we eliminate N-grams with support less than the minimum support as described in Section 2.3.

RNC: Rank N-grams by Confidence. For each surviving N-gram, we compute its confidence using Eqn. 2. This is done in lines 22 to 26. Then we order the N-grams in order of confidence in line 27.

B2L: Convert Blocks in N-grams to Line Numbers. We convert each block in the N-grams back to line numbers using the XSG in line 28.

RLS: Rank Lines According to Suspicion. We traverse the ordered list of N-grams, and report the line numbers in the order of their first appearance in the list. This is done in line 29.

If there are multiple N-grams with the same confidence as the N-gram containing the faulty statement, the best case will be the ordering in which the faulty statement appears in the earliest possible position in the group, and the worst case will be the ordering in which the faulty statement appears in the latest possible position.

4   Case Study

We define the number of lines a programmer needs to examine to find out the fault location as the rank of the program. For example if we have to check α lines to find the fault location of a program, then we say α is the rank of that program. When we are comparing two methods, the method that gives smaller rank is the more effective method. For example, for a program P if method M_1 gives the rank α and method M_2 gives rank β and if $\alpha < \beta$ then it is said that M_1 performs better than M_2. For a program with multiple versions, if methodology M_1 gives smaller ranking for more faulty versions than M_2 then we say M_1 is better than M_2 for that program. Section 4.1 describes the test suites and programs downloaded from [8] used in this study.

4.1   Test Suites

The *Siemens suite* contains 7 programs. The number of faulty versions range from 7 to 41, number of executable statements range from 55 to 216, and number of test cases range from 1052 to 5542. Of the 132 faulty versions, three were not used in our study because one did not have any failing test case and two had faults in header files. The *Space* program has 6218 lines of executable code, 38 faulty versions and 13585 test cases. We did not use 3 faulty versions in our study because there were no failing tests for these versions. The *grep* program has 3306 executable statements, 470 test cases and 18 versions. Compared to [11] that failed to detect any of these faults, we could detect 4 faults in our environment. So we used these 4 versions and also used 2 faults injected by [11], and followed a similar approach to inject 13 more bugs, for a total 19 faulty versions. Manually injected faults are designed to mimic realistic bugs, as described in [11].

4.2   Running the Tests

We conducted our experiments on a Sun Microsystems with 64 bit Intel CPU, 1GB physical memory running Solaris 5.10. We used GCC 3.4.3 and GDB 6.6. For each program, we generated the expected outputs by running the correct program for each test case. Then, we executed the program with the test cases through GDB using a java program to collect the traces. The advantage of using GDB to collect traces is that unlike other studies [6,2] no instrumentation is needed, and we can collect the complete data even if there is a segmentation fault. After data collection, we compared the output of each run with the corresponding expected output and labeled accordingly as passing or failing.

4.3   Applying and Evaluating Our Method

We applied our method on the data collected in Sect. 4.2. For each version, we ran our method for $N = 1, 2, \ldots, 6$ and minimum support of $30\%, 40\%, \ldots, 90\%$ and determined the best case and worst case ranks of the line containig the fault in the source code as described in Section 3.2. From these ranks, we calculated the percantage of code that needs to be examined to find a fault in the best and worst case. From this experiment we found that the best result is obtained when $N = 3$, Minimum Support $= 90\%$, validating our analysis in Section 3.1.

To evaluate our method we compared our results with results from Tarantula [1]. To make the comparison fair we had to collect the data and run Tarantula again because [1] excluded 10 faulty versions and used slightly different number of test cases. We collected the coverage data using a revised version of χSuds [12]. The comparisons of the results are discussed in the following sections.

The Siemens Suite. Fig. 2 shows the comparison between the Tarantula [1] and our N-gram method. The horizontal axis represents the cumulative percentage of code to be examined and the vertical axis represents the total number of faulty versions for which bug can be detected by examining this percentage of

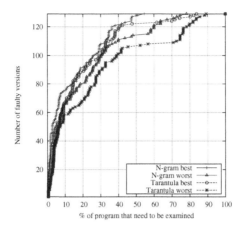

Fig. 2. Comparison between N-gram and Tarantula Method for Siemens suite

code. In worst case N-gram method can discover 80 out of 129 faults by examining only 20% of code while Tarantula can discover only 68 faults from the same percentage of code. Also, in most cases the best case result for N-gram method is better than the best case result for Tarantula, and also worst case result for N-gram method is always better than the worst case result for Tarantula. Also we can see that in worst case N-gram method can discover all 129 faults by examining 78% code while Tarantula has to examine 89% code to discover all faults. Also, we can see from Table 2 that in best case N-gram method performs better than Tarantula method in 120 versions and in worst case our method performs better than Tarantula method in 92 versions.

The Space Program. Fig. 3(a) gives the comparison for Space program between Tarantula [1] and our N-gram method. The axes are same as Fig. 2. In worst case N-gram method can discover 24 faults out of 35 by examining only 1% of code while Tarantula can discover 22 faults by examining that much code. The best and worst case results for N-gram method is always better than the best and worst case results for Tarantula respectively. Also, in worst case N-gram method can discover all faults by examining 20% code while Tarantula needs 32% code for this. For 12 faulty versions out of 35 our *worst* case result is better than Tarantula's *best* case result. Table 2 shows that in best case our method performs better than Tarantula in 21 versions and in worst case our method performs better than Tarantula in 31 versions out of 35.

The grep Program. Fig. 3(b) shows that in worst case N-gram method can discover all faults by examining only 5% of code while Tarantula can discover only 11 faults by examinig that percentage of code. The graph also shows that the *worst* case result for N-gram method is always better than the *best* case result for Tarantula. Table 2 shows that in best case our method performs better than Tarantula method in 17 versions and in worst case our method peforms better than Tarantula method in all versions.

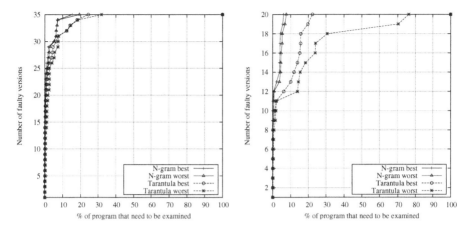

Fig. 3. (a) Comparison between N-gram and Tarantula Method for Space, (b) Comparison between N-gram and Tarantula Method for grep

Table 2. Pairwise comparison between N-gram and Tarantula Method

	Siemens Suite	Space	Grep
Ngram better than Tarantula in best case	120	21	17
Tarantula better than Ngram in best case	4	8	2
Ngram equal to Tarantula in best case	5	6	0
Ngram better than Tarantula in worst case	92	32	19
Tarantula better than Ngram in worst case	28	1	0
Tarantula equal to Ngram in worst case	9	2	0

From the above results we can say that N-gram method outperforms than Tarantula [1] in all of the programs. We also observe from this result that our method perform very well for larger programs and it proves that our method can handle large volume of data than the traditional method.

5   Related Works

In the last few years, a lot of research has been done in this area. In [3], Guo et. al. selected a single passing execution most similiar to a failing trace tried to identify the fault location based on their differences. In [13], Renieris et. al. also find the most similar passing traces but they use nearest neighbor method to measure similarity. Liblit et. al., in [5], described how to collect program execution traces at run time by deploying assertions in the program. They collected only predicate level trace and gave their results at function level. Jones et. al., in their work [1], present a visualization technique using the coverage matrix of the program execution to identify suspicious statements. Denmat et. al. shows in [14] that Association Rule Mining can be applied on coverage matrix. Liu et. al., in their work [2], took each logical expressions as features and tried to detect features that behave differently in passing and failing runs. They also used clustering to detect multiple bugs in [6]. Their method give result in function level. In their research in [4] on software behavior graphs, they used SVM classification to detect suspicious subgraphs, producing a back trace for the fault location. Other works on software behavior graph mining include [15], where Fatta et. al. present their work on finding discriminative patterns based on the failing and passing program execution. Besides test case analysis, researchers also analyze the source code to detect the defect in the source code which may cause software failure, for example, [16,17,18,19,20].

6   Conclusions and Future Works

We have developed a new fault localization algorithm by analyzing the statement sequences of faulty versions. Applying N-gram analysis to fault localization has a very promising future as the results presented in this paper indicate. Using our method, worst case average number of lines to check is 18 in the Siemens suite, 78 for Space and 231 for grep. These results are much better than those achieved by the most standard method Tarantula [1], whose corresponding results are 26 lines, 146 lines and 1488 lines respectively. In all cases, our worst case result is better than Tarantula's worst case result. This shows that our method is both practical and produces better results. Speciallly for larger programs our method produces much better results than [1]. In this study our method only works on single fault, but it can be extended to multiple faults by grouping the failing cases which are caused by same fault and applying our method on these groups.

Research using exact execution sequences, as well as applying data mining to fault localization, is still in beginning phase and there are a lot of avenues to explore and places for improving the results. We are investigating augmenting the execution traces with data flows in order to pinpoint data-driven faults. With software sizes growing with time, processing the huge data collected from test cases will eventually only be possible with data mining methods. Even then, we need to improve our methods to reduce execution time and space. Scalability has to be studied to ensure that it can be applied to large scale software. Also, since it is very common in real life, we need to develop methods to handle multiple faults. It is our belief that research in these directions can help significantly reduce the efforts required to produce fault-free software.

References

1. Jones, J.A., Harrold, M.J., Stasko, J.: Visualization of test information to assist fault localization. In: Proceedings of the 24th International Conference on Software Engineering (2002)
2. Liu, C., Yan, X., Han, J.: Mining control flow abnormality for logic error isolation. In: Proceedings of 2006 SIAM International Conference on Data Mining (2006)
3. Guo, L., Roychoudhury, A., Wang, T.: Accurately choosing execution runs for software fault localization. In: Mycroft, A., Zeller, A. (eds.) CC 2006. LNCS, vol. 3923, pp. 80–95. Springer, Heidelberg (2006)

4. Liu, C., Yan, X., Yu, H., Han, J., Yu, P.S.: Mining behavior graphs for backtrace of noncrashing bugs. In: Proc. 2005 SIAM Int. Conf. on Data Mining (2005)
5. Liblit, B., Aiken, A., Zheng, A.X., Jordan, M.I.: Bug isolation via remote program sampling. In: Proceedings of the ACM SIGPLAN 2003 conference on Programming language design and implementation (2003)
6. Liu, C., Han, J.: Failure proximity: a fault localization-based approach. In: Proceedings of the 14th ACM SIGSOFT international symposium on Foundations of software engineering (2006)
7. Liu, C., Lian, Z., Han, J.: How bayesians debug. In: IEEE International Conference on Data Mining (2006)
8. Do, H., Elbaum, S.G., Rothermel, G.: Supporting controlled experimentation with testing techniques: An infrastructure and its potential impact. Empirical Software Engineering: An International Journal (2005)
9. Agrawal, H.: Dominators, super blocks, and program coverage. In: Proceedings of the 21st ACM SIGPLAN-SIGACT symposium on Principles of programming languages (1994)
10. Han, J., Kamber, M.: Data Mining: Concepts and Techniques. Morgan Kaufmann Publishers, San Francisco (2001)
11. Liu, M.C., Fei, M.L., Yan, M.X., Han, S.M.J., Midkiff, M.S.P.: Statistical debugging: A hypothesis testing-based approach. IEEE Trans. Softw. Eng. (2006)
12. Li, J.J., Horgan, J.R.: χsuds-sdl: A tool for testing software architecture specifications. Software Quality Journal (2000)
13. Renieris, M., Reiss, S.P.: Fault localization with nearest neighbor queries. In: Proceedings of 18th IEEE International Conference on Automated Software Engineering (2003)
14. Denmat, T., Ducass, M., Ridoux, O.: Data mining and cross-checking of execution traces: a re-interpretation of jones, harrold and stasko test information. In: Proceedings of the 20th IEEE/ACM international Conference on Automated software engineering (2005)
15. Fatta, G.D., Leue, S., Stegantova, E.: Discriminative pattern mining in software fault detection. In: Proceedings of the 3rd international workshop on Software quality assurance (2006)
16. Engler, D., Chen, D.Y., Hallem, S., Chou, A., Chelf, B.: Bugs as deviant behavior: a general approach to inferring errors in systems code. SIGOPS Oper. Syst. Rev (2001)
17. Li, Z., Zhou, Y.: Pr-miner: automatically extracting implicit programming rules and detecting violations in large software code. SIGSOFT Softw. Eng. Notes (2005)
18. Chang, R.Y., Podgurski, A., Yang, J.: Finding what's not there: a new approach to revealing neglected conditions in software. In: Proceedings of the 2007 international symposium on Software testing and analysis (2007)
19. Ramanathan, M.K., Grama, A., Jagannathan, S.: Path-sensitive inference of function precedence protocols. In: Proceedings of the 29th international conference on Software Engineering (2007)
20. Li, Z., Lu, S., Myagmar, S., Zhou, Y.: Cp-miner: a tool for finding copy-paste and related bugs in operating system code. In: Proceedings of the 6th conference on Symposium on Opearting Systems Design & Implementation (2004)

Recyclable Connected Dominating Set for Large Scale Dynamic Wireless Networks

Donghyun Kim[1], Xianyue Li[2], Feng Zou[1], Zhao Zhang[3,*], and Weili Wu[1,**]

[1] Department of Computer Science, University of Texas at Dallas,
Richardson, TX, 75080
{donghyunkim,phenix.zou}@student.utdallas.edu, weiliwu@utdallas.edu
[2] School of Mathematics and Statistics, Lanzhou University,
Lanzhou, Gansu, P.R. China, 730000
lixianyue@lzu.edu.cn
[3] College of Mathematics and System Sciences, Xinjiang University, Urumqi,
Xinjiang, P.R. of China, 830046
zhzhao@xju.edu.cn

Abstract. Many people studied the Minimum Connected Dominating Set (MCDS) problem to introduce Virtual Backbone (VB) to wireless networks. However, many existing algorithms assume a static wireless network, and when its topology is changed, compute a new CDS all over again. Since wireless networks are highly dynamic due to many reasons, their approaches can be inefficient in practice. Motivated by this observation, we propose Recyclable CDS Algorithm (RCDSA), an efficient VB maintenance algorithm which can handle the activeness of wireless networks. The RCDSA is built on an approximation algorithm CDS-BD-C1 by Kim et. al. [1]. When a node is added to or deleted from current graph, RCDSA recycles current CDS to get a new one. We prove RCDSA's performance ratio is equal to CDS-BD-C1's. In simulation, we compare RCDSA with CDS-BD-C1. Our results show that the average size of CDS by RCDSA is similar with that by CDS-BD-C1 but RCDSA is at least three times faster than CDS-BD-C1 due to its simplicity. Furthermore, at any case, a new CDS by RCDSA highly resembles to its old version than the one by CDS-BD-C1, which means that using RCDSA, a wireless network labors less to maintain its VB when its topology is dynamically changing.

1 Introduction

Ephremides et. al. first tried to introduce a backbone-like structure in wireless networks [2]. Guha and Kuller firstly used Minimum Connected Dominating Set (MCDS) problem in general graphs to model the problem of computing a minimum size Virtual Backbone (VB) in heterogenous wireless network [3]. Since

---

* This work is supported in part by the NSFC under grant 60603003 and XJEDU.
** This work is supported in part by the NSF under grant CCF-0514796, CCF-0627233, and CCF-0750992.

a smaller size VB is expected to cause less control messages and suffer less from interference, the size of CDS is served as a major quality factor in many previous works [3,4,5,6,7]. Since computing an MCDS is a well-known NP-hard problem, and thus all of existing work present approximation algorithms.

Apparently, establishing a VB brings additional overheads to wireless networks in terms of time and energy. That is, for a wireless network to utilize a VB, a set of nodes has to be selected as a VB and each node in it has to exchange control messages with others to normalize the VB. Therefore, to benefit from a VB, its lifetime has to be long enough so that the profits from it can compensate the losses to build it. Unfortunately, one remarkable characteristic of wireless networks is that topology can be changed frequently due to the mobility, energy exhaustion, or temporal communication error of wireless nodes, which means that we cannot take advantage of VB without a proper strategy to handle the activeness of wireless networks. This problem can be alleviated by minimizing efforts to fix an incomplete VB or by extending the lifetime of it. However, in many cases, the problem is underestimated and computing a new VB is the only way to deal with it, which becomes more inefficient as the wireless network is getting larger and more dynamic.

In this paper, we introduce a new CDS maintenance algorithm for large scale dynamic wireless networks, namely, Recyclable CDS Algorithm (RCDSA) by exploiting CDS-BD-C1 by us [1] whose approximation ratio is 10.359. When a node is added to or an existing node is deleted from current graph, our centralized algorithm recycles the CDS of current graph to get a new one. For this reason, by implementing our algorithm, the communication of two nodes in the same partition will not be disturbed while current CDS is disconnected by a node failure and reconnected again. RCDSA regenerates a new CDS when a node is added within a linear time. In case that current CDS is partitioned by a node deletion, it quickly repairs the broken CDS by adding at most eight nodes. To evaluate the performance of the proposed algorithm, we define average VB size and computation time as the basic performance metric. In addition, to capture the degree of effort for a wireless network to normalize a VB in it, we introduce a new metric, Resemblance Ratio (RR), which evaluates how much a new VB is similar with its previous version. Our simulation results show that the average size of CDS by RCDSA is almost same with CDS-BD-C1, which coincides with our theoretical analysis, but at least three times faster than that in general. Also, the RR of RCDSA is at least 90%, which indicates that much of current control information (i.e. routing path) in each node in current CDS can be reused even after the CDS is reorganized.

The rest of the paper is organized as follows. In Section 2, we define our problem and introduce performance evaluation metrics. We present RCDSA with its theoretical analysis in Section 3. In Section 4, we describe our simulation results and give their analysis. Finally, we make a conclusion and present several future research directions in Section 5.

2   Problem Definition and Performance Evaluation Metrics

We assume every node in a wireless network is homogeneous and use UDG $G = (V, E)$ to represent the network, where V is a set of nodes in the network and $(u, v) \in E$ is a transmission link between node u and v. We use $V(G)$ and $E(G)$ to represent V and E of G. When a node is added or deleted, G is transformed into G'. $M(G)$ represents a Maximal Independent Set (MIS) of G. $C(G)$ is a CDS of G. $N(G)$ is the set of nodes used to link nodes in $M(G)$. That is, $N(G) = C(G) - M(G)$. At last, $Hopdist(x, y)$ is the hop distance between $x \in V$ and $y \in V$ over the shortest path between them and $Eucdist(x, y)$ is the Euclidean distance between x and y. We mention a node in $N(G)$ **useless** if either it is not used to connect MIS nodes or $C(G)$ is still connected without it. Otherwise, we call it **useful**.

In this paper, our goal is to design an efficient VB maintenance algorithm for large scale dynamic wireless networks, while optimizing the size of VB. This algorithm needs to solve a problem to compute an optimal $C(G')$ by using $C(G)$ with a minimal effort. The problem can be seen as a weak MCDS problem because we have more information than what we do in a pure MCDS problem. This problem has to be NP-hard, otherwise we can solve MCDS by starting from a graph with one node, adding one node and computing a new optimal CDS repeatedly. Naturally, the size of CDS is still an important metric. In addition, computation time is an important performance metric since the faster a VB maintenance algorithm for large scale dynamic wireless networks is, the better it can react against a topology change and is more efficient. At last, as we mentioned, the amount of effort (i.e. number of control messages exchanged, energy consumption, and etc.) for a wireless network to normalize a new CDS is an important metric. Intuitively, such effort is directly related to the degree of the change from an old CDS to its next version. For example, when a node is added to current network, if it is adjacent to one CDS node, we can keep using current CDS without incurring any overhead. On the other hand, if one CDS node is deleted and current CDS is partitioned, more control messages will be generated to handle this situation than the former case. As a result, we define the Resemblance Ratio (RR) of a new CDS over its old version to capture the degree of the difference between them, which is defined as $E_{Old \cap New}/E_{New}$, where $E_{Old \cap New}$ is the number of edges which exist in both old and new CDS and E_{New} is the number of edges in the new CDS.

3   Recyclable CDS Algorithm (RCDSA)

In this section, we introduce our centralized algorithm RCDSA. Generally, RCDSA can be divided into following three sub parts: 1) Initial MIS and CDS construction, 2) Handling a new node insertion, and 3) Handling an existing node deletion.

3.1 Initial MIS and CDS Construction

To get $C(G)$ of any G, we use CDS-BD-C1. This algorithm computes $M(G)$ first. To connect any two nearest nodes in $M(G)$, at most two interconnecting nodes are used. Then, $|N(G)| \leq 2(|M(G)| - 1)$, and $|C(G)| \leq 3|M(G)| - 2$. From [7], we have $|M(G)| \leq 3.453opt + 8.291$ for any G, and thus $|C(G)| \leq 10.359opt + 22.873$. Therefore, the approximation ratio of CDS-BD-C1 is 10.359. Before going further, we introduce some theorems that will be used in the rest of this paper.

Lemma 1. *Suppose we have $C(G)$ and every node in $N(G)$ is useful. Then, $|C(G)| \leq 3|M(G)| - 2$ is always true.*

Proof. The hop distance from an MIS node x to the nearest MIS node y is at most three hops. Therefore, to connect nodes in $M(G)$, we need at most $2(|M(G)|-1)$ nodes. Since we are assuming all nodes in $N(G)$ are useful, $|C(G)| = |M(G)| + |N(G)| \leq |M(G)| + 2(|M(G)| - 1) = 3|M(G)| - 2$.

Lemma 2. *Suppose an MIS based CDS of G is partitioned into $P_1, ..., P_n$ by deleting a node in the CDS and $M(G)$ is a valid MIS of G and all nodes in $N(G)$ are useful. Define the distance between two partitions P_i and P_j as $\forall x \in M(P_i) : \forall y \in M(P_j) :: min(Hopdist(x, y))$. Then, the distance between two nearest partition is at most three.*

Proof. Now, assume P_i and P_j are two nearest partitions. Then, there have to be $x \in P_i$ and $y \in P_j$ such that $\forall x : \forall y :: Hopdist(x, y)$ is the minimum. Since the distance between two MIS nodes x and y is at most three hops, the distance between P_i and P_j is at most three.

Lemma 3. *When a node in a CDS is deleted, the CDS can be divided into at most five parts.*

Proof. By [6], in UDG, each node has at most five independent nodes in its neighborhood. Therefore, a CDS can be divided into at most five parts by a node deletion.

3.2 Handling a New Node Insertion

Suppose G becomes G' by a node addition. Then, we may need to compute $C(G')$. Now, we divide every possibility into following two cases and present algorithms to handle them.

- **Case 1 - none of x's neighbors is in C:** set $M(G') = M(G) \cup \{x\}$. Select one of x's neighbor y and set $N(G') = N(G) \cup \{y\}$.
- **Case 2 - at least one of x's neighbors is in C:** if none of x's neighbors is in $M(G)$, set $M(G') = M(G) \cup \{x\}$.

Theorem 1. *In Case 1, $M(G')$ is an MIS. $C(G') = M(G') \cup N(G')$ is a CDS and $|C(G')| \leq 3|M(G')| - 2$.*

Proof. Since x is not adjacent to any node in $M(G)$, $M(G') = M(G) \cup \{x\}$ is still a valid MIS. Because x, a new MIS node is connected with $|C(G)|$ through y, $C(G') = C(G) \cup \{x, y\}$ is a CDS. Now assume $|C(G)| \leq 3|M(G)| - 2$ before adding x to $C(G)$. Then, $|C(G')| = |M(G')| + |N(G')| = (|M(G)| + 1) + (|N(G)| + 1) \leq 3|M(G)| - 2 + 2 = 3|M(G')| - 3$ and thus the theorem is true.

Theorem 2. *In Case 2, $M(G')$ is an MIS. $C(G') = M(G') \cup N(G')$ is a CDS and $|C(G')| \leq 3|M(G')| - 2$.*

Proof. Assume x does not have any neighbor in $M(G)$, since otherwise the proof is trivial. Then, $M(G') = M(G) \cup \{x\}$ is a MIS of G. Since x is adjacent to $y \in N(G)$, $C(G') = C(G) \cup \{x\}$ is a CDS. Now assume that $|C(G)| \leq 3|M(G)| - 2$ was true before x was added to $M(G)$. Then, $|C(G')| = |M(G')| + |N(G')| = |M(G)| + 1 + |N(G)| \leq 3|M(G)| - 2 + 1 = 3|M(G')| - 4$ and thus the theorem is true.

3.3   Handling an Existing Node Deletion

Suppose G becomes G' by a node deletion. Then, we may need to compute $C(G')$. That is, for any $x \in C(G)$, $C(G') = C(G) - \{x\}$ may not be a good CDS of G', which means that $M(G') = M(G)$ may not be an MIS for G' or $C(G) - \{x\}$ is partitioned. To resolve those problems, we proceed following three steps. First, we recover $M(G')$. Then, we execute Algorithm 1 to recognize the number of CDS partitions and nodes included in each partition as well as remove useless CDS nodes in each partition. If we have more than one CDS partition, we choose some non-CDS nodes and add them to $N(G')$ so that $C(G') = M(G') \cup N(G')$ becomes a CDS.

MIS reconstruction. this part of RCDSA is initiated when a node $x \in C(G)$ is deleted. If $x \in M(G)$, set $M(G') = M(G) - \{x\}$ and $N(G') = N(G)$. Now denote Y be the set of x's neighbor nodes. For each $y \in Y$, if y is not adjacent to any node in $M(G')$, then make $M(G') = M(G') \cup \{y\}$. If $x \in N(G)$, set $M(G') = M(G)$ and $N(G') = N(G) - \{x\}$.

Theorem 3. *After the MIS reconstruction phase, $M(G')$ is an MIS of G'.*

Proof. If $x \in N(G)$, then $M(G)$ is a good MIS for G'. Now, suppose $x \in M(G)$. Since by the definition of MIS, every nodes in G has to be in $M(G)$ or adjacent to a node in $M(G)$, and thus the neighbors of x has to be included in one of following two separate sets, $S_1(G)$, and $S_2(G)$. That is, a node s is in $S_1(G)$, if s is adjacent to a node in $M(G) - \{x\}$. Otherwise, s is in $S_2(G)$. Clearly, $M(G) - \{x\}$ is an MIS of $V(G) - x - S_2(G)$. Assume after MIS reconstruction algorithm is executed, we obtain an MIS $M(S_2)$ of $S_2(G)$. Then, obviously, $M(G') = (M(G) - \{x\}) \cup M(S_2)$. Since $M(G) - \{x\}$ and $M(S_2)$ are MISs of $V(G) - x - S_2(G)$ and $S_2(G)$, respectively, and there is no edges between $M(G) - \{x\}$ and $M(S_2)$, $M(G')$ is an MIS of G'.

Algorithm 1. Sweeper - $(G(V, E), COLOR, v_i)$

```
1: color v_i in COLOR
2: if v_i is an MIS node then
3:     for each CDS neighbor of v_i, v_j do
4:         if v_j is not colored yet then
5:             Sweeper (G, COLOR, v_j)
6:         end if
7:     end for
8:     return TRUE
9: else
10:     for each CDS neighbor of v_i, v_j do
11:         if v_j is not colored yet then
12:             T_j = Sweeper (G, COLOR, v_j)
13:         end if
14:     end for
15:     if any of T_j is TRUE then
16:         return TRUE
17:     else
18:         switch v_i to non-MIS node
19:         return FALSE
20:     end if
21: end if
```

Sweeper algorithm. after $M(G')$ is recovered by processing all neighbor of $x \in G'$, we execute Sweeper, a variation of depth first search algorithm. The goals of this algorithm are 1) recognize each CDS partition and 2) remove useless CDS node in each partition. Sweeper assigns the same color number to a set of CDS nodes only if they are in the same CDS partition. It also sweeps useless CDS nodes in each CDS partition. In detail, for each v_i, we execute **Sweeper** (G, W, v_i) if v_i is a CDS node, but not colored yet, where W is the smallest number of unused color.

Theorem 4. *After Sweeper is executed, every CDS in each partition is useful and any two CDS nodes have same color if and only if they are in the same partition.*

Proof. Since Sweeper is a tree traversal algorithm and it visits only CDS nodes, it cannot visit two disconnected CDS nodes within one search trial. Therefore, two nodes in separate partitions will be colored differently. Now assume after Sweep is executed, a subtree of P_i is two connected, where P_i is a partition in a broken CDS. This can happen only if Sweep visits one MIS nodes two times. However, Sweep prevents this from happening by line 4 and line 11. At last, by line 18~19 Sweep deletes any useless CDS node. Therefore, the theorem holds true.

Reconnection algorithm. now, we have at most five partitions and by Lemma 3 and the distance between any two nearest partition is three hops by Lemma 2. Therefore, we need to add at most eight nodes to current $N(G')$ to make $C(G') = M(G') \cup N(G')$ as a good CDS of G'. To select these new inter-connecting nodes, we first reduce each CDS partition into one node and put an edge between them only if they are connected in the original graph through at most two non-MIS nodes. Denote this new graph as $\hat{G}$. Then, we can create an adjacency matrix of $\hat{G}$. Now, our problem to select the interconnecting nodes in G' is reduced to computing a spanning tree in $\hat{G}$, and then a simple tree traversal algorithm like depth first search is good enough to solve this problem. Now, from this solution, we can decide which non-MIS nodes has to be added to $N(G')$ to make $M(G') \cup N(G')$ connected.

Theorem 5. *Assume RCDSA reconnects a broken CDS $C(G)$ and $C(G')$ is a resulting CDS. Then, $|C(G')| \leq 3|M(G')| - 2$ is still true.*

Proof. By MIS construction phase, we have an MIS $M(G')$ of G'. Using Sweeper algorithm, we removed every useless node in each partition. Then, by Lemma 1, $|P_i| \leq 3|M(P_i)| - 2$, where $M(P_i)$ is the set of MIS nodes in P_i. Now assume we have n partitions. By Reconnection algorithm, we add at most $2(n-1)$ nodes to CDS. Therefore, $|C(G')| = \sum_{1 \leq i \leq n} |P_i| + 2(n-1) \leq 3 \sum_{1 \leq i \leq n} |M(P_i)| - 2n + 2(n-1) = 3 \sum_{1 \leq i \leq n} |M(P_i)| - 2 = 3|M(G')| - 2$, and the theorem holds true.

Theorem 6. *The time complexity of RCDSA is $O(n^2)$.*

Proof. To handle a node addition, it takes $O(n)$ time. For a node deletion, MIS recovery requires $O(n^2)$ time. Since Sweeper is a variation of depth first search, it requires $O(E + V)$ time. To recognize the edges between any two partitions, it takes $O(n^2)$ time and to reconnect them, it requires a constant time. Therefore, the time complexity of RCDSA is $O(n^2)$.

4   Simulation Results and Analysis

To evaluate the performance of our algorithm, we compare our centralized algo-rithm RCDSA with CDS-BD-C1. Since we incorporated a mechanism to handle the activeness of wireless network to CDS-BD-C1, these simulation results will show the effectiveness of this approach. For the simulation, we used a desktop com-puter with 2.4Ghz Intel Core2 CPU and 2GB memory. We installed Fedora Core 7.0 by Rad Hat as an operating system. For precise and fair running time compar-ison, we executed each algorithm one by one while only basic demon processes are running on the computer. The implementation of each algorithm exactly follows its description in the literature in terms of procedures and time complexity. We use a 100 by 100 virtual space and randomly deploy wireless nodes. The number of nodes in a network varies from 10 to 100 by increasing 10 per each parameter setting. We set the maximum transmission range of node to 15 and 25. Per each pa-rameter setting, we randomly generated 100 connected graph instances and calcu-lated average CDS size, computation time, and RR. To make our discussion more brief, in Figure 1, we put a tag on each parameter setting. Its interpretation is as follows: DA represents we use RCDSA to handle a node addition. DD and SD mean we use RCDSA and CDS-BD-C1 to handle a node deletion, respectively.

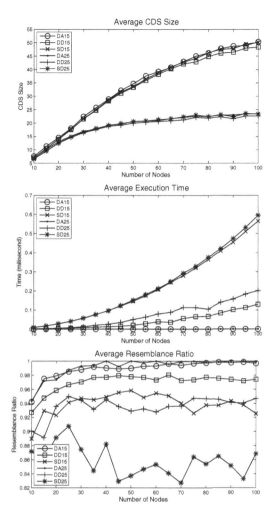

Fig. 1. Each figure shows the comparison result in terms of average CDS size, execution time, and resemblance ratio

The last number 15 and 25 represent the maximum transmission range of nodes in a wireless network in which the simulation is done.

The first graph in Figure 1 shows average size of CDS generated by each algorithm. All curves look almost similar, which coincides with our theoretical analysis that RCDSA has the same approximation ratio with CDS-BD-C1. When the maximum transmission range is longer, we usually have bigger complete subgraph in a given graph G, and thus we have smaller MIS. Therefore, it is natural that the curves in the graph are divide into two groups. The reason that the size of CDS by RCDSA is smaller than CDS-BD-C1 is that when a node is deleted and RCDSA is executed, Sweeper deletes every useless CDS nodes in each CDS partition and this optimizes the final CDS.

The second graph in Figure 1 shows the average running time for each parameter setting. The time complexity of RCDSA to handle a node addition is $O(n)$ and even its structure is so simple. Thus, the shape of the curves for DA15 and DA25 resembles a line. Since CDS-BD-C1 does not have any explicit way to handle a node addition, we do not compare RCDSA with CDS-BD-C1 in this situation. Now let us consider node deletion. If a non-CDS is deleted or CDS is still connected after one CDS node is removed, then we do not need to compute a new CDS, but can use current one. Therefore, in this simulation, we deleted a node such that the remaining CDS nodes are disconnected. The reason that DD is faster than SD is that even though the running time of both algorithms are $O(n^2)$ in theory, DD spends less time due to its structural simplicity. Interestingly, RCDSA shows different performance under DD15 and DD25. In DD, RCDSA identifies every link between CDS partitions, and such links consist of non-MIS nodes. Therefore, when the maximum transmission range is 15, the size of MIS increases and the number of non-MIS nodes decreases and as a result, DD15 is faster than DD25.

Now, let us take a look at the RR of each algorithm. In case of DA, it perfectly maintains current CDS structure and add one node to CDS if necessary. Therefore, naturally, the RR of DA is extremely high as we can see in Figure 1. Based on its property, if CDS-BD-C1 starts from a randomly selected root, its reusability can be very low. To make our comparison fair, we fix the root for CDS-BD-C1 and perform the simulation. In general, RCDSA has higher RR than CDS-BD-C1. This is because in contrast to RCDSA, which uses the most of current MIS to compute a new MIS, CDS-BD-C1 computes a new MIS all over again, and when one node is deleted, the choice of a new MIS over the remaining node can be quite different. At last, when the maximum transmission range is longer, the deletion of one MIS node affects less the rest of CDS, and thus RCDSA has higher reusability ratio in DD25 than DD15. So far, we learn that the execution time of RCDSA increases relatively slower and the RR of RCDSA remains higher than those of CDS-BD-C1's. We also saw that when the maximum transmission range is shorter, the performance of RCDSA is better. From those results, we can conclude that RCDSA is a good VB maintenance algorithm for large size sparse dynamic wireless networks.

5   Conclusion and Future Work

In this paper, we introduced Recyclable CDS Algorithm (RCDSA), 10.359-approximation algorithm to compute and maintain CDS for large scale dynamic wireless networks. By recycling current CDS to build a new one, RCDSA becomes fast and efficient. However, still, RCDSA can be improved. Since RCDSA is a centralized algorithm with limited applications, designing RCDSA as a distributed algorithm can be a good future work. We also consider designing a k-connected RCDSA, where a node can communication with others without being interrupted while current CDS is broken and repaired.

References

1. Kim, D., Wu, Y., Li, Y., Zou, F., Du, D.-Z.: Constructing minimum connected dominating sets with bounded diameters in wireless networks. IEEE Transactions on Parallel and Distributed Systems (2008)
2. Ephremides, A., Wieselthier, J., Baker, D.: A design concept for reliable mobile radio networks with frequency hopping signaling. Proceeding of IEEE 75(1), 56–73 (1987)
3. Guha, S., Khuller, S.: Approximation algorithms for connected dominating sets. Algorithmica 20, 374–387 (1998)
4. Cardei, M., Cheng, X., Cheng, X., Du, D.-Z.: Connected domination in multihop ad hoc wireless networks. In: Proc. of International Conference on Computer Science and Informatics (March 2002)
5. Ruan, L., Du, H., Jia, X., Wu, W., Li, Y., Ko, K.-I.: A greedy approximation for minimum connected dominating sets. Journal of Theoretical Computer Science 329, 325–330 (2004)
6. Wu, W., Du, H., Jia, X., Li, Y., Huang, S.C.-H.: Minimum connected dominating sets and maximal independent sets in unit disk graphs. Theoretical Computer Science 352 (2006)
7. Funke, S., Kesselman, A., Meyer, U., Segal, M.: A simple improved distributed algorithm for minimum CDS in unit disk graphs. ACM Transactions on Sensor Network 2(3), 444–453 (2006)

Locate More Sensors with Fewer Anchors in Wireless Sensor Networks

Hui Ling[1] and Taieb Znati[1,2]

[1] Department of Computer Science,
[2] Telecommunication Program,
University of Pittsburgh, Pittsburgh, PA, USA 15260
{hling,znati}@cs.pitt.edu

Abstract. In this paper, we propose to integrate Out-of-Range information with the multi-lateration scheme to resolve location ambiguities of unknown sensor nodes, which can not gain sufficient reference nodes information due to an insufficient number of reference nodes or low level of network density. The proposed scheme is based on the observation that, if a node, N1, is out of the transmission range of another node, N2, the distance between N1 and N2 must be larger than a given threshold value. This information, referred as "Out-of-Range" can then be used to eliminate location ambiguities of some unknown nodes in Wireless Sensor Networks (WSNs). The simulation results show that the proposed scheme can significantly increase the number of resolved sensor nodes, compared with multi-lateration schemes when the network connectivity is low. In contrast, when node density is high, the proposed scheme can discover the same number of nodes with a smaller number of anchor nodes.

1 Introduction

Wireless sensor networks are envisioned as the key technology for the implementation of a large variety of applications, such as environmental monitoring, disaster prevention, seismic monitoring and tactical surveillance. A network of sensors for seismic monitoring can provide input to active and semi-active vibration dampening systems to make buildings more earthquake resistant.

To realize these applications, geographical location of each sensor node is often required. For instance, when a breach is detected in an under water surveillance network, the location where the breach occurs must also be reported to the base station such that further actions can be taken by users.

The problem of locating each sensor node, referred as "Location discovery", has been extensively investigated for sensor networks and a lot of schemes have been proposed. Most proposed schemes require the location of some nodes in the network to be known in advance. These nodes are referred as anchor nodes. The unknown nodes, then estimate their location after sufficient information are gained through message exchanging with reference nodes. Once an unknown node successfully gains its location knowledge, it becomes a reference node and starts to provide its location information to other unknown nodes in the network.

Y. Li et al. (Eds.): WASA 2008, LNCS 5258, pp. 570–581, 2008.
© Springer-Verlag Berlin Heidelberg 2008

The process continues hop by hop till all nodes resolve their position or no unknown node can resolve its location.

It is worth noting that, during the location discovery process, each unknown sensor node must gain sufficient information, such as the locations of and distances to three or more reference nodes in order to determine its own position. Therefore, to enable the discovery of the locations of unknown sensor nodes, a sufficient number of anchor nodes and degree of network connectivity must exist in the network.

The anchor nodes, however, rely on external devices such as GPS to obtain their locations. These external devices, not only incur additional cost, but also consume a lot of energy. Therefore, the usage of anchor nodes should be limited to maintain a low cost and long life time of the senor networks. In case the number of anchor nodes is small, a high level of network density can also enable the discovery of locations of sensor nodes in the network. The network connectivity, however, tends to decrease as sensors gradually deplete their battery and die. We then investigate how to use the Out-of-Range information to locate more nodes when the level of network connectivity is low, and reduce the number of anchor nodes when the level of network connectivity is sufficiently high.

The rest of paper is organized as follows. Section 2 discusses the related work. Section 3 describes when and how the "Out-of-Range" information is explored for location discovery in sensor network. In section 4, the effectiveness of the proposed scheme is evaluated in a different set of scenarios. Section 5 concludes this paper and discusses future work.

2   Related Work

Range-based location discovery schemes mainly consist of two basic phases: distance (or angle) estimation and distance (or angle) combining. Distance estimation handles how the distance or angle between two nodes is estimated. In distance combining phase, these information is combined together to derive the locations of unknown nodes.

The most popular methods used in distance estimation include received signal strength indicator (RSSI), time based methods (ToA, TDoA), and angle-of-arrival (AoA) technique [1]. RSSI measures the power of signal at the receiver and derives the distance between the sender and receiver, based on the known transmission power and propagation model. Time based methods record the time of arrival (ToA) or time difference of arrival (TDoA) and translate it directly into the distance based on the known signal propagation speed. The AoA system estimates the angle from which signals are received and derives node positions using geometric relationships [2].

In distributed positioning algorithms, unknown nodes only communicate with their one-hop neighboring reference or resolved nodes. Multi-lateration techniques, such as atomic, collaborative and iterative multi-lateration, are then used to estimate the locations of sensor nodes [3][4]. These schemes reduce the number of anchor nodes in the network for location discovery. However, they still rely on a high level of network connectivity to provide sufficient reference nodes information to unknown nodes for location estimation.

The localization problem in sparse networks also draw interests from researchers recently. In [5][6], the conditions for unique localization in networks are studied and used to identify all the localizable nodes in partially localizable networks to prevent flawed location estimations. Furthermore, A special class of sparse network, *bilateration network*, is investigated in [7]. The finite possible location sets of nodes are derived sequentially and some particular edges in the network are then used to sweep location possibilities. It is shown that nodes in bilateration network can be finitely localized using the proposed scheme.

Compliment to the existing effort to discover the locations of sensor nodes in sparse networks, we propose to explicitly explore non-connectivity information, i.e. "Out-of-Range" information, to eliminate location ambiguities of sensor nodes, when sufficient information is not available for multi-lateration, and reduce the number of anchor nodes for location discovery when the network density is high.

3   Location Discovery Using Out-of-Range Information

3.1   Overview

The anchor nodes disseminate their position to neighboring unknown sensor nodes. An unknown sensor node, then measures its distance to each of the neighboring reference/anchor nodes respectively. We assume the distance between two sensors can be estimated using methods such as RSSI or ToA. If more than three neighbor nodes are reference nodes, an unknown node then estimates its own location using trilateration. In addition, the least square method is used to refine sensor node's location in an over determined system. Otherwise, the unknown sensor node sends query messages to non-neighboring nodes to check if they can help to resolve its location using Out-of-Range information. Once its location is resolved, an unknown node becomes a reference node and disseminates its position to other unknown nodes in the network to enable the continuation of the location discovery process.

3.2   Out-of-Range Information

The Out-of-Range information is based on the following observation: if two sensor nodes, N1 and N2, can not hear from each other, then the distance between them must be larger than r1, the transmission range of N1, and r2, the transmission range of N2. In reality, the transmission range of a sensor may be irregular [8]. Therefore, the transmission range from a sensor node depends on where the destination is. However, the observation is still valid if r1 and r2 is replaced with the minimum range over all directions that N1 and N2's signal propagates. The observation is formally defined as following:

$$N1, \ N2 \ are \ not \ neighboring \ nodes \Rightarrow$$
$$dist(N1, N2) > \max(\min(r1_\alpha), \min(r2_\alpha)) \ . \tag{1}$$

For simplicity, let r be $\max(\min(r1_\alpha), \min(r2_\alpha))$ in the rest of the paper.

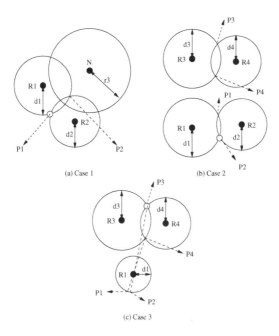

Fig. 1. Using Out-of-Range information to resolve an unknown node's position

In the following, we explain how the Out-of-Range information is utilized to resolve an unknown node's position in several scenarios. In all the following cases, it is assumed that node N is out of the transmission range of node U. Furthermore, it is assumed that the network is connected. Hence, N can reach U through a multi-hop flooding. For simplicity, the other nodes in the network are not shown in Fig. 1.

Case 1: N is a reference node and U has two neighboring reference nodes

In the scenario presented in Fig. 1(a), the unknown node has two neighboring reference nodes, R1 and R2. The distance measured from the unknown node to R1 and R2, is $d1$ and $d2$ respectively. Obviously, there are two possible positions that the unknown node might be, P1 and P2, giving only these knowledge. Let us assume that another reference node, N, exists in the network and the unknown node can not hear from N. Furthermore, P2 is in N's transmission range while P1 is not. Therefore, it can be inferred that the unknown node can only reside in P1 because it would hear from N if it were at P2.

Let (x_N, y_N) be the coordinate of the reference node N, (x_1, y_1) and (x'_1, y'_1) be the two possible positions of the unknown node U, and r be the minimum transmission range of N, N can resolve U's location if:

$$(\sqrt{(x_N - x_1)^2 + (y_N - y_1)^2} > r \;\&\&$$
$$\sqrt{(x_N - x'_1)^2 + (y_N - y'_1)^2} \le r)$$

$$\| \; (\sqrt{(x_N - x_1')^2 + (y_N - y_1')^2} > r \;\; \&\& $$
$$\sqrt{(x_N - x_1)^2 + (y_N - y_1)^2} \leq r) \; . \tag{2}$$

Case 2: N is an unknown node with two neighboring reference nodes and U has two neighboring reference nodes

In the scenario described in Fig. 1(b), an unknown node, N, has two neighboring reference nodes, R3 and R4. Given its distance to R3 and R4, $d3$ and $d4$, N can calculate its two potential locations: P3 and P4. Similarly, the unknown node, U, has two neighboring reference nodes, R1 and R2, and computes its own possible positions: P1 and P2. Furthermore, the distance between P3 and P1 and the distance between P4 and P1 are smaller than U's minimum transmission range, r. Based on the fact that N is not a neighbor of U, U can determine that it must be located at P2.

In general, an unknown node, N, located at either (x_1, y_1) or (x_1', y_1'), can determine the location of another unknown node, U, located at either (x, y) or (x', y'), if:

$$(\sqrt{(x - x_1)^2 + (y - y_1)^2} \leq r \;\; \&\& $$
$$\sqrt{(x - x_1')^2 + (y - y_1')^2} \leq r)$$
$$\| \; (\sqrt{(x' - x_1)^2 + (y' - y_1)^2} \leq r \;\; \&\& $$
$$\sqrt{(x' - x_1')^2 + (y' - y_1')^2} \leq r) \; . \tag{3}$$

Case 3: N is an unknown node with one neighboring reference node and U has two neighboring reference nodes

Similar to case 2, the scenario presented in Fig. 1(c) also describes how an unknown node, N, helps to determine the location of another unknown node, U. This case differs from case 2 in that the unknown node, N, only has one neighboring reference node. In Fig. 1(c), U is located at either P3 or P4. N is located at $d1$ away from the reference node R1. P1 is the farthest point from P4 among all the possible locations N might be. If P4P1 is smaller than r, it can be easily concluded that U must reside at P3, because otherwise U would be a neighboring node of N.

Generally, consider an unknown node, U, located at either (x, y) or (x', y'). Unknown node, N, which is d away from its neighboring reference node, R1, can determine U's position under the following condition:

$$\sqrt{(x - x_0)^2 + (y - y_0)^2} \leq r, \; \forall (x_0, y_0),$$
$$\sqrt{(x_0 - x_{R1})^2 + (y_1 - y_{R1})^2} = d$$
$$\| \; \sqrt{(x' - x_0)^2 + (y' - y_0)^2} \leq r, \; \forall (x_0, y_0),$$
$$\sqrt{(x_0 - x_{R1})^2 + (y_1 - y_{R1})^2} = d \; . \tag{4}$$

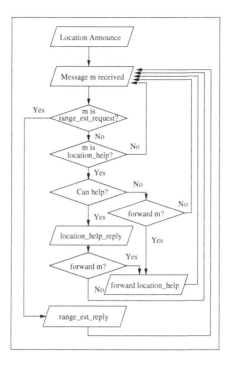

Fig. 2. Localization algorithm at reference nodes

Condition 4 can be simplified into the following equivalent condition after a short derivation.

$$\sqrt{(x - x_{R1})^2 + (y - y_{R1})^2} \le r - d1$$
$$\| \ \sqrt{(x' - x_{R1})^2 + (y' - y_{R1})^2} \le r - d1 \ . \tag{5}$$

3.3   Localization Scheme

Fig. 2 presents the major steps of the localization process executed at a reference node, R. The reference node starts the localization process by announcing its location to neighboring nodes. It then keeps waiting for messages from other nodes. Based on the type of the message received, the reference node, R, responds as following:

- Upon receiving a "Range_est_request" message from an unknown node U, R replies with a "Range_est_reply"
- If a "Location_help" message for U is received, R simply discards this message if it has already processed the help request from U. Otherwise, R checks condition 2 and sends "Location_help_reply" to U if it can determine the location of U using "Out-of-Range" information. If R can not utilize its "Out-of-Range" information to uniquely locate U's position, R decreases the

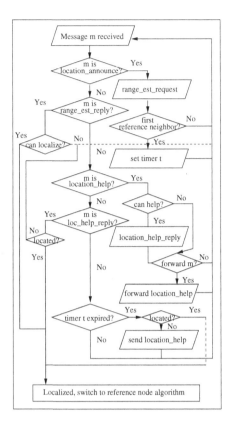

Fig. 3. Localization algorithm at unknown nodes

TTL of "Location_help" message by one and forwards the "Location_help" message to its neighbors if the TTL is bigger than zero.

The main steps of the localization scheme at an unknown node are described at Fig. 3. Each unknown node, U, basically waits for messages from other nodes and acts according to the type of the message as following:

– After receiving a "Location_announce" message from R, U puts R's id and location information in its reference node table. It sends a "Range_est_request" message to R. U also starts a timer t, if the "Location_announce" is the first announce message it receives
– After "Range_est_reply" is received from R, U computes its distance between R and itself. If three or more reference nodes have replied, U can estimate its location and become a reference node and executes the localization algorithm for reference nodes
– If the timer, t, expires and U still can not resolve its location, U initializes the TTL of the "Location_help" message to be h and sends it out to its neighboring nodes

- Upon receiving a "Location_help" message for another unknown node U1, node U, simply discards this message if it has already processed the message. Otherwise it extracts the reference node information in the message and determines if its location information can help to determine U1's position. The conditions of case 2 and 3 at section 3.2 are checked based on the role of U and U1. If U's information can be utilized to determine U1's location, U reply to U1 with a "Location_help_reply" message. Otherwise, U decreases the TTL of "Location_help" by one and forwards the "Location_help" to its neighbors if the TTL is bigger than zero.
- After receiving a "Location_help_reply", U extracts the reply information and resolves its location. If U's location is resolved, U becomes a reference node and executes the localization algorithm for reference nodes

4   Performance Evaluation

4.1   Methodology

The simulation is developed using Glomosim 2.03. A set of different scenarios are simulated to evaluate the effectiveness of the proposed scheme. The simulated network extends over an area of 1000mX1000m. In the simulation, a transmission range of 250m is considered. Furthermore, for simplicity, it is assumed that every sensor has the same value of minimum transmission range.

The proposed location discovery scheme is simulated at the application layer. The initially configured anchor nodes start to broadcast location information at the beginning of simulation. All the messages are delivered using UDP and retransmitted three times if not received. Each node maintains a neighbor table so that it knows if it is out of the range of another node.

4.2   Effect of h

The value of h is critical to the performance of the proposed scheme. On one hand, a big value of h allows an unknown node to have a higher chance to resolve its location ambiguity. However, on the other hand, it also leads to a high level of communication overhead. Care must be taken to configure the value of h.

Fig. 4 presents the number of resolved nodes after the location discovery completes in a network of 24, 28, 32 and 34 nodes. In these scenarios, 4 nodes are initially configured as anchor nodes. The results show that the number of resolved nodes remain the same in most cases. It slight increases in the network of 32 nodes when h increase from 2 to 3. The reason is that nodes multi-hop away may be geographically too far away from the unknown node U to provide any useful Out-of-Range information. The value of h is set to be 2 in the rest of the simulations.

4.3   Performance Comparison

The number of resolved sensors after the location discovery completes is used to measure the effectiveness of the proposed scheme, in comparison to the basic

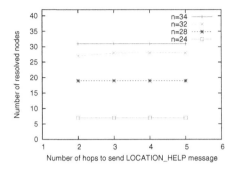

Fig. 4. The effect of h in networks with four reference nodes

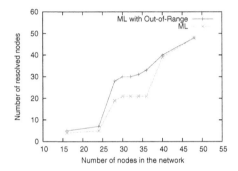

Fig. 5. Number of resolved nodes after location discovery

Table 1. Average node degree g in a network of n nodes

n	16	24	28	30	32	34	36	40	44	48
g	1.8	3.1	4.9	5.0	4.8	4.82	4.83	6.85	6.82	7.3

multi-lateration scheme. The number of additional nodes located using Out-of-Range information depends on the network connectivity and topology. Fig 5 presents the number of resolved nodes after location discovery with Out-of-Range and without Out-of-Range information in a set of scenarios. The number of anchor nodes remains to be 4 in all these scenarios. The average node degree in each scenario is listed in Table 1. It is worth noting that the average node degree does not always increases as the number of nodes increases in the network. It is due to the fact that nodes are uniformly placed over the entire area. In the uniform placement, the area is divided into a number of cells and nodes are randomly placed within each cell. A slight increasing of the number of nodes can result in an additional cell with only few nodes placed in it.

When the average node degree is low, no Out-of-Range information can be used due to the lack of connectivity in the network. On the other hand, when

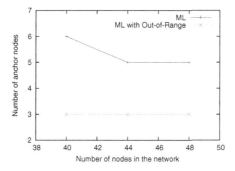

Fig. 6. Number of anchor sensors required to resolve locations of all sensors in the network

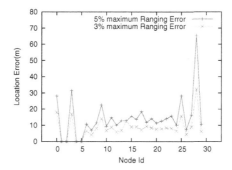

Fig. 7. Location estimation error of resolved nodes

the average node degree is high, no Out-of-Range information is needed since sensors can estimate their locations using reference nodes. In the other cases, the proposed scheme can locate more nodes than the basic multi-lateration scheme. The results show that when the sensor network connectivity starts to decrease, the Out-of-Range information can be used to locate more sensors in the network.

Next, we show how many anchor nodes are required in order to discover locations of all sensors in the network, when the network connectivity is high. As the results in Fig. 6 show, the number of anchor nodes required to discover all sensors in the network can be reduced using Out-of-Range information. The number decreases from 6, 5, 5 to 3 in a network of 40, 44 and 48 nodes respectively.

4.4 Location Estimation Error

Range-based location discovery schemes rely on a ranging technique to estimate locations of sensor nodes. This set of simulations aim to study the sensitivity of location estimation accuracy of the proposed scheme on the ranging errors. Fig. 7 presents the location estimation errors when a 3% and 5% maximum ranging

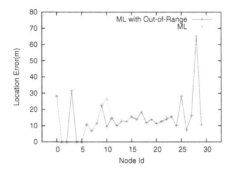

Fig. 8. Location estimation error of resolved nodes with 5% maximum ranging error

error is simulated in a network of 32 nodes. In the simulations, 4 sensors are initially configured as anchor nodes in the network. As expected, the location estimation error increases as the ranging error increases.

Fig. 8 presents the location estimation errors of the proposed scheme and the basic multi-lateration scheme when 5% maximum ranging error is simulated. Similar value of location estimation error is observed at nodes whose locations are discovered by both schemes. Among these additional sensors located by our scheme, some high value of location error is observed due to the accumulation of location errors during location discovery.

5   Conclusion and Future Work

In this paper, we propose to integrate Out-of-Range information with the multi-lateration scheme for location discovery in sensor networks. The Out-of-Range information, based on the fact that if two nodes cannot hear from each other, the distance between them must be larger than a certain threshold value. We then show how the Out-of-Range information at an unknown sensor can be used to determine the location of another unknown sensor in three different scenarios. The simulation results confirm that the proposed scheme can locate more nodes than the basic multi-lateration scheme when the network connectivity is low, and reduce the number of anchor nodes required to locate all sensors when the network connectivity is high. In the future, we plan to investigate how to use mobile anchor nodes to locate these sensors whose locations can not be resolved even using Out-of-Range information in networks with a low level of connectivity.

Acknowledgments

This work is supported by NSF awards 0325353, 0549119 and 0729456.

References

1. Gibson, J.: The Mobile Communications Handbook. IEEE Press, Los Alamitos (1999)
2. Malhotra, N., Krasmewski, M., Yang, C., Bagchi, S., Chappell, W.: Location Estimation in Ad-Hoc Networks with Directional Antennas. In: 25th IEEE International Conference on Distributed Computing Systems (ICDCS), Columbus, Ohio, USA (2005)
3. Savvides, A., Han, C.C., Strivastava, M.B.: Dynamic Fine-Grained Localization in Ad-Hoc Networks of Sensors. In: Annual International Conference on Mobile Computing and Networking (MobiCom 2001). ACM Press, Rome (2001)
4. Savvides, A., Park, H., Strivastava, M.B.: The Bits and Flops of the n-hop Multilateration Primitive for Node Localization Problems. In: 1st ACM International Workshop on Wireless Sensor Networks and Applications (WSNA), pp. 112–121. ACM Press, New York (2002)
5. Goldenberg, D.K., Krishnamurthy, A., Maness, W.C., Yang, Y.R., Young, A., Morse, A.S., Savvides, A., Anderson, B.D.: Network Localization in Partially Localizable Networks. IEEE INFOCOM, Miami, FL (2005)
6. Aspnes, J., Eren, T., Goldenberg, D.K., Morse, A.S., Whiteley, W., Yang, Y.R., Anderson, B.D., Belhumeur, P.N.: A Theory of Network Localization. IEEE Transactions on Mobile Computing 5(12), 1663–1678 (2006)
7. Goldenberg, D.K., Bihler, P., Cao, M., Fang, J., Anderson, B.D., Morse, A.S., Yang, Y.R.: Localization in Sparse Networks using Sweeps. In: 12th Annual International Conference on Mobile Computing and Networking (MobiCom 2006). ACM Press, New York (2006)
8. Zhou, G., He, T., Krishnamurthy, S., Stankovic, J.A.: Impact of Radio Irregularity on Wireless Sensor Networks. In: 2nd International Conference on Mobile Systems, Applications, and Services (MOBISYS) (2004)

Author Index